HISTORY, MAN, AND REASON

MAURICE MANDELBAUM

HISTORY, MAN, & REASON

A STUDY IN NINETEENTH-CENTURY THOUGHT

THE JOHNS HOPKINS PRESS: BALTIMORE AND LONDON

The Johns Hopkins University Press, Baltimore, Maryland 21218
The Johns Hopkins University Press Ltd., London

ISBN 0-8018-1236-4 (cloth)
ISBN 0-8018-1608-4 (paper)

Originally published, 1971
Johns Hopkins Paperback, 1974

For Ann and for John

CONTENTS

It is the purpose of this book to cast light on some highly important aspects of the thought of the nineteenth century. Its scope is not all-embracing, but it ranges more widely than is perhaps prudent: while its central concerns lie within the philosophic tradition, materials drawn from the social sciences, and elsewhere, provide important illustrations of the movements which it has been my aim to trace.

This inclusiveness is not accidental, for what is here at issue is not simply an examination of philosophic modes of thought, but a sifting of presuppositions which were held in common by a diverse group of thinkers whose antecedents and whose aims often had little in common. Thus, after a preliminary tracing of the main strands of continuity within philosophy itself, attention will be concentrated on how, out of diverse and disparate sources, certain common beliefs and attitudes regarding history, man, and reason, came to pervade a great deal of nineteenth-century thought.

In such an enterprise, it is important not to overemphasize the degree of unity which is to be found in the thought of a period. Every intellectual discipline has its own traditions, and in each generation the problems which appear to be most crucial will be likely to stand in some direct relation to that ongoing tradition. In addition, however, any period may be marked by some assumptions or modes of thought which are not confined within the limits of specific disciplines, but tend to spread through the intellectual life of the times. When these are important and relatively novel, and when they are not only pervasive but persist for an appreciable length of time, they may justify us in viewing them as definitive of a particular period, or age, in the history of thought. It is of course difficult to sort out these unifying strands without overlooking the diversity which variations in interests, traditions, vocations, and temperaments introduce into the thought of those who are taken to be representative of the period. Yet, in principle, both the unity and the diversity are there to be discovered, and I

know of no more suggestive way of referring to this fact than through a simile
suggested in a recent book dealing with the age of the Enlightenment:

> The Enlightenment as we can now envisage it is more like a language than a single
> idea, imposing by its very nature certain modes of thought on those who use it, while
> remaining always at the same time an expression, in any actual usage, of particular
> desires and meanings and a response to particular conditions.[1]

If this simile is accepted, it suggests that within the history of ideas there can
be methods which avoid postulating an overriding "spirit of the age" as an explanatory principle, but which may nonetheless lead to the discovery of a greater
degree of unity within a period than, say, the assumptions of A. O. Lovejoy
would lead one to expect there might be.[2] To be sure, such a simile can be used
to suggest a variety of different procedures for dealing with the unity and the
diversity which are present in an age. In this book—for better or for worse—I
have attempted to show how each of a group of otherwise divergent or opposed
thinkers held similar or almost identical beliefs and attitudes concerning the
issues with which I have sought to deal. Since the thought of the same person is
frequently relevant to a variety of issues, the reader will find that certain individuals reappear in several discussions, their thought being examined from
different points of view. While I have made no effort to deal with all aspects of
any individual's thought, I have tried to avoid the distortions which arise if one
merely picks out bits and pieces for illustrative purposes. How well I may have
succeeded, or wherein I have failed, only the reader will be in a position to say.

It should be pointed out, however, that I am here dealing with intellectual
history in a rather confining sense. Almost no mention is made of the major
political and social movements of the age, and of their effects on moral and
political theory. The fact that this is the case should not be taken as signifying
that I believe intellectual changes to be isolated from all other changes which
take place within a society. However, when one is not specifically dealing with
the history of normative political theory, it is perhaps true that sociological factors exert greater influence on the dissemination of philosophic and scientific
views than upon their original formulation and development.

There is, however, one area of intellectual history, the history of economic
thought, which would have been relevant to my task, but which I have had to
avoid because of a lack of competence. Had I invaded that field, or had I sought
to trace the history of legal and political theory, it is more than likely that I
would have had to deal with the social and political scene in a manner which
I have otherwise been able to eschew. Finally, it should be said that, in order to
limit the field of those with whom I have been concerned, I have in general
restricted myself to English, French, and German thought, with almost no
reference to the United States, and none to the rest of the Continent.

[1] Lionel Gossman, *Medievalism and the Ideologies of the Enlightenment*, p. viii.
[2] I have discussed some aspects of Professor Lovejoy's method in an essay entitled "The
History of Ideas, Intellectual History, and the History of Philosophy," in *History and
Theory*, Beiheft v (1964), 33–66.

Because I believe that the views regarding history and man and reason with which I have dealt are philosophically important, and raise pertinent problems for philosophy today, I offer critical discussions of some of these problems, in concluding Parts ii, iii, and iv.

This book was originally begun during the fall semester of the academic year 1953–54, when I was granted a sabbatical leave from Dartmouth College—for which I remain grateful. Much of Parts i and ii were originally drafted then and completed some time ago; had this not been the case, Part ii would have taken into account the parallel work of Robert A. Nisbet in his latest book, *Social Change and History* (1969). A recent research grant from The Johns Hopkins University has been of substantial aid in the final stages of preparing this book. However, my chief debt is to the Center for Advanced Study in the Behavioral Sciences, of which I was a Fellow in 1967–68, and which permitted me to return as a visitor in the summer of 1969. Without the time and the freedom provided by the Center, this book could not have been completed now or possibly at all.

M. M.

I

PHILOSOPHIC BACKGROUND

1

PHILOSOPHIC MOVEMENTS IN THE NINETEENTH CENTURY

1. INTRODUCTION

Until recently, it was almost universally taken for granted that the nineteenth century was a closed chapter in the history of thought. In many respects this is true. Its faith in the reality and inevitability of Progress has been shattered, its science has been transcended, many of its most widely shared social doctrines have been rendered obsolete, and its theological struggles have become museum-pieces. However, there has recently been a marked revival of interest in the intellectual history of the period, and a growing appreciation of its linkage with our own. For example, if one stops to inquire what specifically philosophic movements had the greatest impact upon general thought during the first half of the twentieth century, one cannot avoid naming pragmatism, positivism, and existentialism, and one is hard put to name any others which deserve to be placed alongside them.[1] In justice to nineteenth-century thought it must then be noted that all three of these movements had their origins and growth in that century, and the more recent forms which they assumed were but continuations of their nineteenth-century developments.[2] Similarly, if one inquires as to which contributions in the sciences had most impact upon the first decades of our century, one is again struck by the continuing pervasiveness of nineteenth-century thought. Scientific inquiry was generally regarded as having made its greatest contributions to a new *Weltanschauung* through having given the twentieth century a new understanding of human nature and of social processes. These ostensibly new doctrines were chiefly drawn from cultural anthropology, from Freudian psychology, and from Marxian social analysis. However, they were far less novel than they were thought to be. In fact, they were for the most part extensions and assimilations of doctrines and categories which dominated nineteenth-century thought through a good part of its history.

To be sure, nineteenth-century thought may only have been of controlling influence in the earlier decades of our century; it may be that our present intellectual life is controlled by new interests, new methods, and new assumptions.

3

Thus, a radical break with our recent past may be occurring or may have already occurred; I am inclined to believe that this is the case. However, to establish the existence of such a break, and to characterize it, we need a vantage point from which to see the continuity previously present. It is the ambitious task of this book to provide precisely such a point from which the intellectual history of our immediate past can best be viewed.

The period with which I shall deal may be said to extend beyond the chronological limits of the nineteenth century in both directions. On the one hand, to understand what was new in nineteenth-century thought it is necessary to attend to major intellectual developments which took place in the last decades of the eighteenth century. On the other hand, as I have suggested, dominant modes of nineteenth-century thought have persisted well into the present century, although I shall not in fact discuss their twentieth-century manifestations in any detail. It is my contention that during this period of some one hundred and fifty years there was a greater community of thought than is ordinarily suspected, and I would attribute that communality to the impact of two connected but logically independent discoveries. The first was "historicism," as I shall define that term. The second was a new conception of the relation between the nature of men and the conditions of their social existence, and that conception I shall designate as "the malleability of man." In addition to these ideas, and often in opposition to them, there developed increasing doubt as to the purity and efficacy of human reason. In its extreme forms this tendency manifested itself in a philosophic irrationalism, or rebellion against reason, which has had important repercussions in our own day. It is with each of these tendencies and with their interrelations that we shall be primarily concerned.

The original representatives of this period were extremely conscious of themselves as standing at the threshold of a new age. To cite merely one among many possible representative utterances, the introduction to Hegel's *Phenomenology of Mind*, published in 1807, contains the following passage:

> It is surely not difficult to see that our time is a time of birth and transition to a new period. The spirit has broken with what was hitherto the world of its existence and imagination, and is about to submerge all this in the past; it is at work giving itself a new form. To be sure, the spirit is never at rest but always engaged in ever progressing motion. But just as in the case of a child the first breath it draws after long silent nourishment terminates the gradualness of the merely quantitative progression—a qualitative leap—and now the child is born, so, too, the spirit that educates itself matures slowly and quietly toward the new form, dissolving one particle of the edifice of its previous world after the other, while its tottering is suggested only by some symptoms here and there; frivolity as well as the boredom that open up in the establishment and the indeterminate apprehension of something unknown are harbingers of a forthcoming change. This gradual crumbling which did not alter the physiognomy of the whole is interrupted by the break of day that, like lightning, all at once reveals the edifice of the new world.[3]

Such a sense of standing at a threshold, where a new era opens suddenly before one, is a fairly common phenomenon in social and intellectual history.

There can scarcely be any doubt that at the end of the eighteenth century in Germany and elsewhere there was a self-conscious rebellion against the standards and the forms of thought which had dominated the period of the Enlightenment. However, it is not always true that when convictions and practices which have been widely prevalent are abandoned, a distinctively new and equally dominant set will take their place. In fact, it is usually assumed that after the Enlightenment there was a fragmentation of thought, with no features common to those who rejected its standards. It is my contention, however, that this was not the case. As I shall show, there arose significantly new forms of thought and standards for evaluation in the post-Enlightenment period, and that these not only marked a radically new epoch in intellectual history but came to dominate almost all schools of European thought for something over one hundred years.

To hold that there was this degree of unity in the period with which we shall be concerned—or even to hold that there was a marked degree of continuity between the early half of the nineteenth century and the latter half of that century—is to put forward an unfamiliar thesis, and one which may appear to be patently false. As a preliminary step toward rendering this thesis somewhat more plausible I shall briefly consider the history of philosophy in the nineteenth century. In that connection I shall focus my attention on one fact that has too often been overlooked: that throughout the period there existed only two main streams of philosophic thought, each of which possessed a relatively high degree of continuity, and each of which tended to deal with similar problems, although from opposed points of view. These dominant and continuing movements in nineteenth-century philosophy were metaphysical idealism and positivism.[4]

To be sure, there were individual thinkers, such as Kierkegaard, who are not to be identified with either idealism or positivism. However, it is important to recall that Kierkegaard only began to exert an important influence on European thought at about the time of the first World War, through the early works of Jaspers and of Karl Barth. The case of Feuerbach and of Marx is somewhat different. As representatives of materialism, they stand opposed both to metaphysical idealism and to positivism, and would seem to constitute important exceptions to the view that these were the only dominant and pervasive traditions in nineteenth-century philosophy. Nonetheless, as we shall shortly see, materialism did not present an alternative option to most philosophers in the nineteenth century: the frequently repeated generalization that the latter part of the century is to be characterized as an age of materialism is simply false. This does not entail that Feuerbach and Marx were not in many ways typical of the period; it only signifies that it was not through their systematic philosophy, but through other aspects of their thought, that they were intimately connected with the major intellectual developments of their time.[5] And, like them, Kierkegaard can be taken as providing important insight into the general structure of the period with which we shall be concerned; not because he was representative of its chief philosophic movements, but because he so clearly rejected and combatted some of its basic presuppositions. At this point, however, I shall not deal with these more pervasive aspects of nineteenth-century thought; I wish to confine my attention to movements within the history of philosophy itself. In that history, as I have said, there were only two basic and continuing forms of philosophic commitment, idealism and positivism, and I shall start with a consideration of idealism.

2. METAPHYSICAL IDEALISM

When taken as referring to a form of metaphysical doctrine, "idealism" may be defined in a variety of ways, depending to some extent upon the context in which the definition is to be used. For the sake of offering a rather inclusive, non-technical characterization I would suggest the following: *metaphysical idealism holds that within natural human experience one can find the clue to an understanding of the ultimate nature of reality, and this clue is revealed through those traits which distinguish man as a spiritual being.* Implicit within this characterization is the fact that idealism, like every other traditional form of metaphysics, would regard it as both meaningful and important to speak of "the ultimate nature of reality," thus drawing a distinction between reality and appearance. In using the singular form, "the ultimate nature of reality," this characterization is also intended to suggest that idealists assume some form of oneness in the world, in contrast to doctrines which are ineradicably dualistic or pluralistic. That which is common to all things must of course be present in man; however, the foregoing characterization stresses the idealist contention that we come into closest contact with the nature of ultimate reality through entering most deeply into our own natures, rather than seeking reality in external and apparently alien aspects of the world. In attempting to discover that which is most ultimate, we need rely only upon natural human experience: according to the traditions of metaphysical idealism, we are not dependent upon a revelation to apprehend the truth. Thus, in sum, the metaphysics of idealism finds man's own spiritual nature to be the fullest expression of that which is to be taken as basic in reality.

According to this characterization, an idealist metaphysics would not only be opposed to materialism, but would be distinct from, and opposed to, a variety of other metaphysical systems, such as those of Aquinas or of Descartes. Thus, the above characterization, whatever its inadequacies, should help us to anticipate some of the more specific philosophic and religious convictions which are to be found in nineteenth-century thought. Further, it should help to clarify not only the similarities which exist among various forms of idealism, but the point at which their differentiating characteristics are to be expected. If the preceding characterization is taken as being substantially correct, the most important differences among idealist systems would lie in their conceptions of what constitutes the essential nature of man as a spiritual being, and how we are to apprehend that nature. Consequently, issues concerning metaphysical idealism would, in part at least, be separated from epistemological arguments concerning the independent existence and ultimate nature of material objects, with which they have too frequently become confused.

If we now turn from these generalities and examine the period with which we are to be concerned, it immediately becomes evident that the critical philosophy of Kant does not, in any particular, conform to the characterization of idealism which we have proposed.[6] And this is as it should be. This does not of course imply that the Kantian system did not influence—both positively and negatively —the development of the classic forms of German idealism. It does imply that the sources of that idealism are not to be found in Kant alone. To be sure, it is easy to trace the development of German idealism from Fichte through Schelling to Hegel in terms of technical problems within the Kantian system; these problems did of course have a decisive formative influence on the thought of all of Kant's immediate successors, idealists and non-idealists alike. However, the German idealist movement as it developed at the close of the eighteenth and the beginning of the nineteenth century cannot be adequately interpreted unless it is seen as part of a more general rebellion against the conceptions of man and of nature which characterized the Enlightenment. It was out of new convictions concerning the inner spiritual forces in the individual, in natural objects, and in cultures, and out of a conviction that there was a unity in all of these forces, that German idealism arose. The forms of argumentation within idealism may have originally been parasitic on the Kantian system, but it was not that system, and its difficulties, which can be said to have engendered what was new in this movement.

Once one acknowledges that the classic period of German idealism is not to be construed primarily as an attempt to resolve tensions within the critical philosophy of Kant, one can see that the idealist tradition in Germany did not end with the Hegelian system, and that Schopenhauer—in spite of his avowed relationship to Kant—is to be regarded as an important link in the continuing influence of idealism. To identify ultimate reality with the Will, and not with Reason, is not to give up metaphysical idealism with its distinction between appearance and reality, its emphasis upon the one all-embracing totality, and its faith that this reality is to be interpreted in terms of that which constitutes the inner, spiritual nature of man. For Schopenhauer, this inner nature was poles apart from what Hegel conceived it to be, but it would be a mistake to hold that an identification of man's spiritual nature with his reason (which is in fact Platonic rather than Hegelian), or with his historical and cultural achievements (which is closer to Hegel's own view), is a necessary attribute of idealism. Nor need idealism be pervaded by optimism. When these points are noted, it should be obvious that Schopenhauer stands squarely within the tradition of metaphysical idealism in a sense in which his master Kant did not.

It was not only in Schopenhauer that the tradition of metaphysical idealism persisted in Germany among those who rejected Hegel. To be sure, much of the intellectual life of the period turned away from all metaphysical issues; nonetheless, during the middle years of the century, two philosophers trained in the practice of the empirical sciences, Lotze and Fechner, formulated new and influential systems of metaphysical idealism.[7] It was their aim to provide a means by which idealism could do justice to the mechanical view of nature which other idealists, following Hegel, were ready to condemn. Meanwhile, Schopenhauer's influence continued to spread, and in 1869 Hartmann published his *Philosophy of the Unconscious*, which had an immediate and spectacular success.[8] This success was doubtless in part due to the very great influence of Schopenhauer (or to whatever in the times made voluntaristic pessimism congenial to a wide audience), but it should not be overlooked that Hartmann shared the concern of Lotze and of Fechner, endeavoring to find a means by which the concrete findings of science could be incorporated within the framework of an idealist metaphysics. The task of relating philosophy and the sciences to one another can in fact be said to have been the dominant task of German philosophy in the latter half of the century. As we shall see, the short-lived materialism of Büchner and others had this as its aim; so too did the far more widespread and influential semi-positivistic forms of Kantianism which grew up among Helmholtz and other scientists of the period. At this point it is only important to note that these movements did not in the least obliterate the traces of metaphysical idealism; because of the influence of Lotze in particular, that tradition maintained itself. For example, it is of interest to notice—as one can in the case of Wundt—that when the major scientific figures in Germany in the latter part of the century departed from Kantianism and from positivism, and sought to undergird their thought with metaphysical notions, it was to idealism and not to materialism or any form of metaphysical dualism that they turned.

If we now shift our attention from the German scene to those who represented academic philosophy in France and in England, we do not find that idealism flourished in the earlier decades of the century. In France, Eclecticism was entrenched, and in England the influence of the Scottish school and of Hamilton were especially marked. However, by mid-century—at precisely the time at which it is usually assumed that "scientism" was triumphing in philosophy—we find that, in both countries, metaphysical idealism was for the first time coming into its own. To be sure, the new idealist interests and systems did not wholly dominate the scene; in France the influence of positivism was strong, and in England John Stuart Mill was advocating Utilitarian moral and social philosophy and developing a form of critical positivism in his theory of knowledge. However, by mid-century one of the truly dominant forces in the philosophy of both France and England is to be found in the birth of a strong idealist tradition.

For example, in France, if we trace the course of the Eclectic School against which both the positivists and the new idealists reacted, we can see that it was tending away from its earlier reliance upon the Scottish philosophy toward an idealism which had strong affinities with Schelling.[9] The influence of Maine de Biran, which the Eclectics did much to promote, led French philosophers to be concerned with those problems of the self which eventuated in their characteristic personalistic idealism, emphasizing volitional activity and freedom. For example, it was the adoption of a volitional psychology that led Ravaisson, one of the seminal figures of the time, to reject monistic idealism and embrace spiritualistic personalism.[10] One can also note the extent to which he emphasized the importance of Leibniz' thought, and used Leibnizian doctrines in his evaluations of the thought of other philosophers. A similar tendency toward spiritualistic personalism is to be found in both Renouvier and Lachelier. Each of these philosophers started from a combination of Kantian epistemology and a fundamental concern for concrete human freedom; Renouvier ended his work at the turn of the century with an explicit metaphysics of pluralistic idealism which he himself was willing to term a monadology, and Lachelier's idealism, which contained a far-reaching critique of the ultimacy of causal explanations in our understanding of nature, prepared the ground for much that was to follow in French metaphysical thought.

To what extent the new pluralistic idealism in France was also influenced by the emphasis upon contingency found in Cournot's philosophy of nature and of method, I am not in a position to estimate.[11] However, the same theme of contingency is elaborately expounded by Lachelier's pupil Boutroux in connection with his defense of pluralistic idealism.[12] Within Boutroux's idealism, as he later developed it, there was also contained an interpretation of the nature of scientific thought which merged with developments which we shall trace within the history of positivism. This interpretation of science came to be characteristic of French thought at the turn of the century: it was basic to the thought of Poincaré (Boutroux's brother-in-law), of Milhaud (who was originally a Comtean), of the Catholic Pierre Duhem, and of Bergson. But it is not only important to note the widespread acceptance of this now familiar interpretation of science, it is also important to notice its compatibility with a full-fledged metaphysical idealism, and the affirmation of individual creativity and freedom which was one of the main themes of nineteenth-century French idealism.

We shall later have occasion to refer to Bergson's system in another context. Here it is only necessary to remark that with the advent of Bergson,[13] the course of French philosophy for a time became fixed, his influence augmenting through the first decades of this century. Thus, from the middle years of the nineteenth century well into this century, metaphysical idealism formed a continuing strand in French thought. Whether this idealism was most influenced by Schelling or by Leibniz, or whether indeed a compromise was sought between it and Catholic theism, it had a strong voluntaristic tone which submerged the last vestiges of Hegelianism and tended toward those personalistic forms of idealism which could place emphasis on human freedom.[14]

In England, there was also a continuing strand of metaphysical idealism. The influence of German metaphysical idealism on Coleridge and on Carlyle is well known, and James Martineau's influence, although less frequently noted, was also considerable.[15] When one recalls that it was in 1850 that Mill could regard Coleridge as one of the two recent thinkers (the other being Bentham) whose thought had left the greatest impress on the age, and that it was in 1865 that Stirling published his Secret of Hegel and in 1866 that Edward Caird took up his post in Glasgow, one can recognize that in spite of the dominance of the Utilitarians and the furors of Darwinism, idealism took root within British philosophy in the middle years of the nineteenth century. To be sure, the development of this idealism was slightly different from that which was characteristic of Germany and France, for in Britain, during the course of the century, idealism tended to move from the dominant influences of Kant and Schelling and Fichte toward Hegelianism, while in Germany and France the Hegelian philosophy was left almost wholly behind.[16] In spite of this historically conditioned difference, the aim and the upshot of the idealist movement was in all three cases the same: it constituted a reaction against the philosophy of positivism, asserting the claim that ultimate reality was accessible to man; however, it was claimed to be accessible only if man abandoned the equation of scientific knowledge with truth, looking inward rather than outward for the clues to that which lay behind the realm of nature with which science was destined to deal.

These remarks on German, French, and British philosophy should be sufficient to show to what extent idealism constituted one of the two major strands in nineteenth-century thought.[17] We shall now consider positivism.

3. POSITIVISM

It can be taken for granted that the systems of Comte and of Spencer were of very great importance in the history of nineteenth-century thought; yet if one were to define positivism with special reference to these systems, one would probably reach the conclusion that it was a much less widespread movement than metaphysical idealism had been. A similar conclusion would be forced upon one if positivism were defined solely with respect to the philosophy of science which, late in the century, came to be associated with thinkers such as Ernst Mach. However, there are many respects in which these two forms of positivism do in fact converge. While their programs were marked by sharp differences, the presuppositions which distinguished them from other philosophic positions were in large measure the same.

In order to characterize the positivist position in a manner that will include the systematic positivism of both Comte and Spencer, and will also include the forms of critical positivism represented by Huxley and by Mach, one may proceed as follows. First, positivism rejects metaphysics on the ground that the questions with which metaphysics is concerned presuppose a mistaken belief that we can discover principles of explanation or interpretation which are more ultimate than those which are directly derived from observation and from generalizations concerning observations. For positivists, any attempt to pass from the realm of "phenomena" to a more ultimate reality is a hopeless and unjustifiable enterprise, no matter how deeply rooted the urge to do so may be. However, various positivists have adopted differing positions with respect to the traditional philosophic distinction between the phenomenal and the noumenal. Some have believed it necessary to assume an unknowable reality lying outside of all possible experience; others have denied that there is any such sphere. Still others, with more consistency, have swept aside all discussion of the question since it cannot be formulated in terms which (even in principle) are verifiable within experience. Thus, in so far as its first basic thesis is concerned, positivism

can be seen to have connections with some traditional epistemological discussions: in some cases it has been closely related to a Kantian form of phenomenalism, in others to a philosophy of pure experience, and in still others to a
position which resembles that of Hume.

This first thesis, on the basis of which positivists reject metaphysics, does not
provide a sufficient characterization of what they affirm. What distinguishes
positivists from others who may accept a philosophy of pure experience, or who
accept some form of Kantian or Humean phenomenalism, is a second thesis: that
the adequacy of our knowledge increases as it approximates the forms of explanation which have been achieved by the most advanced sciences. At this point,
of course, other opponents of metaphysics frequently diverge from positivism.
However, to complete the characterization of positivism one further step must
be taken, and that is to note what constitutes an advanced science according to
positivism. Since positivism confines all human knowledge to what has been
experienced or can be experienced, it claims that a science which has freed itself
from metaphysical preconceptions will restrict itself to discovering reliable correlations within experience; it is on the basis of such observed and repeated
correlations that future events can be predicted, and it is on the same basis that
past events are explained. According to this view, a scientific explanation does
not involve appeal to any immanent forces nor to any transcendent entities: to
explain a phenomenon is to be able to subsume it under one or more laws of
which it is an instance. A law, in its turn, is simply a well-authenticated general
descriptive statement of uniformities which have been observed to occur in the
past. Any alternative interpretation of the nature and the aims of the sciences is
rejected by positivism as involving a mistaken metaphysical attempt to transcend
the limits of experience. To summarize, then, positivism may be said to be
characterized by three interlocking theses: first, a rejection of metaphysics; second, the contention that science constitutes the ideal form of knowledge; third,
a particular interpretation of the nature and the limits of scientific explanation.[18]

Taken in this sense, the positivist position was one which was widely espoused
in the nineteenth century. And it is worth noting that its interpretation of science
—which in 1865 Mill could quite properly regard as "the general property of the
age"[19]—even came to be absorbed into the idealist tradition. In tracing the history of the movement, as we shall now do, it will not be necessary to deal with it
in terms of national compartments; it will, however, be necessary to distinguish
between its two branches, which are to be termed the systematic and the critical
forms of positivism.

Systematic positivism, which in its first formulation is to be identified with
Comte, was a distinctively new movement in the history of thought. Other systems, to be sure, had rejected the belief that metaphysical questions were capable
of solution, and other systems had also hailed the discoveries of science as illus-
trating the manner in which truth was progressively being attained. However,
there was genuine novelty in the conception of philosophy which systematic
positivists avowed, and this novelty was recognized. One looks in vain for any
prior modern attempt to transform philosophy into a synthesis of the sciences.

For Comte, Spencer, and others of the school, the task of philosophy became "the organization into a harmonious Doctrine of all the highest generalities of Science";[20] its method was to examine the empirical results attained by all sciences, seeking out the most general laws in each, and bringing these laws together into an integrated pattern of knowledge which was more general than that attainable by any single science. To be sure, neither Comte nor Spencer was able to confine himself to discussions which conformed to this definition of the aim and the method of the new philosophy. However, this fact need not blind us to the originality which they claimed for themselves, and which many were willing to grant them. Whatever their inconsistencies, the conception of philosophy which they represented was a new conception, and they were convinced that the whole of the future belonged to it.[21]

The claim to have discovered a new method and a new aim for philosophy does not of itself explain the impact of systematic positivism on nineteenth-century thought. In addition there was, of course, the prestige which science possessed, and this prestige grew appreciably during the century. Moreover, the thought of both Comte and Spencer was dominated by the view that there had taken place, and was taking place, a progressive development of man and society. This conception, the history of which we shall trace, was deeply rooted in nineteenth-century thought; the fact that both Comte and Spencer placed extraordinary emphasis upon it, helped to ensure that their systems would attain widespread popular influence. If I am not mistaken, there is one further point which must be noted in order to account for the appeal of Comtean positivism in particular. In the eighteenth century it had been an important article of faith that intellectual enlightenment provided a basis through which societies might be transformed. This heritage of the Enlightenment was widely shared in England and in France during the nineteenth century, and was not the property of any one school of thought; however, no other philosophy of history made claims as bold as Comte's concerning the role which intellectual life played in organizing all aspects of society. To those who tended to link intellectual enlightenment and social reform, and who also placed the empirical sciences in the forefront of knowledge, the Comtean system had tremendous appeal. As a consequence, its spread in intellectual circles was out of all proportion to its acceptance and defense as a viable philosophic system.

In noting this connection between philosophy and social reform, one should not overlook the fact that, in general, nineteenth-century positivism was no less closely connected with moral and political issues than was the idealist movement. Looking back upon the nineteenth century in terms of those aspects of positivism which have had the most marked influence on our own thought, it is easy to underestimate the extent to which its theory of knowledge was linked with ideals of social change. However, it is not possible to study Comte's work at first hand without seeing that his *Cours de philosophie positive* is not an isolated treatise on the sciences, their methods and their classification, but is a part of a larger systematic whole the aim of which is moral and social. It must also be noted that a socially directed motivation was intimately connected with the systematic positivism of others, both in France and in England. In England, for example, one finds this motivation in Spencer, and in such lesser representatives of the movement as Lewes and Harrison. It is also worth reminding ourselves that in an account of his reasons for writing his *System of Logic*, Mill laid stress on his hope that it would be of use in combatting false and injurious social doctrines.[22]

Although the systematic form of positivism was frequently accepted at its own evaluation of itself, many philosophers and scientists who themselves shared the basic presuppositions of positivism subjected it to severe criticism. The primary objections were directed against the attempts of Comte and Spencer to provide a rigid codification of the results of the sciences. In the light of the new discoveries which were being made in physics, chemistry, experimental biology, and psychophysics, the attempts of the systematic positivists to find a single all-inclusive system in which all empirical discoveries would fit seemed less and less plausible. Thus, although the views of Comte and of Spencer continued to exert a considerable influence throughout the nineteenth century, particularly in sociology, they did not attract important new adherents from the ranks of scientists or scientifically oriented philosophers.

However, this did not mean that the general movement of positivist thought failed to spread. On the contrary, even as systematic positivism spent its force, there was a remarkable growth in the acceptance of positivist theses regarding the nature of scientific method and an increasing stringency in the interpretation of these theses.[23] On the part of scientists, this tendency was not always connected with a general philosophic position; it sometimes remained a methodological principle only. However, among philosophers and among many philosophically inclined scientists, it did develop into an important philosophic movement which is to be designated as critical positivism. The aims of critical positivism were twofold: on the one hand to analyze the foundations of scientific knowledge, on the other to examine the true sources and meanings of all concepts which tended to be used in an uncritical, metaphysically charged manner, whether those concepts were employed by laymen or by scientists.

This new mode of positivistic thought had an earlier major exponent in John Stuart Mill. In addition to his psychological interest in analyzing the sources of our knowledge in experience and in the association of ideas, Mill was intent upon bringing to the test any unjustifiable common-sense moral or social or metaphysical doctrine. Unlike later critical positivists, he saw no special need to analyze the sources of specifically scientific concepts; he took such concepts to be adequately grounded in experience and adequately justified by the universality of the testimony which experience yielded. Unlike Kant and Hume, Mill did not stress the limitations of science, and it was perhaps for this reason that he was not looked upon by later critical positivists as being a major forerunner of their views. It was, rather, to Kant and to Hume that they tended to trace their lineage.

What led to the new interpretation of science was, I believe, a combination of factors, each of which deserves attention; I shall therefore deal with the history of critical positivism in some detail. The factors which I regard as having been of primary importance in its development were three. First, there arose among practicing scientists a conviction that their investigations needed to be liberated from preconceptions which were metaphysical either in origin or import. They held that so long as their colleagues were interested in upholding or in combatting particular metaphysical positions, scientific inquiry could not be free; nor would it be free so long as there was an uncritical acceptance of concepts to which there clung associations derived from earlier, metaphysical forms of thought. Thus, a positivist interpretation of science was brought forward by scientists themselves in the interest of advancing scientific inquiry. A second source of critical positivism was the rise of interest in what may broadly be termed the psychophysical problem, which was occupying some of the foremost physiologists and physicists of the day. These investigations led many to hold that a positivistic phenomenalism was the only epistemological position in accord with the methods and results of the sciences. Third, there arose in connection with the development of evolutionary theory what may be called a pragmatic interpretation of the human mind, and that interpretation was then applied to scientific thought itself. To illustrate these three factors I shall briefly consider some important, representative figures who contributed to the growth of critical positivism among scientists in the latter half of the nineteenth century.

With respect to the first of these factors let us consider Rankine and Robert Mayer, who were not themselves positivists, but represent those scientists who felt it necessary to adopt a methodological positivism in order to free science from constrictions placed upon it by preceding modes of thought. In their attempts to liberate observation and generalization from the influence of hypothetical, mechanical constructs, their influence lay on the side of a growingly positivistic interpretation of the sciences. Rankine stated his position with respect to a contrast between two types of procedure:

According to the ABSTRACTIVE method, a class of objects or phenomena is defined by describing, or otherwise making to be understood, and assigning a name or symbol to, that assemblage of properties which is common to all the objects or phenomena composing the class, as perceived by the senses, without introducing anything hypothetical. According to the HYPOTHETICAL method, a class of objects or phenomena is defined, according to a conjectural conception of their nature, as being constituted, in a manner not apparent to the senses, by a modification of some other class of objects or phenomena whose laws are already known.[24]

To be sure, Rankine did not wholly reject the hypothetical method, as a positivist would have done; and, as Clerk Maxwell pointed out, he did not abandon a realistic interpretation of science, as contrasted with the phenomenalistic positions adopted by critical positivists.[25] In these respects Mayer's views were similar to those of Rankine.[26] Nevertheless, the insistence of both on liberating empirical inquiry from constrictions placed upon it by hypothetical constructs had an important influence on the development of positivism among later figures in the history of thermodynamics, where positivism had one of its chief centers.[27]

Turning now to a scientist who went beyond Rankine and Mayer, using a full-fledged positivism in defending his objectives and methods of work, we may cite the case of Claude Bernard. In his *Introduction à l'étude de la médecine ex-*

périmentale, published in 1865, Bernard set out to argue that the experimental method applies to living beings no less than to inorganic things, and that determinism characterizes all phenomena associated with life. To support this position it was necessary to discredit vitalism, which constituted the chief opposition to his view. The form in which he cast his attack was to argue that only a critical positivism was consonant with the methods to be followed in scientific inquiry; and this of course precluded in principle all possibility of appealing to vital forces as a means of explaining the functioning of living things. Such an identification of a particular interpretation of science with the possibility of pursuing free and original scientific inquiry, unhampered by past prejudices, was an extremely effective argument at the time. It was on the basis of it, rather than on the basis of philosophical argument, that many scientists, including Bernard, came to accept a critical positivism.[28]

Thomas Henry Huxley presents a second example of the same tendency. While it was undoubtedly true that Huxley drew much from Hume and from Berkeley, and a good deal from Kant (as he interpreted him), it was not primarily on the basis of philosophic considerations that he either put forward or defended a positivistic position. Running throughout his essays one finds emphasis on the lessons which are to be learned from science. The primary lesson was the necessity for acknowledging limitations in human knowledge; a second lesson was the fact that if men scrupulously adhere to the discipline which the practice of science is able to instill, they are capable of pushing back the boundaries of ignorance. Thus, science trains us to recognize what we can and cannot know; its training serves to teach us the necessary rudiments of epistemology. This aspect of Huxley's thought represents a very widespread tendency to interpret critical positivism as the natural outgrowth of accepting and using the methods of scientific inquiry. For those who adopted this view, philosophy was not to be regarded as a means by which the competence or the implications of science could be assessed; on the contrary, science was itself capable of showing the range of problems which men can solve. However, science could exercise this function only so long as it remained free of metaphysical assumptions, and of the vestiges of those assumptions which lay concealed in earlier modes of scientific thought. Thus, the scientists of the period stressed the need for methodological purity, that is, for remaining within the boundaries of those forms of explanation which positivism held to be the only forms which it was legitimate for scientists to use.[29]

I turn now to the second factor which was important to the rise of critical positivism: the development of psychophysics. To be sure, psychophysics does not in itself demand the adoption of any form of positivism; however, at the time, it was widely held to have important implications with respect to the boundaries of human knowledge, and implications for the interpretation of science itself. As an example of a scientist for whom critical positivism was linked to a concern with psychophysics, Helmholtz is especially noteworthy; his own vast contribution to the development of the subject, and his stature as a scientist, made his position particularly significant in Germany. We shall later examine his views in more detail; here it is only necessary to suggest their general import.

Unlike the other philosophically inclined scientists with whom we have just been dealing, Helmholtz did not regard critical positivism as being merely an extension of the method and habits of thought followed by scientists who had freed themselves from a metaphysical heritage; for him, it was a specifically philosophic position which he took to be affiliated to the position of Kant.[30] However, one can scarcely imagine a version of Kantianism more antithetical to the presuppositions of Kant's own thought, for the universal and necessary forms of experience were interpreted by Helmholtz as consequences of the nature of our sensing organs. Thus, his form of phenomenalism rested directly upon the limits of the human organism, not on apriori categories of the mind. Helmholtz developed this supposedly Kantian rejection of metaphysics in an early lecture, on the occasion of his receiving his professorship at Konigsberg. In that lecture he offered an interpretation of experience in which sensations are construed as symbols for unknown relationships; according to him, the specific nature of what we experience is not to be identified with anything existing independently of us any more than the written name of a man is to be identified with that man himself.[31] However, the fact that we can note an orderly connection among our sensations gives us the possibility of knowledge, which is the discovery of patterns of relationship among sensory elements. As Helmholtz recognized, this view of human knowledge ruled out all traditional metaphysical questions, including all philosophic issues concerning epistemological realism and idealism.[32] Thus, as his student Heinrich Hertz later pointed out, Helmholtz assumed that psychophysics was able to establish an epistemological position.[33] This position, which was Helmholtz's version of Kant's Copernican revolution, had a considerable influence throughout the latter part of the century. As we shall later see, it was basic to the claims of DuBois-Reymond regarding the necessary limitations of knowledge; and Lange's influential *History of Materialism*, which was published in 1865, represents a similar physiologically oriented Kantianism. By the mid-seventies an acceptance of this type of position was said by Wundt to have almost been taken for granted in the German scientific community.[34]

The factors which I have already discussed were sufficient to establish a very solid base for critical positivism, but its widespread extension was associated with still another movement in late nineteenth-century thought: this was a new interpretation of science which grew out of a pragmatic, or economical, view of the human mind. According to this view, we have a tendency to order our experience in whatever ways serve to make it most assimilable to our needs, interests, and expectations. To appreciate the radical transformation which this assumption introduced into the interpretation of science, one need only recall the positivism of Bernard or of Helmholtz. For both, there was determinism in nature, and the order of our experience depended upon that determinism. Thus, although we could not know things-in-themselves, it was assumed that the relationships which we found within experience were not attributable to us, but to nature itself. This, for them, was the basis on which the very possibility of science was founded, and they did not inquire on what grounds they, as positivists, had a right to make such an assumption.[35] On a pragmatic-economical view of the human mind, however, even the order which science establishes in experience, and which we are inclined to look upon as an order fixed by nature itself, may be a product of our own tendencies to arrange and summarize experience in a manner useful to us. This conception of the human mind, and its implications for an interpretation of science was presumably accepted by Mach and by others as early as the 1860s, but it was not until the 1880s that one finds the first high water mark of its development.[36] The chief factors which contributed to that development were three.

In the first place, the Darwinian theory of evolution was interpreted as having proved that all aspects of living creatures must have an adaptive function in the struggle for survival.[37] As we see in Darwin himself, this assumption was applied to the evolutionary development of human impulses and human intelligence, no less than to the evolutionary development of bodily structures. Having interpreted the development of man's intelligence in terms of its usefulness in satisfying needs, it was but a small step to the further claim that science itself was to be regarded as a form of adaptation. This connection between Darwin's theory and an acceptance of a pragmatic-economical interpretation of science, as well as of all other knowledge, can be seen in one of the first essays in which Mach offered a systematic statement of the latter view; and in Laas, among others, there is an equally strong emphasis on the ways in which the ordering of experience into a system of knowledge reflects life-serving needs.[38] It should be obvious that this conception of science helped to extend the arguments previously advanced by critical positivists, for its acceptance entailed that even science could not be assumed to have access to relationships existing outside of the domain of experience.

There was a second factor which influenced the development of a pragmatic-economical interpretation of science, adding its weight to evolutionary interpretations of mind. This factor is to be found in the type of analysis of experience which dominated the psychological theories of the period, for example, the views of the associationists, of Helmholtz, and to some extent the earlier views of Wundt. In line with the heritage of traditional British empiricism, it was assumed by associationists and by Helmholtz that all of our everyday concepts, such as our concepts of ordinary material objects, develop on the basis of a series of simple, recurring sensations, some of which ordinarily recur in groups. Past recurrences create tacit expectations regarding future sensations, and when apparently stable groupings are formed we fix them by giving them a name. The fullest application of this general view, extending it to the differentiation between objects and the self, is, of course, to be found in the philosophy of pure experience of Avenarius, but it had also been developed in Mach's influential *Contributions to the Analysis of Sensations* of 1886. The phenomenalistic implications of this type of analysis of perception were not of course new: they had been wholly apparent to Hume and to John Stuart Mill, to name only two. And in Hume, at least, there is recognition of a connection between this analysis and a conception of the human mind which (so long as we leave abstract reason out of account) closely resembles what came to be the pragmatic-economical view. However, it was not central to Hume's concerns to trace the implications of his views of experience for the procedures which should be followed—or should be avoided—by scientists, although there are passages in which he did discuss that issue. In the case of Mach, however, it was precisely here that his major interest lay. One of his aims—which was in line with the whole development of positivism, both systematic and critical—was to purge the sciences of all concepts in which traces of metaphysical assumptions could be found. Another was to show that it was theoretically legitimate to pass back and forth among the data of physics, physiology, and psychology in exactly the ways that Mach's own research, and the research of others, had shown that it was feasible to do. Mach was able to achieve both of these aims by emphasizing the view of the human mind which had, in general, only been implicit in earlier, traditional empiricist analyses of perception: he made that view explicit, and applied it with rigor to the manner in which science itself proceeds. Just as perceptible objects are, in the last analysis, merely the sensory elements which we find often appearing together and to which we attach a name, so scientific concepts, properly conceived, only represent bundles of the elements of experience. This view allowed Mach to argue that concepts such as "force" and "atoms" had no proper place within science; it also permitted him to hold that different sciences are distinguished from one another solely with respect to the manner in which they find it useful to group the elements of experience. According to these assumptions, science is confined to ordering the flow of experiences according to whatever patterns permit us to predict future experiences.[39] This interpretation of science, which was wholly consonant with the dominant psychology of the day, made the pragmatic implications of evolutionary theory all the more plausible, and thus assisted the spread of critical positivism among the large number of scientists who were already predisposed to accept some form of a positivistic view.

This self-criticism and self-limitation on the part of scientists was soon to have consequences unfavorable to the general aims of positivism, for it opened the way to a reintroduction of metaphysics. Those who had previously been attacked by positivists for pursuing metaphysical questions were in a position to point out that scientists themselves no longer interpreted science as a presuppositionless system of knowledge, but as a function of our own practical need to organize experience in some readily manageable form. Thus, the pragmatic-economical interpretation of science deprived positivists of the possibility of offering any objective reasons for their belief that scientific procedures should serve as a model for philosophy or, indeed, as a model for any other form of thought. It was precisely at this point that a strong reaction against positivism, and against other forms of "scientism," set in. However, before sketching the forms which that reaction took, it will be necessary to cite a third factor which helped to show that science was relative to the presuppositions with which it operated, thus undermining the earlier positivist view that science offered an all-inclusive and necessary way of organizing experience. This extension of a pragmatical-economic interpretation arose out of the heavy emphasis newly placed on the roles of hypothesis and theory-construction in scientific method.

Until almost the very end of the century, those philosophers and scientists who subscribed to positivism tended to interpret all forms of scientific theory in terms of generalizations drawn directly from repeated observations. While not all shared Mill's view that inductive inference must proceed from particular to particular, they did tend to regard repeated observations as the source from which any hypothesis useful to the sciences could be derived. However, after the middle of the century, developments in both geometry and physics began to undermine this emphasis on observation, and began to pose very grave problems for those who accepted a strictly positivist view of the sources of scientific knowledge in sense experience. For example, these developments seemed to be wholly at odds with the empiricist interpretations of mathematics given by Mill and by Helmholtz;[40] they also seemed to be at odds with Mach's view, according to which all so-called axioms are the products of instinctive psychological functions which have operated uniformly in the past and have thereby become firmly rooted in our experience.[41] While Mach attempted in *Erkenntnis und Irrtum*, and in other later writings, to defend his epistemological views against all difficulties which had arisen in connection with new, non-observational developments within the sciences, it was not generally conceded that he had been successful in that attempt. Views such as those espoused by Poincaré at the turn of the century became highly influential, and what was then emphasized was not the role of experience in science, but the creative, constructive aspects of scientific imagination in the formulation of hypotheses and of intellectual models.

The philosophic upshot of the new emphasis on constructive imagination which one finds in Hertz and in Poincaré, among others, was not in all respects different from Mach's own view of the general relations between science and experience. Although the assumptions of the two schools concerning the nature of the mind were extremely different, both in fact held that the role of the mind in scientific theorizing was that of selectively ordering experiences in such a way that further experiences could be predicted. Neither held it to be within the scope of science (nor within the power of man) to say that one set of constructs more nearly approximated the characteristics of nature than did another: the test of the adequacy of a scientific theory lay wholly within the results which could be obtained by ordering past and future experiences in terms of that theory. The upshot of such a pragmatic-economical interpretation of science buttressed the view that the human mind, so long as it followed the path of scientific inquiry, could not pretend to a knowledge of the ultimate nature of reality; that, on the contrary, it was only an instrument which selectively ordered its experience according to its own interest in simplicity, coherence, and predictability.

It is precisely at this point that the critical positivist movement became able to meet and merge with the idealist movement. To be sure there were persons in the positivist tradition who remained wholly committed to the general theses of positivism and who, after accepting a pragmatic-economical interpretation of science, refused to acknowledge the legitimacy of attempting to transcend science. But there were others who, at the turn of the century, were equally willing to make this attempt. Some among them sought to reestablish a metaphysics, now that science had not only been shown to be neutral on all metaphysical issues, but had, through its self-criticism, been shown to be necessarily confined to a world of appearances. Among those who followed this path, Bergson was the most influential. However, it was far more frequent to find that once this self-criticism was accepted, philosophers sought to show that since science was limited in its methods, and therefore in the results which it was able to attain, other methods had an equally valid claim to consideration. Thus, in James the pragmatic-economical interpretation of science was closely connected with his willingness to accept forms of pragmatic justification which lay wholly outside of what was traditionally viewed as knowledge. Even more frequently, however, attempts were made to distinguish the method of the natural sciences from other methods of knowledge which had an equal right to be considered as fundamental forms of human understanding. This position did not stem primarily from the pragmatic-economical interpretation of science, but it was able to converge with it. In its origins, it stemmed chiefly from the Neo-Kantian revival and from the growth of interest in humanistic historical studies. These studies, it seemed, demanded a theoretical justification which would show them to be of an equal importance with science. The beginnings of this movement can perhaps be traced as far back as Zeller, in whom we find both the attempt to revive Kant and the attempt to do justice to the place of historical studies in the economy of learning;[42] certainly we find the latter motive strongly represented as early as 1883 in Dilthey's *Einleitung in die Geisteswissenschaften*. However, it was not until almost the turn of the century that the movement reached its height.[43] From then until our own time it has not been unusual to find science interpreted as one of two distinct and equally legitimate means of ordering experiences, although we may here note that the differences between these forms of knowledge have not always been fixed with the precision which one might think was demanded by the importance of the question.

Thus, at the end of the nineteenth century, positivism had turned into a self-criticism of science, largely at the hands of practicing scientists, and the earlier systematic form of positivism had to all intents and purposes lost its hold upon the major streams of thought. What had once seemed to be the philosophic import of the physical sciences no longer carried the same conviction, and the way was open for twentieth-century philosophy to interpret these results in the most diverse fashions, the chief of which were that of setting up other modes of knowing side-by-side with science, or that of restricting the import of science in order to leave room for faith.[44]

4. MATERIALISM

In the two preceding sections we have been at pains to trace the development of the dominant strands in nineteenth-century philosophy. In these discussions of metaphysical idealism and of positivism little mention was made of the doctrine of materialism. However, because it is so frequently claimed that the nineteenth century was a period in which the dominant modes of thought were oriented toward materialism, it will now be necessary to examine the materialist movement. Before attempting to analyze its nature and fix the range and the time-span of its influence, let us first be clear as to some of the causes which have led to the misconception that materialism represents the fullest expression of the dominant modes of thought in the nineteenth century.

There are doubtless many such causes, but one of them is surely the fact that during the nineteenth century there was a tremendous growth in material goods and an enthusiasm for material progress. Since the word "materialism" is sometimes used to connote a concern for material goods as well as being used to designate a particular metaphysical position, and since it has often been believed that the latter position must lead to the former, the two distinct meanings of "materialism" have tended to coalesce. However, there is no necessary relation between these two meanings. Furthermore, if the term "materialism" is to be used to connote an overweening concern for material goods to the exclusion of what might be designated as "moral idealism," then the nineteenth century cannot by any stretch of the imagination be called a materialistic age: it was characteristic of all schools of thought in the nineteenth century—and characteristic of the materialists no less than of the positivists and metaphysical idealists—that they were imbued with "moral idealism." Each school in fact sought to show that its philosophic doctrines were the only sure foundation for moral progress.

It is not with "materialism" in this loose sense of the term that we are to be concerned. "Materialism" has also been said to have characterized the nineteenth century for a specifically philosophic reason: during that century orthodox Christian theism was not held in high repute by a majority of the most influential thinkers. Yet this provides no adequate reason for characterizing the period as an age of materialism. In fact, many nineteenth-century idealists explicitly rejected a theistic position. In general, it was only among those who reacted against Hegelianism that theism came to be included as part of the idealistic position, and even among them this theism was frequently unorthodox. Thus, it is obvious that a rejection of the traditional Christian theist position is by no means equivalent to materialism.

A third, and better, reason for considering the nineteenth century to have been an age of philosophic materialism lies in the fact that during that period there was an increasing number of persons who challenged the traditional dualistic view of the mind-body relationship. As Mill noted in one of his letters,[45] the conventional definition of materialism which was current equated the materialist doctrine with the doctrine that all mental impressions resulted from the activities of the bodily organs. Such a definition of materialism is still sometimes held. However, those who acknowledge the dependence of all mental processes on bodily states need not be materialists, as the examples of Lotze and of other idealists clearly show.[46] And Huxley, too, took such a position, asserting that an acceptance of what he called automatism, and which might have been termed epiphenomenalism, did not entail materialism, and indeed had no specific metaphysical implications.[47] Whether so extreme a position is or is not justified, it is best to avoid using this psychophysiological thesis as a means of defining materialism as a philosophic position. Instead, I shall propose a definition which can serve to make clear exactly where materialism differs from both idealism and positivism.

Unlike positivism, materialism is itself a metaphysical position. Materialists, like idealists, seek to state what constitutes the ultimate nature of reality, and are willing to distinguish between "appearance" and that which is self-existent and underlies appearance. Taken in its broadest sense, materialism is only committed to holding that the nature of that which is self-existent is material in character, there being no entities which exist independently of matter. Thus, in this sense, we would class as a materialist anyone who accepts all of the following propositions: that there is an independently existing world; that human beings, like all other objects, are material entities; that the human mind does not exist as an entity distinct from the human body; and that there is no God (nor any other non-human being) whose mode of existence is not that of material entities.

While this type of characterization of materialism is one which would be very generally accepted, there is a stricter and more precise sense in which that term may be used. In the stricter sense materialists not only deny that there are entities which are not material; they also hold that whatever properties or forms of behavior particular material objects exhibit are ultimately explicable by means of general laws which apply equally to all of the manifestations of matter. It should be obvious that this stricter definition of materialism excludes most forms of a naturalistic metaphysics which accept the doctrine of emergence. For example, what is generally termed "emergent naturalism" would hold that while all entities are material in character, the varying forms of organization which matter may possess give rise to diverse properties and diverse modes of behavior, neither of which can be adequately explained, even in principle, by an appeal to any single set of laws.[48] Strict materialists, on the other hand, put forward the claim that if one had a knowledge of the relevant conditions concerning their forms of organization, all of the diverse forms of organized matter would be explicable in terms of one set of basic laws. Thus, a strict materialism is a reductionist philosophy in a two-fold sense: it not only claims that all entities, however immaterial they may appear to be, have a material basis by means of which they are to be explained, but it also claims that whatever properties these entities reveal are explicable in an identical set of terms, regardless of their apparent disparities. To be sure, even the strictest materialist need not claim, and presumably will not claim, that at any one date the physical sciences have accurately and fully understood the properties of matter. For example, he need not hold (and today could not hold) that the atomism of Boyle and of Newton provided an ultimate explanation of all entities. However, the second element in his reductionism does demand a commitment to the view that there should be one all-embracing and basic science of nature which would, in principle, be capable of explaining all aspects of the behavior of material entities by means of a single basic set of properties, regardless of how these entities are organized. In *traditional* materialist systems, the relevant set of basic properties has usually been identified with the properties which it is the goal of physics to discover, and physical laws (or physical-chemical laws) have been regarded as the basic laws of matter; however, in *dialectical* materialism it is not physics but the method of dialectical explanation itself which is held to serve as a basis for interpreting all manifestations of matter. Thus, dialectical materialism is not wholly reductionistic (in one usual sense of that term), since a full-fledged doctrine of emergence is compatible with it. However, dialectical materialism does go beyond what one usually identifies with the position of emergent naturalism, since it holds that one fundamental set of laws (though these are not identified with the specific laws of physics) is regarded as providing the basic explanation of change at every level of existence.

These distinctions will help to clarify the extent to which there may be said to have been widespread acceptance of materialism in the nineteenth century. If one were to identify materialism with a rejection of mind-body dualism, then materialism was indeed not uncommon: many philosophers and philosophically oriented scientists gave up all attempts to support the view that the human mind was an entity, and that it could function independently of the human nervous system. The positions which were most often adopted with respect to this problem were either a neutral monism or a psycho-physical parallelism, both of which were compatible with positivism, and each of which could also be interpreted as compatible with idealism, as is proved by the examples of Clifford and Wundt. However, if "materialism" is construed in a more usual sense, and is taken as a position which is an alternative to idealism and to other forms of metaphysics on the one hand and to positivism on the other, then there were relatively few materialists in the nineteenth century. One looks in vain for any in France after Saint-Simon, and in England Tyndall stands out as an almost unique example.[49] Only in Germany does one find that materialism represented an important philosophic position.

The reason why this fact has so often been overlooked is that commentators have too frequently accepted the views of those opponents of positivism who refused to acknowledge that there was any difference between positivism and materialism. In the light of the repeated, explicit disavowals of materialism on the part of Comte and Spencer, and on the part of Bernard, Huxley, and Mach, among others, one might wonder how any such confusion was possible.[50] The answer lies in the fact that positivism and materialism had two elements in common: both were opposed to all traditional theologies, and (except for Feuerbach) both held that the sciences represented the most reliable knowledge attainable. It was on the basis of these similarities that those who opposed what was later to be called "scientism" felt justified in identifying positivism with materialism, helping to give currency to the myth that materialism dominated philosophy in the nineteenth century.

Another source of an overemphasis on the scope of philosophic materialism in the nineteenth century lies in a failure to perceive the very marked differences between two originally distinct philosophic movements which existed in Germany. On the one hand, there was a significant materialist controversy which originally centered in the problem of vitalism, erupting in the early 1850s, and giving rise to a series of semi-popular expositions of materialism over a period of some twenty or twenty-five years. On the other hand, there already existed a position which identified itself with materialism, but which had in large measure arisen as a reaction against Hegelian idealism on the part of Feuerbach. In its original form, this position had little to do with most of the metaphysical issues which had always been central to materialism. Thus, in Germany during the period with which we are here concerned, there were two forms of materialism which must be taken into account. Their aims and even their conceptions of philosophy were so disparate that they might never have become related had it not been for the polemical writings of Engels. Since these writings served to interlace the two movements, it will be useful to view nineteenth-century materialism from the perspective afforded by Marxism.[51] However, it should not be forgotten that the two movements were distinct; nor should one overlook the fact that it would be anachronistic to attribute to Marxism in the nineteenth century a philosophic influence comparable to that which it has had in the twentieth.

To understand even the definition of the concept "materialism" which is given by both Marx and Engels, and to understand aspects of their epistemology and of their views of man, one must go back to Feuerbach. The manner in which Feuerbach expressed what he found most objectionable in Hegel was the relation which the latter conceived to exist between thought and being. As Feuerbach never tired of emphasizing, existence precedes thought, and thought arises out of the problems posed by existence. This conviction, which was shared by Marx and by Engels, constituted the primary positive thesis which linked their thought to his. From this it followed that the thought with which they were concerned was the concrete thought of existing individuals, not thought in the abstract, and not thought removed from the problems of existing individuals. That from which they started was, then, the concrete, living, breathing human being, whose thought arises in the course of his struggles with nature, and in his relationships with his fellows. To adopt this starting point, to view thought as arising out of the problems of an organic being's existence, was for them equivalent to being a materialist. This equivalence could, of course, only be maintained so long as they rejected a dualistic view of man's nature, and held that as a part of nature man was in essence a material being whose capacity for thought and for action was a function of the nature of his bodily organs. On this point all three insisted.[52] However, this does not constitute their definition of materialism. Throughout, they define materialism in terms of their opposition to Hegel's system, that is, in terms of the relations between thought and existence.

Now, taken strictly, this is not, as we have seen, an adequate characterization of materialism. In fact, unless one interprets materialism in a very loose sense, Feuerbach cannot be classified as a materialist at all. While he did explicitly reject both idealism and theism, and while he insisted upon the organic basis of thought, his own interpretation of the relation between thought and existence was such as to make him regard all genuine philosophy as being "anthropological" in character, and not metaphysical. The problems of philosophy were for him solely the problems of the nature of man, and these problems were not to be solved by any attempt to push knowledge beyond that knowledge which we can reach through our own specifically human experience.

However one may interpret Marx's own thought, it is clear that Engels goes beyond Feuerbach's starting point and develops a materialistic system of meta-physics. What divides his Marxism from Feuerbach's views was not only the fact that he and Marx developed a sociological interpretation of man's nature, that they rejected Feuerbach's ethics of love, and that they had a hostility to religious modes of thought; more important was the fact that Engels constantly looked to the sciences for a knowledge of nature, and placed emphasis on the need for an understanding of nature in general if we are to attain an understanding of the nature of man. Genuine philosophy was not therefore to be confined to the self-knowledge of man through his personal and historical experience, but was to yield an all-embracing knowledge of existence. For both Marx and Engels the tools for such knowledge were to be found in the empirical sciences: to under-stand himself man could not merely reflect upon his experience, but was forced to employ categories of science. These categories, they claimed, were dialectical categories. Thus Engels held that the materials out of which a comprehensive philosophy could arise were being provided, and would continue to be provided, by the sciences. The tools with which these materials were to be worked into a philosophic system were simply the tools of formal and dialectical logic.

It is at this point that the thought of Engels made contact with that other form of materialism to which we have already alluded: the materialism of Moleschott, Vogt, and Büchner which arose in the early 1850s, and which represented a traditional form of materialism in which all processes were to be explained in terms of physical laws.[53] The position of Engels approached that of these "itinerant preachers of materialism" only with respect to the fact that both claimed to rest their materialistic positions upon science; they diverged in their views of the methods and the conclusions of the sciences. With respect to these conclusions, Engels repeatedly insisted that the most fundamental new discoveries of science—the principle of the transformation of energy, the cell structure of living matter, and the theory of evolution—rendered obsolete a view of nature based upon the science of mechanics. He therefore regarded the materialism of Moleschott, Vogt, and Büchner as residual examples of an eighteenth-century mechanicalism which could not be squared with these new developments. How-ever, the real basis of his charge does not lie in the conflict between an up-to-date and an outmoded knowledge of science, as Engels would have one believe, but in a difference between the two schools with respect to their views of the goal of scientific explanation, and therefore with respect to their views regarding the methods which it was appropriate for science to follow.

Insofar as Marx and Engels viewed all of reality as a developing process, the goal of scientific understanding was for them the elucidation of the place of any phenomenon within this process, that is, the ability to show how it was related to other phenomena out of which it arose, and how it was related to those phe-nomena to which it in turn would give rise. The method of science was therefore conceived as a method in which the concrete and total nature of one type of entity was understood with reference to its relations to the concrete and total nature of other types of entity with which it was developmentally connected. In Moleschott, Vogt, and Büchner, on the other hand, what might be denominated as the classic method of scientific explanation was assumed to be the proper method for science to follow: a scientific explanation consisted in analyzing the concrete events to be explained into a set of specific characteristics, attempting to establish constant relationships among various of these characteristics, and from these relationships deducing by ordinary logic what consequences would follow in any given case. Explanations of this type involve a piecemeal consideration of concrete entities, abstracting specific characteristics from the contexts in which they are embedded and examining them one by one. It also involves disregarding the temporal context in which such entities appear, on the assumption that what holds good of an entity at one particular time will hold good of it, or of any similar entity, at any time. Having tacitly accepted this model of scientific explanation, the non-Marxist materialists then proceeded to generalize on the basis of the results which had been (or which presumably would be) established by science. Their generalizations led to their specifically philosophic view that the total system of nature was one whole in which the place and function of each part was strictly determined by the fundamental laws of matter and energy as formulated by physics and chemistry. It was against this form of reduction that Engels protested. But while he protested on the basis of the claim that their very knowledge of the sciences was inadequate—that they held, in short, to a "mechanical" view of nature—the true basis of his criticism, like that of Feuerbach's criticism of Moleschott,[54] lay in the fact that they had taken the classic model of scientific explanation for their own, while he wished to found a specifically *modern* materialism: that is, a materialism grounded in the belief that nature is a dialectically developing, evolutionary process.[55]

That this furnished the underlying motive for Engels's slighting references to Moleschott, Vogt, and Büchner, is also evident from the nature of his attack on Dühring's metaphysics. Dühring was incomparably more competent as a philosopher than were Engels's other opponents, and he scorned their dilettantism, with its easy reliance upon specific principles which had been utilized in physics, and its failure to be concerned with the problem of knowledge.[56] Yet he, too, shared the traditional materialist position, in which the basic understanding of all nature was to be found in the physical sciences; and he therefore looked upon himself as the continuer of the eighteenth-century materialist tradition, to which he, unlike the dilettantes, would give a fundamental philosophic justification. His language, like the language of Moleschott, Vogt, and Büchner, often suggested a purely "mechanical" view of nature, yet he was thoroughly cognizant of the inadequacies of traditional, atomistic mechanism. What he sought to accomplish was to deal with the problem of the differences between the various gradations of the material world in terms which would make it possible to comprehend all of them through one system of categories.[57] But, to do so, he felt himself obliged to add to the types of concepts which physics employed, and to hold that in physical phenomena themselves there were, for example, self-fulfilling impulses, and that there was a law of opposition and contrast (*Differenz*) which applied equally to inorganic, organic, and mental states. By such means he sought to assimilate the nature of living things, and their evolution, to the nature of matter itself. Since he was not successful in establishing the validity of using such concepts in physics, it sometimes appears as if he, no less than Marx and Engels, was relying upon the doctrine of emergence. Yet this was not his aim. His aim was to show that all of reality, including human and social existence, could be adequately understood in terms of the underlying nature of universal matter, and that this nature could be adequately grasped by human thought if the basic philosophic categories necessary for the physical sciences were uncovered. To this reductionism Engels of course objected, and it is in his attack upon Dühring that his own insistence upon the meaning of modern, or dialectical, materialism becomes most clear. At almost every point in this attack, the genuinely philosophic argument (as distinguished from mere invective) turns upon the fact that for Engels the manifestations of reality cannot be understood in terms of any universal category except that of a dialectical development, and this category makes it impossible to view thought as grasping any eternal structure of things or to regard things as manifesting the same specific properties throughout all of their developments.

In summary of the contrast between the opposed schools of materialism in Germany we may then make the following statements. Feuerbach, Marx and Engels, in their opposition to Hegel, found the essential basis of materialism to be the relation of thought to existence. If one could accept such a definition of materialism, all three could be unambiguously classified as materialists. However, the definition is inadequate, and the self-styled materialism of Feuerbach can only be construed as a form of materialism if one takes the latter term in its broadest sense, that is, as holding that all phenomena have a material basis, and that minds as separate from body—or God as separate from the world of nature— are non-existent. In a stricter sense, Feuerbach cannot be counted a materialist. His main effort was in the first place "anthropological" rather than metaphysical; in the second place, even his metaphysical commitments were not in line with an interpretation of all phenomena in terms of the categories which were adequate to deal with the physical world. In his oft-cited phrase, the type of materialism represented by Moleschott was true of the foundations of human nature and human knowledge, but not of its superstructure: "Rückwärts stimme ich den Materialisten vollkommen bei, aber nicht vorwärts."[58]

The Marxism of Engels, however, represents a materialism in the strict sense of that term. It was his contention that all events were manifestations of the fundamental nature of matter, and that there was one fundamental science which could explain all of these manifestations by means of its grasp of the nature of the material world. This science, however, was not physics, but was the dialectical interpretation of nature and man. In identifying the fundamental science with dialectics, rather than with physics, he departed from traditional materialism, and could espouse the doctrine of emergence: the emergence of new and irreducible

properties in nature was taken to be a manifestation of the fundamental dialectical self-transformations of matter, and an acceptance of these properties did
not therefore collide with materialism.

In Moleschott, Vogt, and Büchner, a more traditional form of materialism was
upheld. For them the definition of what constituted "materialism" was not the
relation of thought to existence, but the problem of whether all aspects of reality
could be analyzed in terms of the categories which the sciences of physics and
chemistry were successfully applying to all inorganic things. They were firmly
convinced that this was not only a possibility for the future, but that it was
gradually beginning to be achieved in their time. It was this faith that lay at the
foundation of their materialism. And it was therefore the growth of critical
positivism, with its interpretation of the necessary limitations of science, that
served to undermine materialism among those who followed the new movements
of thought in the last quarter of the century.[59]

Dühring's brand of materialism had an initial and striking success,[60] but
partly due to the vagueness of his fundamental concepts and partly due to the
unfortunate polemical style which grew out of his personal afflictions, he shortly
lost the influence which he had first exerted, and he is now chiefly known as the
butt of Engels's most savage attack.

Looking back, then, on the materialist movement in the nineteenth century,
one can see that it was of relatively short duration. Even were one to include
Feuerbach among its exponents, it would have first been newly affirmed in the
1840s, and the last of its original as well as influential statements was probably
Dühring's *Cursus der Philosophie*, published in 1875. Were it not for Haeckel's
subsequent popularization of his evolutionary monism, and were it not for the
influence exerted by the political and sociological views of this school, the
materialist movement of the middle years would have been of only antiquarian
interest by the turn of the century: all of the specifically philosophic reasons
which have tended to operate against it in the last decades were by then already
manifest, and were in fact definitive of the new positivism and of the new
idealism. It is for this reason that it is necessary to reject the common view that
the nineteenth century was an age in which materialism flourished. It was almost
totally absent in both England and France. And even in Germany it was not a
movement which had the continuity and the pervasiveness of either idealism or
critical positivism; nor was it fortunate enough to possess any figures of the same
philosophic ability as were represented in both of the other movements.

5. VARIANT VIEWS OF RELIGION

The conventional view of the place of religion in the thought of the nineteenth century holds that science and religion were ranged in open hostility, and
that unremitting warfare was conducted between them. The source of this belief
is to be found in the very obvious fact that the Darwinian theory of evolution
had widespread repercussions on the religious thought of the times, and was

combatted in varying ways, and to different degrees, by a number of theologians. And the thesis can be made even more plausible by identifying the rise of the historical criticism of the Bible with the method of scientific thought—an identification which the historically minded times would not have denied.

This stereotyped interpretation of the place of religion in nineteenth-century thought, and of its relations with science, is one which cannot be accepted. Perhaps the real relations can best be illustrated by a passage from Tyndall who, it will be recalled, probably was the clearest proponent of materialism in nineteenth-century England. In his celebrated Belfast address, Tyndall expressly stated that "the facts of religious feeling are to me as certain as the facts of physics,"[61] and he held that in spite of the fact that many religions, both past and present, are "grotesque in relation to scientific culture," yet they are "forms of a force, mischievous if permitted to intrude on the region of *knowledge* . . . but being capable of being guided to noble issues in the region of *emotion*, which is its proper and elevated sphere."[62] In the same connection he admitted that "without moral force to whip it into action, the achievements of the intellect would be poor indeed."

What led to the stereotyped conviction that the nineteenth century represented an age in which science and religion stood in open hostility was the undoubted fact that science and the historical criticism of the Bible came into conflict with widely held theological doctrines, and that there was a continuing battle concerning the proper interpretation to be placed upon specific teachings of the organized churches. This does not signify that those who were combatting various forms of theological doctrine felt themselves to be combatting religion. In their minds (though not of course in the minds of their opponents) they were combatting certain theological doctrines in the interests of religion itself. At the very outset of the century, Schleiermacher had insisted on separating religion from theology, and this insistence was no less characteristic of most of the theologians of the century than it was of, say, Carlyle, Matthew Arnold, Huxley, and Clifford.

The criticism of theological doctrines on scientific and historical grounds was not, of course, new in the nineteenth century; it was an inheritance from the eighteenth century and was not challenged even by those who were in other respects most opposed to the tendencies of eighteenth-century thought. All of the leading figures in religious thought at the outset of the nineteenth century were fully prepared to distinguish between religious belief and an acceptance of traditional interpretations of the doctrines of the Christian churches. One can see this most clearly in the profound influence which pantheism exerted in the early years of the century. The struggles evoked by this tendency were theological struggles in which those who most vigorously attacked orthodox Christian positions did so on behalf of religion itself. A similar situation arose in 1835. In that year David Friedrich Strauss published his celebrated *Das Leben Jesu*, and from it one may conveniently date nineteenth-century conflicts engendered by the historical criticism of the Bible. However, Strauss was utterly convinced that his criticism of the historical authenticity of the New Testament account of Jesus' life in no way undermined religious faith in the essential truth of Christianity.[63]

The same position persisted among others throughout the struggles which
historical criticism evoked: for example, it was clearly the position of those who
in the 1860s were condemned for unorthodoxy in the two most celebrated cases
in English theology of the century, *viz.*, the heresy trials of the seven authors of
Essays and Reviews, and of Bishop Colenso of Natal. Furthermore, one can see
precisely the same point in the struggles between geology and theology, and
especially in the controversies which followed the Darwinian theory of evolution.
While the orthodox felt that the Darwinian theory was one which undermined
all genuine religious belief, those who used it in order to attack currently accepted theological doctrines did not feel that they were attacking or in any way
undermining what was most significant in religion. Huxley was typical of this
strain of thought, for while he insisted that one must attempt to break up
theological dogma, he wished to do so in order to enable man to start "cherishing
the noblest and most human of man's emotions, by worship 'for the most part of
the silent sort' at the altar of the Unknown."[64] Thus, in all three of the most
notable cases in which nineteenth-century thought came into conflict with the
established churches—in the pantheism struggle, in the growth of the critical
historical treatment of theological documents, and in controversies concerning
evolution—the position of the unorthodox was one in which theological dogma
was being attacked not for the sake of undercutting religious faith, but as a
means of freeing that faith for what were regarded as being nobler and more
adequate forms in which it could find expression.

    In spite of the fact that there was this common feature in all of the major
theological struggles of the century, there was a significant transformation from
the opening of the century to its close. It had been characteristic of German
idealism to stress the unity of art, religion, and philosophy through insisting upon
the identity of that which they revealed.[65] Even though natural science was not
taken to be the highest expression of this unity, it was claimed to be comprehended within it. Yet, writing just after the close of the century, Boutroux found
a striking contrast between earlier views of the relations between science and
religion and those which had come to be widely accepted:

To sum up, the relation between Religion and Science which had established itself in the
course of the nineteenth century was a radical dualism. Science and Religion were no
longer two expressions (analogous in spite of their unequal value) of one and the same
object, viz. Divine Reason, as they were formerly in Greek philosophy; they were no
longer two given truths between which the agreement was demonstrable, as with the
Schoolmen; Science and Religion had no longer, as with the modern rationalists, a
common surety—reason: each of them absolute in its own way, they were distinct at
every point, as were distinct, according to the reigning psychology, the two faculties of
the soul, intellect and feeling, to which respectively, they corresponded. Thanks to this
mutual independence, they could find themselves in one and the same consciousness; they
existed there, the one beside the other, like two material, impenetrable atoms side by
side in space. They had come to an understanding, explicitly or tacitly, in order to
abstain from scrutinizing one another's principles. Mutual respect for the positions
achieved, and on that very account, for each, security and liberty—such was the device
of the period.[66]

One need not agree with Boutroux's assessment of the relations between science and religion in other ages, nor with the suggestion that the relationship which evolved by the end of the nineteenth century was unique in Christian thought. Yet, his general assessment of the trend of the nineteenth-century struggles regarding the relations of science and religion can scarcely be challenged. It is to the task of briefly tracing some of the major factors contributing to this trend that I shall now turn.

So far as the problem of religion was concerned, the heritage which Kant bequeathed his immediate successors, the German idealists, was twofold: in the first place, it involved a critical and largely negative view of traditional interpretations of theological concepts; in the second place, in Kant's system there was a complete cleavage between the realm of pure, or scientific reason, and the realm of the moral and religious. The first of these aspects of Kant's view was willingly accepted by the idealists, but the second was philosophically intolerable for them. To understand their position, it is not sufficient to recall that there were grave technical difficulties within the Kantian system, which they believed that only a new monistic metaphysics could overcome; one must also take into account the appeal which the doctrine of divine immanence exerted upon German thought at the time. One finds that doctrine in Lessing, Herder, Goethe, and Novalis, as well as in Fichte, Schelling, and Hegel. However, it would be impossible to espouse such a view and yet remain within the framework of the Kantian system. According to the latter, the realm of nature as present within direct experience, and as known by science, cannot be considered as a manifestation of the divine: the formative power of the human mind in moulding the alien materials of sensation yields an orderly world, but not a world which manifests within itself a unity which is independent of us and to which we also belong. Nor, according to Kant's view, is there any concrete form of experience through which, within ourselves, we find a unity between the phenomenal and the noumenal; nor are there any concrete circumstances which elicit from us a total response in which all aspects of our nature—and not merely the noetic, or the moral, or the aesthetic—are fully incorporated and fully expressed. In order to see that there could not really be such experiences, according to Kant's system, one need merely think of his attempt to split sensibility from reason, or of his separation of inclination from awareness of duty. In short, Kant's system made it impossible to find any form of ultimate unity within experience, either between man and nature or within man himself.

It was against such a view that Kant's idealist successors revolted. Behind all of their variant technical arguments, each in his way sought that higher unity which was part of the metaphysical pathos of the times, and each sought it in an idealist form of the doctrine of divine immanence. One can see this in Fichte's attempt to make the moral nature of man the clue to the whole of the world of nature; in Schelling's attempt to overthrow Newtonian views (upon which Kant had so heavily relied), in favor of a conception through which man's alienation from nature would be overcome; and, above all, one sees it in Hegel's interpretation of ultimate reality as that which is mediated in all things, but reaches its highest expression in the self-conscious objectification achieved within art, religion, and philosophy. Thus, for all three, man's supreme achievements place him in harmony with the totality of being, and in these achievements he is able to find the clue to reality. For those who identified a doctrine of divine immanence with true religion, this form of metaphysical idealism was itself a religious position. That it was not necessarily an orthodox position did not, of course, trouble them. On their view, that through which man could establish his unity with reality, that through which he could experience this reality in both its magnitude and its inner significance was identical with the truly religious. Thus, the sphere of the religious was enlarged beyond any confines of orthodoxy, and in fact merged not only with philosophy, but with all awareness of whatever was taken to be true or beautiful or good.

As a consequence of this doctrine, not only was there a broadening of the conception of religion, but there was a demand to reinterpret Christian doctrine as being symbolically rather than literally true. The way had already been opened for such an interpretation by Hamann's teachings, and even by Kant's, and it was also made necessary by the sympathetic interest vouchsafed to cultures in which Christian doctrine had no place. Since religious belief was not viewed as a separate compartment of man's nature, the belief in the truth and beauty inherent in the products of these cultures made it impossible to restrict authentic religion to the doctrinal teachings of Christianity. Thus, while Christianity could still be regarded as the highest or most adequate form of religious belief, the specific formulations of Christian theology had to be interpreted as symbols, not as literal transcriptions of matters of fact.

A belief in the idealistic theory of divine immanence, a sympathy for the varieties of religious experience in all cultures, and a willingness to interpret theological doctrine in symbolic terms, was no less characteristic of Schleiermacher than it was of his philosophic and literary contemporaries. However, Schleiermacher radically altered the stream of theological thought by his separation of the religious aspect of experience from both the intellectual and the moral. He sought to define for his contemporaries what constituted the basic phenomenon of religious experience, an experience which he felt to be no less binding because it was autonomous with respect to the intellectual. This basic phenomenon was, of course, to be found in the realm of feeling: the Christian faith is not a body of doctrine, but is a condition of man. Therefore religion is not to be confused with theology. According to Schleiermacher's view, the latter presupposes the religious experience, but religion itself does not need doctrinal expression: it is only because of the needs of the intellect that we must attempt to formulate in theological terms that which is immediately given within religious experience itself.

One can see that such a position could lead to a number of different attitudes with respect to the relations between knowledge and faith. One might, for example, attempt to construct a theology which would interpret Christian doctrine in ways that were satisfactory to the intellect, without seeking to appraise the experience of Christian faith itself. Schleiermacher's own theology may be looked upon as setting itself this goal. However, as Schleiermacher recognized, such an

attempt demanded that theology be separated from philosophy: the intellect was
not to be called upon to pass judgment upon the truth of Christian faith, but
only to interpret that faith. Others, however, were not willing to accept so radical
a separation of philosophy and theology, and they sought to offer a philosophical
basis for the acceptance of that which came through faith. This constituted an
alternative to Schleiermacher's position, and also to the tradition of natural
theology; it consisted in developing a philosophical position in which the realm
of feeling could lay claim to a truth higher than that which arises through the
intellect. One could then defend Christian theology as being guaranteed by, or as
being most consonant with, the spiritual insights to which religious feeling gave
rise. It was in the latter fashion that Jacobi had already proceeded, and which
Coleridge, Hare, and Francis Newman were to follow.

However, there are two other forms which religious thought may take when
religious feeling is held to be prior to and independent of all the propositions
which theology expounds. On the one hand, it can be maintained that all of the
beliefs which are identified with theology are merely "projections" of the fundamental nature of religious feeling. This, in general, was the path followed by
those who, like Strauss and Feuerbach, adopted a mythical or a psychological
interpretation of the historic doctrines of religion. On the other hand, it was
possible to view these doctrines as the reflections of the knowledge and experiences of certain peoples at certain times in the world's history, and to hold
that the importance of religion was to be found, first, within the realm of immediate feeling and, second, in the fruits which this feeling bore. On the latter
view, theological beliefs are not direct projections of feeling; they arise from
sources outside of religion and they undergo change as these external factors
change.

One can see that each of the last two views contains precisely that duality
between science and religion which Boutroux regarded as characteristic of the
development of religious thought in the nineteenth century. But one can also
note that the two views differ with respect to the degree to which they are
potentially hostile to religion. According to the first view, all of the content of
religious belief is to be regarded as error so long as it is interpreted as being anything more than a projection of individual and social feeling. According to the
second view, however, the content of religious belief is a reflection of the state of
knowledge and experience of those who hold to the belief; and in so far as there
is a change in the state of knowledge it is possible to reform religious belief, to
make it no less adequate as an expression of feeling, but more adequate as an
expression of what is known to be true of the world. Thus, on the second view,
one could believe in progress within the domain of religious belief, and one could
seek to reform religion to meet the needs and the knowledge of succeeding
generations.

In the history of nineteenth-century thought one finds that it was the first of
these views, rather than the second, which developed earlier. In Germany it was
chiefly exemplified by Strauss and by Feuerbach, in France by Comte.[67] All three
of these thinkers represented challenges to current Christian orthodoxy, to eight-

eenth century conceptions of natural religion, and to the religious positions generally characteristic of Romanticism and absolute idealism. Each of the latter views—though they were opposed in other ways—had involved a claim that there was a noetic aspect of religion, and that questions of truth and falsity were relevant to religious commitment. However, Strauss, Feuerbach, and Comte rejected this claim. They did point out that the feelings which were associated with traditional forms of religion were capable of generating beliefs about the world, but they insisted that if these beliefs were regarded as statements of matters of fact they were erroneous, and were to be fought. So long as no such cognitive claims were associated with the basic forms of feeling which are present in all religions, these feelings were considered by Strauss and Feuerbach and Comte to be of supreme human importance.

In Comte, for example, a sharp distinction is drawn between the theological, fictive mode of thought, which was to be wholly rejected, and genuinely religious feeling, without which the unity of a good social order cannot be achieved. Similarly, Strauss never abandoned his faith in the value of religious feeling: his devastating criticism of orthodoxy was originally accompanied by his belief in the "eternal truth" of what the myths of orthodoxy symbolized; and even at the end of his life, when he had abandoned Christianity, he, like Comte, attempted to substitute a new faith for the old. And Feuerbach, who was if anything more insistent than Comte and Strauss that the doctrines of Christianity were false, yet regarded religious feeling as that which gives man his worth. In Feuerbach, in fact, one finds an intense religious feeling, and a most passionate affirmation of the value of this feeling, combined with as radical an expression of the theory of the psychological, "projective" origin of religious belief as the nineteenth century has to offer. In his outspoken denial that there is any object outside of man himself which corresponds to the object of religious emotion, Feuerbach's position remains unparalleled until, at the turn of the century, one comes to Durkheim's theory, or, later in this century, to the theory of Freud.

However, the tendency represented by Comte, Strauss, and Feuerbach did not in fact come to dominate nineteenth-century religious thought. It was, rather, the less radical interpretation of the relation between religious feeling and religious belief which exerted the greatest influence. This interpretation, it will be recalled, regarded religious belief as having arisen out of a natural human capacity for religious feeling, operating upon the knowledge and experience available to men at different times and in different places. Thus, religious beliefs were mutable, but each gave expression to that which was taken to be true. Criticism of religious beliefs was necessary in order to bring them into line with current knowledge, but knowledge alone was not sufficient for man: religious feeling was a natural capacity which demanded satisfaction, and was justified by the fruits which it bore.

This attitude was so prevalent among the liberal theologians in England, and among English literary men, that its existence and importance need not be documented through individual discussions of the figures concerned. What may however escape the reader's attention is the intimate connection which existed between this mode of thought and a factor which we have already noted to have been characteristic of the German Romantic and idealist philosophers of religion: the espousal of a belief in divine immanence. Such a belief (as the term is here used) denies that the object of religious worship transcends the world; instead, it finds the object of religious feeling within the totality of nature, of which man is a part. This one-worldly religious conception characterized liberal theologians such as Francis Newman, Seeley, and most, if not all, of the authors of *Essays and Reviews*; it characterized Carlyle, Matthew Arnold, and Tennyson; and it was no less characteristic of philosophers as diverse as Spencer and Bosanquet. For those who held that the object of religious worship did not reside outside the world, but at its heart, the theory of evolution posed no obstacles; indeed, it was possible for some who held this view to identify true religion with a worship of that immanent power which was at work in nature, evolving higher forms of existence, bringing mankind out of crudity, ignorance, and selfishness into altruism, knowledge, and culture. This created a climate of opinion in which the boundaries of what was recognized as religion became greatly enlarged. One finds, for example, that positions characteristic of twentieth-century religious humanism are already explicitly stated when, according to Matthew Arnold, to be religious meant to worship "the Eternal," "the stream of tendency by which all things seek to fulfil the law of their being," "the enduring power not ourselves which makes for righteousness,"[68] and when, in T. H. Green's phrase, "God is our possible or ideal self."[69]

According to such definitions of religion, the age was not an age of irreligion. To be sure, there were those who did not take the noetic claims of religion so lightly, and who, if they were not orthodox, or were unable to struggle to an acceptable compromise with orthodoxy, found it necessary to adopt a position of agnosticism. This, for example, came to be Darwin's view,[70] and it was also the view of Leslie Stephen. However, agnosticism was not widespread, and an openly avowed atheism was even less common. As we have noted in the case of Huxley (who coined the term "agnosticism") and in the case of Tyndall (who was a materialist), religion could be redefined in such a way that it made no noetic claims whatsoever, and the issue of agnosticism or of atheism would thus be bypassed. Such a position seems to have provided a welcome *modus vivendi* between the allegiance felt toward science and the allegiance felt toward Christian belief. This compromise was only possible because religion had antecedently been defined exclusively in terms of feeling. Once this had been accepted, science could be held to yield our most certain knowledge; at the same time, any acknowledgment of the limitations of science (such as one found among critical positivists) would open an adjoining door through which access was given to another domain of existence, in which the endless questionings of the intellect had no place. Thus, poetry could be interpreted as depicting the truths of feeling, and could be apotheosized. And thus, also, the age which saw its chief moral problem as the problem of extending the bounds of sympathetic, altruistic action, could abandon the view that faith in God was either the source or the enemy of the social good, and could instead view God and the social good as synonymous.

Such was the predominant view, during the latter part of the century, among those who had held that the essence of religion was to be found in feeling. There was, however, another tendency in nineteenth-century thought which also served to disengage religion from scientific and philosophic controversy. It consisted in interpreting religion as a manifestation not of feeling but of ideal morality. Although this tendency undoubtedly had other sources as well, it was fed by the strong Kantian revival during the latter part of the century; and just as Schleiermacher may be viewed as the fountainhead of one of these theological tendencies, so Albrecht Ritschl may be seen as the source of the other.

Ritschl, like his predecessor Kant, sought to divorce metaphysics and theology. He attempted to justify his view by holding that since metaphysics had the task of dealing with all forms of being, its categories would have to be applied to the natural world as well as to God. Yet, since he found an absolute cleft between the realms of spirit and nature, and since religion, and all theology, dealt with things of the spirit, the categories of metaphysical thought were inappropriate within the province of theology. However, he also insisted that theology was secondary to, and an adjunct of, the immediate religious experience of man. This experience he found in a self-commitment to the moral ideal. The function of theology became that of interpreting accepted Christian doctrine in terms of the moral faith of a believing Christian. Thus, Ritschl bears a close similarity to Schleiermacher, in spite of the differences between their interpretations of the nature of religious experience. Both found the authority of religion to lie within the sphere of immediate experience; both interpreted that experience as autonomous with relation to theology, seeking through theology merely to explicate its Christian significance; and, finally, both divorced theological questions from the metaphysical questions with which, in their eyes, Christian doctrine had become burdened. Considered in the wider context of modern theology as a whole, one may say that both Schleiermacher and Ritschl stood opposed to what had formerly been regarded as the fundamental thesis of natural theology: that the truth of theism could be established through arguments based upon man's capacity to reach an explanation of the world and of his place within it. Yet neither wholly departed from the traditions of natural theology: it was within experience, and not by revelation, that man could become aware of the truth of Christianity. In this transformation of the very basis of natural theology, the influences of Schleiermacher and of Ritschl converged. Both contributed to the relaxation of demands for theological orthodoxy, since each held that the truth of religion was to be found in the inner nature of religious experience, and that what was important to religion was the spiritual fruit of this experience, not an external conformity with one or another set of conflicting theological propositions. Both also contributed to the willingness to divorce religious commitments from theoretical commitments, since both held that the object of religious worship was inwardly revealed, and could not be found through an examination of that realm of nature and of history with which the methods of empirical and rational inquiry sought to deal.

One can see how this reform of natural theology fostered the compartmentalization of religious and theoretical commitments with which we are here concerned. However, the most extreme degree of compartmentalization was only reached after the development of that form of critical positivism which interpreted theoretic knowledge as symbolic, as a construction of our experience made in the interests of practice and of the economy of thought. Just as Spencer's systematic positivism had permitted him to view both science and religion as two ever-present ways in which man sought to approach and adapt himself to the one Unknowable, so the later forms of positivism saw in the symbols of science and the symbols of religion two different modes of interpreting differing forms of experience, each mode being guided by considerations appropriate to itself. And with the growth of the belief that the realm of nature as depicted by science was different from the realm of man's history and his moral commitments, there came to be an increased emphasis upon a doctrine of the twofold nature of truth. Now, however, the two truths were not separated by the gulf between the natural and the revealed, but were to be found within man's own natural experience: differing objects were to be differently viewed, and even the same object or experience could equally well be regarded from different, purely human, points of view. It was the growth of this spirit, which first came to full flower in James, that may be regarded as the most extreme development of the tendency which dominated the religious thought of the nineteenth century. In spite of the many conservative theologians, and the conservative revivals of the French Romantic reaction and the Oxford Movement, in spite also of the persisting tradition of metaphysical idealism, the most influential strand in nineteenth-century thought was that which attempted to divorce science and religion, and maintain the value of each. Positivism had merged with idealism to limit the domain in which science had authority; and once these limits were generally agreed upon, all schools relinquished the view that religion could intrude into that domain. On the other hand, the scope of religion had been broadened, not narrowed: in giving up its claim to the possession of any literal knowledge, religion came to be identified with whatever ranges of feeling and of moral aspiration were of most significance to man. Thus the assumptions of both natural theology and revealed religion were abandoned, and it was thought that at last a means had been found to effect a permanent reconciliation of science and religion. Set against this background in the latter part of the century, John Stuart Mill's *Theism* seems no less out of touch with his age than had been Kierkegaard's passionate search for orthodoxy in an age dominated by Hegel.

II

*The discussions of every age are filled
with the issues on which its leading
schools of thought differ. But the general
intellectual atmosphere of the time is
always determined by the views on which
the opposing schools agree. They
become the unspoken presuppositions
of all thought, the common and
unquestioningly accepted foundations
on which all discussion proceeds.*

F. A. Hayek, *The Counter-Revolution of
Science*, p. 191

*The study of the history of man is now
put before us as that by means of
which we are to understand man himself,
and know what we ought to do.*

J. Grote, *Exploratio Philosophica*, I, xvii

2

1. The Meaning of "Historicism"

It is generally agreed that one of the most distinctive features of nineteenth-century thought was the widespread interest evinced in history. The manifestations of this interest are not only to be found in the growth and diversification of professional historical scholarship, but in the tendency to view all of reality, and all of man's achievements, in terms of the category of development. This mode of thought was equally characteristic of idealists and positivists. It permeated and softened the materialism of the period; it was also an essential element in attempts to compromise the quarrels between philosophy and science on the one hand and "genuine" religious belief on the other. The use to which the concept of development was put constitutes what I shall term "historicism." The task of the present chapter will be to define the nature of this new mode of thought; in subsequent chapters we shall examine the variant forms which it took, and estimate its validity.

The term "historicism" has been used—and is still being used—in a variety of ways. Among the earlier works which were especially concerned with the history of this complex phenomenon, Ernst Troeltsch's *Der Historismus und seine Probleme* (1922), Karl Heussi's *Die Krisis der Historismus* (1932), and Friedrich Meinecke's *Die Entstehung des Historismus* (1936) are perhaps the most frequently cited. In 1938, in *The Problem of Historical Knowledge*, I put forward a definition of historicism but made no effort to trace its history. Now I wish to return to an elaboration of that definition and to attempt to show the range of its applicability.[1]

Given the variety of characterizations of "historicism" which already exist, the usefulness of any other definition will depend upon how well it unifies and clarifies the phenomena with which others have also dealt. Since almost all writers use the term in a manner which leads them to discuss certain figures as examples of a historicist view, the denotation of the term is to some extent fixed.

Although its connotations vary more widely, they always include reference to a specifically historical way of conceiving the world, and of evaluating its aspects, which first received influential expression in the latter half of the eighteenth century and became prevalent in the nineteenth. However, the thinkers who are invariably classified as clear examples of historicism are representative of a wide variety of philosophic positions, and they spring from diverse intellectual ancestries. For example, Herder, Hegel, Comte, Marx, and Spencer are all generally considered to provide classic examples of historicism, yet their philosophic systems are obviously antagonistic in many fundamental respects. The problem of defining the term is therefore a problem of finding a congeries of characteristics shared by these and other major figures whom historians of ideas would unhesitatingly class as representatives of this mode of thought, and which would at the same time be sufficiently precise to distinguish these figures from earlier writers whose ways of conceiving of the world, and of evaluating it, were different. A definition of the term "historicism" which would be useful in this respect would also be useful in indicating why others, such as Burke, John Stuart Mill, or Carlyle, are in some contexts to be regarded as examples of historicism, while in other contexts they are not. A definition which would serve these functions would be as close as one could come to giving a successful definition of the term. The definition which seems to me to approximate that goal is the following: *Historicism is the belief that an adequate understanding of the nature of any phenomenon and an adequate assessment of its value are to be gained through considering it in terms of the place which it occupied and the role which it played within a process of development.*

In order to suggest how radical a thesis is contained in this position, it will be useful to contrast it with what has often been called "the historical sense," which has also been regarded as characteristic of the late eighteenth and nineteenth centuries. Possession of an adequate sense of history involved being able to shed the prejudices of the day, investigating past events in terms of the conditions under which they actually occurred. More specifically, it involved being wary of assuming that these conditions were identical with conditions which now obtain, or which obtained at some other time. Furthermore, those who prided themselves on a newly discovered historical sense tended to insist that if one is to make a judgment of value concerning any historical phenomenon, one should, in the first place, view it in its own context; and, further, one should avoid assuming that the moral practices or standards of worth characteristic of the present provide the sole basis on which to ground such a judgment. It would surely be admitted today that these principles represent precautions which must be taken if one is to avoid treating past events anachronistically; and an awareness of their necessity for a proper study of history did in fact arise hand-in-hand with the growth of historicism.

However, the two positions are by no means identical. For example, those who would guard against misapprehending history due to our tendency to read the present into the past might none the less hold that individual events or specific periods of history can be understood in their concrete actuality without viewing them as aspects of some larger process of development. It would also be possible to be thoroughly cognizant of the factors which have led to faulty evaluations of past events without holding that moral judgments of historical personages, or evaluations of the achievements of specific periods of history, are to be based on the roles which they played within some longer-range pattern of development. In short, one can be willing to regard as erroneous all judgments which distort the nature of the past because of a faulty historical perspective, and yet hold that our understanding of a historical event, or our evaluation of it, is in the first instance concerned with the nature of the event itself, and not with its place within some process of change. The thesis of historicism, on the other hand, demands that we reject the view that historical events have an individual character which can be grasped apart from viewing them as embedded within a pattern of development. What is, then, essential to historicism is the contention that a meaningful interpretation or adequate evaluation of any historical event involves seeing it as part of a stream of history.

In the following chapters we shall be concerned to trace the various strands of thought which led to an acceptance of this position. However, in order to account for the convergence of what are in other ways radically opposed positions, it will be necessary to examine one concept which was fundamental to all of them: the concept of development.

2. The Concept of Development

The philosophic use of a term such as "development" frequently involves notions which are not included in our ordinary uses of that term. Nevertheless, philosophers rarely use an ordinary term in a wholly arbitrary way, whatever further specifically philosophic meanings they may read into it. For this reason it will be useful to begin by an examination of the manner in which the concept of development was used by nineteenth-century philosophers and then determine what is still the ordinary use of that concept by comparing and contrasting it with our use of the terms "change" and "progress."

The concept of development always involves the concept of change. However, not every type of change is an instance of development. What strikes us as a random, patternless change is not regarded as an instance of development. Furthermore, we do not take all patterned changes—for example, the changing of traffic lights from red to green to red to green—as instances of development. "Development" involves the notion of a change taking place in a specific direction, and, more particularly, it involves the view that what comes later in the process is an unfolding of what was at least implicitly present in its earlier stages. This is the etymological origin of the term, and something of its original significance remains part of its current meaning. There is, then, the suggestion of a linear quality in those processes which we designate as cases of development. It is for this reason that what appears to us as a purely cyclical process would not be characterized as a development, since that which is manifest at the end of the process is not different from that which was explicitly present at the outset. On the other hand, even in a cyclical process we do sometimes single out some particular phase of the process and regard this phase as a development, that is, as an unfolding of such and such a quality up to a specific point in the process as a whole.

It is also to be noted that in speaking of things as developing we frequently read a value connotation into the process, implying that its end-stage is "higher" or better than what was actually present in its earlier stages. Nevertheless, we do not invariably do so. We may, for example, speak of the development of some phenomenon which we consider to be of negative value, as a believer in a free-enterprise system might trace the history of the development of state interference in economic matters. Thus, the concept of development need not always have an evaluative component in its connotation, but it often—and perhaps usually—does so.

Turning now to the concept of progress, it might be thought that we can distinguish the notion of development from the notion of progress by virtue of the fact that while the former need not carry a connotation of increase in value, the latter invariably does. However, so far as ordinary usage is concerned, this does not provide an adequate basis for drawing a distinction between them. For example, there are times at which we speak of the progress of a disease, or speak with regret of the progressive undermining of an idea or of a social system. Thus, use of the term "progress" does not always carry the connotation that what has emerged in the course of a temporal process is of higher value than what was actually present in the earlier stages of that process. Nevertheless, it almost invariably does so when it is used with respect to long-run historical developments, and it can always be assumed to do so when it is used in connection with human history as a whole. To differentiate between the latter use of the term and its other uses, I shall capitalize "Progress" when it is taken to mean that there is a pervasive optimizing tendency in history.

What the terms "development" and "progress" have in common is, then, the idea that a given process of change has a pattern, and this pattern in turn has a directional property. Such a directional property is not, however, simply a question of something succeeding what came earlier, but involves the belief that what was present in the earlier stages becomes more marked or more explicit in the later stages. Such a notion is, I submit, present in both the idea of development and the idea of progress. To be sure, if the original etymological significance of the two words still clung to these terms one could, on that basis, distinguish between development and progress. We would then speak of those processes in which there was an *unfolding* of that which was already at least implicitly present as a case of development, and we would speak of those cases in which there was the element of *advancing* toward something new as progress. However, there seems to be little warrant in either ordinary or philosophic usage for drawing this distinction; and, as we shall soon see, there was no fundamental conflict between the views of those who conceived of history as subject to a law of Progress, and those who, on the analogy of the growth of living things, regarded development as an inherent tendency within cultures to unfold that which was implicit within them.

One further element in our ordinary notions of both development and progress deserves to be noted. Any process characterized as an instance of either is viewed as a relatively continuous process which proceeds not through random variations, but steadily, naturally, and through successive stages toward its goal. What we take to be the successive phases or stages in a developmental or progressive process are successively closer approximations to what we regard as the last stage of that process. This is clear from the fact that if we are tracing a development and find some point in the process at which what has been foreshadowed as the end of the process is temporarily supplanted by a "regression" to an earlier stage, we do not consider the latter as part of the development, but as a hiatus in it. Such a break in the directional process is only regarded as being a phase of the development if what then succeeds the break represents an advance over what immediately preceded that break, rather than being merely a return to the *status quo ante*; in these cases the break is viewed as a phase of the development, constituting a necessary check in the process. It is so regarded because it gave rise to a fuller manifestation of that toward which the process was tending. Thus, "development" and "progress" are both concepts which involve the notion of goal-orientation.

So much for what I take to be our ordinary usage of the term "development" and our ordinary conception of the processes to which this term is applied. It is now necessary to seek out some of the philosophic assumptions which are usually associated with our use of this concept. These philosophic assumptions may not be of great significance with respect to our ordinary uses of the term, but in the context of more technical discussions it is necessary to become acquainted with them.

In the first place it is to be noted that whenever we speak of a development we must always have in mind the idea of *something* which develops. To be sure, this "something" need not be a concrete entity (that is, a "thing" or "substance"); it could, for example, be an attitude, an art form, a disease, or the like. These alternative possibilities introduce a distinction which it is important to draw if we are to understand the fundamental presuppositions of historicism.

To clarify this distinction, consider the case in which a historian writes a specialized history, such as a history of some concept (e.g., "historicism"), or of a literary form (e.g., the novel), or of some attitude or widely shared conviction (e.g., the feminist movement).[2] In such histories we need not suppose that the development that has been traced represents a series of transformations undergone by some substantival entity: the series of events itself is the sole subject of the history. Similarly, if a historian traces the history of sculpture in a given country over a certain period of time, or traces the growth of some form of technology, or the like, he might adopt the same attitude: the true subject of his history is simply the set of related events he has traced. However, histories of this type are sometimes interpreted in a quite different way. Whether rightly or wrongly, there have been those who have tended to view the development of a nation's art or technology as we sometimes view a series of works by a single artist: as successive expressions of a developmental process which occurred within *him*. Were the historian to use this analogy with respect to the series of events which he had established, the development which he traced would not merely be the history of a certain concept, or literary form, or shared attitude in a given country, or area, over a certain period of time; it would be a history of a developmental process taking place within an enduring entity underlying the specific changes. The true subject of development would then be the entity itself, not merely a series of changes.

Now, it so happens that those who embraced historicism used the concept of development in the second of these ways. For them, the observable change in some aspect of nature or some aspect of human endeavor was a symptom of some more basic developmental process: behind the qualitative changes which they could directly observe were changes in whatever basic substance or process gave rise to these qualities. Thus any directional pattern of change in the arts, or in political life, or in technology, was taken as expressive of a pattern of change within a developing entity—for example, in the culture as a whole, or in the spirit of a people, or in Humanity, or Reality.

This conception is not an unnatural one, even if the form in which it has just been stated may make it appear extravagant to the contemporary reader. Surely its defenders might point out that only such a conception is compatible with what we ordinarily mean by "development." That concept, as we have seen, involves the notion of a change which is relatively continuous, instead of proceeding by random variations. If, however, the historian is permitted merely to trace changes with respect to some particular quality without relating the successive manifestations of this quality to some underlying process, is there *real* continuity in what has been traced? To be sure, in time there may be a heightening of the particular quality with which he has concerned himself, but might it not be argued that this in itself does not constitute "real continuity"; that it is, on the contrary, a mere stringing together of beads selected by the historian for the design they will make? On the other hand, if we view a series of changes as phases in one underlying process which manifests itself successively in each of them, then what has been traced is an actual process, not some creation of the historian's interests and imagination.

That it would not be unnatural to argue in this way may also be seen from the fact that we have an inveterate tendency to ask with respect to any change not merely *what* changes, but *why* it changes as it does. If each separate change were taken as the ultimate subject of a historian's account of a developmental process, it is questionable whether we would ever reach a *general* explanation of why the whole series of changes occurred as it did. In some instances the cause of a particular change might be the direct influence of, say, one work of art upon another; in other instances it might be attributed to the impact of the same historical influences on the independent work of two different men; in other cases still other types of explanation might be given. However, the feeling of necessity which we have when we witness the continuity which is present in a process of

directional change seems to suggest that there must be some more basic explanation, some sufficient reason why the whole pattern of change assumed the form it
did. This conviction finds satisfaction in the belief that these changes are manifestations of an underlying process which itself develops according to its own
inner laws.

I am not myself inclined to accept the cogency of these arguments. In tracing
the development of historicism and of other nineteenth-century concepts I shall
not be using the method which they seek to defend. In fact, in the final chapter
of this discussion of historicism I shall criticize the view they represent. Here,
however, it is merely a question of making somewhat more plausible the thesis
that the comprehension of any "genuine" development must be more than a
matter of tracing a succession of changes; that, on the contrary, the historian is
concerned with a developmental process in which some subject manifests itself
in successive forms, each of these forms expressing a tendency which is characteristic of the whole.

3. Two Sources of the Developmental View

It can be said that there were two distinct and presumably opposed sources of
the view that the category of development provided the basic means of understanding reality and human history. One can be identified with the Romantic
rebellion against the Enlightenment, whereas the other was, in some respects, a
continuation of the Enlightenment tradition. The first arose in the late eighteenth century, primarily in Germany; one of its most characteristic features was
its tendency to view historical development on the analogy of the growth of living
things. Though he went far beyond it, it was to this movement that Hegel also
belonged. The second, which involved an attempt to establish a science of society
which would be based on the discovery of laws of social development, had its
first major exponents in Saint-Simon and Comte, and was also represented by
Marxism. However, it is doubtful whether either or both of these tendencies
would have been sufficient to establish historicism as the dominant mode of
thought in the nineteenth century had it not been for Darwin's theory of the
origin of species. Largely as a consequence of that theory, evolutionism became
firmly entrenched as a way of looking at all aspects of the world; and while
evolutionism is not necessarily identical with historicism, when this mode of
thought became dominant, historicism flourished.

Before turning to a consideration of this sequence of events, which will occupy
us in the next chapters, it will be useful to introduce each of the two pre-
Darwinian sources of the developmental view, showing that each had a clear
affinity with historicism. Here we shall first consider the general position of those
who, in opposition to the Enlightenment, tended to use analogies drawn from
the growth of living things as a source of insight into nature and human history.

If we observe the stages in the growth of a plant or an animal, we find that it
appears to be in some degree autonomous with respect to the environment. Under

normal environmental circumstances it seems to develop according to its own nature; if obstacles to its development threaten to block it, it will in many cases surmount these obstacles, continuing to grow until it reaches that state which is the fullest realization of the potentialities which we ascribe to a living thing of its kind. And when, for some reason, it fails to achieve this end, we think of it as "stunted," as precluded from reaching its goal, that is, from the goal which others of its kind, in more favorable environments, were able to reach. This common-sense view is close to the Aristotelian conception of the nature of living things, and it is to such a common-sense view of organic growth that those who used the organic analogy appealed.

Now, if this view of organic growth is taken seriously, then the way in which to explain a particular state of an organism at a particular time is to relate that state to the whole pattern of growth which that type of organism will normally display. Only if it fails to achieve its normal development do we feel the need to invoke *external* factors as the causes for what has occurred. What holds of our explanation of why a particular state has occurred holds also of our explanation of why one particular state has succeeded another: this particular pattern of change is taken as an expression of an inherent tendency in the organism. Once such a view has been adopted, it becomes impossible to explain why any particular state is what it is except through relating it to the pattern of the developmental process as a whole. And this, of course, is the thesis of historicism with respect to the *explanation* of historical events. Similarly, in *evaluating* particular features of an organism, we must view these features in terms of what they contribute to the development and functioning of the organism as a whole; and this too provides a parallel with the manner in which historicism claims that specific events are to be evaluated.

Turning now to the connection between historicism and the views of those who continued the traditions of the Enlightenment, we must take note of a special form of determinism which was accepted by those who sought to establish laws of development. Like most of their predecessors—since Hume's influence was not yet felt—they tended to assume that all natural laws were actual agencies which controlled or governed events.[3] Unlike most of their predecessors, however, they assumed that the laws which would serve to explain social organization and change were not to be derived from a consideration of the psychological dispositions of men, but referred directly to the course of history. Such laws, they believed, defined the direction in which change necessarily proceeds; these laws themselves, it was assumed, controlled the sequence in which events could occur. For those accepting these assumptions, it was not sufficient for a historian to trace the immediate causes of some specific historical change, for these causes were themselves the consequences of the basic underlying law of social development. Therefore, it was the latter which provided the only acceptable basis for the explanation of events which could be regarded as significant for human history. This meant, however, that every event had to be viewed in relation to the direction of the historical process as a whole. Thus, this form of determinism led to an acceptance of the explanatory thesis of historicism.

At this point we can also see how it led to an acceptance of the evaluative form of historicism. In order to be *significant*, an event would have to be an exemplification of the overriding forces inherent in the developmental law: if any event were merely "accidental" and not directly related to the dominant laws of social change, it would not be worthy of attention; it would not have contributed to history at all. Thus, the assumption that there are laws which control the direction of historical change leads directly to historicism, as I have defined that term: to understand or evaluate any phenomenon one must consider it in relation to the place which it occupied and the role which it played within a larger process of development.

It is important to note that this deterministic conception of social change could only be upheld so long as it was assumed that "history" was not in fact a series of different streams, diverging and converging, and frequently affecting one another; but that, instead, all peoples could be said to be part of a single history, the history of Mankind. The latter conception, which had been characteristic of the Enlightenment, was in fact explicitly adopted by Comte, for whom Humanity was actually a substantival entity, "Le Grand Être." It was also adopted by all later social evolutionists who regarded social forms of organization as different stages in a single pattern of evolutionary development. And, as we shall see, this evolutionary view, like the determinism with which it was associated, was a chief factor in the dominance of historicism at the end of the nineteenth century.

Thus, in the period with which we are concerned, historicism tended to spread through all schools of thought. On the one hand, those who rebelled against the Enlightenment on the basis of its mechanical conception of nature and its view of man, tended to conceive of history in terms of analogies with the growth of living things, and this naturally led to an acceptance of historicism. On the other hand, those who regarded themselves as representing a continuing advance in the scientific aims characteristic of the Enlightenment adopted a form of determinism which also led to an acceptance of historicism. It is to the attempt to trace these currents of thought that we shall now turn. In the end we shall re-examine and criticize the usefulness of the organic analogies and the soundness of the deterministic assumptions which we have here only briefly introduced.

3

THE FIRST PHASE OF HISTORICISM:
FROM THE ENLIGHTENMENT THROUGH HEGEL

Because it is now deeply entrenched in our thought, it is easy to forget that the tendency to view all matters in terms of their histories may itself have had a history. In fact, that history has not been a long one. In 1831, in the opening sentences of the first of a series of essays entitled "The Spirit of the Age," John Stuart Mill remarked:

The "spirit of the age" is in some measure a novel expression. I do not believe that it is to be met with in any work exceeding fifty years in antiquity. The idea of comparing one's own age with former ages, or with our notion of those which are yet to come, had occurred to philosophers; but it never before was itself the dominant idea of any age.[1]

What transformed it into a dominant idea was not, I believe, a consciousness that the age was itself undergoing rapid and profound historical change, even though the French Revolution and subsequent political movements deeply affected most of the figures with whom we shall deal. Rather, the new mode of thought seems to have been closely connected with tendencies of a more strictly philosophical sort. As I have already indicated, these were related to views which had been characteristic of the Enlightenment period, and we must therefore first turn to a brief consideration of attitudes toward history within that period.[2]

As we shall immediately see, Enlightenment conceptions of history do not conform to the definition of historicism which was put forward in the preceding chapter. To be sure, if one were to define historicism in terms of an interest in history, and in the concrete rather than the general or universal, as Meinecke's treatment of the rise of historicism suggests one should do, then historicism *did* have its origins within the Enlightenment. However, the modes of explanation and of evaluation which were characteristic of that period were fundamentally different from those which subsequently arose. What was of importance within the Enlightenment for these subsequent developments was, of course, the growth of interest in history within that period. Even more important was, however, the Enlightenment doctrine of Progress.

51

While the main outlines of the origin and development of the concept of Progress are sufficiently well known not to demand discussion here, it will be necessary for us to call attention to certain features which were common to the theories of history of such representative figures as Voltaire, Turgot, D'Alembert, Lessing, and Condorcet. It was through these common features that the Enlightenment paved the way for the development of historicism.

Those who first utilized the doctrine of Progress as the basis for a comprehensive philosophy of history firmly believed that there was a universally valid standard for the assessment of human achievements, and that such a standard was accessible to reason, which was the same at all times and in all places. Yet it was obvious to them that the society in which they lived was not a society ordered in accordance with that standard, and that no society which conformed to the standard had ever been achieved within historic times. Had they believed in Original Sin they would have been furnished with an explanation for the discrepancy between the facts of social existence and the omnipresence of man's ability to discriminate the good from the bad. Or had they doubted that reason was a force which could in the long run control human conduct, they could also have explained the disparity between actual conditions and the rationally grounded ideal. However, they vehemently affirmed the natural goodness of man, and they did not question the efficacy of reason. Instead, they held that the source of the disparity lay in ignorance, and their faith in the efficacy of reason led them to the conviction that ignorance would finally be dispelled.

This conviction was associated with the view, made familiar in the quarrel between "the Ancients and the Moderns," that human history could be regarded as analogous to the development of an individual from infancy to maturity: in the early years there was a lack of the experience necessary for knowledge. It was also partly grounded in an enthusiasm for the great advances which had been made in science and the new possibilities which technology had seemed to open up: the tools for understanding and the tools for social improvement were now being placed within the grasp of mankind. But, above all, the faith in the vincibility of ignorance was merely the reverse side of their faith in reason: men were endowed with the capacity to distinguish the true from the false and the good from the bad, and would never accept a state of ignorance and barbarism if they had the opportunity to know the truth and to live in a state of culture.[3] Thus, for Voltaire and the Encyclopedists the immediate task was one of enlightenment. If superstition, that monstrous offspring of ignorance, could be overcome, then a growth in experience, in science, and in technology, would of itself produce a harmony between the actual and the ideal. The war against superstition was fought on two fronts: the attempt to undermine superstitious explanations of natural phenomena through showing their absurdity, and the attempt to spread a knowledge of those correct explanations of phenomena which science had already been able to achieve. The men of the Enlightenment saw no grounds for doubting that enlightenment was ushering in a new age: mankind could henceforth make more rapid progress toward the ideal.

One sees most clearly in Condorcet the extent to which this eighteenth-century conception of Progress is tied to the ideal of a universal standard for conduct based upon the common possession of reason among all men. Condorcet not only explicitly judged all of the past according to his ideal of enlightenment, but went so far as to periodize history into distinct epochs in terms of their relationship to advances in human knowledge; and he believed it possible to envision the future as the continuation of those tendencies toward enlightenment which he regarded as operative in the past. However, it is important to note that this conception of Progress was by no means identical with historicism. In the first place, unlike historicism, it insisted upon the existence of an eternal standard against which specific achievements and errors were to be measured; in other words, it did not find its standard within the process of historical development itself. In the second place, believers in the doctrine of Progress did not hold that what oc-curred within history must always be viewed in terms of some larger develop-ment: individual periods of history could be adequately known in their actual natures without placing them in the framework of history-as-a-whole. But there were nonetheless two points at which the doctrine of Progress laid the basis for historicism.

The more important of these points was the fact that the doctrine of Progress regarded history as the unfolding of a single process which was not guided from without, but proceeded according to a principle immanent within it. The process itself was the education of Mankind; the agent which furnished the impetus to this process was man himself.[4] In holding to this view, the Enlightenment doctrine of Progress stood opposed to the traditional Christian philosophy of history represented by Augustine and Bossuet. While a Christian philosophy of history could hold that all periods and peoples formed part of the drama of his-tory, it was usually less inclusive. Furthermore, rather than looking upon the fate of Mankind as a single developing whole, it tended to view the manner in which peoples grew, flourished, and perished in terms of the manner in which they obeyed or failed to carry out the Divine Will. And it was also assumed in the Christian philosophy of history that the drama of history would finally come to a close: it had a beginning, a climax, a denouement, and an end. Reward and punishment would be meted out at the end, even more fully than had been the case within the span of the drama. Man's history was not, then, a self-fulfilling process; the reason for its very existence was to be found in a state which lay outside of history.

On the other hand, according to the eighteenth-century doctrine of Progress, an indefinite future opened up before man. All periods and peoples could be placed in the continuing stream of Mankind's development toward higher achievements, and praise or blame was assigned in accordance with the role which individual periods or persons had played in the upward struggle of Man. This process was regarded as having been continuous. There had been setbacks and failures, but the failures had been due to the encroachments of superstition, and even in the midst of the periods of failure man's struggle had continuously gone on. This view of all history as a single process of development, stretching from a remote past toward a remote and a different future, a process which is impelled by a power which is immanent within it, is, as we shall see, also characteristic of the view of history maintained by those who first expounded and then developed historicism.[5]

The second point at which the Enlightenment doctrine of Progress helped to lay the foundations for historicism is to be found in the way in which it widened the scope of what was regarded as historically significant. In general, history had previously been a subject which had only been concerned with what would currently be regarded as political history. Because of the emphasis which the Enlightenment placed upon the intellectual development of mankind, and on the struggle of the intellect against ignorance and superstition, the province of history began to include more of those elements which we should regard as aspects of social and intellectual history. This widening of the horizon of historical writing continued, once it was no longer assumed that the subject-matter of history was to be construed solely in political terms. What came to be viewed as the true subject of history was the total way of life and of feeling of a people.

Voltaire's historical works mark the first self-conscious step in this direction, but parallels to his treatment can be found in Gibbon, in Turgot,[6] and in others. For example, the tendency to interpret the life of a people in terms of factors which extended beyond the sphere of the political is to be found in Montesquieu, whose problem was that of viewing constitutional forms as being themselves related to alternative conditions of life.[7] The attempts of Winckelmann and of Lessing to penetrate the spirit of Greek culture through the works of art which were its expressions are also steps in the same direction. Thus among typical figures of the Enlightenment we find a widespread tendency to include within the boundaries of history a greater diversity of materials than had formerly been included. Yet the scope of the interest evinced in the new types of historical material was still limited by the fact that, in general, these figures shared the conviction that the lucid and eternal dictates of reason served as the basis for an evaluation of the individual and social achievements of man. This conviction tended to force them into a pattern of viewing history as illustrative of the capabilities (and, at times, of the foibles) of the human race. It was not until this standard of evaluation had been severely challenged that the historians of the latter part of the eighteenth century could immerse themselves without restraint in the lives and modes of feeling of the most diverse segments of the past.

Among the many challenges to the standards of evaluation which dominated the thought of the Enlightenment, by far the most radical and influential was that of Rousseau. We need not deal with the manifold ways in which his emphasis upon feeling, and his rejections of the ideal of civilization and of Progress, ran counter to the main streams of thought in the period. What is important to note is that Rousseau himself was not interested in history, and in fact represents a reaction against the growing interest in the actual nature of man's past social life.[8] Yet, by his rebellion against Enlightenment modes of thought and his own emphasis upon feeling and upon "the natural," his influence contributed to a magnificent expansion of that which was considered historically important. When his views of the nature and goal of man's social life came into contact with the expansion of the historical horizon which had been achieved by the Enlightenment (and achieved precisely because of its concern with Reason and Progress), new elements within the pattern of history emerged. Whereas the Enlightenment had considered those forms of thought, feeling, and social cohesiveness which characterized the lives of "simpler" peoples as vestiges of a primitive state of society which was being gradually overcome, the new influence caused men to affirm the necessity and worth of these elements within the fabric of social life, thus focusing historical attention upon them.

Out of this combination of the Enlightenment's expansion of the province of history and challenges to the Enlightenment's standard of what constituted the nature and goal of man's social life, there developed a radically new position. It held that the life of a people is a unitary thing, expressing itself in all laws and institutions, and in all artistic accomplishments; that this unity is achieved because of a unity of feeling which has grown through the traditions and inner needs of the people; and that such a unity of feeling is the soul of the people. Thus the historian's task is that of grasping the inner core of feeling which binds a people together and which manifests itself in all of the accomplishments of that people; it is his aim to see the people as a single, living, historical and history-making entity whose value must be judged in terms of its own inner harmony, not in terms of a rational and universal standard imposed upon it.

It is obvious that such a view constitutes a break with the standards of the Enlightenment. A symptom of this break is to be found in the extent to which a revaluation of the Middle Ages set in. Such a revaluation is to be found in persons who differed from one another as much as did Moeser, Herder, Burke, Chateaubriand, and Madame de Staël. Their revaluation of the mediaeval was a symptom of a change which had been undergone; it was not itself a cause of this change. This can be seen in the fact that each of these figures self-consciously challenged the standards of the Enlightenment on grounds other than those of its neglect of the mediaeval. A similar and associated change is to be noted within the field of political theory. Following the lead of Hume and of others, the concept of a social contract had been abandoned, and states were viewed as natural growths which had their roots in (a) the common nature of men, (b) the nature of existing conditions, and (c) the customs and traditions upon which the people had been nurtured. At first, as one can see in Hume, this did not lead to a denial of the standards which the Enlightenment used in judging the worth of a state: the state's function was to foster the happiness, freedom, and enlightenment of its citizens.[9] Yet, the social contract doctrine (and the whole existing corpus of doctrines within political theory) had been a mixture of supposedly descriptive statements with the expression of a normative ideal. Therefore, when the description of the basis of all civil polities was altered, it was readily assumed that the true nature of these polities also carried implications for the way in which the ideal end of the state was to be conceived. This end could then no longer be viewed wholly in terms of individual well-being: as a natural growth, the state had a being and a goal of its own. States could be regarded not as the products but as the destinies of individuals; they were living, growing things, the embodiments of long traditions, and the bearers of all that bound the individual to his soil, to his family, and to his fellows. On such a view the universal state was a myth, for the appeal to the universal state was based upon the universal reason of man, but the national state was a reality, an embodiment of the feelings and traditions which bound a group of people together. It was to the national state, thus conceived, and to its products that historians came to turn their attention.

This view of the state would not have made the headway which it did had there not already been a challenge to the standards of the Enlightenment. One might of course attempt to hold that the traditionalism of Burke and of Chateaubriand was primarily due to their reactions against the French Revolution, and Moeser's views might be explained as being purely a function of his particular, restricted historical interests. However, it is clear in Herder and in Madame de Staël that their mode of viewing history was linked to their dissatisfaction with their predecessors' conception of the norm of "enlightenment." Madame de Staël, who was in many ways a product of the Enlightenment, attempted to introduce into her consideration of men and societies those forms of "sentiment" and "enthusiasm" which the Enlightenment had disparaged, or for which it had left no room.[10] And Herder, by whom she had been influenced, grounded his conception of history in a religious view of the world which he recognized to be diametrically opposed to the norms which the Enlightenment embraced.[11] In them, as well as in Moeser, Burke, and Chateaubriand, and in fact in all of their successors, the new conception of a *"Volk"* (of the living unity of a people) came to the forefront of attention.[12] The feelings and traditions which bound a people together, and which were expressed in their culture, were not themselves rationally grounded, nor to be rationally justified. Such feelings and traditions sprang from a common language, a common heritage of customs, a common facing of the exigencies of life in a particular locale. As such they were at least as much the heritages of peasants as of cosmopolitan intellectuals or of rulers,[13] and folk-wisdom, folk-tales, and folk-poetry could be regarded as the expressions of the unity which underlay the life and growth of the nation.

This interest in whatever sprang from the common people and was rooted in a common tradition readily merged with Rousseau's conception of purity of feeling as an endowment of man in his primitive and childlike condition. Since those who followed Rousseau[14] also held that the simplicity and integrity of this feeling was sullied by the processes of "civilization" the canons of aesthetic and moral judgment changed. The opposite of refinement was no longer taken to be crudity, but simplicity; and simplicity was linked with the capacity for spontaneity. Sensibility was not the product of cultivation, but was an intense expression of the depths of man's nature as a passionate being. Whatever was unique and individual, whatever was rich and spontaneous, was an expression of this nature, and was of more worth than that which conformed to a universal and intellectualized canon of taste. Genius was not to be limited by formal rules, for these could only serve to hamper the spontaneous expression of those intense feelings through which man was conscious of his unity with nature and with his fellow men. Thus, new heroes were created, new moments in the life of nations were singled out as worthy of admiration, and a new standard was applied to religious institutions and practices. The question of what was important was no longer seen in terms of an opposition between enlightenment and darkness, but between intensity and superficiality, between the spontaneous and the calculating, between that which represented the mysterious springs of creative power and that which the cold light of reasoning could discern.

The separate strands of this new mode of thought all have their individual histories, but they converged in a view of the past which was new. At the heart of this new doctrine was the conception of the *organic* nature of man's social life, and the use of the organic analogy among the thinkers of the last quarter of the eighteenth century suggests two complementary theses. First, it suggests that in dealing with social life we are dealing with a process of change which is analogous to the growth of a living thing. Second, it suggests that the various aspects of social life are to be conceived as related to one another, and to the growth of the whole, as the component parts of a living thing are related to one another and to that thing as a whole. Both theses characterized the period with which we are presently concerned, and in fact tended to dominate all of nineteenth-century thought.[15]

The first of these theses was by no means entirely new. One can find many previous analogies between the growth of a living thing and processes of change within a society as a whole, or within various social institutions. One can also find in the Enlightenment (and before) the idea of the growth of mankind from infancy to maturity. Furthermore, the conception of societies as organic growths was fostered when the Enlightenment rejected the view that man's historical fate was directly controlled by God, holding that the power that made for progress was immanent within Mankind itself. However, these features of the organic analogy, which were present in the Enlightenment, received far greater emphasis from the founders of historicism. On their view, the various aspects of man's social life were as intimately related as were the parts of an organism. Not only was each part organically connected with all other parts, but no part could be understood as a living, functioning thing except by virtue of its relation to the whole of which it was a part. Thus, not only particular institutions were meaningless when they were considered in isolation from one another, but their relationships could be understood only when they were viewed as functioning within a living whole which gave life to each part. That which bound the parts together and animated the whole was the soul of the people. Every aspect of the life of a time was thus instinct with the life of the whole, although some aspects mirrored this whole more fully than did others.[16] No part could be adequately understood in isolation, nor could one assign any value to any part except in terms of its function within that whole without which it could not have been what it was.[17]

Both theses of historicism are obviously involved in this manner of viewing a society. If specific institutions are to be understood only in terms of what they contribute to the societies in which they are embedded, and if these societies are themselves viewed on the analogy of living things, then each institution must be viewed in terms of its place in a pattern of development. Furthermore, one cannot then meaningfully praise or blame institutions, except in terms of the extent to which they promoted or hindered its growth. So long as each culture, or each historical period, was treated as a separate entity, having a life of its own, a full-fledged historicism does not result from this view. It still remained possible to study one historical "organism" in isolation from others, and it would, in principle, even be possible to set up some standard of value against which they might be compared. However, if all historical people and periods are to be seen as portions or aspects of some larger development, then even this possibility vanishes. In Herder we find the first example of such a view.

Herder continually used the analogy of growth, and other analogies from the sphere of living things. He spoke of seeds and plants, of buds and flowers, and used "blossoming" as a root metaphor in his conception of history. Most important of all, he viewed nature as a single developing whole.[18] Starting with the earth's place in the cosmos, he related man to the earth, and the nature of man as an organic being to his nature as a social and historical being. And, finally, he interpreted all history as if it were the growth of a single and marvelous tree, whose branches produced the cultures of mankind.[19]

Such a view was assuredly fostered by the Enlightenment view of the development of Mankind, but even more important was the religious reaction *against* the Enlightenment. This religious reaction we have seen to have been centered in the conception of divine immanence, a doctrine which Herder enthusiastically accepted, and influentially developed.[20]

The relation between the doctrines of divine immanence and historicism is not difficult to see. If all of reality is One, and the Divine is present in all of the manifestations of this One, then what occurs within the process of history is itself a Revelation. Some aspects of the historical process will more fully reveal the nature of the Divine than will others, but this is not because they conform to a human standard of goodness or evil; rather, it is because they more fully reveal the power which operates within all of the manifestations of the Divine. And since God is not a transcendent being, and the human conscience is therefore not a reflection of the specific laws or commands of a transcendent creator and judge, the conscience is fallible if it seeks to approve or condemn isolated acts, failing to plunge below the surfaces of these acts to see them in their relation to God. Thus, because the power of God is within all things, it is the role of man's heart and moral sense to penetrate deeper into the nature of all that exists. Not clarity of judgment, not the voice which commands "thou shalt" and "thou shalt not," but a sense of the dark and the hidden, a feeling of dependence and awe, a worshipful acceptance of the fulness of being, these are the attitudes which put the religious man in touch with the Divine.

For Herder, as well as for others of the time, "the great World-Spirit is the most sublime name for God,"[21] and the inner forces of nature, the hidden drives and secret powers in all things, were the expressions of its essence.[22] But one may note that, in holding this doctrine, those who shared Herder's convictions came into conflict with the religious interpretation of nature which had been held by their predecessors. According to both theists and deists, the laws of mechanics were adequate to describe the mode of operation of the physical world, and these laws were embedded in nature by its transcendent Creator. The German Romanticists and idealists rebelled against both of these theses. They not only conceived of God as the immanent World-Spirit, but attempted to transcend the mechanical view of nature associated with Newton's views. They emphasized those aspects of nature which had not been comprehended within the Newtonian system, such as magnetism, chemical affinities, the formation of crystals, and the inner forces in the lives of plants and of animals. And they went even further, attacking Newton within the sphere of his own mechanical interpretation of nature, and sought to distinguish mechanics from "true physics."[23] For them the ultimate forces in nature were *"living"* forces; and all nature, they found, was to be understood as one process of growth.

It can readily be seen how this doctrine of the self-revelation of the World-Spirit through a process of self-transformations and self-development fostered an acceptance of all of the presuppositions which we have noted as basic to historicism. So far as understanding the nature of anything was concerned, the doctrine of divine immanence made it imperative that one should consider all phenomena as being internally related: not merely related in the sense of being causally connected within one mechanical system but related in essence, since all were manifestations of the one Divine Being. It therefore also led to the view that there were two ways of knowing that which was contained within the historical process: an outer, superficial mode, and a mode by means of which man could penetrate into the hidden inner springs of power from which all things followed. And so far as evaluation was concerned, the principle of divine immanence led to the belief that each thing had its own value, each was an expression of the Divine. It is for this reason that moral judgment came to be viewed as arbitrary, and sympathetic understanding and a reverential attitude toward all forms of culture was held up as an ideal. And, connected with this, we find that there was a transformation of the evaluation of persons and epochs: not morality, but indwelling power was what characterized the objects of the age's praise.

Yet, though we find these tendencies becoming more and more prominent in the period from Herder to Hegel, it is not until we reach Hegel's own system that the full import of historicism is recognized and made the foundation of a complete view of the world. Without summarizing the Hegelian system, we may indicate those points at which Hegel's own thought diverged from that of his predecessors in such a way as to transform historicism into the cardinal principle of a philosophic system, rather than leaving it as a corollary of the doctrine of divine immanence.

In this connection we may first mention Hegel's rebellion against what he took to be the undisciplined Romantic doctrine of feeling, and his insistence that Reason was the sole mode of apprehending the nature of the world. To be sure, it

was under the influence of previous variants of idealism that he transformed the
usual conception of the methods by which Reason operated, viewing the course
which it followed as a dialectical process. But having conceived of Reason in
this way, and having made it the framework of both thought and things, he could
no longer espouse some of the views to which his predecessors had been committed. So far as historicism was concerned, he could no longer hold, as Herder
had done, that each culture was to be regarded as an equally valid embodiment
of the Divine. The dialectical development of the Absolute made each successive
culture a fuller embodiment of the ultimate nature of reality. Nor was there
a constant standard of worth which one could discern within the process itself:
the process was self-justifying, and the births of new cultures, as well as their
tragic deaths, followed the judgment of Reason. The history of the world was,
then, the world's court of judgment.

More importantly still, this conception of the rational dialectical order of the
world precluded the possibility that Hegel could hold, as some of his predecessors
had held, that an understanding of history could be attained by considering either
isolated periods, or even all of human history, without seeing it as a part of the
total process of nature. His predecessors had been ready to believe that by an
empathic act one could understand individual cultures, and that by grasping
them as individual manifestations of the Divine, one could fully appreciate their
natures. But Hegel insisted that one must not only view them in their relations
to the Absolute, but one must view them in their relations to one another, as
logically sequential manifestations of the Absolute. Thus no one culture, taken
alone, would "make sense," even if one were to regard it as an expression of the
absolute World-Spirit, or God; one would have to know it "concretely," as a part
of a single developing process, none of whose aspects we could know until we
had the key of the whole dialectic which would unlock all doors and enable us
to follow the systematic connections among all periods of history. Therefore,
from the point of view of understanding, no less than from the point of view of
value, Hegel represents a complete historicism, systematically applied.

Both the right-wing and the left-wing Hegelians were close enough to Hegel's
historicism to put it to use, but only in the case of Marxian doctrine could one
argue that it continued to be salient. Although the case of Feuerbach is not typical, it is illuminating in this respect. Feuerbach had won his independence from
Hegel by coming to regard Hegel's own system as a historical fact, and therefore
as a system which was to be transcended; however, his own positive position abandoned both the explanatory and the evaluative theses of historicism, and
grounded itself on a non-historical conception of what constituted the essence of
man.[24] Those who belonged to the Hegelian left or right did not deviate so radically from their source, but their interests were no longer primarily metaphysical,
and (with the exception of the joint efforts of Marx and Engels) their thought was
less oriented toward systematization. Thus, while specific areas of thought and
action were still being interpreted in a historicist manner, an encompassing
historicism was no longer stressed. This can be seen in the manner in which both
left-Hegelians and right-Hegelians formulated their political philosophies; it is

also missing in the left-wing school of Biblical criticism, and in the right-wing historians of theology and of philosophy.

As a further symptom of the decline of historicism within German philosophy one can cite the fact that not only were Schopenhauer and Kierkegaard untouched by historicism, but they were powerful antagonists of it. Considering their lack of immediate influence, their attitudes can only be considered as symptoms, not as causes of a tendency to turn away from historicist modes of thought. Similarly, while all forms of Kantianism also tend to be opposed to historicism, it would be a mistake to attribute its decline to a revival of interest in Kant. Rather, to find a causative factor one must turn to developments within the discipline of history itself.

Within the German historical school there was deep opposition to Hegel's attempt to construct a philosophy of history. The opposition between Niebuhr and Hegel was, of course, open and complete.[25] And while Hegel had no occasion to mention Ranke, the latter could not, from the outset, have looked with equanimity on Hegel's attacks on the critical method, and on Niebuhr. In the end, Ranke criticized Hegel: and his own philosophical interpretation of history was utterly opposed to Hegel's historicism.[26] However, long before this time the clash of their methods was apparent. In so far as one followed the critical method of sifting individual national and regional and institutional histories in order to reconstruct an understanding of the past — in so far as one occupied one's self, as did Ranke, with the history of Venice, of Serbia, of the Papacy—the model of a single, linear, developmental process, such as had been demanded by Hegel's philosophy, was seen to be unrealistic. Indeed, as Ranke remarked in an unpublished comment concerning philosophies of history in general, and concerning Fichte's philosophy of history in particular, such views of the past were largely fabrications.[27] In the face of this opposition in method, and given the influence and prestige of the historical school, the historical dimension of Hegel's thought was bound to lose credit, and, with that loss, historicism declined in Germany.

To be sure, historiography flourished, and it was also the case that the members of the historical school, and their successors, tended to use organic analogies in much the same way as the Romantics and the Idealists had done.[28] Nonetheless, given the fate of the Hegelian movement within philosophy, and the rise of the critical historical school, there is no evidence that historicism would have remained a dominant nineteenth-century movement if the second current of thought which we shall trace had not contributed to its spread. As we shall see, even in the case of Marxism the appeal of the historicist theses stems less from the Hegelian tradition than from the infusion of strength which it gained from this second, independent source.

4

THE SEARCH FOR A SCIENCE OF SOCIETY:
FROM SAINT-SIMON TO MARX AND ENGELS

If we are to understand the later development of historicism and the manner in which it merged with a comprehensive evolutionism, we must turn from the Romantics and from Hegelianism to those thinkers who represented a continuation of the intellectual traditions of the Enlightenment and who, on that basis, sought to establish a positive science of social development. The sources of this movement were to be found in France, and not in Germany. Although he had precursors, its first major representative was Claude-Henri de Saint-Simon.

Saint-Simon stands in striking contrast to his German contemporaries. In place of their metaphysical idealism he espoused materialism. In contrast to their rejection of seventeenth- and eighteenth-century science in favor of an organic view of nature, he was an adherent of Newtonianism.[1] Whereas his German contemporaries accepted all spontaneous expressions of the human spirit as manifestations of divine immanence, Saint-Simon did not reject the cosmopolitan ideals of civilization and knowledge which had characterized the Enlightenment. However, he did go beyond all of his predecessors among the philosophers of history of the Enlightenment, including Condorcet, in his stress upon necessity and the governance of inexorable law in human history.

This assumption on Saint-Simon's part stemmed from his general metaphysical position. He believed that man was a machine, like all other parts of nature: a mechanistic microcosm within the great mechanical macrocosm.[2] Furthermore, he believed that human history paralleled man's physiologically grounded individual development.[3] Thus, he was confident that there was a necessity in human affairs, and he credited Locke with having established a general law of human perfectability, which applied both to the individual's intelligence and to the intellectual development of mankind.[4] However, it was through conversations with the physician Burdin, and not from Locke, that Saint-Simon received a suggestion of the precise form which mankind's intellectual evolution had taken.[5] This suggestion, which had also been anticipated by Turgot and was to be more fully developed by Comte, is that mankind has progressed—and each of the sciences has progressed—from a theological to a conjectural or metaphysical stage and then to a positive or genuinely scientific level. What Saint-Simon regarded as needed in the development of the sciences of his own day was that physiology should reach the positive stage of knowledge. He believed that physiology would be able to provide man with a scientifically grounded standard of value, since it could determine his needs; and since Saint-Simon held that the development of the human race paralleled the development of the individual, he believed that there could also be a social physiology which would define the goals of historical development. What these goals were, and in what manner Saint-Simon wished to reform society, is not our present concern. What is important to note is how this developmental necessitarianism was related to historicism in Saint-Simon, since an understanding of this point will considerably facilitate an understanding of the historicism of Comte and of questions which will arise when we consider whether the doctrines of Marx are also to be classified as historicist.

At first glance it may not seem that there need be any connection between historicism and Saint-Simon's view that all things are governed by laws of nature. However, if one construes the laws of nature as regulating a process of development from stage to stage in a continuous series, historicism can scarcely be avoided. For if what transpires is the necessary result of the operation of a developmental principle, then one can only understand any event by viewing it in relation to the law which controlled it; and to relate it to the operation of such a law, one must connect it with what preceded it and what followed upon it. Furthermore, in so far as whatever transpired in the past was part of a necessary process, it would be frivolous to make moral judgments regarding past events: the value of each would be a function of what it had contributed to the process as a whole. While one might still have a tendency to welcome or to deprecate individual occurrences in terms of how they were related to one's own goals, such an attitude could only be justified if one had reason to believe that one's goals coincided with those tendencies which represented the dominant course of history itself. Thus, both the cognitive and the evaluative theses of historicism follow from the assumption that there are laws which determine the direction of historical change. These laws, as we shall see,[6] possess a special logical structure, and it was not necessary for a follower of the Newtonian ideal to affirm that there were any laws which had this structure. Nonetheless, Saint-Simon did insist that there must be laws which controlled the direction of human development, and because of this form of necessitarianism there were a good many points at which he stood in far closer relation to a general historicism than he did to the standards of the Enlightenment. For a fuller development of that species of historicism which is first clearly noticeable in Saint-Simon, one can turn to an examination of the system of Comte.

It is not easy to separate the thought of Comte from that of Saint-Simon, whose secretary and co-worker he originally was. However, even in his earliest works one can find a more radical historicism in Comte's position, and this is especially noticeable in his attacks upon Condorcet, toward whom Saint-Simon had an ambivalent relationship.[7] In Comte's *Plan des travaux scientifiques nécessaires pour réorganiser la société,* which was written in 1822 while he was still an important collaborator in the Saint-Simonian movement, there are a number of pages devoted to an evaluation of Condorcet's thought, and from these pages one can see how widely Comte had diverged from the views of progress which had dominated the Enlightenment.[8]

Like Saint-Simon (although he came to express the utmost contempt for him), Comte attempted to carry out in a more adequate way the task which Condorcet had set himself in his *Esquisse d'un tableau historique des progrès de l'ésprit humain.* Comte held that Condorcet was the first to have seen that a positive science of politics could only be established on the basis of discovering a natural law which would explain the necessary and progressive development of mankind;[9] however, like Saint-Simon, he held that his predecessor had failed in his attempt to grasp the true necessity of history. Comte based this charge on the fact that Condorcet had failed to establish a proper and consistent periodization of history. In addition, he contended that Condorcet had failed to free himself from the evaluative prejudices of the eighteenth century. However, he defended Condorcet against a third possible line of criticism: that he had attempted to predict the future.[10] With respect to this third charge Comte held that it was precisely in this attempt that Condorcet showed his appreciation of the proper basis for a science of politics. The predictions made by Condorcet were vitiated not by any lack of necessity in the historical process, but were due to his inadequate periodization of history and to the non-scientific character of his evaluative standpoint.

With respect to the latter point, Comte held that the eighteenth century had lacked a true historical sense, for it had evaluated past ages with reference to its own preferences, and not with reference to the contributions which these ages had made to the progress of civilization. Thus, for example (and here Comte followed Saint-Simon), its evaluations of theocracy and mediaeval feudalism were faulty. As Comte pointed out, this failure to adopt a proper standard of evaluation gave rise to a paradox in Condorcet's conception of the history of civilization: on the one hand he had emphasized the great superiority of eighteenth-century culture to all previous cultures, regarding the latter as periods of failure; on the other hand he was convinced that there was a law of historical necessity that accounted for the birth of the present out of the past. How, Comte asked, could this be? If the present grows necessarily out of the past, its achievements would themselves have had to be prepared by the past, and past ages could not then be evaluated in a wholly negative manner. It was at this point that Comte explicitly embraced the evaluative thesis of historicism. "We should," he said, "regard institutions and doctrines as having reached, at every period, the greatest perfection compatible with the corresponding civilization."[11] Shortly thereafter, in what can be taken as a rejection of Enlightenment standards, he said: "Instead of regarding the past as a tissue of monstrosities, we should, generally speaking, consider society as having been, on the whole, guided with all the wisdom the situation allowed."[12] This acceptance of the view that a proper evaluation of any institution or doctrine consists in seeing its necessity at a given time, did not lead Comte to a purely neutralist attitude. Like many others who have accepted the historicist thesis, Comte introduced a criterion of value which he assumed to be implicit within the historical process itself: the criterion of progressive development. Thus he distinguished between the period of full vigor of a society, and the period of its decadence; a distinction which was drawn in terms of when that society was a part of the march of civilization, and when it had become stationary. However, Comte did not deduce revolutionary political consequences from this doctrine. Since he believed that all political systems and all forms of social organization necessarily reflected the state of civilization which was present at any time, the attempt to inaugurate political and social changes before new modes of thought had developed could lead only to disorder, not to progress. This characteristically conservative doctrine of Comte's (which signalized a fundamental divergence from the basic economic and social program of the Saint-Simonian movement) was, he believed, the practical import of a positive science of politics. The goal of such a science he had already defined as being that of determining, through an examination of the past, the nature of the social system which the march of civilization tended to produce in the present.[13]

But what was "the march of civilization," as Comte conceived it? To find an answer to this question we must turn back to his first criticism of Condorcet: that Condorcet's periodization of history was faulty. What Comte had found wanting in Condorcet's view of the past epochs of history was its failure to provide a homogeneous principle of classification: each epoch was viewed as having been ushered in by a noteworthy event, but some of these events were industrial, others scientific, and others political. Thus, according to Comte, Condorcet's actual work never passed beyond the practices which characterize literary history, as distinct from scientific history. What Comte regarded as scientific history he then made clear. Since the problem was one of classifying the epochs of history, he urged as a model the methods of classification used by naturalists when they survey the plant or animal kingdoms. In other words, one should start from some overall view of the most general principle applicable to the domain, and subdivide the classes in accordance with the real relations observed among the facts. By carrying through division after division one will end with a hierarchy of concepts which reflect the actually observed relations among the phenomena in question. Thus, an overall conspectus of history must proceed by showing the existence of an articulated pattern in history, rather than by the more usual genetic, narrative method. As Comte said at the outset of this passage: "The distribution of epochs constitutes the most important portion of the plan in a work of this nature, or, to speak more correctly, it alone constitutes the plan considered in its greatest generality; since it determines the principal mode of coordinating the facts observed."[14] Comte, of course, found the overall plan in the same law of the three stages that Saint-Simon had suggested, and it is this law that he then developed in opposition to Condorcet's divisions of history.

The most general principle of classification applicable to the domain of history was, according to Comte, the concept of "states of civilization." The elements of a civilization are the sciences, the arts, and industry, taking each of these terms in its widest sense. Thus, a civilization consists in a particular development of the human spirit and in the corresponding development of human actions on nature.[15] A classification of civilizations must therefore always take as its point of departure the modes of thought which characterize the sciences, the arts, and the industry of a given time and place. Since Comte, following Burdin and Saint-Simon, believed that there was a natural tendency for the human spirit to advance from a fictive to a positive mode of thought, his classification of states of civilization took on a temporal dimension. This emphasis on the temporal dimension sharply differentiated the domain of sociology from all of the other sciences in Comte's system.[16] And he observed that within this temporally oriented science, a valid classification was even more important than in the other domains: an apprehension of particular facts, independently of their relations to other facts, is sometimes useful in other sciences, but is of no use within the domain of politics, where each fact must be grasped in its relation to the continuous and necessary march of civilization.[17] And in this connection it is interesting to note that Comte's emphasis on the unity of history always led him to speak of "Humanity," or "the Great Being," or "the collective organism," as the subject of history: it was not with the specific histories of specific societies that his historical sociology was concerned.[18]

Not only did Comte hold that there was a necessary progression from stage to stage in the evolution of mankind, he also held that this evolution embraced all aspects of human existence. According to his categories of human experience, this meant that the developmental process embraced thought, action, and feeling.[19] At every stage in the course of human development there was a coordination of the intellectual, active, and affective principles in man, and this coordination (which Comte discussed at length in his social statics) provided the necessary and orderly base for the dynamics of historical progress.[20] Thus, for Comte, the development of humanity from its most primitive roots to its highest future attainments represented not merely a necessary development, but a development which included all facets of human experience. Each period of history tended to form a single, unitary whole, and at the same time each was a necessary phase in the overall development of mankind.

Having adopted this consistently monistic view of human history, Comte did not hesitate to draw its necessary epistemological consequences, even though these consequences did not fit with the views of scientific procedure which one would expect from an exponent of positivism.

The first of these consequences was that there is a higher form of historical knowledge than that which proceeds by tracing the specific and detailed interrelations among particular historical events. As we have already noted in connection with his earliest essay, Comte held that the crucial step for historical understanding was to find a general plan in history by means of which the particular facts could be coordinated. Throughout his writings he ascribed greater certainty to the knowledge of the truth of this plan than to any knowledge which could be obtained through an examination of historical records. For example, in arguing that there never has been retrogression in history which was not of a partial and purely temporary sort, he held that what appears to be retrogression is usually the result of "a too detailed exploration" of human history: a concentration of attention on a single element within the undulatory orbit of civilization leads one to suppose that retrogression has occurred, but a tracing of the main trajectory of history quickly serves to correct this erroneous view.[21] Here, as elsewhere, Comte granted positive philosophy a role higher than that granted to empirical science: any particular science becomes complete only by being placed within the larger synthesis of knowledge. It is the synoptic point of view which gives meaning to any element in our knowledge: the highest form of knowledge is not a knowledge of detail, but of overall structure. Thus Comte embraced one of the corollaries which, so far as I can see, always follows from a monistic theory of historical development: an acceptance of the view that there are two ways of knowing, and that the method of detail must be supplemented by that more adequate total vision of the whole, into which each detail can later be fitted.[22]

A second consequence of treating the historical process as a single, necessary, developmental process was Comte's quite unpositivistic introduction of teleology into his explanation of the basis of historical change. What Comte took to be the foundation for the law of the three stages was not (as has often been supposed) the assumption that the individual goes through these stages in his intellectual development, and that the history of mankind necessarily parallels this individual development. Such had been the view of Saint-Simon; and the fact that it has also been attributed to Comte may be due to his well-known statement that the stages of his mental breakdown, and of his recovery, served as a verification of the stages of thought through which mankind passed.[23] However, he could not use a pattern of individual development as a fundamental basis on which mankind's development was to be explained since this would not have been consistent with his doctrine of emergence. Nor would it have been consistent with his conviction that it is not the biological nature of man which determines the forms of social organization, but it is society which determines the social characteristics of the individual.[24] The actual foundation from which Comte sought to derive the necessity of his law of three stages lay in his social statics, which he developed in the second volume of his *Système de politique positive*. There he claimed that the dynamic tendency of history derives from general conditions which are necessary if men are to fulfil each of their three basic faculties: thought, action, and feeling. What he attempted to show was that the conditions necessary for mankind to fulfil these needs are conditions which give rise to precisely the social transitions which the law of development summarizes. In other words, humanity (the collective organism) evolved progressively not because individual human nature changed, but because human nature could only attain its final and proper functioning, its ideal fulfilment, through remaking the forms of social organization.[25] This, of course, introduced a teleological factor into history, and strangely enough Comte did not shrink from its acceptance: throughout his exposition of the dynamics of historical development he appealed to a determination of the present by what was to come. For example, one of his laws of sociological method involved him in holding that the understanding of any event depends not merely upon the past and the present, but in seeing it as a link between the past and the future: "The sound appreciation of every intermediate state is subsequent to that of the two extremes which it is to connect."[26] One can also recognize a teleological element in Comte's view of history in his insistence that a proper understanding of any stage in the history of mankind, as well as of that history as a whole, depends upon examining its "adult state" (i.e., its fullest and final development), viewing its past as a gradual preparation for this stage.[27] This, in fact, is the way in which Comte viewed the successive epochs of civilization: as preparations for what was next to come. Thus, for example, his interpretation of the Middle Ages (which he considered to be the period whose proper appreciation was decisive in forming his own true account of history) was dominated by an attempt to show that it was a necessary preparatory stage for the industrial, positive stage of civilization.[28] In fact, he is quite explicit in stating that we must not look upon history as a mass of events which occurred in the past, for in that way it remains barren; rather, it must be viewed dynamically, as a preparation for what is to come.[29]

The justification (if it be that) for this departure from the model of the laws which characterize the non-human sciences lies in the fact that Comte, as we have seen based his dynamic law of development upon his view of what constituted the normal functioning of the basic faculties present in all men, viz., on the principles laid down in his social statics. But these principles, too, were conceived in a teleological fashion: a proper balance was necessary to fulfil the needs of human nature, and it was toward this self-fulfilment that man naturally tended.[30] Therefore, each historical modification of the basic modes of thought, action, or feeling is related, according to Comte, to the end which is normal for it and which, as normal, will ultimately be attained.[31] As Comte insisted, in order to understand or explain any particular segment of history, one must view it in the context of a larger development, and this contention constitutes an acceptance of the cognitive thesis of historicism.

Comte's acceptance of the evaluative thesis of historicism was closely linked to the position we have just outlined, and we need not deal with it in detail. It will be recalled that in his early criticism of Condorcet, he held that if one were to reach a proper evaluation of events one would first have to understand the necessity which is present within the process as a whole. And since Comte regarded this process as tending toward the full development and harmony of man's potentialities for thought, action, and feeling, each phase of the historical process was judged in terms of what it contributed to that process. Thus, for Comte all events were to be judged, as well as being known, through the place which they occupied and the roles which they played within the stream of human history. It is small wonder then that d'Eichthal, who knew Comte's earliest work, saw a deep affinity between his thought and that of Hegel.

That there was this affinity is also attested by the confluences of their impacts on Taine and on Renan. Looking back on the middle of the nineteenth century, it may seem strange that Comte, the positivist, and Hegel, the idealist, should have simultaneously exerted a profound influence on the same individuals. To be sure, both Taine and Renan were extremely eclectic, and Renan later expressed, in letters to Pasteur, some reservations concerning Comteism as a movement. Yet is it not apparently strange that two men who are quite properly conceded to fall within the positivist tradition should sometimes praise the thought of Hegel in terms no less glowing than that of any Hegelian?[32] The answer lies, I believe, in the fact that Hegel's stress on the continuity, the unity, and the necessity of historical development toward a complete human fulfilment was paralleled in Comte and was shared by those in France and in England who remained within the intellectual traditions of the Enlightenment. As Renan said in *L'Avenir de la science*, which was written in 1848, but not published until much later: "L'histoire, non pas curieuse mais théorique, de l'ésprit humain, telle est la philosophie du XIXe siècle."[33]

The influence of Hegel on positivism was not, however, widespread, even in France: it is in Marxism that one finds the chief point at which his thought merged with attempts to explain social change in terms of scientific laws of development. Although there unquestionably were both positive and negative ways in which Marx was influenced by Hegel, there is room for disagreement concerning the nature and extent of these influences. There is, as we shall see, also room for fundamental disagreements concerning Marx's own interpretation of the laws which explain social change. Both types of question inevitably raise issues concerning the relationships between Marx's earliest writings and his later writings, and concerning the extent to which his views are to be identified with those of Engels, and those held by later Marxists. In approaching these issues we shall first consider the question of Marx's relationship to Hegel.

In 1873, in the preface to the second edition of *Capital*, Marx discussed his indebtedness to Hegel's dialectical method, and he did so in a way that can be taken (and has been taken) to suggest that he had first been influenced by Hegel's philosophy of history. In this passage, when he interprets himself as having reversed Hegel's idealism, he might be thought to be referring to the fact that he had put forward an economic interpretation of history which rested not on the self-development of Spirit, but upon changes in the modes of production. Yet, it is in this same passage that Marx referred to an earlier critical study that he had made of Hegel's dialectic; and this study, as we now know, constituted the third part of his *Economic and Philosophic Manuscripts of 1844*. When one turns to this earlier source one finds that Hegel's primary influence on Marx did not in fact involve any aspects of Hegel's mature views concerning the philosophy of history. Rather, it was from the *Phenomenology of Spirit* that Marx drew his conception of the dialectic.[34] Furthermore, far from interpreting human activities as historically rooted, as Hegel's doctrine of Objective Spirit demands, one finds that Marx's language and whole mode of procedure had been deeply influenced by Feuerbach's concern for the generic nature of man, and for the question of what characterizes the essence of man as a species.[35] To be sure, Marx did insist that man is social. In these contexts his emphasis was similar to Feuerbach's, stressing what might be termed man's generic sociality; unlike Hegel, Marx was concerned with "social being" in general, and not with the relations of men to the concrete nature of the historical situations in which they are placed.[36] Thus, at this point in his development, Marx can scarcely be said to have been engrossed in formulating a science of society, the aim of which would be to discover laws on the basis of which the concrete manifestations of history could be predicted or explained.[37]

However, in the "Theses on Feuerbach," which date from the following year, there is a radical shift in Marx's philosophic position. One major aspect of that shift was his attack on Feuerbach's failure to grasp the importance of concrete historical and sociological influences on men. Another was his emphasis on practice. While this second aspect of his criticism of Feuerbach was wholly consistent with all that Marx had written before, it is not implausible to hold that Marx's contact with Engels's early work—and then with Engels himself—was in part responsible for his new and radical emphasis on the manner in which historical forces shape men. For example, in Engels's "Outlines of a Critique of Political Economy," which Marx had published in the *Deutsch-Französische Jahrbücher* before their first meeting, Engels had applied dialectical concepts to changes in social institutions in a manner which finds no clear parallel in Marx's earlier writings.[38] To be sure, in *Ludwig Feuerbach*, which was written after Marx's death, Engels claimed that the basic principles of the Marxist conception of history, as well as of Marxist economics, are to be attributed to Marx himself.[39] One would think, then, that it would have been Marx who had originally had the sharper historical sense. However, if one compares what each had written prior to their collaboration, the contrast between them is striking;[40] and it is perhaps not unwarranted to suspect that Engels's interest and ability in concrete historical analyses may have had an important influence on the development of Marx's thought.

Whether or not this conjecture concerning the seminal influence of Engels on Marx is sound, it is certainly the case that in 1845 and 1846, beginning with *The German Ideology*, concrete historical argument came to play a major and in fact indispensable role in Marxism.[41] This raises a second question on which there is room for considerable disagreement in interpretation: what relation may be said to obtain between historical materialism, as one finds it in Marx, and those modes of explanation and evaluation which characterize historicism?

In considering this question I shall not be obliged to consider many of the most significant aspects of historical materialism. For example, I shall not deal with the Marxist contention that all other elements in a society depend upon, or are determined by, the means of production and the relations of production within that society. Nor shall I be concerned with the factual truth or falsity of the specific analyses or the historical predictions of Marx. The subject which is to be discussed is simply the logic of explanation and of evaluation in Marxism, and this subject—though far more restricted than either of the other aspects of historical materialism—poses more difficulties in interpretation than are apt to be recognized by some opponents of Marxism, or by Marxists themselves.

A suggestive point of departure for this discussion lies in *The German Ideology*, where historical materialism is specifically formulated as a philosophy of history, and is contrasted with the philosophy of history of Hegel in particular.[42] In developing historical materialism in this discussion, Marx and Engels attempted to illustrate their thesis through tracing epochs in the historical development of Western society, and in doing so laid the groundwork for their subsequent interpretations of the stages in man's economic and sociological development.[43] Although they were not yet in a position to formulate their historical materialism in terms of those more complex analyses of economic processes which Marx developed in *A Contribution to a Critique of Political Economy* and in *Capital*, it is clear that they were seeking to explain historical change in terms of basic economic laws. The problem of analyzing the logic of their mode of explanation turns, then, on how one is to interpret the explanatory laws which they used. In this connection we may recall that in the case of Comte the concept of a law of directional change, such as the law of the three stages, tended to force one to accept both the explanatory and the evaluative theses of historicism. The question now to be raised is whether the laws presupposed by historical materialism are also directional laws, or whether they are not.[44]

Now, if we turn to the preface of the first edition of *Capital*, we find Marx stating that it is his aim "to lay bare the economic law of motion of modern society," and he spoke of the laws of capitalist production as "tendencies working with iron necessity towards inevitable results."[45] Furthermore, in the preface to the second edition of the same work, we find him quoting with approval a Russian reviewer who said: "The one thing which is of moment to Marx is to find the law of the phenomena with whose investigation he is concerned; and not only is that law of moment to him, which governs these phenomena, in so far as they have a definite form and mutual connection within a given historical period—*Of still greater moment to him is the law of their variation, of their development, i.e., of their transition from one form into another, from one series of connections into a different one.*"[46] I have italicized the last phrases of this remark, since they suggest that Marx did in fact believe that there are ultimate laws of historical development, as well as that there are "laws of mutual connection within a given historical period." It is not to be denied that in the rhetoric of *The Communist Manifesto*, as well as in other works up to and including *Capital*, one finds statements which lend plausibility to the view that Marx and Engels actually believed in ultimate and irreducible laws of directional development in human history. On the other hand, when one poses the question of how the analyses of economic processes in *Capital* were thought by Marx and by Engels to be directly relevant to historical materialism, the only tenable answer would seem to be that it was through the operation of these processes at each successive point in time that the directional trends of history were shaped. If this is true, directional laws would *not* be irreducible laws, but would be derivative from the non-directional laws of economic relationships; and this I take to have been the position actually adopted by Marx.

That this is so can best be suggested by quoting further from the review to which I have just alluded, which Marx quotes extensively in the preface to the second edition of *Capital*. The reviewer says:

> The scientific value of such an inquiry lies in the disclosing of the special laws that regulate the origin, existence, development, and death of a given social organism and its replacement by another and higher one. And it is this value that, in point of fact, Marx's book has.

To this Marx himself immediately adds:

> Whilst the writer pictures what he takes to be actually my method, in this striking and (as far as concerns my own application of it) generous way, what else is he picturing but the dialectic method?
> Of course the method of presentation must differ in form from that of inquiry. The latter has to appropriate the material in detail, to analyze its different forms of development, to trace their inner connection. Only after this work is done, can the actual movement be adequately described.[47]

In short, the picture of a dialectical development, proceeding in necessary stages, is what results from tracing the inner connections which have successively developed: the development is not one that follows laws of its own. It is precisely this which Marx seems to be saying when he adds to the above statement:

> If this [detailed analysis] is done successfully, if the life of the subject-matter is ideally reflected as in a mirror, then it may appear as if we had before us a mere apriori construction.

In other words, I take it that Marx is suggesting that a successful reconstruction of the movement of history through step-by-step analysis will make it appear as if history itself followed its own "apriori" necessary laws, as Hegel had believed; whereas, in fact, this is an illusion arising from the very success of a step-by-step analysis.[48] If one were to reject this interpretation of what Marx's actual method of inquiry was, I do not see how one would interpret such chapters of *Capital* as that in which he traced the genesis of the industrial capitalist.[49] Thus, it is my contention that so far as the logic of his argument was concerned, Marx did *not* depart from that classic form of explanation according to which any particular result would be either predicted or explained on the basis of applying general laws to specific historical circumstances: he did not formulate any ultimate laws concerning the sequence of phases through which societies would necessarily pass.[50]

Nonetheless, it cannot be denied that in the development of *Marxism* the modes of explanation which characterize historicism came to be applied. Later Marxists did speak in terms of ultimate laws of historical development, which it was claimed that Marx had established, and according to which it was necessary that all societies should undergo similar evolutionary transformations. As a consequence of this view (which I do not take to have been Marx's own most usual view), all social changes were seen in terms of the places which they occupied in these transformations. To find the primary source of this doctrine one must, I believe, turn to Engels's specifically philosophic writings.

As we have noted, that aspect of Hegel's dialectic which was of preponderating influence on the thought of Marx was to be found in the *Phenomenology of Spirit*, and more particularly in the doctrine of alienation and its stages.[51] However, as one can see in Engels's *Anti-Dühring*, that aspect of the Hegelian dialectic which had most influence on *his* thought was associated with its three basic laws and their manifestation in all phases of reality. Such applications of the dialectic are not evident in Marx's own works.[52] To be sure, in his preface to the second edition of *Anti-Dühring*, Engels referred to the fact that he had read the whole of that manuscript to Marx, and that Marx concurred in its publication. Thus, it would seem that the views which Engels expressed should also be considered those of Marx. Nevertheless, as this passage makes clear, the application of dialectics to the natural sciences was wholly a product of Engels's own studies, and when Engels speaks in the same passage of the fact that it was he and Marx who had rescued dialectics from German idealist philosophy, applying it to the materialist conception of nature and history, the fact that he links a dialectical development of nature with history surely suggests that he is speaking more of himself than of Marx.[53] In fact, in traditional treatments of Marxian dialectics, such as one finds in so orthodox a source as Lenin's "Teachings of Karl Marx," or in M. M. Bober's *Karl Marx's Interpretation of History*, the references to dialectics derive almost exclusively from Engels's *Anti-Dühring* or from two works written by Engels after Marx's death, *Ludwig Feuerbach* and *Dialectics of Nature*.[54] Thus, without accepting the emphasis which is currently being placed on Marx's manuscripts of 1844, and also without in the least denigrating Engels (as is currently the fashion), it is possible to say that Engels's later writings assuredly expand upon the doctrines of Marx, and that in doing so they make these doctrines conform more closely to the very wide and deep strain of historicism which characterized the later decades of the nineteenth century.

That Engels's conception of dialectics involved the assumption that there are laws of directional change is suggested in his famous phrase, "Dialectics is nothing more than the science of the general laws of motion and development of Nature, human society and thought."[55] It was this that he believed to constitute the fundamental connection between Marxism and Hegel's dialectic. In speaking of what was revolutionary in Hegel's thought, Engels said:

> The great basic thought that the world is not to be comprehended as a complex of ready-made *things*, but as a complex of *processes*, in which the things apparently stable no less than their mind-images in our heads, the concepts, go through an uninterrupted change of coming to be and passing away, in which, in spite of all seeming accidents and of all temporary retrogression, a progressive development asserts itself in the end— this great fundamental thought has, especially since the time of Hegel, so thoroughly permeated ordinary consciousness that in this generality it is scarcely ever contradicted.[56]

As a consequence of this view, Engels explicitly drew the following inference as to what form modern scientific explanation should take: it was not to be an analysis of ready-made objects, but of processes, and to understand the concrete nature of such processes we must understand them in their origin and in their development, and in relation to "the interconnection which binds all these natural processes to one great whole."[57] The form of this interconnection was, according to Engels, a dialectical development: one of the mistakes of the earlier form of materialism, which Engels connected with mechanicalism, "lay in its inability to comprehend the universe as a process—as matter developing in an historical process."[58] It was Engels's contention that while the sciences associated with these earlier forms of thought had made gigantic strides, it was unfortunately true that:

The analysis of Nature into its individual parts ... has also left us as a legacy the habit of observing natural objects and natural processes in their isolation, detached from the whole vast interconnection of things; and therefore not in their motion, but in their repose; not as essentially changing, but as fixed constants; not in their life, but in their death.[59]

What Engels meant by understanding processes in their life and development emerges very clearly in his treatment of the law of "the negation of the negation" in *Anti-Dühring*. The question which he there found it necessary to discuss was whether there are not innumerable ways in which a given phase of a process may be negated; whether, for example, if is not equally meaningful to say that a grain of barley is being negated if it is ground up as to find its negation in its germination. To this type of objection Engels answered that such a sequence of events would not constitute a dialectical explanation. In order to explain a process,

I must not only negate, but also in turn sublate the negation. I must therefore so construct the first negation that the second remains or becomes possible. This depends on the particular nature of each individual case. If I grind a grain of barley, or crush an insect, it is true that I have carried out the first part of the action, but I have made the second part impossible. Each class of things therefore has its appropriate form of being negated in such a way that it gives rise to a development.[60]

Thus, to understand any particular phase of an ongoing process, we must interpret that phase in terms of its place in the process: we must not seek to understand it merely as it is here and now, but in terms of that out of which it arose and that to which, in its turn, it will give rise. And since, as we have seen, Engels insisted that all events in nature and history belonged within a single, interconnected series, it was essential to view them not as single instances of change, but in terms of their place in a unitary and all-embracing developmental process.[61]

This monism, embracing both nature and history, has obvious affinities with Hegelian monism, and Engels stressed this connection, never attempting to conceal it. For example, in sketching the background of his dialectical materialism he said:

This newer German philosophy culminated in the Hegelian system, in which, for the first time—and this is its great merit—the whole natural, historical and spiritual world was presented as a process, that is, as in constant motion, change, transformation and development. From this standpoint the history of mankind no longer appeared as a

confused whirl of senseless deeds of violence, all equally condemnable before the judgment seat of the now matured philosophic reason, and best forgotten as quickly as
possible, but as the process of development of humanity itself. It now became the task of
thought to follow the gradual stages of this process through all its devious ways, and to
trace out the inner regularities running through all its apparently fortuitous
phenomena.[62]

Here we do indeed have one of Engels's many expressions of his belief in the
existence of an inexorable law of development, embracing all of human history.
And in Engels no less than in Hegel one finds that this developmental monism
leads to an acceptance of the *evaluative* thesis of historicism.

Such an acceptance is clearly present in the above rejection of what were
presumably the Enlightenment standards of judgment as applied to history. However, in *Ludwig Feuerbach* Engels makes this aspect of his historicism perfectly
explicit when—in terms reminiscent of Hegel—he says:

All successive historical situations are only transitory stages in the endless course of
development of human society from the lower to the higher. Each stage is necessary, and
therefore justified for the time and conditions to which it owes its origin. But in the
newer and higher conditions which gradually develop in its own bosom, each loses its
validity and justification.[63]

However, it would be a mistake to attempt to interpret Engels's acceptance of
either the explanatory or the evaluative theses of historicism solely in terms of
Hegel's influence upon him—important as that influence had been. The Darwinian theory of evolution, with which Engels became acquainted almost immediately upon its publication, also played a crucial role in the manner in which
he phrased his historicist views. One may note the importance of this influence
in almost every passage in which Engels contrasted modern, dialectical materialism with earlier forms of materialism, for Darwinism was repeatedly cited in
this connection. In fact, in his "Speech at the Graveside of Karl Marx," Engels
said:

Just as Darwin discovered the law of development of organic nature, so Marx discovered
the law of development of human history.[64]

It is to the relationship between the theory of evolution and historicism that we
shall now turn.

It is well known, and would in any case be obvious from the reception accorded Darwin's *Origin of Species*, that long before 1859 there had been the liveliest interest in problems associated with transformism, as the theory of biological evolution was then usually named. I have elsewhere briefly sketched the range of scientific problems which provided the background for Darwin's theory and which accounted for the fact that its implications were immediately grasped.[1] Because almost all of these scientific problems had been closely interwoven with theological issues, it was not in the least surprising that the theological implications of Darwin's theory received the immediate and widespread attention that they did.

However, it is neither with the scientific nor with the theological aspects of Darwin's theory that we are here primarily concerned: its relation to historicism at the end of the nineteenth century was primarily associated with attempts to apply analogous concepts of evolutionary development to human traits and to social forms. Now, it is to be noted that, unlike Lamarck, Darwin did not at first explicitly apply his theory to man; one reason was that he wished to avoid the theological objections which he knew a discussion of human origins would provoke.[2] However, he was clearly aware of the applicability of his fundamental concepts to questions concerning man's mental and social life, for in the concluding chapter of the *Origin of Species* the following paragraph appears:

In the future I see open fields for far more important researches. Psychology will be securely based on the foundation already well laid by Mr. Herbert Spencer, that of the necessary acquirement of each mental power and capacity by gradation. Much light will be thrown on the origin of man and his history.[3]

However, it was not until 1871, when he published *The Descent of Man*, that Darwin made public his own views on these questions; by that time, evolutionary conceptions of human origins and human social development were being widely discussed, as is evident in the early works of Maine, McLennan, Lubbock, and Tylor. And, within a very short time, a full-fledged social evolutionism made its appearance and became linked with conceptions of necessity and of progress; it is this congeries of concepts and their relation to historicism that we must seek to understand.

As we have already seen, the idea of general Progress, embracing all of mankind, was deeply entrenched in eighteenth- and nineteenth-century thought; and in Saint-Simon and in Comte there was also an insistence upon the notion of a necessary law of social development. However, in these earlier forms of optimistic and necessitarian doctrines, human history was not seen in terms of a continuation of the same laws which obtained in the non-human realm: with the exception of Herder, the history of mankind was not regarded by any major pre-Darwinian philosopher as representing a continuation of the forces inherent in nature. However, in raising the issue of the emergence of the human species from a non-human ancestry, Darwinism posed inescapable questions for psychology, archaeology, and anthropology. If man had evolved from a non-human ancestry, what were the psychological characteristics which led to the development of social life, at what point in history did such structures as familial organization arise, and did they too undergo a natural, necessary evolutionary development? Similar questions arose concerning the origin, the basis, and the development of other aspects of culture, such as religion. These issues became inescapable as soon as Darwinism was applied to the descent of man from non-human forebears; as a solution for them, full-scale theories of social evolution were proposed.

As a background for understanding the development of social evolutionism, I should like to call attention to three aspects of evolutionary theory in biology. These three points bear no necessary, logical relationships to one another, but they did tend to fuse; and, as we shall later see, each had its parallel in the theory of social evolution, where they tended to merge into the single cohesive doctrine that evolution consists in a necessary and progressive development. The first of the points concerns the use of the comparative method in the field of evolutionary theory. The second consists in the reasons why it was believed that biological evolution had established progress to be a necessary consequence of the laws of nature. The third involves an attempt to understand the manner in which the concept of "a law of nature" was interpreted.

The comparative method must be discussed first. In attempting to establish the fact that biological evolution had taken place, it was necessary for any transformist to use a comparative method: it was not possible to gather observational data concerning the formation of new varieties in a state of nature, nor was it possible to show that new domesticated varieties could take on the character of distinctively new species. The evidence for transformism was therefore bound to be indirect, consisting primarily of comparisons among varieties and species in order to construct a plausible genealogical connection between them. If it were possible to show that a large number of species of a given class of plants or animals resembled each other sufficiently closely—differing only in a continuous series of minor gradations—the assumption that they had had a common ancestry would become plausible. This, of course, was what Darwin's observations on the Galapagos Islands tended to suggest. Similarly, if the resemblances between presently existing species and fossilized remains were sufficiently close to suggest a relationship by descent, this would also suggest that presently extant species were not created in their present form, but had developed over the course of time. Now, it is to be noted that the closer the resemblances, the less abrupt the gradations, and the more "missing links" that could be found, the stronger would be the comparative evidence for transformism. This use of the comparative method in tracing lineal descent was doubtless associated with the doctrine that nature constitutes a Great Chain of Being (as the phrase "missing link" serves to remind us); however, it was also in very large measure due to specifically biological considerations rather than to metaphysical assumptions.[4] Given their conceptions of the causes affecting inheritance, it was necessary to hold—as both Lamarck and Darwin held—that variation must proceed by single, minute changes. For example, it would have run counter to all observation to suppose that there could be any sudden, radical variations due to inherited effects of the use or disuse of specific organs; therefore, *all* variations for Lamarck, and *some* variations for Darwin, could only be regarded as slowly accumulating. The slowness of the process of change was also a corollary of Darwin's doctrine of natural selection: any variation would have to be transmitted to a large number of successive generations before a stable new variety, better adapted to its environment, could begin to be formed.[5] Thus, what took the place of an actual tracing of descent was, necessarily, a comparison of cases. So long as these cases showed marked similarities, and so long as they existed at times and places which either suggested or did not exclude the possibility of common line of descent, they were used in support of transformism. While this comparative method is clearly defensible when one is dealing with biological relationships, it can, as we shall see, become exceedingly strained in its application to social evolutionism.

A similar situation came to obtain with respect to the manner in which the comparative method was used in marshaling another (and far less convincing) type of evidence in favor of transformism. This evidence consisted in applying the comparative method to what were called rudimentary or vestigial organs. The existence of organs having no apparent active function was explained in terms of the vital functions which they had performed in earlier, presumably related species. The justification for viewing them in this manner rested partly on the assumption that every organ exists in order to contribute to the welfare of its possessor (an assumption which, as we have seen, Darwin originally shared);[6] it also rested on the assumption that the stages through which individuals pass in embryological development represent the evolutionary development of their species; thus, organs which are present but are without function were considered to be "vestiges" of a former, ancestral condition.[7] One can note the connection between the comparative method and these interpretations of vestigial organs and of embryological development when Darwin, in summarizing the ways in which he expected his theory to revitalize natural history, said:

Rudimentary organs will speak infallibly with respect to the nature of long-lost structures. Species and groups of species which are called aberrant, and which may fancifully
be called living fossils, will aid us in forming a picture of the ancient forms of life.
Embryology will often reveal to us the structure, in some degree obscured, of the
prototypes of each great class.[8]

Whatever one may think of the use of such evidence for evolutionary theory
in biology, the later application of similar doctrines to questions regarding
social evolution was assuredly less well grounded, and entailed extremely dubious
consequences.

The foregoing remarks on the comparative method as used in establishing the
biological theory of evolution are not intended to do more than scratch the
surface of this complex problem. However, as Erwin Ackerknecht has pointed
out, comparative anatomy was the "glamor science" of the latter portions of the
nineteenth century because of its role in establishing and supporting evolutionary theory.[9] Therefore, it is not surprising that its methods served as the dominant model for the analysis of cultures during the same period.[10] To these matters
we shall shortly return.

The question of progress is to be discussed next. One can readily see how
Darwin's formulation of the doctrine of natural selection tended to sponsor a
belief that the laws of nature inevitably lead to progress. To note this connection
one need only recall some of the passages in the *Origin of Species* which are
most striking from a rhetorical point of view, and which, as a consequence, were
unavoidably influential. For example, at the end of Chapter III, there is the
famous passage which prefigures some of the utterances which were later to
characterize "Social Darwinism":

All that we can do is to keep steadily in mind that each organic being is striving to
increase in a geometrical ratio; that each, at some period of its life, during some season
of the year, during each generation, or at intervals, has to struggle for life and to suffer
great destruction. When we reflect on this struggle we may console ourselves with the
full belief that the war of nature is not incessant, that no fear is felt, that death is
generally prompt, and that the vigorous, the healthy, and the happy survive and
multiply.

This statement serves to suggest that those individuals which, in the long run,
actually do survive are to be considered the *most* fit, and this suggestion became
explicit in the phrase which Darwin adopted from Spencer to characterize the
principle of natural selection: "the survival of the fittest."[11] Strictly speaking,
however, a theory of natural selection only entails that individuals or varieties
which actually were fit to survive and multiply under a specific set of conditions
(including, of course, the individuals and varieties with which they were in
competition) would in fact survive, and that their characteristics would therefore tend to be passed on to future generations. In other words, the principle
of natural selection might properly be phrased as "the survival of the *fit*," not
"of the fittest." Or the principle might have been expressed by using the comparative form: "the survival of the more fit." This would have helped to make

clear the comparative and contextual aspect of the doctrine of natural selection: that, within a specific type of environment, individuals or varieties which, comparatively speaking, were better suited to that environment would tend to survive, whereas—if there were competition among them—those less well suited to the same environment would fail to do so. However, the use of the superlative form, "the fittest," tended to suggest that those which did survive were not merely comparatively better fitted to do so, but that, somehow, they were ideally suited for survival. In other words, use of the superlative tended to conceal something that was actually essential to Darwin's theory: that the process designated by him as "natural selection" always operates within a particular environment, and is therefore relative to the competition and the conditions characteristic of that environment—it cannot be viewed, so to speak, as picking and choosing specimens according to some absolute standard of viability or of perfection.

That Darwin himself did not stress this point may seem surprising, but it is not difficult to comprehend why he failed to do so. His aim in the *Origin of Species* was not confined to establishing the causes by means of which transformism took place; his interest in that problem was derivative from an earlier and continuing interest in the whole history of life upon the earth. Thus, there are two different ways in which one can view the *Origin of Species*, and both correspond to features which are fundamental to that work. On the one hand, Darwin's theory can be viewed as a means of answering a specific set of scientific questions concerning the formation of new varieties of plants and animals, and of how some varieties came to establish themselves and maintain themselves as distinct species. Looked at in this way, there is no necessary connection between his theory and any belief in progress. On the other hand, one can also view the *Origin of Species* as a work which showed that all organic forms developed over the course of time, and that they represent successive stages in a single evolutionary process. When the *Origin of Species* is approached from the latter point of view, it is beyond question that Darwin did believe evolution to be progressive: nature, acting through the survival of the fittest among all forms of life, had gradually, progressively given rise to ever higher forms. The results were such as to fill Darwin with the deepest reverence for the processes of nature: he repeatedly expressed admiration for the marvelously intricate forms of plant and animal life, and above all for the subtlety of their adaptations. The slow, uniform operation of nature's laws achieved goals which far surpassed what human design could have achieved,[12] and the evolutionary process as a whole had given rise to forms which, for Darwin, unmistakably possessed higher beauty and value than those out of which they had arisen.

If one examines the passages in which Darwin most explicitly spoke in terms which served to fuse the concepts of evolution and of progress, one finds that they do not appear in those passages in which he was offering a theoretical account of how new species developed; rather, they are contained in passages where he was speaking of the general history of life upon the earth. It is important to note that in such passages Darwin's evaluative attitude almost always had two contrasting aspects: regret and even distaste was sometimes evoked by the means through which change had been brought about, and by its cost; but in the same passages Darwin confidently welcomed the direction of that change. For example, when he concluded his chapter entitled "Natural Selection; or the Survival of the Fittest" with his famous and extremely influential simile between nature's production of new species and the growth of a great branching tree, Darwin said:

> The affinities of all beings of the same class have sometimes been represented by a great tree. I believe this simile largely speaks the truth. The green and budding twigs may represent existing species; and those produced during former years may represent the long sequence of extinct species. At each period of growth all the growing twigs have tried to branch out on all sides, and to overtop and kill the surrounding twigs and branches, in the same manner as species and groups of species have at all times over-mastered other species in the great battle for life. . . . Of the many twigs which flourished when the tree was a mere bush only two or three, now grown into great branches, yet survive and bear the other branches. . . . Many a limb and branch has decayed and dropped off; and these fallen branches of various sizes may represent those whole orders, families and genera which have now no living representatives, arid which are known to us only in a fossil state. . . . As buds give rise by growth to fresh buds, and these, if vigorous, branch out and overtop on all sides many a feebler branch, so by generation I believe it has been with the great Tree of Life, which fills with its dead and broken branches the crust of the earth, and covers the surface with its ever-branching and beautiful ramifications.

An even clearer expression of Darwin's mixture of evaluative attitudes, and the dominance of his view that, considered as a whole, nature displays a tendency toward progress, is present in the famous final sentences of the *Origin of Species*. There, after very briefly listing the specific laws by means of which evolutionary change was to be explained, Darwin concluded:

> Thus, from the war of nature, from famine and death, the most exalted object which we are capable of conceiving, namely, the production of the higher animals, directly follows. There is grandeur in this view of life with its several powers, having been originally breathed by the Creator into a few forms or into one; and that, while this planet has gone circling on according to the fixed law of gravity, from so simple a beginning endless forms most beautiful and most wonderful have been, and are being evolved.

On the basis of passages such as these, one might expect that Darwin would have regarded it as a law of nature—and perhaps nature's most ultimate law—that all things should progress toward higher forms. However, this was a step which he refused to take. While he did believe that progress was a necessary consequence of the operation of nature's laws, he explicitly rejected the view that the phenomena of life were to be explained by means of a law of progressive development. For example, in his strictures on Lamarck's views, he repeatedly criticized the latter for holding that there is "a law of progessive development," that is, for asserting that there is an inherent tendency toward further development in all living things.[13] Similarly, he repeatedly criticized Nägeli's somewhat different form of such a law, explicitly contrasting it with his own view that adaptations follow from a long series of adaptive changes, not from an inherent developmental tendency.[14] In other words, as Darwin said in a passage which he felt obliged to add to later editions of the *Origin of Species*, "Natural Selection, or the survival of the fittest, does not necessarily include progressive development—it only takes advantage of such variations as arise and are beneficial to each creature under its conditions of life."[15]

This being so, one is forced to wonder why Darwinism was so frequently interpreted as a theory which had established the view that nature's fundamental law was a law of progressive development. Sociological explanations of a Marxian or of a quasi-Marxian sort have sometimes been offered to account for this phenomenon;[16] however, there are factors internal to the history of ideas which provide a more adequate understanding of why even Darwin himself tended to emphasize the progressive aspect of evolutionary processes. Among these factors I shall select only two for consideration. The first is to be found in the influence of the doctrine of the Great Chain of Being. While there were those who followed a mechanical view of nature, derived from Descartes and from the corpuscularian tradition, it is probably fair to say that the doctrine of a Chain of Being (which had Platonic and Aristotelian sources, and was reanimated by Leibniz) did tend to dominate the interpretation of nature immediately preceding evolutionism. According to that doctrine, all forms of life were part of a single, continuous, hierarchical order of species; however, the actual hierarchy outlined by different adherents of the Chain of Being varied according to the criteria which they used in classifying resemblances and differences. This was true even among those who attempted to confine themselves to classifications based solely on specific organic structures, for their results were necessarily relative to the structures on which they had decided to base their classification.[17] However, most writers who employed the concept of a Chain of Being did not in fact confine themselves to a consideration of specific structural similarities; instead, the rather vague criterion of the general, over-all simplicity or complexity which characterized different species was a criterion which was widely used.[18] In addition, such classifications frequently introduced psychological attributes into their systems, and the most important of these attributes was taken to be the assumed intellectual capacities of the various species.[19] If I am not mistaken, it was the introduction of this intellectualistic criterion, and the correlated assumption that man assuredly stands at the apex of the hierarchy of living forms, that helped to conceal, for so long a time, the impossibility of fitting all forms of life into a single, continuous, linear pattern.[20]

Darwin's theory of the origin of species, like Lamarck's theory before it, provided a new basis for the classification of all living forms: classifications were to follow genealogical relationships, and not be expected to form a single linear order. Thus, as we have seen, Darwin used the simile of a great branching tree to suggest the relationship among the various phyla, and the successive differentiations into orders, families, genera, and species. The differences between his simile and that of a Great Chain of Being are both striking and important, and I should not wish to minimize them; nonetheless, there were aspects of the doctrine of a Great Chain of Being which Darwin shared. Chief among them was the fact that when he looked upon nature as a whole, surveying the various forms of life which Nature had produced, these forms did seem to him to present a picture of what was, in general, a hierarchical order. As he interpreted his simile of the Tree of Life, there existed a series of gradations from the lowest, simplest organisms to the highest ones. Where gradations were lacking among extant forms, the fossil record filled-in countless gaps. Thus, one had spread out before him an ascending graded order of forms. Darwin regarded this ordered series as conforming to the serial order in which the various forms of life had successively branched off from what his simile suggested to be the main trunk of evolutionary development. It must be remarked that this vertical trunk, or series of centrally ascending main branches, was surely at least as much a function of Darwin's simile as it was of any evidence which he had marshaled concerning the actual lines of descent of the various organic forms, and of their geographical dispersion. The hypothetical trunk which his simile demanded, and of which all organic forms were the off-shoots, performed within Darwin's theory exactly the same function as did the idea of a single continuous hierarchy of forms in the simile of the Chain of Being: it served as a means of identifying the place of each type of living creature with relation to all others. In this connection it is to be noted that Darwin, no less than his predecessors, constantly referred to species as "lower" or "higher", and his language also disclosed a temporal, progressive note when he distinguished among "lowly" species and those which were "more advanced." [21]

The fact that Darwin used these modes of speech and considered them to be wholly legitimate indicates that he thought of evolution as a single process of development which not only had a single source but grew in a definite direction—a direction which constituted an advance over earlier growth. However, Darwin's explicit rejection of a law of progressive development should have rendered this assumption suspect, unless he had been in a position to show that the factors of variation and of natural selection do make it inevitable that there should be a particular axis along which growth tends to take place. However, Darwin's own treatment of variations asserted that they occur in all directions, and his own use of the concept of natural selection made it clear that selection is always relative to a particular environment. In accordance with these assumptions, one would suppose that instead of having viewed evolution as proceeding along one dominant vertical axis, represented by the main trunk of the Tree of Life, Darwin would have viewed it as developing along a variety of divergent axes, spreading and branching as each individual shoot developed along the lines of whatever variations were most suitable to the particular circumstances of its own environment. To formulate such a conception in terms of a single simile, one might think of the evolutionary process as having been like the spread of ground cover from a single original plant, which had sent shoots in all directions, some of the shoots having taken new root, others having withered and died, and others barely surviving. I do not wish to suggest that such a simile would present a more accurate model of evolutionary change than does the conception of a single, upward-growing tree possessed of innumerable branches, each of which, as it spreads, also tends to grow generally upward. All I wish to point out is that a simile of this sort is no less *compatible* with Darwin's theory of the origin of species, and with his discussions of classification by descent, than is the simile which he actually used. To be sure, one of Darwin's basic convictions would have been omitted from the simile which I have suggested: my suggestion contains no hint that evolution proceeds by ascent. The fact that Darwin conceived of the evolutionary process, when he viewed it as a whole, in terms of upward growth was surely in part a result of the influence upon him of the conception of an ascending hierarchy of forms. This conception, as we have noted, had been built into earlier systems of classification, and it was shot through the whole literature of natural history, and was (as Lovejoy has shown) a dominant traditional assumption in Western thought. It is therefore not surprising that it tended to dominate Darwin's views when he spoke as a descriptive naturalist, even though it had not been legitimized by the theory which he had advanced to account for the origin of species.

I turn now to a second philosophic assumption which, like the doctrine of the Great Chain of Being, may be viewed as a source of Darwin's firm conviction that, taken as a whole, Nature reveals progressive development, not merely an incessant and destructive struggle for existence in which individuals and species arise only to perish. This assumption was theological in character, and was accepted by Darwin throughout his early and middle life; it was also accepted by two of his staunchest defenders, Lyell and Asa Gray, even after he himself had abandoned it. It consisted in the harmonizing of evolution with theism by means of a distinction between God as "the ultimate cause" of the world and the laws of nature as "derivative" or "secondary" causes. It was to this doctrine that Darwin had recourse throughout the years when he was working on the problems which culminated in the *Origin of Species*. Applying the general doctrine of secondary causes to evolutionary biology, the Creator did not separately create the various species of plants and animals, but acted through fixed laws, the operations of which account for the origin of new species. In thus maintaining the divine origin of all natural forms—even though their origin was not attributed to special creation—Darwin was committed to a belief that the general pattern of evolutionary development must be progressive: it could not be a retrograde process or a morally indifferent one.[22]

The doctrine that God's action in the natural world proceeds through "secondary means" had a lineage of considerable authority, and one which Darwin appositely cited on behalf of his own views. One sees this in all three of the epigraphs through which he introduced the *Origin of Species*. The first, from Whewell, was particularly relevant in a work whose aim was to account for the origin of species through the continuous action of nature, rather than through isolated acts of special creation:

But with regard to the material world, we can at least go as far as this—we can perceive that events are brought about not by insulated interpositions of Divine power, exerted in each particular case, but by the establishment of general laws.

The doctrine that these general laws of nature operate always in the same, fixed manner, and that their apparent purposelessness need not contravene belief in divine purpose, was clear in the second epigraph, which derived from another source of unexceptionable eminence, Bishop Butler:

> The only distinct meaning of the word 'natural' is *stated, fixed* or *settled*; since what is natural as much requires and presupposes an intelligent agent to render it so, *i.e.*, to effect it continually or at stated times, as what is supernatural or miraculous does to effect it for once.

And, finally, in defense of the thorough, patient accumulation of a detailed knowledge of nature's operations—and we may recall that more than twenty years of dedicated work had intervened between Darwin's first discovery of the principles of the origin of species and his publication of that book—Darwin cited Bacon's *Advancement of Learning*:

> To conclude, therefore, let no man out of a weak conceit of sobriety, or an ill-applied moderation, think or maintain, that a man can search too far or be too well studied in the book of God's word, or in the book of God's works; divinity or philosophy; but rather let men endeavor an endless progress or proficience in both.

The use of these epigraphs, and Darwin's acceptance of the doctrine of secondary causes, cannot be considered as insincere, that is, as an attempt to adopt the protective coloration of orthodoxy. Not only would such an interpretation be wholly at odds with what we know of Darwin's character and of the history of his religious beliefs, but it would omit the evidence of his notebooks and of his two earlier draft-essays concerning the principles of the origin of species. In each of these places, where the question of public reaction does not arise, we find Darwin accepting the doctrine of secondary causes and advancing in its favor arguments which rest on specifically theological assumptions. For example, in 1837 when Darwin was first moving toward transformism, the following passage appeared in his Note Book, and this passage was used by his son as the epigraph for *The Foundation of the Origin of Species*:

> Astronomers might formerly have said that God ordered each planet to move in its particular destiny. In same manner God orders each animal created with certain form in certain country. But how much more simple and sublime power,—let attraction act according to certain law, such are inevitable consequences,—let animal[s] be created, then by fixed laws of generation, such will be their successors.

Subsequently, the power and sublimity of God's operation through secondary laws was argued, and not merely asserted, in Darwin's essay of 1842. There he pointed out that it is impossible for us to comprehend how all of the various organisms, with their subtle workmanship, should have arisen through the operation of fixed laws, and so we tend to think in terms of separate acts of creation, but our inability to form such a conception does not show that these laws do not exist; it only serves to "exalt our notion of the power of the omniscient

Creator."[23] And in addition to this argument one finds twice repeated in these essays the contention that it would in fact demean our notion of God were we to think he had separately created parasites, organisms that delight in cruelty, animals that lay their eggs in bowels of other sensitive animals, *etc.*;[24] whereas the necessary existence of such animals as products of secondary causes does not do so. And it does not do so precisely because the evolutionary process considered as a whole is good, that is, progressive.[25]

Thus, even though Darwin explicitly rejected the view that there was a law of progressive development, his theological convictions at the time of formulating and elaborating his views concerning the origin of species made it necessary for him to hold that progress would inevitably follow from the fixed laws of inheritance, variability, and natural selection. However, in the years immediately following the publication of the *Origin of Species*, his letters to Lyell and to Asa Gray begin to show doubts regarding his former theistic interpretations of the laws of nature, and his religious position ultimately became one of agnosticism.[26] Had this been his position when he was at work on the writing of the *Origin of Species*, it seems very doubtful that Darwin would have been quite so insistent on the progressive character of the evolutionary process.

To be sure, in the same period, others went even further than Darwin in affirming the inevitability of progressive change, although they did not share his original theological position. Spencer's name comes immediately to mind in this connection, and there also were materialists, such as Büchner, who subscribed to a similar view. To understand the basis on which the doctrine of the inevitability of progress was confidently asserted by those who lacked any theological grounds for asserting it, we must examine their views concerning the status to be ascribed to nature's laws.

In general, one may say that prior to the nineteenth century the dominant modern view of the laws of nature was to regard them as representing the action of physical forces which had originally been implanted in the world by its Creator. For most who shared this view (e.g., for Newton), the nature of these forces was unknowable, and it was not possible to explain why they operate as they do. This invincible ignorance regarding ultimate causes was entirely compatible with holding that through close observation and careful induction men could discover an order among the phenomena of nature, and could use this knowledge for the improvement of life. Thus, the regularity of nature was taken as representing the rules through which divine governance flowed. Because of the attributes of God, there was every reason to hold that these rules or laws must be constant, at all times and places. And, of course, advances in the physical sciences in the seventeenth and eighteenth centuries gave evidence of the great generality, yet the great simplicity, of the means through which the varied phenomena of physical nature were governed. Viewed against this background it is easy to understand how the term "laws of nature" should have been taken to refer to operative principles ingrained in nature, not to formulae discovered by scientists; consequently, one can also understand why it was not felt to be straining language to speak as if these laws served to *govern* actual events, and

that events *obeyed* them.[27] While such modes of speech are now generally rejected, it is not without interest to note that even though a theological interpretation of the laws of nature cannot be ascribed to John Stuart Mill, he attempted
to differentiate between those successful generalizations which are merely "empirical laws" and "the ultimate laws of causation," that is, the basic laws of
nature.[28] Bearing such facts in mind, if we are to understand the position which
was characteristic even of Comte, and certainly of Spencer, we must refrain from
interpreting the status of scientific laws in the manner suggested by Mach, or
Poincaré, or Duhem; we must attempt to think ourselves back into that earlier
tradition from which—in spite of their pretensions—the systematic positivists and
most evolutionists had by no means succeeded in freeing themselves. Only in this
way can we understand why, in the nineteenth century, it was widely held that
one of the basic laws of nature was a law of Progress.

As an example of a view which lies halfway between the traditional, theologically oriented conception of nature's laws and those later forms of positivism
of which Mach may be taken as typical, consider the position of Comte with
respect to this problem. As we have noted, it was one of the basic tenets of his
system to reject the theological interpretation of the laws of nature; he also rejected any employment of the so-called metaphysical concept of "forces." Yet, he
did not cavil at treating scientific laws as if necessity could unquestionably be
attributed to the particular sequences which such laws served to describe. Comte
never examined or sought to defend the basis on which he held this view; like
many of his contemporaries, he seems to have taken it for granted that once
one abandons the appeal to God's purposes as a means of explaining phenomena,
it becomes necessary to assume that the reign of law is absolute.[29] Putting the
matter in terms of Comte's own system, the assurance of uniformity and necessity in the connections among phenomena is simply a question of having passed
beyond theological and metaphysical stages of thought, and of adopting a positive, scientific point of view. What was of most importance to Comte was the
application of this point of view to societies and to their histories. Although
sociology was the last of the sciences to develop, Comte hoped to show that, here
too, one could establish uniformity and necessity—in short, that there were laws
governing history. However, his method was not one of carefully sifting specific
historical events for resemblances and uniform sequences; as one can see as early
as his essay of 1822, he was contemptuous of traditional historiography, and sought
to promote "l'esprit d'ensemble" (in contrast to "l'esprit de détail") as a means of
discovering the large-scale patterns of development in history as a whole. This
method assumed that patterns which had repeated themselves under varying
conditions in the past would in the future repeat themselves, regardless of differences in time and in place (or, as we should say, regardless of differences in
initial and boundary conditions); but this supposition only makes sense if one
thinks of such patterns as representing laws which actually govern the events
which manifest or embody them. That Comte assumed this to be the case, comes
out clearly in Mill's characterization of the general method of the Comteans:

This method, which is now generally adopted by the most advanced thinkers on the Continent, consists in attempting, by a study and analysis of the general facts of history, to discover (what these philosophers term) the law of progress: which law, once ascertained, must according to them enable us to predict future events, just as after a few terms of an infinite series in algebra we are able to detect the principle of regularity in their formation, and to predict the rest of the series to any number of terms we please.[30]

Precisely the same point of view was adopted by Spencer. Like Comte, he took it to be the task of scientific sociology to discover the laws governing the development of societies, and for this purpose he attached little value to traditional forms of historiography, which he regarded as vitiated by concern for the effects of individual actions, rather than a concern for the operations of general laws.[31] To be sure, there were a number of fundamental differences between the positions of Comte and of Spencer regarding the relations of sociology to the other sciences, and also regarding the nature of scientific explanation. However, both insisted that social change was governed by law, that its direction was uniform, and that it proceeded in that direction by necessity; it was this convergence in their doctrines that was of great importance in establishing a mode of thought basic to Social Evolutionism.

The conception of laws as governing phenomena and necessitating the direction of their change is evident throughout Spencer's work; however, it is perhaps most readily documented in his autobiographical sketch of the stages through which his formulation of a general law of Progress developed.[32] The passage in which he describes these stages begins:

In the narrative of my boyhood I pointed out that I early became obsessed by the idea of causation,

and it continues,

... there grew up in me a tacit belief that whatever occurred had its assignable cause of a comprehensible kind. Such notions as uniformity of law and an established order, were of course not then entertained [by me]; but the kind of thinking into which I had been led, and which was in part natural to me, prepared the way for the acceptance of such notions in due time.

In the following pages, Spencer reviewed his earlier works and outlined the development of his views regarding a single, uniform law of necessary progress. He employed such statements as:

The doctrine of the universality of natural causation, has for its inevitable corollary the doctrine that the Universe and all things in it have reached their present forms through successive stages physically necessitated....

and

In *Proper Sphere of Government*, there was shown an unhesitating belief that the phenomena of both individual life and social life, conform to law.... Eight years later increased consistency and definiteness were given to these views in *Social Statics*.... Everything was referred to the unvarying course of causation, no less uniform in the spheres of life and mind than in the sphere of inanimate existence.

This view of the uniformity and the necessity to be found in nature and society was not in the least softened or altered in subsequent passages; indeed, it was made more explicit as Spencer traced the further stages leading up to his mature conception of his law of development, which he associated with "those ultimate laws of force similarly traceable throughout all orders of existence."

Unless it is recognized that there is this form of developmental necessitarianism in Spencer's doctrine—a necessitarianism which is extremely remote from the views of cause and of law which were subsequently associated with critical positivism—it is not possible to understand how he could have justified the application of one and the same law to all aspects of nature and society. This Spencerian belief is what can best be described as "total evolutionism." In using the term *total* evolutionism I wish to designate a doctrine even more comprehensive than one which attempts to show that there has been a constant process of evolutionary change from the origin of our solar system, through the history of the earth, the development of all forms of plant an animal life, man's development of increased mental abilities, and, finally, the development of societies. *In addition to all this*, Spencer promulgated the thesis that exactly the same pattern of development as can be traced within each of the individual series, and which can also be traced in the larger series taken as a single whole, will be found to obtain with respect to all of the more specific phenomena which they include. For example, the very same principle which was held to apply to the history of the sequence of societies was also held to apply to the development of the individual societies included within that series; furthermore, it was held to apply to all of the various aspects of the culture of societies, so that each of these aspects revealed a comparable developmental order, and each aspect within any given society also revealed the same order. Thus, in Spencer's total evolutionism —as in Leibniz' system of monads—each aspect of the whole obeys the same all-pervasive law, and each may be said to be part of a single, immensely dense series progressively unfolding.

This total evolutionism was explicitly formulated by Spencer in 1857 in an essay entitled "Progress: Its Law and Cause." In it he took his clue regarding the law of development from the growth of individual plants and animals, and he formulated this law as "an advance from homogeneity of structure to heterogeneity of structure." He then stated it as his purpose to show

... that this law of organic progress is the law of all progress. Whether it be in the development of the Earth, in the development of Life upon its surface, in the develop-ment of Society, of Government, of Manufactures, of Commerce, of Language, Literature, Science, Art, this same evolution of the simple into the complex, through successive differentiations, holds throughout.[33]

In fact, in his *Autobiography* Spencer attempted to show that the same law even applied to the progressive development of his own system of philosophy![34]

It should be obvious that there are grave difficulties in offering any account of a causal factor which could plausibly be held to be responsible for *total* evolution: yet Spencer sought to offer such an account in terms of the laws of the persistence and transformation of force.[35] However, it seems wildly implausible to hold that this causal factor could not only account for the behavior of physical systems, but could be applied to the history of languages—unless, of course, Spencer could find some intervening laws of connection between changes in, say, syntax, and those physical principles of the transformation of energy which govern the human organism. This was not at all the method which Spencer anywhere employed. Rather, his method was to survey the characteristics of a series of changes in order to "ascertain the character common to these modifications—the law to which they all conform."[36] This method was based upon his unalterable conviction that all phenomena must be governed by some one universal and uniform law. To find such a law, he thought it adequate to proceed as Comte had done: he sought some overt pattern of change which repeated itself in many different types of instance, and he attempted to show through an examination of further cases that this pattern was far more regular than would at first appear. On the assumption that nature's laws are uniform and constantly operative, the more instances of the same pattern of change one could find, the more surely they represented a basic law of nature. Thus Spencer sought confirmation of the law's universality in wider and wider ranges of phenomena. On the assumption that nature always operates in one and the same manner, the more remote were the observed instances, the more they added strength to his law. For example, in the chapter of *First Principles* in which he advanced his "Law of Evolution" in its most basic form, we find him citing a series of the most disparate instances, moving from the evolution of our sidereal system to the progressive integration which he regarded as characterizing the history of music: in each of these areas he found that the universal law of progressive development was confirmed.[37]

I believe that it may be desirable to make just one further remark concerning Spencer's method, in order to elucidate the difference between it and what may be termed the standard method of generalizing in the empirical sciences. The standard method presupposes that laws of great generality represent the operation of factors which can only be uncovered through analysis, and are not given in direct inspection. The basis for this methodological conviction lies in experience, since generalizations based on a collection of resembling instances have always been found to admit of exceptions, if the generalizations are stated with sufficient accuracy; and, in science, a law is not to be accepted if it admits of exceptions. (The dictum, "Exceptions prove the rule," is wholly correct—but only correct—if the verb "prove" is taken in its proper sense of "test.") Thus, any law of the requisite generality will presumably have to relate abstract aspects of concrete events, and not attempt to summarize the characteristics of the events themselves. It was precisely here that both Comte and Spencer failed. For while each thought it legitimate to infer from observed instances to further instances on the basis of resemblances and the postulate of nature's uniformity, they concerned themselves only with what may best be termed physiognomic resemblances, and not with an analysis of the multiplicity of factors present in the concrete cases with which they sought to deal.[38] So convinced was each of the law of progression which he had found, that he did not regard it as counting against his view when negative instances, in the form of a lack of progression, or even retrogression, appeared.[39] The uniformity of nature, and the host of examples of what had been progressive change in the past, were taken as sufficient to establish the direction in which further change was bound to proceed.

The doctrine that all aspects of reality did change, and changed in accordance with law, was taken to be the necessary upshot of the new, historically oriented sciences. We have already noted Engels's insistence on this point, and John Fiske, one of Spencer's American disciples, was no less emphatic:

Now, what does all this drift of scientific opinion during more than two centuries mean? It can, of course, have but one meaning. It means that the world *is* in a process of development, and that gradually, as advancing knowledge has enabled us to take a sufficiently wide view of the world, we have come to see that it is so. The old statical conception of a world created all at once in its present shape was the result of a very narrow experience.... Now that our experience has widened, it is outgrown and set aside forever; it is replaced by a dynamical conception of a world in a perpetual process of evolution from one state into another state.... We can no more revert to the statical conception than we can turn back the sun in his course. Whatever else the philosophy of future generations may be, it must be some kind of a philosophy of evolution.[40]

Should the reader be amused at Fiske's failure to foresee that philosophy itself might soon take quite a different turn, it would be because he has not yet understood the extent to which evolutionism seemed to demand that there be a law of directional change. Fiske would assuredly not have thought of his own system —or of any similar system—as being in any sense final: what was precluded was only that men should ever retrogress to a point where the direction in which change had thus far proceeded would suddenly be reversed. Fiske himself was not a necessitarian,[41] but the idea of controlling, directional laws was part of what he took to be the lesson of the sciences. Similarly, among quasi-materialists such as Haeckel, or materialists such as Büchner and Engels, there was a dogmatic assurance that the direction of change was not only necessary but was universal and irreversible.[42] Even among those whose views were not dominated by philosophic preconceptions to the same extent (such as Andrew Carnegie and Benjamin Kidd), the idea of a necessary, progressive evolutionary development of society seemed to be demanded by the laws which had already brought about other forms of evolutionary change.[43]

6

It is obvious that those aspects of the theory of biological evolution which we have discussed, as well as the prevalence of a belief in an overriding law of historical development, would have been sufficient to engender a theory of Social Evolution. However, that theory, as it developed in the latter part of the nineteenth century, was also fed by other interests and streams of thought. Among these was an interest in comparative law, an interest in the discovery and interpretation of prehistoric artifacts, and an increasing interest in the systematic and comparative study of the beliefs and practices of "the uncivilized races." These interests were not, of course, wholly new. As we have noted, throughout the latter part of the eighteenth century, there had been attempts to formulate a comprehensive view of human history and human progress, and such attempts necessarily presupposed some beliefs—however vague—concerning the early history of mankind. In addition, in the latter part of the eighteenth century, particularly in France and in Scotland, political and social philosophers had attempted to answer specific questions concerning early human history in a more precise way than had formerly been done. While such questions were not entirely neglected during the first half of the nineteenth century, they had become less prominent. Nevertheless, they suddenly came to occupy one of the main centers of interest and debate among social theorists. This interest can be seen in an amazing series of works written by men trained in the law who attempted to reconstruct the nature of ancient law, with special reference to kinship, marriage, and property relations. The materials for such studies were, at first, largely drawn from Greek and Roman sources and supplemented by references to contemporary "savage" tribes, with the latter materials gradually taking on ascendency. As examples of such works and of the rapidity with which they followed one another, only the following need be mentioned: Henry Maine's *Ancient Law* (1861), Bachofen's *Das Mutterrecht* (1861), McLennan's *Primitive Marriage* (1865), and Lewis H. Morgan's studies of kinship, which had begun with his earlier analysis of the Iroquois and which he developed systematically over many years, publishing *Systems of*

Consanguinity and Affinity in 1871 and *Ancient Society* in 1877. Furthermore, these legally oriented works were by no means the only studies which, within this brief span of years, dealt with questions of the early history of mankind. For example, both Tylor's *Researches into the Early History of Mankind* and Lubbock's *Pre-Historic Times* were, like McLennan's work, published in 1865; Darwin's *Descent of Man* and Tylor's *Primitive Culture* were both published in 1871, the same year as Morgan's *Systems of Consanguinity and Affinity*. Thus, questions of social evolution came into prominence only very shortly after the *Origin of Species* had been published. However, it is necessary to repeat that some of these studies—and particularly those deriving from comparative law—were wholly independent of Darwinian theory or of any prior form of evolutionary theory in biology. It is striking, for example, that as late as 1877, in *Ancient Society*, when Morgan was forced to speculate on the characteristics of man in his earliest state, he twice made reference to Lucretius but mentioned Darwin only once; and this reference was only for the purpose of rejecting Darwin's quite cogent argument that promiscuity was not likely to have been the earliest stage in the relations between the sexes in human life.[1] Thus, it is indisputable that full-fledged theories of social evolution could be held, and were held, quite independently of any reference to evolutionary theory in biology.

On the other hand, some discussions of early man were very closely linked with topics connected with the theory of biological evolution. In the first place, the dating of the archaeological discoveries of early stone implements was connected with evolutionary theory, for it rested on similar interpretations of geological and paleontological evidence. Thus it is not surprising to find that evolutionists took the keenest interest in questions relating to the authenticity of the discoveries of Boucher de Perthes at Abbeville, Falconer, Lyell, and Lubbock, among many others, having gone to examine the site itself. The authentication of these discoveries immediately extended the period during which human beings, as makers of tools, had assuredly existed, thus allowing more time to be assigned for the gradual processes of social evolution.[2] The evolutionary context in which this archaeological evidence was discussed is especially clear in Lubbock's *Pre-Historic Times*, for Lubbock was a naturalist and a Darwinian; and in the concluding chapter of that book—a discussion greatly admired by Darwin[3]—the evidences of this connection were unmistakable.

However, there was a second connection between evolutionary theory in biology and social evolutionism which was even more important than the discovery that primitive man was a contemporary of animals long extinct. This was the need to establish some continuity between the mental attributes of the higher animals and those characteristics which could account for man's development of a social form of existence, and for the gradual expansion of social life until it included the whole range of culture. This was all the more important since, as we have seen, the Darwinian view of the mechanisms of evolutionary change demanded that such change should proceed by extremely small variations and very slow modification as to type. To show the possibility of establishing these very slight gradations between the higher animals and the ruder savages was the task which Darwin set himself in the *Descent of Man*. It must be recognized, however, that neither Darwin nor Lubbock linked organic and human evolution into a single indissoluble system, as Spencer had done. And the most careful and influential investigator of cultural development, E. B. Tylor, explicitly separated his own theory of progression as it applied to the elements in culture from "the modern naturalist's doctrine of progressive development," on the grounds that neither his method nor the evidence available to him were "suitable for the discussion of this remoter part of the problem of civilization."[4] Nonetheless, his method did in fact constitute a most striking parallel to the method which Darwin had applied to questions concerning the origin of species, as one can note when Tylor says:

A first step in the study of civilization is to dissect it into details, and to classify these in their proper groups.... What this task is like, may be almost perfectly illustrated by comparing these details of culture with the species of plants and animals as studied by the naturalist. To the ethnographer, the bow and arrow is a species, the habit of flattening children's skulls is a species, the practice of reckoning numbers by tens is a species. The geographical distribution of these things, and their transmission from region to region, have to be studied as the naturalist studies the geography of his botanical and zoological species.[5]

This parallelism should not be taken as establishing an influence of Darwinian theory on Tylor's thought; nor, on the other hand, should it be construed as accidental. Rather, wherever one finds an attempt to establish social evolutionism on an empirical basis, one finds important methodological assumptions similar to those by means of which Darwin had established his theory of the origin of species. Thus, in addition to some instances of a direct influence of Darwinism on social evolutionism, there was an important, indirect, methodological influence: the triumph of the comparative method in biology led to a wholesale and sometimes uncritical use of it in sociology. Even for those who did not regard social evolution as part of a single and total evolutionary process, and even when its truth was not taken to be a corollary of Darwinism, it was widely believed that the only scientifically correct way of understanding man's history was through the use of the comparative method, in which different societies were seen as representing different stages in human development.[6] It is to a consideration of this assumed parallelism between the comparative method in biology and in anthropology that I now turn.

As we have noted, the only evidence which it was possible to muster concerning the origin of biological species was indirect in character: it consisted in inferences drawn from the distribution of resembling forms of plant and animal life, from paleontological evidence, from the existence of rudimentary or vestigial organs, and from the embryological development of the more complex forms of animal life. In the case of cultural change, however, there was a great deal of evidence which was far more direct, since written records, and other cultural artifacts, made it possible to trace many of the very radical changes in practices and beliefs which had occurred in the course of human history. Nevertheless, this information was restricted in scope. For example, little could be discovered concerning those earliest men, whose primitive stone tools gave the merest suggestions concerning their form of life. Furthermore, while explorers, missionaries, sailors, and travelers brought back reports concerning the customs of a host of savage tribes, there was a lack of knowledge concerning the earlier history of these peoples: accurate information concerning their origins was not available, and it was not possible to know what the beliefs and practices of their own ancestors had been.[7] Thus, the historical record was wholly inadequate as a basis for constructing a general history of mankind; if such a history were to be constructed it, like evolutionary theory in biology, would have to rest on indirect evidence.

Now, the assumption that it should be possible to construct a general history of mankind which would include all peoples, regardless of race and of the specific characteristics of their culture, did not face the initial obstacles which had to be faced by the theory of biological evolution. As compared with the enormous differences to be found in the various species of plants and animals, the biological characteristics of man were so similar that it seemed necessary to assume that all of the various peoples of the earth were related to one another.[8] The problem then became one of accounting for both the similarities in the cultures of various groups and for the differences among them. In general, two theories vied for ascendancy: one assumed an original common level of culture in all groups, with the present state of non-civilized races being due to retrogression from an earlier, higher stage of civilization; the other was a progressionist theory, according to which the earliest human forebears started in an extremely primitive condition, that there had been gradual progress, but that not all races had evolved to the same extent. It is somewhat surprising today to note the extent to which leading anthropologists regarded it as necessary to combat the theory of retrogression. Not only was that theory logically vulnerable at many points, as Tylor showed, but almost no positive evidence could be mustered in support of it.[9] A progressionist view, on the contrary, could call on the history of technology, as revealed through archaeological findings, to establish what one might have thought could not be doubted: that there had been a gradual accumulation of skills from prehistoric times to the present. However, while it was a relatively simple matter to trace the main outlines of the earliest forms of technological development in various parts of the world, the problem of tracing the development of the non-material aspects of culture was more difficult. To be sure, the artifacts which were found permitted conjectures concerning the skills which underlay their manufacture, and from these artifacts, plus other remains, inferences could be drawn concerning the domestication of animals, the types of foodstuffs which were presumably eaten, and the like. While this evidence was more conjectural and less detailed than the paleontological evidences for evolutionary theory in biology had been, it was quite solid as far as it went. Nevertheless, its scope was severely limited with respect to the inferences it could yield.

To trace a process of cultural evolution, whether in the material or the non-material aspects of culture, the archaeological method which consisted in comparing items which were found, so to speak, at different "chronological levels," had to be supplemented by comparisons which suggested a geographical spread over time. It will be recalled that one of the methods by which Darwin had laid the foundation for his hypothesis concerning the origin of species was through tracing resemblances among the forms of life to be found in neighboring regions, with particular reference to his observations on the Galapagos Islands. The view that specimens which might otherwise have been regarded as constituting distinct species were really varieties, having a common ancestry, was argued on the basis of a combination of their close resemblances and their geographical distribution. This method, which was independent of paleontological evidence, was precisely the same as the method that was now used in some areas of the cultural domain. In fact, in philology it had already been used before Darwin in tracing genealogical connections among the Aryan (Indo-European) languages, and Darwin had cited this example in connection with the theory of organic evolution itself.[10] The same method now came to be successfully used in tracing relationships among many different cultural phenomena. The results did not immediately establish a great body of information concerning the earliest forms of man's social life, and even with respect to tools and basic techniques the possibility of multiple independent origins posed a major problem which had not really existed with respect to evolutionary theory in biology. Only the gradual, systematic accumulation of evidence could help to overcome these difficulties. In the meantime, however, Tylor—who had contributed very greatly to the formulation of the evidence in a variety of fields, and who recognized the difficulties in the interpretation of this evidence[11]—formulated the concept of "survivals," which served as an analogue in cultural matters to the role played by rudimentary or vestigial organs in the sphere of biology.[12] These survivals he defined as "processes, customs, opinions, and so forth, which have been carried on by force of habit into a new state of society different from that in which they had their original home, and they thus remain as proofs and examples of an older condition of culture out of which a newer has been evolved."[13] In the third and fourth chapters of *Primitive Culture*, Tylor gave a host of examples in which survivals served to establish historical connections which no one would be likely to challenge. However, in some of these examples, and in similar instances in his *Researches into the Early History of Mankind*, he used the concept of a survival in a way which is quite obviously suspect. I shall illustrate this dubious use by the example with which his *Researches* opens.

In the first paragraph of that book Tylor suggests that the jeweled earrings worn by modern European women are to be understood through relating them to forms of decoration which are to be found among contemporary primitive peoples, such as "the rings and bones and feathers thrust through the cartilage of the nose; the weights that pull the slit ears in long nooses to the shoulders," etc. Thus, he remarks, "the modern earring of the higher nations stands not as a product of our own times, but as a relic of a ruder mental condition." Now, what is here of interest is not the question of whether, without further ado, the modern earring is to be understood by placing it in a particular lineage of development, nor whether it actually conforms to Tylor's own later definition of a survival. What is of importance to note is his assumption, as illustrated in this example, that practices to be found among contemporary primitive peoples are to be taken as reliable indices regarding the practices characteristic of the remote ancestors of modern European man.

Tylor was not, of course, alone in making this assumption; it had been taken over from earlier speculative philosophers of history, it was accepted by those concerned with comparative law, with systematic sociology, and with interpreting the archaeological data concerning pre-history. For example, this methodological assumption was perfectly explicit in the full title of Lubbock's book: *Pre-Historic Times, as Illustrated by Ancient Remains and the Manners and Customs of Modern Savages.* And in that work Lubbock, taking his cue from the methods of evolutionary theory in biology, said:

> Deprived, therefore, as regards this period [of pre-history], of any assistance from history . . . the archaeologist is free to follow the methods which have been so successfully pursued in geology—the rude bone and stone implements of bygone ages being to the one what the remains of extinct animals are to the other. The analogy may be pursued even farther than this. Many mammalia which are extinct in Europe have representatives still living in other countries. Much light is thrown on our fossil pachyderms, for instance, by the species which still inhabit some parts of Asia and Africa; the secondary marsupials are illustrated by their existing representatives in Australia and South America; and in the same manner, if we wish clearly to understand the antiquities of Europe, we must compare them with the rude implements and weapons still, or until lately, used by the savage races in other parts of the world. *In fact, the van Damiener and South American are to the antiquary what the opossum and the sloth are to the geologist.*[14]

Now, I do not wish to suggest that Lubbock allowed this analogy to distort his account of contemporary primitive societies, nor that he introjected into genuinely prehistoric times too many speculative conjectures derived from contemporary sources. And Tylor explicitly mentioned the dangers of thinking that the conditions of life among "the savage tribes of modern times" must in all respects resemble the conditions which may have obtained in the early history of the human race.[15] Others, however, had been less cautious. In his essay on "Progress: Its Law and Cause," and throughout his later work, Herbert Spencer assumed that he could reconstruct the early social organization of man in terms of his general law of evolution, and that he could actually document the truth of that law through reference to contemporary primitive societies. Similarly, Comte had believed that one of the means through which he could establish his law of the three stages was by using the comparative method with respect to presently existing societies, among them contemporary primitive societies.[16] The underlying principle of this speculative method of a rational reconstruction of human history has never been more clearly expressed than by McLennan, who—in speaking of the tribes of Central Africa, the wilds of America, the hills of India, and the islands of the Pacific—said:

> These facts of to-day are, in a sense, the most ancient history. In the sciences of law

and society, old means not old in chronology but in structure: that is most archaic which lies nearest to the beginning of human progress considered as a development, and that is most modern which is farthest removed from that beginning.[17]

A partial justification for classifying this widely scattered set of contemporary primitive societies with what McLennan identified as the primitive stage of barbarism is to be found in the fact that written language does not appear in either. Of course, other similarities, such as the degree of development of various forms of technology, can be found. However, in order to reconstruct the history of the human race in terms of traits exhibited by contemporary primitive societies, these societies must themselves be graded in serial order. Although he invoked examples drawn from Africa, America, Asia, and the islands of the Pacific, McLennan did not believe that there were any serious obstacles to discovering such an order. In this connection, he said:

> The preface of general history must be compiled from the materials presented by barbarism. Happily, if we may say so, these materials are abundant. So unequally has the species been developed, that almost every conceivable phase of progress may be studied, as somewhere observed and recorded. And thus the philosopher, fenced from mistake, as to the order of development, by the interconnection of the stages and their shading into one another by gentle gradations, may draw a clear and decided outline of the course of human progress in times long antecedent to those to which even philology can make reference.[18]

In short, he was willing to assume that one did not need actual chronological evidence to classify societies in an order which showed how they had developed from the earliest to the latest.

Precisely the same mistaken assumption was made in Morgan's *Ancient Society*: a classificatory system by means of which social institutions were compared was taken as representing the chronological order in which they had actually developed. The mistake in this view may be easily recognized when one reflects on the following statement made by Morgan in his chapter on "The Sequence of Institutions Connected with the Family":

> Like the successive geological formations, the tribes of mankind may be arranged, according to their relative conditions, into successive strata. When thus arranged, they reveal with some degree of certainty the entire range of human progress from savagery to civilization.[19]

Geological strata are known to be formed by processes following a definite chronological order, and the fossils and skeletons and artifacts contained in them can be dated according to the objective order in which the various strata were laid down. However, in the case of *"arranging"* presently existing tribes in a linear order of development "according to their relative conditions," no such objective measure of sequence is given. In other words, before one should assume that a process of development has proceeded in one direction rather than another, or that it has always proceeded in the same direction, it is necessary to have independent evidence regarding the chronological order of the data which confirm that development; and this is evidence which Morgan did not possess.[20] The point is so obvious that it now seems surprising that an investigator as dedicated and rigorous as Morgan actually was, should have been betrayed into so elementary an error; yet, one finds at least traces of precisely the same error in the far more cautious and penetrating treatment of the evolutionary problem in Tylor's *Primitive Culture.*

The primary reason why such errors occurred is to be found in the presence of assumptions regarding progress which were analogous to the assumptions which had led Darwin and others to look upon biological evolution as being inherently progressive in its over-all tendency. However, there was one additional factor in the case of social evolutionism which calls for special mention: it was the error of comparing the mental and emotional attributes of the adult members of so-called savage tribes with the mental and emotional attributes of children. It is surprising how frequently such a comparison was made. Even Tylor, who employed the comparison with considerable caution, attempting to remain close to facts concerning uses of language, methods of counting, and the like, introduced the topic with the following remarks:

> The trite comparison of savages to "grown-up children" is in the main a sound one, though not to be carried out too strictly. In the uncivilized American or Polynesian, the strength of body and force of character of a grown man are combined with a mental development in many respects not beyond that of a young child of a civilized race.... Few educated Europeans ever thoroughly realize the fact, that they have once passed through a condition of mind from which races at a lower state of civilization never fully emerge; but this is certainly the case, and the European child playing with its doll furnishes the key to several of the mental phenomena which distinguish the highly cultivated races of mankind from those lower in the scale.[21]

When the capacities of savages are compared with those of children, it is easy to draw the further inference that their capacities also throw light on the nature of early man, for it had been widely assumed—as we have already noted in the case of Comte—that the stages through which civilization passes must resemble the stages through which the individual passes in his development toward maturity. In biology, such an assumption seemed to have been more than an analogy, and to have been established as a fact through the evolutionary interpretation of embryology—a fact summarized in the doctrine that ontogeny recapitulates phylogeny. The confusing merger of the latter principle with a comparison of the mentalities of savages and children can be seen in the following passage from Lubbock:

> Savages have often been likened to children, and the comparison is not only correct, but also highly instructive. Many naturalists consider that the early condition of the individual indicates that of the race,—that the best test of the affinities of a species are the stages through which it passes. So also it is in the case of man; the life of each individual is an epitome of the history of the race, and the gradual development of the child illustrates that of the species.[22]

Here Lubbock assumes that contemporary savages represent the early history of mankind, and that the principle of ontogeny repeating phylogeny therefore clinches one's right to compare the capabilities of children and of savages. However, it should have been obvious to a collector of pre-historic artifacts that the characteristics of early man could not possibly have been similar to those of a European child of the nineteenth century. Furthermore, he was aware of various talents possessed by primitive peoples of contemporary times which were sufficiently unusual to evoke astonishment on the part of European travelers; for example, he discussed the skill of Australian natives in their use of spears and boomerangs, a skill which must have been paralleled in constructing these implements. To compare adults who possessed such talents with children of our own civilization would seem to be wholly arbitrary. However, like others of his generation, Lubbock was thoroughly dominated by the conviction that there had been a single progressive direction in evolutionary change, and this conviction fostered the view that contemporary savages represented what were only the first stages of evolutionary change, just as a child represents only a stage in the individual's intellectual, emotional, and moral development.[23] It is the assumptions underlying this progressive conception of evolutionary development that I now wish to examine.

As we noted in the case of Darwin, the interpretation of biological evolution as a progressive development was not primarily a function of the specific mechanisms by means of which he had explained the origin of species, but grew out of his attempt to gain a synoptic view of the total history of life upon the earth. Such was also the case with respect to the theory of social evolution. That theory, as it had developed prior to the nineteenth century, and as it flourished in that century, was not primarily concerned with tracing the specific changes in particular societies, nor with the histories of particular races or cultural communities; rather, it attempted to survey the whole of human development. In the latter half of the nineteenth century this was taken to mean tracing the intellectual and cultural evolution of man from the earliest times when human beings evolved from higher mammalian forms to the present state of civilization in Western Europe.

In tracing this course of development there were, as we have seen, close parallels between the paleontological evidence for organic evolution and archaeological evidence concerning the early development of technology. What is unmistakable concerning this technological development is that, from a stage at which all tools were "rude," "simple," and "primitive," they had developed in refinement, complexity, and efficiency; furthermore, this developmental tendency was not only obvious as a result of the archaeological investigations of prehistoric times, but was clearly evident within the course of recorded history. In addition, all of the evidence suggested that the accumulation of new tools to satisfy diverse needs had been continuing at an accelerating rate. This point was stressed by Lyell and later by Morgan, each of whom claimed that the movement could be assumed to be proceeding at a rate of increase approximating geometrical proportions.[24] Thus, in so far as the development of technology was concerned, there was scarcely any room for doubt that, considering it from an over-all point of view, there had been, and was continuing to be, progress.

With respect to this progressive development, there were at least two points at which it suggested a comparison with Darwin's conception of the over-all pattern of evolutionary development. In the first place, there had in general been an obvious growth from simplicity toward complexity along the axis of time: the earliest artifacts, taken as a group, were far simpler in structure than those which had come late in the historical development of man, just as the earliest fossils indicated simplicity of structure as compared with such late developments as the primates. In the second place, some of the implements which were in use among some primitive tribes closely resembled implements which could be dated as having existed very early in human history; thus, like the still extant branches of some of the earliest forms of plant and animal life, these tribes were taken as representing an early stage in what had in most cases been a general developmental process.

Now, assuming these parallels to have been influential (as there is no reason to doubt that we should),[25] it readily becomes apparent why it was thought that contemporary primitive societies could be regarded as representing an earlier stage in the cultural life of man. Not only was their technology simpler, but the absence of written language and the existence of only rudimentary forms of arithmetical reckoning—to mention only two further items—suggested a comparison between their present state and the earlier stages through which mankind must, at one time, have passed. It then became incumbent upon the social evolutionist to arrange these tribes in a serial order, according to the places which they had occupied in a similar development of forms of marriage, property relationships, religious beliefs, and the like. However, it must again be recalled that evolutionary theory demands that one establish the existence of genealogical connections, not merely that resemblances should be found. Here the social evolutionist encountered grave difficulties, for evidence as to the earlier forms of these institutions was not, in most cases, available. To be sure, there were materials through which the historical backgrounds of European institutions could be traced, for example, through classical and biblical sources; and such knowledge was also becoming increasingly available with respect to even more ancient civilizations. While this was in many cases sufficient to establish particular patterns of developmental connection, it could not possibly prove that wherever there were resembling institutions there must have been genealogical connections. To be sure, in biology the mechanisms of evolution made it likely that marked resemblances were to be attributed to such connections, even though Darwin did acknowledge that there might be contrary cases in which convergence had taken place.[26] In the case of social evolution, however, there was no equally convincing single, or unified, theory of the mechanisms of institutional change; as a consequence, resemblances should not have been taken as decisive indices of historical connections, and an ordering of societies from the supposedly most simple to the most complex should not have been taken as indicative of the order in which social evolution had in fact taken place. In short, even for those who took the Darwinian theory as justifying a progressive interpretation of evolution—an interpretation epitomized in Darwin's own simile of the Tree of Life—there was insufficient evidence to show that there had been an analogous development, which was orderly and progressive, in the history of man's social life.[27] We must therefore ask on what presuppositions this conviction ultimately rested. I find these to have been two: one might be called a spiritual interpretation of man's nature, and the other a conviction that there was consistency and uniformity in all things, human as well as non-human. These two presuppositions may fairly be said to parallel the two presuppositions which we found to be basic in a progressivist interpretation of biological evolution. In that case, as we saw in Darwin, there was a theological motivation for a belief that the new, evolving forms of life had higher significance than those out of which they arose; there was also the presupposition that whatever tendencies one finds uniformly repeated in a sequence of events must be taken as expressive of underlying laws which serve to govern the direction of change. To be sure, the spiritual interpretation of man with which we shall here be concerned was less closely connected with orthodox theology than Darwin's original motivation had been. (In fact, the most orthodox theological position provided strong resistance to every progressionist view of human institutions.) It is also necessary to say that the uniformitarianism of the social evolutionist was generally less harsh than earlier necessitarianism had been. However, as we shall see, the parallel was not insignificant.

As an example of the spiritual presupposition which underlay a progressivist view of social development, I shall cite the conclusion of Tylor's chapter on "The Development of Culture" in *Primitive Culture*:

We may fancy ourselves looking on Civilization, as in personal figure she traverses the world; we see her lingering or resting by the way, and often deviating into paths that bring her toiling back to where she had passed by long ago; but, direct or devious, her path lies forward, and if now and then she tries a few backward steps, her walk soon falls into a helpless stumbling. It is not according to her nature, her feet were not made to plant uncertain steps behind her, for both in her forward view and in her onward gait she is of truly human type.[28]

And, in a more theological vein, we find that after discussing Asa Gray's reconciliation of the Darwinian theory with natural theology, Sir Charles Lyell concluded his treatise on *Geological Evidences of the Antiquity of Man* in the following manner:

It may be said that, so far from having a materialistic tendency, the supposed introduction into the earth at successive geological periods of life,—sensation,—instinct,—the intelligence of the higher mammalia bordering on reason,—and, lastly, the improvable reason of Man himself, presents us with a picture of an ever-increasing dominion of mind over matter.

These sentiments, coming from the most distinguished representatives of their respective fields of scientific inquiry, are not to be lightly dismissed: the evolution of mankind was a progressive development in which the spiritual capacities of the race could be seen as unfolding, and in the long process attaining a new and higher development.

Should such views be considered as mere sentimentality, it is only necessary to recall that, at the time, there was an insufficient appreciation of the capacities of primitive peoples, and because of this there was a widespread feeling of their utter remoteness from modern Western man. In this connection it may be useful to cite Darwin's account of his own reactions to those primitive peoples with whom he came into contact on the voyage of the *Beagle*. In a passage summarizing the impression gained from his voyage, he wrote:

> Of individual objects, perhaps nothing is more certain to create astonishment than the first sight in his native haunt of a barbarian—of man in his lowest and most savage state. One's mind hurries back over past centuries, and then asks, could our progenitors have been men like these?—men, whose very signs and expressions are less intelligible to us than those of the domesticated animals; men, who do not possess the instinct of these animals, nor yet appear to boast of human reason, or at least of arts consequent on that reason. I do not believe it is possible to describe or paint the difference between savage and civilized men. It is the difference between a wild and tame animal: and part of the interest in beholding a savage, is the same which would lead every one to desire to see the lion in his desert, the tiger tearing his prey in the jungle, or the rhinoceros wandering over the wild plains of Africa.[29]

When one bears in mind this vivid reaction to the unfamiliar conditions of primitive life, one can better understand what would otherwise appear to be the unmitigated smugness of a passage such as the following, drawn from Darwin's rejection of the theory of retrogression:

> To believe that man was aboriginally civilized and then suffered utter degradation in so many regions, is to take a pitiably low view of human nature. It is apparently a truer and more cheerful view that progression has been much more general than retrogression; that man has risen, though by slow and interrupted steps, from a lowly condition to the highest standard as yet attained by him in knowledge, morals, and religion.[30]

Thus Darwin, no less than Tylor and Lyell, conceived of progress in terms of a development of man's spirit, and as we see in *The Descent of Man* the social factors which were uppermost in his mind when he considered the nature of human development were not primarily connected with subsistence, family, regulatory organization, property, or technological growth, but with man's intellectual powers and with the foundations of social morality.[31]

Lewis H. Morgan's *Ancient Society* and Spencer's *Principles of Sociology* show evidence of different concerns. Instead of dealing with the progressive development of various specific aspects of human culture, considered topically, they viewed the evolution of mankind as a process in which types of society succeeded one another, and in which it was important to reconstruct the pattern of relationships among the institutions in each type. Thus, unlike some of their contemporaries (e.g., Lubbock), and unlike many later evolutionists (e.g., Westermarck), they did not use the comparative method on isolated fragments of societies: what-

ever their errors with respect to the necessity of establishing chronological and
genealogical connections before claiming to have established an evolutionary
pattern, their theories did not neglect the fact that the various customs and institutions which characterize a given society belong together in a functioning whole.
In this respect Comte may be viewed as one of their forerunners. In addition,
their views paralleled his in the emphasis which they placed on the necessity with
which progress occurred. Neither Morgan nor Spencer regarded progress as being
guided by deliberation, individual decision, or by the moral qualities inherent
in man. For Morgan, progress was both natural and necessary, as we see in the
paragraphs with which *Ancient Society* opens:

> The latest investigations respecting the early condition of the human race, are tending
> to the conclusion that mankind commenced their career at the bottom of the scale and
> worked their way up from savagery to civilization through the slow accumulations
> of experimental knowledge.
> As it is undeniable that portions of the human family have existed in a state of
> savagery, other portions in a state of barbarism, and still other portions in a state of
> civilization, it seems equally so that these three distinct conditions are connected with
> each other in a natural as well as necessary sequence of progress.

Morgan's belief that there was universality in this natural order rested on an
assumption which may be compared to Lyell's uniformitarianism in geology, for
he assumed "that the experience of mankind has run in nearly uniform channels;
that human necessities in similar conditions have been substantially the same;
and that the operations of the mental principle have been uniform in virtue of
the specific identity of the brain in all races of mankind."[32] Furthermore, like the
geologist, he assumed that the processes had gone on in a slow, cumulative manner over very long periods of time, and that, in general, increments to knowledge
were not sudden and discontinuous discoveries, but the results of these cumulative processes. We read, for example, in one of the epigraphs which introduces
Ancient Society that "all the elements of culture—as the arts of life, art, science,
language, religion, philosophy—have been wrought by slow and painful efforts,"
and in another, "Our wondrous civilization is the result of the silent efforts of
millions of unknown men, as the chalk cliffs of England are formed of the contributions of myriads of foraminifera." And at another place Morgan himself
commented, "the phonetic alphabet came, like other great inventions, at the end
of successive efforts..."[33] Throughout his account of mankind's ascent, Morgan
emphasized uniformity and continuity; the accidental, the sporadic, the discontinuous, seem to have no place in his view of the past. And thus, like Comte, his
view of social development seems to be that progress was governed by an inner
necessity; unlike Comte, however, Morgan apparently did not articulate a
philosophic position which served as a means of justifying this assumption.

In Spencer's evolutionism there was, however, an insistence on total evolution
in accordance with one comprehensive law. To be sure, he did not insist that
every society had progressed; in fact, in contrast to other evolutionists, he ceded
considerable ground to those who regarded contemporary primitive societies as

having retrogressed from an earlier, higher state of civilization.[34] Nevertheless, taking an over-all view of the history of specific institutions, as well as of the history of mankind as a whole, he believed in progressive development, with higher types of social organisms emerging, and with more heterogeneity and more complete integration being achieved. If one examines Spencer's sociology in an attempt to discover the means by which he accounted for these processes of evolutionary change, one finds that, at various points, his explanations followed different patterns. Sometimes the changes were explained by an appeal to what were taken to be inherently intelligible psychological factors governing development; sometimes the explanation was in terms of the usefulness of an institution for the survival of the society possessing it; sometimes, on the other hand, the explanations were almost wholly speculative and were dominated by an assumed parallel with what Spencer held to be true in biology.[35] In all cases, however, he claimed that social evolution had proceeded in terms of the one general, overarching law of development. It was by means of this law that he classified all of the various types and constitutions of society, and at the end of that classification he dogmatically stated:

> In this order has social evolution gone on, and only in this order does it appear to be possible. Whatever imperfections and incongruities the above classification has, do not hide these general facts—that there are societies of these different grades of composition; that those of the same grade have general resemblances in their structures; and that they arise in the order shown.[36]

In this statement one sees the mistake which we have already noted in the case of Morgan: the order according to which societies had been arranged by Spencer was not an order which had been established by independent chronological evidence, but was a function of the system of classification which he had employed. Spencer's failure to see this error may, like Morgan's, be attributed to a general conviction that there necessarily was progress in human affairs. Even had he not been predisposed to believe that change is fundamentally progressive, his conception of the nature of ultimate scientific laws would have led him to impose an orderly sequence on all of the different forms of social institutions which he sought to survey. This followed from the fact that he believed that the fundamental laws of nature are concerned with the order in which changes appear, that is to say, he conceived of them as developmental laws.[37] Given the fact that he regarded the institutions of modern Western society as most recent in origin, it was necessary for him to arrange all other institutional forms in an orderly sequence which led up to them. Thus, the system of classification which he adopted appeared to him to constitute a natural and necessary order, and mankind's history was divided by him into stages through which societies had gradually evolved toward their present, more advanced state.

There is a noticeable difference between the necessitarianism which one finds in Spencer's social evolutionism, or even in that of Morgan, and the temper of a progressivist view such as Tylor's. The contrast between these views may merit further scrutiny because of the help it will afford in discussing philosophic issues which are connected with historicism, issues with which our next chapter is to be concerned.

In connection with this contrast it must first be insisted that Tylor was no less convinced than was Spencer of nature's uniformity and of the universal applicability of natural laws. Almost at the outset of *Primitive Culture*, he wrote:

> Our modern investigators in the sciences of inorganic nature are foremost to recognize, both within and without their special fields of work, the unity of nature, the fixity of its laws, the definite sequence of cause and effect through which every fact depends on what has gone before it, and acts upon what is to come after it.[38]

He then argued that one must accept the same assumption with respect to human affairs generally, and, more specifically, with respect to the history of mankind. While admitting that it was not currently possible to establish a philosophy of history capable of "explaining the past and predicting the future phenomena of man's life in the world by reference to general laws," Tylor attributed this inability to the amount of knowledge which was presupposed, not to any inherent impossibility in the task.[39] He therefore chose what he considered to be a narrower field of inquiry, not attempting to deal with history as a whole, but "with that branch of it which is here called Culture, the history, not of tribes or nations, but of the conditions of knowledge, religion, art, custom, and the like."[40] While one can assuredly doubt that this did in fact constitute a narrower field of inquiry, Tylor believed it to be more manageable. While he recognized that there would be difficulties in establishing general laws applicable to the development of culture, this was nonetheless the task which he set himself. It is precisely here that one can note at least an implicit difference between Tylor's view of the nature of such laws and the view which was assuredly characteristic of Comte and of Spencer, and which it is probably also justifiable to attribute to Morgan. The difference lies in the fact that Tylor did not assume that the general laws which could presumably explain cultural change were laws regulating or governing the successive steps in the processes to which they applied. One notes this, for example, in his statement that the field of culture is more manageable than history because the facts can be classified into distinct groups, and these groups can be individually investigated with respect to their distribution, the specific changes which they underwent, and the causal connections existing among them.[41] The same point is evident in Tylor's interest in the problem of whether particular developments were to be attributed to historical contacts or were in all likelihood the results of independent invention.[42] This was not a problem which was relevant to the investigations of those who believed in the necessary, stadial evolution of culture: laws of development were assumed by them to be determinative of the course of change which was characteristic of all societies. Finally, we may note that in most cases in which Tylor made concrete suggestions concerning the types of laws which explain cultural phenomena, these did not define and summarize a necessary direction in which change proceeded; instead, he attempted to show how facts concerning language, myth, magic, and the like, depend upon general principles governing the processes of human thought.[43] Unfortunately, these facts concerning Tylor's views have usually been overlooked, for his position has been chiefly described with reference to his theory of the development of religious belief from animism through polytheism to monotheism. However, even within this field, it is clear that he did not hold that there was a necessary sequence governing the course of all phases of this pattern of development. For example, he pointed out that the notion of a Supreme Deity evolved in different forms among different primitive peoples; he also used culture-contacts and specific survivals to account for differences among those peoples who held roughly similar forms of belief. In short, Tylor's views regarding the evolution of religion consisted in the attempt to classify the wealth of detail regarding different religious doctrines in certain broad categories, and to establish a general chronological order among these categories, as one might establish a chronological sequence in general types of technology; he did not seek to lay down a specific law of stages through which the religious beliefs of each society must necessarily pass.[44]

That Tylor did not hold to a strict form of social evolutionism does not of course mean that he was not a progressionist: as we have already noted, his general interpretation of man as a spiritual being, like that of Charles Lyell, demanded that the footsteps of civilization should not falter. In the case of Tylor, this belief rested on a conviction that all progress depended upon intelligence, and upon the growing uses to which intelligence could be put. Thus, he was convinced that those arts which were useful would not, in general, disappear.[45] Furthermore, he believed that just as one could trace "the history of an upward development" in the arts, so it was also the case that the history of man's mental condition shows "an upward progress, a succession of higher intellectual processes and opinions to lower ones."[46] This progress was, furthermore, linked to a growth in morality, for Tylor was a convinced utilitarian in all aspects of social theory. For example, in the concluding chapter of his *Anthropology*, he first argued that the differences between the lower and higher races of men with respect to their morality rested upon differences in imagination and understanding,[47] and then went on to show that there had been progressive advance not only in moral belief but in all of the major institutional forms by means of which social authority was exercised. In fact, Tylor envisioned modern Western culture as having entered a new stage of progress by virtue of its advances in knowledge. In the concluding paragraph of his *Anthropology*, he said:

Had the experience of ancient men been larger, they would have seen their way to faster steps in culture. But we civilized moderns have just that wider knowledge which the rude ancients wanted. Acquainted with events and their consequences far and wide over the world, we are able to direct our own course with more confidence toward improvement. In a word, mankind is passing from the age of unconscious to that of conscious progress.

Given this belief, one can understand the special value which Tylor attached to ethnological studies. Noting the persistence of custom and the fact that all institutions have their roots deep in the past, the ethnologist was in a position to trace the history of the opinions of the day, enabling his contemporaries to judge which were justifiable, which might still be of limited use, and which were in fact surviving forms of superstition.[48] Thus, on a level far higher than ever before, knowledge was the means through which mankind could continue to advance, with the comparative science of ethnology playing a new and crucial role.

It is not our present concern to trace the decline of faith in progress, whether that faith was based on the theory of natural selection, whether it derived from the idea of an inevitable law of directional change, or whether, as in the case of Tylor and others, it was claimed to be a consequence of a steady improvement in knowledge. Rather, we shall now turn our attention to the manner in which the theory of biological evolution and theories of social evolution were related to historicism.

Were historicism merely a matter of looking at all questions historically, there could be no doubt that every evolutionary theory would involve an acceptance of that thesis, for by definition an evolutionary account of any phenomenon purports to be a historical account. There are, however, two different ways of regarding evolutionary change. One is to regard it as a sum of successive, individual changes, where the pattern which one can retrospectively trace is regarded as being adequately explained as due to specific conjunctions of events at successive points in time. On such a view, evolutionary change is not a function of some inherent tendency for events to succeed one another in any particular pattern. It should now be clear that the mechanisms by means of which Darwin sought to account for the transmutation of species and for the adaptations of organisms to their environments, would have favored this view. On the other hand, it is also possible, in looking back on an evolutionary development, to interpret it as having had, from the outset, a tendency to move in one direction rather than another. Once such a morphic tendency is assumed, and a particular course of development is expected, change in that direction is taken as progressive, whereas an absence of change, or changes occurring in other directions, are considered as instances of stagnation, of retrogression, or as having been, in one way or another, aberrant. As we have seen, this was not an uncommon view with respect to biological evolution; and when Darwin surveyed the whole sequence of living forms, he tended to look upon evolution as a single, progressive process, even though such an interpretation did not actually conform to the mechanisms he invoked in order to explain the changes which had occurred. In fact, it is probably not misleading to say that there always exists a tension between these two ways of viewing a historical process. On the one hand, that which is an object of historical investigation may be regarded as constituting a whole only to the extent to which there existed a particular sequence of events which were causally related; or, on the other hand, such a process may be regarded as a whole which dominates its parts, tending to control what can affect it or what can become a part of it.

These two views have quite different consequences with respect to the explanation of historical events, and also with respect to the evaluation of those events. As we have seen in our discussions of earlier philosophies of history, the assumption that there had been a necessary directional tendency in human history led to an acceptance of historicism. And the theory brought forward by anthropologists, which held that there had been a unitary process of social evolution in material culture and in the development of institutions, had exactly the same consequences. In fact, historicism only declined in anthropology when the tendency to view the human past as a single line of development was abandoned.

The connection between social evolutionism and historicism can readily be seen even in the modified evolutionism of Tylor, who remarked:

> It is indeed hardly too much to say that Civilization, being a process of long and complex growth, can only be thoroughly understood when studied through its entire range; that the past is continually needed to explain the present, and the whole to explain the part.[49]

On the basis of this assumption it would follow that to understand a particular social institution it would not be sufficient to see it in relation to its specific historical antecedents, and in relation to the needs of the people living at a particular place and time; one would have to view it as an aspect in the whole developmental process of which it was only a fragmentary part. As we have noted, this position did not correspond to the actual methods followed by Tylor. However, it did conform to the methodological assumptions which were present in the social evolutionism of Comte and of Spencer, as well as those which we have seen to be characteristic of McLennan and even of Morgan. In each of their theories the manner in which the lineage of a particular phenomenon was established did not consist in tracing its actual historical connections, but in attempting to show what place it occupied in a developmental series which ranged from the simplest and presumably earliest forms to those forms of institutional life which characterize contemporary Western society. That this was indeed the manner in which the comparative method was used as a principle of explanation can be illustrated by a quotation from John Fiske:

> The point of the comparative method, in whatever field it may be applied, is that it brings before us a great number of objects so nearly alike that we are bound to assume for them an origin and general history in common, while at the same time they present such differences in detail as to suggest that some have advanced further than others in the direction in which all are travelling; some, again, have been abruptly arrested, others perhaps even turned aside from the path. . . .[50]

Then, turning more specifically to the results of the comparative method as applied to social evolution, Fiske continued:

> When we have come to survey large groups of facts of this sort, the conclusion is irresistibly driven home to us that the more advanced societies have gone through various stages now represented here and there by less advanced societies; that there is a general path of social development, along which, owing to special circumstances, some peoples have advanced a great way, some a less way, some but a very little way; and that by studying existing savages and barbarians we get a valuable clue to the interpretation of prehistoric times. All these things are today commonplaces among students of history and archaeology; sixty years ago they would have been scouted as idle vagaries. It is the introduction of such methods of study that is making history scientific.[51]

As we have had occasion to note with respect to Comte and to Spencer, this conception of a scientific history—as contrasted with traditional methods of historical inquiry—was characteristic of the new science of society. The laws thus established on the basis of a comparative method were laws of directional change; and it was these, rather than specific historical connections, which were taken as explanatory of the characteristic sequences of major institutional events.

Turning to the problem of the evaluation of specific events, one can readily see the consequences of this assumption. Given a necessary, progressive development, all earlier forms of belief were to be considered rudimentary, or as stages necessary for further advance.[52] Thus, the truth of a belief or the merit of a custom was not evaluated in terms of what was asserted by it, nor in terms of the consequences to which it led, but in terms of the place which such a belief or custom occupied in a larger process of historic development. John Morley summarized both the nature of historicism as a mode of understanding, and also its evaluative implications, in his characterization of what he termed "the Historic Method," saying:

The Historic Method may be described as the comparison of the forms of an idea, or a usage, or a belief, at any given time, with the earlier forms from which they were evolved, or the later forms into which they were developed, and the establishment, from such a comparison, of an ascending and descending order among the facts. It consists in the explanation of existing parts in the frame of society by connecting them with corresponding parts in some earlier frame; in the identification of present forms in the past, and past forms in the present. Its main process is the detection of corresponding customs, opinions, laws, beliefs, among different communities, and a grouping of them into general classes with reference to some one common feature. It is a certain way of seeking answers to various questions of origin, resting on the same general doctrine of evolution, applied to moral and social forms, as that which is being applied with so much ingenuity to the series of organic matter. The historic conception is a reference of every state of society to a particular stage in the evolution of its general conditions.

Then, turning to the evaluative implications of this method, Morley continues:

Character is considered less with reference to its absolute qualities than as an interesting scene strewn with scattered rudiments, survivals, inherited predispositions. Opinions are counted rather as phenomena to be explained than as matters of truth and falsehood. Of usages, we are beginning first of all to think where they came from, and secondarily whether they are the most fitting and convenient that men could be got to accept. In the last century men asked of a belief or a story, Is it true? We now ask, How did men come to take it for true? In short the relations among social phenomena which now engage most attention, are relations of original source, rather than those of actual consistency in theory and actual fitness in practice. The devotees of the current method are more concerned with the pedigree and genealogical connections of a custom or an idea than with its own proper goodness or badness, its strength or its weakness.[53]

I do not propose to enter into dispute concerning the evaluative thesis of historicism, for I believe that if its explanatory thesis can be shown to be false, the foundation for its evaluative thesis will have been undercut. It is, therefore, to a criticism of that explanatory thesis that I shall next turn.

7

HISTORICISM: A CRITICAL APPRAISAL

One problem, with which we have had frequent occasion to deal in the preceding pages, was the prevalent but by no means universal belief among nineteenth-century social theorists that there are laws which determine the direction in which any society or institution will tend to move over the course of time. That belief, as we have seen in Comte and Spencer, to mention only two, was intimately connected with the explanatory thesis of historicism; it will, therefore, be appropriate to open our critical discussion with an evaluation of it. We shall then be in a position to understand that there are interesting and compelling parallels between this sort of scientific necessitarianism and that earlier phase of historicism in which teleological conceptions had been favored, and no attempt was made to establish societal laws.

This meeting of two otherwise antagonistic positions is a phenomenon which has been made familiar by Karl Popper's *Poverty of Historicism* and by Isaiah Berlin's *Historical Inevitability*. However, there is one aspect of historicism which was of special concern to them, but which I shall avoid: the effect of historicist modes of thought on questions relating to individual freedom and responsibility. In my opinion, it was because of their concern with this issue that Popper and Berlin to some extent failed to isolate historicism from a quite different doctrine with which it had been associated: a theory of the nature of societies frequently designated as "holism."[1] To be sure, the connection between historicism and one particular form of "holism" was very close during the period with which we are concerned; however, the two views have not always been jointly held.[2] I therefore regard it as important to separate them, and I shall confine my present discussion to a single topic: whether or not the explanatory thesis of historicism can withstand critical appraisal.[3]

I shall, as I have said, start from a consideration of the position of those who attempted to establish deterministic laws of development, and who claimed it was with reference to such laws that particular instances of historical and social

113

change are to be explained. I shall attempt to establish the fact that it is a mistake to assume that there are any *laws* of the sort which these historicists were attempting to find. I shall then examine the modes of explanation which were characteristic of the first phase of historicism and its teleological approach, raising some issues which have equal applicability to a belief in the existence of directional laws. If these discussions serve to establish the fact that neither form of historicism presents an adequate model for understanding historical events, then it will follow that some of the disturbing ways in which historicists have dealt with questions concerning freedom and responsibility will be recognized to have been misconceived. At that point my discussion will have reached the same type of conclusion which Popper and Berlin were concerned to defend.

1. The Problem of Directional Laws in History

Turning now to the deterministic model of explanation adopted by those historicists who wished to establish a rigorous science of society, let us ask whether or not it would be reasonable to expect that there are any general laws which define a direction of change, which are irreducible, and which would apply to historical and social processes. In speaking of a directional law as "irreducible," I shall be referring to any such laws which would not themselves be explicable through tracing the effects, at successive moments of time, of what I shall term "functional laws." The term "functional," in this connection, derives from the mathematical use of the notion of a function, as when it is said of empirical laws that they state "the functional relationships between the variables."[4] This does not imply that all functional laws must be stated in specifically quantitative terms, as one can see from the fact that we may formulate laws such as the following: "whenever a solid is dissolved in a liquid, the boiling point of the liquid is raised," or "whenever a magnetic rod is broken in two, the pieces are magnets."[5] Since the difference between functional and directional laws does not rest on a distinction between quantitatively formulated laws and those which are not expressed in quantitative terms, it must be sought elsewhere. It will be my contention that this difference consists in the ways in which the relationships which they formulate are themselves related to actual processes of change. Functional laws, I shall hold, express concurrent relationships rather than a series of successive relationships, and they do so even when they deal with processes of change; directional laws, on the other hand, formulate statements which refer to a set of sequential relations.[6]

That there are many cases in which functional laws do, undeniably, deal with concurrent rather than sequential relationships can readily be seen in a case such as Boyle's law, which is one of the most frequently cited paradigm instances of a functional law: the relationship between the pressure and the volume of a gas (at constant temperature) is expressed as a concurrent relationship, not a successive one. However, it is to be noted that Boyle's law does enable us to understand changes over time, even though time does not enter as one of the variables in the law: given a change in the volume, the pressure of the gas will change, and vice versa. Thus, concurrent relationships may serve to explain the successive states of a system. On the other hand, there are cases in which time *does* enter into the expression of a functional law, and yet it is perfectly clear that the law expresses a functional and not a sequential relationship. For example, the time (t) which it takes a pendulum to complete one full swing varies with its length (l),[7] but this relationship between periodicity and length is clearly not to be construed as sequential. I call attention to these cases in order to make two related points, both of which it will be useful to bear in mind in what immediately follows: first, that laws which state concurrent relationships can be applied in the explanation of change, and, second, that it would be false to assume that the presence of time as one of the variables in a law entails that the law is directional rather than functional.[8]

In the foregoing cases, the non-sequential character of the relationships expressed in functional laws should have been obvious. It is also necessary to consider instances in which the factor of time introduces changes in the magnitudes of the other variables. A frequently cited example is provided by Galileo's laws of falling bodies. In such instances it might seem difficult to claim that the relationships which are expressed in functional laws are always to be regarded as concurrent relationships. Nevertheless, it must be noted that what is stated in laws of this type are changes in the magnitudes of other variables *per unit of time*; they do not attempt to trace successive stages in a sequential process. In short, such laws are not, strictly speaking, chronological in character. Thus, although functional laws of this type involve changes in the magnitude of the other variables with respect to time (and thus differ from laws such as Boyle's law), they are like all other functional laws in one fundamental respect: at any moment whatsoever, every functional law formulates fixed relationships which concurrently hold among the variables. It is for this reason that such laws have, following Ferdinand de Saussure, frequently been termed "synchronic laws."

In contradistinction to these functional, synchronic laws, it has become usual to speak of "diachronic laws": laws which seek to establish a necessary sequence of relationships, that is, patterns of change.[9] Such laws may, of course, take various forms, but perhaps the most general way in which one can describe their structure is to say that they attempt to formulate necessary relationships between a series of three or more successive states of an object or system, and in doing so they define the course of changes which (if nothing interferes) such an object or system necessarily undergoes. It is for this reason that I find it most suggestive to speak of them as "directional laws."

Taken in this sense, it is not difficult to find instances of directional laws. The second law of thermodynamics (the increase of entropy in a closed system) would be one; what is usually referred to as Kepler's first law (that of the elliptical orbit of the planets) might be another. As these two illustrations suggest, a directional law may define a tendency to move along a single axis of change, or, on the other hand, it may involve a cyclical form of movement; each of these alternatives, has, of course, been accepted in one form or another by philosophers of history. However, for our present purposes it is not important to discuss the variety of the forms which directional laws may assume, but to try to become clear about the relationships which such laws may be said to bear to functional laws. In this connection I should like to point out that since my concern is with *empirical* laws, the following discussion will not attempt to deal with the special problems which attach to the interpretation of the second law of thermodynamics.[10]

As one or more of the foregoing examples may suggest, what is formulated as a directional law need not be regarded as irreducible; that is, it may be known to be, or conjectured to be, a consequence of the constant operation of functional relationships. Given a set of initial conditions, and assuming that no factors not known to be present will interfere, the constant operation of functional relationships can serve to explain directional processes. For example, Galileo's functional laws explain the constant acceleration of freely falling bodies and the parabolic paths of projectiles, and Newton's laws of gravitation and of motion serve to explain Kepler's directional law of the elliptical orbits of the planets.

It must, however, be noted that the example of what is usually referred to as Kepler's first law has sometimes also been used to show that while it is true that such a law may, at some later time, be explained in terms of the operation of forces described by functional laws, *originally* directional laws can be formulated independently of functional laws; and if they are sufficiently accurate they will be accepted, regardless of whether or not their possible relationships to functional laws are known. While this contention may be true, Kepler's law of the elliptical planetary orbits is probably not a good example to use as a means of establishing its truth. To be sure, Newton's laws were formulated long after Kepler's; in fact, the law of gravitation was taken as partially confirmed through the very fact that it served to explain Kepler's laws. However, it must not be overlooked that while Kepler only discovered his third law at a later time, he published the first two laws simultaneously, and it is likely that what we now call his second law was discovered prior to the first, and in a sense served as its foundation. That law, unlike the law of the elliptical orbits, is clearly a functional, and not a directional law: it ascribes constant equality to the areas swept over by the radius vectors of the planets in equal intervals of time. Moreover, it would seem that Kepler's discovery of this functional law was connected with his conjectures concerning a force emanating from the sun—a force whose constant operation, and whose diminution with distance, make it comparable to Newton's gravitational force.[11] When these historical facts are considered, and when it is recalled that what we now refer to as Kepler's first law did not merely state that the planets moved in elliptical orbits but also stated that the sun stood at one focus of these ellipses, it should be apparent that, in this case, the acceptance of a directional law may not have been independent of prior conjectures concerning functional laws. This, we may note, can have been true even though, at the time, there was no way of showing how one type of law was reducible to the other.

Now, I should not wish to claim that a relationship of this sort holds in absolutely all cases. For example, should we say that someone who, through observation, had learned the life-cycle of a particular species of plant or of insect would feel obliged to press for the reduction of his general description of that life-cycle to the operation of non-directional (i.e., functional) laws? Or, if one can formulate general statements concerning, say, a series of phonetic changes in a group of languages, as is the case in "Grimm's law," would one not be inclined to accept such statements as being wholly legitimate examples of empirical laws, even without the formulation of conjectures as to how they might be shown to result from the operation of factors which can be stated in terms of functional laws? Actually, "Grimm's law" has often been regarded in precisely this way.[12] Given such cases, it might seem most prudent to hold that scientific inquiry should always be free of methodological prejudices, admitting whatever types of laws are useful, and not attempting to force any form of empirical generalization into a mold which had not developed out of inquiry itself. While attractive in other ways, a neutralism of this sort fails to take into account the possibility that there are genuine difficulties in regarding an empirical law which attempts to define a series of directional changes as constituting an adequate explanation of the changes one observes, however regular they may be. It is with at least some of these difficulties that I shall now be concerned.[13]

Let me approach these difficulties through pointing out two basic formal characteristics in which functional laws differ from directional laws. The first is the degree of abstraction from concrete events which is, in general, characteristic of functional laws; the second is the fact that functional laws must be treated as conditional, not as categorical, in their application. What each of these characteristics involves will become clear as we proceed; and we shall see that the difficulties which arise with respect to directional laws are related to the fact that they differ from functional laws in these respects. Thus, we may say that directional laws can be charged with two fundamental errors: the mistake of insufficient abstraction, and the mistake of taking laws to be categorical rather than conditional, in their application. I now turn to a consideration of the degree of abstraction which is characteristic of paradigmatic cases of functional laws.

As a point of departure, let us note that in any case in which we attempt to formulate a functional law that is to be used to explain particular objects, events, or processes, that law must deal with *types* of objects, events, or processes: the relationship which is said to hold must be claimed to hold not only of this particular entity, but of all entities which are of a similar type. This is the first level at which functional laws may be said to be abstractive: they abstract from the times and places of the occurrences with which they deal, designating relationships which hold whenever and wherever the same set of relevant circumstances may occur. However, if such a law is to be of any explanatory significance, it will involve a further degree of abstraction from the events to which it refers: the type of event with which one deals cannot be characterized in terms of *all* properties possessed by any one of its instances, since one could then never effectively generalize from case to case. Thus, any law will not only abstract from the time and place of the instances to which it is to be applied, but will also abstract from many of their characteristics, confining itself to some of their aspects which are not only presumably repeatable in principle, but can be known to be repeated in fact. Even in those cases in which our law-like statements are very crude, both of these levels of abstraction can readily be recognized. If, for example, we explain the fact that a particular object floats or sinks by saying that it is made of cork or of solid iron, we have in the first place said something that presumably applies to all objects of these types; and, in the second place, we have characterized the type in terms of what we consider to be the specific factor which is relevant to its behavior when immersed in water: its composition, not its color, or shape, or size, or the like. Similarly, when we explain the transformations which a particular plant or insect undergoes in the course of its development, referring to the fact that it belongs to a particular species, we not only assume that such developmental changes characterize all members of that species, but we are abstracting from the differences in the environments in which individuals of the species mature, and from whatever differences among individuals (such as size, or variations in color) which we do not regard as essential properties of the species. Thus, there are basic similarities between functional and directional law-like statements, in so far as the first two levels of abstraction in their formulation are concerned.

Nevertheless, it must be noticed that, in some cases, there is a very significant difference between explaining the development of a plant or of an insect in terms of the species to which it belongs, and explaining the floating of a piece of cork or the sinking of a piece of iron through reference to *its* species, that is, with reference to its being made of cork or iron. The cases in which such a difference exists are those in which we attribute the contrary forms of behavior of cork and iron to a specific factor, viz., the light bulk of the one and the heavy density of the other, rather than to the general fact that one is "cork," and the other "iron." In such cases we have abstracted what we take to be a single qualitative factor, and we attempt to explain an occurrence in terms of that factor. On the other hand, when we explain the development of an individual plant or insect by reference to its belonging to a particular species, there is no isolable factor of a similar sort to which we are making reference. It is here that we reach the third and most essential level of abstraction in the classical examples of functional laws. It is because of the fact that there are isolable factors—factors such as pressure and volume, or velocity, time, and distance—which constitute aspects of the most diverse sorts of occurrences, that functional laws can be extremely specific in what they state, and yet be extremely general in their applicability. As one can learn from Galileo's method, the first step that must be taken, if one is to find constant functional relationships, is to resolve complex occurrences into their simple aspects, each of which can be considered in abstraction from the others, however diverse the concrete appearances of these occurrences may be.[14]

Now, I would not claim that, in principle, it is impossible for laws of directional change to be formulated in terms of abstract features, rather than in terms of sequences among complex entities; that it is possible to do so is clear from Spencer's consideration of factors of growth, complexity, and differentiation of function in the most heterogeneous sorts of objects and events. However, it must be pointed out that this has not been the characteristic way in which, in most instances, developmental laws have been formulated. In the social sciences, such laws have in general attempted to establish a particular series of successive stages through which institutions pass, and this has involved tracing, or attempting to trace, the nature of these institutions in previous societies. The only verification which would be possible with respect to such a developmental law, would involve sifting further historical evidence to show that, in all other societies, these stages had also existed, and had existed in the particular order predicted by the law. Thus, such an approach involves "an immediate reference to the historically given reality and to the actual course of events," as Kurt Lewin remarked with respect to an allied mode of explanation, which he termed "Aristotelian."[15] On the other hand, in the Galilean resolution of complex phenomena into their basic aspects, there is an abstraction of particular attributes from the concrete objects or events which possess them: terms such as pressure, velocity, temperature, or mass apply to a host of otherwise disparate objects. Since functional laws are stated in terms of relationships between these abstracted attributes, they are not necessarily tied to specific types of objects or occurrences.[16]

The fact that the method which is characteristic of the modern physical sciences is an abstractive method is now so familiar that it need not be labored; however, it might be thought that another method which does not attain the same level of abstraction, but explains behavior in terms of the concrete natures and differences among species, could (in some cases at least) still hold its own. Thus, it might be claimed that it would be mistaken to abandon the search for laws of directional change, as long as there is any hope of finding such laws. While one cannot entirely reject this position, the issue is not whether one can formulate laws of directional change, but whether such laws are not simply generalizations of what *usually* occurs because of the operation of those factors whose relationships we attempt to state in terms of functional laws. The question is, then, one which concerns the reducibility of one type of law to the other. Yet, even here, the specter of unwarranted dogmatism can easily be raised. As we have already noted, if we are called upon to explain a particular change occurring in some form of insect, we are apt to offer a generalization concerning the developmental sequence of stages through which specimens of that species pass, and we may be at a loss to suggest any means by which to account for this particular change in terms of the effects of functional laws. Although this may be the case, a charge of unwarranted dogmatism is still not in order, for we shall shortly see that directional laws run into very fundamental difficulties when we find what appear to be exceptions to them. Before showing why this is the case, it will be useful to indicate the second general point at which it becomes clear that directional laws must be regarded as fundamentally different from functional laws. This difference can be summarily expressed by saying that functional laws are always conditional with respect to their application, although they are categorical with respect to the relationships which they formulate, whereas directional laws are categorical with respect to their applications, as well as with respect to the sequential relationships which they affirm.[17]

To say that a functional law is categorical with respect to the relationships which it formulates is merely to say that such a law states an invariant relationship between the factors with which it is concerned: for example, wherever and whenever a gas is kept at a constant temperature, its pressure and volume bear a constant relationship to one another.[18] A directional law is, in a similar manner, categorical with respect to the relationships which *it* formulates: whenever and wherever one finds a set of conditions of a specific type, one can say that it will have been preceded or that it will be followed (or both) by some other sets of specified conditions, so that one can trace a series of changes proceeding in a definite direction. Thus, such a directional law is also categorical. However, the two types of law differ in the manner in which they apply to concrete cases. From the knowledge of a functional law, unaided by any further detailed information concerning specific matters of fact, one cannot predict or explain any concrete event whatsoever. Edgar Zilsel stated this point in an exceptionally pithy manner:

Astronomers cannot predict from Newton's law what the position of the planet Mars will be on next New Year's Eve. In addition to the law they need the knowledge of the positions, velocities, and masses of a few celestial bodies at some given time: they need knowledge of "initial conditions" as the physicist puts it. Knowledge of a law, therefore, is not a sufficient but only a necessary condition of prediction.[19]

It is obvious that what Zilsel indicates with respect to prediction also holds of explanation: laws, taken by themselves, do not explain specific occurrences, nor do they explain why other specific events did not occur. Furthermore, it is important to note that we must know not only the initial conditions to which Zilsel makes reference, but also the boundary conditions which obtain in a given situation, that is, whether or not there is some factor, not currently affecting the process, which will later affect it. If one remembers these facts, it becomes obvious that a functional law does not provide explanations or predictions regarding actual events, except in conditional form. Applying Galileo's laws, we can only say that *if* a body situated relatively near the earth were in a position of rest, and were to fall freely in a vacuum, and if its fall were not interrupted, *then* it would have a velocity v at time t. Thus, to explain a specific event, it becomes essential to raise questions as to whether, in fact, these conditions are fulfilled; and when we are dealing with freely falling bodies which are not in a vacuum, in some cases we may not be in a position to say anything at all concerning the distance that some specific object (e.g., a leaf) will traverse, nor what velocities it will attain over any particular intervals of time.

If there were irreducible directional laws, the same stringent limitations would not obtain with respect to them. To be sure, we would have to make some initial observations concerning the state of the system in order to place it in a pattern of developmental stages, but once having made those observations we could ex-trapolate on the basis of the law to say what, in general, had previously occurred within that system, and, furthermore, in what direction the system is tending. It is in this sense that the application of a directional law to actual occurrences may be said to be categorical, not conditional. For example, if there were a directional law defining a sequence of stages in the forms of marriage, then, in order to ex-plain the existence of a particular form of marriage, one would relate that form to its necessary antecedents, and one would also know what subsequent form of marriage might be expected to replace it: one would not account for these changes in terms of specific historical conditions, appealing to the ways in which (under these specific conditions) changes were brought about through the operation of psychological, ecological, or functional factors, or by the effects of external con-tacts. An explanation by means of a law of developmental stages would be analogous to an explanation of why a particular planet follows a particular trajec-tory over one section of its course through appealing directly to the fact that this trajectory constitutes a segment of the planet's elliptical orbit. While such an answer would, under certain circumstances, allay further questioning—and would thus, in one sense, be "an explanation"—what one can regard as its explanatory power is in no way comparable to an explanation which is based on Newton's laws of motion and gravitation, operating constantly over successive moments of time.

It may appear unfair to say that those who believe in developmental laws neglect to take into account initial and boundary conditions, seeking to explain past occurrences and to predict future occurrences through the direct application of such laws. And it must be acknowledged that among contemporary social evolutionists there is some tendency to speak of evolutionary developments as occurring "when conditions permit," or to say that their occurrence depends upon "other factors remaining constant." Furthermore, there is also a tendency, al-though it is rarely made explicit, to relate laws of development to a set of basic functional laws.[20] In spite of these changes in the classical forms of social evolu-tionism, it remains important for us to examine the conception of laws of direc-tional change in its unalloyed nineteenth-century form, since the acceptance of such laws was integral to the dominance of historicism.

What, then, is to be said against laws which do not have the highly abstractive character of functional laws, but seek to deal directly with concrete institutions or societies, and which, in addition, are categorical rather than being conditional in their application? The answer, I suggest, lies chiefly in the fact that these law-like statements fail because of their inability to handle instances which appear to pro-vide exceptions to them. Such instances are of various types, but in each case, as we shall see, the deficiency in the directional law must be compensated by an appeal to factors whose effects can be adequately understood only in terms of functional laws.

Let us start from the fact that there are instances in which, over many succes-sive observations, there appear to be no cases in which the stages of development in some type of biological organism fail to conform to our expectations, and we therefore regard the law of directional change which predicts this sequence of forms as being more than adequately fulfilled. To be sure, there will be cases in which individual members of the species die at some early stage in their development, but we may be convinced on the basis of all previously examined cases that had such an organism lived it would have completed the normal life-cycle. Under these circumstances, premature death would not be taken as providing a counter-instance to the law which had been formulated. However, it is to be noted that such a law would then have to be phrased (or be interpreted) in a conditional form: An organism of type A will, in all cases, go through stages a_1, a_2, a_3, etc., to a_9 (its natural death) unless something intervenes to bring about earlier death. The introduction of this conditional clause is not as trivial as it may at first seem; as we shall find, it entails the consequence that a directional law will not be adequate to explain particular instances of a development independently of the initial and boundary conditions which characterize those instances, Furthermore, the introduction of these conditional factors will show that our explanations of particular instances must be stated in terms of functional relationships, not directional laws.

Take first those cases in which a law of developmental stages will not be fully instantiated because an organism has been killed. To speak of the organism being *killed* implies that something external to its normal organic processes interfered with these processes, inducing its death. This obviously is a case in which the expected boundary conditions were not maintained: something which was not predictable by the law itself interfered to negate the completion of the sequence of stages. But what is equally important to notice is the fact that our explanation of the organism's failure to survive will have to be based on some relationship between the intrusive factor and those processes which normally sustain its life. Thus, in those cases in which organisms fail to develop due to external causes, the exception to the normal pattern will be explained in terms of functional relationships, not patterns of directional change. Similarly, if an organism dies prematurely "from natural causes," our explanations will have to take into account initial and boundary conditions, and will also involve functional laws. In such cases we attribute the shorter life of the organism either to its original constitution or to the effects of what happened to it during the course of its development. Furthermore, in tracing the effects of such conditions, we are not explaining the organism's premature death in terms of a directional law; on the contrary, when something interfered with its normal pattern of development, we are forced to shift our attention from that pattern to special factors which are to be found in this case, but not in others. In all exceptional cases, then, we are led to look for functional relationships as explanations of why the particular directional law, which normally holds, does not hold in these instances.

The fact that exceptional cases must be explained in terms of functional rather than directional laws has a further consequence of major importance: it follows from this fact alone that in normal cases, no less than in unusual or abnormal ones, we must assume that the same set of functional relationships is present and is relevant to what occurs or fails to occur. I do not wish to suggest that we must in all cases *know* what these constant functional relationships actually are, nor how their presence or absence is able to affect the pattern of development which occurs. I only wish to point out that it would be a mistake to assume that such relationships are only needed to explain exceptional cases: the exceptional circumstances could not serve to bring about an unusual result unless, in some way, they deranged, interrupted, excited, or otherwise altered a set of ongoing processes which sustain the usual course of development. Thus, in explaining an abnormal case by appealing to the fact that a specific condition altered some particular process, we presuppose that this process was essential to the usual pattern of development. Consequently, it is through a set of functional relationships, not through a directional law, that we must ultimately explain what occurs in particular instances. We may not be made aware of the need to do so if the pattern of development holds without exception; on the other hand, let there be any dislocation of such a pattern, and we will immediately be forced to take into account the constant operation of functional relationships. Thus, in so far as we are interested in explaining concrete cases (and we do not confine our attention to loose generalizations concerning "what usually happens") we must ground these explanations in functional rather than directional laws.

It may appear doubtful that so strong a conclusion could be established on the basis of examples which are as apparently trivial as the interrupted patterns of development which I have discussed. However, if my conclusion was warranted in these cases, in which the only change in pattern was that occasioned by premature death, it can be expected to apply in all other cases as well. If one bears in mind the differences which exist between functional and directional laws, one can see why functional laws serve to explain concrete instances, whereas directional laws do not. A directional law, it will be recalled, is closely tied to actual concrete cases, seeking to trace a necessary course of sequential developments in these types of instance, wherever and whenever they are found; whereas a functional law abstracts particular types of factors from concrete instances and attempts to state the fixed relationships between these factors. Paradoxical as it may sound, it is precisely because a functional law is abstractive and is *not* directly concerned with actual cases, that it can serve to explain such cases. For, if one tries to generalize about actual events which conform to a given type (say, about all swallows, or all revolutions, or all wars)—and if one then attempts to use such a generalization as an explanation of what occurs in an instance which conforms to this type, one has not advanced beyond a classificatory explanation, which is, of course, where one had actually started. If, on the other hand, one has abstracted a given type of factor from a set of concrete instances, and is able to formulate a functional law expressing a constant relationship between this factor and some other factor or factors, then such a law can serve to explain cases which are extremely different from those through which this relationship had been discovered: genuinely new cases will thus be brought under the law.

In the second place, the fact that functional laws are conditional rather than categorical in their applications entails that not every instance which may at first sight appear to constitute an exception need in fact be a case in which the law

fails to apply: the initial or boundary conditions may be such that the effect
which usually ensues will not do so, even though the law is correctly stated and
is genuinely applicable in this instance. For example, the fact that an object is
at rest on a table, or the fact that balloons may rise, does not signify that the
earth's gravitational force does not affect them precisely as it affects a freely falling body. On the other hand, the categorical manner in which directional laws
are applied, makes it necessary—whenever there is an apparent exception—to
draw a distinction between "normal" and "abnormal" instances. A functional
law, however, does not license exceptions: as we have already noted, it is the
apparent exception which provides the testing ground for the law. As a consequence of this difference, it is possible to say that functional laws, when taken
in connection with the relevant initial and boundary conditions, serve to explain
concrete cases in a way in which a directional law never does.[21] We may summarize this fact in saying that functional laws serve to explain each individual
case because they hold in all cases, whereas a directional law, since it permits of
exceptions, can never tell us why a particular instance was a normal case and not
an exception. Furthermore, in those cases in which it is possible to have a sufficient knowledge of initial and of boundary conditions, a functional law will also
permit us to predict a future event with accuracy, whereas predictions which are
based on a directional law can only be said to hold in normal cases and, as a
consequence of this fact, they fail to provide an adequate basis for prediction in
individual cases.

The points which I have been making have more importance for the history of
the social sciences and for understanding the defects of historicism than might be
suggested by the very simple and crude examples on the basis of which I have
developed this argument. However, our earlier historical survey of theories which
attempted to explain social change in terms of directional laws should suffice to
show that it is no straw man which is here under attack. The theories with which
we have been concerned were necessitarian: they were not content to dismiss
apparent exceptions as due to chance, nor were they couched in probabilistic
terms (that in x percent of the cases a society would conform to a particular
sequence of stages). They attempted to formulate universal laws on the basis of
which it was possible to explain specific transformations which social institutions
had undergone, and to predict the direction in which they would also subsequently move.

It should now be clear why no such laws can be expected to hold in any cases
which are of importance to the understanding of social institutions and social
change. In the first place, it would be unrealistic in the extreme to think that the
history of any social group can be treated as a closed system in which there will
not be any changes in the boundary conditions over protracted periods of time.
Even were we to take the most isolated societies and postulate that there had been
no contacts between them and other societies during a significant portion of their
histories, it would still be the case that because of their interaction with their
natural environments, changes would have been introduced in the amounts and
availability of their food supply, that droughts, disease, and the like, would have

affected the size of their populations in an irregular manner, etc.[22] In the second place, it would be equally unrealistic to assume that the actual conditions obtaining in all societies at any one stage in their development would be so similar as to warrant overlooking their differences. However, if one fails to take into account such initial conditions, it is unrealistic to assume that their subsequent development would also be the same. (For example, it is because we think that all members of the same species are essentially similar, that we expect them to undergo the same pattern of development.) As we have noted, we do in fact take into account differences in initial or boundary conditions when we seek to explain why one society may not have gone through all stages of that pattern which is assumed to be normal. Similarly, one would almost surely have to take such conditions into account to explain why one society developed more rapidly than another, or why there were at least minor variations in the forms which the pattern assumed in different societies. An acceptance of overriding directional laws involves a neglect of such differences in initial conditions: it is mistakenly assumed that such laws necessitate what happens regardless of what differences there may be in the actual conditions obtaining in different societies.

While these two points should be sufficient to undermine the belief in ultimate laws of directional change, the following observations may help us to understand the appeal of such laws. First, the manner in which directional laws are most frequently formulated allows for a number of built-in safeguards against their disconfirmation. For example, while a given sequence of stages in the evolution of social institutions may be prophesied, it is rarely the case that the respective durations of these stages is also prophesied;[23] as a consequence, it remains in many cases possible to assume that a given stage will in the future be forthcoming, although it has been delayed. Furthermore, in those instances in which development has not proceeded in accordance with one's prognoses, it is possible to speak of a social institution as being "a survival," exemplifying arrested development, or of a society as being "a living fossil." To cite merely one further way in which an unwavering belief in a directional law can be squared with a lack of adequate evidence, we may once again cite what we have previously noted with respect to Spencer's method: his tendency to substitute a comparative method for any attempt to trace actual patterns of successive historical change. By the compilation of resembling instances, chosen without regard to their historical connections, it may appear that there had been a single developmental pattern, even though such a pattern would, as we have seen, be likely to have been an artifact of the system of compilation itself.

Each of the foregoing factors has lent some degree of specious plausibility to the thesis that there are laws of directional change in social institutions. However, there is a more important reason why this thesis has continued to remain plausible; it consists in the fact that there are cases in which *functional* relationships foreclose certain possibilities for further development, and open others. For example, in societies in which there is no written language, what we regard as historical knowledge cannot be present, nor can such societies establish the same sorts of reciprocal relations with a literate society as are possible among two or

more literate societies. Similarly, the lack of metallurgy precludes the development of certain other forms of technology, just as the lack of domesticated animals
would preclude certain forms of agriculture. Given such limitations of the
available possibilities, it is not surprising that one can arrange societies in a kind
of serial order which roughly corresponds to steps which can be traced in the
actual histories of those societies for which we have more or less continuous
archaeological and historical records. However, since these changes can be explained in terms of the effects of functional relationships, they are not to be taken
as confirming evidence for laws of necessary directional change. Like the cases
which have already been noted, the sequential order of the individual stages is to
be comprehended as the result of a series of relationships operating concurrently
within a society faced by certain needs and characterized by a particular set of
historically and environmentally generated conditions: it is not the result of a
law defining a set of stages through which any society will assuredly pass.

If this argument has been sound, the explanatory thesis of historicism cannot
be maintained by any one who seeks to understand social institutions and social
change through an appeal to scientific law. Historicism, it will be recalled, involved the belief that, in order to understand any phenomenon, one must view
it in terms of the place which it occupied and the role which it played within a
process of development. We have seen, however, that in order to understand an
actual pattern of development, we cannot view it as a single process formed in
accordance with a directional law; if we are to explain it by means of a reference
to laws, we must do so by showing how particular functional relationships, operating on specific initial conditions, shape each of the successive steps of change.
Once completed, these successive steps may be regarded as having defined some
definite pattern, but that pattern would be a consequence of other forces, and
would not itself represent a directional tendency. Thus, insofar as we wish to use
models of explanation which are derived from scientifically acceptable modes of
explanation, we shall *not* seek to explain any phenomenon by placing it within
the context of a developmental series: we shall, on the contrary, explain every
phenomenon in terms of the specific conditions and the functional laws which,
at each moment of time, was responsible for its being precisely what it was. In
all cases in which such phenomena can be shown to have conformed, with some
degree of regularity, to a directional pattern, this pattern will have its own explanation in repetitive factors, but will not itself serve as the basis for an explanation of what has in fact occurred.

Now, if this is true with respect to those cases in which some clear pattern is
actually discernible (as, for example, a pattern is discernible in the life-cycle of a
plant or of an insect), it is even more clearly true of those cases in which we deal
with complex sets of historical events in which no single pattern is equally discernible, and where—if one were not already committed to the view that there
must be some pattern—no such pattern would in fact be found. In such cases, the
explanatory thesis of historicism would suggest that until some pattern *is* found,
no understanding of particular events would be accessible. Following the classic
model of scientific explanation, this would not be the case: the specific successive

events would be no less fully understandable than they would if they had suggested there was some necessary course of developmental change. Thus, whether or not a pattern seems to characterize the sequence of events with which one must deal, if we are to proceed along the lines of traditional scientific explanation, we must proceed by explaining each event in terms of whatever functional laws are applicable to it, and our explanations will be couched in terms of how these laws, operating within the total set of initial conditions, bring about the successive changes which they do. Thus, instead of seeing the history of specific social institutions, or of specific societies, as implicitly containing any necessary directional tendencies, any such tendencies would themselves have to be explained in piecemeal terms.

2. PROBLEMS CONCERNING PATTERNS OF CHANGE IN HISTORY

The failure of all attempts to understand history in terms of laws of development would have occasioned neither surprise nor dismay in those thinkers whose historicism rested on teleological principles of explanation, and on metaphors of organic and spiritual growth. As a consequence, if we are to criticize their acceptance of the explanatory thesis of historicism, we cannot effectively do so on the basis of the arguments thus far advanced. However, there exist other grounds on which their views may be criticized; and, as we shall see, most of these further objections also apply to those whose historicism had been dominated by the assumption that there are ultimate laws of directional change. This similarity between the metaphysical, teleological view and the scientifically oriented view of human history derives from a single shared assumption: that, in all normal cases, there is a sequence of stages through which development necessarily proceeds. For the one school, such a developmental pattern rested on the fact that there were controlling laws of directional change; for the other, such patterns did not represent any form of external necessity, but was the expression of an inner, autonomous, self-fulfilling tendency.

In order to understand the latter position, it may be useful to start from Aristotle's distinction between that which exists "by nature" and that which exists by other causes. All of those things which exist by nature were taken as having within them an inner impulse to change;[24] and this change was conceived by Aristotle to be purposive, in which the earlier steps in the process were for the sake of that which was to come later.[25] It would be mistaken to assume that this purposiveness was the result of some externally imposed plan; it was by virtue of their own inherent natures that objects tended toward their appropriate goals. In contrast to this Aristotelian view, the form of teleological explanation which was most frequently found in the later seventeenth and in the eighteenth centuries conceived of purpose in nature on the analogy of mechanical contrivances; objects were capable of attaining specific ends because they had been created to do so in accordance with a preconceived plan. In so far as this later form of teleological explanation dominated the interpretation of natural processes, historicism could not arise, for such processes would have had to be understood and evaluated with reference to that plan. Historicism, however, involved the rejection of any such fixed points of reference, and of all external points of view: it was held that the significance of what occurs in a developmental process was to be understood and evaluated in terms of a logic inherent in the process itself. It was the doctrine of divine immanence, in contrast to the doctrine of a divine plan, which helped to introduce this new point of view; it is therefore not surprising to find Hegel praising Aristotle's teleological conception of nature as being nobler than that which had come to dominate modern thought, "for with him the principal point is the determination of [the] end as the inward determinateness of natural things. Thus he comprehended nature as life, *i.e.*, as that which has its end within itself."[26]

There are, it seems to me, two fundamental presuppositions which underlie this Aristotelian and Hegelian conception of developmental processes, and I have already called attention to the first of them in my earlier discussion of one of the ways in which the concept of "development" is used.[27] It consisted in the fact that there was presupposed an underlying substance or subject *which* changes. Thus, a pattern of change conceived in the terms made familiar by Aristotle and by Hegel is not to be construed simply as a sequence of related forms; these successive forms are regarded as having an inherent connection with one another because each of them is viewed as a phase in a single, unified process, and because each expresses some necessary feature of that process.

The second basic presupposition connected with treating history in terms consonant with the Aristotelian and the Hegelian views of developmental processes is the fact that the later stages of these processes were considered as being higher realizations, or fulfilments, of what was only implicit in the earlier stages. To be sure, significant differences existed between the Aristotelian doctrine of the relation of act to potency and Hegel's dialectical emphasis on the role of negation in change. Nevertheless in both cases the end was conceived as representing a higher and more perfect level than had been attained in any of the developmental stages preceding it. This did not entail that, according to Hegel (or even according to Aristotelianism), the value of each of the earlier stages was wholly relative to the value of the end. Since the end could not be attained in one leap, but only through transformations from one stage to the next, each stage had its own value. That value, however, could only be adequately appreciated through understanding how each stage in the development was related to the goal-directed process of which it was a part. And since, as we shall later see, historicism challenged any attempt to separate what was taken to be valuable and what was to be regarded as true, a similar thesis was upheld with respect to historical understanding: it is only in terms of the later stages of development, when latent powers have become fully explicit, that we are in a position fully to understand the nature of a developmental process, and adequately interpret the earlier stages of that process. This familiar teleological theme is, of course, most manifest in Hegel:

> The living substance . . . is that being which is truly subject, or what is the same thing, is truly realized and actual (*wirklich*) solely in the process of positing itself, or in

mediating with its own self its transitions from one state or position to the opposite.... It is the process of its own becoming, the circle which presupposes its end as its purpose, and has its end for its beginning; it becomes concrete and actual only by being carried out, and by the end it involves.[28]

Without reference to such an end, the unity of the process, and consequently the significance of each of its phases, would be lost; for, on Hegel's view, a process consists of an interplay of different moments, but cannot be broken into parts.[29]

Before attempting to criticize the acceptance of these presuppositions by those who conceived of the historical process in teleological terms, I should like to point out that, strangely enough, the same presuppositions were frequently accepted by historicists who condemned both metaphysics and teleology. Consider, for example, Comte's view of history, or that view which came to be characteristic of Marxism. In both cases one finds not only that all of history was treated as a single process, including all peoples, but this process was viewed as the development of man's true social nature, much as Hegel had viewed it as the development of Objective Spirit. Furthermore, both Comte and the Marxists shared Hegel's view that, during any phase of this developmental process, the various attributes of society were organically related to one another, forming a coherent whole. Even the reference to the end of the process as an essential means of understanding its nature was not confined to those who accepted the teleological view: in Comte's system, and in Marxism, the understanding and the evaluation of earlier phases of the historical process demand that we grasp the tendency of history as a whole. Given these similarities between those whose basic philosophic views are in other respects so different, it would seem difficult to find any one point of view from which to criticize the acceptance of their presuppositions. However, it is not impossible to do so. In the first place, I believe that there are unacceptable consequences if one conceives of history as the development of some form of substantival entity, and of historical events as manifestations of this continuing development. Since my objections to such a view will be based on empirical grounds, it can be argued independently of an acceptance or rejection of either set of philosophic views. With respect to the second presupposition— that one must relate the stages of a process to the terminus of that process if one is to understand these stages—I shall show that it too may be criticized without specifically referring to the metaphysical views with which it is most frequently associated. I shall argue that this presupposition, whether held by teleologists or by strict determinists, rests on what I shall designate as the retrospective fallacy.

As we have noted, the view that the processes of historical change represent the successive manifestations of an underlying entity *which* changes has one of its sources in analogies that can be drawn between organic growth and historical development. In the case of organic growth there is, of course, a visible entity which has a life-cycle, and the successive changes constituting this life-cycle are clearly attributes of it. In history, on the other hand, it is by no means obvious what sort of entity can be regarded as underlying the specific changes with which historians deal. There are many histories—of nations, of epochs, and of civilizations, of science or of industry, of the various arts, of legal institutions, etc.—and the question of where one can find *the* subject of history seems to be almost senseless. Yet, one can see that when these various histories are traced out, they are not wholly self-contained, but have connections with one another, and sometimes seem to share in a common development. Readers of Toynbee's *Study of History* will recall that at the outset of that work he sought the proper "unit" for the study of history, and took as its identifying mark that it should be a field of study which would be intelligible in itself. This is to say that such a unit would have its own history, and that the specific changes which would be traced were changes in it. The substantival entities which had a history, and which underlay the detailed changes which historians normally traced, were designated by Toynbee as "civilizations." Others have regarded a *Volksgeist*, or spirit of the people, as the true bearer of history, with the various events in the life of a nation or people as expressions of the continuing unity of that spirit as it manifests itself over time.[30] And for others, as we find in the case of Hegel, the substance of history consisted in the development of the realm of Objective Spirit, with each nation-state that successively achieved greatness representing one of its essential phases. For those who stood closer to the Enlightenment tradition, as did Comte, that which developed was Humanity, which transcended all national boundaries, and which shaped itself through progressive intellectual and moral development; while Spencer conceived of progress in the superorganic realm as a sequence of types of social organization which, like organic species, formed a single evolutionary development, ascending from the earliest and the most primitive to the most recent and advanced. On each of these views, a true understanding of the human past depended upon showing how the specific events which had occurred were related to a single developmental process, with the connections among them being determined by the ways in which each was an expression of that which underlay them all.[31] It was on the basis of such a conception that Hegel, Comte, and Spencer, as well as many others, regarded traditional historiography as lacking in depth, and as lost in superficial detail.

All such conceptions are faced by fundamental empirical difficulties which they cannot overcome and cannot avoid.[32] These difficulties take many forms, but their scope and severity may be suggested by three types of consideration, to which others might easily be added. In the first place, those who look upon human history as representing a single developmental process can be justly accused of not being able to find a place within that process for much that has occurred in the human past. This is not merely that details are omitted from consideration; the conception of a single developmental process does not permit one to view large tracts of the past as having any genuine historical significance at all. Consider, to choose merely one example, the drastic restriction in the scope of history which was characteristic of Hegel's outline of the development of Objective Spirit: not only were vast regions of the world denied any place in that development, but each region which was actually included was regarded as having belonged to the realm of true history during only one period of time. These familiar aspects of his

Philosophy of History were boldly anticipated in a brief section on World History in Hegel's *Philosophy of Right*, from which the following passage is taken:

[A] nation is dominant in world history during [only] one epoch, and it is only once that it can make its hour strike. In contrast with this absolute right of being the vehicle of this present stage in the world mind's development, the minds of the other nations are without rights, and they, along with those whose hour has struck already, count no longer in world history (Sect. 347).

While so militantly forthright a proclamation of a restrictive principle of selection is not to be found in other linear views of historical development, all have involved similar restrictions. And, in fact, it is necessary that they should do so. Putting the matter quite generally, since a linear conception of historical development demands that one view history as proceeding in a single direction, it commits one to looking backward upon the past as if it had constituted a single lineage. Western philosophers of history have seen this lineage in terms of modern Western man, and what could not be regarded as having had a role in his development was not regarded as having been part of the historically significant past. Regardless of what other perspective one may adopt, precisely the same sort of restricted view will follow if one interprets human history as a single developmental process which stretches straight from the past to the present.[33]

Nor can one avoid restricting the scope of the significant past, even if one abandons a linear conception of history, so long as one maintains the assumption that human history is a development inherent in some form of substantival entity. For example, if one regards history as the development of discrete civilizations, as did Toynbee, or if historical events are taken to be the expressions of the spirit of various peoples, each of which has its own birth, its own fulfilment, and its own decline, much that has occurred in human societies will nonetheless be regarded as lacking in genuine historical significance, for it will not have formed part of the life of those entities which are taken to be the bearers of history. For example, it is never claimed that the events in the lives of *all* peoples have manifested a specific *Volksgeist*, nor that any one nation has, throughout its existence, ever maintained the vigor of its spirit; those who hold that the spirit of a people is the true locus of history will therefore regard much of the human past as entirely "dead." The same point is obvious with respect to Toynbee's characterization of civilizations, since not only did he exclude all primitive societies and all so-called arrested and abortive civilizations from his purview, but there exist long periods in the lives of some civilizations which were not counted as belonging to history at all.[34] Thus, even a pluralism of substantival entities excludes from the realm of the significant historical past a great deal that can be the subject of legitimate historical investigation.

In the second place, the variety of features present in any culture are so diverse that one cannot plausibly maintain that all of them are to an equal degree manifestations of a single underlying process. As a consequence, the assumption that historical understanding depends upon relating specific events to some unitary process of development will lead to a neglect of some—and, indeed, of many—of the aspects of life which are present in any particular culture. To be sure, this has not usually been denied by those who depict history as consisting, basically, in a developmental process; what is claimed is that in any society there are many aspects which can be safely neglected by those who seek to understand what has been essential in man's past. This claim has usually been coupled with the view that there is some one central factor—for Hegel the nation-state, for Marxism the means of production, for Comte the stage of intellectual advancement—which dominates the direction of change, and which, over time, molds all other manifestations of culture. Thus, history is regarded as including two quite different sorts of phenomena: those which are of genuine historical importance in either fostering or tending to obstruct historical change, and those which are epiphenomenal only, since they do not play an effective role in the process. It is at this point that conflicts arise between empirical historiography and the types of view with which we are here concerned. In the field of empirical historiography, the question of the relative importance of any event is only to be discovered through tracing its specific effects; that it is an event of a certain type, whether technological, political, intellectual, or artistic, does not suffice to indicate its importance or lack of importance in the network of relationships with which historians are concerned. And, of course, the importance to be assigned to any such event will vary in relation to what particular series of changes is the subject of the historian's account. On the other hand, when history is viewed as a single developmental process, the division of historical phenomena into those which have an absolute importance, and those which do not, becomes a hard and fast distinction; as a consequence, much of what we find to have been historically significant at a particular time in the life of a particular society will be relegated to an inferior historical status on the basis of a prior conception of the nature of history as a whole.[35]

In the third place, the conception of history as a process of autonomous self-development takes inadequate account of the possibility of significant external influences upon any social order. These external influences may take a variety of forms. There is, for example, the phenomenon of cultural diffusion, where that which has been developed elsewhere, and was brought into a society through cultural contact, is assimilated into that society in either an unaltered or an altered form. In such cases there will have been the introduction of an external influence; in most cases it would be difficult to hold that such an element would have been created in either its assimilated form, or in any equivalent form, without cultural contact. There also are cases in which, for example, military invasions change the tempo or the direction of ongoing processes, or in which subjugation and external domination interrupt developments, or extirpate much that had been characteristic of the life of the invaded society. The view that invasions and domination can only kill that which has already outlived its allotted period of vigor (as those who believe that all history represents the effects of inherent developmental patterns tend to suggest), is not a view which has much plausibility. It is certainly not a view which should appeal to those who cite organic analogies, since the lasting effects of a period of drought or of a disease must also be taken into account when one is tracing the development of a specific individual plant or animal.

There also are other, more subtle forms of external influence, which deserve special comment and which may be compared with ecological factors in the environment. For example, a given developmental process may be affected by the fact that a similar process has gone on in another society. In some cases the existence of a parallel development will, if known, serve as the model for imitation and thus instigate or accelerate an imitative process; in other cases it might presumably serve as a warning of what is to be avoided, if possible. Furthermore, there are less conspicuous ways in which parallel forms of development may influence one another; for example, if two societies are tending in a single direction, but have started at different times or are proceeding at different rates, the fact that one reaches a particular stage of development (e.g., in colonization or in industrialization) before that stage is reached by the other, its earlier fruition may permit it to gain a sufficient competitive advantage to allow it to choke off a similar development on the part of its neighbor.[36] Each of these types of fact concerning history is sufficient to show that one cannot interpret historical change solely in terms of autonomous processes of development; taken together, they suggest that the influences which can be exerted by so-called external factors on the processes of historical change are widespread, and that they can be extremely penetrating.

But how, then, shall we conceive of history, if not in terms of developmental tendencies? The foregoing criticisms suggest that if we wish to base our views on the methods and the results which characterize empirical historiography, the human past will not be taken to have been a single developing process, nor a set of such processes going on independently of one another. It will, on the contrary, appear as a very complex web whose individual strands have separate though interlacing histories; as a consequence, no one group of peoples, and no one set of aspects of social life, will be seen as constituting *the* subject matter of history. More specifically, one can say that the complex relations among peoples, whose individual histories may for generations run along independent paths before coming into contact, after which they may or may not again diverge, precludes the possibility of looking upon the past as constituting a single historical sequence. Furthermore, because of the diversity of the elements within cultures, it is also rarely if ever possible to construe all of them as sharing a common developmental pattern: some, which may have been closely connected in their origins, will tend to become independent of one another, others may enter into new relationships, and the pace at which change proceeds in any one series of events may differ greatly from that which characterizes others. Thus, the many individual strands of continuity that must be traced if we are to understand what actually happened in the human past, form an indefinitely complex network. In this network, no event is likely to have a place in only one of the crisscrossing lines of causal connection, and it could therefore be extremely misleading to view specific events solely in terms of the positions which they occupied in one among these strands. It might, for example, be the case that the actual causes of some specific event belong within one strand of facts, while its most important consequences could only be seen if we were to trace its effects in quite a different direction from that which its actual causes might have led one to expect. Or, its causes may themselves be complex, resulting from the meeting of two previously independent lines of development; in such a case, if one were to attempt to understand that event in terms of only one of these two earlier strands, one would necessarily have misunderstood it. Such possibilities are, I submit, left wholly out of account by historicism, which proceeds on the assumption that any event is to be understood and to be evaluated in terms of its place in some particular process of development.[37]

That such an assumption should have been so widely held in the late eighteenth and the nineteenth centuries was connected with the belief that it was possible to look upon Humanity as having had a single history, which embraced all special histories. We have traced some of the forms which that conviction took and have seen that the Enlightenment conception of history, the use of organic analogies, the belief in necessary developmental laws, and the spread of evolutionary modes of thought, all contributed to its nineteenth-century dominance. Nonetheless, it is surprising that during a period in which there had been spectacular growth in almost all forms of empirical historiography, the assumption persisted that there had actually been one single dominant line of development in human history. To explain the persistence of such an assumption we must, I believe, take into account an extremely prevalent human error which is not in the least restricted to speculative thought and which I shall call "the retrospective fallacy."

This fallacy, crudely put, consists in looking at a series of events in terms of its ultimate outcome, interpreting each of the earlier events with reference to that outcome. It is readily understandable that we should have a tendency to do so, for knowing what did in fact eventuate, we seek out the lines of connection between it and previous events, and we are thus led to consider these events in their roles as contributing to what occurred later. Our tendency to view organic growth in this way leads, of course, to a teleological form of explanation. When we view the historical past in the same way, we are led to an acceptance of historical determinism: knowing what occurred, and having traced the steps that led to its occurrence, the chain of events as a whole seems to be characterized by an inner necessity. However, if we do not look at a series of events in terms of that in which this series eventuated, but examine each of these events as it was related to the occasion of its occurrence, the series will present an entirely different aspect. At each step in the series, alternative possibilities may be seen to have been open, and we may find that which of them did in fact materialize was dependent upon the occurrence of extraneous events. Thus, in adopting what may be called a prospectively oriented view, the end of any process of change is to be regarded simply as the result of a sequence of events which *did* occur; it will not provide any point of reference with respect to which the earlier events are subsequently to be interpreted. The retrospective fallacy *is* a fallacy because it rests on the fact that, when we have learned the actual outcome of a series of events, we tend to forget that other conclusions might have been possible: we ascribe a privileged position to that outcome and we view all earlier events as if they had been controlled by it.

The same point may be made in another way, and one which better succeeds in avoiding the problems inherent in questions concerning either teleology or determinism. It may be said that the retrospective fallacy consists in assuming that if we read the past "backwards"—that is, if we start from any particular state of affairs and trace the connections between it and the events which preceded it— we shall arrive at exactly the same view of this series of events as if we had been observing it in the order in which it occurred. In denying that this is the case, I do *not* wish to be understood as suggesting that the causal connections which we find when we look back upon past events could not (in principle) *also* have been seen had we been observing these events in the order of their occurrence. (Were there this difference between the two views, the consequences for historiography would be disastrous.) However, granted that the actual causal connections are in both cases the same, there is at least one very significant difference between a prospective view of events and the manner in which a series of such events appears if we view it retrospectively only: on the basis of a purely retrospective point of view, the past becomes greatly simplified. In looking back from the vantage point of the present, we tend only to take account of connections between actual occurrents, and we are not forced to explore the many possibilities which, at every point in time, remained open for future change if some other events, elsewhere, had not occurred when they did and as they did. Historians are obliged to take such possibilities into account, and are forced to wonder "What would have happened if . . . ?"; but this is merely to say that their method of dealing with the past is not limited to a retrospective point of view. What historians attempt to do is to build up a view of the past which takes into account not only the particular relationships which obtained among those events which did occur, but they seek to establish what factors might have inhibited their occurrence, had such factors been operative at particular times and places. In comparison with the investigation of these relationships, some of which were actualized and others of which were not, a purely retrospective view offers a simplified picture: it is only after the fact that, so to speak, the nap of history seems to lie flat and be uniform in texture. This simplified picture, in which all unactualized possibilities appear never to have been real, leads to the view that there is some form of inherent developmental tendency in events, and that human history has a direction and meaning which escapes empirical historiography.

It should be evident from what has just been said that the acceptance of determinism in history will be characteristic of all who adopt a purely retrospective point of view—it does not depend (as has often been claimed) on an inappropriate application of scientifically oriented forms of explanation to human actions. The proper interpretation of deliberation and choice in human history is obscured if we look upon the past solely in terms of what did eventuate, without tracing each step in the series of events as it happened, seeking out what possibilities had originally been present. Nor is this difference between a retro-spective and a prospective view of events confined to cases which involve human deliberation and choice: in any series of events which does not form a closed system, there is a similar contrast between the unity and necessity which a process appears to have if we view it retrospectively, and the aspect which it presents if we view it as it developed, tracing its course in a step-by-step chronological sequence. The difference may be suggested by an analogy. If one considers a great river system as it appears on a physiographic map, one finds that if one starts from the conclusion, where that system empties into the sea, and follows back along each of its main tributaries, and traces out each of their branches, and follows back along each of the streams which fed these branches, one is always ascending to higher ground. There thus appears to be a unity of principle which gives in-telligibility to the course of the system as a whole. However, should one wish to understand the formation of these river beds in the past, or should one wish to account for the gathering of the waters into a single system, one cannot proceed in that direction: one must start from each of the separate sources, tracing their various channels and junctions, for it is not until they meet that these streams and branches and tributaries form *one* river. That they meet where they do, can only be understood through having followed the course of each, noting the contours of the land and the resistances which at various points diverted them, proceeding along each originally separate stream, along each branch and tribu-tary, following as they gather into a single river, and together reach the sea. In reading history backwards, as in following the course of such a river system in the opposite direction from that which determined the flow of its individual parts, one will be led to a system of interpretation that has little relationship to the principles which were responsible for the end-result which one sees and endeavors to explain.

Once one recognizes the difference between tracing the connections of a series of historical events in the order in which they developed, and viewing them retrospectively only, it is not possible to regard long-term changes as providing a basis on which to understand the specific events which actually occurred: the whole with respect to which these specific events are supposedly to be interpreted actually exists only because of the successive parts which it is alleged to explain. Thus, if what I have said of the retrospective fallacy is true, the explanatory thesis of historicism is left without justification.

We are now in a position to recognize the difficulties inherent in that aspect of historicism which constitutes its evaluative thesis and which, up to this point, we have not specifically discussed. That thesis, it will be recalled, asserts that an evaluation of any phenomenon demands that we view it in relation to what it contributed, or failed to contribute, to the larger processes of development of which it was a part. An acceptance of the moral theory of historicism consequently presupposes that one can, in fact, assign to each phase of man's social life some place in a larger developmental process. The assumption that it is legitimate to construe either the past or the present in terms of any single developmental series is what my preceding arguments have been designed to refute. Thus, if those arguments have been correct, the foundation which the evaluative thesis of historicism presupposes has been removed.

This point is of sufficient importance to deserve further elucidation, paying particular attention to its application to questions of evaluation. Suppose that one traces each step in a series of events in order, examining the conditions under which each occurred, what alternative outcomes appeared to be open, what knowledge was available concerning these possible alternatives, and the like. Having adopted this prospective point of view, and therefore abstracting from the actual results which subsequently occurred, how would one evaluate the patterning of institutions, the decisions which were taken, the competing forces which existed at any particular time? Not knowing what was to occur, one could only evaluate each of the various features of past social life in terms of the particular context in which it actually existed. To be sure, one might later recognize that there had been possibilities for action which were not recognized at the time. However, once a historian places himself in the position of looking at a series of events prospectively, his evaluation of each aspect of the past will be similar in structure to the ways in which we evaluate the situations we ourselves face: we envision various alternatives and assess them in comparison with each other. In contrast to this, those whose evaluations derive from a retrospective point of view assess the various features of past social life with reference to a single linear series whose origins and outcome are already known; thus, they do not judge events in terms of what, at the time, were the actual alternatives, what actions other than those taken might have been preferred to them, or what functions they currently served. Thus, the retrospective point of view actually leads to a form of anachronism: it leads us to look at actions and at institutions not in terms of their own contexts, but in relation to what they inherited from the past and what they bequeathed to the future. Consequently, our evaluations of them are not, strictly speaking, evaluations of *them*; these evaluations derive from our attitude toward that process in which we see them as embedded. For this reason, the evaluative thesis of historicism has always appeared to its critics as presenting a peculiarly perverse and distorted standard of judgment: individual actions and states of affairs are not judged for what they are, but in terms of the extent to which they are believed to have contributed to what has actually come to pass. As Mill said of Thiers, and of others, "they have arrived at the annihilation of all moral distinctions except *success* and *not success*,"[38] and this form of criticism of historicism has been widely shared.

It must be acknowledged that those who accepted the evaluative thesis of historicism were not unprepared to meet such criticisms, for they were no less willing to apply their basic contention to all past standards of evaluation than they were to apply it to other aspects of social life. Thus, Mill's claim that they had annihilated moral distinctions, or my claim that they substituted evaluative attitudes toward the historical process for evaluations of specific institutions or actions, would be countered by *their* claim that whatever standard one might propose for evaluating institutions and actions is itself a standard which developed historically, and is therefore relative to its place in the history of human societies. The only way in which one could escape from an anachronistic evaluation of the past, *they* would claim, would be to view every aspect of human history in terms of the meaning which lies within that process taken as a whole.[39]

To this, I hope, I have already provided a sufficient answer: that it is in fact a mistake to suppose that we can legitimately view the human past as a single developing process. However, so far as the specifically evaluative thesis of historicism is concerned, there is another quite different way in which it can be attacked. That is to show that the view of human nature which it presupposes is mistaken. That view, it will be recognized, involves the assumption that man is almost indefinitely malleable, being formed in and through the changing forms of his social environment. It is to a consideration of the history of that doctrine, and to its criticism, that I shall next turn.

III

THE MALLEABILITY OF MAN

*It is only by historical analysis that we can
discover what makes up man, since it is
only in the course of history that he
is formed.*

Émile Durkheim, *The Dualism
of Human Nature and its Social
Conditions*, p. 325

8

CHALLENGES TO CONSTANCY

In the later eighteenth and throughout the nineteenth century, marked changes developed in what, in a very inclusive sense, can be called the theory of human nature. One such change consisted in a series of challenges to the widely held assumption that human nature is constant. The question at issue was not, of course, whether all men at all times have held the same beliefs and have acted in exactly similar ways: no defender of the constancy of human nature would suppose that such had been the case. However, it was assumed by those who regarded human nature as constant that, underlying the varying beliefs and forms of action of different individuals, there are characteristics common to all men, and that such characteristics are not subject to change. This view had been widely held among moral and social theorists in the late seventeenth and in the eighteenth century, although it was beginning to be undercut by some tendencies in eighteenth-century thought. Later, in the course of the nineteenth century, it was generally abandoned. I shall refer to what took its place as the doctrine of the malleability of man.

As we shall see, a conception of man's malleability may arise from disparate and even opposed streams of thought. So long as what was common to these tendencies was only a negative thesis, consisting in what they denied rather than affirmed, it was possible for them to have a cumulative influence on the presuppositions of the age and yet remain fundamentally opposed to each other. This, I believe, was what occurred in the nineteenth century with respect to the doctrine of man's malleability. What was common to its variant forms was not a shared conception of man, but the purely negative thesis that there are no specific ways of thinking and acting which are so deeply entrenched in human nature that they cannot be supplanted either by the effects of the circumstances in which men are placed or by means of man's own efforts. This view was held in many forms and became a pervasive assumption within nineteenth-century thought.

The almost unlimited faith which the nineteenth century placed in education was a direct expression of the pervasiveness of this belief. If men had been re-

was a direct expression of the pervasiveness of this belief. If men had been regarded as endowed with fixed native capacities, and were believed to have dispositions not subject to change, what could be expected to be achieved through educative processes would doubtless have been seen as important, but it would have been confined within the same limits as had obtained at every earlier stage of man's history. However, it was characteristic of the period to believe that, in a new age, man's individual and social life could undergo almost unlimited change: a radically new order of social relationships could be established, and in that new order there would be fundamental transformations in human nature. This optimism, which was shared by the major reform movements in the century, would have been wholly untenable had there not been a pervasive belief that human nature could change.[1]

As was true with respect to historicism, the belief in man's malleability had roots in the Enlightenment and also had roots in the rebellion against the Enlightenment. Furthermore, like historicism, its dominance in later nineteenth-century thought was in a considerable measure dependent on the uses to which evolutionary theory was put. However, as we shall see, many of its formulations were not actually linked with historicism; therefore, the relationships between these two positions will later have to be indicated.

1. GENETICISM, ORGANICISM, AND MAN AS A PROGRESSIVE BEING

The form of the malleability doctrine to which I shall refer as "geneticism" actually received full expression in the eighteenth century, and did so in the thought of some who, like Helvétius, were in other respects more typical of Enlightenment modes of thought. It arose in connection with associationism, although some representatives of the associationist doctrine (for example, Bentham and James Mill) did not accept the view that human nature changed over the course of time. On the other hand, others believed that the cumulative effects of experience on the formation of character would alter the motives which in the past had been dominant in men.

In order to be more precise in formulating the position which I shall designate as geneticism, and in order to show the way in which experience was assumed able to alter fundamental characteristics of human nature, I shall contrast geneticism and "nativism." In speaking of geneticism I shall be referring to the view that the thought and the actions of individuals can be understood as functions of the particular experiences they have undergone, each person's thought and action being the product of influences brought to bear upon him in the circumstances in which he was placed. In opposition to geneticism, all forms of nativism hold that some instances of thought and action—although not by any means *all*—are to be explained in terms of native propensities inherent in the individual, although these propensities may not become manifest unless evoked by a particular type of situation. Thus, what would count in favor of nativism would be any wholly unconditioned responses, or any instincts, if these were totally independent of past experience, and if they were directly responsible for the specific ways in which individuals thought and behaved. Of course, there could be positions other than geneticism and nativism, as thus defined, which some persons might wish to hold. For example, it might be claimed that all thought and action necessarily involve the interplay of native propensities and past experience. I shall not be concerned with this or other alternatives, for the analysis by means of which I shall attempt to show that geneticism is false should also be sufficient to show that in some cases nativism is true. In other words, I shall argue later that in explaining human action we do not in all cases have to appeal to the formative effects of past experience.

It was precisely this type of nativistic thesis that geneticism sought to deny. Experience was claimed to play a dominant role in *all* aspects of thought and of action, and it was widely claimed, in conjunction with associationism, that, in the course of his experience, an individual acquires wholly new capacities which become, quite literally, a second nature to him. They are to be viewed as a second nature because they become so deeply ingrained in him that they are experienced as wholly natural, as being an essential part of his nature. On the foundation of these new capacities, further transformations are then reared.

This process obviously refers to the ways in which any one individual's nature grows, and is transformed by experience into something which it was not at birth. But how, one may ask, is such a theory of individual development related to the doctrine that, over the course of time, man as a species undergoes changes, and that men have it in their power to effect such changes in the natures of all mankind? It was in this possibility, as we shall see, that those who upheld geneticism were primarily interested.

The manner in which geneticism justified belief in the possibility of radically altering human nature was to hold that, when individuals were transformed through the effects of their own experiences, they would create conditions which would affect the next generation in new ways, and thus further alter the natures of those coming after them. Through slow successive changes spreading through whole communities, old propensities which had been acquired under former conditions would be extirpated, and new ways of acting inculcated. In this explanation of man's malleability, the mechanisms underlying change are obviously conceived in terms of how individuals are formed by their own experiences: the principles of character-formation which are used to explain the changes in human nature are, it may be said, specifically psychological, or "individualistic." Furthermore, such an explanation tends to stress the passivity of the individual in the changes which he undergoes: it is *experience* which forms him, even though he may play a role in forming others by being able to affect (or even to control) the experiences they then undergo.

What I shall term "organicism" rejected this individualistic, psychological account of man's malleability, yet it too emphasized the formative power of environing influences. From the point of view of organicism, it is culture as a complex whole, not specific individual experiences, which creates and changes the natures of men. On such a view, of which Comte, Hegel, and Marx will later be seen to be exponents, human nature may be said to be a cultural product, not a native endowment of those born into the species Man.

In grasping what is essential to the organicist position, one must be careful not to identify it with the more moderate thesis that the knowledge, the values, and the behavior of all persons will always to some extent be influenced by the cultures to which they belong. It would be wholly implausible to deny that such is the case, and I know of no form of nativism which has claimed that cultural influences have no effect on the larger part of man's behavior. However, organicism goes far beyond this moderate thesis. It holds that there are no tendencies or abilities in men which are not affected by cultural influences; that every characteristic which a nativist might assume to be common to men in all cultures is itself penetrated and modified by the effects of society on man. Thus, variations in the knowledge, values, and specific modes of behavior of those reared in different cultures would not be the product of an interaction between constant attributes and variable conditions, as a nativist could hold; on the contrary, such variations would be regarded as due to the direct influence any culture will have on those who participate in its life. Thus, organicism resembles geneticism in stressing the passivity of man, and the formative influence which his environment has upon him.

In fact, in one respect, organicism involves an even more extreme form of the malleability doctrine than is to be found in geneticism. It was necessary for those who accepted geneticism to assume that there are some universally applicable laws of psychology, such as the association of ideas, which serve to explain how the results of an individual's experience become ingrained in him. However, if the organicist thesis is accepted, even this measure of constancy is lost. For example, according to Comte, Hegel, and Marx, all forms of individual behavior which occur in a cultural context must be understood in terms of the nature of that context: there is no science of psychology which can deal with individuals independently of their actual social relationships. For this reason, as we shall see, organicism bitterly opposed the individualistic psychological approach characteristic of geneticism, and the two views should therefore not be confused. Even though neither supported the other, they did have a joint influence, since each contributed to the pervasiveness of a belief in the malleability of man.

In addition to these two types of view, and in contrast to them, there was a third position which I shall term the progressive view of man. It held that, by nature, man is inherently a progressive being. Throughout the period with which we are dealing, there were those who regarded it as certain that a consideration of history showed that there had been basic changes in human nature; these changes, it was held, could not be adequately understood on the assumption that individuals were merely passive, reacting to factors and forces external to them. Emphasis was therefore placed on what men made of themselves; it was as a result of active forces within individuals that mankind as a whole was claimed to advance.

This view, which was probably more widely held than either geneticism or organicism during the *latter part* of the nineteenth century, was expressed in a variety of different and sometimes opposed forms. One form, which was often connected with metaphysical idealism, was to be found in Fichte, at the beginning of the century; it was subsequently revived when English and American philosophers and psychologists rebelled against the basically passive view of the mind characteristic of associationist psychology, and therefore of geneticism. In opposition to associationist doctrines, idealists in particular—but also others—held that the human person is to be regarded as an active moral agent, creating the conditions of self-fulfilment for himself and for others through struggle, through choice, and through aspiration toward ideal ends.

A different form of progressivist doctrine, which had no natural affinities with any type of metaphysical position, stressed the importance of extending the range of human sensibilities, and therefore the range of actions in which pleasure was taken, thus cultivating and socializing man. Unlike the self-realizationist view of ideal ends, of which Fichte was one exponent, this view of man's progressive nature conceived of the *summum bonum* as the enjoyment of those higher pleasures to which men had, over the course of history, learned to be sensitive. Such a view, as we shall see, was not only characteristic of John Stuart Mill, but of Matthew Arnold and Huxley as well.

Still others took a progressivist view of a quite different kind. On the basis of analogies to the development of new biological species, they saw the human species as developing, acquiring new capacities over the course of time. In general, they rejected hedonism, siding with those who regarded struggle and effort as more basic than the desire for pleasure. With few exceptions, they and the metaphysical idealists did not make common cause. Idealists tended to reject the applicability of specifically biological analogies to the spiritual growth of man, and evolutionists did not generally regard the development of the race as a product of an inherent tendency toward self-fulfilment in the individual. According to most evolutionary forms of progressivism, it was the race which progressed, and not necessarily the individuals who happened to be the agents of change. On this view, then, human nature was being transformed, even though the activities of individual human beings might best be explained in terms of fixed instinctive capacities which they inherited.

In spite of these important differences among the various forms of what I term the progressivist view of man, there was enough in common among them to make their position an important tendency permeating a great segment of the thought of the age. This feature, common to all, and definitive of the doctrine as a whole, was the assumption that it was *natural for mankind* to develop new forms of sensibility and new springs of action over the course of history; and it was to be expected that, given the capacities of men, such progress was not at an end. The envisioned development was not merely a matter of cultural advance, or of an amelioration of social evils; it was to be a transformation of man himself, of his own nature.[2]

2. Historicism and Man's Malleability

There are a number of points of contact between historicism and the doctrine of human malleability, but these positions are different and must be distinguished. Historicism is the more inclusive doctrine, since it can, in principle, apply to the explanation and the evaluation of all types of phenomena, rather than being restricted to questions concerning human nature. However, the fact that histor-icism had widespread acceptance tended to foster a belief in man's malleability: if all other phenomena were to be viewed as aspects of a developing process, then human nature might also be regarded not as constant but changing. As we shall see, in the organicism of Hegel, of Comte, and of Marxism, the two doctrines were intimately associated.

Nevertheless, the doctrine of man's malleability does not have any necessary connection with historicism. For example, the view that the forms of thought and action of individuals result from their experience rather than reflect native pro-pensities arose in connection with associationist principles in psychology, yet the modes of explanation and standards of evaluation characteristic of associationism were directly opposed by historicism. Similarly, those who looked upon man as being by nature a progressive being, whose social progress reflected his inherently progressive nature, were not inclined to accept historicist modes of explanation, and in almost all cases they rejected the evaluative principle of historicism as well. Thus, a firm commitment to a belief in mankind's capacity for progress was not by any means linked to an acceptance of historicism, as the examples of John Stuart Mill and of Huxley should serve to make clear.[3]

In the case of theories of the malleability of human nature which were most intimately connected with evolutionary theory in biology, we again find that historicism played an important role. What was characteristic of these theories was that they stressed a phylogenetic point of view: it was the human race that exhibited unmistakable signs of a changing human nature, and it was the race, and its progress, which was regarded as being of primary importance. Thus, whatever effects their experience or changing forms of social organization may have had upon individuals, what was ultimately important about such changes was, quite simply, the way in which they had affected the future of man. Thus, in this case as in others, historicism tended to shift all questions concerning explana-tion from the issue of how a particular result was in fact brought about, to the question of how a particular case was to be construed when seen against a back-ground of some larger process, considered as a whole.

We may therefore expect that in the following discussion the doctrine of man's malleability will sometimes be closely related to historicism, and sometimes the two will diverge. Speaking generally, what I have termed geneticism will be antagonistic to historicism, and so too will many, and perhaps most, forms of the progressivist doctrine of man. On the other hand, organicism and the evolutionary approach to the malleability of human nature will be closely, although not in-separably, linked to historicism—not inseparably, for we shall later see that some more recent forms of organicist theory, such as that represented by Ruth Benedict, is as opposed to the basic tenets of historicism as any theory can be. What bears repeating, however, is the fact that the dominant influence of historicism in the nineteenth century helped to promote widespread acceptance of the view that man's nature is not to be regarded as unalterably fixed, but that at any point in time it can best be understood as being merely one phase in an ongoing process of developmental change.

9

If one considers the history of psychological theories prior to the rise of eighteenth-century associationism, it is clear that they were dominated by what I have termed nativism. Although the effects of experience were not, of course, wholly discounted, it was assumed that there were broad ranges of facts concerning human thought and human action which were directly attributable to native capacities common to all men. Furthermore, it was generally assumed that such capacities were constant, not having changed substantially over the course of recorded time. In spite, then, of a frequent recognition of the transiency of customs, the thesis of man's malleability had not deeply penetrated either the explanation of human behavior or views which were held regarding the history of mankind.

That an acceptance of nativism dominated psychological theories immediately prior to the time when associationism became dominant is a fact that needs only slight documentation. For example, those who belonged to the egoistic schools of political and moral philosophy in the seventeenth and eighteenth centuries were predominantly nativists, for in their accounts of the more complex forms of human action as reflexes of self-interest and foresight, the specific nature of past experience rarely played a decisive role. For these same philosophers the processes of human thought reflected an inherent ratiocinative capacity, the results of which were, in most instances, taken to be independent of the nature of the specific experiences which the individual had previously undergone. In addition, we may note that those who opposed egoism sought to undercut egoistic accounts of human action by multiplying the number of distinct and independent motives attributable to man. In doing so, they greatly reinforced nativism, extending the range of those specific forms of sensibility and of action which were claimed to be independent of prior experience.[1] These were not the only important nativistic tendencies then operative: in France, nativism was, at the time, dominant in the physiologically oriented accounts of human behavior.[2] Nevertheless, it is not our present concern to analyze the various forms of nativism which dominated the philosophy of mind prior to the widespread acceptance of associationism, but to show how a strain of geneticism separated itself off from the hedonistic and generally egoistic psychology of the period, becoming highly influential in establishing a doctrine of the malleability of man.

If one wishes to locate a single source from which modern geneticism derived its greatest power, that source must surely be found in Locke's theory of knowledge. His attack of innate ideas and innate principles was an attack or nativism in the theoretic sphere: all human knowledge depended upon factors given to the mind in the course of experience. However, as we shall see, his successors interpreted his doctrine in a narrower and more radical sense than was justified by the *Essay Concerning the Human Understanding*. The accounts of knowledge to be found in most who expressed their indebtedness to Locke do not assign to the mind's operations the same scope and freedom which one finds in Locke's own doctrine. Nor do most of his successors share his conviction that it is possible to establish a demonstrative system of morality.

Let us first recall what Locke's doctrine actually was. According to him, all knowledge was dependent upon experience, our minds being furnished with no innate ideas. Furthermore, however intricate any man's knowledge might become, all of its original or primitive elements were actually derived from experience: those elements were simple ideas given through the senses, or simple ideas given through introspection (which Locke called "reflection"), or a combination of both. Even though the ultimate and primitive *elements* of knowledge come through experience, it is important to note that not all of the *actual content* of our knowledge can be said to do so. According to Locke, the human mind is active as well as passive. Because we do not merely accept ideas, but compare them with one another, compound them, and abstract from them, much of our knowledge is not a direct reflection or reproduction of what was originally given: the elements of experience are generally rearranged, through the mind's autochthonous activities, and our actual knowledge is the product of such rearrangements. To be sure, when a number of simple ideas go constantly together, we tend to view them as a group, and to denominate them by one name; and in this way our complex idea of a particular material object, or of a specific type of material object, is built up. In such cases, our complex ideas may be regarded as primarily due to the effects of experience. In most other cases, complex ideas do not directly reflect the original presentations of experience, and the second book of Locke's *Essay* is in large measure devoted to the analysis of the latter cases. Among these complex ideas are modes such as number, the modes of place and of time, the conception of power, and mixed modes such as beauty or parricide. There are also conceptions of moral relations, and ideas of collective substances, such as armies. In these cases Locke offers an account of how it is that we can form a particular complex idea. He of course assumes that all such ideas are ultimately grounded in a set of simple ideas which serve as their primitive elements, but the complex idea itself is regarded by him as something different from those elements and not directly attributable to either sensation or introspection (i.e., "reflection").

Unfortunately, Locke himself was not clear on this difference between instances in which the content of knowledge is heavily dependent upon the mind's own activity, and those in which it is more dependent upon the order of experience. Nor was he compelled to draw such a distinction for his chief purposes. However, almost all of his followers came to emphasize the role of experience in determining the actual content of knowledge, and this led to a far more radical geneticism than was present in Locke himself. To that point we shall shortly return. Before doing so, it will be useful to indicate that Locke's account of our moral and religious beliefs raises precisely the same issue: on the one hand, he attributes many of our complex ideas to the activity of the mind operating on the elements given in experience, and, on the other, he emphasizes the role of experience itself in forming some of those ideas.

It is not surprising that there should be this parallel between Locke's theory of morals and of religion and his more general theory of knowledge. The original impetus for the *Essay* came from his interest in reaching some conclusion concerning the possibility of gaining reliable knowledge in the moral and religious spheres, and throughout the *Essay* one can note passages in which moral and religious concerns are important elements in Locke's treatment of some more general argument.[3] In his attack on innate ideas, for example, Locke was at least as much concerned with disproving the innateness of practical principles and religious truths as he was to disprove an apriorist view of logical, mathematical, or metaphysical axioms. However, it is not to be assumed that his attack on the theory of innate ideas led him to deny the possibility of certainty in either morals or religion. On the contrary, his positive theory involved a distinction between the very limited degree of assurance to be attained in beliefs concerning the material world, and the certainty which can be claimed for the truths of morality and religion. On his view, the latter truths are demonstrable. While such demonstrative proofs must be grounded upon elements given in experience, the conclusions which we are capable of reaching are dependent upon man's rationality, not upon the characteristics of that which was originally present in experience. That this was Locke's view is obvious from his use of the cosmological proof for the existence of God; it is also present, as we shall now see, in his complex account of morality.

According to Locke, morality consists in obedience to the rules instituted by men in societies, these rules being a reflection of the basic needs of men and the commands of God. In dealing with such rules and their application to voluntary actions, we are of course dealing with the kinds of complex ideas which Locke terms mixed modes and relations, and these ideas—though ultimately dependent upon elements given in experience—are themselves products of the mind's active powers. To judge whether an action is morally right, one need only consult these ideas: one need not appeal to dictates of conscience, or to a calculation of consequences, or to observation of how men actually behave. In this freedom from any appeal to experience, Locke held that moral reasoning is to be compared with mathematical reasoning: in both, one need only follow out the agreements and disagreements among ideas. (The deficiencies to be found in moral reasoning, as compared with mathematics, Locke attributed to the fact that moral rules have not been defined with equal accuracy.)

It is important to recognize that, while Locke believed that it is possible to attain demonstrative truth in morality and in religion, he was by no means satisfied with many of the moral and religious beliefs which men held. To understand his position, one must distinguish between moral and religious beliefs which are attributable to the use of reason and those which are to be attributed to custom: the former are warranted, but the latter are not. Frequently, Locke speaks of merely customary beliefs as *superstitions*, and denounces them in passages such as the following:

> ... doctrines that have been derived from no better original than the superstitions of
> a nurse, or the authority of an old woman, may at length of time and consent of
> neighbors, grow up to the dignity of principles in religion and morality. For such, who
> are careful (as they call it) to principle children well ... instil into the unwary, and
> as yet unprejudiced, understanding, (for white paper receives any characters,) those
> doctrines they would have them retain and profess. These being taught them as soon
> as they have any apprehension; and still as they grow up confirmed to them, either
> by the open profession or tacit consent of all they have to do with ... come, by
> these means, to have the reputation of unquestionable, self-evident, and innate truths
> (*Essay*, Bk. I, Ch. II, Sect. 22).

It is to be noted that the formation of such superstitious or ill-founded beliefs is not wholly dissimilar from the manner in which custom operates to make us think that we truly understand the nature of a particular material object, or type of material object. In the latter case, too, it is custom that habituates us to regard a particular set of qualities as belonging necessarily together, but there is no demonstrative proof that such qualities will always be found together. In spite of this similarity between the two types of case, Locke did not condemn an acceptance of custom in the case of beliefs concerning material objects as he condemned it in morals and in religion. The reason for this difference is twofold. In the first place, he did not regard the experienced grouping of the qualities of a material object as an arbitrary or accidental grouping: he assumed that it was regularly present because of the properties actually possessed by that which existed independently of our awareness. In the second place, such a custom-engendered view of the nature of material objects—while it is not an adequate view—is sufficient for most of the ordinary concerns of our lives. In the case of moral and religious superstitions, there was not the regularity which was present in our common-sense views of material objects; on the contrary, there was an indefinite variability among the beliefs characteristic of different societies. As he said in the *Essay*:

> He that will carefully peruse the history of mankind, and look abroad into the several
> tribes of men, and with indifferency survey their actions, will be able to satisfy himself
> that there is scarce that principle of morality to be named, or rule of virtue to be
> thought on ... which is not somewhere or other, slighted and condemned by the general
> fashion of whole societies of men (Bk. I, Ch. II, Sect. 10).

Now, Locke was unwilling to accept such variability as the ultimate truth in morality, for he believed in the theory of natural law, which was definitive of

GENETICISM: THE ASSOCIATIONIST TRADITION

certain moral duties, and in the ultimate origin of moral rules in God's commands. Therefore, these variant and alien rules were looked upon by him as constituting moral errors, not as providing justifiable bases for action in the communities which accepted them. They were due to the effects of custom, not of reason.

In this connection it is also relevant to note that Locke held that it was custom, and not their native endowments, which was accountable for the differences among men of different cultures. As he remarked in the *Essay:*

> Had you or I been born at the Bay of Soldania, possibly your thoughts and notions had not exceeded those brutish ones of the Hottentots that inhabit there. And had the Virginia king of Apochancana been educated in England, he had been perhaps as knowing a divine, and as good a mathematician as any in it . . . And if he had not any idea of a God, it was only because he pursued not those thoughts that would have led him to it (Bk. I, Ch. III, Sect. 12).

This contrast between superstition or ignorance on the one hand, and men's capacities to arrive at demonstrative truths in morality and religion when nothing inhibits the full use of their intellectual capacities, could scarcely help but lead Locke to the question of how human beings were to be reared so as to learn to use their faculties aright. *Some Thoughts Concerning Education* was the product of this interest and of the requests of persons seeking his advice concerning the education of their children.[4]

Considering his theory of knowledge, as well as his observations on the variability of moral and religious practices in different societies,[5] it is small wonder that, in this book, Locke should explicitly say of the overwhelming majority of men that

> [they] are what they are, good or evil, useful or not, by their education. It is that which makes the great difference in mankind. The little, or almost insensible, impressions on our tender infancies, have very important and lasting consequences: and there it is, as in the fountains of some rivers, where a gentle application of the hand turns the flexible waters into channels, that make them take quite contrary courses; and by this little direction, given them at first, in the source, they receive different tendencies, and arrive at last at very remote and distant places.
> I imagine the minds of children as easily turned, this or that way, as water itself (Sect. 1–2).

Throughout this work Locke emphasizes the malleability of the individual, both with respect to his body and his conduct,[6] until—in conclusion—he referred to the fact that, in formulating his advice, he had considered the young child "only as white paper, or wax, to be moulded and fashioned as one pleases" (Sect. 216).

It is important to remember that expressions such as these do not have reference to man as a being capable of reasoning: Locke is here speaking of the effects of custom, which he regarded as antithetical to reason. This contrast, which we have now noted in other aspects of Locke's thought, receives what is perhaps its clearest expression in his discussion of the association of ideas. And it is important to understand his position with respect to associationism, if we are to appreciate one of the chief points at which his successors modified his view of the human mind, paving the way for an acceptance of the theory of man's indefinite malleability.[7]

As is well known, Locke added a chapter entitled "Of the Association of Ideas" to the end of Book II in the fourth edition of the *Essay*.[8] In that discussion he consistently treated the association of ideas as something which was by its very nature antithetical to reason. For example, he said:

> Some of our ideas have a *natural* correspondence and connexion with one another: it is the office and excellency of our reason to trace these, and hold them together in that union and correspondence which is founded in their peculiar beings. Besides this, there is another connexion of ideas wholly owing to *chance* and *custom* (*Essay*, Bk. II, Ch. XXXIII, Sect. 5).

The latter connection is, of course, the association of ideas.

If we examine the illustrations of the association of ideas which Locke gives in this chapter, we find that these associations all depend upon associations by contiguity, and not at all upon associations by resemblance. This fact is important, since Locke—like others—found the nature of reason to be the perception of agreement or disagreement among our ideas. Therefore, those cases in which two ideas are associated with one another because of the effects of their resemblances, or because of a contrast between them, could not be used as instances *antithetical* to reason: they would constitute cases in which there was "a *natural* correspondence and connexion ... founded in their peculiar beings." On the other hand, in cases where the presence of one idea evokes another simply because the two ideas have previously been experienced together, there is no "natural correspondence and connexion," and it is not surprising that Locke should contrast such cases with examples of reasoning.[9] Furthermore, in the same chapter, Locke conjectures that those associations which depend upon contiguity are ultimately dependent upon physiological causes, that is, upon "trains of motions in the animal spirits, which, once set a going, continue in the same steps they have been used to";[10] in this respect, too, they are not to be counted among the activities of the mind, but as examples in which it is passive. It is important to take note of such facts, if one is to understand how Locke came to adopt the very extreme position in which he characterized the effects of association as "this wrong connexion in our minds of ideas in themselves loose and independent of one another."[11] On Locke's view, such linkages, being wholly due to contiguity, represent a totally different principle of connection than is to be found when the mind actively employs its discriminatory powers in compounding, abstracting, and relating the materials originally given to it. It is only in the latter instances that we build conceptions which in their degree of abstractness, their generality, and indeed their novelty, represent a level of awareness far different from that represented in the original flow of experience.

It has been of importance for us to stress Locke's doctrine concerning the active, native powers of the mind, for it is primarily with respect to these powers that his theory of knowledge differed from that of his successors. He had prepared the way for their more radical rejections of nativism through his insistence that all of the *materials* of human knowledge must be furnished by experience. However, he stopped short of the view that the mind's own operations were to be interpreted in terms of the effects of experience; thus he stopped short of a thorough rejection of traditional forms of nativism. On the other hand, his successors came to view that which Locke had attributed to the powers of judgment as being due to experience.[12] It is to this radical shift that we must now turn our attention.

In tracing this development, we must first note that Berkeley and Hume, who followed Locke's way of ideas, explicitly rejected his doctrine of abstract, general ideas. This rejection, as one can see in the *Principles of Human Knowledge*, was the first point at which Berkeley felt it necessary to challenge Locke, and his challenge was cited by Hume as "one of the greatest and most valuable discoveries that has been made of late years in the republic of letters."[13] Locke had held that once experience had provided the human mind with simple ideas, the mind could, by its active powers, form genuinely new ideas from these elements. For example, once having touched or seen objects, we could frame the abstract general idea *shape*, which was not to be identified with any of the specific elements on the basis of which it had been formed. And this idea, as an abstract general idea, could itself function as one of the building blocks which the mind used in forming further ideas. Thus, most of our complex ideas (except for those of particular material objects) are ideas in which the original elements from which they were derived play a very small role. The effects of this "pyramiding" activity of the mind can be very clearly seen in Locke's doctrine of moral relations. These relations, it will be recalled, depend upon the conformity of a voluntary action to some moral rule. Now a moral rule relates to types of acts such as *sacrilege* or *parricide*, each of which is an abstract general idea of a mixed mode. While it is true that all of the materials necessary for our conceptions of mixed modes are ultimately derived from simple ideas of sensation or of reflection, these complex ideas are not necessarily tied to the particular simple ideas by means of which we first formed our conceptions of them. Thus, Locke grants the human mind a freedom in its use of experience which Berkeley and Hume came to deny. According to their view, whatever general concepts we use always remain tied to some of the individual simple ideas which originally served as the bases for these concepts. This doctrine brings Berkeley and Hume close to the position of the sensationalist school, in spite of the fundamental differences between their own epistemological positions and the views of most sensationalists.

In addition to this point, it is to be noted that Berkeley and Hume also approached the sensationalist position in the alterations which they made in Locke's theory of the sources of our simple ideas: they eliminated "reflection" as an independent source of ideas, co-equal with sensation. To be sure, the first paragraph of Part 1 of Berkeley's *Principles of Human Knowledge* apparently accepts Locke's view, admitting ideas "such as are preceived by attending to the passions and operations of the mind." Nevertheless, Berkeley did not actually make use of such ideas in his account of the scope of human knowledge. Whenever he departed from a discussion of ideas deriving from sensation, he introduced the concept of our *notions* of spirit. Such notions, however, are not to be construed as analogous

to simple ideas of sensation, for they are not the building blocks out of which
further complex objects of knowledge are formed. In short, the specific ideas
which Locke characterized as original simple ideas of reflection play no part in
Berkeley's system. This unacknowledged alteration in Locke's views became explicit in Hume: many of the ideas to which Locke had referred, Hume denied
that he could find within his own experience; and those which Hume did find,
and called impressions of reflection, he held to be dependent upon prior impressions of sensation. In this he was of course at one with the sensationalists.

The connection between these alterations in Locke's doctrine and sensationalism can be noted in Condillac. While avowing his deep indebtedness to Locke,
and praising his work, Condillac criticized him for having assumed that there are
operations of the mind which are not reducible to sensation.[14] The freedom to
form new ideas, which Locke had believed that the human mind possessed, was
denied by Condillac.[15] As his *Traité des Sensations* suggested, the human being
was no more active in the formation of complex ideas than would be a statue
which had been endowed with no powers other than having the capacity for
sensations: the nature and the sequence of these sensations would be sufficient in
themselves to account for the whole of knowledge.[16] This emphasis on the role of
sensation as the foundation of knowledge is of course continued in later French
thought by Helvétius and by d'Holbach;[17] and in England it is paralleled in the
associationism of Hartley and Priestley.[18]

While Hobbes can rightfully be regarded as the first major figure in the history
of associationism in England, it was not to him but to Locke that the British associationists themselves traced their lineage.[19] For example, in the first chapter of
his *Observations on Man*, Hartley pointed out that the basis of his own doctrine
was a theory of vibrations which derived from Newton, and the theory of association which derived from Locke. To be sure, in the preface to his work, he had
also remarked that he *first* came to consider "the power of association" on hearing
how John Gay had suggested that it might account for *intellectual* pleasures.
However, these remarks concerning his indebtedness to Locke and to Gay do not
involve a contradiction.[20] By his own testimony, Hartley was thirty-one years old
when he heard about Gay's suggested account of intellectual pleasures, but he
assuredly knew Locke's work before that time. Apart from the fame of the *Essay*,
we have his son's testimony on this point,[21] and Hartley himself said that from
Locke "and other ingenious Persons since his Time" he had learned

the Influence of Association over our Opinions and Affections, and its Use in explaining those Things in an accurate and precise Way, which are commonly referred to the
Power of Habit and Custom, in a general and indeterminate one.[22]

His indebtedness to Gay was therefore not one of learning to appreciate the general power of the association of ideas, but something much more specific. Granting Hartley's familiarity with the way in which the association of ideas could explain "the Power of Habit and Custom," Gay's dissertation showed the applicability of the same principle to the formation of the moral sense in man. This

attempt on the part of Gay constituted a decidedly new step,[23] and one which stood in sharp contrast to Locke's disparagement of the effects of association on moral and religious beliefs. Unlike Locke, Gay was not attempting to show that the principles of morality, like the principles of mathematics, form a demonstrative system. He was attempting to square the traditional account of the importance of other-regarding motives in a life of virtue with an acceptance of an egoistic psychology. The rewards and punishments of another life had, of course, often been invoked to do so. However, as Gay noted,

> The generality of mankind do approve of Virtue, or rather virtuous actions, without being able to give any reason for their approbation; and also ... some pursue it without knowing that it tends to their own private happiness; nay even when it appears to be inconsistent with and destructive of their happiness.[24]

It was for the sake of explaining such approbations that Gay invoked the principle of association, appealing to the formative powers of experience to give men standards which others had held to be dependent upon innate moral cognition, or an innate moral sense. In offering this account, he was not, of course, denigrating these approbations: he regarded them as the basis of morality, founded in the nature of man and consonant with the Divine Will. Thus, Gay had transformed Locke's doctrine: the association of ideas was not to be regarded as a source of moral and religious error, but was, on the contrary, the means by which new and praiseworthy motives arose through the effects of experience, with self-interest becoming converted into virtue. Such, one must suspect, is what Hartley saw as "the power" which Gay had discovered in the association of ideas. In Hartley's own work, as his preface tells us, he was interested in tracing the consequences of this power with respect to morality and religion.

In spite of several comparisons which early associationists drew between the association of ideas and the Newtonian law of gravitation, associationism was not, in its origins, an attempt to formulate and validate a specific psychological law. It was not, as Hartley had suggested it should be, an example of "the method of analysis and synthesis recommended and followed by Sir Isaac Newton."[25] Rather, it was the formulation of a principle which served to bridge the gap between the very general proposition that all knowledge derives from sense experience and specific observations concerning reasoning, the use of language, the operation of the imagination, the growth of complex emotions, and the basis of moral beliefs. For example, one may note that Hume was less interested in establishing that associations among ideas follow patterns of resemblance, contiguity, and cause-and-effect, than he was in showing how this view would lead one to treat problems of "Logic, Morals, Criticism, and Politics."[26] Even Hartley, whose interest in the details of the theory of associationism was far greater than Hume's, and who was deeply interested in the physical basis of the association of ideas, was to a very considerable degree motivated by moral and theological concerns.[27] One may also note that Joseph Priestley, Hartley's chief follower, expressed his interest in extending Hartley's system as it applied to questions concerning the conduct of life and "the natural progress and perfection of intellectual beings." In this connection he said of the Hartleian system that "the most important application of Dr. Hartley's doctrine of the association of ideas is to the *conduct of human life*, and especially the business of *education*."[28] Hartley himself had explicitly noted these applications, for he had said:

> It is of the utmost consequence to Morality and Religion, that the Affections and Passions should be analyzed into their simple compounding Parts, by reversing the Steps of the Associations which concur to form them. For thus we may learn how to cherish and improve good ones, check and root out such as are mischievous and immoral, and how to suit our Manner of Life, in some tolerable Measure, to our intellectual and religious Wants. And as this holds in respect of Persons of all Ages, so it is particularly true, and worthy of Consideration, in respect of Children and Youth.[29]

Thus, in its origins, associationism was not what James Mill and especially Alexander Bain later sought to make it, a full-blown psychological system serving to classify and relate all aspects of mental life; it was, rather, a principle used to connect a general epistemological position with more specific issues of intellectual and practical concern.[30] Among these issues, questions concerning the foundations of morality and the relations of morality to religion had an especially important place.

It is no part of my present purpose to trace the history of associationism, except as it bears on the contrast between nativistic and geneticist views of the nature of man. In this connection, one can safely assume from the outset that all associationists accept geneticism to some very appreciable degree. To be sure, associationism demands that we attribute to men certain innate capacities and propensities; among them, of course, are the capacity to receive elementary sensations and the propensity to connect the elements thus given in the specific way or ways summarized by the theory of associations. In addition, most associationists stressed the original, inherent tendency in men to pursue their own interests, seeking pleasure and avoiding pain. However, these may be considered to be general principles which underlie specific forms of action; what associationists denied was not the existence of such principles but the assumption that there were any specific convictions or ways of acting which were natural and independent of experience. Furthermore, associationists attempted to keep even the most general principles to a bare minimum, regarding it as one of the most significant advantages of their theory that it was able to reduce diverse phenomena to a single and all-encompassing law.[31] As Priestley remarked in his criticism of Reid and other members of the Scottish school: "My view in the following inquiry is to relieve dame nature of the unnecessary load which Dr. Reid has laid upon her."[32] Thus, assuming that nature has endowed men with a limited number of simple capacities of a highly general sort, the associationists explained the specific content of human thought and patterns of action in terms of experience. With the exception of Hume, most of the major eighteenth-century associationists made the further assumption that all associations could themselves be accounted for solely through the effects of successive experience, that is, by means of the effects of temporal contiguity.[33]

The doctrine of associationism, as thus conceived, obviously stressed the malleability of individuals, accounting for complex patterns of thought and behavior by an appeal to the ways in which experience had acted upon the individual. All traits which were specifically human were thus assumed to be acquired traits, rather than being "natural."[34] Under these circumstances it would of course be easy to assume—and perhaps today it would be widely assumed—that associationism must have stressed the *diversity* of men, since the formative experiences of different persons would presumably be different. However, this was not in fact the position of the early associationists, other than Locke. As one can see in Hartley, and also in Hume and in Adam Smith, the principles of associationism were first invoked to explain the *similarities* among men, not their differences. In fact, after attempting to show, on the basis of his theory of vibrations, that our complex, acquired ideas may be no less vivid than simple ideas which are due to the direct action of objects upon us, Hartley drew a number of corollaries from that proposition, and among them we may note the following:

Cor. 6. If Beings of the same Nature, but whose Affections and Passions are, at present, in different Proportions to each other, be exposed for an indefinite Time to the same Impressions and Associations, all their particular Differences will, at last, be over-ruled, and they will become perfectly similar, in a finite Time, by a proper Adjustment of the Impressions and Associations.

Cor. 7. Our original bodily Make, and the Impressions and Associations which affect us in passing through Life, are so much alike, and yet not the same, that there must be both a great general Resemblance amongst Mankind, in respect of their intellectual Affections, and also many particular Differences.[35]

Hartley's stress on the element of a great general resemblance among men, rather than on the particular differences among them, can be seen in the fact that from the two preceding corollaries he draws the sweeping conclusion that "association tends to make us all similar."[36]

Should this conclusion be regarded as surprising, one need merely recall that Hartley, like other associationists, had assumed that ideas such as those which we have of individual material objects, and also our ideas of distance in the third dimension, were the effects of a repetition of simple ideas which came to be combined through association. Now, originally, the specific sense-experiences of any one individual might be supposed to differ considerably from the specific ideas received by others, since the original surroundings in which the individuals were placed would be different. However, it was assumed that as an individual's experience increased, the content of that experience would tend more and more to overlap with the experiences of others. As a consequence, it was entirely reasonable for Hartley to hold that the effects of continuing experience would function in an equalizing manner: our characterizations of objects would tend to converge, rather than being disparate, and our ideas of space, being built upon the correlation of our tactile and visual sensations, would also become increasingly congruent. These equalizing effects of experience with relation to the material world were also originally assumed by the associationists to be paralleled by the effects of men's experiences in their social environments.

That which was assumed to function in the social world in a manner analogous to the functioning of material objects in causing sensations was, for most associationists, the tendency of men to pursue their self-interest, seeking pleasure and avoiding pain under all circumstances. While this tendency to pursue only one's own interest would originally lead to conflicts, the painful effects of such conflicts would gradually teach men to refrain from acts of naked and direct selfishness: thus it was claimed that self-interest became transmuted into the pursuit of virtue, that is, into a concern for the good of others. It is precisely this account of the origin of morality that we have noted in Gay, and a not wholly dissimilar one is present in Hartley.[37] While Hume differed from Gay and Hartley in not regarding any one motive as a sufficient basis from which to derive a general account of moral notions, he did share their conviction that it was possible to explain the virtues which underlie social and political life through the effects of experience. As one can see in his account of justice[38] and also in his account of promise-keeping,[39] many of our moral ideas are rooted in social experience and become, as it were, a second nature in man. In such cases, the effects of experience can be seen to lead not to radical differences among men, but to basic similarities in belief and in conduct. Thus, according to Hume, experience instils in us virtues which are as "stedfast and immutable . . . as human nature. And if they were founded on original instincts, could they have any greater stability?"[40]

Associationism did not invariably lead to an acceptance of this view.[41] We find, for example, that Joseph Priestley drew a sharp distinction between the effects of association on the basic patterns of action in men and its effects on ideas of moral right and wrong. Speaking of the first set, which he had illustrated by such actions as grasping, sucking, and blinking, Priestley said:

Who can help admiring the admirable simplicity of nature, and the wisdom of the great author of it, in this provision for *the growth of all our passions*, and propensities, just as they are wanted, and in the degree in which they are wanted through life?[42]

Nevertheless, he differed from those associationists who had stressed the similarity and constancy of men's moral beliefs. Instead, he used the doctrine of associationism to account for the variability in those beliefs.

This opinion of the gradual formation of the ideas of moral right and wrong, from a great variety of elements, easily accounts for that prodigious diversity in the sentiments of mankind respecting the objects of moral obligation; and I do not see that any other hypothesis can account for the facts.[43]

As illustrations of such variability, Priestley cited differences in men's views as to what constituted *justice* or *murder*, and the differences among men with respect to the moral stigma attaching to *lying* and *swearing*. All such differences he attributed to the effects of education, operating through the association of ideas. In drawing such a distinction between the constancy of certain forms of action and the variability in moral convictions due to education, Priestley had been anticipated by Helvétius, whose work represents a consistent attempt to trace the differences among men to the differences in their education.

The general psychological and philosophical views of Helvétius had their origins in that sensationalism and associationism which, as we have seen, arose out of the heritage of Locke; however, the uses to which Helvétius put these doctrines were essentially new. He took as his task that of being the theoretician of what might be called *social education*. Locke's concern with education had focussed upon the upbringing—chiefly moral and intellectual—of a single individual by his parents, and Rousseau's *Émile*, in spite of the range of its implications, was also concerned specifically with child-rearing practices and principles of instruction. On the other hand, Helvétius's theory of education was indissolubly linked to a system of social psychology and an interest in social reform. The background against which his views on these subjects were brought forward in his first major work, *De l'esprit*, was of course furnished by Montesquieu's work, *De l'esprit des lois*. Montesquieu had contended that it was necessary for laws and governments to be in conformity with the characteristics of the people to be governed, and he had attempted to account for differences in national characteristics on the basis of differences in climate.[44] It was this set of relationships which Helvétius attacked in the Third Discourse of *De l'esprit*.[45]

For Helvétius, the characteristics of peoples were not products of the climates in which they lived, but were formed by their education. The conception of education which Helvétius used in attempting to establish this claim was an extremely broad one, including every influence through which an individual acquired new knowledge, beliefs, or skills. It was on this basis that he put forward the claim that no two persons could ever be said to have the same education.[46] And since the laws of a country, and all of its institutions, were among these influences, Helvétius insisted that it was mistaken to think that the laws of a country should conform to the characteristics of a people; their characteristics would always conform with their laws.[47] In justification of this view, and in opposition to Montesquieu's use of climatic differences as a means of explaining national characteristics, Helvétius cited the dissimilarity of the people of modern Greece from those of ancient times. As he said in this connection:

Semblable à l'eau qui prend la forme de tous les vases dans lesquels on la verse, le caractère des nations est susceptible de toutes sortes de formes; c'est qu'en tous les pays, le génie du gouvernement fait le génie des nations.[48]

To be sure, this doctrine is not to be interpreted as a denial of the uniformity of the fundamental psychological principles operative in men: like almost all of his contemporaries, Helvétius assumed that men are all informed by the same types of motives and by the same passions. It was his view that in different ages, and indeed in different sectors of a society,[49] the influence of education resulted in the fact that these passions became attached to different objects. Thus, in spite of an original uniformity among men, the specific values of different cultures were diverse, and not infrequently antagonistic.[50] With respect to intellectual qualifications, Helvétius adopted an analogous view, for it was part of his argument that all endowments which were relevant to intellectual capacity were initially equal in all men, the difference between mediocrity and the highest intellectual achievements being attributable to the effects of education:

> L'homme de génie n'est donc que le produit des circonstances dans lesquelles cet homme s'est trouvé.[51]

While this radical doctrine concerning the effects of education was sufficiently evident throughout Helvétius' first major work, De l'esprit, it was not the explicit subject-matter of that work. However, it was the theme which dominated De l'homme, a work published posthumously because of the furor which had been created by De l'esprit. As Helvétius put the matter, the question which he was attempting to solve in the later work was whether the differences in men's minds (la différence des esprits) is to be reckoned as the effect of differences in organization or in education.[52] And to this question he answered:

> Quintilien, Locke, et moi, disons: L'inégalité des esprits est l'effet d'une cause connue, et cette cause est la différence de l'éducation.[53]

Helvétius' assumption that men are all originally equal by nature, and that their differences are wholly attributable to education, was simply a radical form of a widely held doctrine. One finds Rousseau placing similar emphasis on a native equality in men;[54] this doctrine was also of importance to Hume, whose account of the foundations of political life was predicated upon the fact that all men are nearly equal "in their bodily force, and even in their mental powers and faculties, till cultivated by education."[55] One finds a similar assumption in Adam Smith as well:

> The difference of natural talents in different men is, in reality, much less than we are aware of; and the very different genius which appears to distinguish men of different professions, when grown to maturity, is not upon many occasions so much the cause as the effect of the division of labour. The difference between the most dissimilar characters, between a philosopher and a common street porter, for example, seems to arise not so much from nature as from habit, custom and education.[56]

As we have noted, both Hume and Smith had used this doctrine to account for the similarities in the basic values of different societies, no less than to explain individual and class differences. Helvétius, however, was not fundamentally interested in constructing a theory of the moral sentiments; his interest in psychological theory was bound up with his interest in social reform. At the time, it was Helvétius alone who drew the political and social consequences which were obviously implicit in the theory that the differences among men were primarily due to the conditions under which they lived. Shortly after Helvétius, and largely through his influence, these implications became familiar. One can see his influence on the thought of Godwin[57] and, above all, on the origins and development of philosophic radicalism.[58]

I shall not attempt to trace in any detail the effects of the doctrine of man's malleability on doctrines of political and social reform during this period. Nonetheless, it is important to note the element of what might be called "interventionism," with which these doctrines were connected. This element may be typified in Robert Owen's statement which he affixed as a motto to the title page of *A New View of Society; Essays on the Principle of the Formation of the Human character* (1813):

> Any character, from the best to the worst, from the most ignorant to the most
> enlightened, may be given to any community, even to the world at large, by applying
> certain means; which are to a great extent at the command and under the controul, or
> easily made so, of those who possess the gouvernment of nations.[59]

The same doctrine was present in Godwin, in the Utilitarians, and one might say in almost all who stood for liberal reform.

In order to hold an interventionist view of this sort, it was not enough to suppose that individual men were by nature malleable, taking on the characteristics which their educations impressed upon them. It was also necessary to assume that the power to direct these formative forces were either actually or potentially under the control of governments. Now, those who held this to be the case did not envision—nor would they have embraced—any form of totalitarian state.[60] What regulated their thought was the assumption, which had been characteristic of almost all modern social theory, that the *state* constitutes the central institution in any society, being capable of controlling all other institutions, and is not itself controlled by them. This assumption can be seen in Godwin no less than in Helvétius. For example, in his *Enquiry Concerning Political Justice*, we find that Godwin's first chapter attacks what he takes to be the usually received view that political institutions are primarily negative in nature, and do not exert a positive influence on all aspects of life. Against this view he sets up his own hypothesis that the political institutions of a society shape its people and all aspects of their life. As he says in this connection:

> Perhaps government is, not merely in some cases the defender and in others the
> treacherous foe of the domestic virtues. Perhaps it insinuates itself into our personal
> dispositions, and insensibly communicates its own spirit to our private transactions.
> Were not the inhabitants of ancient Greece and Rome indebted in some degree to their
> political liberties for their excellence in art, and the illustrious theatre they occupy in
> the moral history of mankind? Are not the governments of modern Europe accountable
> for the slowness and inconstancy of its literary efforts, and the unworthy selfishness that
> characterizes its inhabitants? .... If government thus insinuate itself in its effects into
> our most secret retirements, who shall define the extent of its operations? If it be the
> author of thus much, who shall specify the points from which its influence is excluded?[61]

The emphasis which Godwin thus placed on the influence of the state was not, unfortunately, balanced by an equal emphasis on the effects of other social institutions. And in the light of preceding social theory, it is not surprising that such was the case.

Nor is it surprising that those who stood in the direct line of descent from Hartley and Helvétius should have been sanguine about the possibility of radical social reform on the basis of their theory of the state. The utilitarian view of the state, which receives what is perhaps its classic expression in James Mill's article entitled *Government*, held that all governments are founded upon the interests of individuals, and they would not have arisen, nor would they be sustained, were they not instruments for the satisfaction of the interests of individuals. This heritage from the eighteenth century, when coupled with the view that the political institutions of a society constitute its dominant institution, gives the governed the right—and ultimately the power—to mold their own lives. Thus, in opposing the view that men are characterized by the possession of a fixed set of "natural" or inherited traits, geneticism led to the conclusion that through political reform man could be the agent of his own ever-increasing development.

Attractive as this doctrine was to those who shared the eighteenth-century ideals of enlightenment and reform, it met with formidable challenges. These challenges, however, were not directed against the notion of human malleability. Rather, they were directed against the sensationalist theory of knowledge and the utilitarian theory of morals and politics with which the doctrine of malleability had come to be connected. In other connections, and affiliated with other positions, the doctrine of malleability was affirmed in a no less radical way.

10

Was der Mensch sei, sagt nur die
Geschichte.
Dilthey, *Gesammelte Schriften,* IV, 529

In the rise of geneticism, as we have thus far traced it, the approach to social institutions remained essentially what it had been throughout the seventeenth and eighteenth centuries: political and social theory proceeded on the assumption that it was through psychology—i.e., through an analysis of the needs and capacities of individual human beings—that one could both understand and evaluate the forms of institutions which characterized social life. It is not difficult to see why this assumption should have dominated modern attempts to establish a non-theological basis for understanding and evaluting political institutions. That a society was to be construed simply as a set of individuals standing in reciprocal relations to one another was taken to be a truth too obvious to doubt. And the assumption that such a system of reciprocally related parts could be understood by analyzing the forces operative in each of these parts had become thoroughly familiar through the natural philosophy of the seventeenth and eighteenth centuries.

By the end of the eighteenth century, as we have had occasion to note, there had occurred a widespread revolt against the mechanical assumptions of that philosophy, and nature came to be viewed in terms of organic analogies. Such analogies, when applied to the body politic, shifted attention to the notion that the state is a whole, having a life of its own, and is not to be regarded as a sum of individuals, each of whom pursues his own ends. This anti-summative view of the state, which tended to be connected with organic analogies, can be suggested by citing the following passage from Aristotle's *Politics:*

> The state is by nature clearly prior to the family and to the individual, since the whole is of necessity prior to the part; for example, if the whole body be destroyed, there will be no foot or hand, except in an equivocal sense, as we might speak of a stone hand; for when destroyed the hand will be no better than that. But things are defined by their working and power; and we ought not to say that they are the same when they no longer have their proper quality, but only that they have the same name. The proof that the state is a creation of nature and prior to the individual is that the individual, when isolated, is not self-sufficing; and therefore he is like a part in relation to the whole (1253a18–28).

I do not wish to suggest that Aristotle himself drew the moral and political implications from this analogy which were to be drawn from it by many nineteenth-century philosophers. In fact, the essential needs and capacities of individuals were the bases upon which Aristotle's political philosophy rested. This was also the opinion of those who, in the eighteenth century, shared Aristotle's view that the state was a natural growth: while they regarded laws and systems of laws as the results of historical experience, rather than as depending upon deliberate decision and rational compromise, they continued to hold that social institutions were grounded in the needs and the capacities of individual human beings. One sees this in Montesquieu, and one sees it especially clearly in the manner in which the origins and functioning of institutions were explained by Hume, by Ferguson, and by Adam Smith. According to Hume, for example, there were basic traits of human nature which remained unalterable: since it was these traits which explained societies, it was not to be assumed that social institutions could account for them.[1] It was this assumption that was to be challenged by those who stressed organic analogies, for they came to look upon mankind as divided into distinct cultures, each with its own character, and each exerting a formative influence over the minds and the sentiments of those who participated in its life.

The sources of this new doctrine were various, and we shall be dealing with a number of them. What it is initially important to note is their common characteristic: a shift of attention from the individual to the culture into which that individual had been born. Even so radical a defender of the principle of geneticism as Helvétius had been willing to characterize a nation as nothing more than the citizens of whom it was formed, speaking as if these citizens did not themselves have a special character because they belonged to this particular nation, rather than to another.[2] It was the discovery of the distinctiveness of different cultures and of different historical epochs, and of the power which they exercised over the thoughts and feelings of men, that eventually led to the new organicist thesis of the malleability of man.

1. MILL AND COMTE: TWO VIEWS OF A "SPIRIT OF THE AGE"

The beginning of this transition may be signalized by the opening paragraph of John Stuart Mill's essay *The Spirit of the Age*, which we have already quoted, but which is once again apposite:

> The "Spirit of the Age" is in some measure a novel expression. I do not believe that it is to be met with in any work exceeding fifty years in antiquity. The idea of comparing one's own age with former ages, or with our notion of those which are yet to come, had occurred to philosophers; but it never before was itself the dominant idea of any age.

Mill's own sensitivity to this new mode of thought gives us some clues to the sources of the change, and it is to tracing these influences on him that we shall first turn.[3]

In the first place, we may note that in *The Spirit of the Age* Mill argued a point which his father's essay on *Government* had wholly failed to recognize: that each age has its own problems, and that what is possible in one age may not be possible in another. As he put the matter:

To find fault with our ancestors for not having annual parliaments, universal suffrage, and vote by ballot, would be like quarreling with the Greeks and Romans for not using steam navigation, when we know it is so safe and expeditious; which would be, in short, simply finding fault with the third century before Christ for not being the eighteenth century after. It was necessary that many other things should be thought and done, before, according to the laws of human affairs it was possible that steam navigation should be thought of. Human nature must proceed step by step, in politics as well as in physics.[4]

To have come to this view—obvious as it may seem to us—involved a radical break with the assumptions of those theories of government which, like Bentham's, sought to derive the justification of political institutions from assumptions concerning the universality and the constancy of human capacities and human motives.[5]

It had been Macaulay's attack on his father's essay on *Government* that had forced Mill to reexamine his own position. That attack was pithily summed up by Macaulay himself in saying:

Our objection to the essay of Mr. Mill is fundamental. We believe that it is utterly impossible to deduce the science of government from the principles of human nature.[6]

The reason given by Macaulay was that there is in fact no constancy in human nature:

We do not believe that it is possible to lay down a single general rule respecting the motives which influence human actions. There is nothing which may not, by association or by comparison, become an object either of desire or of aversion.[7]

Thus the doctrine of associationism was itself turned against those who, like Bentham and James Mill, purported to derive a theory of government from an associationist psychology. As Macaulay said in his rejoinder to a critic (whom he took to have been Bentham),

Our knowledge of human nature, instead of being prior in order to our knowledge of the science of government, will be posterior to it.[8]

While John Stuart Mill could not accept the premises of many of the arguments brought forward by Macaulay, the two years between Macaulay's attack on his father's position and the publication of his own essays on "The Spirit of the Age" marked a change in Mill's views concerning social institutions. This change did not consist in an abandonment of the principle of utility as the basis for social and political evaluations; the standard of human happiness as the test of the rightness of human conduct, and as the criterion for judging institutions, was never in fact abandoned by Mill. What Mill altered in the Utilitarian doctrine as it had been formulated by Bentham and his father, was the view that an appraisal of institutional forms could be applied to the political life of any society without taking into account the stage of culture of that society, and thus without viewing that culture in terms of a process of historical development. As Mill's *Autobiography* makes clear, there had been two sets of influences—both ultimately Continental in their origins—out of which this revision of his earlier Utilitarianism had developed.[9] Each of these sources of influence could, of itself, have led Mill to use the phrase "The Spirit of the Age," and could have suggested to him the novelty inherent in the uses to which, in his own time, such a phrase was being put.

The first of these sources was that which can best be denominated as a German influence. It comprised the direct influence of Goethe, the influence of Coleridge, and the influence of Mill's friends F. D. Maurice and John Sterling who represented the party of Coleridge. On the whole, it is difficult to assess the strength of this influence, for it is primarily through Mill's retrospective account of it in his *Autobiography* that we have evidence of how it affected him.[10] For example, in that account, he speaks of Goethe's influence upon him, yet it is not possible (so far as I know) to reconstruct precisely what Mill knew of Goethe;[11] nor is it possible to reconstruct enough of the personal doctrine of Sterling to decipher what effects of an intellectual sort his strong personality had upon Mill. It seems safe to assume that what Mill found most significant in what may be designated as "the German influence" on him was (a) that its mode of thought was concrete and historical, instead of proceeding deductively on the basis of psychological assumptions, and (b) that it stressed feeling, and was thus neither simply intellectual nor wholly analytical. That this was what Mill found attractive is not only visible in the relevant passages in his *Autobiography*, but in his characterization of what he called "the Germano-Coleridgian doctrine" in his essay on Coleridge. He said of this doctrine:

> It expresses the revolt of the human mind against the philosophy of the eighteenth century. It is ontological, because that was experimental; conservative because that was innovative; religious, because so much of that was infidel; concrete and historical, because that was abstract and metaphysical; poetical because that was matter-of-fact and prosaic.[12]

He held that it was "the Germano-Coleridgian school" who were "the first (except a solitary thinker here and there) who inquired, with any comprehensiveness or depth, into the inductive laws of the existence and growth of human society.... They thus produced, not a piece of party advocacy, but a philosophy of society, in the only form in which it is yet possible—that of a philosophy of history."[13]

As his subsequent discussion makes clear, what he found particularly noteworthy was the fact that this school recognized the diversity of cultures, and their particularity:

> Every form of polity, every condition of society, whatever else it had done, had formed its type of national character. What that type was, and how it had been made what it

was, were questions which the metaphysician might overlook: the historical philosopher could not. Accordingly, the views respecting the various elements of human culture, and the causes influencing the formation of national character, which pervade the writings of the Germano-Coleridgian school, throw into the shade every thing which had been effected before.[14]

The context of this discussion would make it appear that Mill might have been directly acquainted with Herder's writings;[15] however, other sources make it clear that he was surely not well versed in German philosophy in general. As he told Comte in a letter written as late as 1843, although it was through their views that he had freed himself from the excessively analytic tendencies of Bentham and of eighteenth-century thought, he had never read either Kant, or Hegel, or any other representative of their school.[16] Thus, what he said concerning the new views of culture which had been introduced into modern thought by German philosophy came to him primarily, if not exclusively, at second hand. Such was not the case with respect to the second major Continental influence which affected his theory of government and altered his philosophy of culture; this influence consisted in the Saint-Simonian movement, and the positive philosophy of Comte.

In his *Autobiography*, Mill acknowledged his debt to the Saint-Simonian movement for having given him a new conception of progress.[17] In particular, he was struck by the distinction which its members drew between organic and critical periods in the history of civilization, a distinction which he used in *The Spirit of the Age* as a means of assessing the nature and the needs of his time. Through his contact with the Saint-Simonian movement, Mill had come to know Comte's early work, which had stressed the difference between organic and critical periods,[18] but Comte's chief influence upon him dated from the time that Mill was in the process of completing his *System of Logic,* when he was also reading the later volumes of the *Cours de philosophie positive.* The exchanges of letters between Comte and Mill, which Lévy-Bruhl published, are especially striking as revealing the personal relationships between the two men; but one need merely study Book VI of the *System of Logic,* and in particular the chapter on the historical method ("the inverse deductive method"), to see the extent of this influence. However, what Mill gained from Comte, and wherein he differed, becomes most explicit in the articles on Comte which he later published, in 1865, in the *Westminster Review.* With reference to our present concern—that of understanding the sources of Mill's rebellion against the theory of society which had been accepted by Bentham and by his father—one passage in praise of Comte contained in these articles is of special interest. Mill contrasted the Benthamite and Comtean views, saying:

Since ... the phenomena of man in society result from his nature as an individual being, it might be thought that the proper mode of constructing a Social Science must be by deducing it from the general laws of human nature, using the facts of history merely for verification. Such, accordingly, has been the conception of social science by many of those who have endeavored to render it positive, particularly by the school of Bentham. M. Comte considers this an error. We may, he says, draw from the universal laws of human nature some conclusions (though even these, we think, rather precarious) concerning the very earliest stages of human progress, of which there are either no, or very imperfect, historical records. But as society proceeds in its development, its phenomena are determined, more and more, not by the simple tendencies of universal human nature, but by the accumulated influence of past generations over the present. The human beings themselves, on the laws of whose nature the facts of history depend, are not abstract or universal but historical human beings, already shaped, and made what they are, by human society.[19]

And, very shortly, Mill went on to state his estimate of Comte's contribution in this respect, saying:

> We know not any thinker who, before M. Comte, had penetrated to the philosophy of the matter, and placed the necessity of historical studies as the foundation of sociological speculation on the true footing. From this time any political thinker who fancies himself able to dispense with a connected view of the great facts of history, as a chain of causes and effects, must be regarded as below the level of his age.[20]

Thus, what Mill drew from Comte (in spite of their many more specific disagreements) supplemented what he had learned from Macaulay's attack on his father's theory of government, and supplemented what he had learned from the interest in history among members of the Germano-Coleridgian school. We may further note the essential point at which he held that Comte had far surpassed all predecessors: Comte had specifically attempted to create a social science instead of simply appealing to a collection of historical instances as, Mill felt, Macaulay had done.[21]

However, Mill refused to accept Comte's evaluative standards, and in the second of his essays in the *Westminster Review*, that on "The Later Speculations of Auguste Comte," he made this opposition entirely clear. In that essay he attacked Comte's insistence on the need for unity within a society and his submersion of the individual in the social whole.[22] When one recalls Mill's essay *On Liberty*, it becomes obvious how fundamental this conflict was, and the traces of bitterness in his attack on Comte's system of positive polity are readily understandable. Nonetheless, it would be a mistake to attribute their differences in social philosophy solely to differences in their evaluative standards, or to their ways of envisioning the social needs of their time. It is important to note that the differences between their analyses of social and of political institutions had an important theoretical foundation as well.[23] For Mill, psychological analysis as it had developed within the tradition of associationism was indispensable for understanding all human activities. While it could not, of itself, provide a deductive basis for theories of government, as Bentham and his father had believed, no understanding of the foundations of social life was possible without it. As I have elsewhere tried to show, Mill also believed that standards of good and of evil had their roots in the psychological characteristics of men.[24] Comte, on the other hand, rejected the assumption that there was, or could be, a positive science of psychology. He assumed that any analysis of the human individual which was to be free of fictive and metaphysical modes of thought would necessarily be included within the province of biology: there was not to be any special science of *mind*.[25]

Thus, following the suggestions of Cabanis among others, but basing his views primarily on Gall,[26] he claimed that the moral and mental attributes of individuals were to be understood physiologically. However, he did not conceive of human beings primarily in biological terms: they were social beings who lived their lives within the framework of a set of social institutions, and such institutions always formed a single integrated system, or "social organism."[27] It was from these social systems that individuals received their modes of thought and feeling, and derived the basic beliefs which characterized their common form of life. Therefore, a separate science of psychology had no place in Comte's hierarchy of the sciences: sociology constituted the immediate successor of biology, and was used to explain the differences in the thoughts and the feelings which characterized individuals who belonged to different social systems.

One can readily understand Mill's opposition to Comte with respect to this point. While he had given up the view, held by Bentham and by his father, that social institutions depended directly upon abstract principles of human nature, Mill did not doubt that there were such principles, and that they applied with equal accuracy at all times and places. What he held was that the prior exponents of associationism should have had more interest in the concrete nature of actually existing historical institutions, since these institutions affected the experience of individuals and therefore changed their thoughts and feelings. Such a recognition of the influence of institutions on individuals was a far cry from the position which had been adopted by Comte. For example, according to Comte, men do not at all times think in the same ways: there is a development in the mode of thought from the theological or fictive, through the metaphysical to the positive or scientific, and each of these modes of thought develops historically, spreading successively to different fields of inquiry. For Mill, on the contrary, the basic characteristics of human thought always remained the same: it was solely the material for knowledge, furnished by experience, that changed. Therefore, it was not through an inner historical necessity but through an accumulation and winnowing of experience that increasingly acceptable, positive knowledge was gradually gained. In short, according to Mill, the basic characteristics of human nature were common to all individuals, regardless of when or where they may have lived. While there were very marked differences between individuals who were brought up under different circumstances, these differences were to be attributed to the specific nature of the circumstances: no society could shape an individual in any way other than through its cumulative effects on his experience. A society, according to Mill, was not in any sense an entity independent of the individuals whose activities gave rise to its various structures. The contrary view, held by Comte and by others, is generally denominated as "organicism."[28]

In speaking of "organicism" in social theory, one must proceed with extreme care. The term is an inclusive one which has been used to designate a variety of positions; frequently these have been related, but not all have been concerned with the same questions, nor have all had similar implications. For example, as we have already noted with respect to Aristotle, when organic analogies are used with reference to political and social life, these analogies need not be taken as

suggesting that the nature of individuals is wholly dependent on the characteristics of the particular societies to which they belong. Nor should one assume
that, whenever emphasis is placed upon the unity of an age, there will be a
denigration of individuality, such as one finds in Comte. For example, among
those who influenced Mill, not only Coleridge but Herder and Goethe had
emphasized the principle that the culture of an age possesses organic unity, yet
they had also stressed the creative powers of the individual, and had looked upon
individuality as a principle to be cherished in man. Even those who asserted that
societies are entities which have a reality of their own and are not to be explained
in terms of the actions of individuals, sometimes held that the touchstone of value
is to be found in the satisfactions and fulfilments of individuals. While this can
scarcely be claimed to have been the case in the social philosophies of either
Hegel or Comte, it is possible to regard Marxism as combining organicism with
the view that the ultimate standard of value lies in individual well-being. Or, to
take another example, Spencer had carried out analogies between societies and
organisms in far greater detail than had any of his predecessors, yet his views on
social ethics were militantly individualistic. Bearing these facts in mind, it is
necessary to exercise a high degree of caution in discussing the meaning and implications of organicism in social theory.

The point with which we are here concerned is the question of the malleability
of human nature: whether, in fact, there are fundamental characteristics of men
which are in some measure independent of their social environments—apart, of
course, from those biological characteristics which serve to characterize man as
one among other animal species. Or, put conversely, our question is whether
social environments are to be held responsible for shaping men in all of those
respects which are relevant to their modes of thought and their social actions. As
should be clear from my earlier discussion of the alternative views concerning
man's malleability, I shall use "organicism" to refer to the doctrine that human
thought and action are invariably dependent upon the forms of organization of
social institutions. On some theories this would be to say that they are dependent upon the particular stages of development which the society has reached. As
we have noted, one of the basic reasons why Mill rejected Comte's doctrine was
because it was (in this sense) a form of organicism. This fact serves to suggest what
should in any case be clear—that organicism is to be distinguished from geneticism even though each is equally opposed to nativism. It is with organicism that
we are here concerned.

While it is important to remember that there was, as we have noted, considerable diversity in the views of those who accepted some form of organicism, it is
also important to find an explanation of why, at the time, that view had great
appeal to thinkers who were very dissimilar in other respects. The explanation
lies in the fact that, at the end of the eighteenth century and at the beginning of
the nineteenth, social theorists emancipated themselves from a set of assumptions
which (outside of political economy) had been scientifically sterile, in spite of
their importance in establishing a particular normative point of view. This
emancipation consisted in discovering it was a mistake to suppose that the origins

of any society, or of any widely prevalent social institutions, could be understood through analyzing how individual human beings, when first brought together in a social situation, might be expected to behave. The lack of realism in such an approach becomes obvious as soon as one asks where, outside of groups resembling families or tribes, the individuals who formed societies might have originated. However, the difficulty lies even deeper and was later pointed out by Sidgwick and others.[29] The only materials on which we could draw in order to generalize as to how beings physiologically like ourselves would actually behave if they had had no previous social contacts and no socially acquired experience, would be materials drawn from how men behave when they *are* in a social state. However, such evidence is surely suspect: one has no right to assume that the nature of men living in civil society furnishes a model by means of which we can explain how the institutions of society arose out of some antecedent "state of nature." Or, to phrase the new departure in social theory in a more general manner and more in conformity with recent discussions, it came to be held that facts concerning institutions could not be reduced to facts concerning individual behavior.[30] An acceptance of this position seemed to many nineteenth-century thinkers to justify an acceptance of some form of organicism although, in point of fact, it provided only a necessary and not a sufficient condition for accepting that view. In Chapter 12 we shall have occasion to see that this is true. First, however, it will be useful to examine in what ways this anti-reductionist thesis led a number of major social theorists to accept that view of human malleability which asserts that the nature of men depends upon the nature of the societies in which they have their existence. For this purpose we shall start with Comte, whose thought provides one of the clearest manifestations of the relationship between an institutional approach to social theory and an acceptance of organicism with respect to the malleability of man.

2. COMTE'S ORGANICISM

There are three distinguishable lines of argument by means of which Comte sought to dismiss an individualistic approach to all social phenomena. One of these—though it was by no means the most dominant—was related to a fact that has already been suggested: what we know as human beings are always to be found in a social milieu, and it is impossible to conceive of what we regard as human individuals were they to be stripped of their social inheritance. As Comte repeatedly insisted, a human point of view is a sociological point of view.[31] In this connection we may note that as early as his 1822 essay on the *Plan des travaux scientifiques*, Comte contrasted a biological point of view—even in the case of social animals such as the beaver—with a sociological point of view, and he said in this connection:

No doubt the collective phenomena of the human race, as well as its individual phenomena, must, ultimately, be traced to the special nature of its organization. But the condition of human civilization in each generation directly depends only on that of the preceding, and directly produces only that of the following generation.[32]

In more contemporary terminology, this implies a contrast between the essentially non-cumulative nature of biological inheritance and the cumulative nature of social inheritance.[33] Pressing this point, Comte held that to understand the individual in his capacities as a social being, and not merely as a biological entity, one had to look not at the individual but at the historical process itself: any individual was merely a representative of a stage in the development of social life, an abstraction from the collective being, Humanity, which embraces all men:

> L'homme proprement dit n'est, au fond, qu'une pure abstraction; il n'y a de réel que l'humanité.[34]

In this same vein, contrasting man as an individual with Humanity, le Grand-Être, he said:

> Man indeed, as an individual, cannot properly be said to exist, except in the too abstract brain of modern metaphysicians. Existence in the true sense can only be predicated of Humanity.[35]

In addition to Comte's emphasis on the role of men's social inheritance in making them specifically human, there was a second and even more important reason which led him to insist on the irreducibility of social phenomena to the behavior of individuals: this was his general theory of the hierarchy of the sciences. Since, as we have seen, Comte had rejected the possibility of there being a positive science of psychology, he regarded sociology as the immediate successor of biology in the hierarchy of the sciences. As in other cases, he took what clues he could concerning the nature of any higher science from that which preceded it, though without attempting to reduce the higher to the lower.[36] In this case, therefore, he looked to the fundamental features of organic life for suggestions as to what characteristics might have been developed to an even higher degree in the realm of the social.[37] Now, what Comte had held with respect to biology, as contrasted with the lower sciences, was that the phenomena of life showed a higher degree of mutuality among the parts—or, as we might say, a higher degree of internality of relations among its parts—than did the constitutive elements which formed those wholes which were investigated by the inorganic sciences. Furthermore, he insisted that the genuine elements of which an organic being was composed were its structures, not the chemical elements into which it could be analyzed. Thus, in his analysis of organisms, what he took to be essential was what he termed the consensus in living beings: their mutually related organs which, in functioning together, sustained the organism as a whole. It was this conception that he carried over into sociology; throughout his treatment of social statics, he insisted upon the unity within the social organism.[38] This emphasis, which stands in a clear ancestral relation to twentieth-century functionalism in anthropology, emphasizes (as later functionalism also did) that the elements into which a society is to be

analyzed are themselves social structures, not individuals.[39] It is in this connection
that one can best understand Comte's insistence that the original units out of
which societies grew were not individuals but families.[40] However, it is to be noted
that *later* social developments were not viewed by Comte in terms of families, but
as the development of complex and interrelated institutional structures arising
out of a division of social functions corresponding to social needs.[41] The resultant
whole, Comte insisted, was a unified whole in which each part was related to all
others, and none was independent of the total system of which it was a part:

> De quelque élément social que l'on veuille partir, chacun pourra aisément
> reconnaître, par un utile exercise scientifique, qu'il touche réellement toujours, d'une
> manière plus ou moins immédiate, à l'ensemble de tous les autres, même de ceux qui en
> paraissent d'abord indépendans.[42]

This view constitutes one form of what is sometimes termed "organicism" in
social theory, but it need not necessarily lead to the form of organicism with
which we are here concerned. That is to say, it need not entail that one should
regard all of the basic intellectual and moral characteristics of human beings as
being dependent upon the societies in which they live. A society might be held to
be constituted by a set of institutions which stand in close interrelationship with
each other, and which function as a whole, so that if one institution were to be
changed, the repercussions of such a change would be felt throughout the society
as a whole; but any such society might none the less be construed as an *environment* in which individuals lived, and not as determining the nature of the forces
operating *within* them. To understand why Comte held that a positive science of
social institutions was at the same time a positive science of the mental and moral
characteristics of human beings, we must turn to a third important methodological conviction which had application both to his biology and to his
sociology: the conviction that, in these fields, one must deal directly with total
structures, with phenomena in the aggregate.

The basis of this conviction lay in Comte's maxim that a positive science always
proceeds from the better known to the less well known. While he held it to be true
that in astronomy, and indeed throughout the inorganic sciences, one could best
proceed from the analysis of parts to an understanding of the whole, in the
biology of complex organic systems and in sociology the whole was known with
far more assurance than were the parts.[43] While Comte himself did not believe
that the genuine parts of a social system were the individuals who lived within
that system, the methodological principle which we are here examining would
have been sufficient to rebut anyone who did adopt such a view. He could, for
example, have used this principle against John Stuart Mill, arguing that one
knows much more concerning the nature of a particular, historical social system
than one can possibly know concerning the processes which have gone on within
the individuals and which have molded them to be as they are. And when one
considers Mill's frequent insistence that every experience affects the individual,[44]
one can recognize that the traditional approach of geneticism to the individual's

moral and mental dispositions could not possibly serve as an adequate basis for understanding social phenomena in the large.[45]

However, Comte had another reason for insisting that the priority of our knowledge of the whole to a knowledge of its parts demanded that we view the mental and moral attributes of men as being fully determined by the nature of their societies. For Comte, as we have noted, every social system forms an integrated whole. In that system, the stage of intellectual development which has been reached is of crucial importance: not only religion and government, but all institutions are affected by whether the dominant modes of thought are theological, or metaphysical, or scientific. It is also the case (and this is a point on which, as we have seen, Comte had insisted) that the beliefs which any individual possesses are due to his social inheritance, that is, to the cumulative results of the experience of past generations. Thus, the general categories which determine the thought of an individual will themselves have been determined by the stage of social evolution which his society has reached; furthermore, all of the institutions in terms of which individuals interact with one another will have been shaped by these same modes of thought. Thus one can see why, on Comte's view, it is impossible to understand individuals without relating them to what he conceived to be the progress of mankind as a whole. While it is undoubtedly true that Comte's emphasis on the great collective being, Humanity, and his rejection of all forms of individualism, did spring from fundamental evaluational attitudes of a highly personal sort, it would be misleading—and would lead us to underestimate the importance of organicism in nineteenth-century thought—if we did not also recognize that these convictions had deep intellectual roots.[46] Whatever the errors of Comte's organicism—to which, indeed, we shall later devote some attention— the emphasis which he placed on Humanity had one of its roots in his fruitful recognition of the importance of taking into account the formative influence of social inheritance on all individuals. Furthermore, while others before him had come to look upon social institutions as historical products, he was among the first to see that it was inconsistent with the facts of social inheritance to explain these institutions in terms of some postulated set of pre-existing human needs. The history of mankind thus became the clue to the nature of men, according to Comte; and it is this important doctrine that constitutes one of the points at which his views and the views of Hegel most closely approximate one another.[47]

3. HEGEL

In any attempt to understand Hegel's thought, it is important to recognize that he regarded knowledge as a concrete system: knowledge, properly speaking, was never unsystematic. One can readily see how this view might be engendered. Let it be supposed that if we are to understand any fact we must relate it to other facts; in order to understand these, we must relate them to further facts; and the latter, in turn, must be related to still other facts. On this basis, of course, genuine knowledge would not be gained until one had come full circle and had related all facts, systematically, to all other facts. Put in this manner, the task would appear to be self-defeating; however this appears to be the case only because we have been speaking in wholly abstract terms and have failed to consider what it means to relate one fact to another. Whether a relation be logical or causal, or of any type whatsoever, the ability to relate one fact to another presupposes that we have grasped respects in which they are to be considered as similar, and respects in which they are different. Thus, in seeking understanding, it is inescapable that we shall be concerned with similarities and with differences, and this entails that we are concerned with the specific nature of whatever aspects of the experienced world we are seeking to understand. Thus, the empty abstractness which made the search for systematic connection appear as if it were the pursuit of a will-o-the-wisp was misleading: wherever one might start in a search for understanding, a specific content would be given, and the system being traced would be a concrete system in which similarities and differences, and therefore concrete particularity, would be preserved at every step of the way. Whatever the difficulties within the Hegelian system, and however abstract Hegel's terminology may be, one cannot charge him with lack of concern for the concrete character of various forms of human experience.

Given Hegel's ideal of a concrete system, it is difficult to deal with any one of the aspects of his thought in abstraction from his system as a whole. The best that one can probably do is attempt to make clear both the metaphysical and the empirical reasons which led him to hold the position he did with respect to whatever particular issue one wishes to understand. In the absence of any better alternative, it is this dual method which we shall here follow. First we shall discuss Hegel's organicism in terms of two general metaphysical theses which (among others) run through his system as a whole; we shall then turn to some of the more important empirical considerations from which Hegel drew confirmation for these theses. Each of the metaphysical theses with which I shall deal represents a view which Comte wholly rejected; nonetheless, when we consider Hegel's interpretation of the empirical facts regarding the relations between individuals and social systems, we shall find that his position frequently coalesces with that of Comte, leading to strikingly similar forms of an organicist doctrine.

One fundamental metaphysical presupposition of Hegel's doctrine was that reality, no less than human knowledge, constitutes a single coherent system of mutually related parts. The form in which Hegel maintained this doctrine can be phrased in a variety of ways, but it cannot be phrased more succinctly than it was by Hegel himself in the *Phenomenology of Mind*:

The truth is the whole. The whole, however, is merely the essential nature reaching its completeness through the process of its own development.[48]

From this it follows that to view any particular in abstraction from its relationships to other particulars, and therefore in abstraction from its place within a system, is to falsify its nature, to misconceive it. Or, put in terms of the Hegelian doctrine of relations, no particular constitutes a self-sufficient independent unit:

any particular is what it is only because it stands in relationship to other units, each of which to some degree modifies its nature, just as these are themselves modified in the process. This metaphysical assumption, however one chooses to phrase it, will obviously tend toward some form of organicism, for the self will be constituted by its relationships, not by a set of inherent attributes which it would be possible to investigate by examing the individual in isolation, apart from his activities within a social whole. However, it was not simply this very general metaphysical assumption that provided a basis for Hegel's organicism; there also were more specific metaphysical problems concerning the nature of the self which contributed to it. While the latter were less crucial to Hegel's philosophy as a whole than was his general doctrine of the internality of all relations, they had considerable importance in connection with the topic here under discussion; and the fact that they were less conspicuous within Hegel's system makes it all the more worthwhile to single them out for attention.

In the first place, we may note that Hegel rejected metaphysical theories which regarded mind and matter as belonging to different realms and as capable of existing independently of one another.[49] In rejecting this ultimate dualism, he also rejected two other widely accepted contrasts. One such contrast consisted in the view that the material world was characterized by necessity, but that mind wholly escaped necessity; according to the other, the realm of mind was the inner, subjective realm, whereas the material world constituted an external, objective order of objects and processes whose structures were wholly independent of mind. Against the first of these dichotomous divisions, Hegel insisted that a correct understanding of freedom and of necessity showed that there was no genuine opposition between them;[50] and he took the same position with respect to the traditional dichotomy between self and object. For example, in the *Phenomenology of Mind*, he said:

> Individuality is what its world, in the sense of its own world, is. Individuality itself is the cycle of its own action, in which it has presented and established itself as reality, and is simply and solely a unity of what is given and what is constructed—a unity whose aspects do not fall apart . . . into a world given *per se* and an individuality existing for itself.[51]

In insisting on the interpenetrating unity of self and world, Hegel recognized that it was impossible to attempt to construct empirical laws of psychology which would serve as a basis for understanding the concrete nature of different individuals, since such laws would attempt to abstract the individual from his world. Thus we find him speaking with considerable disdain regarding the possibility of there being an observational science of psychology.[52] He insisted that, in attempting to understand any individual, it is necessary to relate him to his social environment, that is, to shift attention from the realm of subjective to objective spirit; this realm is, of course, the civil society or State, and the historical period to which the individual belongs.

It would be mistaken to suppose that this very important doctrine in the Hegelian system was based solely upon the fact that Hegel rejected the dichotomies which we have noted: that is, between mind and body, freedom and necessity, inner and outer, and between the individual and his world. It is also the case that he at least suggested an analysis of individuals which rendered it plausible to hold that, in the end, their characters and their thoughts were to be interpreted in social terms. This positive analysis constituted Hegel's basic psychology—a theory which should not be confused with the many striking psychological *aperçus* which one finds scattered throughout his works, and most especially in the *Phenomenology of Mind*. In depicting Hegel's basic theory of individual human nature, we are dealing with what must be admitted to be one of the least developed aspects of the whole Hegelian system; in fact, it can only be reconstructed from a variety of discussions which were written from different points of view. In the present context, I shall be content to suggest its general nature rather than to attempt the formidable task of analyzing it in detail.

According to Hegel, if we are to understand the attributes of man as an individual being, it is necessary that he be related to the organic world, although not assimilated to it. Adopting this point of view, it is clear that the unity which is present in the individual's minded-body does not depend upon a set of cognitive capacities (for example, upon any form of transcendental ego), but upon feeling and will.[53] This comes out clearly when, in the *Philosophy of Right*, Hegel says:

> As a person, I am myself an *immediate* individual [*unmittelbar Einzelner*]; if we give further precision to this expression, it means that I am alive in this bodily organism which is my external existence, [and is] the real pre-condition of every further determined mode of existence. . . . As person, I possess my life and my body, like other things, only in so far as my will is in them.[54]

Thus, self is activity, but as activity it reaches out to touch and to seize upon elements in its environment, elements which do not in themselves possess will. The first and essential stage in this extension of the self is, according to Hegel, an appropriation of the external, a making of things into property:

> A person has as his substantive end the right of putting his will into any and every thing and thereby making it his, because it has no such end in itself and derives its destiny and soul from his will. This is the absolute right of appropriation of men over all things.[55]

The extension of the individual's nature to include those external things which belong to him through his appropriation of them is the first step toward the formation of a common will or social condition of existence. Hegel stated this explicitly in the paragraph in which he traced the "Transition from Property to Contract":

> One aspect of property is that it is an existent as an external thing, and in this respect property exists for other external things and is connected with their necessity and contingency. But it is also existent as an embodiment of the will, and from this point of view the 'other' for which it exists can only be the will of another person. This relation of will to will is the true and proper ground in which freedom is existent. The

sphere of contract is made up of this mediation whereby I hold property not merely by means of a thing and my subjective will, but by means of another person's will as well and so hold it in virtue of my participation in a common will.[56]

Thus, in the mutual recognition of that which each has appropriated as an extension of his own will, the common will has its origin. To be sure, the persons concerned may not be overtly aware that property entails a common will, for each person may tend to account for the contracts into which he enters in terms of some private consideration, such as that which is to his advantage. This is one of many instances in which Hegel finds that what, on the surface, appears to be pursued on purely personal grounds manifests a hidden and deeper purposiveness; in this case it constitutes the basis for a genuinely social existence in which the freedom attained is a wider freedom than any individual could attain for himself through his own independent will.

The mutuality which is present in contracts constitutes only the first step from the individual will to the larger will, and to Hegel's insistence that the true nature of the individual is only realized through his participation in a will which is more inclusive than his own. In following Hegel's reasoning with respect to this issue, either of two paths can be taken: one involves tracing the nature of moral custom and the general nature of freedom in the ethical life, whereas the other traces the relations between individual needs and social organization in the family and, more especially, in Civil Society. Each path has the same goal, a consideration of the nature of the State.[57] Since it will be convenient to discuss the nature of morality and of the ethical ideal later, in connection with Hegel's view of the State, we shall follow the second of these alternative paths.[58]

Civil Society (die bürgerliche Gesellschaft), according to Hegel's use of that term, consists of an organized, structured community, carrying on all of the activities necessary for the subsistence of the individuals living within it; it possesses an economic system, a legal system, and means of exercising authority in regulating these systems.[59] Or, as Hegel says at one point, Civil Society may be regarded as that form of state which is based exclusively on need.[60] What it lacks, and what a State possesses, are those forms of political life, embodied in a constitution, through which the unity of a single people becomes a dominant force which expresses itself in all institutions—above all, in art, religion, and philosophy. Yet even in Civil Society, before this greater unity is achieved, individuals have passed beyond a state of independence of one another, and their activities have come to express a will which, in later parlance, is more than the sum of their individual wills. For example, in Section 183 of the Philosophy of Right, Hegel says:

In the course of the actual attainment of selfish ends...there is formed a system of complete interdependence, wherein the livelihood, happiness, and the legal status of one man is interwoven with the livelihood, happiness, and rights of all. On this system, individual happiness, etc., depend; and only in this connected system are they actualized and secured.

Thus, what we have termed "Hegel's basic psychology" consisted in tracing the sequence of forces through which the will inherent in each individual is transformed through his active relationships with others, and finds its expression in the structures of an organized community. According to this doctrine, the real will of the individual merges with a larger whole of which he is and must be a part.[61] Hegel's position is therefore unalterably opposed to all interpretations of human nature which proceed on the assumption that each individual possesses a specific inherent nature, independently of his relationships. Against such an assumption Hegel insisted that an individual is never intelligible in his bare particularity, as merely one of a collection of instances of the human species: each is what he is only because he extends his activity into a world larger than himself, and in his society he becomes one with that world.[62] This doctrine exemplifies the general metaphysical proposition, which we have already noted, that the particular is what it is only because of its relations to other particulars in a concrete system. As we shall see when we consider the empirical basis for Hegel's social and political philosophy, this doctrine finds full expression in the relations existing between the individual and the Nation State.

I now turn to a second metaphysical presupposition which is to be found throughout Hegel's work, and which is equally important in understanding his social and political philosophy. It consists of a doctrine which is fundamentally normative in character, and is summed up in the famous Hegelian dictum:

Was vernünftig ist, das ist wirklich; und was wirklich ist, das ist vernünftig.
[What is rational is actual
and what is actual is rational.][63]

To be sure, at first glance this dictum may not appear to be specifically normative in character, for we are accustomed to think that normative statements will include terms such as "good" or "bad," "right" or "wrong," or make reference to what "ought" to be. However, Hegel heaps scorn on those who moralize, or who disparage the actual by contrasting it with some ideal that they cherish, and which they claim is that which ought to exist. For example, in *The Smaller Logic* he says:

This divorce between idea and reality is especially dear to the analytic understanding which looks upon its own abstractions, dreams though they are, as something true and real, and prides itself on the imperative 'ought', which it takes especial pleasure in prescribing even on the field of politics. As if the world had waited on it to learn how it ought to be, and was not![64]

In the *Philosophy of History* he speaks in the same manner:

Reason is not so powerless as to be incapable of producing anything but a mere ideal, a mere intention—having its place outside of reality, nobody knows where; something separate and abstract, in the heads of certain human beings.[65]

On the contrary, it was his conviction that what *ought* to be was present in the realm of actuality, in the world, for "the truly good—the universal divine reason —is not a mere abstraction, but a vital principle capable of realizing itself."[66]

This position should occasion no surprise if we recall Hegel's doctrine of divine immanence.[67] And, in point of fact, immediately after enunciating his doctrine of the equivalence of the rational and the actual, Hegel said, "The great thing [for philosophy] is to apprehend in the show of the temporal and transient the substance which is immanent and the eternal which is present."[68] This conviction set the task for philosophy in its consideration of the world's history, and Hegel explicitly recognized that fact:

> God governs the world; the actual working of his government—the carrying out of his plan—is the History of the World. This plan philosophy strives to comprehend; for only that which has been developed as the result of it, possesses *bona fide* reality. That which does not accord with it, is negative, worthless existence. Before the pure light of this divine Idea—which is no mere Ideal—the phantom of a world whose events are an incoherent concourse of fortuitous circumstances, utterly vanishes. Philosophy wishes to discover the substantial purport, the real side of the divine idea, and to justify the so much despised Reality of things; for Reason is the comprehension of the Divine work.[69]

As a consequence, Hegel explicitly denominated his *Philosophy of History* as a Theodicy, a justification of the ways of God,[70] and he concluded that work with the paragraph:

> That the History of the World, with all the changing scenes which its annals present, is this process of development and the realization of Spirit—this is the true *Theodicaea*, the justification of God in History. Only *this* insight can reconcile Spirit with the History of the World—viz., that what has happened, and is happening every day, is not only not 'without God,' but is essentially his work.

It is in the light of this doctrine, and not in terms of worship for any actually existing state, that one should interpret Hegel's thought when he makes such extreme statements as "The State is the Divine Idea as it exists on Earth."[71] In this form of assertion, Hegel was not attempting to say that actually existing political structures were not subject to criticism. What he was asserting is that any true state is, in the first instance, to be recognized as an actualization of a spiritual development. This constituted the fundamental positive condition of its existence, regardless of what shortcomings might be present within it.[72] In other words, whatever its faults, a state was viewed as embodying the real will of its members, in which, and through which, their common life and aspirations were fulfilled. Therefore, to think of the state as an absolute external power, against which individuals had no rights, would be to falsify what Hegel attempted to say. Individuals had no special rights against the state simply because the state was that through which individuals first gained that form of life in which one could speak of their rights at all.[73] As we have noted, the foundation of the state ultimately rested upon the conditions necessary to human existence: the will of the individual extended beyond himself, and the exercise of that will established his dependence upon others, and their dependence upon him. Through the growth of a common life, individuals together achieved what they would never have known (let alone what they would have been able to achieve) had it been in their nature to be single, self-enclosed beings, atoms which were unable to become one with another. For Hegel, it was not the family, nor civil society, but the state which brought to fruition this course of development, this sharing in the widest possible spheres a single communal life. Thus, the state is an ethical fabric, woven out of practices which represent the concrete willing of human beings. The divinity of the state is like the divinity of all other things: it springs from its true actuality, not from an other-worldly source. Its ethical justification lies in its own nature. To appeal to a standard of moral rightness against which a state is to be measured is to set up individual consciences against what has indeed made it possible for one to be an individual, and to have a morality, at all.[74]

Thus we come to Hegel's view of the relation between the individual and the state. There are few points at which his doctrine has been so severely criticized, but in some cases that criticism has been based on a failure to comprehend the context in which his views were formulated. The two metaphysical assumptions which we have been examining—the internality of relations, and the identity of the actual and the rational—help to provide such a context, and permit us to understand on what basis Hegel held the views that he did.

As we have seen, for Hegel, no individual thing exists in isolation. In applying this doctrine to man, he insisted that no human being can be understood as human except in his relationships to other persons; and in his philosophical analysis of social existence (as well as on the empirical grounds which we shall shortly examine), Hegel held that this network of interpersonal relationships engenders an organic whole embodying the total culture of a people. It was this whole, and not simply the political sovereign, which Hegel denominated as "the State." We have also noted that, for Hegel, the sphere of the ethical resided in communal life: an individual would be without conscience, and would be without a conception of rights, were it not for the community of which he is part. While an individual might, under these circumstances, meaningfully criticize specific aspects of the institutional organization within any state, Hegel rejected the legitimacy of any attempt to turn against the state itself, and to attempt to discredit the ends embodied in it. For any individual, to claim the right to place some allegedly higher goals in place of those which give the state its very existence would be to destroy the fabric of social life without which the individual would be stripped of all traits that make up his humanity. It is this interpretation of the basis of social life, and of the foundations of morality in social existence, which must be borne in mind when one interprets what Hegel means in saying that "the State is the actually existing, realized moral life."[75]

The foregoing point should be so obvious that, for our present purposes, little further need be said by way of characterizing Hegel's philosophic doctrine concerning the relations of the individual and the state. However, to avoid misunderstanding, it should at least be noted that Hegel's conception of freedom differs radically from the position of those who hold that the individual is free only if he can do whatsoever he may choose to do. For Hegel, such a state of affairs is to be identified with caprice, not with freedom: to be free, is to be unhampered by external constraints in achieving the fullest possible self-realization, and such self-realization is only to be achieved in and through society. As Hegel put the matter in one of his many discussions of it:

> The perpetually recurring misapprehension of Freedom consists in regarding that term in only its *formal*, subjective sense, abstracted from its essential objects and aims; thus a constraint put upon impulse, desire, passion—pertaining to the particular individual as such—a limitation of caprice and self-will is regarded as a fettering of Freedom. We should on the contrary look upon such limitation as the indispensable proviso of emancipation. Society and the State are the very conditions in which Freedom is realized.[76]

As a consequence, Hegel viewed as most free those individuals whose wills coincided most perfectly with the goals of the state, who identified themselves most completely with the larger life of their nations, and did so without hesitation and without tension. Of this relationship he said:

> The State, its laws, its arrangements, constitute the rights of its members; its natural features, its mountains, air, and waters are *their* country, their fatherland, their outward material property; the history of this State *their* deeds; what their ancesors have produced, belongs to them and lives in their memory. All is their possession, just as they are possessed by it; for it constitutes their existence, their being.[77]

This identification of the individual's fundamental nature with the existence and nature of the society to which he belongs constitutes an expression of what I have designated as organicism. However, up to this point we have only been concerned with tracing the way in which some of Hegel's more general philosophic principles led him to adopt that position. Now, in conformity with our earlier suggestion, we shall direct our attention to the more empirically oriented aspects of his social analysis.

It cannot be doubted that Hegel's theory of societies was based on a rich historical background. Of all major philosophers (for I should not be inclined to include Vico in that group), Hegel was the first whose thought was in large measure formed by a study of the history of culture. It is therefore not surprising that throughout his work he analyzed the fundamental forms of human experience as elements in cultural history, and not at all in terms of how particular individuals acquired their skills, their knowledge, and their attitudes. One sees this most clearly in the structure of the *Phenomenology of Mind*. There, in spite of the fact that the work purports to trace the growth of the forms of experience, Hegel did not regard it as necessary to offer explanations of development which took into account the nature of the specific conditions by which individuals were confronted at particular times in their lives. What rendered any such accounts unnecessary was Hegel's assumption that the history of the individual's forms of consciousness would be identical with the history of the forms of consciousness

in the race.[78] Thus, individuals existing at any stage of man's historical development would represent in their own psyches an inheritance drawn from the whole
human past; the stage of thought and of feeling which they would have attained
would be precisely the stage of development that their own culture had achieved.[79]
Thus, Hegel could affirm the unity of the individual and his time, holding that
each person is "the Son of his Nation . . . the Son of his Age,"[80] "a child of his own
time" who cannot possibly "overleap his own age."[81]

The form which this doctrine took in the thought of Hegel should not be
identified with that which was most characteristic of his predecessors and contemporaries. Among them, many tended to look upon the unity of a people or of
an age as a spontaneous expression of feeling; it cannot be said that, in general,
this was Hegel's view.[82] Although he laid no less stress than did Herder upon the
unity of thought and feeling existing within any state at the height of its vital
powers, he regarded such a unity as dependent upon the nature of the institutions
which the people had developed in the course of their history. As one can see in
the concrete analyses contained in Hegel's *Philosophy of History* (as distinct from
the more familiar, theoretically oriented introduction to that work), the unity and
the spirit of a people is grounded in the specific nature of their social institutions,
and in particular in the structure of the state as that is embodied in a constitution.
When one takes note of this fact, Hegel's social philosophy can be viewed as a
form of empirical social theory, and the resemblances between his organicism and
the explicitly formulated sociological theories of Comte and of Marx no longer
remain mysterious.

Like others who upheld organicism, Hegel insisted that any society—even if it
were only a civil society, but more especially if it were a true state—had to be
construed as an entity in its own right. We have noted that in his metaphysical
analysis of the social nature of individuals he had grounds on which to base such
a conclusion, but he seems also to have relied upon the fact that if one is to hold
that a society influences individuals, then one cannot say that only individuals
are real, and the state and its institutions are not.[83] However, even though a
society must be an entity in its own right, Hegel did not suggest that it existed as
a bare external reality, independently of the activities, and the wills of persons:
without the relationships into which persons entered, and the mutuality of their
wills, no social activities whatsoever could exist. The means by which Hegel attempted to resolve this apparent antinomy, to which he had called attention in
the *Phenomenology of Mind*, becomes more clearly articulated in his later
works.[84] In them it becomes apparent that the world of culture, that is the realm
of the objective spirit, has a reality which is independent of the desires of all
particular individuals, even though it depends upon the interactions among their
wills. If a simile which is not alien to some of Hegel's own similes may be used,
the world of culture—i.e., of objective spirit—is like an organism, having
tendencies and goals of its own, different from the tendencies and goals of the
nuclear cells out of which it may have been generated. Using this simile, we may
point out that, when we refer to the various *"members"* of an organism, we are
inclined to think of its organized, differentiated organs—its heart, lungs, eyes,

limbs, etc.—not of its cells, nor of the ultimate chemical constituents of which it is composed; so, too, the true *members* of any state are to be sought in its institutions, not in the individual persons on whose activities its existence may be said ultimately to depend. That this was in fact Hegel's view, the following discussion will attempt to make clear.

Hegel repeatedly referred to the state as an organism, and in one of his most explicit comparisons between it and physical organisms he said:

> The fundamental characteristic of the state as a political entity is the substantial unity, i.e., the ideality, of its moments. . . . Much the same thing as this ideality of the moments in the state occurs with life in the physical organism. Life is present in every cell. There is only one life in all the cells and nothing withstands it. Separated from that life every cell dies. This is the same as the ideality of every single class, power, and Corporation.[85]

In this passage it should be clear that the *members*, whose unity within the state Hegel wished to stress, are not individuals, but institutional structures. Should this be doubted on the ground that Hegel here refers to "moments," not to "members," another passage can be cited:

> The patriotic sentiment acquires its specifically determined content from the various members of the organism of the state. . . . These different members are the various powers of the state with their functions and spheres of action.[86]

Furthermore, throughout the *Philosophy of History*, in those discussions in which Hegel emphasizes the organic unity of the nation state, it is upon the organic connections among its cultural achievements and its institutional structures that he places emphasis, and not (in the first instance) upon a common spirit which animates the individuals who share in the life of the nation state. In fact, when one considers the role of individuals in the dynamics of historical change, one finds that Hegel did *not* emphasize their bonds of unity with one another, nor the harmony of their wills with the goals which were destined to be realized by the nation states to which they belonged. On the contrary, it was "the cunning of Reason" to use the discordant passions and private interests of individuals to accomplish larger designs, of which they remained in ignorance.[87] Such designs were the goals achieved by nation states:

> Thus, the passions of men are gratified; they develop themselves and their aims in accordance with their natural tendencies, and build up the edifice of human society. . . . They gratify their own interest; but something further is thereby accomplished, latent in the actions in question, though not present to their consciousness, and not included in their design.[88]

In the midst of this passage, there appears Hegel's famous aphorism: the individuals have fortified "a position for Right and Order *against themselves*."[89]

The fact that Hegel conceived of social wholes as systems of institutions, rather than as groups of individuals acting in consort, is the first of the two features of his empirical social theory to which it is here important to call attention. The second consists in the fact that he conceived of all of these institutions as being organically related to one another, forming a single interdependent whole. "A State," he said, "is an individual totality, of which you cannot select any particular side, although a supremely important one, such as its political constitution; and deliberate and decide respecting it in that isolated form."[90] This he conceived to be true because he saw the State as "the basis and centre of the other concrete elements of the life of a people—of Art, of Law, of Morals, of Religion, of Science."[91]

Once having accepted this doctrine, affirming that all aspects of cultural life form a single organic whole, we once again come to a point where "organicism," taken as a form of sociological theory, makes contact with what is to be designated as "organicism" with reference to the doctrine of man's malleability. Having accepted organicism in sociological theory, Hegel's other assumptions made it impossible for him to suppose that there were any characteristics of individual human beings which were not to be accounted for in terms of the societies to which they belonged. This follows from the fact that Hegel did not believe it possible to consider specific capacities in abstraction from the concrete forms in which they manifested themselves; for example, he rejected the possibility of investigating modes of thought in abstraction from that which was thought, or seeking to isolate the essential nature of, say, art in abstraction from the actual history of the arts. Such attempts would involve appeals to a false form of generalization which depended upon abstracting common traits rather than grasping concrete universals; they would be merely formal, representing an attempt to deal with form in total abstraction from content. These possibilities were rejected out of hand by Hegel at every point in his system. As a consequence, one could not understand what constituted, say, art or religion or morality apart from their concrete historical manifestations. And since we have now seen that all elements within a culture are mutually related in a single whole, which constitutes the spiritual life of the nation state, it follows that to understand any form of an individual's activity one must view that activity in terms of the culture of his age. However, as we also know, Hegel held that each nation and age represents a different and essentially unique development of spirit:

Every step in the process, as differing from any other, has its determinate peculiar principle. In history this principle is idiosyncrasy of Spirit [Bestimmtheit des Geistes]— peculiar National Genius. It is within the limitations of this idiosyncrasy that the spirit of the nation, concretely manifested, expresses every aspect of its consciousness and will—the whole cycle of its realization. Its religion, its polity, its ethics, its legislation, and even its science, art, and mechanical skill, all bear its stamp.[92]

As a consequence, the very nature of man changes as the World-Spirit develops, and in order to understand men at one time or another one must place them in their appropriate historical contexts, viewing them in terms of their place in a larger process of spiritual development. Thus, Hegel's organicism and his historicism merged with one another; individual human nature, no less than our standards of value for any cultural activity, came to be looked upon merely as moments in a single pattern of development embracing the history of culture as a whole.

4. MARX

Turning our attention from Hegel to Marx, we find the same conviction that man's nature does not remain constant over time, but changes with the basic ways in which societies change. To be sure, in Marx's earliest relevant writings, the *Economic and Philosophic Manuscripts of 1844,* an attempt was made to depict the essential nature of man. However, as I have already suggested,[93] at that point in his intellectual development Marx's conception of human nature was closely linked to Feuerbach's views; consequently, he conceived of man's social nature in terms of direct interpersonal relationships, and not as reflecting the changing forms of social organization under which men's lives were lived in different historical epochs. In these manuscripts, for example, he held that if one contrasted "Society" with individuals, one was dealing with an abstraction only;[94] furthermore, when he praised Feuerbach's materialism, he attributed its correctness to the fact that its basic principle was taken to be the social relationship of "man to man."[95] While this type of interpretation of man's social relationships sometimes reappears in Marx's later works, it only does so in connection with his discussions of a stage of human existence in which alienation has been overcome.[96] In discussing the relationships among men under the historical conditions which actually obtained under different systems of production and different relationships of production, he assuredly did *not* hold that human nature expresses its essence in direct interpersonal relationships, and that social institutions are merely abstractions which rest on these relationships. In fact, as one sees in the sixth and the seventh of his *Theses on Feuerbach,* Marx explicitly rejected Feuerbach's attempt to understand man's nature in terms of generic traits: the concrete natures of human beings were to be understood in terms of actually existing social structures.[97] These two highly relevant criticisms of Feuerbach (which, I should say, are also criticisms of Marx's own earlier views), are stated as follows:

THESIS VI

Feuerbach resolves the religious essence into the human. But the essence of man is not an abstraction residing in each single individual. In its reality it is the whole of social relationships.

Feuerbach, who does not enter upon the criticism of this real essence, is consequently compelled:

(1) To abstract from the historical process and to fixate the religious feeling as something self-contained, and to presuppose an abstract—*isolated*—human individual.

(2) To conceive the essence of man only as "the species," as an inner, inarticulate, *natural* tie, binding many individuals together.

THESIS VII

Feuerbach does not therefore see that "the religious feeling" is itself a *social product,* and that the abstract individual whom he analyzes belongs in reality to a specific form of society.[98]

That these theses did constitute an essential change in Marx's point of view is at least suggested by Engels's retrospective statement·

The step which Feuerbach did not take nevertheless had to be taken. The cult of abstract man which formed the kernel of Feuerbach's new religion had to be replaced by the science of real men and of their historical development.[99]

It was precisely this step which, together, Marx and Engels took in the first section of *German Ideology* in which they set themselves in full opposition to Feuerbach.[100]

The view of man which is boldly stated in the *German Ideology* starts from the fact that, while man's original nature undoubtedly depended upon his bodily organization and on the conditions obtaining in his original environment, what those conditions had been is not known to us; what we do know is that men differ from animals in producing their means of subsistence.[101] Marx and Engels immediately point out that, in producing the means of their subsistence, men not only provide for their physical survival, but create their own form of existence: they enter into specific forms of activity, creating a way of life, and it is this way of life which makes individuals what they are.[102]

After very briefly sketching a history of the forms of organization of social life in terms which refer primarily to the division of labor and to property relations, Marx and Engels return to a discussion of the effects of these forms of organization on individuals. Once again they insist that the characteristics of individuals always depend upon the material conditions under which they produce the means of their subsistence, and these conditions, which are independent of their wills, provide the basic preconditions for all of their activities.[103] That *all* activities are to be included, and not merely those relating to man's material existence, becomes immediately clear, for Marx and Engels continue:

The production of ideas, of conceptions, of consciousness, is at first directly interwoven with the material activity and the material intercourse of men, the language of real life. Conceiving, thinking, the mental intercourse of men, appear at this stage as the direct efflux of their material behavior. The same applies to mental production as expressed in the language of the politics, laws, morality, religion, metaphysics of a people. Men are producers of their conceptions, ideas, etc. . . .
In direct contrast to German philosophy which descends from heaven to earth, here we ascend from earth to heaven. . . . We set out from real, active men, and on the basis of their real life-process we demonstrate the development of the ideological reflexes and echoes of this life-process. The phantoms formed in the human brain are also, necessarily, sublimates of their material life-process, which is empirically verifiable and bound to material premises. Morality, religion, metaphysics, all the rest of ideology and their corresponding forms of consciousness, thus no longer retain the semblance of independence. They have no history, no development; but men, developing their material production and their material intercourse, alter, along with this their real existence, their thinking and the products of their thinking. Life is not determined by consciousness, but consciousness by life.[104]

From this it immediately follows that there could not be a single and unchanging essence of the human species, the same in all existing individuals, as Marx—like Feuerbach—had previously assumed; in fact, Marx and Engels explicitly reject that possibility.[105] Instead, all phases of the life of an individual—even his relationships to nature—were claimed by them to be reflections of the forms of his social existence.[106] In fact, Marx and Engels held that what previous philosophers had attempted to identify as man's inherent nature (*das Wesen des Menschen*) was simply the sum of those productive forces and social relations which constitute the social inheritance of any specific generation.[107]

One can document the same beliefs in Marx's *Poverty of Philosophy*, which was published shortly after the *German Ideology* had been written, as well as in all of the other subsequent works of both Marx and Engels.[108] However, in writings postdating the *German Ideology*, some shift of emphasis in Marx's thought can be traced. The earlier manner in which he and Engels had formulated their position had been dominated by their relationships to Feuerbach and to Hegel, and their questions about man tended to be posed in terms of those issues which, today, are most likely to be discussed under the rubric of "philosophical anthropology." Such questions are, for example, likely to be concerned with man's essential nature or the nature of human consciousness, taking that term as designating the forms according to which men grasp themselves and their world. On the other hand, in the *Poverty of Philosophy*, and in Marx's subsequent works, much greater emphasis was placed on problems which may be said to belong either to the sociology of knowledge (on the development of which Marx had, of course, a preponderating influence), or which apply sociological analyses to other aspects of culture. Thus, for example, in his Second Observation on Proudhon, Marx insisted that the categories of explanation which are used in economics reflect existing social relations, and thus depend upon forms of production.[109] Similarly, in the *Communist Manifesto* there is an attempt to unmask the pretensions to objectivity on the part of the bourgeoisie:

> Your very ideas are but the outgrowth of the conditions of your bourgeois production and bourgeois property, just as your jurisprudence is but the will of your class made into a law for all, a will whose essential character and direction are determined by the economic conditions of existence of your class.
> The selfish misconception that induces you to transform into eternal laws of nature and of reason, the social forms springing from your present mode of production and form of property—historical relations that rise and disappear in the progress of production—this misconception you share with every ruling class that has preceded you. What you see clearly in the case of ancient property, what you admit in the case of feudal property, you are of course forbidden to admit in the case of your own bourgeois form of property.[110]

The implications of such a view for a theory of human nature should be obvious: the thought of individuals, as well as their motivation, is not to be regarded as due to their inherited potentialities and the particular situations in which they are placed: the categories in terms of which they see the world, and the forms of their responses, are dictated by the organization of the society into which they are born. While it is easy to accept such a thesis if it is put forward in an attenuated form, merely holding that every individual is to some degree influenced by the structures of his society and the place that he occupies in that structure, Marx's views cannot readily be interpreted in this fashion. Instead, one must see his views as representing a full-fledged organicism which rejects the possibility of there being a truly general science of psychology, explaining the nature of individual modes of thought and of action through an appeal to the formative powers of social institutions. To understand the radical form in which Marx held such a doctrine, one must examine two aspects of his thought: one philosophical, the other sociological.

The philosophical aspect can be dealt with very briefly. We have already seen that in the *German Ideology* Marx and Engels had claimed that even the manner in which man becomes conscious of his natural environment is a social product, depending upon his relationships with others. This doctrine can, of course, be connected with Feuerbach's views,[111] but it bears an even closer resemblance to the position of Hegel in the *Phenomenology of Mind*: "Individuality is what its world, in the sense of its own world, is."[112] Given this view, the self and its world are not two independent forms of existence, but interpenetrate; and this interpenetration is stressed even more by Marx than it had been by Hegel, because of the Marxian emphasis on *praxis*. As is clear in his *Theses on Feuerbach*, Marx regarded knowledge as an activity in which subject and object were reciprocally transformed; in no case was knowing to be regarded as a disengaged, contemplative relationship.[113] Consequently, all human knowledge will reflect the individual's practical activities, but the world in which men have their concrete existence is always a socially structured world. Thus, it follows necessarily (on the Marxian view) that thought can never be divorced from social structure. Granted this view, the analysis of thought, and of all forms of motivation, will involve an analysis of social structure, and it is therefore to the basic principles of Marx's sociology that we must turn.

There are many alternative ways in which one can proceed in delineating Marx's sociological theories, and I do not wish to claim that those features which I shall now discuss represent the most basic features, nor that the order to be followed is an order representing logical priorities. On the contrary, I am only concerned to develop as much of Marx's sociology as is necessary to understand his views regarding the malleability of human nature under the conditions which have obtained in organized societies during that portion of man's past which is historically accessible, and with which Marx himself sought to deal.

Like Comte and Hegel, Marx believed that each society forms a single, unitary system, the genuine parts of which are its concrete social structures, not the human individuals whose activities enter into and sustain that system. That Marx rejected the view that one could understand societies in terms of the interactions among individuals is clear throughout his works, but it is never more clearly expressed than in those passages in which he separates his social thought from that of earlier political economists who attempted to analyze social relations in terms of individual behavior, and who sometimes went so far as to employ Robinson

Crusoe analogies in their analyses. In the original (but unused) preface to his
Critique of Political Economy, Marx pointed out that an appeal to individuals
pursuing their individual interests cannot possibly serve as a means of understanding the basic forms of social organization, for the pursuit of purely individual interests reflects a form of social life that only came into existence with
the bourgeois revolution. Thus, instead of serving as the basis for a historical
derivation of social organization, the image of primitive hunters and fishermen
attempting to satisfy their own individual needs involves a thoroughly distorted
projection of the historically conditioned nature of contemporary man onto a
remote past.[114] In fact, as Marx remarked, the farther back one goes in history the
less independent individuals appear to be, and the less society appears to be a
means of satisfying private interests.[115] Therefore, if one is to understand communities, one must start from the communities themselves, not from the assumed
nature of individual persons existing outside of particular communities. Furthermore, Marx immediately insisted that one cannot start with abstractions which
concern the conditions of social life *in general*. While it is undoubtedly true that
all communities have certain characteristics in common, he did not consider it
fruitful to speak of these characteristics in wholly general terms: one must always
refer to the particular forms which these characteristics assumed in specific
societies.[116] It was this that defined his historical, institutional approach to all
problems in sociological theory.

In connection with that approach it is also crucial to bear in mind that Marx
held that all institutions in any society tended to form a single, unitary whole.
This view was implicit in his doctrine that the productive forces of any society
provide the foundations of all other phases of its activities. In the preface to his
Critique of Political Economy he put forward this doctrine of substructure and
superstructure in a classic form:

> The sum total of these relations of production constitutes the economic structure of
> society—the real foundation, on which rise legal and political superstructures and to
> which correspond definite forms of social consciousness. The mode of production in
> material life determines the general character of the social, political, and spiritual
> processes of life.[117]

Furthermore, it must be borne in mind that Marx always held that "the production relations of every society form a whole."[118] And, in the latter connection, one
may also note Marx's insistence that "no social order ever disappears before all
the productive forces, for which there is room in it, have been developed; and
new higher relations of production never appear before the material conditions
for their existence have matured in the womb of the old society."[119] This doctrine
presupposes a coherence and internality of relationship among all the forces of
production within a society, and taken in connection with Marx's doctrine of the
relationship between the forces of production and the superstructure, it offers a
view of the essential unity within a society which is strikingly similar to the positions put forward by Hegel and by Comte. To be sure, Marx stressed the conflicts
and tensions within societies to a far greater extent than even Hegel had done.

However, his analysis of the accumulation of the strains introduced by new productive forces coming into conflict with previously existing relations of production, and the manner in which these changes affect the political, legal, and ideological superstructure, obviously presupposed that every society is a single, unitary whole: the strains which build up cannot be confined to any one part of the social organism, but spread through all of its structures.[120] As a consequence, there was no possibility of regarding the various elements in the superstructure as autonomous elements which depended upon how the individuals within any given society responded to the particular intellectual and moral situations which they faced. And, therefore, Marx was committed to holding that the forms of thought and of action were always, and under all circumstances, time-bound; that, as he phrased it,

> The same men who establish their social relations in conformity with their material productivity, produce also principles, ideas and categories, in conformity with their social relations.
>
> Thus these ideas, these categories, are as little eternal as the relations they express. They are *historical and transitory products*.[121]

Given this position, it is small wonder that Marx's thought turned to what we, today, should refer to as the sociology of knowledge, and that for him—as for others since his time—the sociology of knowledge was taken to be a substitute for a psychological investigation of the foundations of knowledge and of action. Like Hegel, and like Comte, the organicism to which he subscribed merged with his historicism; as a consequence, his attempts to understand thought and behavior were couched in terms of a schema of social development, rather than in terms of any general principles of psychological explanation. We shall later be concerned with the weakness of this approach.

11

MAN AS A PROGRESSIVE BEING

*Il me semble que le premier fait qui soit
compris dans le mot* civilisation . . . *c'est le
fait de progrès, de développement; il réveille
aussitôt l'idée d'un peuple qui marche, non
pour changer de place, mais pour changer d'état;
d'un peuple dont la condition s'étend et
s'améliore. L'idée du progrès, du développement,
me parait être l'idée fondamentale contenue
sous le mot de civilisation.*[1]

François P. Guizot

In the history of the doctrine of human malleability we have traced representative forms of two different, fundamentally opposed doctrines, geneticism and
organicism, each of which stressed the formative influence which men's environments have on their natures. However, in the period with which we are concerned,
there were also those who espoused the doctrine of man's malleability, but were
opposed to its predominantly environmentalist forms. Some among them, as we
have noted, stressed man's inherent tendency toward self-fulfilment which, they
believed, would manifest itself naturally, and ever more completely. This was a
form of self-realizationism which we shall discuss in terms of the thought of
Fichte and, among others, of Thomas Hill Green. However, if I am not mistaken,
a more frequently exemplified view of the progressive nature of man was less
antagonistic to geneticism, was explicitly hedonistic, and was not connected with
the metaphysics of idealism. John Stuart Mill was the chief theoretical exponent
of this position which, in slightly varying forms, was widely shared. It was
characteristic of this view to hold that, through the development of forms of
sensibility higher than those which were natural to man in an uneducated and
undeveloped state, human nature had acquired new capacities, and had undergone radical transformations with respect to the old. According to Mill, Arnold,
and Huxley, such changes had not been accidental, nor were they brought about
primarily through external forces: they had been, and were, dependent upon the
efforts of men.

In addition to these forms of progressivist doctrine there was, as we have noted,
a third form which derived directly from evolutionary theory in biology. Since it
arose later, discussion of it will come last. In terms of chronology, it would be
equally appropriate to begin with a discussion of either the self-fulfilment doctrine or the doctrine typified by Mill. However, since the background for a discussion of Mill has already been provided by my discussion of geneticism, and by
our having seen the reasons why he rejected the atomistic view of society which

had characterized the thought of Bentham and of his father (and since, indeed, the very title of this chapter is drawn from Mill)[2] I shall commence my discussion with an account of his views, and of other views related to it.

1. IDEALS OF A BETTER SELF: MILL, ARNOLD, AND HUXLEY

In many ways, as we shall see, Mill represents a continuation of the thought of the Enlightenment, even though his rebellion against the position of Bentham and his father allied him with an important group of its foes. In considering both aspects of his doctrine, it must be remembered that, when we traced the influence on his thought of those whom he termed "the Germano-Coleridgians," our attention was confined to two quite specific points: first, his recognition of the need for a concrete-historical rather than a psychological-deductive approach to history and government; and, second, his recognition of the fact that the views of human nature accepted by Bentham and his father placed too little emphasis on feelings and on the imagination.[3] Both of these points, as we shall soon see, had an important influence on his views regarding human nature. However, these departures from orthodoxy should not be taken as signs that, in other respects, he had abandoned the position of Bentham and of his father. For example, throughout his life, he continued to accept their associationism, not only as a basic doctrine in psychology, but as a foundation for his theory of knowledge. In this connection we may note that, before going on to praise other aspects of Coleridge's thought, Mill explicitly rejected the nativism which characterized his theory of knowledge.[4] Similarly, it is not possible to conceive of Mill as accepting the "Coleridgian" view of moral notions, which (for example) was stated by F. D. Maurice when he held that "in the human mind [there is] a simple and primary idea of the distinction between right and wrong, not produced by experience, but developing itself in proportion to the growth of the mind."[5] In contradistinction to this view, Mill always adhered to the Benthamite principle of utility, even though he modified Bentham's own application of that principle in many important ways.[6] With respect to both his theory of knowledge and his moral theory, one may, then, in general, say that he remained within the tradition of geneticism no less than Bentham and his father had done, yet he so altered the earlier forms of that doctrine that it yielded a quite different picture of the nature of man. In order to understand how this could be the case, we must examine (however briefly) the changes which he introduced in the psychological assumptions of Bentham, and the ways in which he altered, or at least stretched, the system embodied in his father's *Analysis of the Phenomena of the Human Mind*.[7]

In spite of Mill's very great admiration for Bentham's accomplishments, in his essay entitled "Bentham" he severely criticized the limitations of Bentham's temperament, particularly his lack of sympathy for positions and for types of character which were divergent from his own.[8] What has unfortunately been far too little known is that Mill had written another, earlier, anonymously published article on Bentham in which similar and even more damaging remarks were made, but in which those remarks were related to the differences between Bentham's psychological theory and Mill's own psychological views.[9]

Whereas Bentham had supposed that men's actions are always directed toward achieving some future pleasure, or avoiding some future pain, it was Mill's position that men always act in accordance with the pleasantness or unpleasantness of their *present* ideas, whatever these ideas may be. Consequently, unlike Bentham, Mill did not hold that men were always acting under the guidance of what they took to be their self-interest; motives such as patriotism, or benevolence, or a sense of virtue, were no less effective sources of action than was a desire for some future pleasure for one's self. For example, on Mill's view, the only prerequisite necessary for patriotism to serve as an autonomous motive was that the course of action denominated by that name should, through past experience, have become an idea having a positive affective tone (i.e., that it should have become a pleasant present idea), or that lack of patriotism should have become an idea having a strong negative affective tone (i.e., that it should have become positively distasteful).[10] This modification of Bentham's doctrine, which had stressed self-interest, led Mill to say:

> The attempt to enumerate motives, that is, human desires and aversions, seems to me to be in its very conception an error. Motives are innumerable: there is nothing whatever which may not become an object of desire or of dislike by association.[11]

And in one of his extensive notes to his father's *Analysis of the Phenomena of the Human Mind*, Mill said (with perhaps too great praise of the subsections in question):

> The two preceding subsections are almost perfect as expositions and exemplifications of the mode in which, by the natural course of life, we acquire attachments to persons, things, and positions, which are the causes or habitual concomitants of pleasurable sensations in us, or of relief from pains: in other words, those persons, things, and positions become in themselves pleasant to us by association; and, through the multitude and variety of the pleasurable ideas associated with them, become pleasures of greater constancy and even intensity, and altogether more valuable to us, than any of the primitive pleasures of our constitutions.[12]

This doctrine, which holds that what was originally a means to pleasure can become an object desired for itself alone, is an instance of what is now often referred to as "functional autonomy." It was this doctrine (in a hedonistic form) which Mill immediately applied to moral questions; for example, he did so in *Utilitarianism*, where he accounted for the miser's love of money in these terms, seeking thereby to show how our conception of virtue, while ultimately founded on its association with good consequences, can become an end desired for its own sake.[13] However, his application of this doctrine to questions of moral theory need not here concern us. What is important to note is that this psychological doctrine allows for the self-transformation of man: what was originally dominant in the individual's nature becomes transformed by association, and may in fact altogether cease to be dominant as an operative force in that individual's life.

I speak of this as a *self-transformation* of man's nature, but critics of Mill, and of associationism, might point out that, in a strict sense, it is not the individual who transforms himself: he has *become transformed* through the effects of his experience. In short, it might be claimed that the power of remaking the self does not, even on John Stuart Mill's view, lie within the individual; it is a power external to him. Mill explicitly sought to refute this type of allegation in his chapter on "Liberty and Necessity," in Book VI of his *System of Logic*. Whether that argument had the probative force which he assigned to it, I am inclined to doubt; but those doubts, even if justified, are not of crucial importance in the present context. What is important to note is that whether or not any given individual is in a position to change his individual nature, it is assuredly the case that Mill's psychological theory did allow him to hold that human nature does change over the course of time, and that the source of change lies in the actions of men. In any generation, the effects of human action will lead to changes not only in the external conditions of life, but can lead to changes in the *motives* of men in the following generation. Because of these accumulating effects, we may say that it is men who are primarily responsible for what man has become.

This position marked a departure from those earlier views of associationism with which we were previously concerned; among earlier associationists there was no belief that during the course of history man's fundamental motivation could change. Not only were the laws of association held to be constant (as, of course, John Stuart Mill also believed); but each individual had been looked upon in terms of his own experience, and the cumulative effects of the past history of the race tended to be left wholly out of account.[14] In contradistinction to this view, Mill's doctrine of the emergence of new, autonomous motives permitted him to regard history as effecting incremental changes in human nature over successive generations.[15] The mechanism for such changes should be obvious. Forms of conduct which were originally associated with beneficial social consequences would, as we have seen, come to be prized for their own sakes. These evaluations would not have had to be learned anew by each generation on the basis of its own experience of what promoted social well-being; such evaluations would have been a natural and indeed an inescapable part of the education of successive generations. A failure to conform to modes of behavior which had come to be prized would, in some cases, be punished by external sanctions; in all cases, however, the internal sanctions of feeling would have become attached to an avoidance of that which was rejected by others, satisfaction being felt in acting in a socially approved way.[16] Consequently, only a clear recognition that some forms of approved conduct are in fact disadvantageous to society will serve to undermine the authority which derives from their original utility. While Mill did believe that, in some cases, people had become accustomed to accept modes of conduct which had a definite disutility, he had faith that whenever such a disparity between established beliefs and actual utility arose, the exigency of facts and the application of intelligence would force the revision of those beliefs which had lost their original utility.[17] On the other hand, forms of conduct which served to promote happiness would continue to be prized for their own sakes. Thus, Mill's psychology provided him with warrant for his faith in the gradual improvement of human nature.

The form of this improvement was, on Mill's view, primarily a matter of the cultivation of more complex—and, as he often said, *higher* and *nobler*—forms of feeling. To be sure, he held that knowledge also inevitably advanced with experience, but he did not hold that, in itself, knowledge transformed human nature; it was only an instrument by means of which deleterious modes of action could be cleared away, and by which improved social relationships could be discovered and translated into action, giving rise to further improvements.[18] What directly transformed human nature was the manner in which experience affected the sensibilities of men. It increased the depth and the range of their social feelings, making them more sensitive to the rights and the welfare of others, thereby causing that welfare to be a matter of immediate personal concern; and, in addition, it opened to them, for their own immediate pleasure, the more cultivated and complex forms of enjoyment of civilized men.

As we shall very soon see, doctrines of a similar sort were to be found in thinkers as different from one another as Matthew Arnold and Thomas Henry Huxley. However, before withdrawing our attention from Mill, it is necessary to note that his theoretical interests and his practical-reformist interests (which were never wholly unconnected) led him to attempt to establish a new science whose generalizations would throw light on the formation of character under specific types of circumstances. This science, which was to deal with the character both of individuals and of nations, Mill termed "ethology."[19]

According to Mill's usage, ethology was to be distinguished from Psychology, in that the latter dealt with the basic laws of the mind, whereas the former traced the effects of these laws in complex sets of circumstances. While Mill believed that it was in many cases already possible to deduce from the general laws of Psychology what the effects of particular sets of circumstances on the formation of character would usually be, he held that it was necessary to establish "middle principles"—the principles of ethology—if one were to understand "the origin and sources of all those qualities in human beings which are interesting to us, either as facts to be produced, to be avoided, or merely to be understood."[20] His own interest in this field of inquiry had already been made clear in his early essay *The Spirit of the Age*, and a recognition of its importance had been implicit in his criticism of the ahistorical assumptions of Bentham and his father with respect to the theory of government. We may also note that even though he believed that the methods of "political economy" did not rest on a consideration of ethology, but on the principle that "a greater gain is preferred to a smaller,"[21] he was aware of dangers in assuming that such laws held universally, regardless of the character of the people concerned.[22] In fact, throughout his discussion of the social sciences, we see the importance which he attached to the still undeveloped science which he termed "political ethology," that is, "the theory of the causes which determine the type of character belonging to a people or to an age."[23] Of this study he said:

To whoever well considers the matter, it must appear that the laws of national (or collective) character are by far the most important class of sociological laws. In the first place, the character which is formed by any state of social circumstances is in itself the most interesting phenomenon which that state of society can possibly present. Secondly, it is also a fact which enters largely into the production of all other phenomena. And, above all, the character, that is, the opinions, feelings, and habits of the people, though greatly the results of the state of society which precedes them, are also greatly the causes of the state of society which follows them; and are the power by which all those of the circumstances of society which are artificial—laws and customs, for instance—are altogether moulded.[24]

As a result of this conviction, Mill held that a study of the principles of education as applied to social groups constituted the basis for the fullest understanding of history, and provided enlightenment as to those conditions which would best promote the future well-being of Humanity.

It is at this point that one can see that, in spite of Comte's great influence on Mill's philosophy of the social sciences, their views involved diametrically opposed assumptions. Ethology rested upon "psychology" according to Mill; and psychology therefore remained the fundamental social science. As Mill said,

> The succession of states of the human mind and of human society cannot have an independent law of its own; it must depend on the psychological and ethological laws which govern the action of circumstances on men and of men on circumstances.[25]

For Comte, on the contrary, psychology was not an independent science, and the laws of sociology were not in any sense derivative from laws of other sciences. Furthermore, Mill clearly believed that men *could* change their circumstances, and that they could do so deliberately through the powerful tool of education, for it was his belief that "the power of education is almost boundless."[26] As he said in *The Subjection of Women,*

> Of all difficulties which impede the progress of thought, and the formation of well-grounded opinions on life and social arrangements, the greatest is now the unspeakable ignorance and inattention of mankind in respect to the influences which form human character. Whatever any portion of the human species now are, or seem to be, such, it is supposed, they have a natural tendency to be. . . . History, which is now better understood than formerly, teaches another lesson: if only by showing the extraordinary susceptibility of human nature to external influences, and the extreme variableness of those of its manifestations which are supposed to be most universal and uniform.[27]

It was Mill's view that the dominant thought of his own age neglected this fact, and accepted nativism. He attributed this to a failure to pursue an analytical account of the principles of psychology, and believed that this failure was linked to a reaction against the philosophy of the eighteenth century.[28] In his criticism of this aspect of the thought of his age he included not only those who, like the Coleridgians, had come under the influence of German metaphysics, but also Comte, since Comte believed that human nature (and also present differences between the psychological natures of men and of women) was determined by physiological laws. In looking back on the eighteenth century as a time in which the malleability of man was recognized, Mill of course had the traditions of geneticism in mind. While his own doctrine of malleability was, as we have seen, more far-reaching than those of his predecessors, in this respect he represented a continuation of views which had been characteristic of eighteenth-century thought.

With respect to his belief that men could transform their own natures through the application of intelligence, and through the education of the individual, he was also closer to the traditions of the eighteenth century than he was to the or- ganicism of Comte, or of Hegel, or of Marx.[29] For example, unlike Comte, Mill did not believe that there were laws of social change which operated in a necessary manner, independently of men's wills. On the contrary, he was convinced that, with knowledge, men could to some extent control their own destinies. However, he did not base his faith in improvement *solely* on knowledge and deliberate design; as we have noted, the very mechanisms by which changes were brought about in men's nature's were not only capable of being changed, but the laws of association made it inevitable that, over time, they would change. In these changes Mill saw a growth in sensitivity to the needs of others as being capable of over- coming the complete dominance of self-interest. He also believed that past history showed an increasing interest in those forms of enjoyment which were related to ideal, rather than to material, ends. So long as these developments continued to bring about greater happiness in men's social life—as Mill had no doubt that they would—it was a principle of psychology, and not just a pious hope, that men would continue to develop their natures toward less selfish, nobler pursuits.

When one reads Mill's strictures on the society of his time in such essays as that entitled "Civilization," or his discussion of "Individuality, as One of the Ele- ments of Well-Being" in *On Liberty*, it does not seem out of the way to associate his views with those of Matthew Arnold.[30] To be sure, in their discussions of the scope of the state's authority, they appear as antagonists, although perhaps less antagonistic than Arnold had supposed.[31] However, when one notes the profound effect of Goethe's ideals on the thought of Arnold, and recalls the extent to which Mill had modified Utilitarianism to accommodate similar ideals, the possibility of a fruitful comparison, rather than a contrast between them, suggests itself.

The comparison which I wish to draw is, of course, primarily a question of their views regarding human nature; of the possibility of regarding man as a progressive being, capable of transforming himself through the cultivation of his capacities for higher forms of sensibility. In this respect, as I shall show, their views were remarkably similar. To be sure, even here one must note points at which Arnold's views were different from those of Mill. For example, he fre- quently spoke as if the national characters of different peoples—a topic in which he, no less than Mill, was profoundly interested—were a function of racial in- heritance, not of institutions and historical experience;[32] and it is not to be overlooked that Arnold specifically characterized Mill's views as a degenerate form of "Hellenism."[33] Nevertheless, once the views of Mill are disentangled from the stereotypes of Utilitarianism (Arnold, unfortunately, was never able to do this), one can see that Mill and Arnold were in basic agreement concerning the goals of life which it was their hope that the reform of contemporary society could achieve. Various of the similarities and differences between their views, as well as

the actual connections existing between them, have been carefully traced by
Edward Alexander in his *Matthew Arnold and John Stuart Mill*.[34] However, the
specific similarity with which we shall here be concerned needs separate documentation. What must be shown is that, in spite of differences in their backgrounds and general philosophic positions (in spite, for example, of the differences
in their positions with respect to religion and with respect to social reform), the
form of Arnold's belief that human nature is capable of undergoing progressive
change is similar to Mill's. What places them in the same stream of thought,
distinguishing them from most other representatives of their age, was the fact that
both held that the basis for human improvement consisted in the cultivation of
human sensibilities, the effects of which are capable of transforming the lives of
individuals and, through them, the lives of the societies to which they belong.

To establish that this was indeed Matthew Arnold's view, one must first
establish that he did truly believe in progress. This point might be doubted on
the basis of some of his best-known poetry; it might also be challenged because
of his high estimate of Greek thought and his criticism of the state of affairs
which he took to be characteristic of his own time. Yet there are numerous points
at which he expressed an unmistakable belief in progress, and he frequently did
so even when he had been serving as a critic of his time. For example, in spite of
his hostility to contemporary middle-class culture, he saw in that class the possibility for progress, if middle-class education were fundamentally changed. In
this connection he said:

> The truth is, the English spirit has to accomplish an immense evolution; nor, as that
> spirit at this moment presents itself in any class or description amongst us, can one be
> perfectly satisfied with it, can one wish it to prevail just as it is.
> But in a transformed middle class, in the middle class raised to a higher and more
> genial culture, we may find, not perhaps Jerusalem, but, I am sure, a notable stage
> towards it. In that great class, strong by its numbers, its energy, its industry, strong by its
> freedom from frivolity, not by any law of nature prone to immobility of mind, actually
> at this moment agitated by a spreading ferment of mind, in that class, liberalized by an
> ampler culture, admitted to a wider sphere of thought, living by larger ideas, with its
> provincialism dissipated, its intolerance cured, its pettiness purged away,—what a power
> there will be, what an element of new life for England![35]

It was his belief that if the middle class could be brought to a higher level of
culture, it could also serve as an influence in transforming the working class. His
sensitivity to the needs of the latter should not be overlooked. In one passage, for
example, he referred to it as

> ...this obscure embryo, only just beginning to move, travailing in labour and darkness,
> so much left out of account when we celebrate the glories of our Atlantis, now and
> then, by so mournful a glimpse, showing itself to us in Lambeth, or Spitalfields, or
> Dorsetshire; this immense working class, now so without a practicable passage to all the
> joy and beauty of life...[36]

And immediately thereafter, addressing an apostrophe to that class, Arnold said:

Children of the future, whose day has not yet dawned, you, when that day arrives, will hardly believe what obstructions were long suffered to prevent its coming! ... You will wonder at the labour of its friends in proving the self-proving; you will know nothing of the doubts, the fears, the prejudices they had to dispel; nothing of the outcry they had to encounter.... But you, in your turn, with difficulties of your own, will then be mounting some new step in the arduous ladder whereby man climbs towards his perfection; towards that unattainable but irresistable lode-star, gazed after with earnest longing, and invoked with bitter tears; the longing of thousands of hearts, the tears of many generations.

In addition to evidence of this sort, and to the many occasions on which Arnold invoked the concept of progress in his criticism of the culture of his own and of other times, there are passages in which he explicitly stated his own progressivist views. Three of these passages may be quoted, although they are perhaps less typical of Arnold, in being more abstractly phrased. In one Arnold said:

Other creatures submissively follow the law of their nature; man alone has an impulse leading him to set up some other law to control the bent of his nature;[37]

and in another he said,

The only absolute and eternal object prescribed to us by God's law, or the divine order of things, is the progress toward perfection,—our own progress towards it and the progress of humanity.[38]

The third passage which I shall cite deals with the difficulty, and yet the possibility, of man's self-transformation. In discussing the need for a fuller development, Arnold said:

If it is said that this is a very hard matter, and that man cannot well do more than one thing at a time, the answer is that here is the very sign and condition of each new stage of spiritual progress,—*increase of task*. The more we grow, the greater is the task which is set us. This is the law of man's nature and of his spirit's history. The powers we have developed at our old task enable us to attempt a new one; and this, again, brings with it a new increase of powers.[39]

Thus, like Mill, he held that it was possible for man to attain powers not originally part of his nature.

It was because Arnold believed that society had faltered in his own time, that the tone of his writings so often seems anti-progressivistic, as compared with the writings of most of his contemporaries. For example, in discussing what he took to be the dominant characteristic of England in his time, he said:

What brings about, or rather tends to bring about, a natural, rational life, satisfying the modern spirit? This: the growth of a love of industry, trade, and wealth; the growth of a love of the things of the mind; and the growth of a love of beautiful things. ... of these three factors of modern life, your middle class has no notion of any but one, the first.[40]

However, this stricture on the material orientation of contemporary middle-class life should not be taken as suggesting disbelief on Arnold's part in the potentiality of his time for progress with respect to culture. He took it as his task—the task of a critic—to develop such potentialities. In his famous essay on "The Function of Criticism," he characterized criticism as a "disinterested endeavor to learn and propagate the best that is known and thought in the world,"[41] and he believed that by this means the limitations of contemporary standards could be, and would be, transformed. He viewed his own era as "an epoch of expansion," and he expressed not only a hope but a faith in the promise of culture, when, for example, he said

> . . . in spite of all that is said about the absorbing and brutalising influence of our passionate material progress, it seems to me indisputable that this progress is likely, though not certain, to lead in the end to an apparition of intellectual life; and that man, after he has made himself perfectly comfortable and has now to determine what to do with himself next, may begin to remember that he has a mind, and that the mind may be a source of great pleasure.[42]

From Arnold's point of view, a too-absorbing concern for material goods, and all that he described as Philistinism, was not the only source of danger to his age, and to its potentialities for progress in thought and in all aspects of culture; he saw at least equally grave dangers in what he designated as "anarchy," that is, a degree of individualism which to him betokened a failure in a concern for the state. However, in *Culture and Anarchy* it is clear that he did not speak as a traditional political conservative; on the contrary he identified himself as a liberal, but as one who did not belong within the then dominant liberal camp. As he said in his introduction to that volume,

> . . . although, like Mr. Bright and Mr. Frederic Harrison, and the editor of the *Daily Telegraph*, and a large body of valued friends of mine, I am a Liberal, yet I am a Liberal tempered by experience, reflection, and renouncement, and I am, above all, a believer in culture.[43]

What he sought was that men should be moved by forces beyond their individual interests and their class interests; that they should be guided by what he termed their best selves, not their ordinary selves; to ask this was to ask that they should be moved by an ideal of the State. One passage may illustrate this view:

> Well, then, what if we tried to rise above the idea of class to the idea of the whole community, *the State*, and to find our centre of light and authority there? Every one of us has the idea of country, as a sentiment; hardly any one of us has the idea of *the State* as a working power. And why? Because we habitually live in our ordinary selves, which do not carry us beyond the ideas and wishes of the class to which we happen to belong. And we are all afraid of giving to the State too much power, because we only conceive of the State as something equivalent to the class in occupation of the executive government, and are afraid of that class abusing power to its own purposes. . . . By our everyday selves . . . we are separate, personal, at war; we are only safe from one another's tyranny when no one has any power; and this safety, in its turn, cannot save us from anarchy . . .

> But by our *best self* we are united, impersonal, at harmony. We are in no peril from giving authority to this, because it is the truest friend we all of us can have; and when anarchy is a danger to us, to this authority we may turn with sure trust. Well, and this is the very self which culture, or the study of perfection, seeks to develop in us. . . . So that our poor culture, which is flouted as so impractical, leads us to the very ideas capable of meeting the great want of our present embarrassed times![44]

All of this may ring hollow, as if Arnold were totally unaware of the immediately pressing, practical needs of his time. It was with this charge that Frederic Harrison taunted him.[45] Nevertheless, we must in fairness note that (as we have seen) Arnold was aware of the existence of a rising new class, the populace, and he did not regard their needs as being adequately satisfied. Part of his ideal was to remove inequalities; he held that to be placed in a position of inferiority, "to be heavily overshadowed, to be profoundly insignificant, has, on the whole, a depressing and benumbing effect on the character."[46] What he advocated was that culture should animate the life of a whole people, that it should not be confined to any one class.[47] For Arnold, culture was not an aristocratic ideal;[48] it was what we should denominate (in the language of ethical theory) as a *universalistic* ideal:

> And because men are all members of one great whole, and the sympathy which is in human nature will not allow one member to be indifferent to the rest or to have a perfect welfare independent of the rest, the expansion of our humanity, to suit the idea of perfection which culture forms, must be a *general* expansion. Perfection, as culture conceives it, is not possible while the individual remains isolated. The individual is required, under pain of being stunted and enfeebled in his own development if he disobeys, to carry others along with him in his march toward perfection, to be continually doing all he can to enlarge and increase the volume of the human stream sweeping thitherward.[49]

This universalism, as well as Arnold's awareness of the handicaps under which the populace suffered—an awareness not diminished by a recognition that the current ideals of the populace were not ideals which he could accept—provides an exact parallel to what is to be found in the social conscience of John Stuart Mill.

An equally exact parallel exists in their conceptions of that nobility of character which is the goal of the individual's progress. In each case, however, it is difficult to specify the exact content of this ideal. In Mill, it was the ability to find happiness in those higher forms of enjoyment which are specifically human, to lead a life in which narrowness and selfishness have no part, and in which virtue comes to be loved for its own sake.[50] Arnold emphasized similar ideals. "Culture," he said, "places human perfection in an *internal* condition, in the growth and predominance of our humanity proper, as distinguished from our own animality. It places it in the ever-increasing efficacy and in the general harmonious expansion of those gifts of thought and feeling, which makes the peculiar dignity, wealth, and happiness of human nature."[51] As part of this personal ideal, Arnold expressed a deep and abiding concern for the social good:

> . . . the impulses towards action, help, and beneficence, the desire for removing human error, clearing human confusion, and diminishing human misery, the noble aspiration

to leave the world better and happier than we found it,—motives eminently such
as are called social,—come in as part of the grounds of culture, and the main and
pre-eminent part.[52]

In such passages, the similarity between Mill's ideal of nobility of character and
Arnold's ideal of culture shows itself to be very close indeed. If one were to seek a
fundamental difference between them, it would arise in Arnold's stress on well-
roundedness, on what is not improperly identified as a Goethean ideal of character. Thus, in speaking of perfection in human character, Arnold said:

> Perfection—as culture from a thorough disinterested study of human nature and
> human experience learns to conceive it—is a harmonious expression of all the powers
> which make the beauty and worth of human nature, and is not consistent with the
> overdevelopment of any one power at the expense of the rest.[53]

It is unlikely that Mill, in spite of his criticism of any tendency to narrowness,
would have placed as much emphasis as did Arnold on the equipotential development of all sides of one's character, for he recognized sources of strength in
strongly marked elements of individuality. However, if the influence of Goethe
with respect to this particular point separated Arnold from Mill, it separated him
no less from those who, like Fichte and T. H. Green, had ideals of character
which were formed on the model of what he termed "Hebraism," in contrast to
"Hellenism." To understand this point, and to take further note of the affinities
between Arnold and Mill, we must briefly examine what Arnold meant by these
terms.

While he sometimes tended to identify Hebraism and Hellenism rather too
closely with the peoples from whom he took these designative names, one must
conceive of the contrast in broader terms, if one is to be faithful to Arnold's
meaning. In general, Hebraism and Hellenism were taken by him to stand for
two different attitudes, or stances, toward the world. To each of these attitudes
there corresponded a different conception of what was intrinsically of greatest
worth. In contrasting them, he said:

> The final aim of both Hellenism and Hebraism, as of all great spiritual disciplines, is
> no doubt the same: man's perfection or salvation. . . . and this aim and end is august
> and admirable.
>   Still, they pursue this aim by very different courses. The uppermost idea with
> Hellenism is to see things as they really are; the uppermost idea with Hebraism is
> conduct and obedience.[54]

While Arnold not infrequently claimed that true perfection must include both
Hebraism and Hellenism,[55] it cannot be doubted that his own sympathies lay
with Hellenism. To be sure, he sometimes justified his strong advocacy of the
latter by citing the fact that Hebraism had been too exclusively dominant in
England for too long a time;[56] however, what would seem to be a more correct
view of his conception of the proper relationship between them was that the attitude represented by Hebraism, the attitude of moral earnestness and effort, had

been—and remained—a necessary element in progress, but that the end which was to be attained by such exertions, the *goal* of progress, was to be a condition of man represented by those attributes of the human spirit which Hellenism, rather than Hebraism, espoused.

That such was Arnold's view tends to be concealed by his initial characterization of Hellenism as "seeing things as they really are," a characterization which may be interpreted in too narrowly an intellectual sense. To offset this tendency one needs to supplement Arnold's initial description by another of his apothegms concerning these two attitudes toward the world: whereas Hebraism represented *strictness of conscience*, Hellenism represented *spontaneity of consciousness*;[57] and spontaneity of consciousness was never, for Arnold, identified with intellectual activity alone. It was in fact identical with culture,[58] in the honorific sense in which Arnold systematically used that term. That there was this connection, and that spontaneity of consciousness (and therefore Hellenism) was the goal to be attained, can be seen in the following passage, in which Hellenism is identified with sweetness and light—in short, with culture:

> To get rid of one's ignorance, to see things as they are, and by seeing them as they are to see them in their beauty, is the simple and attractive ideal which Hellenism holds out before human nature; and from the simplicity and charm of this ideal, Hellenism, and human life in the hands of Hellenism, is invested with a kind of aërial ease, clearness, and radiancy; they are full of what we call sweetness and light.[59]

What Arnold termed "sweetness and light" were the inseparable components of true culture; by sweetness he meant beauty, and light he identified with intellectual grasp. The culture in which they were combined was not conceived by Arnold as a condition in which individuals pursued these interests in isolation from one another, seeking merely the satisfaction of their own taste and their own curiosity; as we have already noted, Arnold's ideal of perfection included a strong universalistic element, "because men are all members of one great whole." Thus, although he conceived of perfection as an individual development—as did Mill— it was an individual development which was neither self-centered nor self-absorbed. The ideal of human perfection, as Arnold said,

> ... is *an inward spiritual activity, having for its characters increased sweetness, increased light, increased life, increased sympathy.*[60]

Between this ideal and Mill's conception of what constitute the most essential elements in human character, there is no radical dissimilarity. At most, one might say that Arnold believed that it was both possible, and in the end necessary, for any one who was to approximate this ideal to combine all of these traits in a balanced harmony; whereas Mill was very much more willing to hold that, although all were important elements in the ideal, even the most admirable men were apt to combine them in varying degrees. This difference may be considered relatively minor when compared with the extent of their agreement. That agreement not only consisted in their general conception of the elements which entered into individual well-being, but in the fact that, unlike many of their contemporaries, the standard against which they measured progress was solely a matter of that well-being.[61]

An actual and important opposition between the doctrines of Arnold and Mill is to be found in what they considered it necessary to do in order to promote a society in which the well-being of individuals could flourish to a greater extent than was the case in their own time.[62] For Mill, it was necessary and proper for government to intervene wherever the social good was at stake, although he feared the interference of government in the private affairs of individuals, and wished to check the spread of such interference. Arnold, on the other hand, did not believe in the possibility of promoting individual well-being through direct action on the part of the government; however, he did fear the consequences of Mill's attempt to give larger scope to the individual's freedom of action. In both of these respects his position was closer to that of Burke than it was to the views of Mill.[63] One sees this best in *Culture and Anarchy*. In the chapter entitled "Doing as One Likes," he attacked Mill's defense of the individual against the state, whereas in the chapter entitled "Our Liberal Practitioners," he attacked interventionist reform. Near the conclusion of the latter chapter, he stated his own tenets as to how individual well-being was to be achieved, when he said:

> Everything, in short, confirms us in the doctrine, so unpalatable to the believers in action, that our main business at the present moment is not so much to work away at certain crude reforms of which we have already the scheme in our own mind, as to create, through the help of that culture which at the very outset we began by praising, and recommending, a frame of mind out of which the schemes of really fruitful reforms may with time grow.[64]

In appealing to the long, gradualist processes of history to bring about reform, Arnold was appealing to the power of education, and the self-cultivation which it would bring. In the end, it was on this power that Mill also relied. The difference between them lay in whether or not it was necessary, as Mill believed, to enact legislation which would remove the chief obstacles to progress; it would be a travesty of Mill's views to interpret him as believing that the elements of character on which progress depended could in any way be legislated into existence. In fact, he shared Arnold's view that what ultimately counted was something much more positive than government could directly achieve: what counted was the education of individuals not only with respect to knowledge but with respect to their sensibilities, leading to an enlargement of their sympathy and their taste.[65] Ultimately, then, Mill and Arnold represent closely allied positions not only with respect to their ideals of character, but with respect to what they believed to be the conditions necessary for the attainment of a society in which persons having such characters would provide the norm according to which all persons would live. Both recognized that no such society was close at hand, for neither possessed a superabundance of optimism, nor a high estimate of the state of society at the time. Yet, both believed that there was a tendency toward progress, and that in the course of that progress man would have changed his own nature, ridding himself of many of those limitations by which he still remained chained to his earlier nature.[66]

It may appear odd that Thomas Henry Huxley should be linked with Arnold and Mill, since Huxley is correctly identified with Darwinism, and neither Arnold nor Mill was significantly affected by Darwin's thought. Furthermore, even apart from questions directly related to evolutionary theory, Huxley's professional training forced him to lay far more stress on man's biological nature than is even implicit in the thought of Arnold or Mill.[67] The effects of this contrast are particularly striking in Huxley's usual insistence that man can never extirpate, nor can he transcend, those tendencies which are associated with his biological nature;[68] in general, Huxley took the position that it is only possible to exercise continuing control over these tendencies. Furthermore, we may note that Huxley stressed a biological basis for differences in character, which went far beyond Arnold's use of race to explain national characteristics. This was diametrically opposed to what we have seen to have been the view held by Mill, with Huxley claiming that there were fundamental racial differences in intelligence and traits of character between blacks and whites, and similar differences due to sex between men and women.[69] Nevertheless, his beliefs with respect to biologically based differences in potentialities did not lead him to social views which were different from those of Mill: for example, he did in fact side with abolitionism, holding that the domination of one person over another was harmful to both, and in speaking of the rights of women he concluded his essay, "Emancipation—Black and White," by saying,

The duty of man is to see that not a grain is piled upon that load beyond what Nature imposes; that injustice is not added to inequality.[70]

A further contrast between Huxley on the one hand, and Mill and Arnold on the other, may be noted with respect to their views concerning the proper content of education. In numerous essays Huxley propagandized for scientific education as basic to any liberal education, and denounced the traditional emphasis on classical studies. Mill, however, agreed with Arnold in defending the values which they took to be associated with the classics, and both attached far more importance than did Huxley to the role of literature, and particularly poetry, in education.[71] It is possible to overemphasize such differences. Though Arnold attacked Huxley's views with respect to the relative importance of science and the classics, his discussions of Hellenism were not intended to serve as defenses of classical literary culture only. As we have noticed, he specifically defined Hellenism as "the ability to see things as they are," and he connected it so closely with the satisfaction of curiosity that it could include scientific as well as aesthetic culture. Huxley, for his part, did not seek to exclude literary studies from the curriculum, nor did he deny that one function of education was to promote a love of beauty; what he attacked was, primarily, the great proportion of time allotted to such studies and the neglect of the sciences. It would be misleading to underestimate the differences in their views as to what was most essential in education if there were to be an improvement in contemporary society. Huxley not only objected to the heavy emphasis placed on Latin and Greek literature, rather than on the modern literatures, and to the methods used in studying Latin and Greek; in effect, he was also attacking the class bias in such education. Arnold, for his part, did include science among the indispensable aspects of culture, but he was generally using the term "science" in that broad sense in which it is equivalent to "Wissenschaft," and not in the sense which was of primary concern to Huxley. We may also note that, whereas Huxley was energetically and successfully advocating schools which emphasized technical education, Arnold took obvious and quite good-natured delight in satirizing the use of laboratory training.[72] Recognizing this fundamental cleavage, it is probably fair to say that it had two sources. On the one hand, the opposition between them was to some extent (and possibly to a very great extent) dependent on differences between their attitudes toward the social forces which both felt to be transforming England in their time. For Arnold, as for Mill, De Tocqueville's analysis of democracy had indicated very great dangers to the most important cultural values of modern society. Huxley, however, rarely exhibited such anxieties.[73] On the other hand, their opposition also had roots in their views as to what was primary in the sphere of human understanding. As we see in the introduction to *Literature and Dogma*, Huxley was taken by Arnold as a representative of the claim that *knowledge* is of higher value than *judgment*, that "hard reasoning" is the way to wisdom. Arnold, however, was convinced that, for fair-minded men, judgment supervenes upon knowledge, gradually ripening into true understanding without the benefit of any "formidable logical apparatus," such as that with which Huxley wished to equip the young men of his time.[74] The great difference between them on this point is illustrated in the form and the substance of their respective attacks on the religious orthodoxy of their time. Originally, the controversies in which Huxley was engaged centered in his acceptance and defense of Darwin's theory; in those controversies it was inevitable that questions of scientific fact would be of crucial importance. Nonetheless, questions directly related to evolutionary theory played an extremely small part in a majority of his religious controversies: the issues were for him, as they were for Arnold, questions of authority versus the true inwardness of religion. The difference between their modes of argument was immense: for Huxley, it was natural science and detailed scientific scholarship in biblical history that were to be the means for striking off the shackles of ecclesiasticism, whereas Arnold fought his battles almost solely with the weapons of the literary humanist.

Given all of these differences in their backgrounds and views, and their lack of explicit references to one another on many relevant occasions, one might almost suppose that even when they were engaged in similar tasks of biblical criticism, their arguments simply passed each other by, unrecognized. Yet, granted the eminence and the influence of each, such a supposition seems scarcely credible. Fortunately, the exchanges of letters between Arnold and Huxley, concerning Arnold's *St. Paul and Protestantism* and his *Literature and Dogma*, are now relatively easily available.[75] From this and other correspondence one can see that they were not only acquainted, but were on extremely friendly terms.[76] However, our own interpretative task is not one of tracing connections or of drawing detailed comparisons between them, but of seeing to what extent Huxley agreed with Arnold and with Mill in his general views regarding man's nature; and whether for him, too, man could—in Mill's phrase—be designated as "a progressive being."

The answer to this question is less easy to come by than might be supposed. Unlike many of his contemporaries who were identified with evolutionary theory, Huxley had strong reservations regarding the more widely diffused forms of the progressivist view. As two outstanding examples of such reservations, I might cite his regret that Darwin had accepted Spencer's terminology "survival of the fittest" as equivalent to "natural selection," because the superlative form ("fittest") suggested an enhancement of value;[77] and, second, it is to be noted that his view of morality, as expressed in his Romanes Lecture, "Evolution and Ethics," consisted in holding that "social progress means a checking of the cosmic process at every step and the substitution for it of another, which may be called the ethical process."[78] Nonetheless, I believe that it remains true that Huxley's own standard of value did lead him to believe that progress had gone on in the past and could continue (through man's efforts) well into the future. In holding his view, he also held that such progress involved a long, slow transformation in man's nature itself. As will become clear, this transformation was for Huxley—as it was for Arnold and for Mill—a transformation in men's sensibilities, as well as an increase in human knowledge. If there was a difference between Huxley and Arnold or Mill with respect to this point, it lay in the fact that Huxley placed far more stress than did they on the importance of organized knowledge as an instrument of progress.

The place at which one can best find a clear delineation of Huxley's views regarding human progress is in the essay which he wrote as a prolegomenon to "Evolution and Ethics," attempting to

. . . remove that which seems to have proved a stumbling-block to many—namely, the paradox that ethical nature, while born of cosmic nature, is necessarily at enmity with its parent.[79]

In order to remove that stumbling-block, Huxley contrasted nature in an uncultivated state with what is to be found after men have made gardens. In such gardens, he points out,

. . . considerable quantities of vegetables, fruits, and flowers are produced, of kinds which neither now exist, nor have ever existed, except under conditions such as obtained in the garden; and which, therefore, are as much works of the art of man as the frames and glass-houses in which some of them are raised. That the "stage of Art," thus created in the state of nature by man, is sustained by and dependent on him, would at once become apparent, if the watchful supervision of the gardener were withdrawn, and the antagonistic influences of the general cosmic process were no longer sedulously warded off, or counteracted.[80]

Huxley makes clear that he is not denying that "man, physical, intellectual, and moral, is as much a part of nature, as purely a product of the cosmic process, as the humblest weed."[81] This acknowledgment does not contradict the statement that the actions of men can transform other elements in nature: as Huxley indicates, throughout nature there is a strife of forces, and the various manifestations of the same natural processes are often at war with one another. His argument is that man, in cultivating a garden, can stand in opposition to all of those elements in nature which would flourish were it not for the forces represented by man himself. The parallel between the garden and a moral society is pressed even farther by Huxley when he says:

Not only is the state of nature hostile to the state of art of the garden; but the principle of the horticultural process, by which the latter is created and maintained, is antithetic to that of the cosmic process. The characteristic feature of the latter is the intense and unceasing competition of the struggle for existence. The characteristic of the former is the elimination of that struggle, by the removal of the conditions which give rise to it. The tendency of the cosmic process is to bring about the adjustment of the forms of plant life to the current conditions; the tendency of the horticultural process is the adjustment of the conditions to the needs of the forms of plant life which the gardener desires to raise.[82]

Given the fact that we are here dealing with Huxley's own views, "the gardener" in this illustration cannot be interpreted in a supernaturalistic way: he must either stand for the process of natural selection operating within and between societies, or he must be taken as representing man's own deliberate action in fostering conditions which produce "the survival of those forms which most nearly approach the standard of the useful, or the beautiful, which he has in his mind."[83] These two possible interpretations do not involve incompatible alternatives; in fact, Huxley held that both natural selection and deliberate human intervention in natural processes have played a role in the evolution of man as a social being.

With respect to the first of these factors we may note that Huxley held it to be a part of man's biological heritage that he should have gregarious and sympathetic impulses; and, like Darwin, he believed that these non-egoistic springs of action were among the most valuable endowments in the struggle for survival. Thus, natural selection would tend to foster the preservation of these traits. Furthermore, Huxley pointed out that the more closely men came into contact with one another, as they would as their social life developed, the more effectively the sympathetic impulses would operate, and the more scope there would be for man's natural potentialities for imitative behavior. Thus, a social state of existence, in which sympathetic impulses and cooperation could flourish, would gradually and naturally come to supplant a state in which there was a constant and remorseless struggle for existence between individuals.[84] To be sure, Huxley did not anticipate never-ending improvement in this respect. Like Mill and like Arnold,[85] he was deeply troubled by the threat of population growth; he feared that if it were not checked, it would lead to a new struggle for survival, and a consequent tendency to rely on those traits of human character which were most dangerous to the social order.[86] Furthermore, he was aware of the existence of such forces operating within the economic and social conditions characteristic of his own time, the consequences of which were the degradation of large segments of the population in industrialized areas.[87] It was at this point that Huxley found it necessary to rely upon the second factor in social evolution, man's deliberate and intelligent interference in the social process.[88]

One of Huxley's best known similes is that in which he compared nature with a master chess-player, and in which he pointedly argued for the need of an education in the rules of the game, if men were not to be defeated by nature.[89] These rules, of course, are to be discovered by the methods of science, and a failure to advance scientific knowledge would make it impossible for man to intercede successfully in the natural order. Thus, science could confer enormous new powers and practical benefits on society, and Huxley, with great rhetorical incisiveness, made the most of this fact in his superb essay "On the Advisableness of Improving Natural Knowledge." However, the aim of that essay was to show that great as these immediate, practical benefits had been, they were of far less consequence than the effects which science had had in reshaping men's beliefs. Those beliefs were partly intellectual, and partly moral, and in both respects Huxley regarded them as having been instruments of social progress. On the one hand, that intellectual advance which had originally been sought primarily for its practical benefits, had changed men's view of the world and of their place in it. In this connection, Huxley emphasized the importance of such a change with respect to religion, as when, for example, he said:

If the religion of the present differs from that of the past, it is because the theology of the present has become more scientific than that of the past; because it has not only renounced idols of wood and idols of stone, but begins to see the necessity of breaking in pieces the idols built up of books and traditions and fine-spun ecclesiastical cobwebs: and of cherishing the noblest and most human of man's emotions, by worship "for the most part of the silent sort" at the altar of the Unknown.[90]

Connected with this shift in religious attitude and commitment, but even more fundamental, was the moral shift which Huxley held was demanded by the rise of scientific culture. This moral shift was away from authority and to tested knowledge, away from justification by faith to justification by verification.[91] It was this lesson that led him to formulate the position which he named "agnosticism,"[92] and which he insisted involved a moral commitment, not an intellectual one only. Agnosticism held it wrong, both morally and intellectually, "for a man to say that he is certain of the objective truth of any proposition unless he can produce evidence which logically justifies that certainty."[93] In this proposition Huxley was challenging ecclesiastical authority on moral grounds, just as vigorously as he had challenged it on the evidence which it claimed to possess. He found it intolerable that his opponent, Dr. Wace, should seem to be laying claim to moral superiority in the very same sentence as that in which he was saying that Huxley ought to have found it unpleasant to state plainly and forcefully what he actually believed.[94]

For Huxley, such an attitude threatened to block every advance in knowledge; it was as an antidote to that attitude that he formulated the principle of agnosticism. As the magnificent concluding paragraphs of "Agnosticism and Christianity" make clear, Huxley was convinced that it was only through a rigid adherence to this principle that men could free themselves of a hidden inclination to allow personal interest to distort their beliefs, impeding their acceptance of truth. Thus, the principle was of the highest practical importance, and it was applicable not only to scientific inquiry but to the whole range of human choices.[95] It was precisely what Huxley claimed it to be, "a principle which is as much ethical as intellectual."[96]

The justification which Huxley everywhere offered as a basis for this moral commitment lay in its utility, and it would be difficult to interpret his ethical theory in any but Utilitarian terms.[97] His standard of value was always stated in terms of human happiness and, in his most explicit characterization of what constituted social well-being, he said:

> I take it that the good of mankind means the attainment, by every man, of all the happiness which he can enjoy without diminishing the happiness of his fellow men.[98]

After this characterization of the ideal end, Huxley immediately went on to list some of the forms of satisfaction which individuals could enjoy without diminishing the happiness of others, and he gave as his examples the happiness that comes from a sense of security or peace; from the fruits of trade; from art; from knowledge; and from sympathy or friendship. This list, like those instances of the higher pleasures in which Mill found man's chief good to lie, obviously stressed specifically human forms of enjoyment, as distinct from the satisfactions of bodily appetites or specifically sensuous pleasures. This suggests what was in fact the case, that even though Huxley differed from Mill and from Arnold in stressing man's kinship with the rest of the animal kingdom, he did regard the evolutionary process as one in which human beings developed new potentialities, and that it was in the satisfaction of these higher capacities that man's true good lay. This conviction is repeatedly expressed in Huxley's discussions of evolution and ethics, but nowhere more clearly than when he said:

> The primitive savage, tutored by Istar, appropriated whatever took his fancy, and killed whomsoever opposed him, if he could. On the contrary, the ideal of the ethical man is to limit his freedom of action to a sphere in which he does not interfere with the freedom of others; he seeks the common weal as much as his own; and, indeed, as an essential part of his own welfare. Peace is both end and means with him; and he founds his life on a more or less complete self-restraint, which is the negation of the unlimited struggle for existence. He tries to escape from his place in the animal kingdom, founded on the free development of the principle of non-moral evolution, and to establish a kingdom of Man, governed upon the principle of moral evolution.[99]

Thus, like Mill and like Arnold, Huxley conceived of man as a progressive being. While he held that this development was originally rooted in man's biological inheritance as a social animal, and that its growth was at first slow and due to the exigencies of increasing social life, Huxley looked upon the men of modern historical time as beings who, in large measure, have held their fate in their own hands:[100] he regarded applied intelligence as the agency through which the past progress of Western civilization had come, and upon which, alone, the possibilities for future progress depended. In this he differed from many others among his contemporaries whose thought had also been connected with evolutionism and who believed in progress. On the whole, they had tended to regard such progress as inevitable, and had sometimes spoken as if there were a law of evolution, making for progress.[101] Huxley's position was, on the contrary, a steadfast *meliorism*: he insisted that men do have it in their power to remove evils, and to promote good, thus improving the quality of life. In this he was wholly at one with Mill and with Arnold.[102] Furthermore, what Huxley considered as an improvement in the quality of life was, in all essential respects, what Arnold and Mill also took as the standard of improvement: it consisted in the cultivation of men's sensibilities, so that every individual would become increasingly able to find enjoyment in forms of activities which had not existed, or at best could only have existed in a very rudimentary state, during most of the history of the human race. Furthermore, the possibility of a continuing advance lay open to men, if they made adequate use of their opportunities. In a society freed of those debilitating conditions of material deprivation which were all too characteristic of contemporary industrial society,[103] men could increasingly come to find their satisfactions in the pursuit of knowledge, the enjoyment of things of beauty, and through the social affections. In such a society, religion could also increasingly become that which, at its best, it always had been: an inward state, "the reverence and love for the ethical ideal, and the desire to realize that ideal in life."[104] Such an ideal demanded the suppression of man's ruthless egoism, and the cultivation of his more beneficent traits. Huxley regarded this development as one in which, unfortunately, man's susceptibility to pain had also increased. Yet even in stating his belief that such was the case, he showed no more hesitation as to which was the better form of life than had Mill, when Mill was forced to say whether it was better to be Socrates dissatisfied or a pig satisfied. In discussing pain, Huxley said:

> This baleful product of evolution increases in quantity and in intensity, with advancing grades of animal organization, until it attains its highest level in man. Further, the consummation is not reached in man, the mere animal; nor in man, the whole or half savage; but only in man, the member of an organized polity. And it is a necessary consequence of his attempt to live in this way; that is, under those conditions which are essential to the full development of his noblest powers.[105]

Huxley's acceptance of increasing pain as the price of enjoyments not directly connected with the satisfaction of man's physical needs, should suggest the strong kinship between his conception of human nature, and human good, and the conceptions that one finds in Arnold or in Mill. For all three, the standard of worth in human life is a standard which is inherent in man's own potentialities, and is not derived from any external source. The nature of that standard is defined in terms of enjoyment, but in those forms of enjoyment which Mill most

often referred to as "higher" or "nobler," and which were embraced within
Arnold's use of the concept of "perfection." These were enjoyments which depended upon cultivation, which involved a transformation of men from a condition in which they were dominated by appetite and instinct, to a condition in
which knowledge, taste, and a feeling of being at one with others, were the sources
of their fullest enjoyments.

To speak of the standards accepted by Huxley and Arnold and Mill as standards linked to human enjoyment constitutes not only an accurate portrayal of
their basic ethical theories, but immediately separates them from those thinkers
with whom we shall now be concerned. The abrupt transition might be symbolized in the contrast between their views and Carlyle's gospel of work, but the
stream of doctrine with which we are now to be concerned is of such general intellectual importance that it is best not to allow it to become entangled in the
idiosyncrasies of Carlyle's thought. I shall therefore seek to introduce it through
Fichte, who must be considered as one of its most characteristic, although one of
its most extreme, representatives in early nineteenth-century thought.

2. IDEALISM AND ITS DOCTRINE OF SELF-REALIZATION

Fichte and those who stood in what, for convenience sake, I shall refer to as
"his tradition" were no less insistent than Mill, Arnold, and Huxley that the
standard for human conduct was rooted in man's own nature, that its content was
not derived from any external source, and that obedience to it did not depend
primarily upon the threat of sanctions. This, of course, was a heritage which came
to Fichte from Kant's moral philosophy, and came to the age as a whole from the
Enlightenment. It was also agreed that men were able to bring themselves to a
stage of development in which the motives which most pervasively influenced
their conduct could be regarded as evidence that there had been moral progress.
Yet, in spite of these similarities between Mill, Arnold, Huxley, and the idealist
tradition with which we are now to deal, we must immediately note two crucial
points at which they differed. In the first place, Fichte and those who followed
in his tradition rejected hedonism as a standard of conduct: they did not hold
that the objectives which men ought to pursue could best be defined in terms of
the relief of suffering on the one hand, and the cultivation of higher forms of
sensibility on the other. In the second place, they held it to be a distinctive and
essential aspect of human nature that men possess freedom, and that human
action is not to be explained as if it occurred in conformity with causal laws.[106]
These two points of difference had a common root in the basically hormic view
of man's nature that characterized the tradition with which we shall be dealing.
That tradition rejected, and sought to extirpate, all traces of a psychology which
analyzed experience in terms of elements given in sensation; it substituted concepts which suggested that man's nature was dominated by inner dynamic tendencies toward growth. This view is nowhere more extremely stated than in Fichte's
thought, and it is with his formulation of the position that we shall first deal.[107]

It is fortunately not necessary for us to follow the dialectic of Fichte's exposition of his technical philosophy, since his views concerning human nature and man's progress receive their fullest expression in works other than the multifarious expositions of his theory of knowledge.[108] However, since he believed that his system provided a means by which one could move from entirely abstract, necessary principles to a psychological understanding of human action and of the goals of society, it will be useful to take note of what he took to be the ultimate foundation of his system.

As is well known, Fichte was one among many who found it impossible to accept the ultimate dichotomies within the Kantian system, and he radically altered that system through an unrestricted acceptance of the primacy of the practical reason, that is, a primacy of the moral over empirical and scientific forms of experience.[109] In essence, what Fichte actually did was to stress only that part of Kant's doctrine according to which knowledge depended upon the mind's formative powers; he rejected the Kantian view that it also depended upon a faculty of receptivity, that is, upon something being *given*. Instead, Fichte interpreted the mind as wholly active, and the experienced world was taken to be a product of that inner, creative activity; not external *facts* (*Thatsachen*), but the ego's own *acts* (*Thathandlugen*) provided the materials for all that could be thought.[110] In addition, Fichte identified those acts of the ego which were basic to knowledge as acts which expressed the self's own basic moral activity. When one recalls the manner in which Kant had deliberately separated morality from empirical knowledge, assigning to each its own competence, one can recognize the sharp break and the new beginning which Fichte's position represented in the history of modern thought. In a corollary to the first proposition in his *Science of Rights,* Fichte stated his position in terms which closely followed his more abstract statement of the same view in his theory of knowledge:

It is here maintained, that the practical Ego is the Ego of original self-consciousness; that a rational being perceives itself immediately only in Willing, and that it would not perceive itself, and hence would also not perceive the world, and that it would therefore not be Intelligence, if it were not a practical being. Willing is the real essential character of reason. . . . The practical faculty is the inmost root of the Ego; to it everything else is attached, and with it connected (p. 36).

In the *Vocation of Man,* one can see the same position elaborated in more concrete terms, and therefore in a manner more closely related to the issues of moral practice:

In short, there is for me absolutely no such thing as an existence which has no relation to myself, and which I contemplate merely for the sake of contemplating it;—whatever has an existence for me, has it only through its relation to my own being. But there is, in the highest sense, only one relation to me possible, all others are but subordinate forms of this:—my vocation to moral activity. My world is the object and sphere of my duties, and absolutely nothing more.[111]

In the whole tenor of such passages it becomes clear that Fichte's theory of knowledge was primarily a propaedeutic to an exposition of his view of man's nature as a free, creative, moral being. Because of his epistemology, and the metaphysics which followed from it, man could not be considered as a product of an alien and external world of nature: on the contrary, empirical objects, as we experience them, have to exist as they do because of the relationships in which they stand to our own inner being. Furthermore, our being is not under the influence of an external causal law: the necessity which we attribute to the external world has no place in a true conception of ourselves. This emphasis on human freedom was all-pervasive in Fichte's thought; as he said in a letter to Reinhold, who was his predecessor as professor at Jena, "My system is from beginning to end only an analysis of the idea of freedom."[112] Even the world of nature, which may sometimes limit human action, is interpreted by Fichte as being—in an ultimate analysis—that which has existence only because it is needed as a source of opposition and resistance against which men are to struggle and exert the force of their creative energy. To exert this force is to be what one truly is, "for man is his own end,—he should determine himself, and never allow himself to be determined by anything foreign to himself."[113]

The radical nature of Fichte's view of man's freedom expressed in such statements, and in his metaphysics, obviously separates his position from that of Mill and that of Huxley—and it would be difficult to find any strong ties between it and what Arnold believed. No less important, however, and no less intimately connected with Fichte's hormic psychology, was his absolute rejection of happiness as a standard of value. In a passage reminiscent of Spinoza's psychology, and anticipating the standard psychology of self-realization, Fichte said:

An article of food has a pleasant taste to us, and a flower a pleasant smell, because they exalt and enliven our organic existence; and the pleasant taste, as well as the pleasant smell, is nothing but the immediate feeling of this exaltation and enlivenment.[114]

This doctrine was basic to his view of morality, for he held that whatever was moral consisted in the exercise of man's inherent active powers. As he said in another passage which is also reminiscent of Spinoza, but has a different, moralistic twist:

... far from being true that man is determined to moral goodness by the desire for happiness, the idea of happiness itself and the desire for it, rather arise in the first place out of the moral nature of man. Not, *That which produces happiness is good;*—but, *That only which is good produces happiness.*[115]

Not only the rejection of a hedonistic standard separated Fichte from Mill, Arnold, and Huxley, he also differed in his over-riding moralism: there probably has never been another philosopher who so clearly represented the view of life which Arnold designated as Hebraism. For example, in the *Vocation of Man*, Fichte said:

There is but one point towards which I have unceasingly to direct all my attention,— namely, what I *ought to do*, and how I may best fulfil the obligation. All my thoughts must have a bearing on my actions, and must be capable of being considered as means, however remote, to this end; otherwise they are an idle and aimless show, a mere waste of time and strength, the perversion of a noble power which is entrusted to me for a very different end.[116]

The goal of this noble, active power was conceived by Fichte to be a progressive transformation of man to a higher condition of existence; it was this which, in *The Vocation of Man*, he expressed as follows:

> In the mere consideration of the world as it is . . . there arises within me the wish, the desire,—no, not the mere desire, but the absolute demand for a better world. I cast a glance on the present relations of men towards each other and towards Nature; on the feebleness of their powers, on the strength of their desires and passions. A voice within me proclaims with irresistible conviction—"It is impossible that it can remain thus; it must become other and better."
> I cannot think of the present state of humanity as that in which it is destined to remain. . . . Only in so far as I can regard this state as the means towards a better, as the transition-point to a higher and more perfect state, has it any value in my eyes;—not for its own sake, can I support it, esteem it, and joyfully perform my part in it.[117]

The basic clue to the character of that better world is to be found when one recognizes that Fichte held that man's essential self-realization was necessarily incomplete except insofar as it could be completed in and through social existence. For Fichte, man is not merely social by nature, possessing social impulses among his other basic impulses, he is *essentially* social: "Man becomes man only amongst men."[118] While Mill, Arnold, and Huxley would probably not have interpreted this doctrine in as strong as sense as did Fichte, it would not have been wholly unwelcome to them. However, by virtue of Fichte's theory of self-realization, the fact that man was essentially social in nature led to the view that the true goal of human action, man's only true welfare, is not to be found in his own individual fate, but in the progress of the race:

> The Life according to Reason consists herein,—that the Individual forget himself in the Race, place his own life in the life of the Race and dedicate it thereto . . . there is but One Virtue,—to forget one's own personality;—and but One Vice,—to make self the object of our thoughts. . . .
> He who but thinks *at all* of his own personality, and desires any kind of life or being, or any joy of life, except *in* the Race and *for* the Race, with whatever vesture of good deeds he may seek to hide his deformity, is nevertheless, at bottom, only a mean, base, and therefore unhappy man.[119]

The particular content of the Fichtean ideal of the progress of the human race need not occupy us in detail, although one may in passing note that Fichte should be assigned a place of some importance in the history of socialist thought. For our purpose, it is sufficient to be cognizant of the fact that in the ideal state toward which man's sense of perfection inclines him, there would be "*reciprocal* activity, *mutual* influence, *mutual* giving and receiving, *mutual* suffering and doing"; not *subordination*, but *coordination* among *free, reasonable beings*.[120] This internal social harmony was not conceived by Fichte as being restricted to any one nation or any one civilization; in fact, he insisted that if there is to be that ultimate progress of which man is capable, and for which he strives, progress must include all peoples:

... until the existing culture of every age shall have been diffused over the whole inhabited globe, and our race become capable of the most unlimited intercommunication with itself, one nation or one continent must pause on the great common path of progress, and wait for the advance of others. ... [But] when every useful discovery made at one end of the earth shall be at once made known and communicated to all the rest, then, without further interruption, without halt or regress, with united strength and equal step, humanity shall move onward to a higher culture, of which we can at present form no conception.[121]

In this connection we may finally note that Fichte recognized that the achievement of this ideal demanded the self-transformation of men:

Humanity is not so far cultivated in us; we ourselves still stand on the lowest grade of imperfect humanity, or slavery. We ourselves have not yet attained to a consciousness of our freedom and self-activity, for then we should necessarily desire to see around us *similar*,—that is, *free* beings.[122]

If it be asked how Fichte proposed that such a self-transformation in human nature was to be achieved, the answer is that he believed it would follow naturally from man's inherent nature. To be sure, in his own country, at his own time, the requisite tendencies toward growth needed to be fostered by a radically reformed educational system; as the structure of his *Speeches to the German Nation* makes clear, the education of youth is the foundation of the life of a people.[123] However, Fichte recognized that an educational system can only help to develop capacities which are already incipiently present, and in an interesting flight of fancy in the *Science of Rights* he contrasted man's inherent nature with the nature of animal species, holding that men are not suitably compared with animals, but are in some respects more like plants.[124] Unlike animals, they are not equipped from birth with preformed instincts which are sufficient to meet the exigencies of life; men are dependent on others for their early nurture and care, and their development does not proceed in accordance with an inherited pattern. Nature, Fichte says, has allowed the human race latitude for shaping its own destiny, which no animal species ever has.[125] Thus, in this passage as elsewhere, Fichte drew a sharp contrast between man's inherent nature and what is commonly referred to as "man's animal nature:" from the first, man is not an animal, and therefore need not suppress or control an alien animal inheritance. He is by nature a moral being—a being who is free, and freely aspires to a constantly expanding sphere of activity. Thus, for Fichte, the history of mankind is not one in which the fundamental attributes of human nature undergo any change; men simply become better able to express their own essential natures, to realize themselves. However, through this greater self-realization, *Mankind* will have progressed, and the conditions of life will have become such that all men can fully enter into a harmonious relation with one another; they will then be at one with that fundamental principle of Reason which lies behind and beyond Nature and which is indeed the well-spring from which the individual's own free, creative activity comes.

The similarities between the thought of T. H. Green and Fichte are striking, in spite of the differences between the points of departure which characterized their theories of knowledge. Whereas Fichte had attempted to overcome dichotomies within the Kantian system, and thus correct it, Green was not primarily concerned with its outcome; instead, he used Kant's general view of the mind's judgmental activity as a means of attacking the empiricist tradition in British philosophy. As we shall see, he too reached an idealist metaphysics in which nature itself was taken to be an expression of mind; this led him—as it had led Fichte—to reject the view that the mind's activities were subject to natural law, and therefore unfree. Furthermore, like Fichte, he couched his theory of man's basic nature in terms of a striving toward self-realization and, in defending this standard, he too was emphatic in his rejection of hedonism.

All of this constituted a self-conscious attack on the current form of British empiricism. However, it should be noted that Green's was by no means the first such attack within the century: others, both in England and Scotland, had already been influenced by Kant and German idealism, and had attempted to introduce that philosophy into Britain. In this connection, Coleridge and Sir William Hamilton were the outstanding figures, as Mill's testimony bears witness.[126] There also were others: Carlyle, who had been influenced by Fichte as well as by Goethe, and liberal Anglican theologians, such as F. D. Maurice and Julius Hare—both of whom were closely allied with Coleridge—may be mentioned in this connection. Nonetheless, associationism and Utilitarianism remained important and perhaps dominant forces in the interpretation of human nature, partly because of the influence of Mill, and the added influence of Bain in psychology; but perhaps especially because Herbert Spencer, among others, effectively merged an empiricist account of knowledge with evolutionary theory. However, Green's book-length introduction to the works of Hume, which he and T. H. Grose edited in 1874–75, constituted a full-scale attack on empiricist assumptions, and by the mid-1880s, when his *Prolegomena to Ethics* was posthumously published, a new anti-associationist tendency was strikingly evident. This tendency can readily be seen in almost every volume of *Mind* which appeared during that period. Since psychological theory had been intimately linked with ethical theory, both by Utilitarians and by evolutionary theorists, this change had immediate repercussions on ethics, and therefore also on political theory.

The chief documents in this attack on the presuppositions of recent British psychology probably were the first chapters of Green's *Prolegomena* (originally published in *Mind* in 1882), and Ward's famous *Encyclopaedia Britannica* article, "Psychology," which appeared in 1886. Both challenged associationism on the ground that the facts of consciousness presuppose the existence of a perduring self. In attempting to establish this contention, each emphasized the importance of a grasp not of the atomic elements of sensation alone, but an apprehension of relationships. A similar emphasis on the importance of relationships characterized the psychological analyses of William James and of F. H. Bradley, even though neither construed the presence of these relationships within experience as providing a basis for arguing to the necessary existence of a knowing, judging self. However, common to all four was the conviction that experience cannot adequately be interpreted if it is held to consist of entirely separate elements, that is, if relationships are not regarded as equally ultimate constituents of knowledge. The contrast between the new and the old views can be seen in Bain's balanced and appreciative appraisal of Ward's *Encyclopaedia* article. He quoted Ward as saying, with reference to the basic process involved in the individual's psychological development, that

Psychologists have usually represented mental advance as consisting fundamentally in the combination and re-combination of various elementary units, the so-called sensations and primitive movements, or, in other words, in a species of mental chemistry.

To which Bain himself immediately replied:

Not altogether without reason, as it seems to me. Our education from first to last takes principally the form of adding unit to unit, under the retentive or adhesive attribute of our nature, with which we are so marvelously gifted; and any other process is quite secondary in comparison.[127]

Even though Bain remained unconvinced, the effective days of an associationist psychology were at an end in England, and, at the time, the movement found no growing room in America. As we shall shortly see, the emphasis on instincts which was connected with evolutionary theory was of some effect in limiting the claims of associationism; however, as the example of Spencer shows, evolutionism and associationism were not necessarily antagonists. Rather, as I have suggested, what was of paramount importance was an attack on the "atomism" of associationist doctrine. Those who criticized this aspect of the theory—a theory which had relatively little to do with the experimental work on associations and memory which was proceeding in Germany—criticized it for distorting experience because of metaphysical and epistemological preconceptions. For example, William James put the case in the following way:

The traditional psychology talks like one who should say a river consists of nothing but pailsful, spoonsful, quartpotsful, barrelsful, and other moulded forms of water. Even were the pails and pots all actually standing in the stream, still between them the free water would continue to flow. It is just this free water that psychologists resolutely overlook. Every definite image in the mind is steeped and dyed in the free water that flows round it. With it goes the sense of its relations, near and remote, the dying echo of whence it came to us, the dawning sense of whither it is to lead.[128]

This was a point to which James constantly returned, and he labeled a failure to recognize its importance as "the psychologist's fallacy." And in F. H. Bradley's psychological papers one finds the same insistence that relationships are basic among the data of consciousness. For example, in "Association and Thought," Bradley said:

First, the Atomism must go wholly. We must get rid of the idea that our mind is a train of perishing existences, that so long as they exist have a separable being, and, so to speak, are coupled up by another sort of things which we call relations. If we turn to what is given this is not what we find, but rather a continuous mass of presentation in which the separation of a single element from all context is never observed.[129]

I cite both James and Bradley to suggest that this form of criticism was common to those whose views on other philosophic topics might differ very sharply. Even among idealists, such as Green, Ward, and Bradley, an emphasis on relationships was not used in exactly the same ways, nor in the interest of similar metaphysical conclusions. For example, whereas Green used the judgmental grasp of relationships as entailing a self, and made the existence of that self basic to his metaphysical doctrines,[130] Bradley (as we have noted) denied that the relationships found within experience entail any such self. While Ward criticized Bradley's doctrine,[131] he—unlike Green—refused to interpret the self which was presupposed by psychology as providing an adequate basis for any form of metaphysical theory.[132] These are but a few of many illustrations which might have been chosen to suggest that a list of English and American philosophers and psychologists who, at the time, sharply rejected the assumptions of associationism would be both long and impressive. However, it is our aim to trace Green's views on human perfectability, and with reference to this topic he differed profoundly from the other critics whom we have mentioned; and we may note in passing that he also differed significantly from Bosanquet, who became another of the chief critics of associationist assumptions.[133]

Having taken the consciousness of relations as indicative of the existence of a perduring self which is able to apprehend these relationships, and viewing reality as involving a system of relationships, Green was led to the following conclusion:

If by nature we mean the object of possible experience, the connected order of knowable facts or phenomena.... then nature implies something other than itself, as the condition of being what it is. Of that something else we are entitled to say ... that it is a self-distinguishing consciousness; because the function which it must fulfil in order to render the relations of phenomena, and with them nature, possible, is one which, on however limited a scale, we ourselves exercise in the acquisition of experience, and exercise only by means of such a consciousness.[134]

It is noteworthy that Green had introduced the foregoing statement by saying:

The purpose of this long discussion has been to arrive at some conclusion in regard to the relation between man and nature, a conclusion which must be arrived at before we can be sure that any theory of ethics, in the distinctive sense of that term, is other than wasted labour.

Thus, Green's metaphysical idealism was frankly put forward as a basis for a moral philosophy, and the noumenal self which he held to be presupposed by our conceptions of nature was, at the same time, held by him to be a moral self. Of course, this had also been characteristic of the thought of Fichte, with whom Green is too infrequently compared.

For Green, as for Fichte, this metaphysical doctrine meant that the self was not under the dominance of natural causation: its actions did not form a part of a chain of events in which each antecedent is linked to each consequent in an invariant sequential relationship. Rather, he conceived of the self as "a free cause," that is, as an originating agency acting in terms of its own consciousness of self, and of its own ideal ends.[135] When drawing this distinction between natural events and moral actions, Green also distinguished between "cause" and "motives."[136] Since Green believed that it is not possible to construe motives as themselves being dependent on natural causes, he held that, although moral actions could be said to be "determined" by motives, the agent must be said to be free: an agent's actions expressed the character he had made for himself by the ends he had chosen. Whether or not Green's classic statement of this idealist form of the self-determinist position is both self-consistent and tenable is not our concern. What is important in the context of our present discussion is that he should have viewed the self as creating its own character, as making itself by its own choices what it was ultimately to become. While some aspects of this doctrine are noticeable in many other, earlier forms of a self-realizationist psychology— one thinks, for example, of Aristotle on habit—Green's whole moral psychology is couched in terms of this form of progressive self-development. All experience becomes transformed through the moral growth which ensues when men, in concert with one another, pursue ideal ends. These ends, needless to say, do not consist in promoting a life characterized primarily in terms of enjoyment. Like others of his generation, Green had rebelled against a hedonistic psychology, saying of those who held that view:

> Whereas with them the good generically is the pleasant, in this treatise the common characteristic of the good is that it satisfies some desire. In all satisfaction of desire there is pleasure, and thus pleasantness in an object is a necessary incident of its being good . . . but its pleasantness depends on its goodness, not its goodness on the pleasure it conveys.[137]

Similar accounts of the relationship between desire, pleasure, and the good came to be widely accepted, and the dominant moral psychology of the time changed from hedonism to self-realizationism.[138] However, unlike most who later developed the position of self-realizationism, Green's moral psychology was wholly cut off from any naturalistic base: the self which was to be realized did not, for Green, include those organic needs which linked man to the biological realm.[139] Nor did Green attempt to define the content of a life in which the self is increasingly realized, specifying the basic types of needs and desires common to all men. There were many later attempts to build such moral systems, but Green's position followed that of Fichte in holding that man's striving for the good assumed whatever form of growth was necessary to his nature as a moral being. Or, to alter the figure of speech, there were not set channels through which the tendency toward good always flowed. Of course, what constituted the moral good did not, according to Green, consist of a life in which transient and incoherent desires were satisfied; a good life represented a growth in character, and therefore in self-determination toward a desirable end. On the basis of his metaphysical view that there is a divine being working within all individuals, Green held that "the right path" that each should follow is "the path in which [man's consciousness] tends to become what, according to the immanent divine law of its being, it has in it to be."[140] Green not only admitted that such a characterization does not concretely specify the ultimate goal of man's self-realization, but he denied that it is possible to state in any positive terms what such a goal, which he refers to as "the Best," would be. Instead, he appealed to the existence of what might be termed a tropistic tendency in man toward those forms of realization which are better than his current state of being. Thus, while we do not know the Best, we can at any time discern that which is Better, and Green speaks in this connection of

... how man has bettered himself through institutions and habits which tend to make the welfare of all the welfare of each, and through the arts which make nature, both as used and as contemplated, the friend of man. And just so far as this is plain, we know enough of ultimate moral good to guide our conduct.[141]

As this quotation suggests, Green conceived of the Better as involving a growing sense of the needs and aspirations of others, and a widening of the aims of the self. Unlike Mill and Huxley, it was neither through an appeal to needs for co-operation, nor through inborn tendencies such as sympathy, that Green accounted for man's sociality; in fact, he rejected any attempt to offer a genetic account of this characteristic.[142] Instead, he insisted that man's social nature must be taken as a primitive fact. In a manner reminiscent of Fichte's insistence on the social nature of man, Green simply started from the fact that *personality*, as we are conscious of it in ourselves and in others, can only be present in society.[143] This did not imply that he accepted a theory of society in which social institutions were autonomous; unlike Comte, Hegel, or Marx, he insisted that social institutions depend upon the recognition of one personality by another—ultimately depend upon what Green characterized as a relationship of "I" and "Thou."[144] And the standard of value against which society was to be measured was always a standard defined in terms of individual personality. While Green agreed with Fichte in holding that there was an immanent tendency toward a social growth which would include the whole of humanity,[145] the good of the Race was not that which was the proper object of man's aspiration and love: it was with his own self-development, and—as a necessary part of that—with the self-development of his fellow human beings that a man was to be concerned. At this point one can see the difference between Green and his student Bosanquet, to which I have already alluded; for it is probably not unfair to say that for Bosanquet, as for Hegel, the State itself, and its institutions, were expressions of the Absolute, whereas for Green the Absolute was only to be known in and through individual persons, whose autonomy and creative power were its only finite manifestations.

The growth of individuals in history, the growth of their community of spirit, involved a transformation of the whole condition of man's existence, and Green's doctrine can be looked upon as being, indeed, a spiritual Evolutionism. Of that doctrine he said:

According to the doctrine of this treatise, as we have previously endeavoured to state it, there is a principle of self-development in man. . . . He is capable of being moved by an idea of himself, as becoming that which he has it in him to be—an idea which does not represent previous experience, but gradually brings an experience into being, gradually creates a filling for itself, in the shape of art, laws, institutions and habits of living, which, so far as they go, exhibit the capabilities of man, define the idea of his end, afford a positive answer to the otherwise unanswerable question, what in particular it is that man has it in him to become.[146]

3. Evolution and the Malleability of Human Nature

This Spiritual Evolutionism, as I have termed it, was regarded by Green, and by others, as involving a radically different view of man and the world than was to be found in naturalistic evolutionary theories. In this, they were indisputably correct. However, if we do not focus our attention on the question of man's place in nature, but on the present characteristics and future hopes of mankind, the two forms of evolutionism were, in some cases, more nearly similar than opposed. To illustrate these similarities, it will be useful to consider the thought of Darwin and of Spencer.

In approaching Darwin's interpretation of man, it is necessary to bear in mind the conditions under which he put forward his views. In the *Origin of Species* he had deliberately avoided all questions concerning the applicability of his conclusions to the human race, though his work was immediately received in terms of its implications for the interpretation of man.[147] Twelve years later he published *The Descent of Man*, and in it he attempted to establish the view that he had long held, offering evidence to show that there was continuity between man and the rest of the animal kingdom not only with respect to physical form, but with respect to mental powers as well. Now, if we recall Darwin's use of the comparative method, we shall not expect him to start his analysis from any overall characterization of human nature. Instead, we shall expect just what we find: a collection of instances in which specific traits which are supposedly distinctive of human nature can be shown to bear a close resemblance to a series of traits found among non-human species. The range of the traits which Darwin discussed was extremely wide, and he made no pretense of offering either a systemetically constructed list or an exhaustive one; nonetheless, it is possible to interpret what he said as providing a general conception of man's fundamental nature.

In the first place it is clear that, apart from intelligence, Darwin connected many of man's basic traits with the instinctive behavior of animals.[148] Given this assumed connection, one might suppose that his theory of man's nature would minimize malleability: earlier theories of instinct had tended to identify that which was instinctive with that which was universal and necessary, and our more recent conceptions of animal instinct have also emphasized the rigidity of instinctive behavior. However, Darwin's approach was a phylogenetic one, and from this point of view he could easily combine a theory of human nature in which instincts were of preponderating importance in human behavior with the contention that man's nature was subject to important changes over time. The primary mechanism of such phylogenetic changes was, of course, the possibility that there are slight variations among individuals with respect to their instinctive patterns of reaction, that such variations can have a relation to the survival of the individuals possessing them, that they are inherited, and thus that natural selection is brought into play.[149] Furthermore, we must recall that Darwin did not deny that, in some cases, it was possible for individually acquired characteristics to be inherited; therefore, in addition to explanations in terms of chance variations, he was able to hold that habits might sometimes be transformed into instincts, after many generations.[150] For example, in accounting for the sagacity of animals in avoiding traps in those regions in which trapping had long been practiced, he assumed that the results of past learning had been transformed into an instinctive wariness.[151] Regardless of the source of the changes which were introduced, natural selection would of course operate on them; in the course of time, new forms of instinctive behavior would therefore arise, becoming dominant in the species, whether animal or human.[152]

Darwin's emphasis on the role of instinct in human behavior, and his interest in establishing continuity between the higher animals and human forms of behavior, led him to reject a consistently hedonistic account of human motivation. While he attributed some actions to the operation of the factors of pleasure and pain, he did not hold that it was warranted to do so in all cases. For example, after recognizing instances in which fear-reactions were attributable to the effects of pain, he said:

> In many cases, however, it is probable that instincts are followed from the mere force of inheritance, without the stimulus of either pleasure or pain. A young pointer when it first scents game, apparently cannot help pointing. A squirrel in the cage who pats the nuts which it cannot eat, as if to bury them in the ground, can hardly be thought to act thus either from pleasure or pain. Hence the common assumption that men must be impelled to every action by experiencing some pleasure or pain may be erroneous.[153]

Thus, at two fundamental points, Darwin's psychology came into conflict with the traditions which had dominated English and French geneticism: first, in rejecting its emphasis on the individual's acquisiton of distinctively human traits through the medium of his social environment, and second, in rejecting a hedonistic psychology. On the basis of these changes in point of view, Darwin and the Darwinians did not look upon *the individual* as being fundamentally malleable; however, malleability remained characteristic of the race as a race. It is to a consideration of that malleability that we now turn.

In tracing the continuity between human nature and its origins in animal instinct, Darwin devoted most attention to the problems of the development of a moral sense. He did so since it was commonly held that, in this respect, there was an even greater gap between human nature and animal instinct than there was with respect to man's intellectual powers. It was Darwin's aim to show that this gap could be bridged by using the same comparative method and the same explanatory concepts that he had used in accounting for the origin of new species.

To understand the manner in which he proceeded we must understand his conception of human morality. He believed in the existence of a special moral sense or conscience, which he regarded as a component in man's affective and volitional life but not as a source of cognitive insight. His conception of morality also included the acceptance of a non-egoistic moral standard which he identified with the Golden Rule, saying "this lies at the foundation of morality."[154]

Given this general conception of morality, and seeking its remote origins in animal instinct, it was natural that Darwin should have concerned himself primarily with the social instincts in animals. To find continuity between such instincts and the social behavior of men, he could not lay primary stress on the patterns of instinctive action found in birds, ants, bees, etc., with which he had been mainly concerned in the *Origin of Species*. Instead, he focused attention on those forms of behavior among the higher animals which might have a more direct evolutionary connection with social impulses in man. Out of such impulses, when coupled with a higher degree of intelligence, it might then be presumed that man's moral sense had developed. Darwin stated this general hypothesis clearly and explicitly at the outset of his treatment of the origins of the moral sense:

> The following proposition seems to me in a high degree probable—namely, that any animal whatever, endowed with well-marked social instincts, would inevitably acquire a moral sense or conscience, as soon as its intellectual powers had become as well developed, or nearly as well developed, as in man.[155]

The particular instincts on which Darwin placed primary emphasis were not examples of those forms of behavior in which animals hunted in packs or banded together in mutual defense, although he cited such instincts as being of importance to the survival of species, and his use of them did illustrate the fact that instinctive behavior was not necessarily anti-social, as some had tended to maintain. The two forms of instinctive behavior which he regarded as especially relevant to human social behavior were those which, even in speaking of the lower animals, he designated as love and as sympathy.[156] Although he did not attempt to state what characteristic differentiated love and sympathy from other instincts, it is perhaps accurate to say that in these cases Darwin assumed that the animal's behavior was tied to the well-being of some other animal whose actual presence elicited the response. For example, he cited instances of animal attachments to their young as instances of love, and a dog's attempt to defend its master as an instance of sympathy. Unlike instincts which governed hunting in packs, and similar cases (which he often referred to as "special instincts"), love and sympathy were *directly* connected with promoting the good of another individual. Therefore, the presence of this same sort of instinctive reaction throughout a species would tend to establish close bonds among the individuals living in proximity to one another. Darwin also referred to a tendency toward imitative behavior as a factor which could serve to strengthen common forms of behavior within a group. It was out of these basic instincts that he believed morality had originally grown.

The specific steps in that growth need not be followed in detail. With respect to the question of the ultimate origin of an instinct such as parental affection, Darwin was inclined to invoke chance variations and natural selection, since this instinct would have been of help in the struggle for survival.[157] A similar conjecture was offered by Darwin to account for the development of sympathy and of other social instincts. He pointed out that such instincts not only lead to a more gregarious form of existence, but that they tend to flourish and become habitual under these circumstances: thus they tend to be self-reinforcing, or, as we should now say, to continue developing due to positive feedback. Furthermore, as we have noted, Darwin was wholly willing to acknowledge that persistent habits were inherited; thus, sociality would have continued to develop by gradual increments over time. However, Darwin had not established what he had sought to establish: an account of the basis of conscience as an effective influence, among other influences, on conduct. Now, conscience—according to his view of morality—always reflected man's social impulses, not those which were connected with self-regarding instincts; and the question which Darwin therefore wished to answer was how conditions could arise which would make the force of conscience stronger than hunger, and stronger even than the instinct of self-preservation.[158] His answer consisted in holding that the social impulses are actually stronger than impulses such as hunger in so far as they are more persistent. For example, the social impulses constantly maintain themselves, whereas impulses such as hunger are transient, and disappear as soon as they are satisfied; thus, according to Darwin,[159] the reverberations of the social impulses continue, expressing themselves in the discomfiture of conscience, when we have succumbed to a transient impulse. On future occasions, this will help to forestall a repetition of the same behavior. These effects of the social impulses are then reinforced, according to Darwin's account, by the praise and blame of others.[160] Thus, social morality comes into existence.

This by no means concluded what Darwin had to say concerning the moral standard which had thus originated. Adhering to his evolutionary point of view, the specific forms of conduct which were praised or blamed, and which were thus reinforced within any given group, were necessarily those forms of conduct which aided the group to survive. Thus the actual standard of judgment which underlay all moral codes was a standard of the general good of the group, and Darwin contrasted this conclusion with Mill's "Greatest Happiness" principle.[161] To be sure, in the history of the race, many different customs received moral sanction because they contributed to the good of the group under whatever conditions then obtained, and, as a consequence, different societies sometimes praised different virtues and condemned different actions as vices. Nevertheless, there were some general forms of action which would, under almost all circumstances, be either beneficial or deleterious, and Darwin praised Bagehot's articles on *Physics and Politics* for having pointed to the existence of these forms of sanctioned and of prohibited behavior.[162] While such standards were not in most instances originally attributable to man's powers of foresight and reasoning, Darwin readily admitted that our judgments of right and wrong came to be more and more directly related to an apprehension of that which would promote the general good.[163] Any society which maintained standards which did not promote the welfare of the group, or in which ignorance and superstition beclouded man's judgments as to group welfare, were societies which could be criticized by moralists; they were also societies which would not, in the long run, survive. Thus, progressive enhancement of group welfare was a natural accompaniment of the historical process, and while Darwin was not an extreme progressivist,[164] he did conclude his discussion of how natural selection applied to civilized nations with words which we have already quoted:

> It is apparently a truer and more cheerful view that progress has been much more general than retrogression; that man has risen, though by slow and interrupted steps, from a lowly condition to the highest standard as yet attained by him in knowledge, morals, and religion.[165]

In addition to Darwin, there were others who used the principles of individual variation and natural selection to account for long-term changes in human nature, and for social change. As we have already noted, Bagehot used the Darwinian theory to explain why some traits were socially sanctioned and others were not, and Darwin accepted his account. Furthermore, the investigations of Francis Galton, Darwin's cousin, arose out of an interest in questions raised by Darwin,[166] and his book, *Hereditary Genius*, was highly praised by Darwin in *The Descent of Man*. In Galton's later work, *Inquiries into Human Faculty*, in which he reported his research on the capacities of twins, Galton stated the problem with which he was concerned as being that of estimating the relative forces of "Nurture and Nature," and he summarized his conclusion in saying that he had established "the vastly preponderating effects of nature over nurture."[167] This work, which was a primary source of the eugenics movement, fitted very closely with Darwin's own views, for *The Descent of Man* placed far greater emphasis on the effects which inheritance has on the intellectual and moral qualities of individuals than one would today be inclined to do.[168] This emphasis on inheritance, together with the analogy which Darwin always drew between natural selection and selection under conditions of domestication, led to the ideal of a controlled improvement of the human race, which Galton summarized in saying:

> My general object has been to take note of the varied hereditary faculties of different men, and of the great differences in different families and races, to learn how far history may have shown the practicability of supplanting inefficient human stock by better strains, and to consider whether it might not be our duty to do so by such efforts as may be reasonable, thus exerting ourselves to further the ends of evolution more rapidly and with less distress than if events were left to their own course.[169]

In W. K. Clifford's essays, one can find a parallel to Galton's application of Darwinian principles; however, unlike Galton, Clifford applied these principles not to individuals primarily, but directly to societies. As Frederick Pollock informs us, Clifford was one of a group who had been enormously influenced by the concept of natural selection, and wanted to establish on the basis of it "a new system of ethics, combining the exactness of the utilitarian with the poetical ideals of the transcendentalist."[170] In his early exposition of his conception of the development of human nature, Clifford invoked what he took to be a basic biological law, "that the development of an organism proceeds from its activities rather than its passivities."[171] In other words, he regarded change as being induced in an organism from within, and not because of its relation to its environment. This doctrine, which fitted well with the ideal of freedom and self-development which Clifford connected with Mazzini,[172] and with his emphasis on constant growth and development in individual character and in history,[173] also fitted (though only loosely) with Darwin's theory: it minimized any direct action of the environment, and located the primary source of the variability of species in traits possessed by the organisms themselves. While this analogy between their views regarding the sources of variability is only a very loose one, the factor of selection to which Clifford appealed was, precisely, Darwin's own theory.[174] And in his later essay, "On the Scientific Basis of Morals," Clifford emphasized the element of selection in a thoroughly Darwinian manner.

However, there was one fundamental difference between Darwin's theory and that of Clifford. In analyzing moral development, Darwin had placed emphasis on the attributes of individuals, and had tended to regard the survival of a society as dependent upon these character traits. While Clifford accepted Darwin's genetic account of the origins of the individual's conscience,[175] and while he apparently saw no difference between his own theory and that of Darwin,[176] he tended to identify all that was moral with the dominance of what he termed a "tribal self" over the individual self. It was Clifford's conviction that among primitive peoples a sense of group-identity preceded a sense of individuality, and he designated as "Piety" the disposition to give supremacy to those motives which had their origins in the tribal self; in other words, piety was acting for the benefit of the group. On this basis he gave the following account:

The tribe has to exist. Such tribes as saw no necessity for it have ceased to live. To exist, it must encourage piety; and there is a method which lies ready to hand....

If a man does anything generally regarded as good for the tribe, my tribal self may say... "I like that thing that you have done." By such common approbation of individual acts the influence of piety as a motive becomes defined; and natural selection will in the long run preserve those tribes which have approved the right things; namely, those things which at that time gave the tribe an advantage in the struggle for existence.[177]

While this stresses the role of natural selection and social well-being in the development of moral standards, just as Darwin's theory had done, Clifford's account of morality was fundamentally different. He did not seek its roots in the utility of a number of different forms of individual action, such as instinctive tendencies to love and sympathy, or dispositional traits such as courage and self-control, nor in mental capacities such as foresight: morality rested for him on group solidarity, on the dominance of the tribal self. Consequently, when he came to make value judgments, he did not regard particular traits as morally good because they did in fact contribute to the welfare of the social group: they were only morally good in so far as the welfare of the group was the end toward which they were explicitly directed.[178] In the same connection, he distinguished between piety and altruism:

> Piety is not Altruism. It is not the doing good to others as others, but the service of the community by a member of it, who loses in that service the consciousness that he is anything different from the community.[179]

For Clifford, it is piety, not altruism, which is basic to morality.

We can say with some assurance that Clifford's position would have been rejected by Darwin, both as an account of the roots of morality and as a judgment of relative value. Nevertheless, his position was typical of the emphasis of a good many later writers who assumed that the only point of view from which a Darwinian should assess the value of a trait of character or of a form of action, was with respect to the contribution which it made to social survival. To be sure, there were also many writers who interpreted Darwinism in a quite different and incompatible way, holding to a completely individualistic standard of value; on their view, each individual was committed by his nature to ruthless competition with others in a struggle for survival. The opposition of these two views—each of which was fundamentally different from Darwin's own account of morality— suggests the need for characterizing what constitutes the underlying form of explanation which, when applied to man's nature, can properly be called "Darwinian." This form of explanation involves more than an appeal to "natural selection," which, following Spencer, Darwin termed "the survival of the fittest." In addition, it involves an account of the genesis of the particular characteristics upon which the selective process operates. In this respect it is probably fair to say that no account of an evolutionary process is "Darwinian" if it does not hold that new characteristics arise as random variations among the traits of individuals belonging to a particular species, and that such variations are passed on by biological inheritance to the offspring. Finally, we may note that no theory would generally be termed "Darwinian" if it did not include the hypothesis that there is, in some form, a "struggle for survival," that is, that there is competition which does not permit all new variations to survive.

A characterization of this sort obviously excludes some forms of evolutionary theory from being designated as Darwinian; for example, Bergson separated his orthogenetic evolutionism from the Darwinian theory on the basis of his postulate that there is a directional factor in variability, which Darwin had left out of account. Furthermore, if one carefully considers Lamarck's evolutionary theory (and does not equate it with a belief in the inheritance of the effects of use and disuse, which Darwin in some cases also accepted), one finds that the fundamental difference between Lamarck's theory and that of Darwin consists in their conceptions of how the environment operates in fostering the development of new species. According to Darwin's theory, the primary influence of the environment is selective. Apart from some few cases in which he, like Buffon, assumed that it could have a direct effect on the genetic constitution of animals and plants, Darwin held that variations arose independently of environmental influences. Consequently, when one speaks of "adaptation" in Darwinian evolution, one is speaking of how well a particular variety can survive and multiply in the particular environment in which it exists. In a Lamarckian theory, however, the need for adaptation is the basis on which new structures gradually arise, and the lack of a need for a particular structure eventually causes it to disappear. Thus adaptation is a positive factor, being the tendency of an organism, impelled by its inner needs, to grow into closer relationship with its environment. Thus, on Lamarck's theory, there is a tendency on the part of every type of animal to make itself into that which, given a particular environment, it will eventually become. This Lamarckian view of evolution was characteristic of Herbert Spencer's biology, and of his psychology as well.

The role which positive adaptation to the environment played in Spencer's theories was evident in the first edition of his *Principles of Psychology*, a work antedating his *First Principles*. In it he defined life in a manner that then became fundamental to his biology, saying:

The broadest and most complete definition of Life will be—*The continuous adjustment of internal relations to external relations.*[180]

Spencer then developed this concept in terms of an equilibrating interplay of forces, as was demanded by his acceptance of a *total* evolutionism. At a later point in the same work he said:

It is scarcely possible too much to emphasize the conclusion, that all these processes by which organisms are re-fitted to their ever-changing environments, must be equilibrations of one kind or another. As authority for this conclusion, we have not simply the universal truth that change of every order is towards equilibrium; but we have also the truth which holds throughout the organic world, that life itself is the maintenance of a moving equilibrium between inner and outer actions—the continuous adjustment of internal relations to external relations.[181]

Spencer recognized that his theory was fundamentally different from Darwin's, though it could include Darwin's principles as being of some importance in the evolutionary process. In one section of his *Principles of Biology*, Spencer made his position absolutely clear, saying "There must be a natural selection of functionally-acquired peculiarities, as well as of incidental peculiarities";[182] or, in other words, chance variations and natural selection *alone* could not account for the origin of new species—direct adaptation to the conditions imposed by the environment was the primary factor on which change depended.

To be sure, if these adaptive changes were to be effective in bringing about evolutionary change, they had to be transmitted by inheritance; and Spencer, looking at the process of evolution as a whole, rather than considering what could be observed with respect to individual organisms and their offspring, was willing to allow far wider scope to the inherited effects of experience than Darwin had done. This difference is particularly evident with respect to Spencer's views regarding the evolution of mind. While Darwin had, for example, taken most animal instincts to be ultimately dependent on chance variations,[183] Spencer regarded them as compound reflex actions which had grown up through accumulated experience, and were preserved by the inheritance of the effects of that experience.[184] Spencer's theory of the particular way in which experience affected the individual, and hence (ultimately) the race, was through the establishment of an association of ideas. To hold, as he did,[185] that the effects of the association of ideas would be inherited was clearly at odds with earlier forms of geneticism; however, its acceptance becomes somewhat more intelligible when we take into account Spencer's correlation of mental phenomena with the nervous system: if other bodily changes brought about by habit could be inherited, then the effects of an association of ideas, which could be reflected in "the modified nervous tendencies produced by such new habits" could also be passed on to later generations.[186] In fact, we find that Bain, who was the most eminent associationist psychologist of the day, and who did a great deal to relate the traditions of associationism to the growth of physiological knowledge, also believed that simpler and constantly iterated habits, when they were of importance to the animal, could be inherited, since "in virtue of the acquired strength of nervous connections, these might in some degree persist in the germ."[187] Nevertheless, Bain was far more restrictive than was Spencer with respect to the characteristics which could be inherited.[188] For Spencer it was even possible that, within the scope of modern history, new capabilities had developed through habit, and that these capabilities had—within that relatively short time—become inherited traits.[189] Since only those capabilities which represented successful adaptations would eventually survive, it is not surprising that, unlike Darwinians who counted more on chance variations than on adaptive habits as the primary source of inherited variations, Spencer believed that the basic facts of psychology and of biology assured mankind of a continuing cumulative progress.

In addition to the fact that his associationist psychology and his belief in the inheritance of acquired habits provided an explanation of the progressive tendencies of mankind, Spencer explained the sequence of historical change in terms of tendencies inherent within societies themselves. Unlike Darwin, or Galton, or Bain—and with an emphasis quite different from that of Clifford—Spencer's evolutionary account of man's development depended upon his recognition not only of changes in the nature of individual men, but of changes in social institutions.[190] For Spencer, the realm of societal facts was to be characterized as different from the physical and from the organic realms: it was designated by him as "superorganic." Like Comte, or Hegel, or Marx, he held that the phenomena characterizing the structures of society are not capable of being understood in terms of the principles which explain individual actions, even when these actions represent responses to the presence and the actions of other individuals.[191] Thus, according to one meaning of the term "organicism," Spencer might be characterized as belonging to that school of thought. However, as I have already indicated,[192] I am not here using that term with that particular signification; instead, "organicism" is here only being taken to refer to a certain type of theory regarding the relationship which exists between the characteristics of individual human nature and the societies to which those individuals belong. With respect to this issue, Spencer did *not* hold an organicist doctrine, as will now become clear.

Spencer identified a society as a discrete aggregate, of which the aggregated units were individual human beings. Since he believed that the character of any aggregate depended upon the nature of the units of which it was composed, and upon the forces influencing them, it is clear that he did not view an individual's nature as being wholly molded by society. Nor would such a view have been consistent with there being an independent science of individual psychology, in which—unlike Comte and unlike Hegel—he did of course believe. On the other hand, Spencer did not hold that man's nature was constant over time. This was obviously precluded by his insistence on an evolutionary development in which acquired habits became inherited traits. What he held, therefore, was the view that there was a constant interplay between society and its units:

> As soon as a combination of men acquires permanence, there begin actions and reactions between the community and each member of it, such that either affects the other in nature. The control exercised by the aggregate over its units, tends ever to mould their activities and sentiments and ideas into congruity with social requirements; and these activities, sentiments, and ideas, in so far as they are changed by changing circumstances, tend to re-mould the society into congruity with themselves.[193]

This interplay involved a moving equilibrium, since the nature of the individuals would not remain static because of their accumulating experience, and the institutions would likewise be changed by the individuals, and also by external factors, such as changes in the geographic environment. And such a dynamic equilibrium was, of course, precisely what Spencer's total evolutionism demanded: a constant interplay and redistribution of forces. With respect to the applicability of this principle to the relationships between individuals and their society, we find Spencer saying:

> Conformably with the laws of evolution in general, and conformably with the laws of organization in particular, there has been, and is, in progress an adaptation of humanity to the social state, changing it in the direction of such an ideal congruity. And the corollary before drawn and here repeated, is that the ultimate man is one in whom this process has gone so far as to produce a correspondence between all the promptings of his nature and all the requirements of his life as carried on in society.[194]

Once again, it might be assumed that the acceptance of such a standard brought Spencer close to the "organicism" of Comte, Hegel, or Marx. However, once again, it is important to remember—and the extreme individualism of Spencer's social ethics should remind us of the fact—that he placed no less emphasis on the individual than he did upon society as an aggregative organism. Pleasure and pain remained touchstones of value, for they were signs of well-being in the functioning of the individual, and the good of society never supplanted the good of indi-

viduals, according to Spencer's view. Throughout his statement of his theory and
his evaluation of change, both the individual and the social organism maintain
themselves as distinct although interacting elements, both of which are to be considered in understanding the forms of life which have characterized human history. As each has grown, so has the other, and if society is now more developed,
and more progressive, so too is man. While this conclusion is directly deducible
from what Spencer regarded as the ultimate law governing the evolutionary process, he was never wholly arbitrary in his use of that law. As we have noted, his
theories of the association of ideas, of the inheritance of habitual associations, of
the need for adaptation to the environment, and of the interrelation of individuals and the social institutions under which they live, provided what he took
to be an adequate explanation of the vast mass of data which he attempted to
survey, giving scientific support to what from the first he had believed:

> Progress . . . is not an accident, but a necessity. Instead of civilization being artificial
> it is a part of nature; all of a piece with the development of an embryo or the unfolding
> of a flower. The modifications mankind have undergone, and are still undergoing,
> result from a law underlying the whole organic creation; and provided the human race
> continues, and the constitution of things remains the same, those modifications must end
> in completeness. As surely as the tree becomes bulky when it stands alone, and
> slender if one of a group; as surely as a blacksmith's arm grows large, and the skin of a
> laborer's hand thick; . . . as surely as a clerk acquires rapidity in writing and calculation;
> . . . as surely as a passion grows by indulgence and diminishes when restrained; as
> surely as a disregarded conscience becomes inert, and one that is obeyed active; as surely
> as there is any meaning in such terms as habit, custom, practice;—so surely must the
> human faculties be moulded into complete fitness for the social state; so surely must
> evil and immorality disappear; so surely must man become perfect.[195]

When Spencer speaks in this fashion, the term "man" must not be taken as
referring to any individual human being, nor to individuals taken simply as a
collective aggregate, but to a historically developing entity, Man or Humanity;
and this applies also to most of those with whom we have been dealing in discussing either organicism or the doctrine that Man is to be conceived as a progressive
being.[196]

As we have seen, this was a view which was, at the least, different in emphasis
from that held by those philosophers of history in the Enlightenment who discussed the education or the progress of Mankind. Change had been viewed by
them as a tendency to bring about conditions under which truth and happiness,
and the other values of civilization, could be individually and collectively
achieved. Consequently, their emphasis was placed on the goal of the process, on
what was the ideal condition of man. Given their cosmopolitan standards, little
sympathy was evinced for the earlier stages of history, which had to be overcome
before that goal could be reached. It was as a revolt against this and other aspects
of Enlightenment standards of value that another conception of the historical development of man was introduced: cultural diversity was emphasized, as was the
element of tradition which served to bind a people together, giving unity to

historical change. However, on this view of the human race, as one sees it particularly in Herder, the species expressed itself in a multitude of different ways,
but it was not itself a historical entity, a subject which had reality and underwent historical change.[197] On the other hand, according to the metaphysical
idealists, the human condition did not remain the same: the race, as a race, had
developed and, through self-education, brought about not merely a fulfilment of
desires which were already present, but a wholly new condition of man. Thus, for
example, in his *Speeches to the German Nation*, Fichte claimed that through
education mankind would endow itself with a new form: it would actually create
itself, making itself that which it had always implicitly been.[198] And Hegel's
Phenomenology of Spirit actually attempted to trace the stages in such a self-
creation of humanity, in which an increasing depth and comprehensiveness of
the spirit took place.[199]

This general view was not a special characteristic of German metaphysical
idealism; it was, for example, equally characteristic of Comte, and of all who
came under his influence.[200] Furthermore, we may note—not without surprise—
that in spite of Mill's rejection of Comte's social views, he praised the Comtean
conception of Humanity as an object of religious reverence.[201] Totally apart from
that praise, the conception of progressive transformations of human nature was
present throughout Mill's writings; this was, in fact, the point at which, as we
have seen, he profoundly modified the associationist psychology of his predecessors. And after Mill, even independently of biological and sociological evolutionism, there was a tendency toward a historical, developmental psychology of
the human race. One sees this in G. H. Lewes' *Study of Psychology*, in spite of the
fact that his philosophic convictions demanded that he view the human mind as
directly related to the body. The point was put very forcibly when he said,
"Psychology investigates the Human Mind, not an individual's thoughts and
feelings."[202] The manner in which Lewes harmonized these apparently antithetical
views was through his acceptance of the doctrine of emergence. For example, in
the passage just cited he went on to hold that in man "animal impulses are
profoundly modified by social influences, and his higher faculties are evolved
through social needs." And, again, one finds him saying,

Biology furnishes both method and data in the elucidation of the relations of the
organism and the external medium; and so far as Animal Psychology is concerned this is
enough. But Human Psychology has a wider reach, includes another important factor,
the influence of the social medium. This is not simply an addition, ... it is a factor which
permeates the whole composition of mind.[203]

Thus, Lewes' psychology was wedded to an historical consideration of man's
nature,[204] and the psychology of the individual became in effect a psychology of
the General Mind.[205]

Finally, we may note that in the self-realizationism of Wundt, which was relatively far removed from the philosophic presuppositions of Lewes, and certainly
from those of Spencer, the same historical developmentalism was at work. In

Wundt's *Ethics*, which dates from 1886, *development* furnishes the underlying preconception of the whole work.[206] The basis for his actual working out of his theory was in the famous doctrine of *heterogeny* of ends:

...manifestations of will, over the whole range of man's free voluntary actions, are always of such a character that the effects of the actions extend more or less widely beyond the original motives of volition, so that *new* motives are originated for future actions, and again, in turn, produce new effects.[207]

Since Wundt (like T. H. Green) held that the ends which an individual strives to attain are not purely individual ends, it is obvious that his doctrine of the heterogeny of ends opened the door to a belief in an indefinitely extended range of human progress. This belief Wundt consistently maintained. Moral value did not reside in the satisfaction of desires which had the individual's own ends as their goal; it was confined to those desires which were directed toward universal ends.[208] However, it was not merely the universal satisfaction of desire, the general happiness, which man had as his goal; rather, man strove for self-realization through an ever-increasing flow of psychical creations,

...a process in which the individual consciousness bears its part, yet whose final object is not the individual himself, but the universal spirit of humanity.[209]

Thus, "the ultimate end of human morality is the moral ideal, . . . its immediate end is the progressive perfection of humanity."[210] While the individual consciousness plays an all-important part in this progress, Wundt might well have said with Clifford:

Conscience and reason form an inner core in the human mind, having an origin and a nature distinct from the merely animal passions and perceptions; they constitute the soul or spirit of man, the universal part in every one of us. In these are bound up, embalmed and embodied, all the struggles and searchings of spirit of the countless generations which have made us what we are. Action which arises out of that inner core, which is prompted by conscience and guided by reason, is *free* in the highest sense of all; this at last is *good* in the ethical sense. And yet, when we act with this most perfect freedom, it may be said that it is not we that act, but Man that worketh in us.[211]

The belief that one can legitimately speak of Man, or Mankind, or Humanity, as a unitary historical being, as that which transcends every individual, making each of us what we are, was a belief which was among the most distinctive tenets of nineteenth-century thought. Like geneticism and like organicism—with both of which it was not infrequently connected—it rested on philosophic preconceptions which it would be well to examine. And to such tasks we shall now turn.

12

CONSTANCY AND CHANGE IN HUMAN NATURE:
A CRITICAL ACCOUNT

Each of the doctrines which we have now examined rejected the assumption that the basic attributes of human nature were constant, but each invoked a different type of principle to account for the fact that changes in these attributes occurred. Geneticism was concerned with the role of individual experience in the formation of character; organicism, on the other hand, turned its attention to the effects on the individual of the patterns of culture which were characteristic of the times. In short, while both assumed that man's nature was almost indefinitely malleable, the psychological bias of the one contrasted sharply with the historical and cultural bias of the other. This helps to explain how geneticism could flourish within the context of eighteenth-century thought, whereas organicism was linked with the growth of historicism.

The third doctrine which we have been considering, that man is by nature a progressive being, had points of contact with each of the other two views. It resembled organicism, rather than geneticism, in tending to stress the historical development of mankind; on the other hand, it rejected the assumption that societies could change in an autonomous fashion, and therefore, like geneticism, sought a primarily psychological basis for the changing nature of man. However, all forms of the progressivist view rejected the emphasis which both geneticism and organicism had placed on the *plasticity* of human nature, rather than on the individual's active powers. It was this difference which separated John Stuart Mill from the geneticism of prior associationism, and which separated Fichte and Green from organicism. As we have seen, Mill, Arnold, and Huxley, no less than Fichte and Green, held that within man's changing nature there was a power of self-transformation: men had the ability to bestow new capacities upon themselves, actually transforming themselves rather than being transformed. Furthermore, among progressivist theories which used the analogy of biological evolution to explain changes in human nature, emphasis also was placed on the active side of man: only when individuals varied and societies were innovative could the selective process operate and mankind advance. Thus, on all progressivist views, it was not primarily because men could be shaped by experience, but because they tended to bring new forces to bear upon future experience, that human nature itself changed.

These differences among the various theories with which we have been concerned should not be allowed to conceal the point which they had in common: their rejection of the previously dominant nativistic views of the human mind. Instead of regarding variations in human behavior as merely reflecting the ways in which a common set of characteristics expressed themselves under varying circumstances, they held that the characteristics of man's nature had basically changed during the history of mankind, and would presumably continue to change.

In order to analyze this contention in a manner which will be directly relevant to issues that have been important to the social sciences from the nineteenth century to our own day, it will be useful to begin with one of the more recent forms of the malleability thesis, the doctrine which may be designated as *social conditioning*." This doctrine provides a useful point of departure since it combines the psychological approach of geneticism with the cultural approach of organicism;[1] furthermore, it has surely been one of the most pervasive concepts in social psychology in the twentieth century, on both quasi-popular and scientific levels of discussion.

1. THE CONCEPT OF SOCIAL CONDITIONING

One need not trace the history of the concept of "social conditioning" in detail in order to be aware of its origins and of the sources of its appeal. When the doctrine of *conditioning* which had been developed by Pavlov in the early years of the century came to be known in the United States, it became an important force in American experimental psychology, and helped promote the acceptance of behaviorism, through which it had in large measure been introduced.[2] While Pavlov was no less opposed than were the behaviorists to any use of the concept of consciousness in explaining behavior,[3] his primary importance in the development of their views was through the concept of conditioning: his results had suggested that conditioning could provide a well-grounded alternative to instinctivist theories of behavior. Until then, instinctivism had been an important element in early twentieth-century psychological thought, since it was connected with those forms of comparative psychology which had been stimulated by Darwin's evolutionary theory. Furthermore, through the influence of McDougall's *Introduction to Social Psychology* the instinctivist interpretation of human characteristics had come to have widespread popularity in the United States, as well as in England. It was this popularity which the theory of conditioning began to undermine in the 1920s and 1930s.

If we are to understand the development of the concept of *social* conditioning," we must not only take into account the factor of conditioning, which was stressed by the behaviorists, but must also note that within American psychology there were those who placed great emphasis on the role of social interaction in the formation of character. For example, the sociologist E. A. Ross wrote a pioneering work entitled *Social Psychology* (which was published in 1908, contemporaneously with McDougall's book), and his account of human behavior assigned a primary role to imitation and custom, not to instinct. Similarly, in the works of C. H. Cooley and in John Dewey's influential *Human Nature and Conduct*, which was published in 1922, one can see clear exemplifications of the trend toward interpreting individuals as interacting with one another to form a social environment which enters deeply into each individual's nature. This type of socio-psychological theory may be said to represent one form of a theory of social conditioning, but unlike later forms it did not place primary emphasis upon environmental influences in explaining the characteristics of individuals. Instead, as one sees most clearly in George Herbert Mead, it emphasized the factor of an ongoing interchange between the individual and his social environment, through which each formed the other.

The widespread acceptance of this view undoubtedly paved the way for what might be designated as social conditioning in its strictest, narrowest sense: a view which had earlier been exemplified in such works as Sumner's *Folkways* and Westermarck's *Origin and Development of Moral Ideas*, both of which were published during exactly the same period as the social psychologies of Ross and McDougall. The works of Sumner and of Westermarck placed primary emphasis on the diversity of cultural norms, and explained the ideals of individuals in terms of the social group.[4] This theory of moral codes exerted a considerable influence on popular thought, and more than a negligible influence on sociology during the subsequent decades. Nevertheless, the dominance of the theory of social conditioning in the 1930s and subsequently is most properly identified with the impact of a number of anthropological investigations such as Margaret Mead's *Coming of Age in Samoa* (1928), *Growing Up in New Guinea* (1930), and *Sex and Temperament in Three Primitive Societies* (1935), to mention merely one fairly typical series of related studies. In such studies one can see a strong resemblance between the doctrine of social conditioning and organicist views of man's malleability. It must be remembered, however, that anthropologists of this period had rebelled against social evolutionism (and also against cultural diffusionism); as a consequence, they had rejected the possibility of giving historical interpretations of changing schemes of value, as nineteenth-century organicists had done. Furthermore, unlike most earlier organicists, these anthropologists had a strong positive interest in using psychological concepts in explaining the impact of culture on the individual; and for this purpose they made use of the concept of "conditioning," although they first applied it in a loose and very extended sense. Later, under the influence of a special concern with child development, and with the popularity of the theory that differences in culture might be explained in terms of differences in child-rearing practices, the mechanisms of the relevant forms of conditioning were spelled out in somewhat greater detail. However, it is not with these differences among the proponents of various forms of social conditioning theory that we need here be concerned: what I first wish to establish is that no form of such a theory can legitimately hold to an indefinite malleability in human nature. What I have to say in this connection will shortly be seen to be relevant to most of the doctrines which were characteristic of geneticism and of nineteenth-century organicism as well.

To establish this point, let us consider the conditioning experiments which Pavlov himself originally performed. In conditioning a dog to salivate at a specific sound, it was necessary that this sound should have been repeatedly connected with the presence of food; obviously, if food were not itself capable of inducing salivation, it could not serve as a vehicle for the conditioning process. To be sure, what constitutes an unconditioned response in any particular set of trials may itself have been due to prior conditioning. For example, it is a conditioned response that an animal salivates at the mere sight of food; and this conditioned response can serve as a basis for further conditioning. However, the regress cannot be indefinitely extended: there must eventually be some unconditioned response (in this case, salivation when food is present in the dog's mouth) upon which the conditioned response is based. Furthermore, as Pavlov quickly discovered, conditioned responses do not persist through an indefinite number of repetitions without being restored through re-conditioning. Thus, it is clear that conditioning presupposes the existence of native tendencies to react in specific ways: not *every* response can be a conditioned response.

Pavlov not only admitted this fact, but insisted upon it. His system depended upon there being a relatively large number of unconditioned reflexes, and among those which he discussed we find not only reflexes of grasping, and of salivating when food is placed in the mouth, but also unconditioned reflexes which he designated as reflexes of purpose, of freedom, and of slavery (as when puppies fall on their backs in the presence of larger dogs).[5] On the other hand, J. B. Watson attempted to cut down in drastic fashion on the number of unconditioned responses which psychologists would have to postulate in order to explain behavior. This attempt served to forward the belief that human beings were almost indefinitely malleable, and Watson himself drew this conclusion from his theory. Nevertheless, neither Pavlov's experimental work, nor Watson's assumptions regarding the existence of complicated chains of conditioned responses, provided concrete help in explaining the actual differences in social behavior with which anthropologists were concerned. Still, the views of Pavlov and Watson had already had sufficient impact to make it appear that "conditioning" was a synonym, or almost a synonym, for "learning." Under these circumstances, it was assumed that the differences in attitudes, beliefs, and behavior which anthropologists described were to be explained in terms of "social conditioning."[6]

In contrast to the classical form of conditioning theory characteristic of both Pavlov and Watson, one must take cognizance of what is termed "instrumental conditioning," the conditioning process primarily associated with the name of B. F. Skinner.[7] This form of conditioning theory is undoubtedly closer to what most persons have meant when they have spoken of "social conditioning." According to it, a conditioned response develops and becomes stable, or it is extinguished, because it has led to what can be designated as reward or punishment.

For example, in the experiments of Thorndike, or in those of Skinner, a cat comes to be conditioned to pull a string, or a rat to press a lever, because in past trials these actions have led to obtaining food. In short, the conditioning process is instrumental to the attainment of a state which the organism naturally seeks, or one which it would naturally avoid. On such a theory the initial success, or initial failure, might be construed as having resulted from trial and error, or from chance; in that case, the only *un*conditioned factors which would be needed to explain the process of conditioning would appear to have been the animal's tendency to pursue or avoid that which served as reward or punishment. Yet, even in such cases, what is involved is somewhat more complex than initially appears, for in instrumental conditioning the tendency to pursue or avoid that which serves as reward or punishment actually has two facets. On the one hand, the animal's behavior would not be what it was in the absence of some specific drive or propensity (the term to be used is not particularly important): for example, it is obvious that a condition of deprivation with respect to hunger or thirst is presupposed in many animal experiments. On the other hand, conditioning also demands that the satisfaction of such a drive or propensity will result in reinforcement: the animal must be assumed to have a tendency to repeat whatever acts led to the satisfaction of its drive.[8] As an example of this second type of factor, we may refer to Thorndike's "Law of Effect," which was phrased in terms of states of affairs which were *satisfying* or *discomforting*; and others have referred to this type of factor as the "tension-reduction" of reinforcers, or as "drive-reduction." While the theories connected with the use of these terms are not identical, each of the terms is meant to refer to some generic factor in conditioning. However, any such generic factor is to be distinguished from specific drives or propensities, such as hunger, thirst, or a tendency to activity. These two types of factors may be said to serve quite different explanatory functions. As Skinner has argued, if one is attempting to discover general laws of conditioning, one need not catalogue and classify the different forms of behavior presumably connected with different propensities—a task which he characterized as "the botanizing of reflexes."[9] On the other hand, this should not lead one to neglect the fact that in every instrumental conditioning experiment some drive or propensity *is* presupposed: it is not sufficient merely to appeal to the general concept of reinforcement (or to one of its equivalents) when analyzing the factors which must be present if conditioning is to occur. Thus, instrumental conditioning presupposes elements in behavior which are themselves unconditioned, just as classical Pavlovian theory had done.

It is at precisely this point that one can see a major cause of failure in vaguely formulated theories of "social conditioning." Those who have been identified with this doctrine have not been sufficiently concerned with the fact that conditioning presupposes aspects of behavior which are essential to the occurrence of conditioning, and are not themselves products of it. It is, of course, possible that these unconditioned factors might differ widely from individual to individual, with very little similarity among them; however, I know of no one who would regard this as a plausible suggestion. Nor would most psychologists, sociologists, or anthropologists be inclined to expect a high degree of variability in native endowment when the populations of different societies are compared. In fact, those who have laid greatest stress on the concept of social conditioning have been especially inclined to insist on the unity of mankind with respect to inherent capacities, and have generally rejected explanations of cultural differences which postulate differences in biological inheritance. Thus it would not be consistent for them to suppose that the process of conditioning involves widely different propensities in people belonging to even the most widely differing cultures. They generally fail to make this explicit. Instead, they emphasize the fact that what serves as an effective reward or punishment in one society may not do so in another. This is a fact which no one is likely to deny. However, from it we cannot legitimately infer that the propensities of people in different cultures are themselves different, for exactly the same propensity may be satisfied by different objects. It is the differences among these objects which theories of social conditioning have stressed; unfortunately, they have not also been concerned with the particular propensities which must be present if conditioning is to take place at all. We shall later be in a better position to estimate the significance of the variability of specific rewards and punishments; at this point it is only important that such variability should not be permitted to obscure the fact that whenever something serves as a reward or a punishment, there is presupposed some definite type of propensity, in the absence of which it could not function either as a reward or a punishment.

This conclusion should be sufficient to throw fundamental doubt on any thesis which affirms the indefinite malleability of human nature. Nevertheless, it does not fully uncover the flaws in the general theory of social conditioning. To do so, one further preliminary step must now be taken: it must be shown that the theory of conditioning does not commit us to holding that there is only a restricted range of basic propensities in human nature. Once this is acknowledged, it will quickly become evident why social conditioning only remains plausible as long as it remains vaguely stated.

From a number of points of view it might be considered theoretically satisfactory if one could successfully hold that the only unconditioned responses in human beings could be reduced to some very small number, and it might seem to be maximally satisfactory if there were only one type of unconditioned response. Perhaps the most persistently prevalent theory which has attempted to explain all human action in terms of a single causal factor has been psychological hedonism. Originally, hedonistic theories of motivation were phrased in a manner that emphasized the universality of a desire for pleasurable experiences: for continuing in a state of hedonic satisfaction, or for achieving as much future pleasure as one could. The differences among the variant forms of this general type of hedonistic theory should not be minimized; however, each was a theory which treated the desire for pleasure (or for the avoidance of pain) as a specific propensity regulating all behavior. It was assumed either to do so directly, or because new desires and aversions could be built into us through the pleasures and pains which we had experienced in the past. Nevertheless, as we noticed in discussing

Fichte and Green, pleasure is frequently only a by-product of the satisfaction of desire, rather than being that which itself elicits the desire. It is therefore not plausible to hold that our only propensity is that which directs us to seek pleasure.

There is another form of hedonism which supposedly avoids this difficulty. It was held by Locke and, as we have noted, it was the view which John Stuart Mill adopted in opposition to Bentham's psychology. According to it, the decisive factor in motivation is the pleasantness or unpleasantness accompanying present ideas, not a desire for future pleasures; it has therefore often been referred to as "psychological hedonism of the present moment." Unlike the more traditional form of psychological hedonism, this theory does not hold that there is only one fundamental propensity in human nature; in fact, it does not refer to specific propensities at all. Rather, it suggests that affective tone provides the common denominator which is present whenever action follows one course rather than another; it is thus roughly comparable to more recent explanatory concepts, such as "the law of effect." Unlike them, this form of hedonism does not lend itself to the explanation of animal behavior, nor does it serve to explain those forms of human behavior which do not include deliberate choice: it is surely not on every occasion that, before acting, we envision some future state of affairs, and are led to act as we do because our idea is either agreeable or not.[10] Therefore, it would be self-defeating for those who may wish to explain all human behavior in terms of some single common denominator if they were to accept this form of hedonism. Furthermore, it is important to note that, even in those cases in which the theory might be applied, it does not serve to explain the existence of our drives or propensities: if we were not attracted or repelled by an envisioned state of affairs, the idea of that state of affairs would not be pleasant or unpleasant to us. Therefore, like the law of effect, the theory would not offer a *sufficient* explanation of the springs of action: appetency remains irreducible to the concepts of pleasure and pain.

If this point may now be taken for granted, we can turn to the question of whether the drives, propensities, or appetites which are not themselves engendered by conditioning, but which must be presupposed in order to explain it, are to be assumed to be highly restricted in number, or whether it is plausible to assume that there are many such tendencies. In order to answer this question, no extensive "botanizing of reflexes" is demanded. When we consider the general nature of the experimental method (which is most effective when only one factor is varied at a time), we can understand why, in conditioning experiments, every effort is made to elicit responses which presuppose only one very specific native propensity, in order that all variations among the responses will be attributable to the process of conditioning itself. Thus, only hunger will be presupposed in one particular set of experiments; in another, only thirst. For the same reason, environmental conditions must be carefully controlled in a stimulus-response experiment, so that the responses elicited are—in so far as possible—limited to those directly involved in the conditioning. Bearing these methodological demands in mind, one can readily understand why the units of behavior in conditioning experiments tend to be restricted to relatively simple elements. However, the same propensities which are essential to the conditioning process under artificially controlled conditions are, of course, known to enter into far more complex forms of behavior in both animals and humans. Hunger, for example, gives rise to food-seeking behavior which can be much more complicated than pressing a treadle or running a maze. What is said of hunger can also be said of thirst; or it can be said of any other propensity used in animal conditioning. It is to be noted, however, that these are themselves different propensities: hunger is not to be identified with thirst, nor is either to be identified with the avoidance of electric shock.[11] Furthermore, hunger and thirst and shock-avoidance by no means exhaust the list of propensities which have been used in conditioning experiments. As H. F. Harlow and his associates, as well as others, have shown, the satisfaction of curiosity can be as effective a reward as is food when monkeys are being conditioned; manipulation as well as exploratory behavior have also functioned in this way in animal experiments. Given even this degree of variety of drives, propensities, or appetites, all of which are sufficiently specific to provide a basis for animal conditioning under experimental conditions, the range of unconditioned propensities which might reasonably be assumed to be present among animals would be rather wide;[12] among men, there is reason to believe, it would be very wide indeed.

The assumption that the repertory of human propensities may be wider than that of animals demands some defense. Against that assumption, some might be inclined to invoke C. Lloyd Morgan's well-known canon. In his pioneering work in comparative psychology in 1894, Morgan stated his canon as follows:

In no case may we interpret an action as the outcome of the exercise of a higher psychical faculty, if it can be interpreted as the outcome of one which stands lower in the psychological scale.[13]

This methodological principle has led to the supposition that all complex forms of behavior can be analyzed in terms of compounding factors which are simpler in character; and it must be admitted that, in many cases, the results of such analyses have been wholly adequate. However, it is worth noting that Morgan tended to look upon his principle as a necessary consequence of evolutionary theory, as one can note in his use of the terms "higher" and "lower."[14] Interpreting it in this fashion, one can presumably drastically reduce the number of different factors which must be invoked to explain the behavior of the higher animals; thus, Morgan's canon would seem to conform to the principle of Ockham's razor, avoiding the multiplication of different "entities." In general, animal psychologists have tended to interpret the canon this way, and have not been tempted to challenge it. On the other hand, one should notice that this canon makes the explanation of the behavior of the so-called higher animals far more complex than it might otherwise be presumed to be: in explaining what are designated as higher processes in terms of compounding those which are lower, one does save *entities*, but in doing so, one multiplies the steps through which such an explanation must proceed. Therefore, if Ockham's razor is interpreted as commending the simplest *explanation*, it would not necessarily constitute an endorsement of Morgan's canon. Now, I do not believe it possible to hold that one should always seek simplicity in explanation at the cost of multiplying entities, nor that one should always proceed in the opposite direction; on the contrary, I am inclined to believe that the relative adequacy of either procedure must be decided from case to case. Nevertheless, in the context of this discussion of Morgan's canon, and of the presuppositions of the processes of conditioning, I wish to argue that it is not necessary, in principle, for us to assume that the number of independent unconditioned propensities in human nature must be restricted to very few.

Evolutionary theory does not demand that such should be the case. In fact, when Darwin analyzed animal instinct in the *Origin of Species*, he assumed that these inherited changes in behavior could be explained by the same factors as changes in bodily organs; in both cases, natural selection acted upon individual variations and, over the course of time, gave rise to new forms. Thus, it is wholly consonant with Darwinian theory to hold that new and more complex forms of behavior are due to changes in the constitution of organisms, rather than being complex resultants of simpler patterns of reaction. In fact, considering the evolutionary changes in the nervous systems of the higher animals, it might even be considered surprising were there no characteristics of human behavior which were without counterparts among many of the lower animals. Evolutionary theory does not force us to suppose that the only distinctive characteristics of new species will be anatomical features which are readily apparent, and that no changes in the propensities and behavioral capacities of these species will accompany the other changes which they have undergone.

To be sure, if one were to say that the propensities of men were absolutely different from those of any other animals, one would be making a claim that would be regarded as implausible by evolutionists. This would also be true if the lines of kinship which one claimed to trace between the psychological characteristics of men and other animals did not in general conform to the lines of biological descent that evolutionary theory has established. Neither claim is here being made. The only point at issue is whether evolutionary theory does not permit us to suppose that along with those psychological traits in which men and other animals resemble one another there may not be a number of inherited capacities which are crucial for the analysis of human behavior, but which are not possessed by most other species; and whether, among these, there may not also be some not possessed even by those animals most closely resembling man.[15] It seems to me not in the least implausible to hold that such is the case.

However, there is a rather widespread tendency to assume that the basis for every unconditioned drive or reflex, and for every inherited capacity, must be connected with some specific organ or structure, as hunger is often assumed to be connected with the stomach, sex with the genital organs, reflexes with specific neural connections, etc.[16] Once this assumption is made, any attempt to enlarge the number of man's propensities beyond the limit of those ascribed to other animals is likely to encounter difficulties, since the supposedly relevant anatomical features of men will have close analogues among other species. However, the assumption is one which should not be made. Totally apart from the doubt which attaches to the analysis of either hunger or sex in these terms, it will be recalled that Pavlov believed it necessary to assume unconditioned reflexes of freedom, of power, and of slavery, which are not related to specific organs. While he firmly believed that every response, whether conditioned or unconditioned, did depend upon neural mechanisms, he did not insist that it was necessary to discover them in order to decide that a particular form of behavior was conditioned, or that it was an unconditioned response. The same point has, of course, been a basic methodological principle in B. F. Skinner's work, which involves a self-conscious attempt to avoid any physiological assumptions whatsoever, let alone assumptions which relate to specific anatomical organs. One can in fact be as reductionistic as one likes with reference to the physiological foundations of behavior without assuming that every basic drive must be connected with a specific organ or with a specific neural connection. Therefore, the similarity of man to other animals with respect to anatomical structure is largely irrelevant to the question of what are the basic propensities of human nature.

Bearing this in mind, and in order to make the following discussion more concrete, I should now like to propose that among men's basic propensities there is one which was most commonly designated as "pride" by eighteenth-century moral psychologists, but which might better be termed *self-esteem*. I place no special emphasis on singling out this particular propensity for attention, and it would not be fundamentally damaging to the points which I wish to make if one could show that it happens to be a response acquired through experience, by means of conditioning.[17] What I wish to illustrate is the fact that while self-esteem is surely not a derivative of the specific propensities which are used in the experimental conditioning of animal behavior, and while we are not likely to attribute it to animals,[18] nor likely to be able to find any specific anatomical or neural basis for it, it is itself an important factor in influencing human behavior; furthermore, it is especially important in what is referred to as "social conditioning."

Consider, for example, the manner in which praise and blame can be used in guiding the actions of children. Casting these facts into the terminology used in conditioning theory, we may say that the rewards and punishments which serve as reinforcements with respect to some social actions often consist in having other persons praise us or blame us. Nevertheless, if we are to derive satisfaction from another's praise, or to be troubled by his blame, we must first have an inclination to be thought well of by others. This is in principle no different from the fact that food can only serve as a positive reinforcer for a rat because that rat, without being conditioned, is the sort of organism which (under the conditions of the experiment) has strong food-seeking propensities. Similarly, we are the sorts of organisms whose social conditioning would not proceed as it often does, if we were not affected by self-esteem, and if we were not also tied to others by bonds which make their feelings toward us relevant to our own self-feelings. Thus, the efficacy of self-esteem in social conditioning is closely tied to the existence of what has often been loosely designated as *sympathy*. Yet self-esteem and sympathy are not the same, for either can function independently of the other. In the particular case with which we are here concerned, that of conditioning by means of praise or blame, both propensities must be assumed to be present: there must be an urge to think well of oneself, and, in addition, there must also be bonds of affectivity which relate us with others, in order that it should happen that what they may think of us will influence what we think of ourselves.

Of course, there are cases in which self-esteem and sympathy may not enter into what is often designated as "social conditioning." In some cases, we have learned to pay attention to the good or bad opinions of others through having learned that it will be of some special advantage for us to do so: in such cases, we are primarily interested in assuring ourselves of future rewards, or seeking to avoid overt punishment. However, we are not always thus motivated. There are phenomena such as being offended by others, and "being offended" is different from being physically hurt; yet both types of being "hurt" are effective conditioners. In fact, each type seems to be effective in all societies of which we have careful reports; it might therefore be safe to assume that each is equally to be regarded as rooted in man's nature, rather than itself having been "socially conditioned."

To be sure, those who have stressed social conditioning have placed great emphasis on the fact that individuals in different societies manifest sympathy or self-esteem, or other similar states, under very different sets of circumstances; they have also stressed the fact that the forms through which such attitudes express themselves differ widely. That there is such diversity is a fact which, as I have admitted, no one would be inclined to deny. The question, however, is whether sympathy or self-esteem could be conditioned *into* an organism if either were originally absent; and, if so, upon what unconditioned responses such a process of conditioning would rely. To make a plausible case for holding that either is in fact a product of prior conditioning, one must be in a position to suggest how the conditioning proceeded: as we have seen, neither Pavlovian nor instrumental conditioning can take place unless unconditioned propensities are present and serve as a foundation for the conditioned responses. However, it is worth noting that even if traits such as sympathy or self-esteem are probably not explicable in terms of conditioning, such traits can be *removed*, or rendered generally inoperative, through conditioning. For example, in describing experimentation on a particular dog, Pavlov showed that what he designated as an unconditioned reflex of freedom could be removed through a process of conditioning.[19] In this case, as in many others, there is an asymmetry between the possibility of conditioning "in" and conditioning "out": the fact that a person can be trained *not* to be sympathetic under certain circumstances does not prove that he was first rendered capable of feeling sympathy by any analogous process of conditioning.

Taking this into account, we are in a better position to understand some aspects of the variability which characterizes different societies. Given similar propensities, we may expect that the occasions on which these propensities will be exhibited may (in some cases at least) be affected by the manner in which rewards and punishments were distributed under roughly similar circumstances in the past. Some of these rewards and punishments might have been deliberately assigned within the society; others might have arisen independently of conscious design. In either case, certain standardized forms of behavior could result; but these forms of behavior might be expected to vary from one society to another. That such variability could occur, and could nonetheless be consistent with the presence of the same propensities in all societies, should be obvious from the fact that even propensities such as hunger and thirst can be satisfied by different objects, and from the fact that sexual drives can be satisfied in variant ways. In the case of a propensity such as self-esteem, the occasions which would provide for its gratification, or occasion its frustration, would be myriad: it is difficult to imagine any object which might not, on some occasion, be experienced as having a direct connection with a person's self-esteem. Granted these facts, it would be astounding if there were not radically different ways in which different societies (each of which had developed through a different history in a different environment) rewarded or punished the various ways in which specific human propensities were satisfied.

Or, to put the matter differently, in terms more closely related to the theory of conditioned responses: different forms of behavior will be reinforced in different societies, just as different animal responses are reinforced in different experiments. Nevertheless, we must in every case assume the existence of particular propensities which are satisfied in the course of these experiments, or reinforcement would not occur. Similarly, when one says that particular social responses are either rewarded or punished, there must be preexisting propensities with reference to which something serves as a reward or a punishment. It is these preexisting, underlying drives or tendencies which are neglected in the usual, vaguely formulated, statements which hold that men are indefinitely malleable, being formed by social conditioning. As soon as attention shifts to the propensities which must be postulated in order to account for conditioning itself, the plausibility of the thesis of complete malleability quickly disappears. One will then become aware of some needs which human beings must have been able to satisfy in order that they could survive, either individually or as a species. Any such needs could not, of course, be assumed to have been engendered by *social* conditioning, since their existence, and the means of satisfying them, would be presupposed if social life were to be possible at all. Furthermore, if one assumes that psychological characteristics tend to be the same in all individuals belonging to the same biological species, varying around some fairly constant biologically based norms, the postulate of indefinite malleability suffers further loss in plausibility. What then becomes important, of course, is to explain the degree of variability which one finds in human behavior from society to society. Our consideration of conditioning theory suggests a way in which this variability can be explained. Differences in the conditions accompanying the exercise of any propensity will lead to differences in the ways in which that propensity will be expressed; at the same time, however, it will not be possible even to begin to explain the behavior if one does not first acknowledge the existence of the propensity itself. Since, as we have seen, even in the most restricted forms of animal experimentation various different propensities account for the conditioning which takes place, one would expect that under non-experimental conditions (in which neither the propensities nor the environments are rigidly controlled) an interplay of factors would be present and a greater degree of variability in individual responses would therefore occur. Thus, even were one to assume that the processes of conditioning are the sole factors involved in learning,[20] the thesis of indefinite human malleability would be erroneous in the form in which it was espoused both by those subscribing to geneticism and by those who accepted organicism.

First, let us consider the difficulties in geneticism, in so far as it is a theory of malleability.[21] It will be recalled that geneticism viewed the development of individuals as shaped by the specific nature of their experiences, each person being the product of the series of influences brought to bear upon him in the circumstances in which he was placed. The model on which this theory of character was originally based was the doctrine of the association of ideas, according to which all knowledge could be traced back to a series of ideas inscribed on the mind by experience. To be sure, neither Hobbes nor Locke had accepted associationism in this form, and there were various differences among other associationists. However, the standard manner of treating the association of ideas as an explanatory principle was to hold that the mind was fundamentally passive in acquiring knowledge, the primary connections among our ideas being dependent upon the order and frequency of their presentation. Now, it is to be noted that the principle of the association of ideas would not, of itself, account for the formation of a person's character, for while it might be assumed to account for his thoughts, it would only account for his behavior in so far as his thoughts were responsible for his behavior, either directly or indirectly. Therefore, in accounting for the sum total of an individual's behavior, some principle in addition to the association of ideas was called for. As we have noted, this principle was generally taken to be one or another form of egoistic impulse, the most common interpretation of such an impulse being hedonistic: that every person, on all occasions, is motivated by a propensity to favor that which brings pleasure or avoids pain. Given the assumption that men are so motivated, and that associative connections have been formed between particular states of affairs and past pleasures or pains, every individual's tendency to behave in one way rather than another can be explained in terms of the effects of his past experiences: the order and frequency of occurrence of the elements in his past experience will account for the associations among his ideas and for the fact that he seeks or avoids certain objects. Thus it is his past which will make him into whatever he becomes.

Our preceding analysis of "social conditioning" should have been sufficient to show that this classic associationist form of geneticism is basically misleading. Even if it were true that a propensity to favor pleasure over pain were regarded as the decisive factor in every instance in which any individual behaves in one way rather than another,[22] it would still remain the case that in many such instances this hedonic propensity can come into play only because the individual has other propensities as well. As we have seen, these propensities must themselves be unconditioned, just as it is assumed that the tendency to favor pleasure over pain is a native, unconditioned propensity. Thus the attempt to explain the total character of a person through the effects of past experience upon him is a program which simply cannot be carried through.

To be sure, we have admitted that the effects of experience will have a great deal to do with how an individual's propensities will be channeled, and in this sense every individual may be said to be malleable in some degree. This follows from the fact that different objects are capable of satisfying the same propensity. Of course, the types of object capable of doing so are sometimes relatively restricted; not everything, for example, can serve as a foodstuff and allay the hunger of human beings. In other cases, however, the range of potential satisfiers seems to be almost indefinitely extensible, as we noted with respect to self-esteem. Yet, even in the latter type of case, the propensity itself is not an effect of learning, nor can its first manifestations be held to be: the effects of experience can only come into play after there has been some actual experience in which that particular propensity was or was not satisfied, and whether it was then satisfied would have been dependent on forces operating then, not in the past. This point is so obvious that it probably appears not worth saying; yet it is highly important, for it applies in every case, and not merely in the case of what is taken to be the first instance in which some propensity comes into play. This fact is easily over-looked because the effects of experience are often so obvious in influencing the choices which we make. However, in all cases in which anything that we choose proves to be either satisfying or dissatisfying, it has that character here and now, not in the past. It is, then, because of a direct relationship between a present state of affairs and a present propensity that we find something satisfying or not. While past experience may strengthen a propensity which we already had, and while it may also have established the fact that a particular type of action can satisfy a particular propensity, this by no means proves that present satisfactions are derivative from past satisfactions. In short, satisfaction is not itself a product of learning, even in those cases in which learning may help to explain how we came to seek satisfaction in one quarter rather than another. It is a confusion with respect to this point that accounts for the fact that variations in the forms of expression of a propensity have led so many people to hold that where a person finds satisfaction is merely a matter of how he has been trained. This, as we have seen, was unfortunately the lesson which was drawn by the later associationists and, more recently, by those who have sought to explain human behavior in terms of "social conditioning." Both schools have inferred, from the variety of the changes in behavior which can be traced to learning, that the only stable psychological factors in human nature are very general, contentless principles according to which the individual's nature is affected by his experience. That such a view should have been held prior to the rise of evolutionary biology is more readily understandable than that it is still widely held.

2. The Limits of Organicism

Up to this point we have directed our attention to that form of the malleability thesis which rests on psychological grounds, that is, we have been concerned with geneticism. It is now necessary to consider the views of those who have argued for the same conclusion on the basis of the history of human development. This, as we have seen, was a position which Comte and Hegel and Marx held in common. Each held that human nature is not constant, but changes as the forms of human social life change. On their view an understanding of the nature of a person is not to be gained through tracing the specific series of experiences which make up his personal history, as geneticism held; rather, we must approach the individual through first understanding the dominant cultural forces in the community to which he belongs. Since this approach to the fundamental forms of human be- havior did not rest on the concept of conditioning, nor on any direct analogue of it, the foregoing argument cannot be assumed to provide a cogent reason for re- jecting the organicist version of the malleability thesis.[23] Furthermore, if we are to show in what precise respects the malleability thesis is mistaken, we must dis- engage it from other issues with which it may sometimes be associated. For ex- ample, organicism is not necessarily connected with the belief that there is an evolutionary pattern to which all social institutions must themselves conform. While these two doctrines were not adequately separated in the thought of Comte, Hegel, or Marx, Durkheim's sociological theory provides a case in which it is easy to see that the arguments in favor of organicism can be wholly independent of considerations which presuppose an evolutionary point of view.[24] In what follows, I shall therefore treat the question of organicism as a problem in sociological theory, separating it from those developmental questions with which it was frequently entangled in nineteenth-century thought.[25]

There is one presupposition basic to all forms of organicism. It consists in hold- ing that, even though the existence of human societies presupposes the existence of individuals, no society is simply an interacting aggregate of individuals: societal facts are irreducible to facts concerning the beliefs, desires, habits, actions, etc., of the individuals on whose activities the existence of the society depends.

There are a number of different but interlocking ways in which one can attempt to establish this thesis; in another place, I have argued for it through attempting to show that the ways in which any individual behaves are dependent upon the status which he has in a society, and the roles he is called upon to play.[26] Though I continue to believe my argument to have been correct, and to be the most basic means of establishing this contention, it will here be useful to proceed in another manner since, in the present context, we are also dealing with questions concern- ing the psychological characteristics of man. The point of departure which I here choose is the fact of social inheritance.

No human being is self-sufficient at birth; he or she is dependent on others, and the ways in which he or she is cared for, and what he or she is taught, depend upon the customs of the ongoing society into which he or she was born. On the basis of this fact, Comte emphasized the dependence of the individual on previous generations, that is, on the history of mankind as a whole.[27] Durkheim's state- ment of the same point was made in a non-historical way: every individual is constrained by the society into which he has been born, its institutions are ex- ternal to him, not being dependent upon his will. Thus, Durkheim spoke of societal facts as objective, not subjective; as being "things."[28] They are, as he said, inherited by the individual through his education;[29] moreover, they have coercive power over him, "they impose themselves upon him, independent of his individual will."[30] This externality and objectivity was the basis on which Durkheim argued against any attempt to reduce societal facts to the thoughts and actions of individuals: what is true of any given individual is true of every individual—each is constrained by societal facts, and indeed, within any given society, each is constrained by the same set of facts, by a system of punishment, by a system of kinship, etc. Therefore, one must resist the temptation to suppose that societal facts can be reduced, *seriatim*, to an aggregate of interactions among individuals: it is the pattern which is all-important, and it is the pattern which constrains every individual within the society. In short, when we are dealing with institutions, it is grossly misleading to say that we are dealing with nothing more than a set of interactions among individuals, for these individuals are not simply reacting to each other; it is to the institutional pattern of action, which each has learned, that each is reacting.

In seeking to describe the difference between the sphere of individual thought and action and the nature of institutions, Durkheim appealed to the concept of "collective representations." While it is not difficult to understand why he did so, the term immediately gave rise to misunderstandings and needless debate.[31] For our purposes, we shall avoid his terminology and speak of institutions, using that term to refer to all aspects of a society which, in consonance with Durkheim's main line of argument, are not reducible to the behavior of individuals. That there are such aspects is a point on which I am in agreement with Durkheim, and also, of course, with Comte, Hegel, and Marx.

One standard objection to all forms of this thesis is that the elements on which every aspect of social life depends are to be found in the activities of individual human beings; that a society is simply a group of people living and working together. Or, differently put, it is claimed that a society is, simply, its members. Durkheim denied this proposition, constructing a defense in terms of the doctrine of emergence, as that doctrine had been applied in chemistry and in biology.[32] However, in order to defend Durkheim's general position, it is not necessary to follow him along this brambly path. Instead, one can show that the objection itself rests on a fundamental mistake: that it assumes that when one says of a group of individuals that they are "members of a society" we mean to affirm that a society is composed of individuals who are its constitutive elements or parts. However, if we are to make sense of the fact that a particular society cannot be said to have undergone a change, as a society, because a king dies or a presidential term expires, we cannot say that it is individual persons who are the constitutive elements of societies; rather, it is the roles which individuals play that compose a society's "parts." Roles, however, are defined by institutions; and while roles may be inherited, ascribed, or won by individuals, they are not identical with the individuals who function in them, nor are individuals identical with their roles.[33] If this is not already obvious, the reader need merely take account of the fact that, when we describe the differences between two societies, we do not describe specific individuals who live in those societies; we describe each society as a system of roles, taking into account the different roles which any one individual can assume; that is, we describe societies in institutional terms.

There are, of course, other standard objections to the type of thesis which Durkheim maintained, in defense of which the preceding argument was constructed. Some are based on epistemological grounds (e.g., "How can we know institutions except by observing individual behavior?"); others are based on quasi-metaphysical grounds (e.g., "How can institutions be said to be real, except in so far as they exist in the behavior of individuals?"). I shall not attempt to deal with such objections here. In my opinion, the preceding argument is decisive as an answer to the view that institutions *must be* reducible to the behavior of individuals, and this view is one on which, to some extent, most formulations of both the epistemological and the metaphysical objections rest. As I shall now show, the argument which I have given is also decisive as an argument against *organicism*.

There is no paradox in holding that the same argument can function in defending the irreducibility of societal facts and also function as a counter-argument against organicism: as I have already remarked, the thesis that institutions cannot be reduced to the behavior of individuals is a *necessary* presupposition of organicism, but this irreducibility does not provide a *sufficient* condition for organicism's truth.[34] We shall now quickly see that this is the case.

In arguing that it is not individuals who are the constitutive elements in a society, we saw that it was necessary to distinguish between individuals and their roles. While we saw that this distinction ensures the irreducibility of societal facts, it also establishes the point that the individual cannot be identified with whatever social roles he may play. In fact, we have already noted in passing that any one individual plays a number of different roles; and, of course, different individuals in the same society often play exactly the same roles. This does not serve to make the two individuals one, nor does it suggest that they will closely resemble one another in temperament or ideas, nor in all aspects of their behavior, merely because they have the same social roles to play. This point is obvious if one simply considers how the individual personality of a president or a king may affect the functioning of a society, even though the description of that society, as a society, does not change merely because one president or king has succeeded the other: unless the effects of their personal differences change the institutional relationships within the society, the fact of a royal or a presidential succession does not force us to describe the society in different terms.

Should the foregoing point seem in any way doubtful, we may return to the fact from which we started in explaining Durkheim's views. Every individual, as he insisted, is born into an ongoing society, and the duties which he is to perform are something external to himself; they are defined by law and by custom, and must be learned.[35] However, it is a human individual who learns what these laws and customs are, and the capacities necessary for social learning—for coming into one's social inheritance—must be innate. For example, one such capacity is the ability to use languages: whatever characteristics underlie this ability must be inherited before any particular language to which the child is exposed can be learned. What is true in this case is true also in others: members of the human species must possess certain psychological characteristics not possessed by other species, for only our species has developed a form of existence which is entirely dependent on the transmission of learned modes of behavior. Thus, underlying all cultural differences between societies, there are similarities in inherited capacities which are not themselves explicable in social terms.

A similar point can be made through a comparison of individual persons, rather than through the contrast between humans and other species. We find significant variations in the capacities of different persons. Even if it were never the case that the variations which we note are *solely* attributable to the individual's biological inheritance, there can be no doubt that there are some inherited differences in the capacities for learning which different individuals possess. Such differences would not themselves be attributable to the social roles which people assume in the course of their lives.[36] Therefore, in so far as Durkheim's type of position depends upon the fact that individuals are molded by their social inheritance acquired through an educative process, it does not establish a complete malleability of human nature: the capacities for learning which human beings possess are not themselves functions of the societies in which they live. Rather, we are forced to say that, in order to understand the nature of human beings in any society whatsoever, we need a science of psychology which is independent of sociology. This, as we saw, was a point which Comte, Hegel, and Marx all denied.

Durkheim differed from them in believing in a science of psychology which would investigate the connections among "individual representations," as distinct from "collective representations." Nonetheless, he drastically restricted the scope of those phenomena with which psychological explanations are usually assumed to be concerned: wherever the subject-matter of thought involved what he termed "collective representations," he assigned the question of why individuals thought in that way to the province of sociological explanation, not to psychology. This procedure is most apparent in the introductory and concluding chapters of *The Elementary Forms of the Religious Life.*

It is not easy to state Durkheim's position with respect to how society influences human thought without using his concept of "collective representations;" nonetheless, I shall once again avoid using that term because of the confusions which it tends to invite. Putting the matter quite generally, what Durkheim attempted to establish was that the forms of life characteristic of a particular society constitute the sources for whatever is common in the ways in which its individual members think. He held this conviction not only with respect to moral and religious beliefs, but with respect to the categories of time, space, causality, and the like. In fact, he held that whatever appears to us as a priori, rather than as being based upon our individual experience, is a product of the form of life of our social group.[37] As he said in speaking of the categories, "Not only is it society which has founded them, but their contents are the different aspects of the social being." He illustrated this general dictum by saying:

It is the rhythm of social life which is at the basis of the category of time; the territory occupied by the society furnished the material for the category of space; it is the collective force which was the prototype of the concept of efficient force, an essential force, an essential element in the category of causality.[38]

In speaking in this way, Durkheim did not intend to suggest that the rudimentary forms of temporal and spatial experience were socially acquired; in an immediately subsequent paragraph he admitted that such forms of experiencing were undoubtedly found in animals as well as in human beings. What he wished to establish was the fact that our general conceptual frameworks of space and time—that is, the ways in which we organize the experienced world—are a function of the forms of life characteristic of our society. Time, he held, is organized and measured by the recurrence of rites and public ceremonials; space is given its coordinates of right and left, up and down, north and south, in terms of values attributed to specific regions by the society, and in some societies the totality of space is conceived according to the same plan which characterizes the manner in which the tribal community is divided.[39] Furthermore, Durkheim attributed the concept of *totality* itself, which he regarded as performing a crucial role in building up the conceptual frameworks of space and of time, to a sense of the social group as a totality.[40]

The concrete evidence which Durkheim offered in favor of this radical thesis was really very slight, even if one were not to challenge any of his interpretations of that evidence. The basis on which he rested his case was less a matter of empirical evidence than of one particular argument: that concepts could not originate in the experience of individuals, for they would not then be universally shared by the members of a society. In advancing this argument, Durkheim contended that each individual's experience was fluid rather than fixed, and was different from the experience of others; consequently, any concepts originating in that experience would not be applicable beyond the scope of the individual's own experience.[41] Yet, as Durkheim pointed out, the concepts which individuals use, and the language in which these concepts are embodied, impose themselves upon individuals, and are socially shared. Thus, he argued, their source must be sought in the group itself. If this argument holds of concepts generally, then it holds most especially of those concepts which are to be regarded as categories, by means of which we organize all of our experience. These categories, Durkheim remarked, have so great a stability and impersonality "that they have often passed as being absolutely universal and immutable." To this he added:

Also, as they express the fundamental conditions for an agreement between minds, it seems evident that they have been elaborated by society.[42]

If one wishes to understand why this seemed evident to Durkheim, one may turn to his essay "The Dualism of Human Nature and its Social Conditions," which was acknowledgedly written to help clarify *The Elementary Forms of the Religious Life*. In that essay Durkheim's psychology is explicitly stated, and is summarized in the following way:

Our intelligence, like our activity, presents two very different forms: on the one hand are sensations and sensory tendencies; on the other conceptual thought and moral activity. Each of these two parts of ourselves represents a separate pole of our being, and these two poles are not only distinct from one another but are opposed to one another. Our sensory appetites are necessarily egoistic: they have our individuality and it alone as their object. . . . [Conceptual thought] and moral activity are, on the contrary, distinguished by the fact that the rules of conduct to which they conform can be universalized. Therefore, by definition, they pursue universal ends. . . . A sensation of color or sound is closely dependent on my individual organism, and I cannot detach the sensation from my organism. In addition, it is impossible for me to make my awareness pass over into someone else. I can, of course, invite another person to face the same object and expose himself to the same effect, but the perception that he will have of it will be his own work and will be proper to him, as mine is proper to me. Concepts, on the contrary, are always common to a plurality of men.[43]

Any such sharp separation of sensations and concepts is, of course, open to challenge, as is the supposition that "sensory tendencies" are always egoistic, and that the privacy of sensations entails a variability from individual to individual which the individual's grasp of a concept does not. It was these epistemology-ridden assumptions of Durkheim's psychology which made him assume that the universality which we attribute to our basic concepts establishes the fact that they have a social origin, and are not to be understood except in social terms.

Even if the foregoing objection were to be rejected by those who follow Durkheim, it can be shown that there are other respects in which the views which he put forward in *The Elementary Forms of the Religious Life* presuppose constant and universal psychological factors in human nature, in spite of all that he said to the contrary. Consider, for example, the distinction which Durkheim drew between *the sacred* and *the profane*. It was this distinction which, he held, was at the root of all forms of the religious life. It was his contention that

All known religious beliefs, whether simple or complex, present one common characteristic: they presuppose a classification of all the things, real and ideal, of which men think, into two classes or opposed groups, generally designated by two distinct terms which are translated well enough by the words profane and sacred (*profane, sacré*). This division of the world into two domains, the one containing all that is sacred, the other all that is profane, is the distinctive trait of religious thought.[44]

This, however, presupposes a constant feature in human experience, based upon a trait common to all men: it is not a feature of some societies, and not of others, nor is it a characteristic which has no basis in human nature, as such. This can be noticed in the manner in which Durkheim assumed a psychological interpretation of religious commitment:

If we give the name delirious to every state in which the mind adds to the immediate data given by the senses and projects its own feelings into things, then nearly every collective representation is in a sense delirious; religious beliefs are only one particular case of a very general law. Our whole social environment seems to us to be filled with forces which really exist only in our own minds.[45]

This is obviously a generalization concerning a psychological fact, and it is a fact essential to the distinction which is drawn in all societies between the sacred and the profane—if one accepts Durkheim's views. A similar psychological generalization is evident in the statement which Durkheim made in accounting for the origins of totemic symbolism, when he said:

> That an emblem is useful as a rallying-centre for any sort of group it is superfluous to point out.

And he explained this dictum in the following terms:

> If left to themselves, individual consciousnesses are closed to each other.... It is by uttering the same cry, pronouncing the same word, or performing the same gesture in regard to some object that they become and feel themselves to be in unison.[46]

Such generalizations underlie the whole of Durkheim's explanations of the effects of societies on individuals. Yet such generalizations are psychological in character, not sociological: they are not facts concerning social organization, facts external to individuals, that is, they are not what Durkheim denominated as *things*. Instead, they are *processes* by means of which he sought to explain why societal facts appear as external, and are capable of influencing human behavior. Such processes are psychological, and if Durkheim's theory of religion is actually correct, they are universal. Thus, they themselves would not be explicable through reference to the particular forms of social organization which are present in some places, and not in others.

Exactly the same point can be made with respect to Durkheim's classic study, *Suicide*. The correlations which, for example, he found between European suicide rates and religious affiliations established his point that suicide bears a significant relationship to institutional factors. However, according to his own etiology of suicide, this connection was mediated by psychological factors, the suicide rate varying inversely with the degree of integration of the religious society to which individuals belong.[47] Or, quite generally put, in all societies individuals tend to commit suicide when subjected to particular strains which derive from a lack of integration in the social groups through which their lives are organized. The needs which induce such strains are *psychological* needs, and are universal. What is not attributable to these psychological needs are the particular forms of organization according to which such needs are satisfied, or because of which they fail to be satisfied. These forms of organization cannot be directly attributed to the needs, precisely because they are *not* universal, but vary from society to society. Thus, for example, in *Suicide* Durkheim presupposed that individuals have a need for integration into a group, and for support from the group; of course, he recognized that there are various types of groups capable of lending such support, and that their efficacy varies in different countries. Similarly, in *The Elementary Forms of the Religious Life* he argued, as we saw, that a distinction between the sacred and the profane is universal, but the specific forms of the religious life vary enormously. Now, if one is to understand the behavior of individuals in any given society one will have to take into account both the psychological needs of these individuals and the specific forms of social organization which channel the ways in which those needs are satisfied, or because of which they remain unsatisfied. It will therefore be necessary to take into account both psychological and sociological factors, and neither will prove to be reducible to the other.

It is important to acknowledge that the views of Durkheim, as well as those of Comte, Hegel, and Marx, provided a historically important corrective to earlier attempts at purely psychological explanations of societal facts. However, it is one thing to show that the facts of history and of social organization are not to be explained in terms of universal psychological principles, and another thing to establish that there are no such principles. I have used the example of Durkheim to illustrate the difference between these two theses, for in his case the hiatus is particularly apparent. I shall now illustrate the same general point through reference to the sociological theories of Marx.[48]

Let us first concede, for the sake of the argument, that the systems of belief, the approved forms of attitude, the categories of interpretation and explanation, and, in general, all aspects of the intellectual and moral life of a society reflect the modes of production and the class structure characteristic of that society. Even acknowledging this to be true, it would be a mistake to suppose that there is no room for an independent science of psychology. This is the first point which I wish to establish.

In speaking of systems of beliefs, approved forms of attitudes, categories of interpretation—or, in short, "ideologies"—one is speaking of what it is that a particular group of individuals accepts as true, what they regard as good, etc.: that is, one is speaking of the content of their beliefs. An analysis of this content may be the task of the historian, anthropologist, or descriptive sociologist; it is not the task of the psychologist. Nor is it a primary task of psychologists to correlate differences in the content of socially accepted beliefs with specific forms of social structure. Rather, the central problems of psychology have involved attempts to find and to apply general explanatory or interpretative principles to the experience and the behavior of individuals. Different branches of psychology have specialized in different phases of their subject, but all have had as their first task that of establishing general principles. In short, they have not been primarily concerned with differences in the specific nature of the experience and behavior of different individuals. This can be seen even when, for example, a psychologist attempts to explain why the thoughts of a particular individual continually revert to certain materials, or why an individual repeatedly behaves in some particular way; it is not with the content as such that psychologists are in such cases primarily concerned, but with the principles which account for its repetition.[49] To choose another example, the psychologist who is concerned with learning, with memory, or with perception will not be involved in describing what is learned, remembered, or perceived. To be sure, the nature of that material may in some cases affect the processes themselves, as one finds in comparing the learning of nonsense syllables with the learning of other materials. Nevertheless, it is still not the case that the psychologist is interested in the content as such; rather, he is interested in the ability, attempting to establish the principles which best describe its modes of operation.

Translating this into terms which are relevant to Marxian thought, one can say that, even if it is assumed that everything that Marx said about the relation of ideologies to the economic substructure were true, there would still be adequate room for the science of psychology. This would not merely be a psychology concerned with problems of learning, or perceiving, or of any other field which might be supposed to have restricted import for problems of social organization. Psychologists have investigated the ways in which social pressure can influence conformity in the expression of opinion, and some have claimed that it influences conformity in perception itself; they have also investigated the effects of various forms of deprivation on thinking, and some of the ways in which alienation or frustration affect the personality of individuals. No one, I take it, would hold that generalizations concerning such matters would necessarily conflict with Marxian analyses of the relationships between ideologies and social organization. Furthermore, in Marx's own writings (even apart from the early *Economic-Philosophical Manuscripts*), one finds at least implicit psychological generalizations, and these generalizations were not meant to apply to some forms of society but not to others. For example, it would be a mistake to interpret Marx as having held that men's reactions to alienation or to oppression count for nothing in the historical process; and he did not treat such reactions as if they were simply causal consequences of a particular set of historically conditioned institutions. Or, to use a related example, it would not be plausible to interpret Marx as believing that individuals seek equality only because their societies have antecedently instilled ideals of equality in them. At this basic level of human experience, his theories actually presupposed the existence of attributes of human nature which were not derived from specific forms of social organization.

Unfortunately, Marx failed to recognize this fact. Whether because of the influence of Hegel upon him, or for some other reason, he too readily assumed that if one can show that great changes have been brought about in men's beliefs and attitudes by institutional changes, then one can abandon the supposition that there is anything constant in human nature. Yet it should be apparent from ordinary experience that changes in our beliefs and attitudes do not necessarily reflect changes in our abilities: for example, it is frequently the case that, when our convictions change, it is not because the form of our thinking has changed, but because we have acquired new knowledge, or because we have been exposed to new modes of experience. Therefore, if changing social institutions provide new modes of experience (as they undoubtedly do), one would expect such changes to be reflected in differences in the content of generally accepted beliefs. Thus, Marx was undoubtedly correct in holding that beliefs and attitudes are deeply influenced by the social institutions under which men live, and he was undoubtedly correct in criticizing Feuerbach's interpretation of religion for overlooking this fact; but this does not in itself prove that men change in all fundamental respects as their institutions change. Thus, the new insights of Marx and of Engels, in the *German Ideology* and elsewhere, which established connections between economic and ideological factors, should not have led to an advocacy of the view that an interpretation of man's nature has to be couched in exclusively sociological terms. This was the first point which I wished to make clear.

Turning now to Marx's sociological analysis itself, there are a number of problems which arise with respect to the relationship between the superstructure of a society and its economic substructure, and one among these problems is directly relevant to questions concerning constancy and change in human nature. That problem is, whether the modes of production and the relations of production in a given society determine the *existence* of some particular element in the superstructure, or whether their influence upon such an element is limited to *altering* it in one direction or another. The very important difference between these two interpretations of the substructure-superstructure relationship—a difference which Marx himself appears to have overlooked—may be illustrated by the following cases.

First, take the question of the organization of familial life. One can readily admit that in every society the structure of the family will be deeply affected by the modes of production of that society, and that changes in these modes of production will be reflected in changes in the conditions of familial life. However, the fact that all societies possess some form of family-structure is not itself to be explained merely in terms of the needs people have to produce the means of their subsistence: sexual controls, and the protracted period of dependency of the human offspring, must also be taken into account. Thus, it would not be plausible to seek to explain the existence of the institutionalized structures of familial organization solely in terms of the economic substructure, no matter how deeply changes in the substructure may penetrate particular forms of family organization. To explain the universality of this institution, an appeal must be made to some constant factors in human nature. On the other hand, there may also be cases in which a particular type of institution has been present in all societies, but in which its existence is not to be explained in terms of some particular set of biological or psychological factors. According to some interpretations of religious institutions (including that usually attributed to Marx himself), religion does not spring from any basic human need; on the contrary, it is held that these institutions reflect the interests of a particular social class, and are designed for the sake of consolidating power and social control. Although such an interpretation of religion is surely suspect, it does illustrate the fact that one should not too readily assume that any type of institution which is to be found in all societies is one which exists to fulfil some specific type of biological or psychological need. And, quite obviously, if there are institutions which exist in some societies and not others, *their* existence will have to be explained in historical or sociological terms, and not in terms of factors which can confidently be taken as representing universal human needs.

On the other hand, when we turn to the question of how one is to explain *alterations* in particular institutions, rather than the existence of the institutions themselves, the situation is quite different. We have already noted that the type of sociological analysis which Marx's doctrine of substructure-superstructure offers may do much to explain changes in family organization, even if it cannot serve to account for the existence of the institution itself. On the other hand, when we consider any institution which is not universal, and whose existence must therefore be explained in historical or in sociological terms (or in both), it must not be assumed that every alteration in such an institution is to be explained only in these terms. However important may be the specifically economic factors which Marxist doctrine uses in explaining historical change, it is nonetheless true that psychological factors may also have to be taken into account. For example, we have already remarked on the fact that Marx himself implicitly assumed that at the most basic level of experience men will react in similar ways, rebelling against deprivation and oppression; and we may note that the existence of this tendency in human nature was an essential assumption in his analysis of the growth of class-consciousness and of revolutionary activity. This is not to say that this particular factor would, of itself, allow one to explain the forms which that revolutionary activity would take; nor would it be decisive with respect to the success of any revolution: Marx's contentions concerning the importance of specifically sociological factors in revolutionary situations would not be affected by what I have just been saying. All that it is necessary to note is that, in such a case, psychological forces as well as sociological forces are responsible for historical change.

That alterations in institutions may be brought about by a combination of psychological and sociological forces makes it plausible to suggest that there may also be many cases in which the manner of functioning of an existing institution is to be explained in the same way, rather than in terms of either factor alone. We have already noted that such is the case with respect to family organization, since the very existence of the institution depends upon universal factors in human nature, but the forms of the institution depend upon historical and sociological factors. The same interplay of these disparate factors can be noted in other cases as well. Consider some particular institution which is characteristic of our own society, but not of all others; for example, consider the system of elective representative government, either as it exists in the United States or in its more general form—as a system which has come to be characteristic of modern Western-style democracies. The particular way in which such a system functions cannot be understood apart from historical and sociological factors; among these factors one may wish to include precisely those which Marx was concerned to analyze in his doctrine of substructure and superstructure. However, even on a Marxian basis, psychological factors would have to be taken into account in order to explain the functioning of this institution; and this would be true even if Marx were wholly correct in thinking that there are no universal psychological characteristics to be found among men. For we are not in this case attempting to explain the *existence* of this institution, and we are not attempting to explain an institution which is universal. We are also not trying to explain how this institution has changed. What we are trying to explain is how such an institution functions here and now. To do so, even in Marxist terms, we need to take into account the historically and sociologically conditioned forms of thought characteristic of the bourgeois class. Even though these particular modes of thought are the products of forces residing in the substructure, it is through them that contemporary political activities are carried on. What is said in this respect of political institutions can be said with equal force regarding any other institution which Marx would care to designate as part of the superstructure of a society.

It might be tempting to hold that the foregoing point can be generalized without limitation, and to say that in explaining *every fact concerning any society* one must take into account psychological as well as historical and sociological factors. This might seem tempting since it is undoubtedly true that it is only through the activities of individual human beings that any of the ongoing processes of a society are carried on. Nevertheless, for reasons which I shall not here attempt to adduce, I believe that this sweeping generalization should be resisted; and nothing that I have said would entail that, whenever some relationship between two institutions—say, between the growth of scientific technology and changes in industrial organization—is to be explained, one must necessarily introduce psychological factors into such an account. What I have argued has been more restricted in scope. I have argued (1) that there are some cases in which the existence of a particular type of institution in all societies presupposes common factors in human nature, but (2) that the universality of a particular type of institution does not necessarily rest upon such factors. (3) I have also argued that, in explaining changes in institutions, it is sometimes necessary to invoke both psychological and sociological factors, and (4) I have suggested that in many cases the ways in which a specific institution functions may also have to be explained in terms of both sets of factors. It should be apparent that, if these theses are accepted, they will severely limit the claims of Marx, or of Durkheim, or of others who uphold organicism, and they will involve us in often appealing to psychological, as distinct from sociological, generalizations.[50] Yet these claims do not in any way serve to undercut the important contributions made by those who rebelled against the individualistic and psychological approach of geneticism, and who established once and for all the importance of historical studies and the irreducibility of societal facts.

3. SELF-REALIZATION AND THE ILLUSIONS OF PROGRESS

In the foregoing sections, we have seen reason to doubt two types of argument which have stressed the indefinite malleability of human nature. One had attempted to show that tendencies to think, to feel, and to act in one way rather than another are to be explained in terms of the individual's personal history; the other held that such tendencies were primarily attributable to the nature of the society in which the individual lives. According to both views, whatever tendencies might be assumed to be the possession of individuals from birth were of the most restricted and rudimentary kind; either pain-avoidance or biologically-based needs would be examples of them. On the other hand, our various skills, our beliefs, and our attitudes, and all of the complex sentiments that characterize our emotional lives, were looked upon as having no basis in our natures until they became ingrained in us through external influences.

As we have noted, there was another view which was characteristic of nineteenth-century thought: that man is by nature a progressive being. While this view was held in various forms, in general they shared the belief that mankind had undergone a self-transformation through forces rooted in the individual's nature; furthermore, they all tended to hold that the talents and powers of individuals were capable of continuing to transform virtually all aspects of men's social existence. Changes which had been achieved, and were still to be achieved, were regarded as constituting mankind's progress. They were progressive not merely in the sense that men were gradually learning better ways of mastering their environments and achieving their goals, but in the sense that these goals were themselves becoming higher in value. Thus, human nature was viewed as changing, with new and nobler ends coming to dominate the lives of individuals.

As we saw in discussing the thought of Fichte and Green, one form of this doctrine stressed the concept of self-development, or self-realization, taking it to be the most important key to understanding man's intrinsic nature. While this concept was intimately connected with an idealist metaphysics in both Fichte and Green, it could also be held on other grounds; for example, in Nietzsche as well as in others, it was connected with a biologically-oriented form of voluntarism. Regardless of these differences, self-realizationism always involved an outright rejection of a hedonistic psychology; it also involved a rejection of nativism. In the present context, it is the latter aspect of the doctrine which is of primary importance. In accounting for the ways in which human beings think and act, the self-realizationist thesis did not appeal to isolated principles of explanation, as nativism inclines to do; rather, it sought a single underlying tendency toward growth and self-development which manifested itself in all human activities, expressing itself in multifarious and ever-changing ways. Before examining the general thesis that progressive change is a fundamental characteristic of the human race, we shall first consider the difficulties in self-realizationism as a psychological concept.

When stripped of its metaphysical associations and treated as a basic psychological concept, the notion of self-realization or self-development is unfortunately empty. If one considers how the concept would be used in interpreting individual development in the case of an infant, this emptiness becomes immediately apparent; and the same lack of significance attaches to it as a psychological principle if one attempts to apply it to any other stage of a person's life. Let us first illustrate the point with respect to the infant.

The biological processes in an infant do, of course, tend to sustain its life and promote its growth, and they lead to the successive development of new forms of activity. However, these processes are not under the control of a general tendency toward self-development. The specific propensities which the infant exhibits—sucking, swallowing, yawning, sleeping, grasping, kicking, stretching—may *lead to* self-development, but they are not to be explained as being engendered by a tendency toward that end. To think that they are, would be to fall once again into what I have termed "the retrospective fallacy."[51]

Nor is the situation different if we look to the psychological forces in a person at any stage in his later development, rather than focusing on the basically organic needs of the infant. Every person, whether young or old, has concrete particular ends which he seeks, which are associated with his present wants and desires, and it is in terms of these particular ends that we must understand his choices. If it is the case—as it often is—that a person has an ideal of the self toward which he wishes to develop, that too is a particular end which is presently desired. To say, however, that he desires "self-development," or "self-realization," without indicating what he regards as being an instance of self-development for him, is to speak in terms which lack meaning. To be sure, a person may sometimes actually say that he wants to realize himself, but when he speaks in this way, he generally has in mind some set of conditions which he wants to have removed, because they presently inhibit him from getting what he wants; or he may have in mind certain capacities which he hopes to be able to develop, in order that he may in the future attain some presently envisioned ends which he is not yet in a position to achieve. In such cases, the concept of self-realization has meaning, but it has this meaning because it actually refers to concrete particular ends which are to be attained: it is not to be interpreted as if it were being sought as an independent end in itself.

This fact was not always noted. In Nietzsche's voluntarism, for example, self-surpassing was interpreted as an end-in-itself; in Bradley's *Ethical Studies* we are told that men never aim at particular ends, but that they always actually aim at that whole which is their true self.[52] These two positions—though they have been influential—were by no means typical of self-realizationist doctrines. If one examines such standard texts of the period as those of Paulsen, of Muirhead, of James Seth, or of Mackenzie,[53] one sees that they did not deny the *psychological* fact that desire is related to concrete, particular ends which are heterogenous in nature; what they were concerned to establish was a specifically *ethical* thesis which they put forward in opposition to hedonism and in opposition to Kant. Their thesis was that the good is to be conceived in terms of the fulfilment of desire, not in terms of pleasure nor in terms of the Kantian conception of duty. It was also essential to their view that men's desires can only be adequately fulfilled when they are harmoniously integrated within the individual, and when, through a growing sense of community, the good of each individual is also brought into harmony with the good of others. I shall not attempt to estimate this specifically ethical thesis, for it is only with psychological questions concerning man's nature that we are here concerned. In this connection, I need merely point out that all ethical self-realizationists admit that it is unfortunately possible for particular persons to fall short of the ideal, obsessively pursuing very restricted ends, permitting selfishness to override communal good, and the like. Thus, it would not be correct to say that all individuals, as a matter of fact, are to be regarded as dominated by a tendency toward progressive growth; this is rather claimed for them only when they are "at their best," when they exhibit health in the life of the will. Such, at least, is the way in which one must interpret the doctrine of self-realizationism which tended to dominate Anglo-American philosophical theories of conduct at the turn of the century.

In point of fact, running through this form of self-realizationism, there was a premise concerning man's nature that often entered the argument, but was seldom singled out for attention, perhaps because it was thought too obvious to be designated as a fundamental principle of human action. It was the principle that there must be some consistency in the manner in which we behave, that in acting today we feel constrained not to negate what we strove for yesterday, unless we now find ourselves to have been mistaken: in short, that in behavior no less than in thought, we avoid disjointed sequences, the absence of continuity, and whatever is completely random or disordered. This characteristic tendency, which, as I say, was implicitly present in the theory of human nature held by self-realizationists, is not, of course, a concrete particular desire; instead, it provides a principle of connection among these desires. As such, it helps to explain the development of a stable self which tends to grow in one way rather than another; and it does so without making the assumption that every concrete desire is to be interpreted as merely one manifestation of the single, all-inclusive desire for self-development.[54]

If the foregoing suggestion commends itself to the reader, it will be obvious that there is no necessary connection between stressing the so-called hormic aspects of human nature and interpreting human nature as being essentially *"progressive"* in character. Consequently, the view that men's natures become radically transformed over time, with primitive impulses subjugated or extirpated, and a new race (psychologically speaking) being born, is a view of human history for which historical evidence must be supplied. Unfortunately, the evidence for the progressivist thesis, though it was widely accepted, was extremely weak.

That evidence consisted in assuming that all societies could be arranged in a single evolutionary order in which contemporary non-literate societies represent the comparatively early stages, with development moving in a linear fashion toward the highly literate, scientifically and technologically advanced societies of the contemporary world. This evolutionary hypothesis was not severely challenged until Franz Boas's essay "The Limitations of the Comparative Method of Anthropology" in 1896, and the influence of his essay was apparently not felt for some time. However, there can now be little doubt that the comparative method, as it had been used by anthropologists, was not based on historical evidence, but was forced to rely upon preconceived theories as to what stages there may have been in the history of mankind. In this respect, it differed markedly from the manner in which the comparative method had contributed to the theory of organic evolution. In biology, evolutionists had well-grounded geological and paleontological evidence on the basis of which they could trace the sequence of species, but there was no historical evidence of comparable weight upon which social evolutionists could rely in structuring their views of the past. Consequently, when they assigned particular places in an evolutionary sequence to various

contemporary non-literate societies in North America, Africa, or Oceania, class-
ing them as "survivals" of earlier forms, they were unable to show from what
particular earlier societies their descent was to be traced.[55] In fact, so long as one
did not depart from the evidence, no general movement of social evolution could
be discovered. To be sure, one could say that, in certain areas of the world (for
example, in Western Europe and in those regions to which European influence
had spread), it was possible to trace a sequence of changes in specific respects:
there had been growth in literacy, in science and in technology, there had been
specific changes in certain forms of social institutions, such as the forms of family
organization, or ownership of land, and the like. Now, regardless of what judgments of value one might make with respect to these changes, it remained an open
question as to whether *other* societies would be assumed to possess a tendency to
develop in the same ways. In fact, the evidence on this question would appear to
have been negative. Contemporary non-literate societies were acknowledged not
to have done so, nor had the vast societies dominated by religions other than
Christianity which existed in the East; yet all of these were assumed to be older,
not younger societies. Therefore, the progressive nature of man could not be
established on the basis of historical evidence any more than it could be established through an appeal to the psychological concept of self-realization. Yet this
progressive view was nonetheless widely held, and we must seek to understand
why this was so.

While one can find a variety of more specific influences at work, one fundamental reason why nineteenth-century thought, from Comte and Hegel through
Spencer, was dominated by the theory of a progressive course of social evolution
is to be found in the growth of interest in what might be called a rudimentary
form of comparative history. When it was recognized that societies were not artifacts designed by individuals in order that they could secure their own ends, but
were the products of cumulative historical change, attention was shifted from the
desires and interests of individuals to the growth of social institutions. Social
theorists sought to compare institutions, and to locate their place in the history
of the human race. Just as it was of historical interest to know what sorts of
implements pre-historic man possessed, and to trace how these implements
changed over time, so it would be of interest to trace similar changes in religion,
in family organization, and in all other aspects of social life. Thus, the point
of view which was adopted did not seek to explain any specific society in all of its
concreteness, as later anthropologists attempted to do; instead, a vantage point
was chosen from which it was thought that one could trace the development of
different institutional forms, and could thereby place different societies along a
single developmental scale. This assumed the unity of the human race, that the
human race does indeed have a single history. This assumption had of course
been characteristic of eighteenth-century views of Progress, no less than it was a
presupposition of most historically oriented thought in the nineteenth century.
We shall now show that, far from being obviously true, it is a theory which should
be regarded as highly suspect.

I do not wish to be taken as suggesting that it is necessary to assume that the human species arose in different places, and at different times, from different non-human or semi-human progenitors. This issue, which has often been heatedly debated, is irrelevant to the point which I wish to make. Let us therefore accept the contrary assumption: let us suppose that the whole human race has a single biological ancestry which (in theory) can be traced back to a single place of origin, with all of the progenitors of what we now know as human beings having been of common stock. Still, human beings have spread throughout the world, and wherever they now exist, they live in organized societies. The question is whether we should say that all of these societies have a common history, and it is clear that we should not. Even though my present assumption commits us to saying that there was some point of remote time when the ancestors of all presently existing men existed together, and even were we to suppose that these men then had some one common form of social life, what has happened since that time is that various groups have split off, have taken up residence elsewhere, and each has had a history which (over some stretch of time) is different from the history of the others. Thus, it would be grossly misleading to say that the whole human race has had the same history. In fact, we must say that the contrary is the case, and that all societies have to some extent had their own quite different histories.

Once this is granted, the supposition that mankind is inherently progressive will lose its plausibility. Whatever standard of progress we accept, it will assuredly not be true that we shall find all societies exhibiting progress. Even with respect to the actual history of any one society, it is not likely that we shall find that there has been only one directional tendency throughout the entire course of its history. What we may more reasonably expect is that, whatever standard we choose to apply, there have been times at which that society has progressed, and other times during which it has regressed; and there may be stretches of time during which there were no significant changes with respect to the particular criteria by means of which we estimate progress. What is in this respect true of each society would assuredly be true were we to examine them all.

At first glance, this conclusion might seem to be wholly sceptical with reference to questions of value; however, such is not the case. To be sure, if one were to maintain that our judgments of value rest on the movements of history, then the lack of a single directional tendency within all history would entail that we would be left without a way of knowing what is good or bad, right or wrong. However, as I have obliquely suggested, a belief in progress is not established *through* history, but it is brought *to* history. This should have been abundantly clear in the progressivist views and the social criticism of Mill, Arnold, and Huxley. It was also clear in the self-realizationism of Fichte and Green. It was even true, as we have seen, of the organicism of Comte, of Hegel, and of Marx, whose standards of what constitutes social well-being were not actually deduced from history, but were critically applied to it. But what, one might then ask, could be the source of such standards?

If our earlier arguments against theories of social conditioning were correct, the answer should be obvious: these standards have a basis in the specific propensities, interests, and needs which are basic in human nature. To be sure, we have not attempted to designate a list of inherent tendencies upon which all judgments of value may be supposed to be based, but we have mentioned some tendencies which surely have relevance to the moral standards which one finds in any community. We have noted pain-avoidance and the existence of biological needs; we have noted the existence of sympathy and of self-esteem; and in discussing self-realizationism we have also noted a tendency to be uncomfortable with inconsistencies in our actions. Any such admittedly heterogeneous list of presumably unconditioned propensities might be greatly expanded, and while those which I have just mentioned may not unreasonably be supposed to have some fairly direct connections with the fact that we make moral judgments, and with the actual nature of the moral judgments which we make, there will be others which it would not be plausible to suppose to be directly connected with the moral life. For example, as we noted, curiosity appears to be an unconditioned propensity in some animal species, and may perhaps be so among men; yet its relevance to the fact that we make moral judgments at all, or that we make the moral judgments that we do, would appear to be so slight as to be negligible. Thus, the relationship between morality and the existence of native propensities is likely to prove complex, not simple.

Furthermore, in saying that the source of the fact that we make moral judgments lies in our psychological dispositions, and in suggesting that these dispositions may also be reflected in the actual nature of the moral judgments we make, I am not denying that the social matrix is also an important influence on the specific moral codes which individuals and groups accept. As I noted in the case of self-esteem, the concrete forms of behavior through which self-esteem can be satisfied, or even be expressed, will vary according to the society in which the individual lives; it is well-known that, under certain circumstances, even extreme self-abnegation can greatly enhance self-esteem. As I have sought to point out, the channeling of our propensities, and the precise nature of the things that we seek or that we avoid, cannot be understood without taking into account the societies in which we live. Nor would it be sufficient merely to cite the general conditions dominant in our society: account must also be taken of the roles which we play and of our own individual experiences as well as of any particular dispositional traits of temperament which we may have inherited. Yet, all of these elements of variability among men should not be taken as suggesting that there are no basic psychological traits which they have in common, regardless of differences among their societies, and regardless of differences in their life-histories. If our earlier arguments have been correct, these basic forms of unconditioned responses, these common propensities and basic human needs, are also of importance in determining the course of human development.

It should now be clear that there is no necessary antagonism between some features of geneticism, some features of organicism, and some of the types of propositions concerning human nature and moral psychology which nativists have always sought to uphold. For example, in comparing geneticism and the form of nativism which has here been defended, the primary difference lies in the fact that geneticism, in both its classic hedonistic-associationistic form and in recent behaviorism, has attempted to restrict the native dispositional traits of men to an absolutely minimal number. As we have seen, there are reasons which make it doubtful that any such radically restrictive attempts will be successful; and we have seen no methodological reasons which would justify that they should be made. To be sure, one can find reasons of a specifically historical sort which account for the attacks of the associationists upon prior forms of nativism; there were other historical reasons why behaviorists held the positions they did. Going back to the situation in which the associationists found themselves, one can indeed sympathize with the attacks which they directed against the supposedly apriori character of all basic intellectual and moral propositions. However, scepticism regarding the claims of apriorists need not lead to the conclusion that the only basis on which human experience is to be explained is through pleasures and pains, and through the effects of associations among our ideas. The range of our experience and our capacities of thought need not be assumed to have so narrow a compass.

If we now compare organicism with the form of nativism which is here being defended, there need be no incompatibility in what they affirm, but only in what they deny. The irreducibility of societal facts to facts concerning individual behavior can be accepted; the relativity of different forms of institution to different periods of history can also be accepted; all that has been denied is the assumption that these facts entail that we reject the possibility of any stability in human nature, and therefore reject the possibility that there can be a generalizing science of psychology. These rejections had their sources in historicism, and in the belief that the history of mankind is a single and unitary process; they were not made necessary by what was in fact one of the great intellectual achievements of the late eighteenth and of the nineteenth century. This was, first, the discovery that the character of social institutions is to be historically understood, rather than interpreted in terms of that which was constant in human nature; and, second, that these institutions do have an influence upon the characters of individuals, helping to determine all that they can become.

IV

THE LIMITS OF REASON

Human Reason has this peculiar fate that
in one species of its knowledge it is burdened
by questions which, as prescribed by the very
nature of reason itself, it is not able to
ignore, but which, as transcending all its
powers, it is also not able to answer.

Immanuel Kant, *The Critique of Pure Reason,*
Preface to the First Edition

13

CRITIQUES OF THE INTELLECTUAL POWERS OF MAN:
THE IDEALIST STRAND

The reader may have been surprised that up to this point three extremely significant figures—Schopenhauer, Kierkegaard, and Nietzsche—have not been discussed. To be sure, of the three only Schopenhauer had an important influence during the period with which we have been concerned. However, that has not been my reason for delaying discussion of them; rather, it has been because the basic presuppositions of their thought did not in most respects relate to the movements we have traced. Each, for example, was extremely hostile to historicism; each also rejected the conceptions of human nature which were characteristic of geneticism and organicism. With respect to the view that man is by nature a progressive being, nothing was more alien to the thought of Schopenhauer and Kierkegaard. However, in the case of Nietzsche, one finds fairly strong resemblances to idealist forms of the progressivist doctrine, as well as obvious resemblances to biologically oriented theories. Nonetheless, the basic presuppositions of Nietzsche's thought can be seen most clearly in relation to the issue with which we shall now be concerned: To what extent can reliance be placed on the human intellect as a means of knowing ourselves and the world?

Given this topic, it is a temptation to focus one's attention almost exclusively upon Schopenhauer, Kierkegaard, and Nietzsche, since they adopted positions which were far more extreme than those of most of their contemporaries. Nevertheless, to do so would lead to a false estimate of the extent to which there had been a deeply critical attitude toward the intellectual powers of man in many phases of thought, almost throughout the nineteenth century. To confine our attention in this way would also involve stressing what subsequently became highly influential, rather than that which was most influential at the time. Therefore, before approaching the radical, voluntaristic critiques of the intellect which are to be found in Schopenhauer, Kierkegaard, and Nietzsche, I shall examine two other tendencies in the nineteenth century, each of which attempted to show in what ways the intellectual powers of man were necessarily limited. The earlier of them arose in connection with developments within idealism and religious thought; the second was linked to reformulations of the basic tenets of positivism in the latter half of the century. The present chapter and that which follows will deal with these two tendencies, although in each case I shall confine my attention to fewer figures than the scope and the importance of the tendency would justify. As we shall see, both will provide help in understanding some aspects of the related but more radical positions of Schopenhauer, Kierkegaard, and Nietzsche.

As a general background for the discussions with which the present chapter is concerned, we must note one development within psychology which was important for what followed. This was a change in the traditional categorization of mental activities, involving a new theory of the fundamental faculties of the mind. Instead of the view that all specifically mental activities belong either to the Understanding or the Will, a third distinct and coequal faculty was recognized— that of *Feeling*.[1] The concept of "feeling" was almost immediately applied to a host of different aspects of mental life, and no one usage established itself as standard. However, all of these uses involved reference to that which is "subjective," whereas the Understanding was interpreted as dealing only with that which is in some sense "objective." As a consequence, a sharp antithesis was drawn between the aspects of experience which belonged within each of these faculties: it was widely held that our *intellectual* powers are only concerned with that which exists in the external world; all that concerns the inner life of man can only be apprehended in and through Feeling. On this basis it was claimed that there is a fundamental difference between two spheres of knowledge: those cases in which we are solely interested in objective, non-human knowledge, which is the proper sphere of the Understanding, and the rest of our experience, in which Feeling and Will are also engaged. Thus, there arose a series of challenges to the view that intellectual analysis and the canons of logic are the best ways of comprehending man and his place in the world.

1. JACOBI AND FICHTE: THE SUPRASENSIBLE

Among those who denied that we can rely upon intellectual analysis to provide an adequate way of interpreting human experience, one obvious and important starting point for our discussion is to be found in Kant's theory of knowledge.[2] As we shall see, it was dissatisfaction with that theory which helps to explain the positions of Jacobi and of Fichte, who represent the first type of critique with which we shall here deal.

If we approach Kant's system through the distinction which he drew between phenomena and noumena, it is obvious that he was attempting to establish the existence of limitations in the knowledge which it is possible for us to attain. Yet, as the epigraph to this section of our study attests, Kant recognized that there is in us a constant urge to attempt to transcend these limitations. In the technical terms which he used in this connection, our Understanding (*Verstand*) is unable to yield the ultimate knowledge which our Reason (*Vernunft*) seeks to possess. In seeking to show how this predicament was to be resolved, Kant held that what drives us to try to transcend the limits of human knowledge are moral convictions and religious concerns: were it a matter of our intellectual interests only, it would not be important to speculate about anything which may lie beyond the boundaries of experience. While Kant himself was deeply sympathetic with the moral and religious commitments which he regarded as underlying traditional metaphysics, he refused to allow such commitments to confuse issues concerning the certainty and the extent of our actual knowledge. (Nor did he hold that either morality or religion needed to be buttressed by metaphysical claims.) Therefore, he held that, when we speak of *knowing*, and not of morality or religious faith, only those concepts which have an application within the world of experience are legitimate. Thus, it was Kant's claim that it is only through the Understanding, and not through Reason, that we know all that we can ever *know*.

Ironically, it was against this restrictive conclusion that some of Kant's successors used his own distinction between the Understanding and the Reason. According to Kant, the sphere of the Understanding is the world as it appears under the forms of space and time, and as it is organized by those categories which the human mind necessarily imposes upon experience. This his successors admitted. However, they rebelled against assuming that all knowledge is restricted to what the Understanding, thus limited, can apprehend. To extend the limits of what we can legitimately accept as true, they appealed to what Kant had rejected: Reason's authority to decide those ultimate questions. Of course, they differed from Kant in their interpretations of "Reason." Unlike him, they did not regard our Reason as an illegitimate extension of concepts borrowed from the Understanding; they held it to be an essentially different and more profound faculty of the human mind. Sometimes, but not always, they identified this faculty with Feeling. In all cases, however, they regarded Reason as distinct from, and opposed to, those forms of thought which depend upon sense-experience, and they rejected the view that truth was to be obtained by means of the methods and the categories which had accompanied the rise of the modern physical sciences.

As Arthur O. Lovejoy has pointed out, Jacobi was actually the first among the successors of Kant to use the latter's distinction between the Understanding and the Reason in a manner which altered the degree of authority to be assigned to each.[3] In an examination of what he took to be the unsatisfactory outcome of Kant's critical philosophy, Jacobi placed the blame on Kant's willingness to allow the Understanding to arbitrate the moral and spiritual claims which were made by Reason. In opposition to Kant, he insisted that the correct relationship between the two faculties was that it was Reason which had the right to evaluate the conception of the world which our Understanding provides.[4] Although he did not formulate this position in Kantian terms until 1801, all of Jacobi's earlier works had made use of an equivalent distinction between two faculties of cognition in man, attempting to establish the same conclusion regarding the authority to be assigned to each.[5] For example, in his famous letters to Moses Mendelssohn concerning Spinoza, Jacobi held that any attempt to establish a philosophic system through the employment of man's power of reasoning led to atheism and necessitarianism. On the other hand, he claimed for man the possession of another faculty, which he designated as faith (*Glaube*). Through this higher power, we have a direct intuition (an *Ahnung*) of the suprasensible, which allows us to affirm God's existence, human freedom, and immortality. Had we not this higher power, we would be driven by a rigorous course of reasoning to accept the Spinozistic system, according to Jacobi.[6]

When Jacobi reformulated this contrast between the intellectual powers of men and their innate capacity for suprasensible intuition, stating it in terms of an opposition between the Understanding and the Reason, he not only altered Kant's view of the relative authority of these forms of thinking; he also radically changed the meaning to be assigned to the term "Reason" itself. In fact, almost the only features common to the contrast which each drew was the fact that both he and Kant denied that the Understanding could provide answers to any questions concerning the existence of God, the freedom of the will, or the soul's immortality; and both agreed that this was what Reason attempted to do. In contradistinction to Kant's use of that term, Jacobi did not regard Reason as a tendency in us to extend the concepts which characterize the Understanding beyond the boundaries of sense experience; for him, Reason had nothing to do with concepts, nor with the ways in which the Understanding functioned, nor with any ratiocinative process whatsoever.[7] On the contrary, what Jacobi referred to as "Reason" was a special form of *feeling*. To be sure, it was feeling which in its responsiveness to spiritual truths was in some way different from other feelings; Jacobi described this difference in characterizing feelings which were directed to the suprasensible as being *objective* and *pure*.[8] This characterization of them as a form of objective aesthesis tended to connect them with the Kantian doctrine of sensibility, of a faculty of receptivity in man, and Jacobi in fact insisted that man has a sensibility for that which cannot be sensed (*ein Sinn für das Uebersinnliche*)[9]—a position which Kant, of course, absolutely denied. In stressing the element of feeling, Jacobi was also stressing the immediacy of our sense of the suprasensible, and he repeatedly compared it with the beholding of that which is presented to our bodily senses.[10] These two forms of presentation he took to be our only sources of truth; and he contrasted the Understanding with them. Unlike the senses and unlike that awareness of the suprasensible which he called our Reason, the Understanding lacked immediacy, proceeding deductively through the use of concepts. Jacobi regarded this parallel between the senses and Reason as warrant for holding that the Understanding could never be used to cast doubt upon the intuitions of faith: just as he believed that it is impossible by means of argumentation to undermine convictions which are based upon the testimony of sense experience, so he held that it is not really possible to offer argumentation sufficient to dispel the authority of faith.[11] It was in this way that he completed what he took to be his task of correcting the upshot of Kant's system, freeing the concerns of Reason from those tests of truth imposed by the Understanding, and showing that the conception of the world which depends upon the Understanding must be made subservient to a higher truth.

This way of attempting to defend the claims of religion against probings by the critical intellect has had many parallels, both in earlier and in later religious thought. However, from our present point of view, it is not the upshot of Jacobi's position which is of primary significance, but the more specific objections which he raised against the Understanding, and against philosophy itself.[12] Among these objections are asseverations that were frequently echoed by later thinkers, some of whom may have been influenced by Jacobi, although others undoubtedly were not.[13]

To understand Jacobi's attack on the Understanding, and upon philosophy, we must bear in mind that he did take seriously the supposition that Spinoza's system was the only consistent conclusion that could be reached so long as one were willing to confine oneself to canons of proof acceptable to the Understanding. However, the logical necessity which he attributed to the Spinozistic system had led Spinoza to an acceptance of complete determinism in nature, a determinism which negated teleology and also the freedom of the individual's will. These were two principles of Reason which Jacobi regarded as absolutely true.[14] Therefore, the more consistent a philosophy is, the farther it departs from the truth.[15] In trying to illuminate the nature of existence, philosophy only succeeds in concealing it, according to Jacobi; it attempts to offer *proofs*, which depend upon concepts and upon demonstrative inference, whereas an apprehension of the truth comes through feeling and needs no proof.[16]

If it should then be asked what can be achieved by philosophy, or by any science which, like philosophy, uses the Understanding, Jacobi's answer is an entirely negative one. In 1799 in a letter to Fichte, and in almost identical words when he was attacking Schelling twelve years later, Jacobi condemned all systematic knowledge (i.e., all forms of *Wissenschaft*), characterizing the attempt to gain such knowledge as a mere playing of games through which we while away our time, without advancing the cause of truth by one iota.[17] What is lacking in these games is any genuine content, that is, any contact with actual, substantive reality (*eigentliches, wesenhaftes Daseyn*).[18] Because of this lack, these games are complete within themselves, and we can therefore become masters in them. When we turn to reality, however, each of us only comes into possession of it in so far as he is able to experience it within himself—as it comes alive, subjectively, in him.[19] In short, the contrast between the games of our intellects and the actuality of existence is, for Jacobi, a contrast between the emptiness of concepts and that concrete individuality which is not grasped by means of concepts. The Understanding, he claims, always seeks to reverse the proper order of knowledge, assuming that species exist prior to individuals,[20] or (as later thinkers have put the point) that essence precedes existence. In opposition to this tendency, in a very impassioned discussion of the weakness of Kant's system, Jacobi argued that we are directly acquainted with individuality in ourselves, in our own living and thinking and feeling; and that we can never conceptualize this mode of experience. Thus, for Jacobi (as later for Kierkegaard), truth is subjectively grasped; the attempt to get behind phenomena by the categories of the Understanding is not only delusive, but is a complete reversal of our natural knowledge, of that indwelling Reason through which the truths of faith are revealed.[21] Thus, when it is asserted by those who rely upon the Understanding that freedom is an illu-

sion, and when they look upon Divine Providence as a philosophic *problem*, they
have lost touch with the true sources of our knowledge, since for actually existing
individuals freedom is no illusion, Divine Providence no problem: these are the
truest and most fundamental of all of our thoughts, and are known directly
through feeling.[22] This, then, is the beginning and the end of Jacobi's positive
doctrine: knowledge is not established through proofs, but through that inner
awareness in which reality is revealed to us, and it is always with reference to the
primacy of this awareness that any other noetic claims must be estimated.[23]

By this time it should be clear why, when Fichte's *Vocation of Man* appeared,
Jacobi should have raised the charge of plagiarism. The relations between the
two men were extraordinarily complex, with frequent and strong expressions of
sympathy between them, yet with Jacobi consistently rejecting Fichte's claim to
have founded a *science* of knowledge.[24] However, in his *Vocation of Man* Fichte
was not attempting to construct a system, but was offering a popular exposition
of the truth to which his *Wissenschaftslehre* had led.[25] Therefore, the mechanics
of his system—to which Jacobi had objected—were barely visible, and the respects in which their conclusions were similar became very evident. Each had
taken his point of departure from the world as pictured by those who had held a
complete scientific determinism, and each regarded as intolerable the denial of
human freedom which that view entailed. Fichte differed from Jacobi in attempting to show that the solvents of a critical epistemology, which was largely
Berkeleian in spirit, could overcome the Spinozistic view of nature and of man's
place in nature; however, the resulting position failed to offer him any positive
belief which he could accept. Thus, like Jacobi, he rejected the critical intellect
entirely, not only in science, but in philosophic analysis; and like Jacobi, he insisted that men do possess some other organ through which truth is to be apprehended. Like Jacobi, Fichte designated this organ as a basis for faith (*Glaube*).

These similarities are sufficiently striking for us to place Jacobi and Fichte
side-by-side within one movement which sought to disparage the critical intellect,
and all knowledge stemming from it, avowing the absolute primacy of values, and
identifying these values with morality, freedom, and religious faith.[26] Nevertheless, this movement had two sides, and while Jacobi represented one, Fichte
represented the other. For Jacobi, as well as for some of his contemporaries in the
Romantic movement in Germany, and for Coleridge, the higher truths which
come through Reason involve a receptivity, a form of direct revelation (an *Offenbarung*); for Fichte, on the other hand, moral affirmation and assertive commitment are the source of all spiritual truth. In fact, it was action, and not knowledge,
nor any form of feeling, which, according to Fichte, constituted man's true Vocation. For example, when he had rejected all analyses which deny reality to man's
creative self, Fichte proclaimed:

I have found the organ by which to apprehend this reality, and, with this, probably
all other reality. Knowledge is not this organ:—no knowledge can be its own foundation,
its own proof; every knowledge presupposes another higher knowledge on which it is
founded, and to this ascent there is no end. It is *faith* ... which first lends a sanction to
knowledge, and raises to certainty and conviction that which without it might be mere

delusion. It [*faith*] is not knowledge, but a resolution of the will to admit the validity of knowledge. . . . All my conviction is but faith; and it proceeds from feeling (*Gesinnung*), not from the understanding.[27]

If it be asked whether, or in what sense, an act of faith is self-justifying, Fichte replies that it cannot be argued about: it is self-justifying for those who have actually felt the necessity of that faith, and only for them.[28] However, the necessity which is involved in an act of faith is not to be regarded as an externally imposed necessity, but as the inner, moral necessity of the individual's own being. What Fichte may be said to have been holding is that faith should not be regarded primarily in terms of any relationship to knowing or to not-knowing; rather, it is a form of action, a commitment. For him, the essential attribute of that commitment was that, in committing oneself, one is able to establish by one's spontaneous endeavor the very freedom which one wishes to be able to affirm.[29] From this freedom all else followed: the Spinozistic world-picture was known to be false; the sceptical doubts of philosophers were seen to be only a game; and thought could become harnessed to a higher moral purpose, through which the progressive self-development of mankind would attain its ultimate goal. Thus, in Fichte as in Jacobi, we find it claimed that truth and value are ultimately reconciled, once the false claims of the critical Understanding have been rejected. The content of those aspirations which are embodied in the ideas of Reason need not be merely postulated, as they were in Kant's system, but can be decisively affirmed. Once this step is taken, it is not possible to look upon the Understanding as being finally authoritative, even within its own sphere of operations. On the contrary, for Fichte and for Jacobi, the Understanding is not to be regarded as a legitimate form of knowing, but is a form of not-knowing (*Unwissenheit*), which only a higher cognitive faculty, or an act of affirmation, can cure.

2. HEGEL: THE INTELLECT VS. REASON

It may appear perverse to suggest that Hegel, who is generally regarded as an arch-rationalist, belongs among those nineteenth-century philosophers who offered a critique of the intellectual powers of man. Nevertheless, in speaking of these powers we are speaking of particular individuals, not of the Infinite Reason. Furthermore, in speaking of them, we are referring to those forms of thought which Kant and his successors identified as being characteristic of the *Understanding*, not of any supervenient faculty. In this sense, as we shall see, Hegel set relatively narrow limits to the knowledge which the human intellect can attain.

In this respect Hegel may be compared with Jacobi and Fichte. In fact, like them he was explicitly attempting to rectify an error which each believed Kant had committed in claiming that knowledge must invariably conform to the categories according to which men's understanding organizes that which is given to sense. On the other hand the emphasis which Jacobi and Fichte had placed on feeling, and on the personal and inward, as a means of escaping Kant's position, was wholly foreign to Hegel's mode of thought. Instead of seeking a second source of knowledge within the individual, in feeling and in faith, he sought to establish a position in which Reason was shown to complete the process which the Understanding first undertook, but which it could not complete. This contrast between his view and theirs may be documented if we first turn to a series of early studies entitled *Glauben und Wissen* in which Hegel attacked their views as well as the views of Kant.[30]

In these studies Hegel explicitly claimed that what was common to Jacobi and Fichte, as well as to Kant, was that each had adopted "subjectivity" as his starting point, and it was in relation to this fact that Hegel attacked their views regarding faith and knowledge. The religious spirit, he held, seeks to affirm ideas which concern the ultimate nature of reality; however, in analyzing knowledge from the point of view merely of the subject, instead of in terms of both subject and object, each had made it impossible to speak of reality as it is in itself. Therefore, their systems could not satisfy the religious spirit. For example, Kant had limited the sphere of knowledge to the sensible realm, refusing to concede that the idea of God, the highest idea of Reason, had cognitive import; Jacobi had restricted our contact with reality to subjective feeling, a mere sense, or instinct, of something which cannot be conceptually grasped; and for Fichte, all knowledge ended in not-knowing and in a flight to unsupported faith.[31] Hegel regarded these views as involving a "dogmatic metaphysics of subjectivity" which was no less objectionable than the "dogmatic metaphysics of objectivity" which Kant had attempted to overthrow.[32] In terms similar to those that Schelling was then using, but in a manner forecasting his own future synthesis, Hegel was pleading for an approach to reality which would overcome the dualism of "subjective" and "objective" by abandoning the use of purely formal categories, and by rejecting what he regarded as the emptiness of a purely formal morality.[33] The system toward which he was striving was one in which *thought* and *things* were so related that neither was alien to the other: the necessity inherent in the ways in which the actual world develops was a rational necessity, and he claimed that those who separated the subjective from the objective had misread both the nature of thought and the nature of things.

The conviction that nature and history exhibit the same rational necessity which controls thought was what Hegel later expressed in his aphorism, "What is rational is actual and what is actual is rational."[34] Reason, he held, is "the Sovereign of the World."[35] Bearing such expressions in mind, it might be assumed that Hegel did not belong among those who stressed the limitations of man's intellectual powers. This assumption would be false. When Hegel speaks of "*Reason*," he is not speaking of the intellectual processes characteristic of individuals, of their powers of *reasoning*; actually, he is not speaking in terms of individuals at all. For example, it is "the cunning of Reason" that men's passions and their egoistic desires achieve historical ends which they had not anticipated and toward which their actions had not been directed. Such ends, in fact, differ completely from those which they expected to achieve.[36] Throughout the realm of human history, according to Hegel, change proceeds according to a dialectical necessity, the outcome of which cannot be foreseen. What has happened in a nation's history cannot even be comprehended—it can only be directly lived by the participants—until its results have started to sink into the past. It was this doctrine to which Hegel gave expression when he said,

As the thought of the world, it [Philosophy] appears only when actuality is already there cut and dried after its process of formation has been completed.... The owl of Minerva spreads its wings only with the falling of dusk.[37]

The foregoing use of some of Hegel's more famous aphorisms should be sufficient to show that his basic conviction concerning the dominance of Reason in the world did not entail any particularly exalted view of the individual's intellectual powers. The same point can also be more systematically stated in terms of his rejection of the Kantian doctrine regarding the Understanding and Reason. Like Jacobi and Fichte, Hegel criticized Kant for limiting our claims of knowledge to the Understanding; like them, he held that Reason has higher authority: "It is Reason, the faculty of the Unconditioned, which discovers the conditioned nature of the knowledge comprised in experience."[38] Yet there was one respect in which Hegel was less like Jacobi and Fichte, and more like Kant: according to him, Reason is not a wholly different mode of cognition from the Understanding, for it does not consist in feeling rather than thinking, nor is it based on a flight from the Understanding through a commitment of faith. What Kant had held, as we have noted, was that Reason involves an extension of the categories of the Understanding beyond their normal and legitimate use. For Hegel, too, there was a discernible relationship between Reason and the Understanding. In his case, Reason was a development and fruition of what had been merely implicit in both Sensibility and the Understanding: it had higher authority precisely because it developed in a systematic and coherent form that which had been limited, and therefore erroneous, in them.[39]

The fault of the Understanding, according to Hegel, was its *abstractness*, a vice which assumed various guises. For example, he said:

Thought as *Understanding*, sticks to fixity of characters and their distinctness from one another: every such limited abstract it treats as having a subsistence and being of its own.[40]

Now, Hegel admitted that it is natural to suppose that knowledge must begin in this way:

In theory, knowledge begins by apprehending existing objects in their specific differences. In the study of nature, for example, we must distinguish matters, forces, genera, and the like, and stereotype each in its isolation ...[41]

However, he denied that thought can legitimately call a halt at this point. The predicates by means of which we characterize objects are logically related to one another; objects themselves do not exist in isolation, but affect one another; change rather than fixity is a characteristic of nature and of history; consequently,

Hegel contends, if we are to grasp reality in thought, we must leave the logic of the Understanding behind, accepting the dialectic of Reason: the truth, Hegel insists, is not in the parts, but in the whole.[42]

It is precisely at this point that we can grasp the fact that, when Hegel speaks of "Reason," he definitely is *not* speaking of the cognitive processes of any actual individuals, but in terms of what is really a world-historical process.[43] If the truth is in the whole, it will not be found in what any one person thinks, for that thought necessarily reflects his culture; and it will not be in what is represented by that culture, for each culture represents only a stage in the development of human history: it is *Mind* that embodies Reason, not the thought of any particular individual. This, of course, is precisely the way in which Hegel treated the history of philosophy, which, in his system, represented Reason coming to full consciousness of itself.[44]

The importance of recognizing the true locus of that to which Hegel refers as Reason lies in the fact that he did not claim that the way in which men actually think *is* rational: everyone is usually immersed in the world of sense, and therefore tends to accept the categories of common-sense, and the modes of explanation characteristic of the empirical sciences; thus, in general, men fail to transcend the inadequate modes of thought which characterize the Understanding.[45] To be sure, those modes of abstract, analytical thought which are characteristic of the Understanding have not been without their use, according to Hegel: the contradictions to which they give rise have paved the way for higher forms of synthesis which the dialectic of Reason achieves.[46] However, it is in Reason—it is not in the thought of the individual thinker, as such—that truth is attained. Thus, far from being a pan-intellectualism, Hegel's doctrine of Reason locates rational necessity in the world-historical process itself, not in what individuals and cultures have taken to be self-evidently true.

This point may be made even more evident if we consider another aspect of Hegel's interpretation of the nature of individual thought and action. This aspect is perhaps most evident in his treatment of "intelligence" in the *Encyclopaedia of the Philosophical Sciences*.[47] Intelligence, Hegel tells us, is not primarily receptive (*aufnehmend*) but essentially active (*thätig*), and it is inseparably connected with will; to separate intelligence from will, or (as is often done) to attempt to separate the Understanding (*Verstand*) from the sentiments (*das Herz*), is to engage in false abstraction, for neither has a fixed and separate existence of its own.[48] Hegel insisted on abandoning any sort of faculty psychology, or any other compartmentalization of mental activities. Thus, in contrast to his predecessors who (he claimed) had distinguished between perceiving, representing, recollecting, imagining, remembering, and thinking as basic elements in cognition, Hegel insisted on an internal relatedness among these activities. So, too, did he insist on an interpenetration of thought and will. In fact, "Mind" *as* abstract intelligence was not, according to Hegel, actual at all; it is only as will that "the mind steps into actuality; whereas as cognition it is on the soil of notional generality."[49] However, it is to be noted that thought is itself embodied in all aspects of men's wills: in the preface to the second edition of his *Science of Logic*, Hegel speaks of

Logic as entering into all the natural behavior of man—into feeling, perceiving, desiring, into needs and impulses—rendering this behavior specifically human, bringing it to consciousness as ideas and purposes.[50] Yet, none of this is Reason itself, for in speaking of the individual's thought, feeling, and will, we are still speaking of what exists in the realm of Subjective Mind. Reason only comes to full consciousness in the realm of Absolute Mind, and in Hegel's system there is, so to speak, no bridge by means of which one can pass directly from what any individual thinks to a true conception of Reality. It is only through the whole process of development of the human spirit, which is designated by the term "Objective Mind," that one can move from the thought of any particular person to that which is true in itself. Thus, there is a sense in which Hegel's system interprets the individual as being far more restricted in the knowledge to which he can lay claim than was the case in the positions adopted by Jacobi and by Fichte. While both had rejected the ultimacy of all the knowledge which depended upon the Understanding, which men had generally trusted as a guide to truth, each claimed that there was another path open to all individuals by means of which genuine understanding could be attained. Hegel denied that any such path exists: within his system there are no short-cuts to truth which any individual can take. The truth is in the whole, in the self-development of Spirit. While that is a process in which individuals participate, they often (and perhaps usually) participate in the fundamental activity of Spirit without being aware that they are doing so. This, in fact, is what we have noted with respect to "the cunning of Reason" in history, and with respect to the relationship between Civil Society and the wills of individuals.[51] In short, it may not be too much to say that Hegel believed that individuals generally participate more deeply in the life of the Spirit when they are not consciously directing their wills to that end, than when they attempt to identify their activities with what they take Spirit to be.

If one seeks a common denominator in the rebellion of Jacobi, of Fichte, and of Hegel against Kant's position, one can find it in the fact that not only did each seek in his own way to overcome the dualisms inherent in the Kantian system, but each sought to put an end to the critical, analytic spirit of the Enlightenment. Each held that, if knowledge were confined to that which can be grasped through the categories of the Understanding, and if these categories can only be validly applied within the range of that which can be presented in sense-experience, then the loftiest insights of the human spirit would be lost. In short, this revolution took the form of asserting that the Understanding not only does not have a monopoly on truth, but actually distorts and debases our conception of reality.

3. MAINE DE BIRAN: *Le sens intime*

In a quite different philosophic environment in France, Maine de Biran affords an interesting, roughly contemporaneous parallel to the attempts of Jacobi and of Fichte to escape the confines of the Understanding.[52] Like them, but unlike Hegel, he turned inward in order to escape those limitations of knowledge which are due to our reliance on the external senses and to our intellectualistic habits of thought.

The point of departure for Maine de Biran's views was not, of course, the critical philosophy of Kant; as is well known, his position developed slowly, in a succession of transformations, out of problems posed by the sensationalistic theories of Condillac and of Condillac's followers, the Ideologues. In fact, his acquaintance with Kant's philosophy was chiefly second-hand, coming through his friend Ampère and through commentaries of somewhat doubtful value.[53] To be sure, Maine de Biran did show some interest in the Kantian theory of knowledge, but his own analysis of experience was not deeply affected, either positively or negatively, by Kant's position.[54] It was only subsequently that he spoke with enthusiasm of Kant, and that was with respect to the latter's moral theory and doctrine of freedom.[55] This is not surprising, for the theme that runs through all of Maine de Biran's works is a rejection of the view that knowledge is confined to that which has a basis in sensory experience: in ever-increasing measure, he insisted that the ultimate source of our conception of reality is to be found in the human self as we know it inwardly, through acts of volition. It is to this fact, and to its implications, that we shall now turn.

The task which Maine de Biran set himself in his earliest philosophical work, *Influence de l'habitude sur la faculté de penser* in 1803 still stood within the traditions of Condillac and the Ideologues. However, the element of originality in that prize-winning essay involved an important departure from Condillac's views. Although one can find lines of thought in Cabanis and in Destutt de Tracy which are suggestive of the direction in which Maine de Biran was to go, it was only he who followed this line until it developed into a definitely new theory of knowledge. Unlike Condillac, who had believed that all of the elements to be found in experience are provided by our capacity to receive sensations, Maine de Biran insisted that motor activity is to be distinguished from sensation, and that it, too, provided some of the basic components which are present in experience.[56] In this connection, he introduced the notion of active impressions and, more particularly, the notion that there is an unanalyzable sense of effort. It was in calling attention to this sense of effort, and to its relation to our tactile experiences, that Maine de Biran first developed his fundamental belief that knowledge of existence depends upon our volitional nature.[57] During the succeeding decade, in a series of psychological writings, he continued to develop this position, treating the subject in greater independence from Condillac, and with increasing emphasis upon its epistemological consequences. We need not follow these changes in detail.[58] What is important is to call attention to those particular aspects of Maine de Biran's thought which led him to draw an ever-sharper distinction between the methods of the understanding which are directed only toward the world of sense, and the awareness of an inner world of experience through which reality is to be interpreted.[59]

In 1804, as seen in the introductory section of *De la décomposition de la pensée*, Maine de Biran had fully acknowledged what he regarded as the Baconian ideal of carrying on an analysis of experience without seeking to establish ultimate metaphysical causes for the phenomena to be analyzed. However, in developing his own position regarding the distinction between active internal impressions and passive sensations, he did in fact adopt a very explicit metaphysical thesis. He stated it as his view that passive sensations have their basis in our organisms, or else in external sources (i.e., in something which is material), but that our active impressions have *their* basis in the self.[60] Similarly, three years later, in his essay for the Berlin Academy, he sharply criticized those whose methods of analysis did not take cognizance of the differences in the sources of our experience, and who treated our active internal impressions in the same way as they treated sensations coming from outside ourselves. He held that it was only among the latter types of experience (and not among those which involved the *"sens intime"* through which the self is given) that classifications and laws have relevant applications.[61] Further-more, as he developed his system in his *Essai sur les fondements de la psychologie*, Maine de Biran equated the differences between these two forms of knowledge with a difference between two sides of man's nature: a moral, spiritual side, and man's passive, bodily self.[62]

The full exploitation of this contrast was not evident until 1813, when he wrote *Rapports des sciences naturelles avec la psychologie*. In that work, Maine de Biran took exactly the same path as had those in Germany who had claimed that in addition to the Understanding there was a faculty of Reason, or belief.[63] One sees this extension of his theory of knowledge most clearly when—in terms which parallel Fichte's *Vocation of Man*—Maine de Biran contrasts that form of scien-tific naturalism which regards man as being subject to a complete cosmic deter-minism with the contrary assumption that man rises above the forces of nature through his possession of thought and of will.[64] And, in his later works, this same theme becomes even more pronounced. Thus, in his *Nouveaux essais d'anthro-pologie* we find Maine de Biran insisting, in terms reminiscent of Pascal, that man is a twofold being, subject to two different kinds of laws: while he to some extent resembles other sentient animals, and is subject to the laws which char-acterize their existence, he also possesses self-awareness, and is capable of creating the forms of his own existence.[65] That man does have both of these sides to his nature is, according to Maine de Biran, simply a fact which we must accept.[66] What he then wished to show was that, once this fact has been recognized, it is mistaken to suppose that the nature of a human being can be understood in terms of precisely the same principles which are adequate for an understanding of the non-human realm.[67] In this connection, Maine de Biran acknowledged that while the physiological sciences could deal with the influence of the nerves and the brain on those aspects of human behavior which were comparable to animal be-havior, he denied that one could find a similar connection between our nervous system and specifically human forms of thought and action. At this point he claimed that one must acknowledge an absolute *hiatus* which the natural sciences would never be able to bridge.[68] He was in fact exceptionally critical of the claims of progress which were being made on behalf of modern science. He contrasted earlier explanations of human behavior which had invoked spirits and demons, and a multiplicity of different principles, with the purported simplicity and clarity of the views held by scientists in his own day; and it was the latter that he challenged. He accused modern physiologically oriented science of distorting facts concerning human action to make them appear to conform to preexisting theories, with which they did not in the least conform.[69] On his view, there was an absolute gulf between the characteristics of the internal world of man and the characteristics of the natural world, and this difference the sciences could never successfully conceal.[70]

In his last years, as is shown in his *Journal* and in the *Nouveaux essais d'anthropologie*, Maine de Biran began to introduce into his analysis of man a level of experience even higher than the inner life of thought and of will. It is at this point that the parallel between his views and the views of Jacobi becomes most plain. Maine de Biran denominated this higher level as the life of spirit (*vie de l'esprit*), distinguishing it from the merely psychological realm (*vie humaine*), just as he had distinguished the latter from the merely organic (*vie animale*).[71] In the life of the spirit, which was the religious life, man was linked to God by a capacity for receptivity: the expression of will which was integral to the internal life of human consciousness, no longer appeared to be the highest stage of being to which men could attain. Rather, absorption in God, the loss of a sense of the importance of selfhood, constituted the marks of the highest spiritual state.[72] At this level, it would seem, our cognitive faculties no longer appeared to Maine de Biran to be either self-sufficient or wholly satisfying: it was through aspiration toward the infinite, the eternal, the beautiful, the perfect—an aspiration which was not simply a matter of intellectual knowledge or of choice, but of *love*—that human experience was adequately fulfilled.[73]

Having thus briefly traced the development of Maine de Biran's views, we are in a position to consider how these views might have been expected to affect (and did in fact affect) the attitudes toward the intellectual powers of man of those French philosophers who looked upon him as having blazed a new philosophic path.[74]

In the first place, it is clear that in his rebellion against Condillac and in his modification of the theories of the Ideologues, Maine de Biran rejected the view that sensation is either the sole or the primary source of human knowledge. Thus, like Jacobi and Fichte, he could not accept the Kantian dictum that all knowledge ultimately presupposes our capacity of receptivity in sensibility: an internal sense, unrecognized by Kant, was of at least equal importance. Like Fichte, although unlike Jacobi, Maine de Biran identified this internal sense with the volitional aspect of human experience. However, what is of primary interest to us in this context, and what relates Maine de Biran to both Jacobi and Fichte, is his rejection of the view that the concerns, the methods, and the achievements of the natural sciences provide an adequate basis for an interpretation of reality. Each claimed that there were domains of spiritual activity which the modes of explanation modeled on the natural sciences could not explore; and Maine de Biran, like Jacobi, identified this realm of spirit with the Christian faith.

It was not the orthodoxy of Maine de Biran's final position through which his primary influence was exerted; rather, it was through his criticism of the conceptualizations of science, and his rejection of the abstract generalizations which he regarded as being embedded in ordinary language and scientific discourse. This was an important influence on Ravaisson, on Lachelier, and on Paul Janet; it can best be seen in Bergson's acknowledgement of Maine de Biran's contribution to French philosophy.[75] In discussing Maine de Biran, Bergson remarked:

A l'opposé de Kant (car c'est à tort qu'on l'a appelé le Kant français), Maine de Biran a jugé que l'esprit humain était capable, au moins sur un point, d'atteindre l'absolu et d'en faire l'objet de ses spéculations. Il a montré que la connaissance que nous avons de nous-même, en particulier dans le sentiment de l'effort, est une connaissance privilégiée, qui dépasse le pur *phénomène* et qui atteint la réalité *en soi*, cette réalité que Kant déclarait inaccessible à nos speculations.... Bref, il a conçu l'idée d'une métaphysique qui s'élèverait de plus en plus haut, vers l'esprit en général, à mesure que la conscience descendrait plus bas, dans les profondeurs de la vie intérieure.[76]

It was in both of these respects—the transcendence of the phenomenal, and the discovery of a foundation for metaphysics in the experiences of the inner self—that Maine de Biran resembled both Jacobi and Fichte, and could (in post-Kantian terms) be said to have held that the limits of our knowledge are not identical with the limits of the Understanding. It was through this doctrine that Maine de Biran paved the way for the main stream of anti-positivistic philosophy in France in the nineteenth century.

14

IGNORAMUS, IGNORABIMUS: THE POSITIVIST STRAND

Just as a physicist has to examine the telescope
and galvanometer with which he is working; has to
get a clear conception of what he can attain with
them, and how they may deceive him; so, too, it
seemed to me necessary to investigate the capabilities
of our power of thought.

Hermann von Helmholtz[1]

The strand which we have just followed in nineteenth-century thought was concerned with the failure of the critical, analytic understanding to grasp what is essential in man and what is essential with respect to his place in the world. In Germany, as we saw, it originally arose out of Kant's distinction between the Understanding and the Reason, and involved a rejection of his view that all knowledge is based on sensibility and conforms to the categories of the Understanding. The movement which we shall now examine arose in the mid-nineteenth century and returned to a position which was in this respect similar to that of Kant: our knowledge is circumscribed by the limits of sensibility and by the manner in which our minds organize that which is immediately presented to us.

Unlike Kant, however, those with whom we shall now deal did not hold that the categories are native to the mind; rather, they regarded them as acquired in the course of experience. Even more importantly, they differed from Kant in the stress which they placed on the fact that all human knowledge is circumscribed by the limits of sensibility. For Kant, this was a general epistemological limitation, demarcating the line between knowledge and belief; for the forms of positivism with which we shall now deal, the limitation was translated into basically physiological terms: our knowledge is necessarily limited by the nature of our sense-organs. In this respect, they not only differed from Kant but from earlier positivists; for example, neither Comte nor Mill formulated his views regarding the limits of knowledge in terms of the nature and limitations of our sense-organs. After the middle of the century, this was one the characteristic marks of positivism among scientists and scientifically oriented philosophers. As a consequence of it, these later positivists placed heavier stress than had Comte or Mill upon the distinction between that which is knowable and that which exists in itself. They justified the distinction by appealing to the fact that knowledge depends upon sense experience, and what we are capable of directly experiencing is a function of the sense-organs we possess.

One should not assume that this physiologically oriented form of phenome-nalism[2] is nothing more than an extension of the epistemological uses to which physiological data had often been put: for example, we are not here dealing with explanations of particular illusions in terms of the nature and the conditions of the sense-organs. Rather, a general epistemological position is put forward on grounds which derive from the positive sciences, and in this case from the physiological sciences in particular.[3] This fact was insisted upon by Helmholtz, and the structure of Spencer's *Principles of Psychology*, in its radically rewritten second edition, affords clear evidence that such was also his view. In this shared view they were by no means alone.

In order to understand why this form of phenomenalism should have gained widespread acceptance, several factors must be taken into account. In the first place, the general position of phenomenalism had already been widely accepted, and did not have to be established as a new and unfamiliar view. To return to a doctrine of the limits of positive knowledge seemed to many an easy and welcome step. This was not only true of German reactions against post-Kantian philosophy, as one can note in Helmholtz;[4] it was also congenial to those in England who had been influenced by Comte, or were sympathetic to Mill in his attack on Hamilton, or who were influenced by Hamilton and by Mansel, or who—as in the case of Spencer—had been influenced by each of these. Nevertheless, the fact that phenomenalism was a familiar type of position is not sufficient to explain why it was taken to have been established by developments which had occurred within the natural sciences. Here the specific influence of positivism upon scientists played an important role. It will be recalled that positivism held that genuine knowledge of a systematic sort can only be established by scientific means; there-fore, it followed that if epistemological issues were to be definitively settled, they would also have to be settled by this means. While Helmholtz, Spencer, and others, such as Huxley, did not rigidly adhere to this position, their identification of reliable knowledge with scientific method was sufficiently strong to have led them to discuss epistemological issues in terms of the results which contemporary science had achieved. It is precisely at this point that the impact of the physio-logical sciences on epistemological issues is most clearly seen, for it was at this time, in the mid-century, that there was an important confluence of physical theory and physiological investigations. As a consequence, physiological investiga-tions were fully incorporated into the body of the positive sciences, and had to be taken into account in any attempt to understand the relationships between man and the natural world.

In this connection, the views of the eminent physiologist Emil DuBois-Reymond are enlightening. His famous phrase "ignoramus ... ignorabimus" provided the conclusion for a lecture in which he had not only attempted to show the limits beyond which scientific understanding could not go, but in which he had vig-orously defended the truth of a mechanistic account of the world.[5] Before turning our attention to his more eminent contemporary, Helmholtz, it will be useful to characterize DuBois-Reymond's view.

The first point to be noted is the fact that DuBois-Reymond placed physiology squarely within the framework of a mechanical world-view, which he characterized in terms of a strict Laplacean form of determinism. That he did so should not be construed as suggesting that he was blindly taking over a traditional form of philosophic materialism; rather, in part at least, his position had been formed by a major theoretical advance in the empirical sciences: the formulation of the principle of the conservation of energy. In this connection one should recall that two of the formulations of that principle—those of Mayer and of Helmholtz— had originated within the context of physiological problems: in fact, Helmholtz's essay on the subject stemmed from his opposition to the vitalism of Stahl.[6] Thus, when DuBois-Reymond argued that there is one set of laws which is basic for all nature, and these are the laws of theoretical mechanics, he was speaking of what he regarded as a necessary consequence of a major scientific revolution which had taken place in his time.[7] The same attitude is to be found slightly earlier, in 1865, in Kirchhoff's rectoral address "On the Goal of the Natural Sciences," in which he had stated that there could be no understanding of the complex processes occurring in plants or animals until they were reduced to the principles of theoretical mechanics.[8] In 1869 Helmholtz expressed a similar view in a lecture to a scientific congress which he entitled "The Aim and Progress of Physical Science." Considering the success of Helmholtz and DuBois-Reymond in their experimental work on nerve impulses, and the monumental treatises on physiological acoustics and optics which Helmholtz was able to construct, the view that physiology belonged among the physical sciences seemed to have become secure. Given the developments within theoretical mechanics, this meant that physiological processes must conform to the basic laws of mechanics, and vitalistic explanations were therefore to be regarded as wholly false.[9] That this doctrine of the unity of all science should have been accepted at the time was not, then, merely a vestigial metaphysical prejudice: it seemed warranted as a conclusion to be drawn from empirical investigations in physiology and from the basic principles of physics itself.

It is precisely at this point, where all natural phenomena are held to conform to the fundamental principles of mechanics, that DuBois-Reymond claimed that one is forced, for the first time, to say "ignorabimus." His point was that we shall always remain in ignorance of why these ultimate forces act as they do: we can never understand "matter" in itself, nor "force" in itself, but we only know them through their manifestations. To be sure, when DuBois-Reymond spoke in this way, he was obviously supposing that a distinction is to be drawn between how things manifest themselves and what they actually are in themselves. It might then be thought that he was himself indulging in "metaphysics." However, the fact that he did draw this distinction was a consequence of what I have characterized as a physiologically oriented phenomenalism. It was his contention that the world in itself lacks all of the *qualities* which it appears to have as we experience it: what we experience depends upon the ways in which our nerves are affected, and this means upon molecular processes going on within the nerves themselves, regardless of how these processes were caused.[10] Thus, the world conceived in physical-mathematical terms, and the world known in direct experience, seem to bear no relation to one another. To be sure, *if* we could discover the relationship between nerve processes and the qualities to which they give rise, we could escape this predicament. However, it is precisely at this point, when the question arises as to how nerve processes are related to conscious experiences, that DuBois-Reymond found himself forced to say *ignorabimus* for the second time. Thus we cannot know the world as it exists independently of how it *appears* within our experience; all that we can say of such a world is that all events in it are in principle predictable on the basis of a single set of absolutely uniform laws, the laws of theoretical mechanics.

I need scarcely point out that this acceptance of Laplace's formulation of a complete determinism combines rather oddly with phenomenalism. Yet the belief that these doctrines could be combined was characteristic not only of DuBois-Reymond, but of Helmholtz and Spencer. However, unlike DuBois-Reymond, each offered a theory of knowledge which, if not entirely satisfactory, did recognize some of the difficulties, and did attempt to overcome them.

1. HELMHOLTZ: SCIENCE AND EPISTEMOLOGY

On the occasion of Helmholtz's seventieth birthday, he was presented with a book of essays written in his honor, *Beiträge zur Psychologie und Physiologie der Sinnesorgane*; this volume carried as its epigraph a quotation from one of his essays which, in translation, reads: "a metaphysical conclusion is either a false conclusion or a concealed experimental conclusion."[11] No more succinct statement of his basic positivism could be given. However, it is just as important to note the respects in which Helmholtz differed from some other positivists, as it is to see to what extent he agreed with their rejection of metaphysics. While he held that all knowledge is to be drawn from experience, and is to be confirmed through experience, he did not hold that such confirmation is ever direct. Therefore, as we shall see, he did not regard it as meaningless to speak, for example, of forces in nature which lie behind observable phenomena;[12] in this respect, he differed very radically from others whom one regards as "positivists." To understand why he rejected any theory which restricts our knowledge to that which we are capable of verifying through direct sense-experience, one must understand his views regarding the physiology of the senses.

A basic factor in his position derived from the views of his teacher, Johannes Müller, concerning "specific nerve energies." According to that theory, the afferent nerve fibers of the different sense modalities each have their "specific energies" so that regardless of how they may be stimulated—whether through external or internal causes—they excite the appropriate type of sensation. On this view, to cite simple cases which were cited by Müller, auditory sensations may be caused either by sound-waves emanating from an object or by a blow on the head, just as pressure on the eyeball, and not merely the stimulation of light, may cause sensations of color. The importance of this doctrine for the theory of knowledge consists, of course, in the fact that there cannot be assumed to be any qualitative resemblance between the cause of a sensation and the sensation itself. Helmholtz was very explicit in drawing this inference from Müller's theory, even though he rejected the semi-Kantian manner in which Müller himself had used it. For example, in a series of lectures on "The Recent Progress of the Theory of Vision," delivered in 1868, we find him saying:

> We have already seen enough to answer the question whether it is possible to maintain the natural and innate conviction that the quality of our sensations, and especially our sensations of sight, give us a true impression of corresponding qualities in the outer world. It is clear that they do not. The question was really decided by Johannes Müller's deduction from well ascertained facts of the law of specific nervous energy. Whether the rays of the sun appear to us as colour or as warmth, does not at all depend upon their own properties, but simply upon whether they excite the fibres of the optic nerve, or those of the skin. . . . The most complete difference offered by our several sensations, that namely between those of sight, of hearing, of taste, of smell, and of touch . . . does not, as we now see, at all depend upon the nature of the external object, but solely upon the central connections of the nerves which are affected.[13]

Or, as he says in another place, when discussing the extension of Müller's point of view to processes occurring within systems of nerve fibers in a single modality:

> In this case it has been shown that no kind of physical similarity whatever corresponds to the subjective similarity of different composite light of the same colour. By these and similar facts we are led to the very important conclusion that our sensations are, as regards their quality, only *signs* of external objects, and in no sense *images* of any degree of resemblance.[14]

Yet, Helmholtz held that "apprehension by the senses supplies after all, directly or indirectly, the material of all human knowledge."[15] Obviously, there were epistemological difficulties here which demanded solution. One among them was the problem of explaining how our senses could supply us with adequate information concerning material objects if all of the data of which we are conscious depend upon what goes on, so to speak, within our own skins.

The problem would be insoluble if what we demand is that our senses should provide us with images of independently existing material objects: however, it may perhaps be done away with if what we mean by a knowledge of material objects is a reliable system of signs which represent the relationships among the entities which our signs are taken as signifying. This was the path which Helmholtz followed:

> An image [he said] must be *analogous* to the original object; a statue, for instance, has the same corporeal form as the human being after which it was made. . . . In the case of a *sign* it is sufficient that it become apparent as often as the occurrence to be depicted makes its appearance, the conformity between them being restricted to their presenting themselves simultaneously. The correspondence existing between our sensations and the objects producing them is precisely of this kind.[16]

According to Helmholtz, the difference between languages as systems of signs, and sense-perception as a system of signs, is that the system of our sensations is not arbitrary, but is in fact a universal language of which there are not diverse families or differing dialects: it is the mother tongue of nature itself.[17] Different people, he held, receive the same sensations from the same objects, and at different times an object which has not changed will excite the same sensations in us. Thus, the system of the sensations which are caused by objects will conform to the relationships existing within the field of those objects.

To be sure, one feature of the doctrine of specific nerve energies would seem to render the assumption of such a conformity dubious: as we noted, it was held that quite different types of stimuli can cause similar sensory excitations; thus, for example, a blow on the head can give us visual or auditory sensations. However, Helmholtz incorporated such facts into his theory by distinguishing between our awareness of sensory data and our perception of objects. For example, in his lectures on "The Recent Progress of the Theory of Vision," which summarized the more general views developed in his *Physiological Optics*, he distinguished sharply between the *sensations* of sight, which depend upon how the eye is affected, and *perceptions* of sight, which depend upon unconscious inferences based upon past experience. Sensations, as such, can never be mistaken, but they may be mistakenly interpreted when we take them as signs of the existence of external objects. Furthermore, they may give rise to *illusions*, which depend upon faulty inferences due to the presence of unusual circumstances in the conditions under which sensations are presented to us:

When the modes of stimulation of the organs of sense are unusual, incorrect ideas of objects are apt to be formed; which used to be described, therefore, as *illusions of the senses*. Obviously, in these cases there is nothing wrong with the activity of the organ of sense and its corresponding nervous mechanism which produces the illusion. Both of them have to act according to the laws that govern their activity once for all. It is rather simply an illusion in the judgment of the material presented to the senses, resulting in a false idea of it.[18]

He states his explanation of such illusions in the case of vision by means of the following rule:

We always believe that we see such objects as would, under conditions of normal vision, produce the retinal image of which we are actually conscious.[19]

Taking these doctrines into account, we may say that what constitutes veridical perception is, simply, our capacity to infer, on the basis of normal past experience, how different sensory excitations are connected with one another, so that they form an interrelated system of signs, or cues. The unconscious inferences which are involved do not differ, according to Helmholtz, from *logical* inferences, except superficially, by virtue of the fact that logical inferences can be formulated in words, whereas the implicit inferences of perception only make use of sensations, and of the memory of past sensations.[20]

When Helmholtz spoke of perceptual judgments in this way, what he had in mind was the fact that every such judgment consists in an *induction* based upon past experience: like Mill, whose logical theory influenced him,[21] Helmholtz was attempting to give what he termed an "empiristic" (*empiristische*) account of all human knowledge, showing that neither "intuitionistic" nor "nativistic" hypotheses had to be invoked in order to account for any aspects of our experience. In this connection we may note that, like Mill, he also offered an empiristic account of mathematics; this account, it is to be noted, included a consideration of non-Euclidean geometries. In a series of essays, he set himself the task of explaining how it is that, on the basis of imaginative experience, we can formulate various types of non-Euclidean systems, although our spatial experience is such that Euclidean geometry seems intuitively certain to us.[22] In this field, as in all others, what Helmholtz wished to reject was the theory that there is "a pre-existing harmony of the laws of mental operations with those of the outer world"; it was his aim "to derive all correspondence between mind and matter from the results of experience."[23]

It would seem that, if this were his aim, he was still in epistemological difficulties. As we have seen, he had rejected the idea that our sense-experience, which is the sole source of our knowledge, could be assumed to *resemble* the external world: knowledge consisted in a set of usually reliable signs, or cues, as to simultaneities and sequences within what we experience. How then could Helmholtz establish *any* form of correspondence between what is experienced and what exists independently of us? The answer to his question lies in the fact that, unlike Hume, or Mill, or Comte, he believed that experimental science must be interpreted as establishing that phenomena are the effects of *causes* which are not themselves directly experienced, and that such an interpretation is legitimate even though the effects which we experience do not resemble their causes. We must now attempt to state what sort of justification Helmholtz was able to offer for his view.

We may start from a point which would not have been challenged by Hume, by Mill, or by Comte: Helmholtz's insistence that knowledge does not consist in an accumulation of observations, or facts, but in the discovery of regularities, or laws, within experience. Phrasing this in terms of experimental science, Helmholtz said:

> Isolated facts and experiments have in themselves no value, however great their
> number may be. They only become valuable from a theoretical or practical point of view
> when they make us acquainted with the *law* of a series of uniformly recurring
> phenomena, or, it may be, only give a negative result showing an incompleteness in our
> knowledge of such a law, till then held to be perfect.[24]

At this point Helmholtz took what was the decisive step in his theory of scientific method: he held that those systematizations of facts which are to be considered as laws of nature can be distinguished from systematizations which are imposed upon facts by our own interests, speculative tendencies, or needs. As examples of arbitrary and subjective systematizations he mentioned the Linnean system of classification, as well as the arrangement of materials in an encyclopedia.[25] The difference between such systematizations and the procedures of science was that in the first cases the orderliness depended upon the principle which was used to construct the system, whereas in *science*, Helmholtz held, the order is not imposed upon the data, but must be discovered through careful, systematic examinations of the conditions under which phenomena recur. This distinction was formulated by him in the following crucial paragraphs:

> A law of nature . . . is not a mere logical conception that we have adopted as a kind of *memoria technica* to enable us to more readily remember facts. We of the present day have already sufficient insight to know that the laws of nature are not things which we can evolve by any speculative method. On the contrary, we have to *discover* them in the facts; we have to test them by repeated observation or experiment, in constantly new cases, under ever-varying circumstances; and in proportion as they hold good under a constantly increasing change of conditions, in a constantly increasing number of cases and with greater delicacy in the means of observation, does our confidence in their trustworthiness rise.
>
> Thus the laws of nature occupy the position of a power with which we are not familiar, not to be arbitrarily selected and determined in our minds, as one might devise various systems of animals and plants one after another, so long as the only object is classification. Before we can say that our knowledge of any one law of nature is complete, we must see that *it holds good without exception*, and make this test of its correctness. If we can be assured that the conditions under which the law operates have presented themselves, the result must ensue without arbitrariness, without choice, without our cooperation, and from the very necessity which regulates the things of the external world as well as our perception. The law then takes the form of an objective power, and for that reason we call it *force*.[26]

The conception of "force" in which this argument eventuates is obviously not the same conception as that which Hume and others have criticized, for Helmholtz is not claiming that he sees, or otherwise experiences, transfer of power between any observed phenomena. That to which he is appealing is an experienced difference between those cases in which we find that we can arrange observations in any order we may choose, in which we can manufacture new data or obliterate others, etc., and, on the other hand, cases in which we find that we are not able to do so. Thus, that to which he is appealing is similar to that to which Kant appealed in his analysis of causation: the distinction between an objective order of sequence and one which is under the control of the subject. In other words, what Helmholtz is taking to be a sign of *force* is a resistance or recalcitrance in the *sequences* which are to be observed among phenomena; he is *not* assuming that he directly observes one phenomenon offering resistance to another, nor offering resistance to him. The only manner in which he knows of "objective power" or "force" is through the degree of regularity which is to be found in relations among phenomena: he never claims to know it "in-itself."

We are now in a position to understand the next step in Helmholtz's analysis: he takes such underlying and unexperienced forces to be *causal necessities*. Once again we may note that he is not claiming that he directly experiences a relationship of cause and effect: causes are *not* experienced, but are what underlie those regularities which we discover in phenomena, which are universal and do not fall under the control of our wills.

Helmholtz summarizes this entire theory of science in one brief paragraph which we are now in a better position to understand:

> Our desire to *comprehend* natural phenomena, in other words, to ascertain their *laws*, thus takes another form of expression—that is we have to seek out the *forces* which are the *causes* of the phenomena. The conformity to law in nature must be conceived as a causal connection the moment we recognize that it is independent of our thought and will.[27]

In this paragraph, seen against the background of the foregoing discussion, the following points may be singled out for attention: (1) The aim of science is that of comprehending natural phenomena, not merely accumulating observations and classifying them. (2) This involves formulating laws concerning observable regularities which do not admit of exceptions. (3) The fact that these regularities are not malleable by our thought or will is what leads us to characterize them as objective powers or *forces in nature*. (4) Such forces are what we refer to as the causes upon which phenomena depend. However, there is a final point which is not explicitly stated in this paragraph, but which must be stressed, for it provides the basic philosophic postulate of Helmholtz's whole theory of science: (5) To relate a natural phenomenon to a law of nature *is* to comprehend it: there is no further, more ultimate form of understanding than that which scientific laws provide. Thus, we have no secret access to the powers of nature; we know them only through their observable effects.

Helmholtz's acceptance of this final proposition might be thought to render nugatory all of his claims regarding "the forces of nature," which constitute the unobservable causes of observed effects; knowledge would seem to be reduced to a discovery of correlations among the immediately given presentations of the senses. However, this would involve attributing to Helmholtz a position diametrically opposed to that which he did in fact accept. He held that, in order to decide what knowledge we can obtain by means of the presentations of the senses, we must rely upon physics and physiology. Furthermore, he regarded the laws of these sciences as being concerned with relationships which are not directly presented in sense-experience, but can only be established by experimental means. To fail to use such inferences would be to continue to assume that traditional philosophic modes of analysis, which he believed to have been sterile, should take precedence over the methods of science. On Helmholtz's view, the sciences themselves were now in a position to examine the reliability of our senses, and thus formulate an adequate theory of cognition.[28] His conviction that such was the case rested on his belief that, through the research in which he and others were participating, the sciences were beginning to be able to formulate an interlocking system of physical, physiological, and psychological laws, which would be able to establish interconnections between processes in the external world, the sensations correlated with them, and the perceptions to which such sensations, on the basis of past experience, give rise. On the basis of a knowledge of these interconnections, it would no longer be epistemologically significant that we should have to admit that our sensations are not *images* of the external world, but only *signs* of

relationships which obtain within it, and between it and us.[29] Since these signs
are not arbitrary, or in any way imposed upon experience by us, since on the
contrary they represent the necessary ways in which our organs function, there
is no reason to describe the world of our experience as "false." From both a
practical and a theoretical point of view, the system of relationships which we can
discover within experience is in every way reliable, and is to be denominated as
knowledge.[30]

Were one to claim that we still need to ask what lies behind such a system of
relationships and is accountable for it, one would be raising metaphysical questions which cannot possibly be given a scientific answer. In response to such questions one would not only have to answer *"ignoramus"* but *"ignorabimus."*
However, for Helmholtz as for DuBois-Reymond, the tasks of science were sufficiently broad, including all natural phenomena, whether physical or mental, so
that the limits of verifiable knowledge would presumably never be reached. To
give up the search for answers to unanswerable questions would not only be to
free ourselves from unnecessary burdens, but it would open the way for considering those questions to which answers can be found. Among such questions there
are not only those which concern the science of physics, but those which refer to
organic phenomena and to the phenomena of mind. Once metaphysical dogmas
are cleared away, the latter questions, too, can be answered by methods appropriate to science, and a unified system of scientific laws can be expected to result.[31]
It was to the advancement of this task that Helmholtz's own prodigious scientific
researches had been directed, and it was this ideal which he sought to elucidate
and to justify through his theory of knowledge.

2. HERBERT SPENCER: THE LIMITS OF THE KNOWABLE

In its original form, Spencer's *Principles of Psychology*, which first appeared in
1855, had a quite different orientation from its radically revised second edition,
the first volume of which appeared in 1870, the second volume being issued in
installments which were completed in 1872. In the fifteen-year interval, Spencer
had formulated his conception of a system of Synthetic Philosophy, and had
published *First Principles* and the *Principles of Biology*. It was therefore natural
that the second edition should have emphasized the place of psychology in the
system of the sciences, and should have been concerned with applying the universal law of natural phenomena to psychological processes. Although we are not
here concerned with this systematic elaboration of Spencer's views, in attempting
to understand his theory of the scope and the limits of human understanding we
cannot rely upon the unsystematic organization of the first edition, with which
Spencer himself was dissatisfied.[32] Fortunately, Spencer was able to include almost
all of the materials of the first edition, which was oriented toward problems of
cognition, within the systematic framework of the second edition, providing a
clearly articulated theory of knowledge in which a deterministic world-view can
presumably be reconciled with a positivistic rejection of metaphysics. In this

respect, as we shall see, the conclusions of Helmholtz and Spencer were essentially similar, in spite of the great differences between their methods of inquiry.

Even in the first edition of the *Principles of Psychology*, Spencer connected the fundamental characteristics of mental life with what he took to be the essential attribute of life-processes: that, in living things, there is "the continuous adjustment of internal relations to external relations."[33] In the first edition, however, attention was not devoted to the nature of the nervous system; it was only later that Spencer came to recognize it as providing the means by which there could be a continuous adjustment between psychological processes and changes in the environment. In the second edition of the *Principles of Psychology* his point of departure therefore became a physiological consideration of the nature and functioning of the nervous system. In this physiological analysis, Spencer identified afferent stimuli with molecular motions, insisting that physiological accounts should rigorously exclude all reference to consciousness.[34] These motions were not to be identified with sensations, for the latter are "feelings," that is, conscious states. If, then, there were to be a science of psychology, there must first be a science which would deal with the relations between nervous stimulation and conscious states: in the absence of such a science one would either be confined to physiology, not dealing with consciousness at all, or one would be at a loss to show how the relations within consciousness were correlated with changes in the environment. The intermediary science was termed "aestho-physiology" by Spencer; its aim was to collate the objective phenomena in the nervous system with the data of consciousness, which are known to us only through introspection.[35]

While Spencer's discussion of aestho-physiology is at some points very general and rather obvious, dealing with correlations between our ability to experience various sensations and the fact that we possess a certain type of nervous system, he also attempted to formulate some concrete principles of correlation between changes in experience and measurable changes in the excitation of the nerves. For example, he suggested a correlation between the after-effects of the stimulation of a nerve and the after-effects to be found in sensation; he also suggested that there are quantitative correlations between the strength of nerve-impulses and the degree of feeling which we experience.[36] Thus, what Spencer termed aestho-physiology dealt with many of the conventional problems of psychophysics. In addition, he believed that its findings applied not merely to sensations, but to the other large class of "feelings" designated as "the emotions."[37] In all cases, aestho-physiology had the same task: to correlate the data of consciousness with physiological reactions, not attempting to interpret either in terms of the other but attempting to depict whatever systematic connections existed between them. Spencer described this function in the following terms:

Aestho-physiology has a position that is entirely unique. It belongs neither to the objective world nor the subjective world; but taking a term from each, occupies itself with the correlation of the two. It may with as much propriety be included in the domain of physical science as in the domain of psychical science; and must be left where it stands, as the link between them.[38]

Since Spencer's time it has become customary to include within the province of psychology the inquiries which he assigned to aestho-physiology. Spencer himself did not do so, because his conception of psychology was of a very special sort. Since he wished to relate psychology to what he regarded as the universal nature of living things, he emphasized the adjustment of internal relations to external relations, not the relations between physiological states and consciousness. Thus he was interested in correlating connections between feelings with connections existing between phenomena in the external environment. Aestho-physiology, which connected feelings with physiological processes *within* the organism was therefore dealing with what was only an intermediary link: its existence as a science was a precondition of there being a science of psychology, but it did not belong within psychology itself.

The task of psychology was, then, that of correlating two distinct types of proposition: one type would assert a connection between two events in the external world, the other would assert a connection between two sensations or other subjective phenomena. Spencer said:

[A psychological proposition] is not the connection between the internal phenomena, nor is it the connection between the external phenomena; but it is *the connection between these two connections*. A psychological proposition is necessarily compounded of two propositions, of which one concerns the subject and the other concerns the object; and cannot be expressed without the four terms which these two propositions imply. The distinction may best be explained by symbols. Suppose that A and B are two related manifestations in the environment—say the colour and taste of a fruit; then, so long as we contemplate their relation by itself, or as associated with other external phenomena, we are occupied with physical science. Now suppose that a and b are the sensations produced in the organism by this peculiar light which the fruit reflects, and by the chemical action of its juice on the palate; then, so long as we study the action of the light on the retina and optic centres, and consider how the juice sets up in other centres a change known as sweetness, we are occupied with facts belonging to the sciences of Physiology and Aestho-physiology. But we pass into the domain of Psychology the moment we inquire how there comes to exist within the organism a relation between a and b that in some way or other corresponds to the relation between A and B. Psychology is exclusively concerned with this connection between (AB) and (ab)—has to investigate its nature, its origin, its meaning.[39]

Since he conceived of the task of psychology in this way, Spencer's psychological system consisted in developing the theory of associations in a manner that extended to all feelings, whether simple or complex, and of then accounting for how such associations are correlated with connections between phenomena in the external world. His theory of associations added little that was new to the associationism of his time; what was new was his hypothesis of the inherited effects of past associations, so that in the history of the race—and not merely in the history of each individual—more and more complex and reliable associations came to be formed. It is not with this clearly untenable psychological system that we must concern ourselves; it is rather to the characteristic nature of its epistemological implications that I wish to direct attention.

In this connection, the first point to be noted is that Spencer, like Helmholtz,

denied that we have any right to assume that there is a qualitative similarity between our sensations and their causes in the external world. Helmholtz's argument in this respect had taken the doctrine of specific nerve energies as its point
of departure; Spencer's basic position derived from a contrast between the characteristics of molecular motions in the nerves and the qualities of which we are
directly aware in experiencing colors, sounds, shapes, odors, etc. In discussing
aestho-physiology, Spencer held that, while we are bound to acknowledge that
feelings are always correlated with nerve impulses so that the two can only be
held to be "the subjective and objective faces of the same thing," yet we are unable
to comprehend their relationship to one another: the qualities of our sensations
seem utterly different from the molecular motions, or "nerve shocks," which they
accompany.[40] Therefore, since nerve action serves as the necessary intermediating
link between the sensations we experience and the external environing world,
the disparity between the two sides of the aestho-physiological relationship precludes us from regarding sensations as being qualitatively similar to what exists
independently of us.

In addition to this basic fact, Spencer's discussion of aestho-physiology pointed
out another reason why we cannot identify what we experience with what exists
independently of experience. Although he held that there is a correspondence
between the strength of our feelings and the strength of the nerve impulses which
underlie them, he denied that there is a one-to-one correspondence between the
strength of these nerve impulses and their external exciting causes. As he pointed
out, prior stimulation often tends to diminish later reactions to stimuli of equal
strength; therefore, a strict correlation between nerve impulses and feelings entails that there is an actual disparity between feelings and events in the external
world.[41]

These arguments, which were drawn directly from aestho-physiology, were not
those upon which Spencer chiefly relied when attempting to show that the sensations which we experience are not similar to what exists independently of us.
Rather, he cited more traditional forms of epistemological arguments to show that
there are variations in the ways in which the organs of different types of organisms
react to external stimuli; furthermore, he pointed out that in the case of each
individual our sense organs differ in their responsiveness to stimuli, depending
upon their sensitivity and upon their condition at any particular time. On the
basis of such arguments, Spencer held that it is entirely mistaken to suppose that
our sensory experience directly mirrors the qualities of objects which are external
to and independent of us. Furthermore, he argued that not only the content of
specific sensations was relative to the nature and condition of our sense organs,
but that the relationships which we experience among sensations are subject to
the same type of relativity. Thus, even the spatial and temporal relations which
we experience, and the differences which we can discriminate with respect to sets
of feelings, are not to be identified with sets of relationships which exist independently of us. These arguments, which Spencer mobilized in chapters entitled
"The Relativity of Feelings" and "The Relativity of Relations between Feelings,"
led him to formulate a general proposition which he claimed was a truth "familiar

to all students of Psychology," that "though internal feeling habitually depends upon external agent, yet there is no likeness between them either in kind or degree."[42]

This is, of course, similar to the conclusion reached by Helmholtz. However, unlike Helmholtz, Spencer was primarily a philosopher. He felt obligated to offer a defense of epistemological realism against the attacks which could be expected to be leveled against him by those who might claim that under these conditions it was illegitimate to defend realism at all. In both the first and the second editions of his *Principles of Psychology*, he argued against Berkeley and Hume, attempting to show that, if one were to establish the position that our sensations do actually depend upon the nature and conditions of our sense organs, and if one set out to show that they cannot therefore be interpreted as being identical with what exists in the external world, one could only do so on the basis of realistic assumptions. In short, it was Spencer's claim that interpretations of sense-perception which presume to establish subjectivism are self-refuting, since arguments designed to establish the principle that our sensations are subjective phenomena always presuppose realistic assumptions: if realism is false, we cannot in fact establish any disparities between what we directly experience and what, in naive experience, we regard as existing independently of us.[43]

The question, of course, immediately arises as to what form of realism Spencer believed to be tenable, and we find that it was a realism which closely resembled the position that Helmholtz had reached. Spencer designated this position as "Transfigured Realism," characterizing it as "one which simply asserts objective existence as separate from and independent of subjective existence. But it affirms neither that any one mode of this objective existence is in reality that which it seems, nor that the connexions among its modes are objectively what they seem."[44] Nevertheless, there was one form of correspondence between subjective and objective existence which, Spencer believed, could be affirmed, and that was what may best be regarded as an isomorphism between the set of systematic relationships within experience and the set of relationships existing independently of us. Spencer illustrated this form of correspondence by a diagram of a cube and its perspective projection on a cylinder. The shape of the surfaces, and the relationships among sides and angles, all have a different form in the projection from that which characterizes their relationships in the cube, but there is a systematic connection among them which corresponds to the systematic connections existing in the object itself.[45] Thus, on Spencer's view, our sensations and the directly experienced relations among these sensations, cannot in any case be assumed to be *images* of the nature and the relationships of independently existing objects: to believe the contrary would be to disregard what physics, physiology, and aesthophysiology establish concerning the nature of external objects and the forms of our reactions to them. On the other hand, to deny a systematic connection between what occurs within consciousness and what occurs in the physical world would be to deny the accumulated evidence of the regularity of nature which these same sciences provide. Spencer termed this interpretation of sense experience "transfigured realism" and he held it to be the only sound alternative to that

"crude realism" which was incompatible with a knowledge of science.[46] He believed that, at the same time, it could escape the incoherence of scepticism which
assumed the existence of an independent, external world even when it was arguing against our right to believe in such a world.

It might seem inconsistent for Spencer to have held a position which he himself designated as a form of realism, and yet refer to reality as being "the Unknowable." However, we have already seen that a comparable position was characteristic of both DuBois-Reymond and of Helmholtz; in explicating Spencer's
view, we shall once again find that he, like them, showed an extreme degree of
confidence in scientific knowledge, although he combined that confidence with
asseverations concerning the fact that all human knowledge has outer limits
which it cannot in any case transcend.

Spencer, like Helmholtz, regarded his realism as having been established on
scientific grounds. To be sure, he recognized that it constituted a specifically
philosophic position, but it was a position characteristic of a *positive* philosophy,
and differed entirely from the positions of those who were to be designated as
"metaphysicians."[47] According to the Kantian heritage which Helmholtz and
Spencer shared, metaphysics involved the attempt to form conceptions of reality
which transcended the bounds of all possible experience, whereas the sciences
were taken to be formulations of systematic connections to be found within
experience. Thus, for Helmholtz and Spencer, there could be sciences of matter
and of mind, and of the relationships which exist between data of consciousness
and changes which occur within the organism; however, there was no way in
which one could formulate any conception of what "Matter" or "Energy" is in
itself, or what "Mind" is in itself, or whether one is merely a product or appearance of the other.[48]

For Spencer, all knowledge depended upon observation and proceeded by assimilating particular facts into wider and ever wider generalizations. Basically, of
course, all of the concepts used in such generalizations ultimately depend upon
sense-experience, but he held that it was possible and also necessary to extend
these concepts beyond what was originally presented in that experience. We form
what he referred to as "symbolic conceptions," as when, for example, we combine
our image of an object of spherical shape with the experience of seeing ships sail-
ing over the horizon, and come to conceive of the earth as a sphere.[49] This process of forming symbolic conceptions involves both a simplification of what is
originally given in sense perception and an extension of the given to what has not
been directly given at all. Spencer regarded this as a wholly legitimate process,
without which we could form no generalizations and could discover no general
laws. However, symbolic conceptions are only legitimate when it is possible to
bring them back into touch with observations, either through direct sense-perception or through showing that the predictions which they enable us to make are
actually fulfilled.

Using this basic theory of knowledge as a touchstone, we can see why Spencer
believed that his "transfigured realism" could be regarded as scientifically warranted, whereas any attempt to make statements concerning what reality is in-

itself necessarily transcends the limits of knowledge. His epistemological realism could be regarded as having been originally suggested by everyday experience, where our ability to receive impressions rests on the unimpaired functioning of our sense-organs; where that which we experience often varies with the conditions under which we experience it; and where it becomes obvious that different persons experience what we take to be the same object in dissimilar ways. The science of physiology translates these crude generalizations concerning the functioning of our sense-organs into terms of molecular motions in the nervous system; physics and chemistry, along with physiology, serve to relate these nerve impulses to what occurs in the external world. Aestho-physiology provides correlations between sensory content and nerve impulses. It proceeds from an analysis of the individual sense-modalities to wider generalizations concerning the ways in which all sensory experience is correlated with appropriate changes in the nervous system. Finally, psychology, which concerns itself with our complex mental processes, shows how the linkage among our thoughts corresponds with linkages occurring in the external world and accounts for this correspondence in what Spencer took to be a scientifically satisfactory way: through the theory of a biological inheritance of the effects of past experience.

In all of this argument, Spencer would say, he had not left the firm ground of confirmed observations: what are admittedly symbolic conceptions (such as molecular motions in the nerves, or correlations between the stimulation of the retina by light and sensations of sight) are conceptions which are confirmed by the predictions which they permit us to make. Science would be transcended and metaphysics would set in if one tried to form any conception of *how* motions in the nerves "produce" sensations, or *how* complex associations of ideas can lead to those efferent nerve-impulses which eventuate in action. To attempt to go behind the verifiable correlations between these utterly different types of concept would be to introduce notions which it is not in any way possible to verify within experience. Thus, Spencer's doctrine of when symbolic conceptions are legitimate, and when they are not, provided him with a way of avoiding traditional metaphysical issues concerning the mind-body relationship, and at the same time allowed him to claim that epistemological conclusions, like all other warranted philosophical conclusions, follow directly from the systematic study of relationships among the data of experience. That there was one widest generalization which included all facts, one fundamental law of nature, Spencer had no doubt: this law of developmental change could, he believed, be established through a synthesis of the sciences.[50] It was only with respect to the traditional questions raised not by scientists but by metaphysicians that he, like DuBois-Reymond and Helmholtz, would have said *"ignoramus, ignorabimus."*

3. Ernst Mach and the Economy of Thought

In moving from the type of position accepted by both Helmholtz and Spencer to that accepted by Mach, we encounter a new interpretation of the limits which are to be assigned to human thought. It will be recalled that Helmholtz and Spencer denied that our experience directly mirrors what exists in nature independently of us; however, they both held that the relationships which we gradually come to find within experience can be regarded as corresponding to relationships which characterize nature itself. Both assumed that as the sciences advance, and all facets of experience are more carefully investigated, this correspondence becomes more and more reliable; in this sense it may be said they held that truth is to be construed in terms of a *correspondence*, i.e., a correspondence between the systematic connection among our ideas and a set of relationships existing in nature itself.[51] This assumes, of course, that the relationships which we find among experienced entities when we follow the methods used in empirical enquiry are not artifacts created by those methods, but are controlled by relationships existing independently of us. It was precisely this assumption that came to be challenged with increasing frequency by philosophers of science. It is with one such challenge, that of Ernst Mach, that we shall now be primarily concerned.[52]

Unlike Helmholtz and Spencer, Mach demanded that we confine our assertions about nature and about ourselves to statements which refer to elements given within experience, avoiding all assumptions concerning that upon which experience depends. In interpreting this injunction, one must note what it was that Mach regarded as being directly given in experience. On his view, that by which we are confronted is not a world of *objects*, and we do not experience ourselves as something different from these objects, standing in various relations to them; rather, he took experience to be constituted by free-floating "elements," that is, by data which do not entail the existence of anything else, but are simply *there*, within experience. Furthermore, it was Mach's view that the manner in which these elements came to be organized, forming our conceptions of the world, is not determined by characteristics intrinsic to the elements themselves; rather, ways of organizing them develop during the course of human experience according to the interests or purposes which take shape within us. On this assumption, the question of what constitutes truth must be answered by offering some criterion by means of which we can discriminate better from worse principles of organization among the elements making up our experience. Mach held that the sciences, correctly interpreted, furnish the clearest example of a satisfactory criterion, and on this basis he formulated his theory of "the economical nature of thought." It is in connection with this doctrine that his views differ markedly from those of earlier positivists, and that they are most clearly related to other tendencies in later nineteenth-century philosophy; for that reason it will be helpful to see how he came to develop his position regarding the economy of thought.

If we consult Mach's various sketches of his intellectual development we can trace the main stages in the process leading up to his acceptance of the view that our conceptions of the world rest, in the last analysis, on the principle of the economy of thought.[53] At the age of fifteen he had read Kant's *Prolegomena to any Future Metaphysic*, and it had made a profound impression upon him; however quite suddenly, two or three years later, he came to believe that the Kantian assumption of things-in-themselves was an unnecessary and empty assumption, and at this stage he moved toward an acceptance of Berkeley's idealism.[54] However, he tells us that an interest in the physiology of sense-perception, as well as the study of Herbart, soon led him to abandon Berkeley's position for one more nearly akin to that of Hume, although he did not yet know Hume's work.[55] This shift, we may conjecture, involved the abandonment of the notion of a substantial self, or ego; a step which was in line with his previous abandonment of the conception that there is some Kantian "Unknown-X" behind the sensory qualities which we experience.[56] This extension of his position in the direction of a pure subjectivism presumably took place prior to his receiving his doctorate in 1860. Between that time and 1864, when he received a professorship at Graz, two independent and highly important influences helped to develop his later philosophy of science. On the one hand, in lectures concerning physical theory which he gave as a Privat-Dozent in Vienna, beginning in 1861, he became convinced that ideals of simplicity in explanation had been of the greatest importance to Copernicus, Galileo, and Newton; this, he tells us, was one factor which prepared the way for the later development of his theory of the economy of thought.[57] Less obviously connected, but conceivably of even greater later importance, was Mach's concern with the problems of psychophysics after the appearance of Fechner's *Elemente der Psychophysik* in 1860. He had already been interested in allied problems, studying the Doppler-effect in relation to sound and colors, and for a time he increasingly occupied himself with psychophysics. In fact, he delivered a broad-ranging series of lectures concerning these problems, and although he later denigrated their value, we may note that in the course of them he criticized Helmholtz's position from a point of view which, apparently, he never abandoned.[58] If I read him aright, what Mach rejected was Helmholtz's view that, in general (i.e., under normal circumstances), differences among the qualities of our sensations represent differences among the causes of the nerve impulses which are connected with these sensations—a doctrine which would allow for the type of correspondence theory of truth which I have attributed to both Helmholtz and Spencer. In opposition to this assumption, Mach argued that, since different antecedents might give rise to similar nerve impulses, the qualitative distinctions among sensations should be correlated with ascertainable changes in the sense organs, not with the postulated *causes* of these changes.

From this point on, as his various publications show, Mach became more interested in the physiological bases of sensations in the sensing organs; in these investigations, his method consisted in directly correlating relationships between physiological stimulation and sensory experience, rather than tracing a physiological chain of causes that could be said to have a particular sensory element as its ultimate effect. This, he felt, permitted him to unify all of the data relevant to psychophysics in a single continuum, whether these data were usually classified as belonging within the province of physics, or psychology, or physiology. For example, the events with which physicists deal when they deal with light emanating from a particular source would be directly correlated with how the eye reacts to such light, and since Mach was correlating sensations with events occurring on the sensing organ, he could move easily back and forth between the sensation "yellow," a physical source of yellow light, and the reaction of the eye to such light. Thus, psychophysics relied on objective correlations, not on a chain of causal links in which one would first be tracing a series of physical events, then a series of physiological events, and finally mention a specifically psychological event: "this sensation of yellow." It was this conception of a unified, objective science which was the position which Mach later developed at length in his *Analysis of Sensations*.[59] While there is no evidence that, at the time, he had already formulated his position in the full-fledged epistemological fashion which characterized that later work, the method which he had developed for dealing with psychophysical problems can be considered as having paved the way for an acceptance of the principle of the economy of thought: it rid psychophysics of the mind-body problem which had provided a background for it in Fechner's work, and, even more importantly, it rid psychophysics of hypotheses involving unobserved causal relationships, such as those which had been assumed by Helmholtz.[60]

While Mach did not publish any statement concerning the principle of the economy of thought until his essay on *The History of the Principle of the Conservation of Energy* (1872), the idea itself took shape for him during this earlier period, while he was still at Graz (1864-67). As he tells us,[61] it had two sources: on the one hand, it was suggested by discussions with his colleague and friend, Emanuel Hermann, who was an economist; on the other hand, it derived from a Darwinian-inspired view that there is a struggle for survival among scientific conceptions. As Mach himself notes in this connection, originally these were entirely independent ideas. The ideal of simplicity in scientific explanations, which had already impressed him, became associated with what appear to have been Hermann's views, developing into Mach's contention that scientific laws are simply marvelously economical means for describing observed phenomena. On the other hand, what he drew from the Darwinian concept of a struggle for survival was a way of interpreting the history of thought. As he tells us in the same passage, he used this notion in his University lecturing at Graz. In one popular lecture on the velocity of light, dating from this period, he expressed his Darwinian position in the following way:

It will now perhaps be clear to you that new thoughts do not spring up suddenly. Thoughts need their time to ripen, grow, and develop in, like every natural product; for man with his thoughts, is also a part of nature.

Slowly, gradually, and laboriously one thought is transformed into a different thought, as in all likelihood one animal species is gradually transformed into new species. Many ideas arise simultaneously. They fight the battle for existence not differently than do the Ichthyosaurus, the Brahman, and the horse.

A few remain to spread rapidly over all fields of knowledge, to be redeveloped, to be again split up, to begin again the struggle from the start. As many animal species long since conquered, the relicts of ages past, still live in remote regions where their enemies cannot reach them, so also we find conquered ideas still living on in the minds of many men. Whoever will look carefully into his own soul will acknowledge that thoughts battle as obstinately for existence as animals.[62]

While this position is not incompatible with holding that when we develop a scientific law we are simply finding a shorthand way of describing experience, the connection between the two views is not immediately evident. It is to establishing their linkage that we must now turn.

Mach himself gives us the clue as to their connection when he speaks of his view as a biological-economical view of thought, holding that all thought serves *adaptive purposes*.[63] In two popular lectures entitled "The Economical Nature of Physical Inquiry" and "On Transformation and Adaptation in Scientific Thought," which date from 1882 and 1883, as well as in his *Science of Mechanics*, which was published in the latter year, he held that the fundamental characteristic of the mind is that it organizes experience in ways that prove to be useful. In fact, in the former essay, Mach goes so far as to praise Schopenhauer's view that the will creates the intellect for its own purposes.[64] Although this way of speaking of "will" and "intellect" is not compatible with Mach's more mature views, as developed in his *Analysis of Sensations* and elsewhere, from this point on he stressed the fact that thought functions as a means of adaptation by organizing experience in whatever ways make it most manageable.[65]

One form of organizing the "elements" given in experience is, of course, to regard them as clustered into more or less permanent objects, among which one's own body is one such object. The importance of the conception of permanent objects, to which changes can be related, was expressed by Mach in his *Science of Mechanics* when he held:

All ideas of conservation, like the notion of substance, have a solid foundation in the economy of thought. A mere unrelated change, without fixed point of support, or reference, is not comprehensible, not mentally reconstructible (p. 504).

It was on this basis that he accounted for the fact that, in ordinary experience, what we are interested in are *objects,* viewed as permanent, and this relative permanency of clusters of elements becomes more stable through our useful habit of designating them by single names, and grouping them together in single thoughts.[66] According to Mach, such supposedly permanent entities, whether they be "bodies" or "ego," are "only makeshifts, designed for provisional orientation and for definite practical ends."[67] This organization of elements into our conception of permanent things naturally involves viewing the elements in terms of spatial relationships; in order to account for the particular spatial organization they display, Mach again appealed to biological functions, holding that our perceptual space is organized to fulfil the adaptive needs of the organism.[68]

If one asks how the individual human being has time to acquire these deepseated and lasting modes of organizing experience in the short span of his earliest years, Mach answers in the same vein as did Spencer: all of the basic assumptions which appear as "instinctive" to us, represent the funded experience of the race, "bequeathed to us as an heirloom by our forefathers." In this connection Mach said:

Such primitive acts of knowledge constitute to-day the solidest foundation of scientific thought. Our instinctive knowledge, as we shall briefly call it, by virtue of the conviction that we have consciously and intentionally contributed nothing to its formation, confronts us with an authority and logical power which consciously acquired knowledge even from familiar sources and of easily tested fallibility can never possess. All so-called axioms are such instinctive knowledge.[69]

Nevertheless, in spite of the compelling character of such instinctive knowledge, and in spite of its undoubted usefulness for the ordinary adaptive purposes of life, Mach did not place total reliance upon it. In fact, from the point of view of the sciences, it was a hindrance and not a help. In the *Analysis of Sensations* and in *Erkenntnis und Irrtum*, as well as elsewhere, he argued against accepting the hidden metaphysical axioms of common-sense when one is engaged in constructing an adequate and unified system of scientific knowledge. For example, he felt it imperative for scientific purposes to reject our common-sense contrasts between self and object, or between particular sensations and permanent things, both of which he recognized to be of definite utility within everyday experience; however, from the point of view of advanced scientific investigations, both were prejudices and definitely disadvantageous.[70] What was at stake in scientific investigation was not the direct adaptation of the human organism to the environing world, but the successful unification of experience within a single economic system which permits us to codify, recall, and anticipate experience. Only by possessing such a system can we overcome the limitations of human memory, and acquire a stock of knowledge adequate for all of our purposes. The methods developed by the sciences, in particular their ability to summarize regularities in experience by means of mathematically formulated laws, provided the solution to this problem. It was in this context that Mach remarked that science itself could be regarded as a problem concerning *minima*: how one can achieve the most complete summarization of facts with the least possible expenditure of thought.[71] This economical function of science was what led to its biological usefulness. Thus, in spite of the fact that it contravened the powerful, instinctive metaphysics of common-sense, science performed important adaptive functions, permitting us to recall and anticipate experience in far more satisfactory ways than our everyday modes of thought permit us to do. Thus, Mach interpreted science in an ultimately biological way:

The biological task of science is to provide the fully developed human individual with as perfect a means of orientating himself as possible. No other scientific ideal can be realized, and any other must be meaningless.[72]

It is at this point that we note how sharply Mach's thought diverged from the realistic assumptions of Helmholtz and Spencer, for while each of them also regarded human thought as performing an adaptive function, neither identified the goal of science with the performance of that function. Rather, each regarded science as capable of deciphering relationships in nature, and of finding causal laws to explain the existence of these connections among phenomena. For Mach, however, the connections among phenomena which are described by the sciences are consequences of the theories through which we organize these phenomena, rather than reflecting independently existing facts. Thus, for example, he said:

> A theory, indeed, always puts in the place of a fact something *different*, something more simple, which is qualified to represent it in some *certain* aspects, but for the very reason that it is different does *not* represent it in other aspects. . . .
>
> Only in rare cases will the resemblance between a fact and its theoretical conception extend *further* than we ourselves postulate. . . . As a general rule we have every reason to distinguish sharply between our theoretical conceptions of phenomena and that which we observe. The former must be regarded merely as auxiliary instruments that have been created for a *definite* purpose and which possess permanent value only with respect to that purpose.[73]

And in even more extreme form, and in contrast to the beliefs of DuBois-Reymond, Helmholtz, and Spencer regarding the uniformity of nature, Mach explicitly said:

> Suppose we were to attribute to nature the property of producing like effects in like circumstances; just these like circumstances we should not know how to find. Nature exists once only. Our schematic mental imitation alone produces like events. Only in the mind, therefore, does the mutual dependence of certain features exist.[74]

In this respect, Mach's views departed radically from earlier forms of positivism and merged with the ever-growing stream of philosophers who abandoned the view that through the methods of the sciences we can uncover relationships in nature which exist whether we know them or not, and which are what they are, however we may choose to describe them.[75] From Mach's point of view, the abandonment of this conception of the sciences was to be welcomed rather than deplored, since it abolished with a single stroke the assumption that human knowledge was necessarily limited in the ways in which DuBois-Reymond, Helmholtz, and Spencer had assumed it to be. Issues as to how consciousness is related to the body, or what accounts for the ways in which matter behaves, were to be regarded as fictitious problems, and they did not therefore place arbitrary limits on how far scientifically organized knowledge could proceed.[76] Thus, from Mach's point of view, the range of science was indefinitely extended: it could organize the elements of experience in whatever ways proved to be most fruitful in storing up and codifying that experience for the purpose of anticipating and adapting to future events. While this open-endedness has obvious attractions, one may legitimately wonder whether Mach's theory of the economy of thought does in fact do justice to either the recalcitrance of the ways in which experience presents itself to us, or to the implications which are to be drawn from a biologically oriented theory of the human mind. It is with these questions, among others, that our concluding chapter will be concerned.

15

In the two preceding chapters we were first concerned with those who rebelled against the claim that all of man's knowledge is limited to what can be represented in sense-experience, and we then examined the views of others who insisted that there is no escape from this fact, and none need be sought. As we have seen, those who sought to escape these limitations appealed to forms of knowing which are not dependent upon the senses and the analytic understanding; the others used the limitations of sense-experience in order to discredit speculation concerning any questions more ultimate than those with which the empirical sciences can deal. We turn now to a third tendency in nineteenth-century thought which was more radical, though less pervasive, than either of these: it consisted in a voluntaristic rebellion against reason.[1] Among those who most clearly embody such a rebellion, Schopenhauer, Kierkegaard, and Nietzsche have been of exceptional influence on subsequent thought, and it is only with them that we shall here be concerned.

The term "voluntarism" is generally used in characterizing theories which hold that *the will* is more fundamental than the intellect in some particular domain of experience; however, "voluntarism" may be interpreted in a more radical way, as holding that the will is not only more fundamental or important than the intellect, but that the latter is always under its dominion and control. It is in this stronger sense that I shall be using the term.

In order to understand what such a position entails, we must note that when voluntaristic theories speak of "the will" they are not referring collectively to specific cases of choosing, of desiring, of seeking or avoiding, and the like. Rather, they consider "the will"—whether it is taken in the sense of the will of an individual, or in some larger metaphysical sense—as the unitary source of all such activities, which underlies them and manifests itself in and through them. As Schopenhauer said in this connection, "Every individual act of will is a specimen of the Will, in which the entire Will reveals itself."[2] Thus, the will is not conceived by the voluntarist as a "faculty," or set of capabilities, but as a single power or force expressing itself in multiform ways. The ways in which such a power is capable of channeling and controlling thought have been variously interpreted by different voluntarists, as we shall see in examining the views of Schopenhauer, Kierkegaard, and Nietzsche. Were we to examine the views of others who also belong within the tradition of voluntarism, we would become acquainted with still other ways in which it has been claimed that the will exercises control over thought. What makes it particularly significant to discuss Schopenhauer, Kierke-gaard, and Nietzsche together is not that each presents a different and important view of the nature and the power of the will; rather, it is the fact that each was led by his form of voluntarism to disparage the authority of reason within its own traditional province, rejecting the canons of rationality as adequate tests of truth. Because of this common feature in their otherwise disparate doctrines—a feature not to be found, for example, in the thought of Sigmund Freud—whatever in-fluence each has had on recent thought has tended to reinforce the influence of the others, in spite of the fact that their moral and metaphysical views were fundamentally opposed. Thus, together, they and those whom they have influenced have had an overwhelmingly important influence on mid-twentieth century thought.

1. SCHOPENHAUER: THE WILL AND THE INTELLECT

The uniqueness of Schopenhauer's system does not derive from any excep-tionally novel insights, but from the manner in which he was able to weave ex-tremely diverse strands of thought into a single encompassing system. As is universally recognized, one of these was the negative side of Kant's critical philosophy: the claim that our knowledge is necessarily limited by the categories inherent in the mind's activity. It was this negative side which, as we have seen, other successors of Kant, such as Jacobi, Fichte, and Hegel, had accepted in so far as the Understanding was concerned, but which they sought to overcome by appealing to another source of knowledge. In this respect, Schopenhauer clearly resembled them, even though it was not to "Reason" that he appealed. Attention has frequently been directed to this similarity between his view and theirs. How-ever, there is another, less frequently noted similarity among these post-Kantian philosophers. Kant's doctrine of the Understanding not only stressed the limita-tions of human knowledge, but it had a positive side which was of at least equal importance, and this positive side was not only rejected by Jacobi, Fichte, and Hegel, but by Schopenhauer as well.

By the positive side of Kant's doctrine of the Understanding, I refer to the fact that he regarded himself as having validated the universality and necessity of the basic structure of empirical knowledge. For Kant this meant that objectivity is to be ascribed to the perceptual world; furthermore, it meant that mathematical modes of thought and the causal forms of explanation characteristic of science had been proved to apply, without exception, to all aspects of human experience. Yet, as we have seen, post-Kantian idealism had challenged both our natural reliance on sense experience and the validity of the conceptualizations of the mathematical and physical sciences. In this respect, Schopenhauer also shared the views of those who had been attempting to overcome Kantianism. Thus, in spite of his claim to a close affinity with Kant, he was in agreement with those who rejected Kant's belief that all which is worthy of the title of *knowledge* is to be attained through the Understanding. Unlike Kant, but like those for whom he always expressed contempt, Schopenhauer held that any philosophy which sought to justify the forms of experience which depend upon the Understanding would be substituting illusion for truth.

These similarities do not, of course, suggest that Schopenhauer agreed with Jacobi, Fichte, or Hegel regarding the ways in which the confines of the Understanding could be overcome. Nor should they lead to the assumption that his views regarding the empirical natural sciences would be the same as theirs. In each previous case, it will be recalled, an attack on the Understanding also involved some form of attack on the adequacy of the sciences; however, as we shall see, Schopenhauer's stance with respect to the sciences was fundamentally different. This fact has often been overlooked because he insisted that space, time, and causation are only applicable within the world as representation; and the world as representation was regarded by him as being—from a metaphysical point of view—a world of illusion. Consequently, it is easy to assume that Schopenhauer would have been forced to adopt as negative an attitude toward the empirical sciences as one finds in Jacobi or Fichte, and that his judgment of the merit of purely empirical research would have been even more severe than that of Hegel. For the same reason, one might also expect Schopenhauer to have held that the empirical sciences, by their very nature, must be metaphysically irrelevant. This, in fact, has been a widely held interpretation.[3] However, such an interpretation makes it difficult to understand the way in which Schopenhauer used physiologically based considerations in originally propounding his position, or how he could later have made appeal to the work of empirical scientists as a means of supporting his views.

Of course, it would be possible to charge that he was, in this respect, wholly inconsistent, merely snatching at whatever data the sciences might happen to bring within reach. Such will not be my interpretation. Summarily put, I shall hold that since Schopenhauer regarded all phenomenal objects as expressions of one underlying reality, which is the Will, it was legitimate that he should have regarded some empirical investigations as being, in principle, metaphysically relevant. To be sure, the sciences could not tell him that there *was* any form of ultimate reality behind appearances; nor could the sciences have established that, if there were, this reality was Will. To establish these points, he appealed to his own immediate consciousness of his body as will. This I do not deny. Yet, having established the metaphysical basis of his system in this manner, he was able to regard some empirical investigations as providing metaphysically relevant information, although other investigations did not. He had no interest in any phenomena in which a direct manifestation of will was not discernible, even though he held that they, too, in some concealed manner, must be expressions of Will.

However, in all cases in which it appeared to scientists that observed phenomena could only be adequately interpreted as expressions of a hidden force which he could regard as Will, Schopenhauer was provided with data which could find a place within his system. In other words, on the assumption that some aspects of the phenomenal world manifest Will more clearly and explicitly than do others, it is easy to understand why Schopenhauer should have been interested in scientific investigations of them. Furthermore, when one bears in mind that it is through the experience of one's own body that he held we discover the nature of Will, it is not surprising that the sciences which attempted to deal with the active powers in living things should have occupied a very special position in his system. Nor was this privileged position assigned to them only in works such as his essay *On the Will in Nature*, and in the addenda to *The World as Will and Representation*; as I shall first attempt to show, his basic epistemological theory was a highly modified form of Kantianism, resting to a very great extent on physiological foundations.

Because Schopenhauer claimed to be a follower of Kant, it is easy to overlook how un-Kantian his epistemological starting point actually was. In the very first sentence of *The World as Will and Representation* Schopenhauer espoused a subjectivism which Kant always rejected: "The world is my representation"; or, as an earlier translation put it, "The world is my idea."[4] This un-Kantian form of subjective idealism was then made more explicit through invoking the authority of Berkeley and of Vedanta philosophy. Nevertheless, Schopenhauer was not in fact a Berkeleian any more than he was a Kantian, for he immediately went on to assert that *what* we are conscious of is always a state of our own bodily organs: we do not know a sun and an earth, "but only an eye that sees a sun, a hand that feels an earth."

At first glance, this doctrine appears to be hopelessly confused, for Schopenhauer would of course hold that all of our bodily organs themselves belong to the world of *Vorstellungen*, or representations, and he explicitly states this belief within the next two pages.[5] However, it would be unfair to suppose that he was unaware of what looked like so flat a contradiction, or that he did not believe there was an adequate way of overcoming it. His answer depended on maintaining that we are not merely aware of our bodies through experiencing them as we experience other objects, through sense-perception; we are also directly aware of them in our consciousness of them as Will. It was, of course, by this means that Schopenhauer sought to escape the limits of knowledge prescribed by the Kantian doctrine of the Understanding; for him, as for Jacobi, Fichte, and Maine de Biran, there was "a way from within" that was more direct and revelatory than sense-perception could be. This basic and frequently repeated aspect of Schopenhauer's system receives one of its clearest expressions in an essay entitled "On the Possibility of Knowing the Thing-in-Itself," which was added to *The World as Will and Representation* in its second edition:

> If our perception, and thus the whole empirical apprehension of the things that
> present themselves to us, is already determined essentially and principally by our cognitive
> faculty and by its forms and functions, then it must be that things exhibit themselves

in a manner quite different from their inner nature, and that they therefore appear as through a mask. This mask enables us always merely to assume, never to know, what is hidden beneath it. . . .

In consequence of all this, on the path of *objective knowledge*, thus starting from the *representation*, we shall never get beyond the representation, i.e., the phenomenon. . . . So far I agree with Kant. But now, as the counterpoise to this truth, I have stressed that other truth that we are not merely the *knowing subject*, but that *we ourselves* are also among those realities or entities we require to know, that *we ourselves are the thing-in-itself*. Consequently, a way *from within* stands open to us to that real inner nature of things to which we cannot penetrate *from without*.[6]

In contrast to the views of Jacobi, Fichte, and Maine de Biran, Schopenhauer identified this immediate inner consciousness of ourselves as thing-in-itself with our awareness of Will *within our own bodily organs*. In order to interpret this aspect of Schopenhauer's doctrine correctly, it is necessary to consider in some detail the physiological basis on which it rested.

That Schopenhauer's thought had a physiological orientation should not be surprising when we recall that he enrolled as a medical student in Göttingen, and that both there and in Berlin he spent a considerable proportion of his time in the study of the sciences.[7] Furthermore, although his first work, his doctoral dissertation, remained in much closer conjunction with Kant's thought than did any of his later works, in it Schopenhauer assumed—contrary to Kantian doctrine —that the only direct or immediate object which we are capable of experiencing is our own body.[8] However, this doctrine did not emerge into full prominence until his consideration and revision of Goethe's theory of colors. The importance of Schopenhauer's formulation of his own physiological theory of colors, as constituting a turning point in his thought, is often overlooked because his doctoral dissertation on *The Fourfold Root of the Principle of Sufficient Reason* is usually only examined in the radically rewritten and expanded form in which Schopenhauer republished it thirty-four years later: as a consequence, it is generally assumed that the whole cast of his thought was determined as early as his dissertation.[9] However, in his revision of Goethe's theory, one for the first time finds the development of a physiological type of theory which subsequently played a major part in his philosophical views. As he himself pointed out, his revision of Goethe's theory consisted primarily in having transformed it from a physically oriented theory into one which was strictly physiological.[10]

In the introduction to *On Sight and Colors*, in which he developed his theory, Schopenhauer mentioned Descartes, Locke, and Sextus Empiricus as precursors of the view that "the colors with which objects appear to be clothed" are only in the eye of the beholder.[11] As he had suggested in his doctoral dissertation, it is only because the mind orders experience under the apriori form of causality, that we attribute these colors to objects existing externally in space. What was novel in the way in which Schopenhauer developed this doctrine was his interpretation of sensation itself. Unlike Descartes and Locke, he did not treat the sensing organ as a receptor which merely served to transmit stimuli to the mind: sensation depended, according to Schopenhauer, on *activity* within the sense-organ. It was an indubitable truth of physiology, he insisted, that sensibility is never pure passivity; that it is always a *reaction* to a stimulus.[12] To be sure, we are not conscious of the reaction of our organs as distinct from the stimuli which affect them, but Schopenhauer held that the presence of consciousness is not a reliable clue to reactions which are present within the organism. This conviction, too, had an empirical basis in the physiology of Schopenhauer's time. In his early notebooks, we find that he was aware of the distinction being drawn between "sensibility" and "irritability"; and in the second edition of *The World as Will and Representation*, Schopenhauer laid considerable stress on this distinction, and frequently cited Albrecht von Haller with whom the distinction is to be connected.[13] One can readily see why this distinction was regarded as important by him. "Irritability" signified that an organ which does not possess the capacity for *sensation* may nonetheless possess the capacity to react to stimuli. Such an organ can absorb materials which are beneficial to the organism, and reject those which are harmful; furthermore, it does so without the organism's being conscious of these inner responses. Such activities, which proceed without the intervention of consciousness, undoubtedly helped to buttress Schopenhauer's conviction that even sensibility itself is to be regarded as a form of organic reaction, and not as a form of mere receptivity.

At this point, Schopenhauer's emphasis was clearly different from Kant's, since for Kant sensibility was the capacity for receptivity. The differences become even more striking when one notes the other ways in which Schopenhauer altered Kant's analysis of perceiving. Like Kant, he believed that the materials of sensibility are organized under the forms of space and time, and in accordance with the category of causality; however, Schopenhauer treated space and time as categories rather than as forms of intuition, and he reduced Kant's table of categories from twelve to one: causality. By virtue of these changes, Schopenhauer was able to hold that it is the causal category which leads us to experience reactions which take place within our sensory organs as existing in objects external to us: the causal category is, so to speak, the mechanism through which we project what goes on in eye, or hand, into a sun, an earth. It is important to note that for Schopenhauer, unlike Kant, this is not to be taken as involving an act of judgment, for judgments involve concepts, and Schopenhauer wished to effect a complete divorce between *perceiving* and *conceiving*.[14] One can note this difference in the fact that Schopenhauer held that these apriori categories are exhibited in the behavior of the higher animals, as well as by human beings, and of course neither he nor Kant held that animals had the capacity to employ concepts.[15] Schopenhauer had in fact self-consciously set himself to change the Kantian theory of categories in precisely this way, for by banishing conceptualization from acts of perception he was able to divorce all that pertained to man's intellect from what was immediately present in sense-experience.

On the other hand, Schopenhauer seems not to have been equally aware of how radically he was altering Kantian doctrine in another respect: he interpreted the categories of space, time, and causality as being the results of the way in which *the brain* functioned. To interpret the categories physiologically, as reflections of a particular form of complex cerebral system, would have been anathema to

Kant; yet this was Schopenhauer's position. A striking statement of it—and one which shows how little he appreciated Kant's position—is the following:

The world as representation, as it exists extended in space and time and continues to move regularly according to the strict rule of causality, is primarily only a physiological phenomenon, a function of the brain that brings this about on the occasion of certain external stimuli, it is true, but yet in accordance with its own laws. Accordingly, it is already a matter of course that what goes on in this function itself, and consequently through it and for it, cannot possibly be regarded as the quality or nature of things-in-themselves.... Just as Locke claimed for the organs of sense all that comes into perception or apprehension by means of sensation, in order to deny it to things-in-themselves, so Kant, with the same purpose and pursuing the same path, showed everything that makes real *perception* possible, namely space, time, and causality, to be brain-function. He refrained, however, from using this physiological expression, to which our present method of [objective] consideration necessarily leads us.[16]

Thus, what we have as an analysis of perception in Schopenhauer is, as I have said, a definitely physiological theory. Our sense organs receive stimuli (from whence Schopenhauer never says), and the organ *reacts* to them. However, they are not experienced as the reactions of the organ itself: through the mechanisms of the brain, these reactions are projected and appear as external to us, located in a space and at a time which also are functions of the physiological nature of the human brain. It is the brain, then, which creates the phenomenal world: the world of representations is a cerebral product. Over and over, Schopenhauer speaks in these most un-Kantian terms.[17]

Should it be objected that Schopenhauer has no right to speak realistically of the brain, since it—like all other bodily organs—must be considered part of the phenomenal world, he would answer that *no organ is phenomenal only*. Any bodily organ is phenomenal in so far as it is regarded as existing as one among other objects which can be seen, touched, measured, weighed, etc.; but every bodily organ also has its own inner activity, and this activity is an expression of a will which animates the organism as a whole. If this general position is adopted, it of course follows that, even though the brain can be viewed as one among many phenomenal objects, it also possesses some form of inner activity which bears a relation to the will of the organism as a whole. This, of course, entails that we should not interpret the phenomenal world as merely representing the results of cerebral activity, but as being a product which, to some degree, expresses the underlying force of will which animates us. This, as we shall see, is actually Schopenhauer's view.

It may appear pure fantasy to hold that the entire phenomenal world is a product of some force within us, identified as Will; yet if this represents a fantasy, it was not unique in Schopenhauer, as Fichte's theory of knowledge serves to suggest. However, in the case of Schopenhauer we may best explicate what he held by again appealing to his views regarding the nature of organisms. In this case the relevant doctrine—which will itself doubtless first appear as mere fantasy —was Schopenhauer's familiar view that every physiological organ *"objectifies"* some form of inner will, and the body as a whole is an objectification of will.

Thus, in a famous passage, he said: "The whole body must be nothing but my will become visible" and, in addition, "The parts of the body must correspond completely to the chief demands and desires by which the will manifests itself; they must be the visible expression of these desires. Teeth, gullet, and intestinal canal are objectified hunger; the genitals are objectified sexual desire . . ."[18] Remarks such as these are not merely incidental to Schopenhauer's doctrine, for on this thesis—when it is generalized—there rests his whole theory of grades of objectification in nature, and, therefore, his doctrine of knowledge through the aesthetic contemplation of the Platonic Ideas. It is therefore of some importance to the interpretation of Schopenhauer's manner of philosophizing to understand whether there was anything which might have seemed to him to provide an adequate justification of this view.

For those acquainted with Lamarck's theory of the transformation of species, Schopenhauer's position is bound to have a familiar ring. It was the essence of Lamarckian theory that the adaptation of different species to their environments was not a consequence of providential design, but came about through natural causes; he also held that these causes were to be found in *the needs* of different types of organism in relation to their environments. Because of the internal needs of an organism, new rudimentary organs would begin to develop, and as these structures were used in successive generations they expanded and became part of the bodily organization of that type of animal; whereas organs which were not needed were not used, and degenerated and gradually disappeared. Thus, in terms of Lamarckian theory, the structures of a species were not merely variable but were essentially plastic, being formed over successive generations in response to forces within individual organisms, as these organisms actively sought sustenance and satisfaction of the other necessities of life.

In his essay *On the Will in Nature*, Schopenhauer discussed Lamarck's doctrine, comparing and contrasting his own views with it.[19] At one very important point he rejected Lamarck's view, but this need not obscure for us the other points at which they were in close agreement. Like Lamarck, he pointed out the striking facts of "the adaptation of each animal for its mode of life and outward means of subsistence," and he noted that it is because of facts of this nature that the teleological proof of God's existence was invoked.[20] Like Lamarck, he of course rejected any providential explanation of adaptations; it is also to be noted that he specifically entertained and rejected what was in essence the later Darwinian way of explaining adaptations: that particular structures arise, as if by chance, prior to the adoption of the way of life for which they are needed. Like Lamarck, Schopenhauer insisted that the form of organization of an animal reflects its pre-existing needs. In this connection, he remarked that "in many animals, during the time they are growing, the effort of will to which a limb is destined to minister, manifests itself before the existence of the limb itself, its employment thus anticipating its existence"[21]—an assumption that is present throughout Lamarck's discussions of the origin of new organs. Thus, both Lamarck and Schopenhauer held that the actual structures which any type of animal possesses are really to be explained as the outward manifestations of inner needs. This congruence between his own view and the view of the biologist to whom, in this discussion, he referred as "the immortal Lamarck," would surely permit Schopenhauer to claim that his doctrine of an objectification of will in animal organs was wholly consistent with biological theory. At this point we may also note that a tendency to explain all external manifestations in terms of inner forces was a trait characteristic of the *Naturphilosophie* of the whole idealistic period.[22]

The special feature of Lamarck's theory which Schopenhauer attacked was his view that the origin of new organs was a slow process, proceeding by minute degrees over successive generations. Schopenhauer claimed that were this the case, any species would have died out before it had produced the organs which were needed for its survival. In opposition to Lamarck's gradualism, Schopenhauer apparently held that the underlying Will-in-nature expressed itself in variegated ways, immediately fitting each type of organism with those organs which fulfill its needs. And, speaking metaphysically, Schopenhauer argued against gradualism in another way: the Will which underlies the existence of all forms of organization cannot be considered as operating successively, for it is not subject to the category of time.[23] Speaking in this way, it is irrelevant whether the various forms of objectification of the Will succeed one another temporally or not: each is an immediate outward expression of the one underlying Will, and is not therefore adequately explained through tracing a sequence of developmental stages, as Lamarck and other evolutionists had sought to do.[24] Thus, Schopenhauer was critical of Lamarck, yet without abandoning what was most essential in the way in which Lamarck interpreted the facts of comparative anatomy: structures arose out of inner forces which were conceived as impulse and need.

At this point one can begin to see a definite physiological basis for what is the crucial question in our concern with Schopenhauer: the extent to which, and the ways in which, he regarded thought as subservient to will. The whole of the world of perception, we may recall, depends upon our bodies, on sensing organs reacting to stimuli, and on brain-functions which impose an order on what is given in sense. However, as we have just seen, Schopenhauer also holds that all organs of the body are objectifications of will, answering to need. This must then be true of sensing organs, and also of the human brain to which the sensing organs are, as it were, appendages. Therefore, the whole phenomenal world must, in some way, be a reflection of the organism's needs, since it is a product of the activity of these organs. It is with this general relationship between the will and the phenomenal world that we shall first be concerned. We shall then be in a better position to interpret those features of Schopenhauer's views regarding thought and will which are more usually emphasized in accounts of his system.

As we have noted, Schopenhauer distinguished human beings from animals in terms of man's ability to form concepts. Both humans and animals experience a world of representations, even though these worlds should not be assumed to be identical, since there are differences between the sensory organs of various types of animals and of men. Among the higher animals, as well as for men, the world of representations is ordered according to spatial, temporal, and causal categories. On the basis of what is thus presented, men are able to form concepts, that is, "representations of representations"; because of this ability they, unlike animals, are lifted above particularity and immediacy in their experience of the phenomenal world.[25] On the other hand, these concepts always remain pale simulacra of the percepts from which they derive: perception is the source of all concepts which we form, and it is only in relation to perception that concepts retain their significance. Schopenhauer constantly reiterates this point; for example, in introducing his discussion of conceptual thinking, he says:

> As from the direct light of the sun to the borrowed reflected light of the moon, so do we pass from the immediate representation of perception, which stands by itself and is its own warrant, to reflection, to the abstract, discursive concepts of reason (*Vernunft*), which have their whole content only from that knowledge of perception, and in relation to it.[26]

Even though Schopenhauer stressed the derivative status of concepts, he attributed important functions to them. He held that our ability to lift specific representations out of the stream of immediate experience, forming concepts of them, underlay memory and language. Furthermore, once these abilities were present, it was possible and indeed necessary for men to seek explanations of what is given in representations.[27]

All of this Schopenhauer attributed to the manner in which the human brain functions. Just as it is the brain and its sensory organs which give rise to the world of representations, so the brain, through its own internal activity, forms representations of these representations, connecting them with one another in explanatory systems according to one or another of the fourfold forms of the principle of sufficient reason. As Schopenhauer remarked in a slightly different connection, the brain itself is the quarry for the materials on the basis of which Reason seeks to construct explanations of the world.[28] This interpretation of the relation of the brain to man's intellectual activities is apparent throughout his work, for Schopenhauer repeatedly spoke of the human brain as the objectification of the intellect, and of the intellect as being simply the way in which this organ functions.[29] However, since he held that every organ is a manifestation of will, and stands in the service of will, it was necessary for Schopenhauer to decipher the way in which the existence of a world of representations and our drive to offer explanations of that world could be of service to the will in man. Contrary to what is often said when exclusive emphasis is placed on his distinction between the phenomenal character of our representations and the world as Will, Schopenhauer did attribute a degree of life-serving significance to the world of representations, and even to our attempts to grasp that world through the abstractions of thought.[30]

To understand Schopenhauer's position regarding this point, it is necessary to note that he granted a degree of autonomy to the operations of the intellect: the brain, unlike the sexual organs, did not function under the direct and immediate needs of the organism as a whole. Thus we find Schopenhauer frequently contrasting the genitalia and the brain, as constituting the two poles of human activities,[31] the one being the most immediate manifestation of the will in the organism,[32] the other the most removed from the demands of the will-to-live. Thus, in a passage in which he was specifically discussing the brain, Schopenhauer said:

> The more complicated its organization became through higher development, the more manifest and specially determined became its needs. Therefore, a wider range of vision, a more accurate comprehension, a more correct distinction of things in the external world in all their circumstances and relations were here required. Accordingly we see the powers of representation and their organs, brain, nerves, and organs of sense, appear more and more perfect, the higher we ascend in the order of animals; and in proportion as the cerebral system develops, does the external world appear in consciousness ever more distinct, many-sided and complete. The comprehension of the world now demands more and more attention, and ultimately to such an extent that at times its relation to the will must be momentarily lost sight of, so that it may occur the more purely and correctly. This quite definitely appears first in the case of man; only with him does a *pure separation of knowing from willing* occur.[33]

To be sure, here as elsewhere, Schopenhauer immediately went on to state that *ultimately* the functioning of the brain is subservient to the will: that "the last step in extending and perfecting the brain, and thus increasing the powers of knowledge, is taken by nature, like all the rest, merely in consequence of the increased *needs*, and hence in the service of the will."[34] However, in man, the brain does have a degree of autonomy from the will in its manner of functioning, and Schopenhauer even speaks of its spontaneity, attributing the processes of reasoning to this factor.[35] It would therefore be a mistake to regard Schopenhauer as having assumed that all intellectual processes are under the direct and immediate dominance of the needs of the organism.

In his explanations of how the intellect exercises life-serving functions, Schopenhauer does not speak in directly pragmatic terms: once again he stresses autonomous activities and not merely those instances in which thinking is under the immediate control of forces which represent the will.[36] This can be seen in his account of why it is necessary that man should be conscious, rather than only possessing blind impulse as do other forms of life. The complexity of the human body is such, Schopenhauer claims, that it has a variety of needs, and if these are to be satisfied, they must be focused, as it were, in one point, rising from mere sentience into consciousness.[37] This is all the more necessary in man because, in contrast to animals, his actions are not successfully controlled by instinct, and intellect is needed for the sake of attaining ends which are essential for self-maintenance and for propagation.[38] This theme is frequently reiterated by Schopenhauer, even though he also points out that, in some cases, taking thought is a hinderance to skillful action.[39] For example, even when he contrasts the abstractness of reason with perception, and argues that all of the basic content of reason must have a perceptual source, he nonetheless insists on the usefulness of abstract knowledge for action:

> All safe preservation, all communicability, all sure and far-reaching application of knowledge to the practical, depend on its having become a rational knowledge, an

abstract knowledge... Every continuous coordinated and planned activity must start
from fundamental principles, i.e., from an abstract knowledge, and must be guided
in accordance therewith.[40]

Nor is it only with respect to *action* that the abstractness of reason is useful:
science, too, depends upon reason, and Schopenhauer is perfectly explicit in
holding it to be of advantage to man.[41] To be sure, in the discussion which follows
one such passage, the advantage may appear to be somewhat doubtful, for he
offers a highly restrictive interpretation of the method of science, according to
which it differs from other forms of reasoning and always proceeds from the universal to the particular.[42] However, if one puts aside that special interpretation of
science and turns to his more general discussion of abstract knowledge (which
includes science, but has greater scope), the advantages which abstraction confers
on our thinking are clear. Even though Schopenhauer insists that original discovery must rest upon immediate insight into the concrete and particular, thus
relying on the presentations of sense, the abstractions of reason also receive their
due. For example, he says:

There is only one thing, the concept, which is not subject either to that instantaneous
vanishing of the impression, or to the gradual disappearance of its image, and is
consequently free from the power of time.[43]

Shortly thereafter, he says:

We can judge the inestimable value of *concepts*, and consequently of the faculty of
reason, if we glance at the endless multitude and variety of things and conditions
coexisting and succeeding one another, and then reflect that language and writing (the
signs of concepts) are nevertheless able to afford us accurate information about everything
and every relation, whenever and wherever it may have been, in that comparatively
few concepts concern and represent an infinite number of things and conditions. In
our reflection, *abstraction* is a throwing off of useless luggage for the purpose of
handling more easily the knowledge to be compared and manoeuvred in all directions.
Thus, much that is inessential, and therefore merely confusing, in real things is
omitted, and we operate with few but essential determinations conceived in the
abstract.[44]

Of course, in interpreting such passages, it is important to remember that
abstractions are, so to speak, twice removed from reality. Not only are they
derived from, and remain dependent upon perception, but perception itself deals
only with the phenomenal world: the Will which underlies appearance cannot
be known by means of the Understanding nor can it be known by Reason. Yet
this does not affect the point with which I am here concerned: that Schopenhauer
is not to be interpreted as holding that the intellect is always directly subject to
the will. "Reason," he says, "appears in contrast to man's other faculties"; we
distinguish between the rational and the irrational, and this means that what we
designate as reason has a different mode of operation than anything which is to
be ascribed to impulse and will.[45]

One reason why Schopenhauer's doctrine of the autonomy of abstract thinking is often overlooked is that he says that *in the last analysis* the intellect, like every other feature of the world, is a manifestation of will, and therefore subject to its dominance. This domination does not entail an immediate and direct control of thought by will. The relationship can be clarified if we again return to Schopenhauer's biologically oriented doctrine of the objectifications of the Will in nature, with which we were previously concerned. The *brain*, as we noted, is to be regarded as the objectification of the *intellect*; on the other hand, the *organism as a whole* is the objectification of will.[46] Thus, the brain may function in ways which are different from the ways in which other organs, objectifying other needs, will function, and we may attribute a degree of autonomy to it. However, the brain's functioning obviously depends on the functioning of the organism as a whole, and in that sense the intellect, *in the end*, is utterly dependent upon the will which manifests itself as the organism's will-to-live.

This relationship can also be traced in the way in which Schopenhauer describes how, for a time, the intellect can control human behavior, taming the will, but cannot ultimately suppress it and falls under its domination:

The intellect strikes up the tune, and the will must dance to it; in fact, the intellect causes it to play the part of a child whom its nurse at her pleasure puts into the most different moods by chatter and tales alternating between pleasant and melancholy things. This is due to the fact that the will in itself is without knowledge, but the understanding associated with it is without will. Therefore the will behaves like a body that is moved, the understanding like the causes that set it in motion, for it is the medium of motives. Yet with all this, the primacy of the will becomes clear again when this will, that becomes, as we have shown, the sport of the intellect as soon as it allows the intellect to control it, once makes its supremacy felt in the last resort. This it does by prohibiting the intellect from having certain representations, by absolutely preventing certain trains of thought from arising . . .[47]

While one may wish to stress the fact that in such passages Schopenhauer speaks of how the will sometimes interferes with intellectual processes, one should also bear in mind that what is involved—as Schopenhauer said in introducing this particular passage—is an *interplay* of two fundamentally different types of force within us; he is not accounting for experience in terms of only one force of which all else is simply an epiphenomenal reflection.

To be sure, Schopenhauer's own words sometimes tend to conceal the fact of such an interplay, as when he speaks of the intellect as the servant of the will, and when, in this context, he holds that it is subconscious will which controls the association of ideas.[48] Furthermore, it becomes easy to assimilate his psychological theories to more recent forms of voluntarism when one finds him stressing unconscious motivations, and returning again and again to examples of how they sometimes control thought.[49] In these as in other respects, his relationships to Nietzsche and to Freud are too obvious to be overlooked. Nevertheless, it would be a distortion of Schopenhauer's views regarding the scope and limits of the intellect if all aspects of thinking were to be interpreted as expressions of will. Philosophy itself would in that case lose the privileged position which Schopenhauer, unlike Nietzsche, accorded it. Although Schopenhauer held that truth is not directly accessible to the understanding or to reason, but depends upon our own immediate experience of will, the elaboration of this truth can only be undertaken by reason; furthermore, its truth consists in its conformity with what we discover in the world, not in its satisfaction of demands of the will.[50]

In fact, few philosophers—even including Spinoza—have placed greater emphasis on the liberation that comprehensive understanding brings.[51] Knowledge is not only capable of controlling the ways in which the individual's will finds expression under varying circumstances,[52] it is also capable of temporarily freeing us from the will through the contemplation of the Platonic ideas which are objectified in the hierarchy of nature and made manifest in art. More importantly, a true grasp of the suffering which arises through the restless, unceasing striving of the Will is a form of knowledge that leads to the final annihilation of the Will itself.

If, then, we are to understand in what sense Schopenhauer's philosophy represented a rebellion against Reason—as indeed it did—we cannot say that it was because he interpreted all reasoning as being only a manifestation of will: *that* form of voluntarism was, in general, foreign to his thought. Instead, his voluntarism was metaphysical; he rebelled against the fundamental principle of Rationalism, that reality has an inherent logical structure such that the laws of thought are also the laws of things. On the contrary, reality itself is arational: its nature can only be appreciated through what stands at the opposite pole from that which, in our own experience, we know as intellect—it is Will. For this reason Schopenhauer remarks that among all philosophers it is Anaxagoras who represents his direct opposite, "for he arbitrarily assumed a *Nous*, an intelligence, a creator of representations, as the first and original thing."[53] Schopenhauer, on the contrary, regarded reason as present only in man, a mere epiphenomenon in reality as a whole. While, as we have seen, he regarded the human intellect as being of use to men, nonetheless, as he points out in this same passage, what men can accomplish by using their intellectual powers is insignificant and clumsy as compared with what is elsewhere present in nature. That for which we are indebted to understanding and to reason is primarily self-consciousness: through them we have knowledge and are not "forever in the presence of inscrutable forces." However, it is not through the understanding or the reason that we gain access to these forces. While these faculties provide self-consciousness and present us with a phenomenal world which is useful in fulfilling the needs of the will, they fail to reveal the inner nature of Will itself. Only our direct inner experience of our bodies suffices for this: the way lies from within.

Schopenhauer's metaphysics of the Will is so familiar that we need not discuss it here. What is of significance is merely to show in what fashion his metaphysics determined his view of the basic insufficiency of the intellect. As we have seen, it was not Schopenhauer's view—though it has often been held to be so—that the intellect is to be distrusted because it is directly controlled by the will. On the contrary, he believed that in most instances the intellect functioned in its own relatively autonomous manner, and was of positive use to man in doing so. Nevertheless, all of the materials of the intellect depended, as we have noted, on what is given in representations, and our representations are only ejects of the brain. In order to understand the will as it exists in us, we cannot look to these ejects, but must directly experience our own bodily activity as a feeling or striving; however, we obviously do not experience the brain itself in this way. The brain stands at the opposite pole from the organs of sex or of hunger, in which the life-force of the organism as a whole is most clearly expressed. Thus, it is in the immediate experience of *these* organs, and not through the characteristic functioning of the brain, that we know the world as Will. In fact, the projection of a world of representations might even be said to serve as a partial concealment of the existence of Will, for so long as we are absorbed in simply tracing the relations among these representations, we do not become aware of that which underlies them.

At this point one can see why Schopenhauer held that the abstractions of reason, even when useful, could not possibly be taken as indicative of the nature of reality. They were even farther removed from reality than were the immediate perceptions upon which they depended, for perception involves sensation, and sensation involves the active response of the sensory organ to a stimulus: thus it involves will. However, the grade of will which is involved in sensing does not, as will, generally reach the threshold of consciousness: instead of being aware of the eye, it is the sun we say that we see. Naturally, if the will actually present in the reacting eye is not present to our consciousness, then it surely cannot be experienced within the picture which is projected. Thus, when we attend to the world as perceived, and not to the basis of these acts of perception themselves, we lose all possibility of coming into contact with *will*. This being true of *perception*, it is obviously true of all conceptual thought, for concepts are but representations of representations, ideas of ideas: they are in effect drained of the life-force which makes it possible that they should exist.

These, to be sure, are not Schopenhauer's forms of expression, but I have sought to explain how his account of sense-perception, and his belief in the absolute dependence of concepts on the representations of sense, made it inevitable that he should hold that all intellectual activity, even when it is useful, takes us away from reality instead of guiding us toward it. This has, of course, become a familiar theme, which we find affiliated with other positions in late nineteenth and twentieth century thought. In the case of Schopenhauer, as I have attempted to show, it follows from the acceptance of a metaphysics of a life-force; it was because of that metaphysics (which, to some extent, was itself attached to a reading of science), that Schopenhauer, like Bergson, set strict limits on the reach of the intellect.[54]

2. KIERKEGAARD: THE SUBJECTIVE THINKER

If we are to trust Kierkegaard's account of how to judge his work as an author, it is to be said that his total productivity from first to last was related to the task of becoming a Christian in a society which was purportedly Christian.[55] Thus, it would be false to treat the stages in his authorship as representing different stages in a spiritual development: on his own account he was always primarily a religious author, focusing with great intensity (but nonetheless often secretly) on a single problem, on what becoming a Christian truly involves. It must be said that when *The Point of View for my Work as an Author* reveals secret hints of this motivation in works which were apparently otherwise motivated, his claim is not unbelievable.[56]

Nonetheless, however sharply focused Kierkegaard's aim may have been, what he found it necessary to attack was multifarious. Furthermore, the literary, psychological, and satirical elaborations of his basic themes led him into further byways. Therefore, only to consider Kierkegaard as a religious thinker would be to oversimplify his position, and it would also obscure much that he has come to represent in modern thought. To be sure, even if we *were* to confine our attention to his religious thought, he would still represent a powerful and decisive figure in the modern rebellion against reason, for no other person in the nineteenth century so sharply rejected the *reasonableness* of the religious beliefs to which he was committed. Of course, during the nineteenth century it was not generally held that religion was based on reason, nor that its importance was to be vindicated by argument; nevertheless, if religious convictions were to be deemed acceptable, they had to be considered rationally credible. During the period, many different paths were followed by those who believed that it was both possible and necessary to reconcile reason and religion; however, Kierkegaard may be said to have rejected them all. It was essential to his view that Christianity should be literally true in its claims, and yet that it should not be considered as reasonable in any sense of that term.[57]

While Kierkegaard's attack upon the relationship between reason and religion was extremely radical, what makes him of greater importance to recent philosophy is the fact that he applied his critique of reason to all spheres of human life. That he should have done so was inevitable, since he denied that religion is confined within some sealed compartment of the individual's life: what is not religious is, of itself, anti-religious, and is to be judged by the standards religion sets. As a consequence, Kierkegaard was far more radical than those who only deny reason's competence to assess religious beliefs; he belongs within the far smaller class of those who have, in one way or another, rebelled against reason itself.

In tracing this aspect of his thought we must not treat Kierkegaard as if he had been primarily a technical philosopher. Like Schopenhauer, he was of course contemptuous of professorial philosophy;[58] however, he went further and even rejected the possibility that any philosophic systematization of experience was worthy of belief.[59] Thus, if one were to consider Kierkegaard primarily as a philosopher, judging him by philosophic standards, one would not only be misapprehending his motivation, but would inevitably treat him with less consideration than he deserves. Still, when we examine many of the polemical discussions which were necessary to the defense of his own positive religious commitments, we find him adopting positions of a specifically philosophic sort. Since he obviously did not take these arguments lightly, we must examine them. At the same time, his presentation so frequently enmeshes them with social criticism and with satirical portraits of his age, or with what appear as little better than apostrophe or invective, that the thread of philosophic thought often seems to be lost. If, then, Kierkegaard is not to be regarded so digressive as to be wholly chaotic in his doctrine, we must seek to understand how this mixture of modes comes about. It is to this problem that I shall first turn.

In the first place—and this will scarcely be open to challenge—one can say that Kierkegaard's thought does have a single focal point, to which he always returns. This, as he tells us, is his conviction that the category of individuality is the ultimate category of being and of worth.[60] Since this conviction can manifest itself in many forms, and since Kierkegaard held that it cannot be demonstrated by argument, it is not surprising that even when one discounts his literary elaborations, psychological excursions, and satirical playfulness, his philosophic style should fail to conform to the practice of others.

It was not only because of the nature of this central doctrine, and its indemonstrability, that Kierkegaard placed philosophic arguments in contexts in which they would not seem to most philosophers to belong. Another reason lay in the fact that he, like Hegel, assumed that logical principles directly manifest themselves in concrete facts (though these logical principles were, of course, very different from those of Hegel). Thus, he could easily pass back and forth between abstruse philosophic propositions and satirical observations on the motives and the behavior of men. It is because of such transitions that one gets the impression of flightiness in his arguments. However, the transitions are intelligible as soon as one sees that they rest on the assumption that the same dialectic which underlies thought finds expression in motives and actions. To illustrate this fact, I select a series of passages extracted from the main line of Kierkegaard's argument in a lengthy literary review entitled *The Present Age*. The review begins in satire:

Our age is essentially one of understanding and reflection, without passion, momentarily bursting into enthusiasm, and shrewdly relapsing into repose.

If we had statistical tables of the consumption of intelligence from generation to generation as we have for spirits, we should be astounded at the enormous amount of scruple and deliberation consumed by small, well-to-do families living quietly, and at the amount which the young, and even children, use. . . .

Nowadays not even a suicide kills himself in desperation. Before taking the step he deliberates so long and so carefully that he literally chokes with thought. It is even questionable whether he ought to be called a suicide, since it is really thought which takes his life. He does not die *with* deliberation but *from* deliberation. . . .[61]

According to Kierkegaard, such an age, which is reflective and passionless, transforms everything into "a feat of dialectics":

. . . it leaves everything standing, but cunningly empties it of significance. Instead of culminating in a rebellion, it reduces the inward reality of all relationships to a reflective tension which leaves everything standing but makes the whole of life ambiguous: so that everything continues to exist factually whilst by a dialectical deceit, *privatissime*, it supplies a secret interpretation—that it does not exist.[62]

How, one must ask, does it manage to accomplish this? Kierkegaard's answer—and here we come to the point of my comment—is that it is accomplished by *abolishing the principle of contradiction*!

> The present age [Kierkegaard says] is one of understanding lacking in passion, and has therefore abolished the *principle of contradiction*. By comparison with a passionate age, an age without passion *gains in scope what it loses in intensity*. But this scope may once again become the condition of a still higher form, if a corresponding intensity assumes control of the extended field of activity which is put at its disposal. The abolition of the principle of contradiction, expressed in terms of existence, means to live in contradiction with oneself. The creative omnipotence of the differentiating power of passion, which makes the individual completely at one with himself, is transformed into the extended scope of reflective understanding: as a result of knowing and being everything possible, one is in contradiction with oneself, i.e., nothing at all.[63]

To illustrate what happens in the ordinary course of men's lives when the principle of contradiction is regarded as "abolished," Kierkegaard goes on to describe "talkativeness."

> What is *talkativeness*? It is doing away with the vital distinction between talking and keeping silent. Only some one who knows how to remain essentially silent can really talk—and act essentially. Silence is the essence of inwardness, of the inner life. Mere gossip anticipates real talk, and to express what is still in thought weakens action by forestalling it. But some one who can really talk, because he knows how to remain silent, will not only talk about a variety of things but about one thing only, and he will know when to talk and when to remain silent.[64]

What, we must now ask, is the connection which links a satirical portrait of a population without passion and the supposed abolition of the principle of contradiction, or links the abolition of the principle of contradiction with an emptiness of self and mere talkativeness? Kierkegaard's underlying assumption was that the principle of contradiction, which Hegel's system claimed to have superseded, was essential to individuality: if individuality was ultimate, the principle of contradiction was ultimate, and only if the principle of contradiction is ultimate can it be true that *this* is not *that*, one thing is not another, and individuality can be preserved.[65] Thus Kierkegaard, no less than Hegel, looked upon a logical principle as definitive of relationships among concrete existents. For this reason, I submit, he found no difficulty in making immediate application of a philosophic position to a concrete particular, or equating a psychological aperçu with a philosophic proposition.

This is not to say that Kierkegaard's basic philosophic theses cannot be discussed in other terms and cannot be compared with the positions of Hegel and others; I have here only attempted to explain why he found it acceptable to have his discussions of typically philosophic issues move as they did. Had he been more free of the dominance of the Hegelian system, not all problems concerning truth would have been so rigidly identified with questions concerning principles of thought. In this connection we may note that even Socrates, the counterfoil to Hegel in Kierkegaard's writings, is really the Socratic spirit, a mode of argument, not a source of particular insights.[66] Thus Kierkegaard continually takes abstract principles as representatives of particulars, and takes particulars as embodiments of principles, in spite of what one might perhaps expect on the basis of his existentialism: his insistence on the separation of the realm of essence from existence. There is no contradiction here. The principles to which Kierkegaard appealed were not construed by him to be abstractions of reason, belonging within the realm of possibility, but were what he took to be the actual dialectic through which the thought of an existing person proceeds.

There is one further point to be noted concerning Kierkegaard's mode of presenting his position, and that is the personal tone of voice with which he speaks. Regardless of the pseudonyms he used—which, of course, pose problems of interpretation in particular works, and for his work as a whole—Kierkegaard's manner rests on the assumption that author and reader can be brought into a direct or personal form of communication: the discourse itself is not an objective entity which is to be considered as having first been written by one and then read and judged by the other.[67] Since it was essential to Kierkegaard's personality that he should stand out in all his uniqueness, and since he sought to bring the reader to a consciousness of the value of uniqueness, whatever served to make an issue more personal was brought into play. Thus, arguments which could be expected to appeal to all who strip themselves of idiosyncratic modes of thought are precisely the arguments which Kierkegaard disdains to use. Every person whom he wishes to address is to be equal to him in individuality and uniqueness, and therefore cannot be addressed through some mode of discourse which purports to be objective, independent of the individual, and common to all.

These remarks on the philosophic style of Kierkegaard's thought are not only designed to explain why it is impossible to find sustained argument in even his most philosophical works,[68] but to illustrate the intensity with which the category of individuality animated all that he did. As he said in the second appendix to *The Point of View for my Work as an Author*:

If this thing of 'the individual' were a trifle to me, I could let it drop; indeed, I should be delighted to do so and should be ashamed if I were not willing to do it with the most obliging alacrity. But such is far from being the case. For me—not personally, but as a thinker—this matter of the individual is the most decisive thing...
... With the category of 'the individual' is bound up any ethical importance I may have. If that category was right, if that category was in place, if I saw rightly at this point and understood rightly that it was my task (certainly not a pleasant nor a thankful one) to call attention to it, if that was the task given me to do, albeit with inward sufferings such as certainly are seldom experienced, and with outward sacrifices such as a man is not every day found willing to make—in that case I stand fast and my works with me.[69]

It is from this point of view that Kierkegaard attacked bourgeois society and the conformist attitudes of the day,[70] but it is with his philosophic position, not with his social criticism nor his attack on "Christendom," that we must be concerned. Since Kierkegaard always tended to define his own position as *an existing thinker* through a contrast with *speculative thought*, and since he tended to identify speculative thought with Hegel and the Hegelian system, it is with his criticisms of "the System" that we can most readily begin.

Among the many criticisms, there are some which would be applicable not only to Hegelian forms of thought, but to any philosophic system, and for our purposes these are the more important ones. Yet it is also enlightening to see which aspects of Hegel's particular system were the special targets of Kierkegaard's attack. These may be summarized under three headings: Hegel's logic, his views regarding the sphere of the ethical, and his treatment of Christianity.

With respect to logic, Kierkegaard's complaint was that logic, as such, has nothing to do with movement: it cannot seize the moving, and its categories do not generate movement. Therefore, he says that what is regarded as "Hegel's unparalleled discovery, the subject of so unparalleled an admiration, the introduction of movement into logic, is a sheer confusion of logical science."[71] One reason which Kierkegaard gives for his position is that the concepts of pure logic (as contrasted with existential thinking) are abstractions, and deal with possibilities only; movement pertains to *existence* and not to possibilities. Or, as he sometimes put it, possibilities are merely grasped conceptually, *sub specie aeterni*, and can therefore have nothing to do with becoming.[72] Or, to shift from the nature of concepts to the logical relationships obtaining among them, we find Kierkegaard arguing that the necessity which is present in logic does not pertain to existence; it is a logical connection of *ground and consequence* which has nothing to do with becoming, that is, with something coming into existence.[73] To be sure, Kierkegaard readily admits that his own existential logic, with its strict antithesis of either-or, does not apply in the world of essences; in the realm of pure thought "leaps" are not made, and only abstract relationships of ground and consequence hold. What he objects to in Hegel's logic is that it should have been assumed to be possible to introduce becoming into the world of pure thought, bridging the gap between essences and concrete existence: for Kierkegaard that gap must not be bridged, for the logic of essence has *nothing* to do with the logic of existence.[74]

There is a further Kierkegaardian criticism of Hegel's system which was specifically connected with Hegel's logic, although Kierkegaard tended to speak as if it would be true of any philosophic system whatsoever, which it is not. This criticism consisted in the fact that the Hegelian system was not finished, and could never be finished if it were to deal with existence, and not merely essences: any system-builder who seeks to include his own system-building within that system is obviously caught in Tristram Shandy's paradox. Kierkegaard often makes sport of Hegel because of this fact.[75] However, the difficulty is peculiarly Hegelian, and not universal among systematic philosophers, for it was Hegel's contention that in each successive stage of thought reality stands more fully revealed. Therefore, to postpone the end is to postpone the full meaning of what has gone before, and Kierkegaard is surely not unjustified in saying:

It is ridiculous to treat everything as if the System were complete, and then to say at the end, that the conclusion is lacking. If the conclusion is lacking at the end, it is also lacking in the beginning, and this should therefore have been said in the beginning. A house may be spoken of as finished even if it lacks a minor detail, a bell-pull or the like; but in a scientific structure the absence of the conclusion has retroactive power to make the beginning doubtful and hypothetical, which is to say unsystematic.[76]

In another passage he phrased this criticism in a more pointed way, claiming that the Hegelian system inevitably led to scepticism, if one took seriously the fact that its completion was necessarily lacking.

According to Hegel, truth is the continuing world-process. Each generation, each stage of this process, is valid; and yet it is only a moment of the truth. Unless we here allow ourselves to introduce a dash of charlatanry, which helps out by assuming that the generation in which Professor Hegel lived, or the generation which after him plays the role of the *Imprimatur*, is the last generation, we are all in a state of sceptical uncertainty.... [because] only the next following generation can know what the truth was in the preceding generation. The great secret of the System ... is pretty much the same as the sophism of Protagoras, that everything is relative; except that here everything is relative to the continuing world-process.[77]

Considering the teleological impetus of Hegel's system, this objection assuredly had ample justification.

We come now to the second point at which Kierkegaard raised objections against the Hegelian System, the place which that system accorded to the ethical sphere of existence. On several occasions, Kierkegaard objected to the introduction of an ethical term in Hegelian logic, as when Hegel spoke of "the bad infinite."[78] However, that relatively trivial point, although not unconnected with Kierkegaard's sharp distinction between the ethical and the logical, is not the one with which we are here concerned. Rather, we must attempt to understand what Kierkegaard had in mind when he said that, regardless of how many theoretical flaws may be found within the Hegelian system, its fundamental error was that it ignored the ethical element in the individual's existence.[79]

The meaning of this challenge becomes clear as soon as we contrast Kierkegaard and Hegel with respect to where each thought that the ethical dimension of life is to be found. As we have seen,[80] Hegel held that the ethical resides in the fabric of society; the individual's moral life consists in playing his part in the life of the community which has enabled him to become what he is. For Kierkegaard, the ethical is the sphere of the individual's own existence *as an individual,* involving his personal responsibility for whatever choices he makes. These choices, Kierkegaard holds, are made in complete freedom, and our judgment of them is not to be based upon circumstances or consequences. Thus we find Kierkegaard saying:

...whatever a man may accomplish in the world, even to the most astonishing of achievements, it is none the less quite dubious in its significance, unless the individual has been ethically clear when he made his choice, has ethically clarified his choice to himself. The ethical quality is jealous for its own integrity, and is quite unimpressed by the most astounding quantity.[81]

The realm of "quantity" which Kierkegaard here rejects is that which is judged to be *historically* significant. Whatever range of significance any act may have for world-history is regarded by Kierkegaard as ethically irrelevant, since it depends upon external circumstances, not upon the individual's own act of choice. In fact, Kierkegaard not only draws a sharp contrast between what is of world-historical significance and the nature of the ethical, but he also argues that if one looks at one's actions in terms of historical tendencies one is likely to become—in a literal sense—*de*moralized. Under these circumstances, he says,

> . . . people no longer have any will for anything except what is world-historically significant, no concern for anything but the accidental, the world-historical outcome, instead of concerning themselves solely with the essential, the inner spirit, the ethical, freedom.[82]

Or, as Kierkegaard said in speaking of the ethical demands of Christianity:

> Christian heroism (and perhaps it is rarely to be seen) is to venture to be oneself, as an individual man, this definite individual man, alone before the face of God, alone in this tremendous exertion and this tremendous responsibility; but it is not Christian heroism to be humbugged by the pure idea of humanity or to play the game of marvelling at world-history.[83]

Thus, for Kierkegaard, the Hegelian system, which looks upon the individual's moral life in terms of his place in a community, and then interprets social life as part of the progressive unfolding of the historical process, constitutes an outrageous attack on all individuality. Furthermore, it constitutes an attack, Kierkegaard holds, on all that is essential in Christianity.

Kierkegaard had no opportunity of knowing Hegel's early theological writings. When he attacked Hegel's view of Christianity it was not these that he was attacking, nor was he attacking the doctrine of religion in *The Phenomenology of Spirit*. Rather, it was the later writings which he apparently had in mind.[84] His most explicit attacks on Hegel's interpretation of Christianity are closely linked to his general attack on speculative thought; however, as we shall see, his opposition was also rooted in the fact that Hegel submerged the ethical and religious in the world-historical process.

According to Kierkegaard, the fundamental error of speculative thought in its attempts to deal with Christianity is that it treats Christianity as if it were a speculative system, comparable to other speculative systems. It therefore assumes that it should be possible to mediate between Christian doctrine and other speculative doctrines, finally embracing its truth, along with all other truths, within a single speculative system. It was precisely this assumption that Kierkegaard challenged:

> The question of what Christianity is, must first and foremost be determined before there can be any question of mediation. But speculative philosophy makes no move in this direction. It does not first set forth what philosophy is, and then what Christianity is, to see whether the entities thus made to confront each other admit of a mediation; it does not make certain of the identity of the respective parties before proceeding to reconcile them. If speculative philosophy is asked what Christianity is, it replies at once: Christianity is the speculative interpretation of Christianity. It does not trouble

to inquire whether there is anything in the distinction between a something and an interpretation of this something.[85]

Kierkegaard himself held that there is an absolute distinction between what Christianity is and what a speculative system is:

> Christianity is not a doctrine but an existential communication expressing an existential contradiction. If Christianity were a doctrine it would *eo ipso* not be an opposite to speculative thought, but rather a phase within it. Christianity has to do with existence, with the act of existing; but existence and existing constitute precisely the opposite of speculation.[86]

This opposition parallels the general opposition between the spheres of essence and existence which we shall shortly examine. What Kierkegaard attacked was speculative thought, claiming that it led to a complete distortion of actual experience. For example, in an entry in the *Journals* in which he had been attacking Hegel's system, we find him saying:

> And now what about Christianity, how has it been dealt with? I entirely agree with your disapproval of the way in which every Christian concept has been so sublimated, so completely volatilised into a sea of fog that it is impossible to recognize it again. To such concepts as faith, incarnation, tradition, inspiration, which in Christianity must be referred to a particular historical fact, it has seemed good to philosophers to give an entirely different general meaning whereby faith becomes immediate certainty, . . . tradition has become the summary of a certain world experience, whilst inspiration has become nothing but the result of God having breathed the spirit of life into man, and incarnation nothing else than the existence of one or other ideas in one or more individuals.[87]

These philosophic reinterpretations of doctrines such as the incarnation rob them of all direct meaning for existing individuals, according to Kierkegaard. Thus, he claims that his age, with its reliance on speculative thought, has "transformed Christianity into a philosophical doctrine that asks to be understood, and [has] turned being a Christian into a triviality."[88]

Because Kierkegaard regarded the ultimate question facing him as one of being —or, rather, as one of *becoming*—a Christian, he rejected Hegel's attempt to interpret Christianity as a moment in the unfolding of Absolute Spirit. While Kierkegaard did not pose this issue in explicit terms in his *Philosophical Fragments*, it assuredly served as part of the context of that work.[89] What was at issue in the *Fragments* was the relation in which a Christian must stand to the central event of Christian history, the Incarnation. The relationship, Kierkegaard holds, is one of contemporaneity: every believer must, in his faith, be contemporaneous with Christ. This difficult doctrine, which is an ultimate paradox of Christian faith, obviously contradicts the Hegelian notion of the ultimacy of the historical process through which the Absolute successively reveals itself. The presence of the eternal God as an individual man in history occurred only once, and occurred for all time. It is referred to by Kierkegaard as the Moment, and the individual, regardless of his era, is contemporaneous with this Moment through his faith.[90]

The same point is made, but in a different and more inclusive way, when Kierkegaard, in the conclusion to *Fear and Trembling*, very simply says:

> The highest passion in a man is faith, and here no generation begins at any other point
> than did the preceding generation, every generation begins all over again, the subsequent
> generation gets no further than the foregoing.[91]

In fact, in contradistinction to Hegel, Kierkegaard sometimes says that the task
of later generations is even more difficult than was that of the earlier. He regarded
this as the case when one lived in a so-called Christian society, for in "Christendom" what it means to be a Christian is often confused with other, quite contrary
things.[92] And, according to Kierkegaard, the intellect itself poses an obstacle to
faith because it seeks to rob men of inwardness and passion. Thus he says:

> In the nineteenth century it is not easier to be a Christian than it was in the first age,
> on the contrary, it has become more difficult, especially for the cultured, and it will
> become more difficult from year to year. The predominance of intellect in the man of
> culture, and the direction toward the objective, will in his case constantly cause
> resistance against becoming a Christian, and this resistance is the sin of the intellect:
> lukewarmness.[93]

Since man cannot wholly abandon the intellect, what role can it play? Obviously,
it cannot render Christianity intelligible, yet it does have a role. At one point, in
summing up what he had aimed to accomplish in his *Concluding Unscientific
Postscript*, Kierkegaard said:

> Since it is in fact the highest attainment to become and continue to be a Christian,
> the point of it [intellectual effort] cannot be to reflect upon Christianity, but only
> *by reflection to intensify the pathos* with which one continues to be a Christian.
> And it was about this [point that] the whole work has turned.[94]

This estimate of the place of the intellect in human life is obviously not merely
a part of Kierkegaard's attack on the Hegelian system, but constitutes an attack
on all philosophic systems. In this general attack, Kierkegaard used several forms
of argument which can be separately considered, even though each is only a variation on his basic theme: that, so far as human beings are concerned, systematic
connection is only to be found in the sphere of abstract thought—while a *logical*
system is possible, an *existential* system is not.[95] In this connection, it is necessary
to say "so far as human beings are concerned," since Kierkegaard explicitly holds
that "Reality itself is a system—for God."[96] However, to think that an existing
individual could comprehend reality as it appears to God would be impious,
were it not merely comical. The three specific Kierkegaardian arguments which I
shall in this connection examine are: first, the major one in which he used the
distinction between essence and existence as a means of attacking all philosophic
systems; second, one which relies on the fact that every speculative system has as
its author an existing individual; and, third, that every system contains tacit presuppositions which cannot be systematically proved.

Turning to the first of these points, it is clear that Kierkegaard had a firm grip on the necessity of distinguishing between universals and concrete existents, and that—in his less radical statements—one can scarcely disagree with him as to what constitutes the starting point for human knowledge. For example, in the *Philosophical Fragments,* he says:

I always reason from existence, not toward existence, whether I move in the sphere of palpable sensible fact or in the realm of thought. I do not for example prove that a stone exists, but that some existing thing is a stone. The procedure in a court of justice does not prove that a criminal exists, but that the accused, whose existence is given, is a criminal. Whether we call existence an *accessorium* or the external *prius,* it is never subject to demonstration.[97]

Yet it is assuredly doubtful whether either Hegel or any other metaphysician would deny this, save in the case of God's existence. The burden of Kierkegaard's argument actually rested not on the fact that metaphysical systems are formulated in terms of that which is *general,* but upon the alleged fact that no conceptual system can seize the *temporal.* That which is "general," consisting in "abstractions," is claimed to provide an inadequate basis for human understanding because concepts exist *sub specie aeterni,* and therefore are not involved in becoming.[98] However, Kierkegaard fails to establish that the general cannot apply directly and unambiguously to that which is not only actual, but involves *process:* one need merely think of the general concept of, say, "metabolic processes" to find an adequate counter-example. At this point the Kierkegaardian position unfortunately has next to nothing to recommend it, unless Platonic prejudice and Hegelian failures can be considered arguments.

The second argument on which Kierkegaard bases his attack on philosophic systems consists in the argument that every system, as a system, aims to be all-inclusive, but inevitably fails, since the system-builder himself stands outside it. As Kierkegaard put the matter in one place:

Existence must be revoked in the eternal before the system can round itself out; there must be no existing remainder, not even such a little minikin as the existing Herr Professor who writes the system.[99]

In an effort to escape this inescapable fact, Kierkegaard charges, systematic philosophers speak as if "speculative thought," in the abstract, were capable of formulating a system; they forget that it is they who have formulated it. This he repeatedly ridicules as a form of comic absent-mindedness.[100] His point, thus phrased, only has validity if one accepts one or more of a number of assumptions, and there are three such assumptions which we find Kierkegaard more than willing to make. First, he assumes that a philosophic system can only be said to be all-inclusive if it can take note of all actual existents, and not merely of whatever characteristics are to be found in each and every existing thing. Naturally, because of his rejection of abstractions, and his interest in concrete existents, this was an assumption Kierkegaard made. Second, the fact that the system cannot ever be complete because it cannot "include" the person who formulates it, is

only damaging if one accepts the Hegelian assumption that "every scientific problem within the great field embraced by science has its definite place, its measure
and its bounds, and precisely thereby has its resonance in the whole."[101] This,
too was an assumption which Kierkegaard—for reasons opposed to those of Hegel
—was willing to accept. Finally, the existence of the system-builder was conceived by Kierkegaard as a threat to the completeness of the system because he
assumed that contingency is always present where there is existence, and what
cannot yet be known by an existing thinker will inevitably threaten what he has
said in the past.

Once it is recognized that Kierkegaard's ridicule of system-building rests on
assumptions of this sort, his argument may remain effective against Hegel, but it
would lose most of its sting if he attempted to direct it against, say, Aristotle,
Spinoza, or Descartes. Nevertheless, the third of his arguments to which I have
alluded would appear to be a more generally effective form of attack. It consists
in the contention that all philosophic systems must rest upon presuppositions
which cannot be proved within the system.[102] Let us assume that this contention
is true. The question arises as to why it should have been regarded by Kierkegaard
as destructive of the whole enterprise of system-building. Part of the reason consists, of course, in the fact that he tended to identify system-building with Hegel's
system, and he agreed with Trendelenburg that Hegel had failed in his attempt
to construct a presuppositionless system.[103] However, the full reason lies deeper.
In holding that there were no presuppositionless systems, Kierkegaard also assumed that whatever presuppositions were present sprang from the problems of
the individual's own existence, and were not at all the sorts of logical and
intellectual problems with which philosophers asserted they were really concerned. Thus, for example, in opposition to the Hegelian system, he contended
that "a resolution of the will is required to end the preliminary process of reflection," and that "only when reflection comes to a halt can a beginning be made;
and reflection can be halted only by something else, and this something else is
something quite different from the logical, being a resolution of will."[104] As one
can see throughout Kierkegaard's work, he insists that if thought is to have vitality
it must spring from the existential commitment of the philosopher himself, as a
whole being.[105] When, on the other hand, a thinker seeks to divorce himself from
existence, he becomes pitiful. (Though, he may also be comic.) As Kierkegaard
says:

> While a genuine human being, as a synthesis of the finite and the infinite, finds his
> reality in holding these two factors together, infinitely interested in existing—an abstract
> thinker is a duplex being: a fantastic creature who moves in the pure being of abstract
> thought, and on the other hand, a sometimes pitiful professorial figure which the
> former deposits, about as when one sets down a walking stick. When one reads the story
> of such a thinker's life (for his writings are perhaps excellent), one trembles to think
> of what it means to be a man.—And when you read in his writings that thought and
> being are one, it is impossible not to think, in view of his own life and mode of
> existence, that the being which is thus identical with thought can scarcely be the being
> of a man.[106]

It is here that we encounter Kierkegaard's special form of voluntarism. Not all thought and action spring from passion, but all that possess vitality and significance do. Social and religious conformism, as well as intellectual abstraction, are empty and insignificant because they lack passion; and so too are all other activities which are directed outward, relying upon what appears to be objectively certain. The only sphere in which there is intensity and passion is the sphere of the individual's own inward consciousness of himself and his existential situation, forced to make choices and standing alone before his God.

It is in the light of this distinction that the famous Kierkegaardian passages on subjectivity and truth must be read:

When the question of truth is raised in an objective manner, reflection is directed objectively to the truth, as an object to which the knower is related. Reflection is not focussed upon the relationship, however, but upon the question of whether it is the truth to which the knower is related. If only the object to which he is related is the truth, the subject is accounted to be in the truth. When the question of the truth is raised subjectively, reflection is directed subjectively to the nature of the individual's relationship; if only the mode of this relationship is in the truth, the individual is in the truth even if he should happen to be thus related to what is not true. Let us take as an example the knowledge of God. Objectively, reflection is directed to the problem of whether this object is the true God; subjectively, reflection is directed to the question of whether the individual is related to a something *in such a manner* that his relationship is in truth a God-relationship. . . .

Now when the problem is to reckon up on which side there is most truth, whether on the side of one who seeks the true God objectively, and pursues the approximate truth of the God-idea; or on the side of one who, driven by the infinite passion of his need of God, feels an infinite concern for his own relationship to God in truth . . . the answer cannot be in doubt for anyone who has not been demoralized with the aid of science. If one who lives in the midst of Christendom goes up to the house of God, the house of the true God, with the true conception of God in his knowledge, and prays, but prays in a false spirit; and one who lives in an idolatrous community prays with the entire passion of the infinite, although his eyes rest upon the image of an idol: where is there most truth? The one prays in truth to God though he worships an idol; the other prays falsely to the true God, and hence worships in fact an idol.[107]

Thus, what is essential in truth is the passion with which a belief is inwardly seized, or *appropriated*, by the individual, by *one* individual.[108] What others may hold is irrelevant to an existing individual; it is his obligation to grasp his own nature and condition, and the only access to this involves his turning inward.[109]

In interpreting these crucial aspects of Kierkegaard's position, it is necessary to grasp that what is involved in inwardness is not a faculty of "feeling," in the sense of affectivity, but is, rather, passion, interest, will. This is, of course, evident in his treatment of the aesthetic category; it also provides a basis for the connection between an aesthetic mode of existence and the realm of abstract intellectual knowledge, for both lack what is basic in existence, passionate concern.[110] This concern *is* present in the ethical, and is what distinguishes it from mere knowledge;[111] it expresses itself in the Promethean striving which Kierkegaard regards as giving ethical meaning to life:[112]

The question is what existing human beings, in so far as they are existing beings, must needs be content with: then it will be evident that the ideal of a persistent striving is the only view of life that does not carry with it an inevitable disillusionment.[113]

It does not carry disillusionment with it since, according to Kierkegaard, it is the striving itself, and its wholeness, not its goal, which is important:

The principle that the existing subjective thinker is constantly occupied in striving, does not mean that he has, in the finite sense, a goal toward which he strives, and that he would be finished when he had reached this goal. No, he strives infinitely, is constantly in process of becoming.[114]

Thus, we must renounce the need to have things finished and completed: we must, as existing beings, forever remain within becoming, for that is what existence is.[115]

Yet, the passion which evinces itself in striving *can* be fulfilled even if no goal is set: the highest form of this passion is faith. To exist in a God-relationship, to become and remain a Christian, takes an enormous and never-ceasing energy of will. It is this which Kierkegaard holds to be the highest form of existing which any individual can attain; like any form of existing it cannot be attained once and for all, but depends upon an inward appropriation of the Christian paradox, against which reason rebels. When this is attained, one does not *know* the truth: in the Kierkegaardian language which we have quoted, one is *in* the truth. To be in the truth is the ultimate, passionate, inwardness of one's faith, which no one can share. A grasp of this fact, and its elaboration in his philosophic and religious writings, can be identified with that which Kierkegaard, in his earliest *Journals*, sought: an idea for which he could live and die.[116]

3. NIETZSCHE: VALUE AND TRUTH

Nietzsche's writings, unlike those of Schopenhauer, do not confront us with a metaphysical system, nor do we find that, like Kierkegaard, he looked upon himself as having a single task and a single thesis. His writings fall into relatively distinct periods as his interests and his self-image changed, and in this respect, too, he differed from them. In spite of such changes, and in spite of his aphoristic manner of writing, there was a considerable degree of unity in Nietzsche's thought; this is evident, for example, in the fact that throughout his life those whom he cherished as enemies remained generally the same.[117] To be sure, there are issues with respect to which he sometimes contradicted himself, and there were some themes which he took up only briefly, and then dropped. However, the themes and issues to which he constantly returned form a web of interconnecting positions whose mutual support give the system of his thought its tensile strength.

Within that system one might choose to emphasize Nietzsche's moral psychology, and his attacks on both Christianity and what he took to be a herd morality; one would thereby be led to consider his own moral commitments. In many ways, this is perhaps the most interesting and significant set of strands in his thought. However, in the present context, it is not with Nietzsche as moralist, but with his views regarding reason and truth, that we are concerned. To be sure, there is an important although not immediately obvious connection between these aspects of his thought. Nietzsche's theory of truth depended upon what may be called the principle of the primacy of value; and since he approached questions of value through psychological analyses, the questions which he raised concerning truth were formulated in psychological terms. So, too, were the questions he raised regarding morality. Thus, whether one approaches his thought from the side of his moral concerns or with respect to the question of truth, one will find that they have a common source in his voluntaristic psychology. As Nietzsche said in *Beyond Good and Evil*, "Psychology shall be recognized again as the queen of the sciences. . . . psychology is now again the path to the fundamental problems."[118]

The doctrine that psychology is fundamental to the theory of knowledge has, of course, been held in many forms, some of which we have noted in the post-Kantian positivist tradition. Within that tradition, and within the tradition of British empiricism as represented by Locke and by Hume, psychological theory was regarded as relevant to epistemology in so far as it analyzed the *sources* of human knowledge. In the case of Nietzsche, the issue was entirely different: he was concerned with the *motivation* of knowledge, of our interest in truth. As he said in the very first paragraph of *Beyond Good and Evil*:

> The will to truth which shall still tempt us to many a venture, that famous truthfulness of which all philosophers so far have spoken with respect—what questions has this will to truth not laid before us! What strange, wicked, questionable questions. . . . Is it any wonder that we should finally become suspicious, lose patience, and turn away impatiently? that we should finally learn from this Sphinx to ask questions too? *Who* is it really that puts questions to us here? *What* in us really wants truth?
>
> Indeed we came to a long halt at the question about the cause of this will—until we finally came to a complete stop before a still more basic question. We asked about the value of this will. Suppose we want truth: *why not rather* untruth? and uncertainty? even ignorance?

This is clearly an issue which echoes questions raised by Schopenhauer concerning the function of knowledge in the life of the race; and perhaps even more clearly it recalls Kierkegaard's manner of posing the question of truth—not objectively, but subjectively, in terms of what is of ultimate concern to an existing individual.[119] However, these and other affinities should not be allowed to conceal the great difference which exists between Nietzsche's approach and theirs. His philosophy may be said to have more closely resembled that of Feuerbach in its motivation, being a form of *anthropology* in Feuerbach's sense of that term: unlike Schopenhauer and Kierkegaard, he looked upon the world only in its relation to man, ultimately rejecting all truths which claimed to refer to anything existing independently of human experience.[120]

Because of Schopenhauer's actual influence on Nietzsche, it is easy to overlook, or to minimize, this striking difference between their conceptions of philosophy. However, as the preface to *Beyond Good and Evil* should serve to make clear, the difference was fundamental. There, Nietzsche attacked philosophers for dogmatism, for system-building; and, remembering Kant, it is not possible to read this passage, with its constant reiteration of the concept of "dogmatism," without taking it as an attack on the whole metaphysical enterprise. If Nietzsche's opposition to Schopenhauer were not sufficiently clear from this alone, it could not fail to become clear through the two examples he used as illustrations of dogmatic metaphysics: they were the two systems most highly regarded by Schopenhauer, the Vedanta philosophy and Platonism. To these supposedly discredited metaphysical systems Nietzsche added Christianity and characterized its doctrines of the soul and of a timeless good as "Platonism for 'the people'."[121] Although this characterization, and some of Nietzsche's diatribes against Christianity, would not have touched the existential faith of Kierkegaard, his insistence on a philosophy which stressed man's immanence in nature could not fail to have done so.[122] For Kierkegaard, the center of existence does not lie within man, but in God, with whom each man must establish a personal relationship. For Nietzsche, *God was dead*, and existence could only have meaning insofar as man gave it meaning: it is man who is the creator of values.[123] Among these values is "truth," and Nietzsche interpreted truth as he interpreted all other values, in terms of answers to human needs.

To speak of truth in these terms would seem to suggest that he accepted a straightforward pragmatism, according to which whatever beliefs are of positive value are to be denominated as true, and any beliefs which have negative values are, because of that fact, false. However, to interpret Nietzsche's theory of truth in this openly pragmatic fashion would be to misread him; in doing so, one would fall prey to what Nietzsche called "the typical prejudgment and prejudice which give away metaphysicians of all ages," the assumption that *opposites*, such as truth and error, or selfishness and selflessness, are actually independent of one another, and do not spring from a single root.[124] Nietzsche sought to discover and then to uncover this root, which he regarded as a task for psychologists, and one which would only proceed successfully when unhampered by the usual philosophical dichotomies. Thus we find him using locutions such as the following: "*Truth* is the kind of *error* without which a certain species of life could not live. The value for life is ultimately decisive."[125] While a pragmatic thesis is obviously involved in the claim that *value for life* is what is decisive in what we regard as true, it is also the case that the statement involves some aspect of a correspondence theory of truth, since Nietzsche could not otherwise have spoken of useful beliefs as *errors*.

If Nietzsche is not to be regarded as hopelessly confused in making such a statement, we must take seriously his assertion that truth and error are not to be regarded as opposites, and must seek the common root from which both spring. This root is to be discovered when we find Nietzsche saying:

> The falseness of a judgment is for us not necessarily an objection to a judgment; in this respect our new language may sound strangest. The question is to what extent it is life-promoting, life-preserving, species-preserving, perhaps even species-cultivating.[126]

Once again, this might appear to be a straightforward pragmatism were it not for the fact that he speaks of the *falseness* of judgments which serve life.

In trying to straighten this out, one might be tempted to say that Nietzsche was suggesting that particular errors were true for some beings, but not for others; that these could be called "falsehoods" or "errors" because they were not true *in themselves.* To speak in this way would be to fall into the same type of mistake as that of which Nietzsche accused philosophers who spoke of "things-in-themselves." There not only is no way in which such a thing-in-itself could be known, but every conception of "things" is relative to us as knowers. Similarly, there can be no truth-in-itself: there are no facts without interpretation, no truth which is not true for someone.[127] Therefore, it would be wholly unacceptable to treat Nietzsche's theory of truth as if it committed him to any usual form of correspondence theory.

A way out of this apparent impasse opens when we raise the question of *for whom* a true belief is true. Nietzsche, one should remember, always distinguished between the strong and the weak, the healthy and the sick, the yea-saying and nay-saying. Using this dichotomization of human beings, a generally consistent (though not always clearly expressed) theory of truth can be found in Nietzsche. "True" and "false" have a meaning which is not relative to belief, just as "good" and "bad" have a meaning which is not relative to contemporary (and, in Nietzsche's opinion, perverse) standards of "good" and "evil"; furthermore, in questions of truth, as in questions of morals, the only authentic standard is that which the strong, in their strength, can accept, and which the weak seek to distort. Those who fear life set up protective illusions for themselves, and call them "truth," but in reality they are unconscious lies; the strong directly grasp the truth in their own being, so long as they remain undeceived by what the weak call "true." Thus, *truth* and that which is life-enhancing *for the strong* are one and the same; what protects the weak is *not* the truth, but the unconscious self-deceptions which their weakness leads them to project. Then, in imitation of the strong, they call these deceptions "the truth," just as in the moral realm they call the projections of their own weakness "good."

This interpretation corresponds to Nietzsche's thesis that truth and falsity have a common root: when we understand the dynamics of the will, we see that they are not genuine opposites.[128] Like Freud, whose thought he here closely resembles, the difference is one between a healthy and a distorted expression of the same underlying force.[129] This interpretation of Nietzsche's general views regarding truth and falsehood receives confirmation when it is applied to his more specific views regarding philosophy itself.

It was one of Nietzsche's important aims to unmask past philosophic systems, showing that the claim of philosophers to embody pure, disinterested objectivity was mere pretense. In opposition to any such claims, he contended that "most of the conscious thinking of a philosopher is secretly guided and forced into certain channels by his instincts." To this he added, "Behind all logic, and its seeming sovereignty of movement there stand valuations or, more clearly, physiological demands for the preservation of a certain type of life."[130] Such assertions might be taken to mean that Nietzsche attempted to explain particular philosophic systems in terms of the instinctual needs of their creators, or in terms of needs for the fantasy fulfilments of secret drives; or, perhaps, as compensations for early forms of deprivation, or as the effects of certain child-rearing practices, or the like. Such interpretations of philosophic thought have become familiar to us, and not infrequently one finds Nietzsche speaking in similar terms. For example, he sometimes related the thought of a particular philosopher, such as Kant or Spinoza, to hidden wishes or to particular psychic maladies;[131] there is also the well-known passage in which he wrote:

> Gradually it has become clear to me what every great philosophy has so far been: namely, the personal confession of its author and a kind of involuntary memoir.[132]

However, this passage should not be taken as suggesting that a philosophy springs from particular personal deformations of character. What Nietzsche holds is that every great philosophy springs from some basic attitude toward life, some value predispositions. Unlike most more recent psychologists, he did not seek to account for these basic attitudes by means of reference to specific biographical factors: his usual view was that, from birth, individuals represent different personality types.

Nietzsche's unmasking of traditional dogmatic metaphysics rested on exposing the hidden fears of the type of personality who created such systems. On his view, the whole enterprise of traditional philosophy had rested on a single, unhealthy, all too common, psychic need: a need to escape from the world of sense, of becoming, and of immediacy—in short, an attempt to escape from all that is real. According to Nietzsche, philosophers have actually been afraid of the real, and have therefore sought to denigrate it, just as the Christian, out of *ressentiment*, denigrates strength. In opposition to that which actually is real, the philosopher claims to find another, higher form of reality, which he then names "reality"; therefore, whatever actually *is* real comes to be regarded as "appearance." In *The Twilight of the Idols* Nietzsche offers his clearest and most concise attack on this philosophical perversion, summing it up in four propositions:

> *First proposition.* The reasons for which "this" world has been characterized as "apparent" are the very reasons which indicate its reality; any other kind of reality is absolutely indemonstrable.

> *Second proposition.* The criteria which have been bestowed on the "true being" of things are the criteria of not-being, of *naught*; the "true world" has been constructed out of contradiction to the actual world: indeed an apparent world, insofar as it is merely a moral-optical illusion.

> *Third proposition.* To invent fables about a world "other" than this one has no meaning at all, unless an instinct for slander, detraction, and suspicion against life

has gained the upper hand in us: in that case, we avenge ourselves against life with a phantasmagoria of "another," a "better" life.

Fourth proposition. Any distinction between a "true" and an "apparent" world—whether in the Christian manner or in the manner of Kant (in the end, an underhanded Christian)—is only a suggestion of decadence, a symptom of the *decline of life.*[133]

Thus, once again we see that value-categories determine what we take to be true and false: the sick and the decadent claim to find truth in another world, whereas those who possess their natural strength, and enjoy the freedom that it brings, recognize the falsity in all forms of other-worldliness.

The interpretation which I have given concerning Nietzsche's theory of truth and error not only serves to elucidate his attitude toward philosophy, but serves to explain the rather complex and ambivalent attitude which he came to adopt toward the sciences. To be sure, there was one relatively brief period when Nietzsche considered the natural sciences as the great liberating force of the age;[134] however, as one sees in *Beyond Good and Evil*, and in many entries in *The Will to Power*, it came to be characteristic of his later attitude that the sciences—apart from his type of psychological analysis—were to be viewed merely as one way in which men tended to order their experience. When viewed in this way, the value of science depended on the needs which it served. Thus, when science was directly in the service of life-needs, Nietzsche viewed it as a wholly justifiable enterprise, but when an attitude of detachment and pseudo-objectivity underlay it, Nietzsche ridiculed it, and railed against it.

As examples of Nietzsche's view of the general character of science, the following statements may be chosen:

It is perhaps just dawning on five or six minds that physics, too, is only an interpretation and exegesis of the world (to suit us, if I may say so!) and *not* a world-explanation.[135]

And, in his notebooks, dating from the same general period, Nietzsche said:

The entire apparatus of knowledge is an apparatus for abstraction and simplification —directed not at knowledge but at taking possession of things.[136]

Or, to choose merely one further, somewhat later, example:

Not "to know" but to schematize—to impose upon chaos as much regularity and form as our practical needs require.

In the formation of reason, logic, the categories, it was *need* that was authoritative: the need not "to know," but to subsume, to schematize, for the purpose of intelligibility.[137]

All of this Nietzsche was willing to accept as necessary for some of the purposes of life—for assimilating experience. In fulfilling this task, scientists showed an attitude of mind which he always found acceptable: a drive to appropriate and conquer.[138]

On the other hand, he regarded the "respectable" scientist, "the scientific average man," as one whose life depended upon a lack of internal strength; such a man possesses no drive to appropriate and conquer, but uses knowledge as a protective shield. Nietzsche painted his portrait in the following colors:

> Let us look more closely: what is the scientific man? To begin with, a type of man that is not noble, with the virtues of a type of man that is not noble, which is to say, a type that does not dominate and is neither authoritative nor self-sufficient....

What such a person seeks, according to Nietzsche, is "constant attestation of his value and utility which is needed to overcome again and again the internal *mistrust* which is the sediment in the hearts of all dependent men and herd animals."[139] In short, what lies at the root of the scholarly or scientific search for *objectivity* is a lack of strength which shows itself as an unwillingness to take risks. According to Nietzsche, caution of this type fails to serve the interests of life.

Even at its best, when it is necessary for the assimilation of experience, science was not regarded by Nietzsche as offering a satisfactory way of interpreting the world. He held that there is "no limit to the ways in which the world can be interpreted; every interpretation [is] a symptom of growth or decline."[140] By the time he had fully formulated this position, he had become critical of the views of nature which were based on the methods characteristic of the natural sciences. Although he still regarded science as a necessary means of assimilating and schematizing experience, its methods were actually inimical to all of the characteristics which he identified with vitality and with growth.

The most evident way in which this can be illustrated is through what Nietzsche says concerning general concepts, without which, of course, scientific generalization would be impossible. In his early essay on "Truth and Lie in an Extra-Moral Sense," he wrote:

> Let us ... give special attention to the formation of concepts. Every word immediately becomes a concept, inasmuch as it is not intended to serve as a reminder of the unique and wholly individualized original experience to which it owes its birth, but must at the same time fit innumerable, more or less similar cases—which means, strictly speaking, never equal—in other words, a lot of unequal cases. Every concept originates through equating what is unequal.[141]

This was a view which he never changed. Furthermore, he claimed that the basic categories through which we apprehend that which we take to be real involve us in thinking of what we experience as static, denying that individuality and becoming are ultimately real. Thus, in speaking of "species" and of other *forms* which we ascribe to the world, he says:

> The form counts as something enduring and therefore more valuable; but the form has merely been invented by us; and however often "the same form is attained," it does not mean it *is* the same form—what appears is always something new, and it is only we, who are always comparing, who include the new, to the extent that it is similar to the old, in the unity of the "form"....

One should not understand this compulsion to construct concepts, species, forms, purposes, laws ("a world of identical cases") as if they enabled us to fix the *real world*; but as a compulsion to arrange a world for ourselves in which our existence is made possible: we thereby create a world which is calculable, simplified, comprehensible, etc., for us.[142]

The distortions of reality which are involved in every attempt to grasp it by means of general concepts and static forms were, according to Nietzsche, especially obvious in the natural sciences. The world-view of the sciences which he set himself to challenge was what he characterized as *mechanism*. Although he regarded atomistic materialism as having been amply refuted,[143] the conception of causal necessities in nature was still, on his view, being erroneously maintained. He regarded this as a form of mythologizing, as is evident in the following passage:

One should not wrongly reify "cause" and "effect," as the natural scientists do (and whoever, like them, now "naturalizes" in his thinking), according to the prevalent mechanical doltishness which makes the cause press and push until it "effects" its end; one should use "cause" and "effect" only as pure concepts, that is to say, as conventional fictions for the purpose of designation and communication—*not* for explanation. . . . It is *we* alone who have devised cause, sequence, for-each-other, relativity, constraint, number, law, freedom, motive, and purpose; and when we project and mix this symbol world into things as if it existed "in itself," we act once more as we have always acted—mythologically.[144]

In this passage, Nietzsche was not only attacking the belief in mechanical *forces*, but also the idea that the laws of physics were in any sense isomorphic with independently existing relationships in nature—as most positivists of his period still held. As he said in a notebook entry of approximately the same date:

It is an illusion that something is *known* when we possess a mathematical formula for an event: it is only designated, described; nothing more![145]

Such descriptions, though they might be effective in *summarizing* experience, failed to *shape* it, or to bestow meaning upon it. It was precisely because the mechanical world-view failed in this respect that Nietzsche rejected it. For example, in the passage from *Beyond Good and Evil* which I have just quoted, where he attacked the notion of causal necessities as a form of mythologizing, he completely rejected the notion of determinism as applied to human choices, saying, "the 'unfree will' is mythology; in real life it is only a matter of *strong* and *weak* wills."[146] In the following section, he then sought to explain precisely why physicists had come to ascribe uniformity to nature and speak of "nature's conformity to law." This arose, he asserted, out of a "plebeian antagonism to everything privileged and autocratic," and was a secret, unconscious form of concession to "the democratic instincts of the modern soul."[147]

This extravagant interpretation of modern science, which Nietzsche (as was often the case) attempted to defend as a philological insight, need not be taken seriously; however, what lay behind it became more and more clear in his notebooks. The whole quest for "truth," for arranging facts even when such arrangements served the needs of life, became distasteful: the task was to change life, not describe it. In one entry, which we may without distortion abbreviate, Nietzsche said:

> The ascertaining of "truth" and "untruth," the ascertaining of facts in general, is fundamentally different from creative positing, from shaping, overcoming, willing.... To introduce a meaning ... to posit a goal and mold facts according to it: that is, active interpretation, not merely conceptual translation.[148]

It is in terms of this contrast that one can best understand Nietzsche's view of the limitations of science. Even when science enables us to assimilate experience, its service to life is restricted; what was of primary importance on Nietzsche's view was not merely "adjustment," but the *enhancement* of experience. Just as he regarded the Darwinian concept of "a struggle for *survival*" as a debased version of the "will to *power*,"[149] so the usefulness of the schematizations of science were lacking in truth when compared with creative insights which could transform life. Unlike those whom he called "philosophical laborers," and "scientific men," Nietzsche believed that true philosophers could actually shape existence, imparting meaning to it.

> *Genuine philosophers ... are commanders and legislators*: they say *"thus* it *shall* be!" They first determine the Whither and the For What of man ... With a creative hand they reach for the future, and all that is and has been becomes a means for them, an instrument, a hammer. Their "knowing" is *creating*, their creating is a legislation, their will to truth is—will to power.[150]

Since, as we have seen, truth is what enhances the power of the strong, even though science (because of its usefulness) must be acknowledged to be superior to those traditional forms of metaphysics which spring from a need to escape from life, it cannot be considered as "true" once one compares it with genuine philosophy. Thus, we may say that, at its weakest, traditional philosophy is worthy only of contempt; that science is more worthy of respect; but that only the creative philosopher who, in Nietzsche's phrase, "philosophizes with a hammer," takes possession of truth.[151]

Immediately, one would appear to face the question of whether there has ever been, or could ever be, more than one genuine philosopher; of how, if there were, the truths they would create could be expected to harmonize. To such a question, Nietzsche's answer is of course obvious: there can be as many genuine philosophers as there are truly great individuals capable of grasping and transforming the values by which men live, and there is no reason to assume that their views *should* harmonize. Each such philosopher would say, with Nietzsche:

> "My judgment is *my* judgment:" no one else is easily entitled to it....
> One must shed the bad taste of wanting to agree with many. "Good" is no longer good when one's neighbor mouths it. And how should there be a "common good"! The term contradicts itself: whatever can be common always has little value. In the end it must be as it is and always has been: great things remain for the great, abysses for the profound, nuances and shudders for the refined, all that is rare for the rare.[152]

This is Nietzsche's doctrine of *perspectivism*, which he took to be "the basic condition for all life."[153] One cannot possibly escape from one's own perspective, and it is a symptom of mistrust in oneself, and therefore a symptom of weakness, to attempt to do so:

> The objective man [Nietzsche says] is indeed a mirror: he is accustomed to submit before whatever wants to be known, without any other pleasure than that found in knowing and "mirroring"; he waits until something comes . . .
>
> The objective man is an instrument, a precious, easily injured and clouded instrument for measuring and, as an arrangement of mirrors, an artistic triumph that deserves care and honor; but he is no goal, no conclusion and sunrise, no complementary man in whom the rest of existence is justified, no termination—and still less a beginning, a begetting and first cause.[154]

The strong affirm their own perspectives openly, recognizing that the world is what they can create from their own point of view, in their own image, in terms of their own values:

> Every center of force adopts a perspective toward the entire remainder, i.e., its own particular valuation, mode of action, and mode of resistance. . . .
>
> The world, apart from our condition of living in it, the world that we have not reduced to our being, our logic and psychological prejudices, does not exist as a world "in-itself"; it is essentially a world of relationships; under certain conditions it has a differing aspect from every point; its being is essentially different from every point; it presses upon every point, every point resists it—and the sum of these is in every case quite incongruent.[155]

To attempt an escape from such a conflict of perspectives and interpretations is to seek to escape life. Those who are strong will not thus abdicate, and those who are strongest fully know that the world as they interpret it *is* true, for "*the criterion of truth resides in the enhancement of the feeling of power.*"[156] Nietzsche would deny that such feelings of power would be present in the weak when they disparage the values of the strong, and there would therefore be no truth in the slanders they perpetrate against life. Even when those who are weak band together and succeed in gaining dominance over the strong through a perversion of the scale of values, one cannot say that they have transformed their timidity into strength, nor their falsehood into truth. Thus, for Nietzsche, truth remains a positive value: it is that which is life-enhancing—but not for everyone. Only that which is life-enhancing for the strong is to be denominated as the truth.

Although the preceding discussions have been concerned with "the limits of reason," I have not attempted to state what was common to the various positions I have examined, some of which were in complete and obvious opposition to one another. In fact, their presuppositions were so different that one might doubt there could have been any widely shared assumption, or common denominator, among them. Even if this had been so, and each had limited the scope of the human intellect in a wholly different way, the effect might have been cumulative, with each having given an added reason for challenging the intellectual powers of man. However, the sources of their criticisms were by no means so disparate as they initially seem.

While I should not wish to claim that there was any single assumption common to all of the nineteenth-century critics of the intellectual powers of man, I do find a characteristic which was very widespread in the thought of those with whom we have been concerned, and this particular feature tends to distinguish them from others, such as Locke and Hume and Kant, who had also set limits to the scope and powers of human reason. This feature is to be found in a distrust of the conceptual aspect of thought, a doubt that the concepts we employ in the sciences and in the practical affairs of everyday life are really adequate to the tasks which we ordinarily assume they perform. To be sure, none of the positions with which we have dealt denied that the conceptual element in empirical thought can be of use, in one way or another. The value attached to such uses varied, as we have seen, but all of those with whom we have been concerned agreed with respect to one point: our empirical concepts do not adequately delineate the characteristic features of what it is that we take them as representing. For example, our ordinary ways of conceptualizing experience were taken by some to be poor imitations of those species of knowledge which were genuine and concrete; they were regarded by others as ways in which, due to our limitations, we symbolize relationships which we cannot concretely apprehend; they were also interpreted as representing an order which we are led by our own needs to impose upon that which we experience. In none of these cases was conceptual knowledge claimed to be adequate, even by those who regarded it as the only knowledge we have.

We have seen the various arguments and motives which led a highly diverse group of thinkers to reach the foregoing conclusions, but I now wish to focus attention on a very specific point which helps to explain the fact that, in spite of their differences, they did reach this common negative conclusion. There was, I believe, a widely shared, but erroneous, philosophic assumption which made these attacks on the adequacy of our empirical concepts seem plausible, or even obviously true. In the Romantic movement in the late eighteenth and nineteenth centuries, and subsequently in other movements as well, it was assumed that genuine knowledge necessarily involves some form of immediate apprehension, in which what we know must be both directly present and grasped in concrete detail. On this view, if one is to know anything with which one is not presently in immediate contact, it must originally have been immediately known and must now be "*re*-presented," that is, brought back again, in its immediacy, in all of its concreteness. If one accepts this assumption, any knowledge which merely *represents* an object, without *re*-presenting it, is never adequate: it merely stands for, or symbolizes, that which we seek to know.

It is to a critical examination of this assumption, which was common to those whose views I have discussed, that I now wish to turn.

1. IN DEFENSE OF ABSTRACTIONS

I should not wish it supposed that I am ready to defend all abstractions, nor that I have sympathy with all cases in which abstractions have been used as counters in the processes of thought. The following defense of abstractions will be limited in scope. Essentially, it consists of two theses which, although independent, help reinforce one another. First, I shall point out that it is mistaken to suppose that the elementary data of direct experience include only what is concrete and particular, and not elements which are general in character, covering a range of instances. Then, I shall argue that when we deal with some of the qualities and relationships of objects or events in abstraction from others, we are not necessarily distorting the actual nature of that which we are seeking to understand.[1] If these two theses are accepted, the critiques of reason which have been examined will have lost much of their force.

Whether we take investigations of animal or of human discriminations as our point of departure, it is evident that, in many cases, what is immediately apprehended in direct sense experience are not the specific simple qualities which Locke, Berkeley, and Hume had regarded as the ultimate building blocks of knowledge. In the light of twentieth-century psychology, atomistic sensationalism must be abandoned, and whatever can be said to be "given" must be taken to have some degree of complexity, if it is to allow for the relational determination which is evident in all—or, to be cautious, in almost all—perceptual processes.[2] For example, we must now say that what is "given" in visual experience includes figure-ground relationships, and also includes contrasts of brightness and color; it includes patternings and groupings, and the texture of surfaces, as well as a host of other features for which the theories of Locke, Berkeley, and Hume had no adequate place. Nor is vision unique among the sense-modalities in this respect: in all cases, what is given cannot be reduced to simple ideas (or to what Hume termed simple impressions), atomistically conceived. It is precisely at this point, when we examine what must be regarded as directly given, and not inferred, that we discover how deceptive it is to contrast the immediacy of perception with the "abstractness" of concepts.

To illustrate this fact, let us consider characteristics of shape. It must surely be acknowledged that all animals, including men, discriminate some configural patterns from others without benefit of prior training; in fact, much subsequent learning is dependent upon a native ability to do so. However, in the apprehension of a pattern, what is very frequently discriminated is not that pattern in its specificity, but a configuration of a particular type, that is, one which covers a range of instances. Thus, for example, we discriminate horizontal patterns from vertical ones, or triangles from squares, or S-curves from circles, but what we notice in these discriminations is not necessarily that which is unique and distinctive in a particular instance, but what is characteristic of patterns of that type. In other words, perceptual experience does not necessarily consist of the awareness of a specific determinate quality, but is often the awareness of what W. E. Johnson designated as "a determinable":[3] that is to say, we are aware not of *this* triangular shape, but of the *triangularity* of this shape. Similarly, in the case of colors, we are often aware of something as being red, while not noticing the precise shade of its redness. Furthermore, we may have a more accurate impression of the relations between two qualities than we possess of the specific natures of these qualities themselves. For example, we may clearly perceive the difference in two shades of gray without being able to identify either shade when it is again presented. Such a direct and primitive apprehension of relationships, rather than an apprehension of the specific nature of presented qualia, may also be exemplified in sense-modalities other than vision, as is obvious when one considers our judgments of heavier-than, or louder-than, or the like.

All of these facts make it difficult to hold that, in sense experience, the given must be assumed to include only what is concrete and specific, and not traits which are general and apply to a wide range of instances. However, for those who may be unconvinced by appeals to psychological theory in questions which concern epistemological issues, a brief consideration of Berkeley's attack on abstract general ideas may prove useful.

In Section XII of the Introduction to his *Principles of Human Knowledge,* we find Berkeley offering the following account of how we arrive at general ideas:

> An idea, which considered in itself is particular, becomes general by being made to represent or stand for all other particular ideas of the *same sort.*

The italics, we may note, are those of Berkeley; nonetheless, he did not specify what he meant by the phrase "of the same sort." Furthermore, he did not comment on what is involved when we recognize that two particular ideas *are* of the same sort. To be sure, in the preceding paragraph he had said:

A word becomes general by being made the sign, not of an *abstract* general idea, but of several particular ideas, any one of which it indifferently suggests to the mind.

Although the qualifying adverb *"indifferently"* plays a crucial role in this sentence, its meaning is not wholly clear. While Berkeley might be taken to have meant that a word becomes general when it suggests *any* of a number of particular ideas to the mind, this interpretation is implausible, since a word may suggest a variety of utterly different ideas to the mind on different occasions. For example, in different contexts, "fire" may suggest ideas related to mortar-fire, or to a fire in a fireplace, or it may suggest "Run!". Rather than accept this implausible interpretation, the term "indifferently" must be taken to mean that a word becomes general *if it does not matter* which of several particulars its use suggests to the mind. If we then ask under what conditions this actually *is* a matter of indifference, the answer must be that it is indifferent only when the particular ideas are "of the same sort": that is, when they resemble one another in precisely that respect which the word is taken to signify. Thus, even though Berkeley avoided acknowledging the fact, his account of general ideas actually presupposed that we can and do recognize features which two or more particulars have in common. This involves acknowledging that general characteristics, such as "triangularity," and not merely specific particulars, such as *"this* figure" are immediately present and recognized in perceptual situations.

The significance of this conclusion is limited: it does not suggest that the resemblances and differences of which we take note in immediate experience provide the basis for *all* of the conceptual elements of which we make use in either the sciences or everyday life. It might therefore be argued that many of the latter do not reflect autochthonous elements within that which is experienced, but are determined by our needs, interests, biases, and socially acquired habits of mind. Nevertheless, although our conclusion is limited, it is not for that reason unimportant. The thesis that I have attempted to establish is that, even in those cases in which we may be said to have "knowledge-by-acquaintance," our experience is not confined to the specific and particular: general characteristics, or determinables, which are features common to a whole range of objects, are significant elements within direct experience, and are not addenda to it. Thus, although concepts are general, they need not for that reason be contrasted with that which is immediately *given.* Among them, some refer to characteristics which, although general, are as directly present to us as are any of the specific qualia in and through which we are aware of them.

To be sure, some critics of conceptual thought might acknowledge this fact and yet say that if we are to claim that we actually grasp the nature of a concrete individual thing, we must grasp it in its particularity and uniqueness: in so far as we describe it through the use of features which it has in common with a variety of other things, we are not really aware of *its* precise nature.

This conviction, rather than any theory of the actual origin of concepts, was undoubtedly what led Nietzsche to say that "every concept originates through equating what is unequal."[4] In a similar vein, Bergson contended that

> The concept can symbolize a particular property only by making it common to an infinity of things. Therefore it always more or less distorts this property by the extension it gives to it.[5]

Shortly thereafter, in a related passage, he said:

> An empiricism worthy of the name, an empiricism which works only according to measure, sees itself obliged to make an absolutely new effort for each new object it studies. It cuts for the object a concept appropriate to the object alone, a concept one can barely say is still a concept, since it applies only to that one thing.[6]

If this view were to be accepted, conceptual thought could never adequately grasp concrete existents; and this conclusion was, of course, precisely the one that Nietzsche and Bergson, among others, sought to maintain. However, if one asks how it might be shown that conceptual thought necessarily distorts the nature of that which exists, the answer is obvious: we must possess another means of knowing objects in their full, concrete actuality. Both Nietzsche and Bergson believed that we do possess such means.

It is not part of my present purpose to criticize their views regarding the sources of the knowledge upon which they felt it necessary to rely: to do so would lead us far afield, since Nietzsche and Bergson were not in agreement with respect to the nature of this knowledge, and if we were to consider the views of Schopenhauer, or of Maine de Biran, further difficulties would arise. However, there was one assumption which was common to their views, and was also characteristic of Hegel and Kierkegaard: each held that whatever is ultimately real cannot be decomposed into a multiplicity of independently variable aspects or parts.[7] From this conviction each drew the inference that reality cannot be grasped through concepts, since any concept refers to only one of the many aspects of any existing object. Conceptual thought must therefore proceed in piecemeal fashion, considering first one and then another of the various aspects or relationships of those objects with which it seeks to deal. But this, it is claimed, is precisely what destroys the unity of that which is real.

It must immediately be pointed out that this inference is fallacious. The unity of objects, or the interpenetration of their parts, does not entail that knowledge of such objects will necessarily be inadequate if acquired through first considering one aspect of the object and then another, tracing each of the interrelationships of these aspects as they exist in the whole. The assumption that such knowledge is necessarily inadequate rests on a confusion in which it is supposed that whatever is true of an object must also be true of our knowledge concerning that object.

It is not difficult to show this supposition to be mistaken: if it were accepted it would lead to ludicrous conclusions. For example, I may know that an object weighs two pounds, but my knowledge weighs nothing at all. Similarly, I may know that I am now at home, sitting at my desk, and that yesterday I was in New York; however, to *know* this is not itself a matter of either sitting or traveling. Or, if these illustrations should be rejected as frivolous, one need merely point out that, when we come to know that some specific event occurred in the past, the date and the location at which that occurrence took place are different from the date and place at which we have acquired our knowledge concerning it. Once we draw this necessary distinction between characteristics pertaining to our knowledge and the characteristics of that which we know, the inference drawn by Bergson and others can be seen to be illegitimate: it does not follow from the fact that an object may not be made up of independently variable aspects or parts, that our knowledge of such an object cannot be made up of a series of independently known propositions referring to these aspects or parts.

In order to illustrate the contrast between the characteristics of knowledge and the features of that to which knowledge refers, let us briefly consider how it is that we gain knowledge of any object which has a high degree of internal relatedness among its parts—for example, a complex living thing. We may agree that if we were to attempt to *decompose* any complex organism by breaking it up into separate parts, we should have destroyed it. Furthermore, we may fully recognize that the attempt to alter some one of its parts would involve altering the characteristics possessed by many, or all, of its other parts. Nevertheless, our *knowledge* of its nature does not constitute the same sort of unitary whole. This may be suggested in at least two different ways. First, our knowledge concerning how organisms function, and how various of their parts are interrelated, has increased bit by bit, by a process of accretion, as biology, biochemistry, and biophysics have advanced. These advances have, in many cases, established the existence of previously unsuspected interrelationships among the parts of organisms: one case in point might be the growth of our knowledge of the regulatory functions of the endocrine glands. The demonstration of such interrelationships should be welcomed by those who insist on the unity of the organism as a whole. Yet the fact that these results have been achieved in a step-by-step fashion illustrates the difference between the characteristics of our knowledge and the characteristics of those objects and events which we seek to know: the growth of knowledge proceeds piecemeal, and will doubtless always remain incomplete, but that which we seek to know does not change its characteristics as our knowledge of it continues to grow.

A second way in which it may be shown that we must distinguish between the characteristics of our knowledge and the characteristics of that to which our knowledge refers lies in the fact that, even when we are dealing with objects such as organisms which have a high degree of internality of relationship among their parts, it is not only legitimate but necessary to consider their various features individually, in abstraction from one another, rather than to attempt to understand the object in all of its concreteness, as a single individual whole. This may be illustrated by the fact that, if we are to establish some specific interrelationship between, say, the functioning of heart and lungs, we must examine their functioning in a variety of different cases, in abstraction from whatever other differences may be present in these cases. For example, we must show that regardless of differences in skin color, or body weight, or differences between male and female—and, indeed, regardless of whether the subject is a human or non-human primate—the ways in which heart and lungs function are mutually dependent. This signifies that, in order to establish this close mutual dependence between two organs, we must consider these organs in abstraction from many of the other characteristics of the organism. In fact, if one were to reject all attempts at abstraction, regarding such abstractions as necessarily involving distortions of what actually exists, one could not establish the correct belief that the parts of many wholes do interact in specific ways, and one would have no basis for saying that their functioning *as wholes* depends upon a specific set of complex interactions among their parts.

The distinction which is to be drawn between the unity which may characterize any object and the ways in which we discover this unity might be illustrated in a host of other ways, but I shall select only one. I shall choose an example from perception. It is a fact that there are many cases in which some of the discriminable features of a perceived object affect one another, and yet we are only able to discover their connection by considering these features separately, relying upon precisely the sort of abstractive method of analysis which Nietzsche and Bergson, among others, would have us shun.

Such a case is as follows. We all know that, in attempting to match a color, the perceived shade of the color may vary according to the size of the sample, most colors appearing darker in small samples than large. The fact of this relationship—and of analogous relationships between size and shape, or, in tones, between pitch and loudness—does not mean that color and size, shape and size, or pitch and loudness are not discerned as different discriminable aspects of what we perceive. They clearly are, yet they also affect one another. When, in our example, we place the large and the small samples of the color side by side, we recognize them to be identical in shade; we then attribute our original mistake to the difference in the sizes of the samples, and not to a difference in their color. Thus, our grasp of the interrelationship between different attributes of a particular object involves abstraction from the object itself and consideration of its abstracted aspects under alternative sets of conditions. It is not immediate perception, apart from abstraction, nor is it immediate intuition that serves to reveal the hidden interplay of a perceived object's various attributes. Rather, it is through a comparison of instances with respect to some of their features, and not with respect to others, that we must in such cases proceed. Thus, although the various perceived characteristics of an object may be intimately connected, and mutually dependent, our knowledge of these connections is in most cases acquired piecemeal, by abstraction, comparison, and generalization: in short, in precisely those ways which were disparaged by Nietzsche and Bergson, and by others before them who rejected the methods by means of which the analytic intellect proceeds.

Bearing in mind what I take it we may now regard as established—that a distinction is to be drawn between the characteristics of objects and our knowledge of these objects—we may return to a fact which has previously been noted: that, in direct experience, we are aware of general characteristics or determinables, and not merely of specific determinate qualia. Returning to this point, we are in a position to say that, while it is doubtless true that *objects* have determinate qualities, our *knowledge* need not be considered inaccurate because it does not include or reproduce these qualia, but deals with the determinables which are presented in and through them. Of course, if a person were to claim that he had, in his mind's eye, a perfect replica of that which he had experienced, then his claim would be well-founded only if he did possess such an image, which was accurate down to the least detail. However, the knowledge which we claim concerning any object is rarely, if ever, of this kind. That fact may be illustrated by the following example which, although trivial, not only can serve to suggest that our claims to knowledge do not depend upon our being able to conjure up exact images of what we have experienced, but will also serve to emphasize once again that what is true of an object need not be true concerning our knowledge of that object.

On my desk there is a stapler which I recently bought, and which I used only a moment ago. I have a rough idea of how heavy it feels; I know that I would say that its color is grey; I can quite clearly recall the sort of sound it usually makes when I use it, and I can recognize another slightly different sound which signifies to me that I have just used the last staple it contains. I also have an idea of its shape and its size, and I could draw a rough sketch of its approximate outline. I know that it is a Bostitch stapler, and I assume that the name is imprinted somewhere on it, but I do not know how or where. I know something about its parts, but some are bolted together, and I do not know what is concealed; and even among those parts which I can see, and which I have now carefully inspected, there are some whose functions I do not understand.

In the foregoing remarks it should not be difficult to say where I am laying claim to knowledge, and where I am not. I can be said to know that my stapler is grey, and that it is relatively heavy compared with one which I formerly owned. However, when I claim that I know this much about it, I am not claiming to have so precise an idea of its color that I could pick out a shade of grey which would exactly match it, nor that I can recall just which of its parts are chrome, and not grey. Nor do I claim to have an accurate recollection of the exact shape and size of the stapler, nor of its heft. Thus, what I may be said to know about such an object is not necessarily determined by the clarity and the detail of the images which I can conjure up when I try to picture it. What I know respecting these characteristics may be said to be *general*: it is a knowledge of the general features of the object, not a knowledge of its precise details. Such knowledge is also in one sense *relative*: it is accurate only to the extent that it correctly states the difference between this particular object and other objects which differ from it in color, in shape and size, and in weight. However, knowledge which is both general and relative, in these senses, may in another sense be both precise and absolute: the claim I make that, for example, my stapler is grey, and not brown or green, is a very specific claim about this particular stapler, and it is a claim which is not to be interpreted as being anything less than exactly true.

The same point may be made with reference to other aspects of what I claim to know about the stapler, and what I admit that I do not know. When, for example, I say that it is a Bostitch stapler, my knowledge is also general and relative, for I know nothing about the manufacturer except this brand name, and I use the name only to distinguish the type of stapler I own from those bearing other names. Yet, this is knowledge which, in another sense, is also both precise and absolute: it is knowledge on which I can rely when I next buy a box of staples. Furthermore, the fact that I know my stapler is a Bostitch, and yet do not know how or where the name is imprinted on it, clearly shows that not all of our knowledge is directly related to our ability to conjure up distinct images of what can be learned through sense-experience. This fact is even more obvious in my statement that I have inspected all of the visible parts of the stapler, and I do not understand the functions which some of them serve. Any knowledge of an instrument, such as a stapler, must be said to include some knowledge of how its parts function when it performs whatever it was designed to do. However, even in the case of so simple an instrument as a stapler, this is not knowledge which comes through inspection alone; it presupposes familiarity with the ways in which objects of various kinds interact; it is quite general, and is of the sort with which, in more exact form, the science of mechanics is concerned. Such knowledge, being general, involves an appeal to determinables, and does not merely refer to what is true of an object having precisely these determinate characteristics. Nor should it be thought—as followers of Nietzsche and Bergson might be inclined to suppose—that this is true only in those cases in which we are dealing with mechanical contrivances: it is equally true of our getting to know how the organs of living things function, for this knowledge, too, does not come through immediate experience alone.

From the foregoing illustration we can extract the conclusion that knowing is not to be identified with directly apprehending objects in all their specificity, in complete and concrete detail; it is often a matter of understanding their relations to other things, how they function under different conditions, and the like. To be sure, there are occasions when the clarity, the accuracy, and the degree of specificity of our images *are* highly important to us; they are important when, for example, we are trying to sort objects which closely resemble one another, or when we wish to buy something which will be aesthetically congruous with objects we already possess. On the other hand, primary importance often attaches to the recognition of the generic characteristics of an object: to know in advance what is to be expected of something, we must know what has occurred when other things of the same type have been placed in similar situations. Thus, what we seek to know is frequently directed toward what is common to many instances, not what is confined to any one case. While it would be arbitrary to hold that such is always our goal, it would be equally arbitrary to claim that we have knowledge only if we are able to grasp the concrete individuality of specific instances in all of their detail.

Once this is recognized, it is not necessary to treat with distrust those determinables which I should be inclined to call "perceptual universals." To be sure, they are *general*; however, as we have just remarked, not all knowledge involves the possession of exact replicas of objects before the mind's eye. Furthermore, they may be *relative*, for they may only be precise to the extent that they allow us to know an object in terms of the ways in which it resembles or differs from others; nevertheless, in recognizing the similarities and differences which are present in objects, we can be said to have knowledge of these objects. Nor need perceptual universals be distrusted because they refer only to certain aspects of objects, and are thus *"abstractions"*: there is much that I can know about any object without knowing everything that is to be known about it—I may know its color better than I know its shape, or its shape better than its color, and I can also know how some parts of it function without knowing the functions which other parts perform. This may even be true, as we have noted, in those cases in which the parts are connected, and might not be able to function independently. There is surely nothing surprising about this fact, once one recognizes that the characteristics of our knowledge need not be the same as the characteristics which are possessed by the actually existing objects to which our knowledge refers.

There have been those in the history of thought who reject such a view, insisting that to have knowledge is to become one with the object, whether through loss of self as in the mystic experience or through self-assertion and an act of appropriation. Bergson and Nietzsche are striking examples of these disparate ways of emphasizing immediacy, but each type of position can be held in less extreme forms. For example, the Bergsonian contrast between intuition and intellect had a milder counterpart in Dilthey's distinction between understanding *(Verstehen)* and explanation *(Erklärung)*; surprisingly enough, one can also note a resemblance between Nietzsche's assumptions concerning knowledge and the views of Croce and Collingwood regarding what is essential if we are to understand the past. However, the full force of the doctrine of immediacy, and an accompanying disdain for conceptual knowledge, has only been felt where the existentialist movement, with reliance upon Kierkegaard as well as upon Nietzsche, has gained a dominant position in twentieth-century thought. Yet, in one form or another, a distrust of conceptual knowledge has become characteristic of much recent thought: it has come to be widely claimed, in a variety of different contexts, that we only make use of abstractions, and that we only appeal to common traits within that which we experience, in order to render experience manageable. In short, it is assumed that we overlook the concrete in favor of the general, and we neglect the unique for the repeatable, only for the sake of an economy of thought which is directed not to understanding but to practice. When a view of this type is accepted, both the generalizations upon which we rely in daily life, and the generalizations which it is crucial for the sciences to attain, are construed as reflections of subjective interests and needs, projected onto nature; they are not accepted as reflections of traits which belong to the world, being present whether we know them or not.

While there are many factors which help to explain why this general doctrine has become so widely diffused in contemporary thought, there is one which should not be overlooked: positivism itself turned toward a pragmatic-economical view of thought. Thus, we again find an instance in which philosophically incompatible tendencies within the nineteenth century served to reinforce each other, combining their influences to create a climate of opinion which, in this case, continues to maintain much of its authority today.

To be sure, when Ernst Mach and other positivists put forward a pragmatic-economical interpretation of thought, they did not do so for the sake of making room for an alternative method of knowledge; rather, Mach sought to loosen the bonds of common-sense assumptions and give the sciences free play to organize all experience in whatever ways might prove to be scientifically most fruitful. It was precisely this fact which has since provided arguments for those who wish to attack the adequacy of scientific modes of explanation: what is *scientifically* most fruitful need not, they claim, be identified with what is true. This form of argument has often been supported by appealing to evolutionary considerations not wholly different from those to which Mach appealed: the human mind is an instrument which serves to fulfill our needs, and cannot be regarded as an organ whose purpose it is to reveal the essential structure of the world.[8] Of course, Mach rejected the supposition that, independently of human experience, there is any such structure inherent in nature to which knowledge must seek to conform. On his view, it is solely with respect to how successfully the organization of experience fulfils our needs that truth and falsity are to be judged. It is this cardinal tenet of Mach's view that I here wish to challenge. Of course, it is not possible at this point to examine all of the major philosophical issues which such a question involves, but there is, I believe, one relatively simple method of undercutting his position by showing that his assumption of two fundamentally different ways of organizing experience, corresponding to two different types of need, is false.

It will be recalled that Mach's analysis of experience aimed at overcoming the common-sense assumptions which he regarded as standing in the way of a unification of physics, psychology, and physiology. Chief among them was the distinction which we ordinarily draw between the self and material objects. To overcome this distinction Mach argued that all material objects are merely relatively permanent complexes of the simple elements of experience, and the self is only another such complex. Thus, it was not necessary to regard different sciences as dealing with fundamentally different kinds of data; psychology, physics, and physiology differed only with respect to which sets of relationships among these elements were selected for investigation. In such investigations, scientists were to confine themselves to what is directly observable, that is, to actual elements present in experience; for example, Mach claimed that physicists should not appeal to inferred entities, such as atoms, in order to explain the relations among the phenomena they observe. He held that, if the sciences succeeded in purging themselves of all metaphysical assumptions, the relationships which they would be able to establish would cohere in a single unified system.[9]

Had this unity actually been achieved, it would have been purchased at a considerable cost, since it would have engendered a severe conflict between scientific modes of explanation and beliefs which we regard as fundamental in everyday life. Of course, there are conflicts between the sciences and our ordinary beliefs which are not particularly troublesome: anyone can think of instances in which he has accepted a scientific explanation even though it conflicted with a belief which had always seemed to him obviously true. In such cases, what is involved is merely giving up one belief for another. What Mach regarded as "metaphysical" in our ordinary conception of the world was the basic assumption that there are material objects existing in their own right, independently of experience, and that much of our experience itself depends upon them. Thus, what he asked that we relinquish were not merely particular beliefs about specific matters of fact, but the entire framework into which all aspects of our ordinary conceptions of experience fit. Mach was not, of course, unaware of how drastic a change he was introducing into conventional patterns of thought; he was, in fact, anxious to accept it as a means of bringing about a unification of the sciences. However, in his analysis of this change, he failed to take note of some of the consequences which his position actually entailed.

To become aware of these consequences, one should first note that the scientist himself lives in the everyday world. This is not only true whenever he is outside his study or his laboratory, but is also true when he is working in them: his pen, his desk, his laboratory equipment, all appear to him as permanent material objects, existing in their own right. Furthermore, the objects on which he performs his experiments are not the ultimate "elements" of which Mach spoke, for we never encounter any such element except as being embedded with other elements in a complex whole. Thus, when Mach remarks that in physics one correlates a color with a luminous source, his statement stands in need of expansion: what is correlated is the color-aspect of a surface, located at a particular place, with some aspect of the light originating from a particular source, such as a sodium lamp or a lithium lamp. Similarly, when one correlates the color which one sees with the stimulation of the retina, which is identified by Mach as a specifically psychological problem, one is again not speaking of a correlation between two ultimately simple, immediately presented "elements," but is speaking of some aspect of the relationship between a visible surface and light focussed on the retina after having been reflected from that surface.[10] Thus, the correlation of elements, which Mach considered to be the essential task of any science, actually takes place within a more complex matrix of relationships. When this is recognized, and one does not speak as if the sciences correlated free-floating, isolated bits of experience called "elements," there is in fact no such sharp contrast as that which Mach drew between the ways in which the sciences organize experience, and the basic patterns in which objects appear to us to be organized in everyday life.

In addition to Mach's misleading characterization of the sciences as dealing only with relationships among *"elements,"* there is a further feature of his discussions of scientific inquiry which tends to conceal the similarities which exist between the organization of our everyday experience and the relationships with which the sciences deal. In stressing the unity of the sciences, Mach spoke of how the differences between physics, psychology, and physiology were simply differences in the ways each organized experience, not differences in the ultimate nature of the materials with which they dealt. At least so far as the present discussion is concerned, let this contention be granted. In granting it, we are not committed to any particular view regarding the ways in which physical, psychological, and physiological explanations are themselves related. Therefore, even though it may be true that the materials of all three sciences are similar, and all three types of explanation can consequently fall into place within a single system, the relationships among these types of explanation might be determined by the nature of experience, and not be under our control. Yet Mach's discussion of the unity of the sciences never brings this fact to light. In speaking of how one can pass back and forth among the sciences, first establishing one set of relationships among elements and then establishing another, he did not point out that, when we come to link up these relationships with one another, there is in each instance a definite order in which we must proceed, regardless of what had been the order of their discovery. For example, in the case already mentioned, in which one correlates red with the fact that the luminous source is a lithium and not a sodium lamp (a physical explanation), and one also correlates the sensation of red with retinal stimulation (a psychological explanation), these explanations are coherent: *however,* they are only coherent if ordered in an appropriate way. It is not the sensation red, as correlated with retinal stimulation, nor is it the red surface that I see, which is used to explain the luminous source. In fact, it is clear although it is not made explicit in Mach's own account that the luminous source provides the explanation of the color, of the retinal stimulation, and of the sensation "red." When the existence of such an order is recognized, the supposed disparities between the organization of our everyday experience and the organization of the elements of experience by the sciences tend to disappear.

In considering Mach's general position, it becomes apparent that one reason why he insisted so strongly on there being a fundamental difference between the forms of organization characteristic of the world as it appears in everyday experience and the relationships which scientists discover when they analyze experience was that he believed that our ordinary experience is dominated by the practical adaptive needs of the organism, whereas thought in the sciences is dominated by purely theoretic needs.[11] If this contrast were accepted, there would, in fact, be two different and fundamentally opposed accounts of the relationships among the elements given in experience, and two different and opposed criteria of truth. Mach often spoke as if this were so, and one can see how easy it is to fall into this manner of speaking when one contrasts all that we take for granted in ordinary experience with the careful way in which individual factors are isolated and analyzed in the experimental sciences. Regardless of this contrast, it is not reasonable to suppose that there is in fact an opposition between the patterns of thought and standards of truth used in laboratories, and the ways in which we think and sift evidence in the ordinary concerns of everyday life. Clearly, scientists do not lead a Dr. Jekyll–Mr. Hyde existence: if they did, this fact would be thoroughly familiar through the accounts of scientific inquiry which have been written by practicing scientists. Also, it is clear that the problems scientists set themselves often arise in the course of everyday experience; furthermore, in a vast majority of cases, one test of the answers which are proposed is whether they are confirmed by direct experience. Nevertheless, Mach was insistent that the world of science should be kept separate from the everyday world. One reason was his belief that the explanation of why the world appears to us as it does in everyday experience is to be found in the Darwinian theory: were it not for our *vital needs*, our sensations would not be grouped as they are, as if they constituted objects independent of us, and so on. On the other hand, scientists structure experience in terms of specifically *scientific needs*, not as a means of adjustment. Therefore, Mach held that the two worlds must be kept separate.

However, this is a most implausible account of why our experience is organized as it is. It would only be tenable if one were to assume that the way in which the world appears to us is a cumulative heritage, bequeathed to us by the experiences of our remote ancestors: no individual, in the course of his own early development, would be able to acquire, through a process of trial and error, the complex structuring of experience which Mach describes as characteristic of our everyday beliefs. To be sure, the fact that we survive does show that the way in which we apprehend the world is not disastrously maladaptive. However, in seeking to explain why, in everyday experience, the world appears as it does, one should not resort to general speculation concerning the evolutionary process: instead, one should make use of the experimental findings of the interlocking sciences of physics, physiology, and psychology, since it is a false interpretation of Darwinian theory to assume that whatever does in fact serve our practical needs must have originated in order to do so.[12]

The foregoing considerations should serve to cast considerable doubt on Mach's assumption that the element of order in our experience, whether in the sciences or in everyday life, is a function of our own purposes or needs. At the same time, they lend support to the views of Helmholtz and Spencer, both of whom held that there are close connections between the order which is present in everyday experience and the forms of order which can be established by the empirical sciences. Unlike Mach, they treated these connections as causal: our experience reflects relationships which exist in nature because it is upon the existence of these relationships that the structure of experience depends. Once this view had been accepted by them, it may seem surprising that both Helmholtz and Spencer should have insisted that we can never justifiably claim to know what nature is truly like in itself. Their argument was based on the fact that, as soon as nature is reflected within our experience, we know only what we experience, not nature itself.[13] They justified this restrictive argument by holding that, since all knowledge is ultimately based upon sense-experience, it will be limited by, and in fact be determined by, the nature of our sense-organs. Therefore, when we take into account the fact that we might have had quite different sense-organs, which would have pictured the world in quite different ways, it is not legitimate for us to assume that the world, in itself, has those particular characteristics which we are inclined to attribute to it.[14]

This theme is a familiar one, but taken as an argument regarding the limits of knowledge, it is not—as I shall show—one which either Helmholtz or Spencer should have used. Nor would they have used it, had they not shared the common assumption that all *"genuine"* knowledge must include an immediate apprehension of something directly given, that is, an intuition of the concrete, and not merely an understanding of relationships which have been established by inference. Kant, it will be recalled, had held that concepts are empty whenever they lack concrete content furnished by sensibility, and in this respect Helmholtz's views replicated his: since we do not directly apprehend the relationships which underlie the forms of order present within our experience, we cannot be said to *know* these relationships, no matter how well attested their modes of operation may be. In the case of Spencer, the same assumption was operative. He held that we constantly attempt to stretch what was originally presented in sense-experience, but the symbolic conceptions we form only maintain their validity in so far as a concrete, sensuous element is still included in them. Thus, for both Helmholtz and Spencer, the fact that what we directly experience is relative to the nature of our sensing organs led to the conclusion (without further argument) that we can never adequately grasp the nature of objects as they exist in their own right, independently of us.

This was a strange and, indeed, a self-contradictory conclusion for them to have drawn. Both Helmholtz and Spencer had insisted that what we directly experience never portrays the characteristics of that which exists independently of us. This fact they took to have been adequately established by the combined efforts of the sciences. However, having trusted the inferential methods of the sciences to establish this point, both Helmholtz and Spencer then reversed themselves and spoke as if it were a *defect* in knowledge that we do not directly experience the world as it exists independently of us. Instead of speaking in this way, it would have been more consistent, and also more accurate, if each had given praise to the sciences for having established the fact that it is only through inquiry and inference, and not through direct experience, that we attain precise and well-authenticated knowledge of those relationships which give structure to nature and define our own place in the world.

Perhaps it is too much to expect that they should have done so, for it is difficult to acknowledge that beliefs which rest only on inference, and which must be acknowledged to be fragmentary in their scope, can not only be more inclusive, but also more accurate and detailed, than beliefs which appear as self-authenticating because they refer to our immediate experience. Yet, if we do not falsely identify the characteristics of knowledge with the characteristics of that which we seek to know, there is no reason to assume that scientific knowledge distorts reality merely because it does not reproduce it; nor any reason to suppose that we should be able to say in advance that there are limits beyond which it would be impossible to extend our knowledge of ourselves and the world.

2. A CRITIQUE OF VOLUNTARISM

It is now time to turn from the widespread dissatisfaction with man's reason which was based on a distrust of conceptual thought, and consider the radical voluntarism which, although it was to be found in only a few nineteenth-century thinkers, has subsequently become a powerful intellectual influence on our time.

In the last half-century the rebellion against reason has taken many forms; to an alarming degree, unreason may be said to have permeated our lives. To what extent this could have been due to the theories with which I shall here be dealing, I am unprepared to say. Many who write intellectual history seem to attribute a direct social efficacy to ideas which I find it doubtful that ideas, in most cases, possess. However, it is undeniable that the ideas with which we shall now be concerned have had a considerable influence, for they have become standard assumptions in many disciplines, and have directly and profoundly influenced literature, religion, and the arts. Under these circumstances, it is surely the case that their effects, channeled through these media, have been felt in more ways, and in subtler forms, than one can now readily trace.[15] It is no part of my task to show how this may have come about. The view with which I am here concerned is restricted in scope, no matter how widespread its ramifications have been. What I wish to consider is the doctrine represented in different forms by Schopenhauer, Kierkegaard, and Nietzsche, that our thought is always to be interpreted in terms of its relation to the goals of the will.

This doctrine had obvious, even though mistaken, connections with nineteenth-century evolutionary theory; these connections will later occupy us. However, if we are to understand its present influence, we must connect it with two more recent tendencies which have, for some time, dominated psychology. The first has been the assumption that motivational forces underlie all other psychological processes, exerting a hidden but controlling influence on them. It has been because of this assumption that psychological views such as those held by Schopenhauer, Kierkegaard, and Nietzsche have not only been revived but have seemed to be of special contemporary relevance. In this revival it has been necessary to excise the metaphysical pessimism of Schopenhauer, the Hegelian background of Kierkegaard, and the egoism of Nietzsche, in order to refashion their thought to the mood of the times. What has not needed alteration has been their anti-intellectualism, their insistence that reason is not, and cannot be, disinterested. That this insistence should have struck a familiar chord is understandable when one considers recent psychology. Not only has the widespread influence of Freudian theory made this seem obviously true, but experiment after experiment has been designed to show the ways in which motivational factors influence perception and learning, and only rarely has emphasis been placed on the ways in which motivation is relative to that which is perceived, and to that which is believed.

In addition, under the influence of Freud, and under the quite different influence of Dewey, personality theory and American social psychology have emphasized the view that human nature is not to be understood in terms of specific, discrete modes of reaction, but as a whole. In such a whole, the elements have been taken to be mutually dependent and mutually compensatory. This has led to an almost wholesale rejection of earlier views, which had accepted a variety of motivational forces, largely independent of one another. When the autonomy of different facets of human nature is minimized in this way, and when this doctrine is coupled with a motivational bias, it becomes obvious that thought must be interpreted in terms of that which satisfies the needs of the self: any independence which we are inclined to ascribe to our thought-processes, and which they often seem to possess, will be denied. Because of this denial, the psychological views of Schopenhauer, Kierkegaard, and Nietzsche appear up-to-date, even though—if one examines their views in any detail—their assumptions and arguments are riddled with error.[16] In what follows, I shall not be concerned with such errors; rather, I wish to deal with the central thesis itself—that we must assume thought to be dominated by the forces of will.

There are many ways in which such a position can be criticized. The particular path which I here wish to follow is to show that it is not plausible to assume that all of the characteristics of human nature are to be interpreted as expressions of any single underlying force, such as voluntarism identifies with "the will." As I have already pointed out, it is mistaken to assume that we can explain either animal or human behavior without appealing to a plurality of drives, propensities, needs, or desires.[17] In that connection I used curiosity as an example of an autonomous motivational factor on the basis of which experiments in animal conditioning have been successfully carried out.[18] Once we regard curiosity in this way (and if we can assume that members of the human species also, under some conditions, behave in a way that exhibits curiosity), then the interest which we take in our environment need not be construed as an expression of some other, more basic, practical or psychic need. Curiosity would itself be one of our propensities, and its satisfaction would be a need. Or, if one wishes to avoid the term "curiosity," then the exploratory behavior or inquisitiveness of animals and of humans might be substituted for it: the need to satisfy these propensities would not call for further explanation in terms of the concept of "will." Thus, on the view I am here suggesting, I am not seeking to get rid of the hormic side of behavior: on the contrary, in these particular cases I am emphasizing it.[19] What I am rejecting is the appeal to a further explanation of these propensities through invoking some different and supposedly more basic propensity. In short, I wish to hold that they—no less than hunger and thirst—may be regarded as autonomous.[20]

This, I submit, is wholly in line with evolutionary theory. To be sure, there was a time when it was held that most (or all) specific drives, such as hunger and thirst, are expressions of another more basic instinct, the instinct of self-preservation. One even finds that Darwin occasionally used that term. However, there was a basic confusion in appeals to an instinct of self-preservation: that which followed from being able to satisfy a drive was mistakenly regarded as the goal of the drive itself. To illustrate the distinction that should have been drawn, one may note that we do not normally eat in order to preserve our lives, but the fact that hunger leads us to eat does serve to keep us alive. Similarly, it is not in order to preserve the human race that we have sexual relations, although it is true that the continuity of the human race depends upon the existence of sexual impulses. In fact, it was never made clear just how the generalized instinct of self-preservation in the individual, or in the race, was related to specific instincts or drives; furthermore, it would be difficult to think of any inherited mechanism which could be responsible for self-preserving actions which are as different from one another as are eating and sleeping or breathing and jumping out of the path of an oncoming vehicle.

Fortunately, we are no longer forced to cope with those who appealed to an instinct of self-preservation to account for the actual behavior of animals or men. However, another form of pseudo-teleology is still to be found in popular thought concerning evolutionary theory. It consists in the assumption that traits only originate and become established in so far as they have some value as a means to survival; therefore, their continued presence suggests that, if we are to understand them, we must do so with reference to biologically based needs. Applying this position to human thought, our intellectual capacities would have to be interpreted in terms of the needs they fulfill: they would have to be regarded as tools for survival. Thus, thought would be viewed not in terms of ends of its own, but in terms of what it contributes to various forms of adjustment.

This widely held view, which has long been associated with evolutionary theory, does not in fact derive any support from that theory. Any propensity, or other trait, might arise and be preserved even if it failed to contribute to the adjustment of a specific type of organism in its environment. As Darwin himself came to recognize, it is not necessary that a particular trait have positive survival-value;[21] the theory of natural selection only requires that none of the traits which characterize a species shall have consequences which consistently interfere with the survival and the self-reproduction of individuals possessing those traits. Seen from this point of view, it should be obvious that curiosity might be a basic and enduring characteristic of animals and men, whether or not it had any positive survival-value for the species possessing it. All that evolutionary theory requires is that—in any given environment—curiosity, or any similar trait, should not have consequences which markedly interfere with the continuing survival and the self-reproduction of individuals possessing that trait.

Once this lesson has been learned, much that has been written concerning the intellect as a tool for survival will be acknowledged to need re-thinking. However, not all who have stressed the practical nature of thought, and the influences which our needs, our desires, and our values have upon it, have emphasized merely biological survival. Thus, we shall have to consider their views in more general terms, and not with special emphasis on evolutionary theory.

Let us then go back to the point which I earlier made: that we cannot interpret animal or human behavior without appealing to a plurality of drives, propensities, needs, or desires. Not all of these will, of course, have anything to do with understanding man's intellectual powers. However, if we may assume curiosity to be one among the native propensities of man, it would presumably be a factor to take into account when analyzing the nature of thought. Naturally, it would not have to be considered the only such factor. It might, for example, elicit a process of thought without controlling it. Furthermore, it might not be the only factor capable of eliciting thought, and I should reject the assumption that it is. For example, there obviously are cases in which thought is called forth by our need to escape from some situation which is immediately painful. In other cases it may be oriented toward remote ends, and its function may be to calculate the means by which these ends can be attained. In still other cases we may merely be curious. That it may be mere curiosity which, in some cases, originally arouses thought can be illustrated by two well-known examples which Dewey used for another purpose: (a) we may seek to understand why, in the bow of a ferry-boat, there is an odd sort of pole, resembling a flagpole, but jutting out almost horizontally; or (b) we may be curious to know why, when one is washing dishes, soap bubbles first form outside the rim of an inverted glass and then slip back into it.[22] While both examples were designed by Dewey to establish the view that thinking is problem-solving, they also show that, in some cases, it may be nothing more than curiosity which originally sets the problem which is to be solved.

At this point, we can take one further step which leads even farther from the goal-oriented interpretation of thought which Dewey, as well as the radical voluntarists, held to be true. What we have termed "curiosity" may be viewed as a hormic aspect of man's nature, that is, as some form of propensity or drive. However, like other propensities and drives in human and animal nature, it is not always present and active; it often evinces itself only when it is triggered by a factor in the environment. For example, although it is true that we begin looking for food when we are hungry, it is also sometimes the case that the sight of food leads to a craving to eat; similarly, the sex drive of animals is, in many cases, triggered by very specific perceptual cues. When we consider the case of curiosity, the strangeness of an object may be one such cue. This, however, directly relates the source of our curiosity to our knowledge and our beliefs, *not* to another propensity, drive, or need. This illustration, however crude, can serve as a paradigmatic case of the manner in which our motivation is often directly affected by our immediate perception and by what we have learned. Such cases stand in contrast to those occasions in which motivation is basic, modifying both perception and learning. As I have pointed out, recent psychology has unfortunately tended to emphasize only the latter sort of case.

In opposition to this tendency, we may further note that whatever may be the inciting reasons for our thinking, the manner in which thought actually proceeds is not necessarily a function of the factors which served to evoke it. When we try to extricate ourselves from a painful situation, we may need to rely on conjectures, assumptions, a careful scrutiny of evidence, deductive inference, and the like, no less than when we are attempting to solve a scientific problem. This fact is important to note, for it indicates that, in interpreting the nature of thought, one cannot assume that what gives rise to it will also control it. Thus, even if (contrary to fact) it were true that the source of all thinking lies in the will, neither the way that we think, nor what determines the validity of our thought, can be assumed to be determined by characteristics of willing. To be sure, what has been referred to as "the will" may sometimes lead us to accept or reject the conclusions of our thought: some thoughts are—sometimes, for some persons—too unpalatable to bear, and they are denied in one way or another. Here, it would seem, the will exerts itself, just as Schopenhauer, Kierkegaard, and Nietzsche insisted. However, it would obviously be false to attribute all error to the effects of the will, as if fatigue, or dizziness, or arteriosclerosis had no consequences for thinking.[23] It would be even more misguided to forget that we draw a distinction between valid and invalid forms of thinking. Schopenhauer himself acknowledged the distinction, although he held, as we have seen, that in the end the demands of the will overcome the intellect. Kierkegaard, in his own way, also recognized a domain in which the intellect was, for a time, free of the influence of the will, that is, when our thought is directed to possibilities only, not to existence. However, both rejected the principles which guide thought in these realms, regarding these principles as being out of touch with reality. In part, this was because they insisted that there must be a fundamental unity in the nature of man: one force alone must dominate him. Since it was obvious to them (as it also must be to us) that men do not live by intellect alone, they identified this force with the individual's will.

Similarly, as I have suggested, there has been a marked tendency among social psychologists, and among those psychologists who are concerned with personality theory, to assume that, if the self is to constitute an integral whole, our actions cannot spring from a great variety of diverse sources, as earlier psychologists had assumed. They have instead sought to establish the view that there is a fundamental unity underlying all different propensities, each of which is related to the others in an interlocking system of forces. As a consequence of this assumption, thought cannot be supposed to proceed along lines of its own, according to its own principles: it too expresses the whole system of the individual's needs.

There is, of course, no reason to assume that an individual human being might not achieve integration of his impulses, even if they spring from wholly different sources and even though, in many instances, there may be potential conflicts among them. It should be remembered that not all propensities are at every moment active, since each is capable of being temporarily satisfied. Furthermore, in many cases they only arise because of the presence of specific inciting conditions in the environment. When these facts are recognized, it is not necessary to assume that individuals will be constantly torn to pieces merely because they possess a host of different drives. To be sure, in some cases, persons may suffer extremely because there are conflicts among their drives; in other cases, individuals are able to achieve a measure of integration in their lives. In neither of these cases can one plausibly assume that all facets of human nature are mutually connected, and that all act to fulfil an interconnected set of biological and psychological needs. Instead, it would seem more in accord with the facts to hold that there is a pluralism of motives and forces in human beings, and that many of them are relatively independent of the others. This, I submit, would also be more consistent with evolutionary theory, which has recently been given lip service more often than it has been treated with the respect it deserves. On strictly evolutionary grounds it would seem implausible to assume that the forms of behavior characteristic of all species are to be interpreted, as Schopenhauer and Nietzsche supposed, as variant forms of a single force, rather than being unique combinations of different factors which, taken together, happened to make them viable in the particular conditions surrounding them. Once this point of view is adopted, there is no reason to suppose that intelligence is not itself a special principle which has evolved, enabling the higher animals and men to fulfil their needs under the conditions imposed by their environments. That it will be adequate to our present needs must be our hope, but it is more difficult to preserve this hope than was once the case. This helps account for the fact that the rebellion against reason has become so pervasive an influence in our time.

3. CONCLUSION: THE NINETEENTH CENTURY AND THE PRESENT

If there has been any one factor which, more than others, has led to a revolutionary shift in twentieth-century thought and which has involved a break with those nineteenth-century movements which still dominated the earlier years of this century, it has been the loss of belief in Progress. If we look for the causes of this change, we of course find a number of doctrines which constituted challenges to progressivist assumptions. For example, social evolutionism had been generally abandoned by the leading schools of anthropology; we can also say that, in so far as scientists and philosophers had given up the idea that laws *govern* events rather than merely describe them, there was no longer reason to suppose that human history necessarily followed a definite, determined course. However, these specifically intellectual reasons, even if multiplied many times, are surely not adequate to explain the disappearance of a belief which had been as pervasive as had the belief in Progress throughout the nineteenth and early twentieth century. To account for its disappearance, one must take cognizance of the experience of the first World War, especially in Germany, and of the widespread social and political upheavals which began in the 1930s and have continued unabated ever since. Such experiences have left little room for the earlier forms of optimism which, on the whole, dominated Western thought since the Enlightenment.

With the loss of belief in Progress, historicism also lost a hold on recent thought, and this connection has not been accidental. To be sure, historicism was not originally associated with the doctrine of Progress, as that doctrine had been present in the Enlightenment. In fact, the two positions had been opposed, with those who adopted historicist views challenging the methods of explanation and the standards of evaluation which were characteristic of the Enlightenment, Nevertheless, when faith in Progress was lost, historicist modes of thought likewise tended to disappear. Why this should have been the case is readily explained.

Consider the mode of evaluation of historical events which historicism entails. Its evaluative thesis demands that we refrain from setting up any form of external standard against which to judge the historical process, but that we be reconciled to those tendencies which dominate historical change; in short, that we accept the view that the history of the world is the world's court of judgment. However, insofar as we cannot in fact be reconciled to that which has occurred and is occurring, this standard will not only appear to us as false, but as shameful. We then find ourselves forced to seek an explanatory understanding of historical events which differs from that of historicism: it is no longer possible to view such events simply as phases in some larger tendency of history. One looks instead for mistaken choices, unfortunate accidents, and a host of other critical factors, in order to explain how something which might have been attainable has escaped use; one attempts to establish, in concrete detail, why particular events occurred as they did. Seen in this way, history no longer appears as a single developmental process in which each phase plays an essential role, subservient to the whole. Thus, when belief in Progress is abandoned, historicist explanations also tend to be abandoned. Or, to put the same point in a different way: the nineteenth-century form of the doctrine of Progress had emerged from an acceptance of historicism, and was widely taken to be one of its necessary corollaries. The fact that this corollary subsequently proved to be unacceptable is at least one major reason why the whole historicist system of which it had been a part has also been rejected as unacceptable. In this respect, at least, there appears to be a sharp break between the intellectual presuppositions of the nineteenth and early twentieth century, and those which dominate thought today.

On the other hand, loss of faith in Progress has not seriously undercut belief in the malleability of man, which is still generally accepted. However, the ways in which the doctrine of malleability has been used have drastically altered because of loss of faith in Progress, Formerly, malleability in each of its forms had offered hope for the future: since man's nature was not unalterably fixed, it seemed possible that through education and social reform, through the growth of civilization, and through the evolutionary process itself, there could be ever-increasing accomplishment for each and for all. However, in the light of the devastating experiences of this century, the social forces which shape men no longer appear as benign, nor as being subject to control; consequently, the fact that the social environment exercises a formative influence on human nature is not seen as a reason for hope but as a reason for dismay. In short, the doctrine of malleability has recently come to be regarded as a threat to the individual, not as a foundation for the future progress of Mankind.

In order to find examples of the view that the accepted norms of social life pose a threat to all that is essential in the individual, one need not confine one's attention to doctrines which developed in the mid-twentieth century: among those whom we have discussed, Kierkegaard and Nietzsche also provide striking examples. To be sure, neither accepted the doctrine of man's malleability: both regarded human nature as having characteristics which neither society nor experience can change. Nonetheless, each held that, if intensity of passion or of will is lacking, the effects of society completely distort the individual: for Kierkegaard, individuals then become transformed into a crowd, and for Nietzsche, all that is noble in man becomes hopelessly corrupt. This anti-social individualism seems to me to account for a good deal of the present influence of both Kierkegaard and Nietzsche. However, those who have accepted this aspect of their doctrines have also tended to suppose that we are formed by our environments; and these two positions seem ill-suited to each other. To be sure, those who currently hold the doctrine of man's malleability regard it only as a theory concerning a matter of fact, and not a doctrine involving any judgment of value, whereas their rejection of any social norm which threatens the inviolability of the individual constitutes a moral appraisal. It may be worth commenting that, when beliefs concerning matters of fact stand in such sharp opposition to moral convictions, it is not surprising that those who accept both positions should feel themselves engaged in a desperate personal struggle against the society which they regard as having formed them. Such was not the view of those who had earlier accepted the doctrine of man's malleability, for whom it offered hope for the future.

Finally, we turn to the question of how the limits placed on reason in the nineteenth century are related to the dominant views of our time. Here I detect no essential change, Unlike historicism, which has been abandoned, and unlike the doctrine of man's malleability which, although still espoused, no longer retains its earlier significance, there seems to be continuity with respect to what are taken to be the uses and the abuses of reason. For example, the views of both Jacobi and Kierkegaard have obvious counterparts in contemporary theology; similarly, intuitionist and existentialist critiques of objectivity, and of all conceptual thought, remain prominent; even within the philosophy of science, the similarities between presently dominant views and the positivism and pragmatism of the late nineteenth and early twentieth century are more obvious than are the differences which separate them. Since these are tendencies which I have been inclined to criticize, I do not find the lack of change encouraging, any more than I find hope in those more recent movements in Anglo-American philosophy which possess somewhat greater novelty.[24]

My dissatisfaction stems from the fact that I fail to find in *any* of these positions an adequate appreciation of what the analytic understanding, using abstraction and generalization, has been able to accomplish. Among those who attempted to set limits to reason, attention was focused on whatever factors supposedly limit the range and the power of the intellect; equal attention was not paid to the question of why the analytic understanding has enabled us to attain the knowledge which we in fact possess. To account for the range and the exactitude of our knowledge is, I submit, no less serious a question for a theory of knowledge than are any questions concerning the limits which human knowledge may not be able to transcend. In fact, it may be said that theories of knowledge which rest on assumptions incompatible with giving an adequate account of why we have been able, through observation and inference, to extend the scope and the accuracy of our empirical knowledge, are theories which cannot in the end be maintained. For this reason, I believe that the nineteenth-century views of the intellect which have here been examined will, before long, be unacceptable. When this occurs, our philosophic horizon will be radically altered, and we shall then be free of still another aspect of nineteenth-century thought.

PART I—PHILOSOPHIC BACKGROUND

CHAPTER 1. PHILOSOPHIC MOVEMENTS IN THE NINETEENTH CENTURY

1. To be sure, Bergson had a strong and widespread influence on the thought of the twentieth century. The main impact of his work came through his views regarding science and the limitations of the intellect. At these points he had much in common with nineteenth-century French idealism and with pragmatism, and his thought also opened the way to a broad acceptance of existentialism in France. However, the metaphysical aspects of his work had a lesser influence, and Bergsonian spiritualism did not become a major movement in twentieth-century thought.

2. It might be claimed that this is not true of existentialism, since Kierkegaard's influence affected the main currents of philosophy and theology only during the period following the First World War. However, the basic theses of existentialism are to be found not only in Kierkegaard, but in Feuerbach, Marx, and Nietzsche, and in other nineteenth-century figures. (Cf. Paul Tillich, "Existential Philosophy," *Journal of the History of Ideas*, V [1944], 44–70.) In fact, it is important to note that, with the exception of Nietzsche's works, almost all of the presently canonical writings of existentialism were published between 1807 and the late 1840s.

3. Translated by Walter Kaufmann, and to be found in his *Hegel: Texts and Commentary*, p. 20. This is far more accurate than the Baillie translation, where the passage appears on p. 10; even so, it loses a good deal that is in the original, cf. vol. II, p. 18, of the Glockner edition (Jubiläumsausgabe), 1928.

For quotations from Kant, from Fichte, and from Schelling which might also have been used as representative of the point which I have wished to make, cf. Kroner, *Von Kant bis Hegel* I, 1–4; also cf. Feuerbach, *Gedanken über Tod und Unsterblichkeit* (1830), in *Sämmtliche Werke*, I, 8–9.

4. Höffding is one of the few historians of philosophy who recognized the pervasiveness and the continuity of these two streams of thought in nineteenth-century philosophy. As readers of his *History of Modern Philosophy* know, he designated them as "romanticism" and "positivism," and their continuity pro-

vided the basic pattern by means of which he organized the second volume of that admirable work. However, Höffding did not note the common presuppositions which underlay many aspects of these otherwise opposed movements. It is with some of these common presuppositions that we shall later be concerned.

5. It may appear arbitrary and tendentious to distinguish between philosophy as a technical subject and other intellectual developments, but such a distinction seems to me wholly justified. Philosophy, like art or religion, has its own history, and that history is not to be confounded with the history of ideas or of *Weltanschauungen*. For a preliminary discussion of some of the methodological problems involved, see my article "The History of Ideas, Intellectual History, and the History of Philosophy," in Beiheft 5 of *History and Theory* (1965).

6. In Kroner's valuable book, already cited, the period of German Idealism is interpreted as spanning forty years, from the publication of Kant's *Critique of Pure Reason* (1781) to the publication of Hegel's *Philosophy of Right* (1821). For Kroner there was a sharp break after Hegel, and the characteristics of the period then came to a close (*Von Kant bis Hegel* I, 1–6). However, his characterization of idealism (I, 7–10) was aimed at defining "the idealist school" in such a way that one could trace a direct line of descent from Kant through Hegel. Such a characterization seems to me at once too broad and too narrow: too broad in its inclusion of Kant, too narrow in its assumption that idealism is to be characterized primarily in terms of a restricted movement in early nineteenth-century German philosophy.

7. Lotze's first relevant work, *Metaphysik*, was published in 1841; Fechner's *Nanna* was published in 1848 and, more importantly, his *Zendavesta* in 1851. Both men continued to develop their systems, and each published what was probably his more important metaphysical work in 1879.

8. According to Höffding, in the five years succeeding the publication of von Hartmann's *Philosophy of the Unconscious*, fifty-eight works dealing with his philosophy were written (*History of Modern Philosophy*, II, 533). For Büchner's puzzled disappointment at the decline of materialism, see his *Am Sterbelager des Jahrhunderts*, p. 9.

9. Cf. Ravaisson's treatment of Eclecticism in his admirable and influential *La philosophie en France* (1868). This work was itself one of the major influences on the French idealist movement of the latter part of the century. It is also characteristic of the self-evaluation of the Eclectics that the third volume of Ferraz' *Histoire de la philosophie en France au XIXe siècle* (1887) should have been entitled *Spiritualisme et liberalisme*. It may also be noted that in 1857, in *Les philosophes français du XIXe siècle*, Taine regarded Eclecticism as a species of Idealism.

10. E.g., *La philosophie en France*, pp. 258–62, *et passim*.

11. There are of course interesting parallels between Cournot and specific doctrines of the idealists. On this point, cf. Parodi, "Le criticisme de Cournot," especially pp. 474–75; also, cf. Parodi, *La philosophie contemporaine*, in which Renouvier and Cournot are compared with respect to their interest in the problem of the limitations of science.

12. See the conclusion of *La contingence des lois de la nature* (1874). As in the

case of Ravaisson, who was also his teacher, Boutroux manifested great interest in Leibniz, whose *Monadology* he edited, contributing a long introduction.

In the development of Boutroux's thought there is a striking difference between his earlier exposition of the factor of contingency and the exposition which one finds in his *De l'idée de loi naturelle* (1895). It is difficult to estimate whether this difference was due to the manner in which Cournot had developed his own thought in *Materialisme, vitalisme et rationalisme* (1875). There would also have to be considered the mutual influences of Boutroux and the Tannerys, and of Boutroux and Poincaré. Given the importance of Boutroux as a teacher, and his close relationship to other important figures in the philosophy of science, one would think that there should be more interest in his thought than has recently been shown.

13. It is often forgotten that Bergson published his *Essai sur les données immédiates de la conscience* (translated into English as *Time and Free-Will*) in 1889; a second edition was published in 1898, and thereafter new editions followed in rapid succession. When one considers the date of this publication, as well as its content, one sees in how close a relationship he stood to the continuous tradition of nineteenth-century French idealism. (Cf. Benrubi, *Les sources et les courants de la philosophie*, II, 741, *et passim*; and Parodi, *La philosophie contemporaine*, p. 254, *et passim*.)

14. The denial of freedom which was felt (with some justice) to be implicit within French positivism, doubtless also contributed to the French rejection of Hegel. (One notes that Ravaisson was impressed by the manner in which Schelling's late lectures stressed human freedom; cf. *La philosophie en France*, p. 264.)

15. For an interesting letter from Mill to Martineau, cf. *Letters of John Stuart Mill*, I, 62.

With respect to Martineau's earlier relations to Mill, and for the development of his idealism, see Martineau's preface to the first edition of his *Types of Ethical Theory*.

16. Martineau's reaction against Hegelianism was, I believe, the nearest approximation in England to the changes taking place within idealism in Germany at mid-century, and to the French idealist movement. Like the latter movement Martineau insisted upon the concepts of freedom and personality as ultimate, and therefore regarded Hegelianism as a threat.

In Green, of course, the same two concepts played an important role, but his system represented a merging of Kantian and Hegelian elements, rather than the development of a personalism. Apart from Martineau, we find the development of personalism most clearly exemplified in Seth's *Hegelianism and Personality* in 1887, in some of the contributions to *Personal Idealism* (1892), and in James Ward, who was greatly influenced by Lotze. McTaggart's pluralistic idealism was, in his own eyes at least, closely related to Hegel.

In Sir John Herschel, at an earlier date, we find the rudiments of a monadology, but I am not aware of any influence which his views on this subject exerted. (Cf. his essays "On Atoms" and "On the Origin of Force" in his *Familiar Lectures on Scientific Subjects*.)

17. As is universally recognized, metaphysical idealism was far and away the dominant strand in nineteenth-century American thought, and was extremely widespread in Italy as well.

18. Cf. Mill's statement of what Comte took to be the essential nature of the Positive Philosophy: "We have no knowledge of any thing but Phenomena; and our knowledge of phenomena is relative, not absolute. We know not the essence, nor the real mode of production, of any fact, but only its relations to other facts in the way of succession or similitude. These relations are constant; that is, always the same in the same circumstances. The constant resemblances which link phenomena together, and the constant sequences which unite them as antecedent and consequent, are termed their laws. The laws of phenomena are all we know respecting them. Their essential nature, and their ultimate causes, either efficient or final, are unknown and inscrutable to us." (*The Positive Philosophy of Auguste Comte*, pp. 7–8.)

Those acquainted with Kolakowski's *The Alienation of Reason: A History of Positivist Thought* will note two major differences between his characterization of positivism (pp. 2–10) and that offered here. (1) While stressing the first and third features which I have discussed, Kolakowski omits the second; as a consequence, he links Locke and Berkeley (among others) with the positivist tradition, and places Hume squarely within it. (2) He regards non-cognitivism in value-theory as a defining characteristic of positivism, yet neither Comte nor Mill represents non-cognitivism as he defines it. In addition, and perhaps most importantly, we differ in the fact that he fails to distinguish between the methods and aims of systematic positivists and critical positivists.

19. *The Positive Philosophy of Comte*, pp. 9–10.

20. G. H. Lewes: *Biographical History of Philosophy*, II, 654.

21. The followers of Comte did not necessarily attribute finality to his system. In spite of his self-evaluation, and in spite of how highly they rated his achievement, it was the new method rather than his system itself which evoked their unbridled confidence. One sees this not only in Littré (cf. Benrubi: *Les sources et les courants de la philosophie contemporaine en France*, I, 23–25), but in Lewes (*History of Philosophy*, II, 640–41).

22. Cf. J. S. Mill: *Autobiography*, pp. 157–59.

23. Cf. Antonio Aliotta: "We must distinguish two periods in the history of positivism: of these the first is marked by a dogmatic belief in physical science, which is set up as a model for every form of knowledge; the second, dating from around 1870, goes still farther, and subjects science itself to searching criticism in order to eliminate any traces of metaphysics which might be sheltering themselves beneath the cloak of experimental theories." (*The Idealistic Reaction against Science*, p. 53.)

24. William J. M. Rankine, "Outlines of the Science of Energetics" (1855), *Miscellaneous Scientific Papers*, p. 210. Cf. Robert Mayer, *Ueber die Erhaltung der Energie*, especially Letters X and XIII, written in 1844.

25. Cf. Tait's Memoir prefixed to Rankine's *Miscellaneous Scientific Papers*, p. xxix.

26. Cf. Mayer, *Ueber die Erhaltung der Energie*, especially letters I, III, and V.

27. Ernst Cassirer tended to identify the mid-century developments in physics

with the overthrow of a realistic interpretation of science (cf. *The Problem of Knowledge*, Ch. 5), but Rankine, Mayer, and others of the period should really be counted as precursors of that change, not its representatives. In this connection, it is to be noted that Cassirer made his point through citing (in the main) Ostwald and Helm, who belong to a later generation.

One can also see the fallacy of identifying the mid-century developments in physics with the later overthrow of a realistic interpretation of science if one considers the more philosophical passages in Clerk Maxwell's writings. To be sure, Maxwell not infrequently expressed impatience with metaphysics; for example, he characterized a metaphysician as "a physicist disarmed of all his weapons—a disembodied spirit trying to measure distances in terms of his own cubit, to form a chronology in which intervals of time are measured by the number of thoughts they include, and to evolve a standard pound out of his own self-consciousness." (Lewis Campbell and William Garnet: *The Life of James Clerk Maxwell*, p. 436.) It is also true that one can find statements in Maxwell which anticipate the economical view of thought which was later associated with Mach's form of critical positivism. While these statements appear to have had a certain influence on Boltzmann and others, it can scarcely be said that Maxwell consistently espoused critical positivism. He never extended such statements through to their full implications, and he was himself frequently absorbed in discussing metaphysical issues. (Cf. Campbell and Garnet, Ch. 8 and Ch. 14.) The most famous of these discussions is to be found in his essay "Molecules" (1873), where he was led from a consideration of molecular structure to a proof for the existence of God. (Cf. *Scientific Papers*, II, 361–78.)

28. For illustrations of Bernard's thought with respect to the preceding points, see in particular the following sections of his *Introduction à l'étude de la médecine expérimentale*: Part I, Ch. II, Sect. IV; Part II, Ch. I, Sects. I and IX; and Part III, Ch. IV, Sect. IV.

29. Kirchhoff, who was regarded by Mach as one who anticipated his own position (cf. "On the Principle of Comparison in Physics," in Mach's *Popular Scientific Lectures*), seems to have subscribed to a view of the sort here discussed. The following passage from Ludwig Boltzmann's account of Kirchhoff's scientific aims is revealing in this respect:

Nicht kühne Hypothesen über das Wesen der Materie zu bilden und aus der Bewegung der Moleküle die Bewegung der Körper zu erraten, ist das Ziel, sondern Gleichungen zu bilden, welche frei von Hypothesen möglichst getreu und quantativ richtig der Erscheinungswelt entsprechen, unbekümmert um das Wesen der Dinge und Kräfte.—Ja, in seinem Buche über Mechanik will Kirchhoff sogar alle metaphysischen Begriffe, wie den der Kraft, als Ursache eine Bewegung, verbannen, er sucht bloss die Gleichungen welche den beobachteten Bewegung möglichst genau entsprechen. ("Kirchhoff" [1887], *Populäre Schriften*, pp. 70–71.)

30. Cf. *Helmholtz's Treatise on Physiological Optics*, III, 2 and 35–36. Also, cf. *Popular Lectures on Scientific Subjects*, II, 230. Of course, Helmholtz explicitly rejected Kantian views regarding our perception of spatial relations (for example, cf. *Physiological Optics*, III, 17–18, 36, *et passim*) and regarding the status of geometrical axioms (cf. *Popular Lectures*, II, 68 and *Wissenschaftliche Abhandlungen*, II, 640–60).

31. Cf. *Wissenschaftliche Abhandlungen*, II, 608. (For a further discussion of this view, cf. pp. 293–94 and 297–98, below.)

32. Cf. *Die Thatsachen in der Wahrnehmung*, pp. 24–40; also, *Popular Lectures*, II, 284–85.

33. Cf. Hertz's lecture on the occasion of Helmholtz's seventieth birthday (1891), in Hertz: *Miscellaneous Papers*, especially pp. 335–37. It is to be noted that at the end of this passage Hertz expressed a degree of scepticism with respect to the view that epistemological claims legitimately followed from psychophysics. Hertz's own views more nearly approached a true Kantianism, as one sees in his *Principles of Mechanics*, for example on pp. 1–3 and 296–307. (Cf. also Cassirer's discussion of Hertz and Mach in *The Problem of Knowledge*, pp. 105–8.)

34. Cf. Wilhelm Wundt: *Ueber den Einfluss der Philosophie auf die Erfahrungswissenschaften*, p. 6.

35. This assumption is perfectly explicit throughout Bernard's *Introduction à l'étude de la médecine expérimentale* (1865), and is equally clearly expressed in Helmholtz's lecture in 1869 "The Aim and Progress of Physical Science" (translated and reprinted in his *Popular Lectures on Scientific Subjects*). As we shall later see, it was also characteristic of the views of DuBois-Reymond.

36. Lange, in his treatment of ideals, anticipated it in 1865, and in various places it was also suggested by Clifford; in fact, in Clifford's series of lectures entitled "The Philosophy of the Pure Sciences," delivered in 1873, one finds an expression of each of the three reasons which I single out as the primary reasons why a pragmatic-economical view was held (Cf. William K. Clifford, *Lectures and Essays*, I, 301–36).
    According to Höffding, Mach himself had actually arrived at his economical interpretation of science as early as 1863 (cf. *Modern Philosophers*, p. 116), and had regarded Kirchhoff and Maxwell (though perhaps with little justification, as I have indicated) as his forerunners. Though Mach may well have arrived at this view earlier than the 1880s, it was at that time that he came to develop it in a whole series of lectures and books. (For Mach's own later account of the development of this aspect of his thought, cf. *Die Leitgedanken meiner naturwissenschaftlichen Erkenntnislehre*, pp. 1–6.)

37. To this day it is insufficiently recognized that this is not in fact an implication of Darwin's theory. All that his theory entails is that no factor which is markedly deleterious will persist. In the *Descent of Man* (1871) Darwin explicitly recognized the error of assuming that every new factor must be of positive value in order to persist, and he attributed that error to the difficulty of abandoning his earlier teleological habits of thought (cf. *Descent of Man*, I, 146–47). In the second edition Darwin rearranged his order of discussion, and this passage is to be found two paragraphs prior to that section of Chapter II which is labeled "Conclusion." The original passage in the *Origin of Species*, which it was obviously Darwin's aim to correct, appears in Ch. VI, p. 212, shortly before the concluding summary, and contains a reference to Paley.

38. Cf. Mach's "On Transformation and Adaptation in Scientific Thought" (1883), pp. 215–17.
    Cf. the following statement from Ernst Laas: "Nicht bloss die Wahrnehmungen wechseln: auch die Vernunft ist wandelbar. Alles Denken ist ein Mittel, das Leben den Lebensbedingungen anzupassen; der Erfolg bestimmt seinen Werth" (*Idealismus und Positivismus*, III, 671). Vaihinger, of course, pushed this view even

farther. Although his work was not published until later, its composition dates from the same period.

39. In addition to his *Contributions to the Analysis of Sensations* and his lecture "On Transformation and Adaptation in Scientific Thought," which have already been cited, the following other works of the same period are to be especially recommended as giving insight into his philosophic thought: "The Economical Nature of Physical Inquiry" (1882) and "On the Principle of Comparison in Physics" (1894), both of which are republished in his *Popular Scientific Lectures*. In addition, his classic *Science of Mechanics* (1883) is directly relevant.

40. Mill's analysis of mathematics is to be found in Part II, Ch. 5 and 6, of his *System of Logic*; for Helmholtz's discussions of geometry see his *Wissenschaftlichen Abhandlungen*, II, articles 77, 78, 79, and for his discussion of arithmetic see III, article 129, of the same collection.

41. Cf. "On the Economical Nature of Physical Inquiry," in *Popular Scientific Lectures*, p. 190.

42. Cf. *Ueber die Aufgabe der Philosophie und ihre Stellung zu den uebrigen Wissenschaften* (Heidelberg, 1868).

43. Cf. Windelband: *Geschichte und Naturwissenschaft* (1894), republished in his *Praeludien*; Rickert: *Die Grenzen der naturwissenschaftlichen Begriffsbildung* (1896) and *Kulturwissenschaft und Naturwissenschaft* (1899); also Croce: "La storia ridotta sotto il concetto generale dell'arte" (1893), reprinted in *Primi Saggi* (Bari, 1919).

44. Among other examples of this movement at the turn of the century are to be found Balfour and Boutroux. Cf. Balfour's development of his earlier criticism of "scientific philosophy" (*A Defense of Philosophic Doubt*, 1879) in his *Foundations of Belief*, for example, pp. 243 and 301. Cf. Boutroux's development from *De la Contingence* (1874) to *La Science et la Religion dans la Philosophie contemporaine* (1908).

45. Cf. *Letters of John Stuart Mill*, II, 286.

46. As Pollock pointed out, Clifford's views were such that they would "in a loose and popular sense be called materialist," even though Clifford in fact accepted a form of metaphysical idealism. (Cf. Pollock's biography, prefixed to Clifford: *Lectures and Essays*, I, 50.) Although Pollock does not thus state it, the causes of this erroneous ascription of materialism to Clifford would have been the two which we have mentioned: an attack on Christian orthodoxy and an attempt to hold, in Mill's terms, that "toutes nos impressions mentales resultent du jeu de nos organes physiques." These are in fact the two most important grounds upon which Hutton criticized Clifford. (Cf. *Criticisms on Contemporary Thought*, vol. I, essays 26 and 27.)

47. "On the Hypothesis that Animals are Automata," pp. 243–45.

48. There are two points concerning the doctrine of emergence to which I should here like to call attention: first, that it can be associated with a vast variety of otherwise very different philosophic positions, and, second, that it is not a

doctrine which was new in the twentieth century, as has often been supposed by
those who identify it with the thought of Samuel Alexander and C. Lloyd Morgan.

One can find idealists such as Hegel, materialists such as Marx and Engels,
positivists such as Comte, non-dualists such as Alexander and R. W. Sellars, and
dualists such as Lovejoy and Broad, all holding doctrines of emergence which
(with the exception of Hegel's) were remarkably similar. Thus, it is a mistake to
treat the concept of emergence as if it were necessarily associated with an interest
in metaphysics, or with a particular metaphysical position, or with a denial of
mind-body dualism.

The foregoing remark should also be sufficient to suggest that an acceptance of
the doctrine of emergence was prevalent in all schools of thought in the nineteenth century. It is of special interest to note that in Book III, Chapter V of his
System of Logic Mill gave the first careful analysis of the difference between the
principle of the "Composition of Causes" and what he called "chemical causes."
G. H. Lewes developed the first full-fledged natural philosophy which was based
upon the principle of emergence in his *Problems of Life and Mind* (especially
in Volume II), which appeared in 1874–75; and it is said that it is to him that we
owe this use of the term "emergence." Among the many other instances of an
acceptance of emergence in the nineteenth century one further example may be
noted, for it also serves to illustrate the way in which that doctrine migrated
freely from system to system. Claude Bernard accepted a doctrine of emergence,
holding that the living was not reducible to the non-living, and it was this
doctrine—and not his positivism, nor his arguments for an experimental science
of medicine—that was of primary influence on the next generation of philosophers, most of whom used this aspect of his thought in support of some form of
idealist metaphysics. (Cf. Ravaisson's treatment of Bernard in *La philosophie en
France*, pp. 125–27, *et passim*, and Bergson's "La philosophie de Claude Bernard,"
in *La pensée et le mouvant*. For one of Bernard's own clearest statements of his
doctrine, cf. *Leçons sur les phenomènes de la vie*, I, 50.)

49. For Tyndall's position, see his well-known lectures, "The Scope and Limit of
Scientific Materialism" (1868), and the "Address Delivered before the British
Association in Belfast" (1874), which was then published with additions.

In support of the view that Tyndall's position was the chief manifestation of
materialism in England, one may cite James Martineau's exchanges with him, as
well as the accounts of these exchanges in Hutton's *Aspects of Religious and
Scientific Thought*, essays 10 and 11, and Tulloch's "Modern Scientific Materialism," in *Modern Theories in Philosophy and Religion*.

To be sure, in 1851 the *Letters on the Laws of Man's Nature and Development*
by Henry George Atkinson and Harriet Martineau caused something of a scandal.
The position they represented was akin to that of the German materialists of the
time. However, within two years Harriet Martineau published her translated
abridgment of Comte's *Positive Philosophy*, and the influence of Atkinson was
no longer significant.

It is finally necessary to note that in England the working-class movement seized
upon the eighteenth-century thought of Tom Paine, and Paine's influence persisted in the Secularism of Bradlaugh and Holyoake. However, this can scarcely
be taken as indicating that materialism had established itself as an important
philosophic movement in England.

50. In this connection, the following representative passages may be listed:

(1) Comte, *System of Positive Polity*, I, 40–41.
(2) The concluding section in all editions of Spencer's *First Principles*.

(3) Claude Bernard's *Introduction to the Study of Experimental Medicine*, p. 66.

(4) The concluding remarks in Huxley's essay "On the Physical Basis of Life" (1868), in *Collected Essays*, vol. I.

(5) Mach: *The Analysis of Sensations*, p. 12.

51. In what follows concerning the doctrines of Marx and of Engels I wish to avoid current controversies over whether or not one can assume that Marx subscribed to that form of dialectical materialism which one finds developed in Engels' *Anti-Dühring* (1878) and would have subscribed to Engels' *Ludwig Feuerbach und die Ausgang der klassischen deutschen Philosophie* (1888), which are the two texts of greatest relevance to what follows. While I am inclined to believe that current interpretations of Marx's own thought are too much under the influence of the *Economic and Philosophic Manuscripts of 1844*, I shall attempt to phrase my remarks in such a way as to leave it as an open question how one is to relate the philosophic position of Marx to that of Engels.

52. It is, I believe, a mistake to view Feuerbach's early attack on Dogurth (1838), in which he took a fundamentally dualistic view of the mind–body relationship, as being consistent with the views which he came to develop as soon as he had completely rejected Hegel. However, in *From Hegel to Marx*, Sidney Hook interprets Feuerbach in this way. On the basis of his other writings of this period, I should agree with the interpretation of Jodl in *Ludwig Feuerbach*, Ch. I.

53. The following are perhaps the most characteristic and significant works of these three materialists: Moleschott, *Kreislauf des Lebens* (1852); Vogt, *Köhlerglaube und Wissenschaft* (1854); Büchner, *Kraft und Stoff* (1855).

54. "Was für ein Unterschied zwischen dem 'Atheismus,' den ich lehre, und dem 'Materialismus' Vogt's, Moleschott's und Büchner's ist? Es ist lediglich der Unterschied zwischen Zeit und Raum, oder zwischen Menschengeschichte und Naturgeschichte. Die Anatomie, die Physiologie, die Medizin, die Chemie weiss nichts von der Seele, nichts von Gott u.s.w.; wir wissen davon nur aus der Geschichte." Letter to Bäuerle, in *Briefwechsel und Nachlass*, II, 188.

55. In his *Ludwig Feuerbach*, Engels says:

The old metaphysics which accepted things as finished objects arose from a natural science which investigated dead and living things as finished objects. But when this investigation had progressed so far that it became possible to take the decisive step forward of transition to the systematic investigation of the changes which these things undergo in nature itself, then the last hour of the old metaphysics sounded in the realm of philosophy, also. And in fact, while natural science up to the end of the last century was predominantly a *collecting* science, a science of finished things, in our century it is essentially a *classifying science*, a science of the processes, of the origin and development of these things and of the interconnection which binds all these natural processes into one great whole (p. 55).

Cf. also the contrast drawn by Engels between "mechanical" and "modern" materialism in *Herr Eugen Dühring's Revolution in Science*, pp. 31–32.

56. Cf. *Cursus der Philosophie*, pp. 56ff.

57. Cf. *Das Werth des Lebens*, pp. 102ff., and the passage in *Cursus der Philosophie* (p. 104) which Engels selected as the passage through which he attacked

Dühring's natural philosophy of the organic world (*Herr Eugen Dühring's Revolution,* opening of Ch. 7).

58. *Briefwechsel und Nachlass,* II, 308.
   On the relations between Feuerbach and Moleschott, cf. A. Levy, *La Philosophie de Feuerbach* (Paris, 1904).

59. As Lenin recognized, the most important philosophical enemy of dialectical materialism was critical positivism, and he therefore attacked Mach and Mach's followers in *Materialism and Empirio-Criticism* (1909).

60. In 1876 Vaihinger looked upon Hartmann, Dühring, and Lange as the three outstanding newer philosophers (cf. his *Hartmann, Dühring und Lange,* p. 4), and in the *History of Modern Philosophy* (1894) Höffding selected Dühring as one of the five German philosophers of the period from 1850 to 1880 to whom he devoted individual discussions, the others being Lotze, Fechner, Hartmann, and Lange, all of whose names remain far more familiar to us.

61. *Address Delivered before the British Association in Belfast,* p. 4.

62. *Ibid.* pp. 63-64. Also, cf. the preface to Hennell's *Inquiry Concerning the Origin of Christianity* (1838) in which Christianity is regarded as "an elevated system of thought and feeling," but one which must be freed of "fables." By Tyndall's time, "free-thinkers" regarded Christianity as an elevated system of feeling, but not of thought.

63. Cf. the preface to *Das Leben Jesu,* and the appendix to its second volume. To be sure, Strauss's position later changed, as can be seen in *Der alte und der neue Glaube* (1865); by that time his religious position had shifted toward pantheism.

64. "On Improving Natural Knowledge" (1866), in *Collected Essays,* I, 38.

65. As Höffding pointed out, "Beim Eintritt in das neunzehnten Jahrhundert war die Verbindung von Religion, Philosophie und Kunst die Losung in der Welt des Geistes. Man hegte den begeisterten Glauben, dass die Wahrheit Eine sei und dass alles Wertvolle, gleichviel, auf welchem Gebiete und in welcher Form es auch auftrette, in dieser Einen Wahrheit inbegriffen sei, wenn man sich nur offenen Sinnes in sie vertiefe." (*Sören Kierkegaard als Philosoph,* p. 11.)

66. *Science and Religion in Contemporary Philosophy,* p. 35. Boutroux, of course, sought to overcome this dualism.

67. There does not seem to have been any independent analogue to this position in England. To be sure, the works of Strauss and of Feuerbach were widely known through the translations of George Eliot; Comte, of course, had a significant number of followers.

68. Cf. Arnold, *Literature and Dogma,* Ch. I, Sect. 4 and 5. (*Prose Works,* VI, 189-201.)
   Fiske, in *The Idea of God as Affected by Modern Knowledge* (1885), takes up and utilizes Arnold's phrases as defining the object of his own religious worship.

69. Cf. Otto Pfleiderer: *Development of Theology*, p. 345.

70. Cf. my article, "Darwin's Religious Views," *Journal of the History of Ideas,* XIX (1958), pp. 363–78.

PART II—HISTORICISM

CHAPTER 2.   THE NATURE AND SCOPE OF HISTORICISM

1. In the article "Historicism" in the *Encyclopedia of Philosophy* I have subsequently discussed some of the alternative ways in which the term has been used. That article also includes a brief chronological bibliography.

2. I have elsewhere sought to deal in a preliminary way with some of the problems raised by what I would call "special histories." (Cf. "The History of Ideas, Intellectual History and the History of Philosophy," in Beiheft 5 of *History and Theory*.)

3. Countless instances of this assumption can be found in the early nineteenth century, but it will be well to cite Sir John Herschel's *Preliminary Discourse on the Study of Natural Philosophy* (1831) since that work was the most notable and influential discussion of inductive logic and the philosophy of science to appear in the nineteenth century prior to the works of Whewell and Mill. In it there are many statements such as the following, in which Herschel is speaking of chemical compounds which are yet to be discovered.

> No chemist can doubt that it is already fixed what they will do when the case occurs. They will obey certain laws, of which we know nothing at present, but which must *be* already fixed, or they could not be laws. . . . This is the perfection of a law, that it includes all possible contingencies, and ensures implicit obedience,—and of this kind are the laws of nature. (#26)

The persistence of this identification of scientific laws with controlling forces, as well as its theological background, can also be seen (for example) in remarks made by Darwin at the end of the *Origin of Species*. There he spoke of his theory that species were not independently created, but were produced by secondary causes, as being better in accord "with what we know of the laws impressed on matter by the Creator"; further, one finds him speaking with awe of those complex relations among living forms which have "all been produced by laws acting around us."

CHAPTER 3.   THE FIRST PHASE OF HISTORICISM

1. *The Spirit of the Age*, p. 1.

2. In this chapter I shall only be dealing with those aspects of the Enlightenment which are directly relevant to the problem of historicism. Defining historicism as I do, much that would be considered relevant on a definition such as Friedrich Meinecke's will also be omitted.

3. For an illustration of each of these points, cf. Turgot: "Second Discours sur le progrès" (1750) in *Oeuvres*, II, especially pp. 52–64. Lessing's *Die Erziehung des Menschengeschlechts* (1777 and 1780) also clearly represents the first and third of

these points; however, in Lessing the emphasis on science and technology is lacking.

4. Cf. the concluding sentence of Voltaire's *Essai sur les moeurs*: "Quand une nation connaît les arts, quand elle n'est point subjuguée et transportée par les étrangers, elle sort aisement de ses ruines, et se rétablit toujours."

5. Quite characteristically, Lessing's general position with respect to the philosophy of history may be regarded as an intermediate position between Enlightenment views and those views which came to be characteristic of the following generation. Since they contain features present in both, it may be of interest and help to offer a brief summary of them.

Like other Enlightenment thinkers, Lessing regarded the process of history as one in which there had been progress, and he also believed that this progress was to be regarded as the education of mankind. However, he was not wholly opposed to some form of a doctrine of Revelation. What he did was to reinterpret the traditional doctrine of a Divine Revelation in history in such a way as to make it compatible with the Enlightenment doctrines regarding (1) the efficacy of natural reason, (2) the natural goodness of man, and (3) the possibility of an indefinite progress. He did this by holding that in the education of mankind, as in the education of a child, there must at some stages be guidance by a superior power. The truths that are given by this authority are then capable of being understood in their true significance by the maturing mind. Therefore, Revelation is, so to speak, a pedagogical technique, and is merely a transitional stage within the process of genuine education: it must finally be assimilated by man's natural reason and moral sense until it is no longer taken on authority, but is discerned to be a natural truth. Such were the revelations given in the Old Testament and given through Christ. And since Lessing also held the Enlightenment doctrine that there is an indefinitely long future open to man, he also suggested the possibility of further Revelations.

This doctrine, then, shared the Enlightenment view that history was a continuing process of development toward a higher state of human life, an indefinite growth from childlike crudity to intellectual and moral enlightenment. And while Lessing admitted Divine guidance within the process, this guidance was only genuinely effective because man himself had the innate power to assimilate for himself the real truth which it contained.

The point at which Lessing broke from the Enlightenment view of Progress was not so much in his granting a role to Divine guidance in history, but in his refusal to assume that the ultimate goal of this indefinite Progress was discernible. Unlike Condorcet, he did not assume that the nature of man's perfect state was capable of being defined in advance. The very fact that he suggested the possibility of a further Revelation entailed that the present could not be projected into the future: the highest achievements of Mankind were still in the future. This represents not only a break with the Enlightenment tradition but a break with the orthodox Christian philosophy of history, in which the drama of history comes to a close with the transformation of history into the timeless world of eternal life. Lessing's sense of an indefinitely long process of future education, and his religious reverence for this process itself, is much closer to the spirit of those who, as we shall later see, grounded historicism in the doctrine of divine immanence.

6. Cf. the preliminary sketches of Turgot's proposed universal history given in *Oeuvres*, II, 209–352.

7. One sees Montesquieu's influence on a new, broadened conception of national history in figures such as Madame de Staël (cf. the introduction to *De l'influence des passions sur le bonheur des individus et des nations*), and in Moeser (cf. Meinecke: *Die Entstehung des Historismus*, Ch. 8). For Herder's view of the greatness and limitations of Montesquieu, cf. *Auch eine Philosophie der Geschichte zur Bildung der Menschheit*, in *Werke*, V, 565–66.

8. Cf. especially *Émile*, Bk. IV. This characteristic is also to be noted in the structure of his political theory, as compared with that of most of his contemporaries.

9. Even in Herder the standard is an individual standard: it is the *Glückseligkeit* of individuals, not of the state. (Cf. preface to *Ideen zur Philosophie der Geschichte der Menschheit*.) It is only in later figures that such a standard is abandoned.

10. For Madame de Staël's coupling of the Enlightenment doctrine of the perfectability of man with her new emphasis upon feeling, and her recognition that this emphasis runs counter to the former treatment of history, cf. especially the preface to the second edition of *De la littérature*. For her acceptance of the importance of feeling, cf. especially *De l'Allemagne*, Part 4.

11. E.g., "Naturlich dass die ersten Entwicklungen so simpel, zart und wunderbar waren, wie wir sie in allem Hervorbringen der Natur sehen. Der Keim fällt in die Erde und erstirbt: der Embryon wird in Verborgenen gebildet, *wie's kaum die Brille der Philosophen apriori gutheisen wurde*, und tritt ganz begildet hervor; die Geschichte der frühesten Entwicklungen des menschlichen Geschlechts, wie sie uns die älteste Buch beschreibt, mag also so kurz und apokryphisch klingen, dass wir vor *dem philosophischen Geiste unsere Jahrhunderts, der nichts mehr als Wunderbares und Verborgenes hasset*, damit zu erscheinen erblöden: eben deswegen ist sie wahr." *Auch eine Philosophie der Geschichte zur Bildung der Menschheit* (1774) in *Werke*, V, 477f. [The italics are mine.]

Cf. also the passage (p. 507) where Herder, speaking of Providence, says, "Philosoph im nordischen Erdenthale, die Kinderwaage deines Jahrhunderts in der Hand, weisst du es besser als sie?". Also cf. remarks in the preface of his *Ideen zur Philosophie der Geschichte der Menschheit*.

For his attempt to assess his century as a whole, cf. the concluding pages of the same work.

12. Cf. Adam Müller, who held to the organic nature of the state, "ein grosses, energisches, unendlich bewegtes und lebendiges Ganzes" (*apud* Meinecke, *Die Entstehung des Historismus*, II, 379). Also, Heinrich Leo: "Der Staat ist eine lebendige Einheit d.h. hier: ein sittlicher Organismus" (*Lehrbuch der Universalgeschichte*, VI, 782).

13. Cf. Herder: *Auch eine Philosophie der Geschichte*, in *Werke*, V, 571.

14. As one example of Rousseau's influence, cf. Herder's praise of him in his youthful poem, *Der Mensch*.

15. The extent to which the organic analogy was used as the basis for interpreting history can be seen in Troeltsch's long chapter on "Organologie" in *Der Historismus und seine Probleme*.

16. It was not uncommon to assume that in a living thing some one of its organs better mirrored the nature of the organism as a whole, than did others. Like many other doctrines of the time, this probably developed out of Leibniz's monadology, and it was also compatible with the growth of interest in physiognomic characteristics such as one finds in Herder. As late as 1857 we find Haym saying (as if it were an obvious and universally accepted truth): "Wie man an dem höchsten Organ den Charakter des ganzen Organismus anschaulich machen kann ..." (*Hegel und seine Zeit*, p. 2.). As we shall see, this view had affinities with the metaphysics of Schopenhauer.

17. Moeser's views on this point are most clearly expressed in the preface to the first edition of the first part of his *Osnabrückische Geschichte*. Herder continually emphasizes it, and it leads him to his doctrine of the necessity for *Einfühlung* as a means of understanding the past. (Cf. *Auch eine Philosophie der Geschichte zur Bildung der Menschheit*, in *Werke*, V, 502.)

18. "Alles ist in der Natur verbunden: ein Zustand strebt zum anderen und bereitet ihn vor." (*Ideen zur Philosophie der Geschichte der Menschheit*, Bk. V, Ch. 6, in *Werke*, XIII, 194.)

19. E.g., *Ideen zur Philosophie der Geschichte der Menschheit*, Bk. VII, Ch. 1.

20. Cf. the influence of his *Gott*, a series of dialogues addressed to the quarrel over Spinoza. For one of the many examples of the way in which his conception of "the tree of history" is related to the doctrine of divine immanence, cf. *Auch eine Philosophie der Geschichte*, in *Werke*, V, 512–13.

21. In a letter written in 1770, *apud* Burkhardt's edition of Herder's *God*, p. 8.

22. One may note how he, like others of the period, was fascinated by magnetism (cf. the Fifth Conversation in *God*), and by the forces of growth in plants and in animals (cf. *Ideen zur Philosophie der Geschichte der Menschheit*, Bk. III, Ch. 4).

23. Cf. Hegel's criticism of mechanics in his doctoral dissertation, *De orbitis planetarium*, written under the influence of Schelling: "Was Newtons Begriff der Physik gewesen ist, geht ja daraus allein schon hervor, dass er sagt, man würde vielleicht, wenn man sich physikalisch ausdrücken wollen, statt Anziehung richtiger Stoss sagen. Wir dagegen sind der Ueberzeugung, dass der Stoss in die Mechanik, nicht aber in die wahre Physik gehöre." (*Dissertatio philosophica de orbitis planetarum*, in the Lasson edition, I, 353.)
Again: "Gottes Wirken aber ist weder äusserlich oder mechanisch, noch willkürlich oder zufällig; deshalb muss man festhalten, dass die Kräfte, von denen behauptet wird, dass Gott sie der Materie gegeben habe, dieser auch wahrhaft innewohnen und die Natur, das immanente und innerlich Prinzip der entgegengesetzten Kräfte der Materie ausmachen. Die Mechanik aber scheut vor diesem Prinzip zurück; sie versteht weder von Gott, noch von wirklicher Kraft, noch von dem Innerlichen und Notwendigen etwas...." (*Ibid.*, pp. 381–82.)

24. This is apparent throughout Feuerbach, but is most clearly manifested in the first chapter of *The Essence of Christianity*. As we shall later note, it constitutes one of the main points of Marx's attack in his "Theses on Feuerbach."

25. For documentation, cf. Simon: *Ranke und Hegel*, pp. 26–28.

26. Cf. the posthumously published work *Ueber die Epochen der neueren Geschichte*, dating from 1854. The following passage comes from the first essay:

> In Jeder Epoche der Menschheit äussert sich also eine bestimmte grosse Tendenz, und der Fortschritt beruht darauf, dass eine gewisse Bewegung des menschlichen Geistes in jeder Periode sich darstellt, welche bald die eine, bald die andere Tendenz hervorhebt und in derselben sich eigentümlich manifestiert.
>
> Wollt man aber im Widerspruch mit der hier geäusserten Ansicht annehmen, dieser Fortschritt bestehe darin, dass in jeder Epoche das Leben der Menschheit sich höher potenziert, dass also jede Generation die vorhergehende vollkommen übertreffe, mithin die letzte allemal die bevorzugte, die vorhergehenden aber nur die Träger der nachfolgenden wären, so würde das eine Ungerechtigkeit der Gottheit sein. Eine solche gleichsam mediatisierte Generation würde an und für sich eine Bedeutung nicht haben; sie würde nur insofern etwas bedeuten, als sie die Stufe der nachfolgenden Generation wäre, und würde nicht in unmittelbarem Bezug zum Göttlichen stehen. Ich aber behaupte: jede Epoche ist unmittelbar zu Gott, und ihr Wert beruht gar nicht auf dem, was aus ihr hervorgeht, sondern in ihrer Existenz selbst, in ihrem eigenen Selbst. (Ranke, *Weltgeschichte*, VIII, 177.)

In Leo Strauss' *Natural Right and History* it is claimed that the rise of historicism is attributable to the German historical school (cf. pp. 13 ff.). While part of the difference between my view and that of Strauss is attributable to variant characterizations of historicism, we also differ very appreciably with respect to the views which we attribute to the founders of the historical school.

27. Cf. quotation in Alfred Dove's foreword to Ranke's *Ueber die Epochen der neueren Geschichte*, in *Weltgeschichte*, VIII, 162–63.

28. Cf. Troeltsch's discussion of the use of the organic analogy among the members of the Historical School in *Der Historismus und seine Probleme*, pp. 277–307.

CHAPTER 4.   THE SEARCH FOR A SCIENCE OF SOCIETY

1. In this respect Saint-Simon's followers departed from his basic philosophic presuppositions. They distinguished between critical and organic periods in the history of thought, and opposed the critical periods, including those on which Saint-Simon's thought had been dependent. (Cf. *The Doctrine of Saint-Simon; An Exposition [First Year, 1828–29]*. Translated by George G. Iggers. Boston: Beacon, 1958.)

2. Cf. *Oeuvres*, VI, 66–67. [*Introduction aux travaux scientifiques du XIXe siècle*, Tome I, Second Ouvrage, Deuxième Section.]

3. Cf. "De la physiologie appliquée à l'amèlioration des institutions sociales," *Oeuvres*, V (Part I), 175–78. Also *Oeuvres*, VI, 133. [*Introduction aux travaux scientifiques du XIXe siècle*, Tome II, Episode No. 9.]

4. Cf. his foreword to *Introduction aux travaux scientifiques du XIXe siècle* (*Oeuvres*, VI, 14). The same point is repeated at the beginning of the discussion of Condorcet (*Oeuvres*, VI, 54).

5. *Mémoire sur la science de l'homme*, in *Oeuvres*, V (Part II), 25–27 and 45–46.

6. Cf. Ch. 7, below. For a fuller discussion of alternative types of laws which might be applicable to social change, cf. my article "Societal Laws," *British Journal for the Philosophy of Science*, VIII (1957), 211–24.

7. *Oeuvres*, VI, 54–66. [*Introduction aux travaux scientifiques du XIXe siècle*, Tome I, Second Ouvrage, Première Section.]

8. Comte republished this essay, as well as his other early essays, in a general appendix to his *Système de politique positive*. It is that source, in its English translation, that I shall cite.

In some respects, Comte was less than fair in his criticisms of Condorcet, but in what follows I shall remain close to Comte's own exposition.

9. *System of Positive Polity*, IV, 570. Other important passages in which Comte acknowledges his debt to Condorcet are III, xviii–xix, and IV, 27.

10. Comte's discussions of these three points are to be found in the Appendix to the *System of Positive Polity*, IV, 570–77.

11. *Ibid.*, IV, 575.

12. *Ibid.*, IV, 575.

13. *Ibid.*, IV, 571.

14. *Ibid.*, IV, 570.

15. *Ibid.*, IV, 554.

16. Comte claimed that he distinguished dynamics from statics throughout his system, and not with reference to sociology only. (Cf. *Cours de philosophie positive* [XLVIIIe Leçon], IV, 317–18.) He specifically cited his treatment of biology in this connection. However, his equation of anatomy with statics and of physiology with dynamics was artificial, as is clear in the XLe Leçon of the same work. Therefore, it is not until the level of sociology that Comte really considers dynamic laws.

17. *System of Positive Polity*, IV, 571.

18. Cf. Lévy-Bruhl, *La philosophie d'Auguste Comte*, p. 299–300.

Saint-Simon anticipated Comte (and perhaps influenced him) in speaking of humanity as a single entity, having an existence of its own. (Cf. Saint-Simon, *Oeuvres*, V, Part I, 177–78 and 180.) Although earlier writers, such as Turgot and Condorcet, had accepted a doctrine of the unity of human history, I find no unambiguous evidence that they ever regarded the noun "Humanity" as having reference to an individual substance rather than a collective substance. In fact, Condorcet states that his method is one of choosing and combining facts from the histories of a number of different peoples in order to construct "l'historie hypothétique d'un peuple unique, et former le tableau de ses progrès." (*Esquisse d'un tableau historique des progrès de l'esprit humain*, in *Oeuvres*, VI, 19.) Thus, it would appear that Humanity constitutes what we might call "a construct" for Condorcet, not what Comte regarded as "le Grand-Etre."

19. E.g., *System of Positive Polity*, I, 6–7, and III, 13–14.

20. Cf. *ibid.*, III, 2–3.

21. *Ibid.*, III, 60. As we shall later see, a similar view is to be found in Spencer.

22. The most revealing of the methodological passages concerning this matter is the passage already cited in Comte's early essay in which he criticized Condorcet. In discussing the importance of classification in biology he said, "In a word Classification then becomes merely the philosophic expression of Science, the progress of which it follows. To know the classification is to know the science, at least in its more important portion." (*Ibid.*, IV, 571.)

23. Cf. *System of Positive Polity*, III, 62–63. In justification of the following interpretation, the following passage may be cited:

It is therefore only by the positive study of human progress as a whole that we can discover the real laws of the mind. When these are once found, the individual life furnishes the best possible verification of them, since the individual and social growth must always be essentially similar. When by observing the progress of the Race I had discovered the law of the three stages, a study of the Individual afforded me a most useful confirmation of it. But I might have observed the Individual for ever without making the original discovery. (*System of Positive Polity*, III, 38–39.)

24. Cf. the following statement:

The systematic study of man is logically and scientifically subordinate to that of Humanity, the latter alone unveiling to us the real laws of intelligence and activity. (*Ibid.*, IV, 162.)

In further support of my interpretation, see the letter of June 19, 1842, from Comte to Mill stating that it is only through sociology that a proper understanding of intellectual and moral development can come, and that to approach such problems from the point of view of the individual is false. (*Lettres inédites de John Stuart Mill*, p. 75–76.)

25. Cf. *System of Positive Polity*, II, 4–6, and III, 8, where he says of the volume devoted to his social statics:

The general results of the last volume may be thus summed up;—the normal type of Human Existence is one of complete unity. All progress therefore, whether of the individual or of the race, consists in developing and consolidating that unity.

26. *Ibid.*, III, 52. Cf. II, 296.

27. E.g., *Ibid.*, III, 39; cf. II, 148.

28. Cf. *Ibid.*, III, 52 and 353. Also, II, 99 and IV, 13.

29. Cf. *Ibid.*, IV, 4.

30. Cf. *Ibid.*, III, 60.

31. E.g., *Ibid.*, III, 8–9.

For an extended discussion of normality in which Comte leans heavily on the views of Broussais cf. *ibid.*, II, 359–63. However, it would seem extremely doubtful that Broussais' principle justifies the use to which Comte put it. Also, cf. *ibid.*, II, 350.

32. Cf. Taine: *Philosophes français du XIXe siècle* (1st ed.), pp. 126–27. For a

later passage in which the contributions of Hegel and of Comte are assessed, cf. *Histoire de la littérature anglaise*, V, 273–78. For Renan's view, cf. *L'Avenir de la science*, pp. 172–73.

It is also worth noting that as late as 1870 both Taine and Renan joined in an appeal in the *Journal des Debats* to have a monument erected at public expense for Hegel.

33. *L'Avenir de la science*, p. 132.

34. "One must begin with Hegel's *Phenomenology*, the true point of origin and the secret of the Hegelian philosophy." (*Economic and Philosophic Manuscripts*, p. 146.) That it would be mistaken to view the *Phenomenology* as constituting even an embryonic philosophy of history has been made clear by Jean Hyppolite. (Cf. *Genèse et structure de la phénoménologie de l'esprit*, I, 42–53.)

To be sure, prior to the manuscripts of 1844, Marx did concern himself intensively with Hegel's *Philosophy of Right*. Two documents bear witness to this: an essay which was intended to serve as introduction to a paragraph-by-paragraph analysis of that work, and a sizeable chunk of that never-completed analysis. However, neither of these documents concerns itself with Hegel's general philosophy, nor with his conception of world history, even though a preliminary sketch of the Hegelian philosophy of history appeared as the concluding section of the *Philosophy of Right*.

The only other passage which seems relevant to a possible Hegelian influence on Marx prior to 1844 is to be found in a long letter to his father concerning the course of his studies at the University of Berlin. This letter, dated November 10, 1837, shows interests and even forms of speech which are readily related to the Hegelian intellectual atmosphere which was doubtless present at the University, but the remarks on Hegel himself do not suggest that Marx was intent upon studying Hegel's works at that time.

35. Among the many examples of this, cf. *Economic and Philosophic Manuscripts*, pp. 105 and 109–10.

In the same connection, it is interesting to note that in a letter to Feuerbach, written on August 11, 1844, Marx expressed himself in a way that leaves no doubt that he shared Feuerbach's view that it was legitimate and important to speak in terms of the generic nature of man. (Quoted in Cornu, *Marx et Engels*, III, 140, note 1.)

36. For example, cf. *Economic and Philosophic Manuscripts*, pp. 103–5.

37. It is doubtless for this reason that the manuscripts of 1844 have the influence which they currently do among those who have a greater interest in discussing the condition of man than in establishing scientifically fruitful generalizations concerning social processes.

38. In the same connection it is worth noting that in his early essay, just mentioned, Engels treated Adam Smith and the classical economists in a typically historicist fashion, relating their theories to the social developments and needs of their times; whereas Marx's treatment of classical economics in the manuscripts of 1844 bears no trace of this historicist interpretation, even when he is citing Engels. (Cf. *Economic and Philosophic Manuscripts*, pp. 178–79 for Engels's discussion, and pp. 67–68 and 94–95 for that of Marx. For Marx's later view, which coincided with Engels's, cf. *Poverty of Philosophy*, p. 105.)

One of the more systematic statements of Marx's views on the social nature of man, which postdated his acquaintance with Engels but stems from this early period, is to be found in a letter to P. V. Annenkov in 1846. (Cf. pp. 152–54 of *Poverty of Philosophy*, to which that letter is appended.) And in the *Poverty of Philosophy*, in 1847, Marx wrote: "M. Proudhon does not know that all history is a transformation of human nature" (p. 124). It is this view—which stands in sharp contrast to the position maintained in the manuscripts of 1844—that characterizes Marx's position throughout his later writings.

39. *Ludwig Feuerbach*, p. 52, note.

40. The early works by Engels which are especially relevant are two of his essays entitled "Die Lage Englands," which he contributed to *Vorwärts* in 1844, and the study which he had already made of the English working class and which was shortly to appear.

41. An interpretation of the difference between the manuscripts of 1844 and *The German Ideology*, which runs parallel to my view but which is written with a different biographical and evaluative intent, is to be found in Tucker, *Philosophy and Myth in Karl Marx*, pp. 165–67.

42. Cf. *Werke*, III, 37–39 and 48–49.

43. Cf. *ibid.*, III, 50–77.

44. Karl Popper's interpretation of Marx is one striking example of the claim that Marx undoubtedly accepted historicism. One of Popper's definitions of "historicism" is that it holds that "the method of a science of society is the study of history, and especially of the tendencies inherent in the historical development of mankind." (Cf. *The Open Society*, p. 661, note 2, paragraph 2a. Cf. also *The Poverty of Historicism*, p. 45.) However, the textual evidence which Popper offers in support of the view that Marx held this position is wholly insufficient. Popper's case really rests on conflating two quite different beliefs: a belief in prediction, which Popper designates as "historical prophecy," and an acceptance of laws of directional change. That these beliefs need not be connected can be seen from the fact that Popper cites as an example of "historical prophecy" the prediction of a typhoon (*The Poverty of Historicism*, p. 43), but such a prediction need surely not involve the acceptance of any irreducible laws of directional change. One notes that the basis for this error lies in Popper's original characterization of "historicism," where he simply lumped together, without in any way explaining the conjunction, a belief in historical prediction and a belief that there are rhythms, patterns, or laws that underlie the evolution of history (*The Poverty of Historicism*, p. 3). This conflation of views which are in principle separate is a mistake that Popper failed to correct in *The Open Society*. Yet it is to be noted that in those chapters of the latter work in which he attempts to offer a careful reconstruction of Marxian analysis (Ch. 18, 19, 20), Popper does not show that Marx actually based his views on the acceptance of ultimate and irreducible laws of sequence among historical phenomena.

One notes the same confusion between an acceptance of the possibility of predicting future events in history and a belief in ultimate laws of directional change in Popper's discussion of Mill. And here one may find even greater fault with his documentation. For example, in *The Poverty of Historicism* (p. 118), Mill is directly quoted as holding that one can predict future historical events in a manner analogous to the projection of an algebraic series, and Popper even italicizes this statement. However, in the passage cited, Mill is describing "historical speculation in France," and as the immediately succeeding sentences show, he does not himself subscribe to the view that there are ultimate and irreducible laws of development. He does, however, hold that given ultimate laws of human nature, and a knowledge of historical conditions, one can presumably make reliable predictions about the future. Had Popper not conflated prediction with laws of development, his argument for holding that Mill's position is really comparable to that of Comte (or to that which he attributes to Marx) would have collapsed.

45. *Capital* I, 14 and 13, respectively.

46. *Ibid.*, I, 22. The reviewer was Professor A. Sieber of Kiev. (Cf. translator's note in Bukharin, *Historical Materialism*, p. 70.)

47. *Capital*, I, 24-25.

48. My interpretation of this last statement (which is precisely the point at which Marx introduced his discussion of Hegel) is wholly in conformity with the criticism which Marx and Engels made of Hegelian teleology when they discussed it in *The German Ideology*. There they said:

> Die Geschichte ist nichts als die Aufeinanderfolge der einzelnen Generationen. . . .
> während das, was man mit den Worten "Bestimmung," "Zweck," "Keim," "Idee" der
> früheren Geschichte bezeichnet, weiter nichts ist als eine Abstraktion von der späteren
> Geschichte, eine Abstraktion von dem aktiven Einfluss, den die frühere Geschichte auf
> die spätere ausübt." (*Werke*, III, 45.)

49. Volume I, Ch. 31. The following chapter, "Historical Tendency of Capitalist Accumulation," does contain passages (e.g., I, 835 and 836-37) concerning the inevitability of historical change which have often been cited as evidence that Marx believed in the determination of history by some overarching directional law. For example, Popper cited one of them (although with a mistaken chapter reference) in his article "What is Dialectic?" (p. 424). However, these passages, too, are most plausibly interpreted as summarizing trends which are governed not by directional laws but by the successive operation of non-directional laws on current situations. Thus, although Marx undeniably believed in the prediction of future social developments, he did not base his predictions on the existence of ultimately irreducible directional laws. In this connection it is also useful to remind ourselves that whereas Hegel did believe in inevitable directional tendencies in history, he rejected the possibility of making specific predictions. (To attempt to do so would be to contradict what Hegel took to be the fundamental character of philosophy. Cf. *Philosophy of Right*, pp. 10-12.) Thus, in the case of Hegel, no less than in the case of Marx, Popper's conflation of historicism and predictability in history can be seen to be mistaken.

50. This is also the view of Lichtheim, who concludes his discussion of Marx's historical materialism by saying:

> In any event Marx himself—unlike some of his followers—deduced the necessity of
> socialism not from any general theory of history, but from the analysis of 'the capitalist
> mode of production' and its social counterpart: bourgeois society. (*Marxism*, p. 152;
> cf. p. 256.)

It may be added that many contemporary forms of "Marxist humanism" tend to overlook this distinction in their attacks on what they misleadingly call the "positivist" interpretation of Marx. Consider, for example, the following account of the views of Antonio Gramsci, as interpreted by M. Marković:

This historical, basically humanist approach is clearly incompatible with the still prevailing (dogmatic and) positivist interpretation of Marxism. The essential feature of this [latter] interpretation is a purely ideological attempt to reduce Marxism to indubitable scientific knowledge about the existing reality and its development. There is no doubt that every truly progressive, contemporary, social movement must seek to base its program on truth, on objective knowledge about the historical possibilities of changing the given social reality. However, change is often possible in several directions, social laws at best are trends only, knowledge of them cannot be indubitable, and, most important of all, genuine revolutionary action must sometimes oppose prevailing trends and try to realize marginal historical possibilities which better correspond to the needs of the broad masses of people. (Marković, "Gramsci on the Unity of Philosophy and Politics," p. 335.)

It is my claim that Marx actually did attempt to offer a system of "indubitable scientific knowledge," but that this system was based on economic analysis (on the basis of which changes were predictable, from point to point), not on establishing general laws of necessary sequential development. Thus, in my opinion, the proper mode of criticizing Marx's necessitarianism is not to say that "laws at best are trends only," but to consider such other issues as (1) what further information is needed (in any science) for making concrete predictions, once a general law has been established concerning a general type of occurrence, and (2) whether Marx was correct in his views regarding the role of economic factors in social organization and social change.—A revolt against "positivism" and "necessary laws," in the name of "humanism," fails to provide a satisfactory basis for either a historically accurate account of Marx's thought (and of its distortions by others) or for an appraisal of it.

51. Cf. *Economic and Philosophic Manuscripts*, pp. 150–51.

52. It is to be noted that when, in the preface to *Capital*, Marx speaks of having coquetted with Hegelian modes of expression (I, 25), the conception which was involved remained that of alienation, not of historical transformation.

53. It seems to me that Lichtheim is wholly correct when, in speaking of Engels' *dialectical* materialism, he says:

The resulting medley of philosophy and science constitutes what has come to be known as 'dialectical materialism': a concept not present in the original Marxian version, and indeed essentially foreign to it, since for the early Marx the only nature relevant to the understanding of history is human nature. For the later Engels, on the contrary, historical evolution is an aspect of general (natural) evolution, and basically subject to the same 'laws.' The contrast could hardly be more glaring. (*Marxism*, p. 245.)

With respect to the term "dialectical materialism," we may note that it seems to have been introduced by Plekhanov. (Cf. Acton, *What Marx Really Said*, p. 31.)

54. It is to be noted that in his preface to the first edition of his book, *Karl Marx's Interpretation of History*, M. M. Bober says: "In this essay Marx and Engels are treated like one personality."

55. *Anti-Dühring*, p. 155.

56. *Ludwig Feuerbach*, p. 54. Earlier, in a review of Marx's *Contribution to a Critique of Political Economy*, Engels offered the following appreciation of Hegel —which, in my opinion, illustrates the difference between his own relationship to Hegel and that of Marx:

> Was Hegel's Denkweise vor der aller andern Philosophen auszeichnete, war der enorme historische Sinn, der ihr zugrunde lag.... Er war der erste, der in die Geschichte eine Entwicklung, einen innern Zusammenhang nachzuweisen versuchte, und wie sonderbar uns auch manches in seiner Philosophie der Geschichte jetzt vorkommen mag, so ist die Grossartigkeit der Grundanschauung selbst heute noch bewundernswert. (*Werke*, XIII, 473–74.)

57. *Ludwig Feuerbach*, p. 55.

58. *Ibid.*, p. 37.
There is one brief passage in *Capital* in which Marx himself contrasts a correct form of materialism with "the abstract materialism of natural science, a materialism that excludes history and its process" (I, 406, note 2). This phrase would seem to suggest that Marx advocated "dialectical materialism," a scientific materialism that would apply dialectical concepts to the physical world. While there is nothing to exclude the possibility that Marx would have subscribed to Engels's views in this respect, the passage itself does not warrant that inference. Both its context and the sentence as a whole make it clear that the specific criticism of "the abstract materialism of natural science" which Marx is here expressing is its failure to deal with *human* history, the history of human social relations.

59. *Anti-Dühring*, p. 27. Cf. also, pp. 28 ff.

60. *Anti-Dühring*, p. 155. For a suggestive discussion of the multiform meanings of the negation of the negation in Engels, cf. Hook, *Reason, Social Myths, and Democracy*, pp. 184–95. For Hook's criticism of dialectic as explanation, *ibid.*, pp. 195–226 and 250–66.

61. "Thanks to these three great discoveries [the discovery of the cell, the transformation of energy, and the Darwinian theory] and the other immense advances in natural science, we have now arrived at the point where we can demonstrate as a whole the inter-connection between the processes in nature not only in particular spheres but also in the inter-connection of these particular spheres themselves, and so can present in an approximately systematic form a comprehensive view of the inter-connection in nature by means of the facts provided by empirical natural science itself." (*Ludwig Feuerbach*, p. 56.)

62. *Anti-Dühring*, p. 30.

63. *Ludwig Feuerbach*, p. 22.
As this quotation suggests, Engels (like Hegel) assumed that the later stages in a dialectical development are always of higher worth than the earlier: while no morality has an absolute validity, that which represents the forces which lead to the overthrow of the present and give shape to the future, is the higher form of morality. (Cf. *Anti-Dühring*, p. 104.)

64. In a brief communication in *Encounter* (March, 1967), bearing the heading "From Hoax to Dogma: A Footnote on Marx and Darwin," Shlomo Avineri suggests that the parallel between Marx and Darwin which Engels emphasized, and

which later Marxists and anti-Marxists have taken for granted, actually originated as "a hoax." He bases this interpretation on a letter from Marx to Engels (December 7, 1867) which suggests in detail how Engels should review *Das Kapital* in order to place that review in a journal edited by a liberal who was a great admirer of the Darwinian theory. The letter does establish that the review must be termed "a hoax." However, it does not of itself establish what Marx's own attitude toward Darwin and Darwinism actually was. With respect to that question, I wholly agree with Avineri that Engels was an enthusiastic Darwinian (except for Darwin's reliance on Malthusian doctrine), and that Marx was not. However, Avineri badly overstates his case with respect to this difference.

In the first place, Marx's letter to Engels, dated December 19, 1860, was more positive in its tone than Avineri's description of its content would lead one to believe. Marx actually said of the *Origin of Species*: "Obgleich grob englisch entwickelt, ist dies das Buch, das die naturhistorische Grundlage für unsere Ansicht enthält." That statement can scarcely be characterized as merely expressing the view that the book "is very helpful." In the second place Marx in effect repeated his original appraisal of Darwin in *Capital* itself. In attempting to analyze the difference between "tools" and "machines," and in speaking of the need for a history of technology, Marx says: "Darwin has interested us in the history of Nature's Technology, i.e., in the formation of the organs of plants and animals, which organs serve as instruments of production for sustaining life. Does not the history of the productive organs of man, of organs that are the material basis of all social organization, deserve equal attention?" (*Capital*, I, 406, n. 2). In short, the Darwinian problem was seen by Marx as analogous to a fundamental problem in his own theory, but one which he did not himself attempt to solve. To be sure, neither in this passage nor elsewhere does Marx suggest that the Darwinian theory should be applied in historical analysis, nor that social change is to be construed as an extension of the processes of biological evolution; however, a *parallel* was drawn between Marxism and Darwinism. It remained for Engels to assert that this was more than a parallel, that the two theories were rooted in a common soil—the dialectical version of materialism.

CHAPTER 5.   EVOLUTION AND PROGRESS

1. Cf. "The Scientific Background of Evolutionary Theory in Biology," *Journal of the History of Ideas*, XVIII (1957), 342–61. Reprinted in Wiener and Noland, *Roots of Scientific Thought*, New York: Basic Books, 1957.

2. Cf. the following postscript which appears in a letter which Darwin wrote to Lyell at the time he was preparing to send a manuscript of the *Origin of Species* to his publisher, Murray:

P.S. Would you advise me to tell Murray that my book is not more *un*orthodox than the subject makes inevitable. That I do not discuss the origin of man. That I do not bring in any discussion about Genesis, &c., &c., and only give facts and such conclusions from them as seem to me fair.... (*Life and Letters of Darwin*, I, 507).

Cf. also *Descent of Man*, p. 1.

3. *Origin of Species*, p. 559. (The reference to Spencer does not appear in the first edition, but the purport of the passage was the same.)

In his autobiographical account of his life, Darwin stated that he had been convinced that the evolutionary doctrine applied to man as soon as he had become convinced of its truth with respect to other species (i.e., in 1837 or 1838).

It was therefore a matter of intellectual honesty, he felt, to add the above paragraph in the *Origin of Species*. (Cf. *Life and Letters of Darwin*, I, 75–76; also, II,
58.) In that paragraph, Darwin was of course referring to the first edition of
Spencer's *Principles of Psychology*, which had appeared in 1855. The second edition, which formed part of Spencer's "Synthetic Philosophy," was radically altered, and did not appear until 1870.

4. I do not wish to deny importance to the metaphysical background which Lovejoy traced in *The Great Chain of Being*. (Cf. especially Ch. VIII on eighteenth-
century biology and Ch. IX on the temporalization of the concept of a Chain of
Being.) For example, one can see this influence in Lamarck, who explicitly related
his doctrine to Bonnet's view "that there exists a sort of scale or graduated chain
among living bodies" (*Zoological Philosophy*, p. 12). Furthermore, Lamarck's
own theory rested on the assumption that "in all nature's works nothing is done
abruptly, but that she acts everywhere slowly and by successive stages" (*ibid.*, p.
46). This temporal form of the axiom *natura non facit saltum* doubtless owed a
great deal to the conception of a Great Chain of Being, but it can also be interpreted as an expression of the uniform and constant action of laws of nature. Such
a conception did play an important role in Lamarck's thought, and in the case
of Darwin it is obvious that the expression *natura non facit saltum* must be so
interpreted. For example, when he spoke of it as a canon which "every fresh addition to our knowledge tends to confirm" (*Origin of Species*, p. 540), he explicitly
connected its truth with the uniform and constant laws of variation and natural
selection (cf. also *Origin of Species*, p. 304). The difference between the static
conception of *natura non facit saltum*, which had been connected with the
doctrine of a Great Chain of Being, and its temporal interpretation as due to the
constant action of the laws of nature can be clearly seen in Darwin's discussion of
the theory of classification. (Cf. *Origin of Species*, Ch. XIV, especially pp. 476
and 482–84.)

5. The foregoing considerations seem to me to have been overlooked by Kenneth
Bock when he argued that Darwin's acceptance of minute steps in evolutionary
change was not dictated by available evidence, but that it derived from the
doctrine *natura non facit saltum*. Bock is indeed correct that it found no support
in the evidence provided by the geological record, but if Darwin's views regarding
variation and regarding inheritance are taken into account, it is surely understandable why he should have cited the imperfection of the geological record as
the reason for our failure to find minute, intervening steps in the course of
evolutionary development. (For Bock's discussion, cf. "Darwin and Social
Theory," p. 125.)

6. The relationship between original utility and the existence of rudimentary
organs was made explicit by Darwin in a letter to Lyell in answer to criticisms
made by the latter. (Cf. *Life and Letters*, II, 9.)
   For my reference to the later change in Darwin's views, cf. Ch. I, note 37.

7. The doctrine that (in Haeckel's phrase) "ontogeny recapitulates phylogeny"
was associated with transformism almost from its beginnings. For example, cf.
Chamber's *Vestiges of the Natural History of Creation*, pp. 149–51. In this connection it may be remarked that the very title of Chambers's anonymous book
was a significant clue to its content.

8. *Origin of Species*, pp. 557–58.

9. "On the Comparative Method in Anthropology," p. 119.

10. It was through the influence of Franz Boas's attack on the comparative method that the use of that method in establishing social evolution was finally overcome. Boas's crucial article, "The Limitations of the Comparative Method of Anthropology" (republished in Boas's *Race, Language, and Culture*), was published in 1893 but its effects were not immediately noticeable. Boas's position became dominant primarily through its influence on the distinguished group of American anthropologists who were his students.

In connection with this article, it is to be noted that some of Boas's objections to the comparative method might also be applied to some instances of Darwin's own use of that method. For example, in the chapter on instinct in the *Origin of Species*, Darwin's discussion of the slave-making instinct in ants assuredly failed to offer evidence sufficient to suggest that the variations of form in this instinct could be used to reconstruct a probable line of descent.

11. On Darwin's indebtedness to Spencer for this phrase, cf. *Origin of Species*, p. 63, and Darwin's letter to Wallace, July 5, 1866 (*Life and Letters*, II, 229–30).

12. In speaking of the adaptations which must arise when a plant or animal is placed in a new environment, and must therefore gain an advantage over a new set of competitors, Darwin said:

It is good thus to try in imagination to give any one species an advantage over another. Probably in no single instance should we know what to do. (*Origin of Species*, p. 79.)

Yet, of course, this is constantly being accomplished in nature through the workings of constant laws.

The same point was made by Darwin in his 1842 and 1844 drafts of his theory; cf. *Foundations of the Origin of Species*, p. 14 and pp. 94–95.

13. Cf. Darwin's remarks in the prefatory note to the sixth edition of the *Origin of Species* (p. xxii), in which he gives a historical sketch of earlier views regarding the origin of species. The same criticism appeared as early as 1844 in a letter which Darwin wrote to Hooker (*More Letters*, I, 41) and is repeated in the *Origin of Species* itself (cf. p. 128). Surprisingly enough, Darwin found himself forced to return to it in a letter to Lyell which was written as late as 1863. (Cf. *Life and Letters*, II, 198–99.)

14. Cf. *More Letters*, II, 376. For other discussions of the same point, cf. *Origin of Species*, p. 227 and *More Letters*, I, 286, 311, 344.

15. *Origin of Species*, p. 129. (For an explanation of the insertion of this passage as an answer to objections drawn from retrogression in the evolution of animal forms, cf. *More Letters*, I, 164–65.)

The same point was most emphatically stressed by Darwin in 1862 in a letter answering objections raised by Hugh Falconer. In that letter he not only rejects a law of *progressive* development, he also rejects the notion that there is "some unknown law of evolution by which species necessarily change" (*More Letters*, I, 208).

16. As an example of a suggested correlation between social and political changes and the acceptance or rejection of evolutionism I might cite some recent remarks of Leslie A. White:

It may be significant to also note that evolutionism flourished in cultural anthropology in a day when the capitalist system was still growing: evolution and progress were the order of the day. But when, at the close of the nineteenth century the era of colonial expansion came to an end and the capitalist-democratic system had matured and established itself securely in the Western world, then evolution was no longer a popular concept. On the contrary, the dominant note was "maintain the status quo". . . .

But antievolutionism has run its course and once more the theory of evolution is on the march. Again, it may be significant to note that this is taking place in a world which is once more undergoing rapid and profound change. The so-called backward nations in Africa and Asia are rebelling against the white man and colonialism. (Foreword to Sahlins and Service, *Evolution and Culture*, pp. vi–vii.)

One scarcely knows what to make of such facile correlations. To attribute the original flourishing of social evolutionism to the mood of a growing capitalism and not to mention the tremendous intellectual impact of the theory of biological evolution—let alone other influences which, as we shall see, one is forced to take into account—is to denigrate the scientific seriousness of those who sought to establish social evolutionism. Furthermore, White's attempt (*ibid.*, page v) to connect the criticisms of evolutionism made by Boas and Herskovits with specific tendencies in the history of capitalism, and not to mention their actual political and social views, is not only superficial but grossly unfair.

It should be obvious that some adaptations of Darwinism to discussions of political issues may be explicable in the general manner which is suggested by White; for example, works such as Richard Hofstadter's *Social Darwinism in American Thought* make it apparent that there were connections of this general type. However, it should be equally obvious that there is a difference between explaining the rise and spread of a scientific theory and explaining the non-scientific uses to which that theory has been put, or might be put.

17. This was one of Darwin's most basic objections to the so-called "Natural System" of classification, and he used it as an argument to support his own theory of genealogical classification. (Cf. *Origin of Species*, Ch. XIV, pp. 476–84, and also his earlier discussion in the draft essay of 1844, *Foundations of the Origin of Species*, pp. 198–213.) So far as I am able to ascertain, Darwin did not share the philosophical objections to the reality of species which one finds in, say, Locke, Condillac, and Buffon, and which played so large a role in Lamarck's arguments for transformism.

18. One can note the effect of this aspect of the Great Chain of Being in Lamarck's theory of transmutation:

Nature has produced all the species of animals in succession, beginning with the most imperfect or simplest, and ending her work with the most perfect, so as to create a gradually increasing complexity in their organization. (*Zoological Philosophy*, p. 126.)

The same emphasis on an ascending order of complexity is found in Chambers's hypotheses concerning the serial order of development in plants and animals (cf. *Vestiges of the Natural History of Creation*, pp. 145–55, *et passim*), as well as in the anti-transmutation doctrines of Progressionists such as Hugh Miller.

19. Cf. the quasi-biological but actually psychological ordering of forms suggested by Soame Jenyns in the late eighteenth century:

Animal life rises from this low beginning in the shell-fish, through innumerable species of insects, fishes, birds, and beasts, to the confines of reason, where, in the dog, the monkey, and chimpanzè, it unites so closely with the lowest degree of that quality in man, that they cannot easily be distinguished from each other. From this lowest degree in the brutal Hottentot, reason, with the assistance of learning and science, advances, through the various stages of human understanding, which rise above each other, till in a Bacon or a Newton it attains the summit. (Cited by Lovejoy, *The Great Chain of Being*, p. 197.)

For a brief discussion of the intrusion of psychological criteria into zoölogical classifications, and for references to Isidore Geoffroy St. Hilaire's criticism of this, cf. Lyell, *Geological Evidences of the Antiquity of Mankind*, pp. 473–76.

20. It is not to be assumed that the doctrine of the Great Chain of Being completely dominated the classification of organic forms among those who rejected transformism. In the second decade of the nineteenth century, in opposition to Lamarck, Cuvier attacked the conception of a single lineal series of animal forms in *Le règne animal*; so too did Augustin de Candolle.

21. Darwin used such expressions throughout his writings, but rarely faced the theoretical issues involved. There is one point at which he appears to have started to do so; it occurs in that section of Chapter IV of the *Origin of Species* which is entitled "On the Degree to which Organization Tends to Advance." The section begins with what might be construed as an argument for the necessity of advance:

Natural selection acts exclusively by the preservation and accumulation of variations, which are beneficial under the organic and inorganic conditions to which each creature is exposed at all periods of life. The ultimate result is that each creature tends to become more and more improved in relation to its conditions. *This improvement inevitably leads to the gradual advancement of the organization of the greater number of living beings throughout the world* (p. 127; italics added).

If these sentences were to be construed as an argument designed to show that there must necessarily be a general advance from "lower" to "higher" organisms, it would clearly be fallacious, for the improvement of each species is relative to its own environment, and the existence of a single directional line of advance in all forms of life would not be a necessary consequence of summing these separate improvements. However, Darwin did not commit this fallacy; in fact, he simply abandoned the argument at this point.

22. It was of course possible to claim that the whole of *human* history was a retrograde process, and to do so within the framework of theological orthodoxy, since moral retrogression would accord with the myth of the Garden of Eden and the doctrine of Original Sin. This, as we shall later note, was in fact the line taken by Archbishop Whately and then by the Duke of Argyll. In the *Descent of Man* Darwin discussed their views only briefly, but their earlier impact must have been considerable, if we may judge from the necessity felt by Tylor, Lubbock, Morgan, and others, to rebut them. I am not aware, however, of any Christian theological justification for assuming that the non-human world was marked by a general retrograde tendency.

23. *Foundations of the Origin of Species*, p. 52.

24. Cf. *ibid.*, p. 51 and p. 254.

25. The view presupposed is, of course, reminiscent of Leibniz: one can affirm that this is the best of all possible worlds and yet acknowledge the existence of events which assuredly would have to be designated as evil if they were considered in and of themselves. Thus, in the creation of parasites, considered apart from the

necessity of nature's general laws, evil would have been created; however, in so far as they follow necessarily from laws which work toward good ends, they are not to be considered as evil.

26. I have sought to trace this development in "Darwin's Religious Views," *Journal of the History of Ideas*, XIX (1958), 363–78. More thorough, documented discussions of the doctrine of secondary causes, of the views of Lyell and Gray, and also of John Herschel, are to be found in that article. (Should the reader wish to consult a letter belonging to the period in which Darwin's attitude toward secondary causes had begun to change, he might refer to one written to Lyell in 1861, published in *More Letters of Darwin*, I, 193–94.)

I regret that I formerly underestimated the extent to which, earlier in his career, Darwin had thought there were positive arguments in favor of the doctrine of secondary causes. It has been my aim to rectify that error here, by means of my comments on the epigraphs to the *Origin of Species* and on the quasi-theological arguments which are to be found in the last pages of the drafts of 1842 and 1844.

27. For an influential expression of this traditional view, the reader may consult a work admired by Darwin, Sir John F. W. Herschel's *Preliminary Discourse on the Study of Natural Philosophy*, which was first published in 1830—the same year as that in which Comte published the first volume of his *Cours de philosophie positive*. For Herschel's clearest statements of his views on the subject of nature's laws, cf. Part I, Ch. III, especially sections 26 to 29, 32, and 33. Comte's views will be discussed below.

28. Cf. *System of Logic*, Bk. III, Ch. XVI ("Empirical Laws"), *et passim*.

29. Buckle may be said to have resembled Comte in this respect. As he formulated the issue, the crucial question was "Are the actions of men and therefore of societies, governed by fixed laws, or are they the result either of chance or of supernatural interference?" (*History of Civilization in England*, I, 6.)

On the extent to which others who belonged within the positivistic tradition assumed a necessitarian position which was not always compatible with their positivism, cf. my discussion of Claude Bernard and of Helmholtz in Chapter 1, p. 16.

It is against this background that we can best understand why the idealistic rebellion against Positivism in France took the form of attempting to establish contingency in nature as well as freedom of the will.

30. *System of Logic*, Bk. VI, Ch. X, Sect. 3, p. 633.

31. Cf. especially *The Study of Sociology*, Ch. 2. It is of significance to note that this brief popular work had a tremendous impact on the development of American sociology. (Cf. the remarks of Charles H. Cooley, quoted in Hofstadter, *Social Darwinism in American Thought*, p. 20.) Also, cf. "The Social Organism," in *Essays: Scientific, Political and Speculative*, I, 266, and *Education*, pp. 64–71.

For useful references to the views of Comte and Spencer on the issue of history *vs.* sociology, and for a general discussion of this problem in the nineteenth century, cf. Kenneth E. Bock's monograph, *The Acceptance of Histories*.

32. His account of these stages is to be found in his *Autobiography*, II, 6–16.

It will be noted in what follows that Spencer, unlike Comte, used the concept of cause, and assumed that every uniform sequence had to be causally explained through the operation of some more general law—until the most basic law, governing all phenomena, was reached. Stimulated by the doctrine of the conservation of energy, and by the equivalence and transformation of diverse forms of energy, Spencer formulated his ultimate causal law as a law of force. It should be obvious that there would have been few positions in the philosophy of science more unacceptable to Comte than a *reductionism* which attempted to find a single all-embracing law explaining *why* things happen as they do, and expressing such a law in terms of the general concept of *Force*, which—in itself— is admittedly Unknowable.

In an essay entitled "Reasons for Dissenting from the Philosophy of M. Comte," Spencer attacked Comte's rejection of causal explanation, but a far more detailed attack was given by his disciple John Fiske in *Outlines of Cosmic Philosophy*, Part I, Ch. VII. However, Fiske gave credit to Comte for inaugurating a revolution in philosophy by advancing the thesis that there was a necessary evolutionary order of intellectual development.

33. *Essays: Scientific, Political, and Speculative*, I, 10.

An even earlier formulation of his belief in the indivisible unity of the progressive evolutionary series is to be found in the first edition of his *Principles of Psychology*, which he published in 1855 but later thoroughly revised. One particularly striking passage is the following:

> Thus, it will be manifest, that from the lowest to the highest forms of life, the increasing adjustment of inner to outer relations is, if rightly understood, one indivisible progression. Just as, out of the homogeneous tissue with which every organism commences, there arises by one continuous process of differentiation and integration, a congeries of organs performing separate functions, but which remain throughout mutually dependent, and indeed grow more mutually dependent; so, the correspondence between the phenomena going on inside of the organism and those going on outside of it, beginning, as it does, with some simple homogeneous correspondence between internal and external affinities, gradually becomes differentiated into various orders of correspondences, which are constantly more and more subdivided, but which nevertheless retain a reciprocity of aid that grows ever greater as the progression advances. The two progressions are in truth parts of the same progression.... As the progress of organization and the progress of the correspondence between the organism and its environment, are but different aspects of the evolution of Life in general, they cannot fail to harmonize. And hence, in this organization of experiences which we call Intelligence, there must be that same continuity, that same subdivision of function, that same mutual dependence, and that same ever-advancing *consensus*, which characterize the physical organization (p. 485).

Spencer was not alone in holding to the doctrine of total evolutionism, although he undoubtedly provides the most extreme example of it. One finds that a similar doctrine is enunciated at the outset of Haeckel's *History of Creation*, where he says:

> The scientific theory set forth in [*Origin of Species*], which is commonly called Darwinism, is only a small fragment of a far more comprehensive doctrine—a part of the universal Theory of Development, which embraces in its vast range the whole domain of human knowledge (I, 1–2).

34. *Autobiography*, II, 13–14.

An analogy between intellectual development and other forms of development which appears to be equally fantastic is to be found in *Principles of Sociology*, I, 80–81, where Spencer compares the processes of bodily nutrition in lower and higher animals with less intelligent and more intelligent forms of "intellectual assimilation."

35. As a matter of accuracy, it should be pointed out that in the comparatively early essay which I have quoted, the ultimate cause of evolutionary change was not yet formulated by Spencer in terms of the laws of the transformation of energy; rather, it was phrased in the dictum that "every active force produces more than one change—every cause produces more than one effect." (*Essays: Scientific, Political, and Speculative*, I, 37.) However, since Spencer abandoned the earlier formulation without abandoning his earlier list of areas in which progress was evident, the following criticism should not be considered as biased.

36. "Progress: Its Law and Cause," in *Essays: Scientific, Political, and Speculative*, I, 9.

37. Cf. *First Principles*, Ch. XIV. (For the sidereal system, p. 318; for music, p. 336.)
It might be claimed that my statement of Spencer's method is unfair, since I stress only the diversity of instances, and neglect the element of systematic order in his argument. However, the order existed more in the table of organization of the fields to be covered than in systematic discussion of any of the individual fields. Should this be doubted, I ask the reader to turn to his essay "The Social Organism" (in *Essays: Scientific, Political, and Speculative*, I, 265–307) and note the analogies which Spencer finds between the organic and the superorganic. His use of these analogies involves a constant shifting in point of reference, for some were drawn from embryological development, others from the functioning of specific organs in adult individuals, others from the behavior of colonies of individuals, and others from the evolution of species. Furthermore, in each of these different types of case, he made indiscriminate reference to the most diverse sorts of plants and of animals.

38. Spencer's method of deriving a law which can be applied to complex phenomena (in this case, a law applicable to societies) was described by Fiske as follows:

> Minor perturbing elements must for a time be left out of consideration, just as the inequalities of motion resulting from the mutual attractions of the planets were first passed over in the search for the general formula of gravitation. The discussion of endless minute historical details must be reserved until the law of social changes has been deduced from the more constant phenomena, and is ready for inductive verification. A law wide enough to form a basis for sociology must needs be eminently abstract, and can be found only by contemplating the most general and prominent characteristics of social changes. The prime requisite of the formula of which we are in quest is that it should accurately designate such changes under their leading aspect.
> Now by far the most obvious and constant characteristic common to a vast number of social changes is that they are changes from a worse to a better state of things,—that they constitute phases of Progress. (*Outlines of Cosmic Philosophy*, III, 281–82.)

39. Spencer accounted for such cases by pointing out that in both biological and social evolution developmental change depends upon a combination of inner and outer factors; thus, forms which remained in equilibrium with external conditions would not progress. (For example, cf. *Principles of Sociology*, I, 95–98 and *First Principles*, p. 588.) However, if one examines Spencer's statement of the law of evolution and his application of it to concrete cases in *First*

Principles, one can see that he did not in fact usually make reference to the external factors which should have been treated as co-responsible for any development which took place.

An answer which, on the whole, must be considered a more adequate answer on the part of those who believed in the necessity of progress, is to be found in the fourth lecture of Büchner, *Die Darwin'sche Theorie.* That lecture makes clear how widespread was the dissatisfaction with the belief in the inevitability of progress. Büchner's answer to challenges regarding stagnation and retrogression was to deny that progress should be thought of in terms of a single linear series; instead, he used Darwin's simile of the great, branching Tree of Life. Progress was claimed to be clearly discernible in evolution as a whole, though not in the history of each of its offshoots. (Cf. pp. 222–23 and 247–48.)

40. John Fiske, *A Century of Science,* p. 35. For a comparable passage from Engels's *Ludwig Feuerbach,* cf. p. 74, above.

41. Cf. *Outlines of Cosmic Philosophy,* III, 282–89.

42. As its title indicates, Haeckel attempted to offer a new cosmogony in his *History of Creation: or, the Development of the Earth and its Inhabitants by the Action of Natural Causes.* Its scope, however, was less broad than its title. Its principal theme was that there are two basic laws which are the necessary consequences of natural selection: a law of differentiation and, second, "the law of *Progress* (progressus) or *Perfecting* (teleosis)." It was held that these laws governed the course of development of plants, of animals, and of mankind, but the cosmogonic details were not filled-in. (Cf. vol. I, ch. XI, p. 277.)

Büchner shared the same ambition to give a single comprehensive evolutionary interpretation of the world as a whole, and we have already alluded to Engels's attempt to unify all aspects of reality through dialectical materialism. What I especially wish to call to attention in Büchner and in Engels is the manner in which they conceived of laws as governing or necessitating particular events. For this purpose I may quote from the preface to the first edition of *Force and Matter,* where Büchner says that the rise of the empirical sciences makes it "daily more evident that both the macrocosmic and the microcosmic worlds obey at every state of their genesis, existence, and subsidence, the *mechanical* laws which lie in the very nature of things". (p. vi.) (Cf. also the two chapters in which he discusses the immutability and the universality of natural laws.)

The following passage from Engels is a relatively extreme one, but it does illustrate the fact that Marxists have often tended to look upon laws as "controlling" and "dominating" events:

In the world of nature, where chance seems to rule, we have long since demonstrated in each separate field the inner necessity and law asserting itself in this chance. But what is true of the natural world is true also of society. The more a social activity, a series of social processes, becomes too powerful for men's conscious control and grows above their heads, and the more it appears a matter of pure chance, then all the more surely within this chance the laws peculiar to it and inherent in it assert themselves as if by natural necessity. . . . and still to this day the product rules the producer; still to this day the total production of society is regulated, not by a jointly devised plan, but by blind laws, which manifest themselves with elemental violence, in the final instances in the storms of the periodical trade crises. (Engels, *Origin of the Family,* p. 159 f.)

43. The following passages from Kidd's *Social Evolution* may serve to illustrate his position:

But let us deal first with the necessity for progress. . . . Progress is a necessity from
which there is simply no escape, and from which there has never been any escape since
the beginning of life (p. 35).

The inevitability of progress derives, according to Kidd, from the principles of
rivalry and selection, and he continues:

With whatever feelings we may regard the conflict it is, however, necessary to remember
that it is the first condition of progress. It leads continually onwards and upwards.
From this stress of nature has followed the highest result we are capable of conceiving,
namely, continual advance toward higher and more perfect forms of life. . . . The law
of life has been always the same from the beginning—ceaseless and inevitable struggle
and competition, ceaseless and inevitable selection and rejection, ceaseless and inevitable
progress (pp. 38–39).

And with respect to the inevitability of progress in social development Kidd
says:

Nor can there be any doubt that from these strenuous conditions of rivalry the race as
a whole is powerless to escape. The conditions of progress may be interrupted amongst
the peoples who have long held their place in the front. These peoples may fail and fall
behind, but progress continues nevertheless. For although the growth of the leading
shoot may be for the time arrested, farther back on the branch other shoots are always
ready to take the place of that which has ceased to advance (p. 57 f.).

In order to avoid misunderstanding, it must be pointed out that Kidd, like
Darwin, strongly believed in the efficacy of altruism, and that his emphasis on
competition did not lead him to defend economic or political *laissez-faire*.
For a discussion of Carnegie, and illustrative quotations, cf. Hofstadter, *Social
Darwinism in America*, pp. 31–32.

The influence of Darwin, and of biological analogies, on German sociology
is discussed in Barth's *Die Philosophie der Geschichte*, pp. 243–87.

CHAPTER 6.   SOCIAL EVOLUTIONISM

1. For the references to Lucretius (one tacit and one explicit), see *Ancient
Society*, pp. 12–13 and 25; for the reference to Darwin, see p. 357. Darwin's
discussion of the problem is to be found in the *Descent of Man*, II, 324–47. It
is to be noted that in this passage Darwin actually accepted, rather than rejected,
the theory of promiscuity advanced by Morgan, Lubbock, and McLennan, on
the grounds that they seemed to have offered adequate evidence for it; he simply
rejected the view that promiscuity could plausibly be thought to have been the
very earliest form of sexual relationship among the remote ancestors of man.
But Morgan refused even this concession, preferring his own reasoning as to
what must have been true among the gregarious animals (cf. p. 424).

It is also of interest to note that McLennan's use of a comparative-evolutionary
method was quite independent of evolutionary theory in biology. On this point,
cf. J. W. Burrow, *Evolution and Society*, pp. 230–34.

2. For a brief sketch of Boucher de Perthes's contribution, and mention of
those who had visited the scene, cf. Lubbock, *Pre-Historic Times*, pp. 342–46.

An important step in the expansion of the human time-scale was Lyell's
careful summation of the evidence in *Geological Evidences of the Antiquity of
Man* (1863), though this work left Darwin uncomfortable because of the reservations regarding the theory of descent which it contained. (Cf. *Life and Letters*,
II, 193–202.)

3. Cf. *Life and Letters*, I, 220.

4. *Primitive Culture*, I, 37. In the preface to the second edition, published two years later (i.e. in 1873), Tylor said:

It may have struck some readers as an omission, that in a work on civilization insisting so strenuously on a theory of development or evolution, mention should scarcely have been made of Mr. Darwin and Mr. Herbert Spencer, whose influence on the whole course of modern thought on such subjects should not be left without formal recognition. This absence of particular reference is accounted for by the present work, arranged on its own lines, coming scarcely into contact of detail with the previous works of these eminent philosophers (pp. vii–viii).

In fact, the only other points at which Tylor refers by name to Darwin and to Spencer relate to specifically ethnographic concerns.

There is one point at which Tylor makes use of language reminiscent of the doctrine of competition for survival which had been made familiar by Darwin. (Cf. *Primitive Culture*, I, 69.) However, as we shall later note (p. 108, below), Tylor's usual explanation of progress in institutions depends upon growth in the arts and in knowledge, not directly upon competition.

5. *Primitive Culture*, I, 7–8.

It is to be noted, however, that Tylor is here referring to naturalists in general, not to Darwin; and that he does not pose the ethnographer's task as one of accounting for the origin of the species with which he deals.

In connection with the similarity between Tylor's methodological assumptions and those of Darwin, it is relevant to note the enthusiasm with which Darwin greeted *Primitive Culture*. In a letter to Tylor (whom he evidently did not know), he wrote:

My dear Sir,—I hope that you will allow me to have the pleasure of telling you how greatly I have been interested by your 'Primitive Culture,' now that I have finished it. It seems to me a most profound work, which will be certain to have permanent value, and to be referred to for years to come. It is wonderful how you trace animism from the lower races up to the religious belief of the highest races.... How curious also are the survivals or rudiments of old customs.... (*Life and Letters*, II, 331).

As R. H. Lowie points out, there was the same parallelism of methodological assumptions in the case of A. Lane-Fox Pitt-Rivers (*History of Ethnological Theory*, pp. 19–20). For an account of the origins of the Pitt-Rivers ethnological collection, cf. Tylor, "How the Problems of American Anthropology Present Themselves to the English Mind," pp. 90–91.

6. This parallelism of method is a factor which has been generally overlooked in attempts to assess the relationships between social evolutionism and the theory of evolution in biology. For two strikingly opposed estimates of the influence of Darwinism on social evolutionism, the reader may wish to consult Kenneth Bock's "Darwin and Social Theory," which minimizes that influence, and Morris Ginsberg's "Social Evolution," which emphasizes it.

7. As Lubbock pointed out in *Pre-Historic Times* (pp. 424 ff.), even with respect to relatively recent events the testimony of non-literate people was apt to be grossly unreliable.

8. To be sure, there were those who argued that different races represented different species of a common genus, rather than varieties of a common species.

However, not only did this view run counter to Biblical authority, but it failed to meet the usual tests as to what constituted distinct species. The view seems in fact to have been more common in earlier periods than it was in the mid-nineteeth century.

9. Tylor summarized his own view, which was a more cautious version of the progressionist hypothesis than was shared by many of his contemporaries, in saying:

> History, taken as our guide in explaining the different stages of civilization, offers a theory based on actual experience. This is a development theory, in which both advance and relapse have their acknowledged places. But so far as history is to be our criterion, progression is primary and degradation secondary. (*Primitive Culture*, I, 38.)

As he pointed out in this passage, "culture must be gained before it can be lost."

It is interesting to note that he had earlier, and more briefly, discussed the same issue in both the seventh and the concluding chapter of his *Researches into the Early History of Mankind.* That he should have felt it necessary to return to the issue, and to place the discussion of it in a more prominent position, shows that the degradation theory had not suffered eclipse in the intervening years.

One finds the same topic discussed in Spencer's *Principles of Sociology*, in Morgan's *Ancient Society*, and in two lengthy appendices to Lubbock's *Origin of Civilization*, where the arguments of both Whately and the Duke of Argyll are examined. It is also discussed, though only briefly, in Darwin's *Descent of Man*, I, 174–77.

10. Cf. his discussion of classification in Ch. XIV (p. 484) of the *Origin of Species.* In *Geological Evidence for the Antiquity of Man*, in 1863, Lyell devoted the whole of a chapter to developing the analogy, and Darwin returned to it in *The Descent of Man*, I, 57–59.

11. For one of his discussions of the theoretical problem posed by the possibility of multiple independent origins, cf. *Researches into the Early History of Mankind*, pp. 275 ff.

12. In "The Doctrine of Survivals: The History of an Idea," Margaret T. Hodgen argues that Tylor's conception of "survivals" is independent of the Darwinian view. I should not be inclined to challenge her thesis, nor her emphasis on the extent to which Tylor was reacting against Whately, but the methodological parallel nonetheless remains.

In his discussion of Tylor, J. W. Burrow points out that both McLennan and Spencer had used the concept of "survivals" prior to Tylor, although they had not used that term. He speaks somewhat contemptuously of the fact that "it was left to Tylor to make survival-hunting one of the major anthropological activities" (*Evolution and Society*, pp. 240–41). I trust that what has been said gives a fairer picture of the methodological importance of "survival-hunting."

13. *Primitive Culture*, I, 16.

It is of interest to note that a clue to the fact that a given custom is to be considered a "survival," and is in this respect to be compared to a vestigial organ, is that it purportedly performs no useful function in the culture in which it survives. (Cf. Tylor, *Primitive Culture*, I, 71, *et passim.*)

14. *Pre-Historic Times*, pp. 427–28 (italics added). Also, compare the opening

paragraph of Lubbock's *Origin of Civilization*, as well as passages cited by R. H. Lowie from Letourneau and from Pitt-Rivers (*History of Ethnological Theory*, p. 20.)

The customs of contemporary savages were also sometimes compared with *fossils*, rather than with the present descendants of extinct species. For example, in discussing Morgan's theory of a primitive state of promiscuity, Engels says: "The primitive social stage of promiscuity, if it ever existed, belongs to such a remote epoch that we can hardly expect to prove its existence *directly* by discovering its social fossils among backward savages." (*Origin of the Family*, p. 28.) Also, cf. Lubbock, *Origin of Civilization*, p. 1.

15. Cf. *Researches into the Early History of Mankind*, pp. 379–80.

16. In the Martineau abridgment of *The Positive Philosophy*, one finds the following discussion of one use to which Comte puts the comparative method:

I begin with . . . a comparison of the different coexisting states of human society on the various parts of the earth's surface,—those states being completely independent of each other. By this method, the different stages of evolution may all be observed at once. Though the progression is single and uniform, in regard to the whole race, some very considerable and very various populations have, from causes which are little understood, attained extremely unequal degrees of development, so that the former states of the most civilized nations are now to be seen, amidst some partial differences, among contemporary populations inhabiting different parts of the globe. . . . From the wretched inhabitants of Tierra del Fuego to the most advanced nations of western Europe, there is no social grade which is not extant in some points of the globe. (*Apud* Teggart, *The Idea of Progress*, p. 383.)

17. From *Primitive Marriage*, reprinted in *Studies in Ancient History*, p. 3.

18. *Ibid.*, pp. 3–4.

19. *Ancient Society*, p. 422.

20. To be sure, Morgan believed that kinship terminology, which no longer represented the realities of family organization, could provide a clue as to an earlier form of family organization. (This, in his system, afforded a parallel to McLennan's interpretation of the past through symbolic acts.) However, even were one to accept Morgan's interpretation of this evidence, it is clear that his fairly elaborate divisions of the history of mankind from savagery through barbarism to civilization went far beyond anything that such evidence could confirm. In fact, the order which he introduced in his reconstruction of human history rested heavily on inventions and discoveries, and on the subsistence techniques associated with them; but the pattern according to which he arranged these materials had not been established on the basis of independent evidence comparable to the evidence which was provided by the geological strata in which fossil remains or artifacts were found.

Morgan's emphasis on technology and on subsistence techniques, together with his assumptions concerning the *gens* as a form of social organization prior to the political state, accounts for the enthusiasm of both Marx and Engels for his theory of human history.

21. *Researches into the Early History of Mankind*, p. 106. Also, cf. *Primitive Culture*, I, 31.

22. Lubbock, *Pre-Historic Times*, p. 570. In his answer to the Duke of Argyll's theory of degeneration, Lubbock used the same illustration, though in that case it is not entirely clear that he tied the two actually independent principles so closely together. (Cf. *Origin of Civilization*, p. 360.)

23. Lubbock perhaps represented a more extreme instance of this tendency than did many of the other anthropologists of his generation, for the provincialism of his moral notions was more rigid than most. Lubbock's attitude was not, however, exceptional when compared with attitudes commonly found among laymen.

As one illustration of the narrowness of his views, I quote the opening paragraph of his chapter on religion in *The Origin of Civilization:*

The religion of savages, though of peculiar interest, is in many respects, perhaps, the most difficult part of my whole subject. I shall endeavour to avoid, as far as possible, anything which might justly give pain to any of my readers. Many ideas, however, which have been, or are, prevalent on religious matters are so utterly opposed to our own that it is impossible to discuss the subject without mentioning some things which are very repugnant to our feelings. Yet, while savages show us a melancholy spectacle of gross superstitions and ferocious forms of worship, the religious mind cannot but feel a peculiar satisfaction in tracing up the gradual evolution of more correct ideas and of nobler creeds.

24. Lyell argued as follows:

We see in our own times that the rate of progress in the arts and sciences proceeds in a geometrical ratio as knowledge increases, and so, when we carry back our retrospect into the past, we must be prepared to find the signs of retardation augmenting in a like geometrical ratio; so that the progress of a thousand years at a remote period may correspond to that of a century in modern times. (*Geological Evidences of the Antiquity of Man*, p. 377–78.)

And Morgan said:

Human progress, from first to last, has been in a ratio not rigorously but essentially geometrical. This is plain on the face of the facts; and it could not, theoretically, have occurred in any other way. Every item of absolute knowledge gained became a factor in further acquisitions, until the present complexity of knowledge was attained. (*Ancient Society*, p. 39.)

25. I wish to reiterate that while it is necessary to acknowledge the influence of evolutionary theory in biology on social evolutionism, the latter view not only could be held independently of the former, but was so held. For example, on the basis of archaeological evidence alone, we find that in 1843 Sven Nilsson, in the preface to his *Primitive Inhabitants of Scandinavia*, contended that one is unable "properly to understand the significance of the antiquities of any individual country without at the same time clearly realizing the idea that they are the fragments of a progressive series of civilization, and that the human race has always been, and still is, steadily advancing in civilization." (Cited by Tylor, *Primitive Culture*, I, 62.)

26. This was in answer to a criticism made by H. C. Watson; cf. *Origin of Species*, pp. 131–33.

27. "There were two reasons why these early anthropologists could not achieve a solid success similar to that of Darwin. . . . The first of these reasons is that Darwin inherited a highly accurate, solid, and comprehensive classification of

animals and plants which had developed by systematic coöperation among biologists since Linnaeus, more than a century before. As against this, the would-be anthropologists had a helter-skelter miscellany of travelers' tales and missionaries' accounts, from which obtruded some picturesque features . . . somewhat like elephants' trunks and armadillos' armor in pre-Linnean natural history. An added difficulty became clear only gradually: the family tree which outlines the history of life is throughout a one-way affair: once two life forms have diverged a very little, they cannot ever reassimilate or merge again. But culture, without genes or genotypes, and floating through and out from phenotypes, is protean in its sources." (Kroeber, "Evolution, History, and Culture," p. 11.)

28. *Primitive Culture*, I, 69.
Tylor's formal statement of his progressivist view reads as follows:

> The present comparatively narrow argument on the development of culture . . . takes cognizance principally of knowledge, art, and custom, and indeed only very partial cognizance within this field, the vast range of physical, political, social, and ethical considerations being left all but untouched. Its standard of reckoning progress and decline is not that of ideal good and evil, but of movement along a measured line from grade to grade of actual savagery, barbarism, and civilization. The thesis which I venture to sustain, within limits, is simply this, that the savage state in some measure represents an early condition of mankind, out of which the higher culture has gradually been developed or evolved, by processes still in regular operation as of old, the result showing that, on the whole, progress has far prevailed over relapse. (*Primitive Culture*, I, 32.)

29. *Journal of Researches*, p. 504. Cf. page 205 describing his first contact with the natives of Tierra del Fuego.

30. *Descent of Man*, I, 176–77.

31. For example, in speaking of the conditions of progress in civilized nations Darwin says:

> We must remember that progress is no invariable rule. It is most difficult to say why one civilized nation rises, becomes more powerful, and spreads more widely than another; or why the same nation progresses more at one time than another. We can only say that it depends on an increase in the actual number of the population, on the number of men endowed with high intellectual and moral faculties, as well as on their standard of excellence. Corporeal structure, except so far as vigor of body leads to vigor of mind, appears to have little influence (*Descent of Man*, I, 170).

In another passage (I, 160), in dealing with uncivilized nations, he also mentions climate. The lack of emphasis upon the nature and structure of social organization—though various of its aspects are at times mentioned—is most striking.

32. *Ancient Society*, p. 15. Also, cf. Morgan's preface, pp. 5–6.

33. *Ancient Society*, p. 34, note 2.

34. Cf. *Principles of Sociology*, I, 97–98.

35. As examples of the first of these types of explanation, most of the phases through which he traced the history of religion may be cited (*Principles of Sociology*, Part I, Chapters 9–25), as well as his treatment of ceremonials (*ibid.*, Part IV). Some aspects of his account of the relations between the sexes are good

illustrations of his use of the concept of survival-needs (e.g., his discussion of promiscuity in Part III, Ch. 5). In connection with an assumed biological parallel as helping to flesh out speculative conjectures, one may note his account of the family (cf. Part III, Ch. 9, Sections 319 and 320 in particular).

It is probably fair to say that the same three types of mechanism were invoked by Spencer in his sociological explanations from the very beginning of his career. For example, in *Social Statics*, the first may be illustrated by his account of the relationship between general conditions of life and the development of social sympathy (cf. pp. 448–51); the second is present throughout his discussion of the need for adaptation as basic to human life and progress (e.g., Part I, Ch. 2); and the third is evident in the analogies which he draws between societies and organisms (e.g., pp. 493–97).

36. *Principles of Sociology*, I, 556.

37. Like Hegel and a number of other nineteenth-century philosophers, Spencer conceived of reality as a process. For him the most ultimate laws of science were not laws of interrelationships between specific types of factors (such as mass and distance, pressure and volume) which had been abstracted from concrete events; rather, they were the most general laws which described the direction in which processes flowed. For example, in recapitulating his views, Spencer wrote:

The decomposition of phenomena into their elements, is but a preparation for understanding phenomena in their state of composition, as actually manifested. To have ascertained the laws of the factors is not at all to have ascertained the laws of their co-operation. The question is, not how any factor, Matter or Motion or Force, behaves by itself, or under some imagined simple conditions; nor is it even how one factor behaves under the complicated conditions of actual existence. The thing to be expressed is the joint product of the factors under all its various aspects. Only when we can formulate the total process, have we gained that knowledge of it which Philosophy aspires to. (*First Principles*, p. 284.)

(The fact that Spencer uses the term "Philosophy" rather than "Science" is not material in the present context, since the method of explanation which he deemed appropriate for philosophy was only a wider extension of the method of science.)

Further examples of his emphasis on understanding phenomena through viewing them in this historical manner, as aspects of a process of change, are to be found in the opening pages of the subsequent chapter of *First Principles*, on "Evolution and Dissolution."

38. *Primitive Culture*, I, 2.

39. *Ibid.*, I, 5.

40. *Ibid.*, I, 5.

41. Cf. *Ibid.*, I, 5–9.

Tylor's attempt to establish causal connections between specific elements of culture is mostly clearly seen in a paper published in 1889 in the *Journal of the Royal Anthropological Institute* entitled "On a Method of Investigating the Developing of Institutions; Applied to Laws of Marriage and Descent." In it he attempted to show that statistical methods can be applied in the same manner in anthropology as in other sciences, serving to establish linkages between species of facts. While Tylor did attempt to use these causal linkages as a basis for reconstructing a developmental sequence, this merely reinforces the point which I here wish to make: he held it to be the task of ethnographical inquiry to establish the direction in which change had in each case proceeded, and he did not assume that there was any general law which served to define what that direction would be.

42. In the opening chapters of both *Researches into the Early History of Mankind* and *Primitive Culture*, Tylor explicitly raised the question of whether similarities among the elements of culture in different societies are to be treated as resulting from independent invention or historical contact. He accepts the fact that both may occur. And throughout his works one finds him interested in which of these means should be used to explain the similarities which he noted. (For example, cf. his *Researches into the Early History of Mankind*, p. 204 and p 274; also his much later lecture, "How the Problems of American Anthropology Present Themselves to the English Mind," pp. 86–90.)

43. For example, see *Researches into the Early History of Mankind*, p. 3, where he states the method which he will follow in Chapters II to V and in Chapter VI of that work. On magic and the association of ideas, cf. *ibid.*, pp. 116–39; *Primitive Culture*, I, 115–16; "On Traces of the Early Mental Condition of Man," pp. 396–98.

44. The clearest statements regarding Tylor's evolutionary view of religion are to be found in the latter half of Chapter XVII of *Primitive Culture*. It is in the very same discussion that one can best see that he is not attempting to formulate a universally applicable, irreducible law of historical sequences. (For example, cf. II, 336, as well as his treatment of forms of dualistic religion in that chapter.)

45. Cf. *Researches into the Early History of Mankind*, pp. 190–91 and 374–75.

46. Cf. "On Traces of the Early Mental Condition of Man," p. 391.

47. Cf. *Anthropology*, pp. 407–8. This view regarding advance in morality is far less cautious and more sanguine than Tylor's treatment of the same subject in *Primitive Culture* (cf. I, 28–31). However, it need not be taken as representing either the results of popularization or an alteration in view, for the earlier, more cautious statement did in fact end with the following conclusion:

> Altogether, it may be admitted that some rude tribes lead a life to be envied by some
> barbarous races, and even by outcasts of higher nations. But that any known savage
> tribe would not be improved by judicious civilization, is a proposition which no moralist
> would dare to make; while the general tenour of the evidence goes far to justify the
> view that on the whole the civilized man is not only wiser and more capable than the
> savage, but also better and happier, and that the barbarian stands between.

48. Cf. *Primitive Culture*, II, 445 and 451–53; also, "On Traces of the Early Mental Condition of Mankind," p. 398.

49. *Researches into the Early History of Mankind*, p. 2.

50. *A Century of Science*, pp. 29–30.

51. *Ibid.*, p. 33.

52. For example, Spencer opens a discussion of the special creationist doctrine, as applied to life, in the following way:

> Early ideas are not usually true ideas. Undeveloped intellect, be it that of an individual or that of the race, forms conclusions which require to be revised and re-revised, before they reach a tolerable correspondence with realities. . . .
> If illustrations be needed, the history of every science furnishes them. The primitive notions of mankind as to the structure of the heavens, were wrong; and the notions which replaced them were successively less wrong. . . . The interpretations of mechanical facts, of meteorological facts, of physiological facts, were at first wrong. In all these cases men set out with beliefs which, if not absolutely false, contained but small amounts of truth disguised by immense amounts of error.
> Hence the hypothesis that living things resulted from special creations, being a primitive hypothesis, is probably an untrue hypothesis. (*Principles of Biology*, I, 333–34.)

53. These two passages come from Morley, *On Compromise*, pp. 28–31.

It is of interest to note that Herbert Spencer, who used a genealogical method, defended it as follows:

> Inquiring into the pedigree of an idea is not a bad means of roughly estimating its value. To have come of respectable ancestry, is *prima facie* evidence of worth in a belief as in a person; while to be descended from a discreditable stock, is in the one case as the other, an unfavourable index. The analogy is not a mere fancy. Beliefs, together with those who hold them, are modified little by little in successive generations; and as the modifications which successive generations of the holders undergo do not destroy the original type, but only disguise and refine it, so the accompanying alterations of belief, however much they purify, leave behind the essence of the original belief. (*Essays, Scientific, Political, and Speculative*, I, 208.)

Chapter 7.   Historicism: A Critical Appraisal

1. The term "holism," as used in this connection, is Popper's rather than Berlin's. Popper characterizes its meaning in the following way:

> [According to holists,] the objects of sociology, social groups, must never be regarded as mere aggregates of persons. The social group is *more* than the mere sum total of its members, and it is also *more* than the mere sum total of the merely personal relationships existing at any moment between any of its members. (*Poverty of Historicism*, p. 17.)

In the writings of Popper and others, "methodological individualism" is usually taken to be the antonym of "holism."

2. As I have elsewhere endeavored to show, not every social theory which conforms to Popper's definition of holism need involve an acceptance of laws of directional change. (Cf. "Societal Laws," *British Journal for the Philosophy of Science*, VIII [1957], 211–24.) For this reason, I believe that Popper's general attack on holism is to some extent beside the point, so far as historicism is concerned. However, this does not affect the validity of those of his arguments which are specifically directed against the existence of laws of directional change. Those arguments and my own run along parallel lines; however, the forms in which they are cast differ rather markedly.

3. The problems connected with holism which were of special concern to Isaiah Berlin will later arise in connection with my discussion of "Organicism" in Part III of this book.

4. I borrow this from Bergmann and Spence, "Operationism and Theory Construction," as reprinted from the *Psychological Review* (1941) in Melvin H. Marx: *Psychological Theory*, p. 57.

5. I select these examples from Hempel, *Philosophy of Natural Science*, p. 54, who cited them in a group of standard examples of natural laws. In the same group he also cited laws which were phrased in terms of quantitative relationships. It seems to me correct not to draw a distinction between the two sets of cases, even though our ability to state a law in quantitative terms will greatly aid us in inferring the precise nature of its consequences when it is applied in concrete cases.

It might be held that the second of the foregoing examples (viz. the law concerning magnets) is neither a functional law nor a law of directional change. I believe that it can best be interpreted as derivative from functional laws, and that it is surely not a law of directional change. My interest in it in the present context is confined to the fact that it affords a clear example of a law which is not quantitative in character.

6. It is tempting to try to state the difference in terms of whether or not *time* enters into the relationship as one of its variables, and this was the way in which it was stated by Edgar Zilsel in his interesting article, "Physics and the Problem of Historico-Sociological Laws" (p. 573). I previously attempted to delineate the difference in a similar way. However, as the following discussion will suggest, such a formulation is inadequate.

A formulation of the difference which parallels that which is here given is to be found in L. J. Goldstein's distinction between *causal* and *developmental* theories in anthropology. (Cf. "Theory in Anthropology: Developmental or Causal?", pp. 154–55, *et passim*.)

Arthur W. Burks has pointed out to me that one can formulate physical laws, such as those which concern the path of a beam of light, in terms of either a *causal* theory or a *minimizing* theory (viz., in terms of angles of incidence and reflection, or in terms of minimizing the time of transit); and that the two formulations would be equivalent. Burks suggests that the differences between mechanical and teleological explanations in biology may be of this kind. (Cf. his forthcoming book *Cause, Chance, and Reason*, Sect. 4.2.2.) Whether or not this suggestion is correct, the distinction which he draws is different from that which I am drawing in distinguishing between functional and directional laws: his is actually a distinction between two types of functional law. This can be seen in Burks's own formulation. The path which a beam of light follows is explained on the minimizing theory in terms of "the law of least times"; that law, however, is not (in my sense) a directional law since it does not define a particular direction of change (viz. the actual path of this beam of light, or of any beam of light), but states a general condition to which any path of a beam of light, regardless of its direction, will conform.

7. $t = 2\pi\sqrt{l/g}$, where g stands for the acceleration of a freely falling body.

8. For a brief statement of the notion of a functional law, and of the two subtypes here under consideration (as represented, for example, by Boyle's law and by Galileo's law), cf. Nagel, *Structure of Science*, pp. 77–78. The distinction between these sub-types is often formulated as a distinction between "laws of coexistence" and "laws of succession" (cf. Hempel, *Aspects of Scientific Explanation*, p. 352). The use of the latter phraseology unfortunately blurs the dis-

tinction between the general characteristics of functional laws and the class of laws which Nagel calls "developmental" and which I am designating as "directional."

Gustav Bergmann's more complex classification, in which he distinguishes cross-sectional laws, process laws, developmental laws, and historical laws, raises a number of important points with respect to my treatment of the following issues, but I shall not undertake to discuss them. It is only essential to point out the following: (1) what he calls "process laws," I call "functional laws," and what he calls "developmental laws," I call "directional laws"; (2) if what follows is sound, it would strongly argue in favor of Bergmann's own prognosis that what he terms "historical laws" will prove to be expendable, being reducible to process laws, at least in all cases which are relevant to history, the social sciences, and psychology.

9. De Saussure's contrast between *synchronic* and *diachronic* approaches in linguistics has become most familiar through its use by theoretical anthropologists; it seems to have been introduced into anthropology by Radcliffe-Brown. Within anthropology, however, it has led to some unfortunate controversies; for example, the charge has often been made that a synchronic approach necessarily neglects factors which bring about change. I therefore prefer the term "functional" to "synchronic," since (as we have seen) one class of functional laws does explicitly take into account rates of change. I also prefer to avoid the term "diachronic," since what have usually been called diachronic studies have not usually been concerned with establishing laws concerning successive states: for the most part, they have been attempts to trace individual sequences of change.

10. I assume that neither the law of the conservation of energy nor the law of increasing entropy are empirical laws, in spite of the importance of their consequences for empirical science.

However, there is some reason to think that the primacy which I shall assign to functional laws in other cases had a parallel in the formulation and the earlier interpretations of the second law of thermodynamics. (Cf. Mach's historical essay "On the Principle of the Conservation of Energy," especially Sect. III [*Popular Scientific Lectures*, pp. 160–65]. Also, cf. Lord Kelvin's "On a Universal Tendency in Nature to the Dissipation of Energy," and his analysis of Carnot's theory in his earlier paper "On the Dynamical Theory of Heat," especially Sections 7–14. The latter papers are contained in the first volume of Lord Kelvin's *Mathematical and Physical Papers*.)

11. Cf. Rufus, "Kepler as an Astronomer," pp. 19–21. Also, Holton, "Johannes Kepler's Universe," pp. 199–200.

12. However, as modern linguists have pointed out, the changes formulated in Grimm's law are "merely historical," applying to a particular set of sound changes in a particular language, or group of languages, over a given period of time. For example, Sapir points out that "a phonetic law applying to a particular sound in the history of English applies only to that sound within a given period of time and by no means commits itself to the development of the same sound in other languages" (Sapir, *Selected Writings*, p. 72). (Also, on Grimm's law, cf. Bloomfield, *Language*, pp. 14, 348, and 368.) Putting the matter in the brief technical form which we owe primarily to Nelson Goodman, Grimm's so-called "law" would not qualify for designation as a law because (as

Sapir points out) it would not serve to support subjunctive conditionals, i.e. statements of the form "If there were to be an *x*, it would be followed by a *y*." (For a brief statement concerning this requirement of a natural law, cf. Hempel, *Philosophy of Natural Science*, pp. 55–57.)

A more recent example in which some persons have been strongly tempted to hold that it is possible to formulate basic laws of directional change, is to be found in discussions of stages in economic growth. While I should not be inclined so to regard them, the reason is different from that which obtains with reference to "Grimm's law." In the present case, the difficulty is that such laws do not appear to be irreducible: on the contrary, as often formulated, they seem to depend upon functional laws. To choose one illustrative example from a particularly well-known book, consider the first three factors which W. W. Rostow cites as providing the foundation for his theory of economic growth: each suggests that the basis for predictions of growth is to be found in functional laws. (Cf. *Process of Economic Growth*, pp. 17–18.)

Among the cases in which it has been claimed that irreducible directional laws concerning individual and social behavior have actually been established, Piaget's developmental psychology probably represents the clearest effort to formulate universal laws which, if true, would support subjunctive conditional statements. (For a useful formulation of Piaget's theory, cf. J. H. Flavell, *The Developmental Psychology of Jean Piaget*.)

13. The following discussion must be considered as exploratory only. To my surprise, I have not been able to find any systematic, extensive treatment of the issue by philosophers of science. To be sure, others have dealt in more detail, and far more carefully, with some of the specific issues which will arise in what follows: for example, I shall deal only very cursorily with the complex issues concerning the characteristics of scientific laws. (For more careful discussion, cf. Nagel, *Structure of Science*, Ch. 4, and Hempel, *Aspects of Scientific Explanation*, pp. 264–70, 335–47, *et passim*.) However, the relevance of such discussions to the question of the relationship between functional and directional laws is rarely considered in an explicit fashion: for example, neither Nagel nor Hempel devotes more than a paragraph to this general issue. (Cf. Nagel, p. 76, and Hempel's discussion of Clark Hull on intervening variables, pp. 204–5.)

Perhaps the mostly closely related attempts to perform the same sort of analysis which is here undertaken are in Popper's *Poverty of Historicism* (especially, pp. 116–30) and in Leon J. Goldstein's article, "Theory in Anthropology: Developmental or Causal?". However, each of those treatments not only involves other issues, but is less general than what follows.

14. The level of abstraction with which I am here dealing is sometimes indicated by saying that we should be concerned with the genotype, not the phenotype, when we seek to explain events. This analogy from genetics is suggestive, and should put social scientists on their guard as to the danger of trying to find laws which apply directly to phenomena such as "revolutions" or "migrations," which represent "phenotypes." Nevertheless, I am inclined to avoid the use of these terms, since the differences between the relations of phenotype and genotype are utterly different from the relations between concrete occurrences and the isolable factors through which these occurrences are explained.

15. Cf. Kurt Lewin, "The Conflict between Aristotelian and Galilean Modes of Thought in Contemporary Psychology," p. 150. There is much in the first section of Lewin's article that bears on the topic here under discussion.

16. In this connection we may note that implicit in John Stuart Mill's discussions of why we do not place assurance in what he terms "empirical laws" is the fact that they are insufficiently abstractive. (Cf. *System of Logic*, Bk. III, Ch. XVI, especially Sect. 4; and Bk. VI, Ch. V, Sect. 1.)

In the same connection, and of great relevance to current discussions, I might point out that the difficulty which W. H. Dray found in Hempel's "covering-law" model of explanation rested on the fact that, in one instance at least, Hempel had spoken as if the deductive-nomological model of explanation demanded that we find law-like generalizations concerning such complex actual occurrences as migrations. However, as I have elsewhere pointed out, it is not plausible to expect to find such generalizations in either the physical or the social sciences; the general laws which are of importance to historians are of the same abstractive type as functional laws in other areas of investigation. (Cf. my article, "Historical Explanation: The Problem of Covering Laws," *History and Theory*, I [1961], 229–42.)

17. To avoid confusion, I should point out that in using the terms "conditional" and "categorical" I am not referring to differences in the grammatical forms of sentences: the expression "For any x, if x is A then x is B" is equivalent to "All A is B."

18. I refer to Boyle's law in its original form for illustrative purposes only; the emendations which it has undergone do not alter the point here being made.

19. Zilsel, "Physics and the Problem of Historico-Sociological Laws," p. 567.

20. One can note this in Leslie A. White's theory, although his emphasis on the course of evolutionary development tends to conceal the crucial role played in that theory by assumptions concerning specific functional relationships between "the substructure" of technology and "the sociological stratum." This ambivalence in his theory can perhaps be most clearly seen in an essay on "Energy and the Evolution of Culture," which is Chapter 13 of his *Science of Culture*.

Similarly, as one sees in Goldstein's critique of M. H. Fried's evolutionary theory of social stratification and the state, the evolutionary sequence which Fried attributes to this range of phenomena rests on functional relationships operative at successive points in time. (Cf. Leon Goldstein, "Theory in Anthropology: Developmental or Causal?", especially p. 165.)

It remains unclear how the two types of law, with their fundamentally different sets of formal presuppositions, can be brought together: this issue is one to which contemporary evolutionists in anthropology have apparently failed to devote their attention. In this respect they differ from Comte and from Spencer, whose views on the relations between "statics" and "dynamics" represent, in some measure at least, an attempt to come to grips with this problem.

21. Because of his influence on contemporary anthropological theory, I feel obliged to point out the error in a statement made by Evans-Pritchard, which is diametrically opposed to what has just been said. Evans-Pritchard says:

The search for diachronic laws was for a time abandoned in a search for synchronic laws; but it is precisely, as I think Comte saw, the diachronic laws which must first be established for they alone can validate the synchronic laws. (*Anthropology and History*, p. 2.)

Whatever may be the merit of his interpretation of Comte on this point, this statement is assuredly confused. As its context makes clear, Evans-Pritchard's real point is that, in order to validate a synchronic law, one must observe that a change in one variable brings about a change in the other. But this is a matter of observing (and measuring) particular instances of change; it is not a matter of establishing a law which permits one to trace successive stages of development as Comte and others had sought to do.

22. In this connection we may note that the second law of thermodynamics, which might be taken as an example of a fundamental and irreducible directional law, is explicitly phrased with reference to closed systems. No society, as I have just pointed out, can be thought of as constituting such a system.

23. This is for example true in the case of Julian H. Steward's evolutionism (cf. his *Theory of Culture Change*, p. 27), and in Piaget's theory of developmental stages (cf. Flavell, *The Developmental Psychology of Jean Piaget*, p. 20).

24. Cf. *Physica*, Bk. II, Ch. 1.

25. Cf. *ibid.*, Bk. II, Ch. 8, especially 199a7–30.

26. *Lectures on the History of Philosophy*, II, 157.
    The *Jubiläumsausgabe* of Hegel's works uses a different text which explicitly connects his view with that of Aristotle; for that reason, it is worth quoting:

> Des Aristoteles Begriff von der Natur ist vortrefflicher, als der gegenwärtige; denn die Hauptsache ist bei ihm die Bestimmung des Zwecks, als die innere Bestimmtheit des natürlichen Dinges selbst. Dass die neueste Zeit darüber das Vernünftige hergestellt, ist nichts anderes, als eine Wiedererweckung, Rechtfertigung der aristotelischen Idee (XVIII, 342).

27. Cf. above, Part II, Ch. 2, Sect. 2, pp. 45–46.

28. *Phenomenology of Mind*, pp. 80–81.
    It is interesting to note that the same view was held by Marx. In the original introduction to his *Critique of Political Economy*, which was found among his economic manuscripts and published posthumously, there is a passage in which he claims that the significance of earlier institutional forms can only be understood in terms of that into which they later developed. I shall quote this passage in its original form:

> Die bürgerliche Gesellschaft ist die entwickeltste und mannigfaltigste historische Organisation der Produktion. Die Kategorien, die ihre Verhältnisse ausdrücken, das Verständnis ihre Gliederung, gewährt daher zugleich Einsicht in die Gliederung und die Produktionsverhältnisse aller der untergegangnen Gesellschaftsformen, mit deren Trümmern und Elementen sie sich aufgebaut, von denen teils noch unüberwundne Reste sich in ihr fortschleppen, blosse Andeutungen sich zu ausgebildeten Bedeutungen enwickelt haben etc. Anatomie des Menschen ist ein Schlüssel zur Anatomie des Affen. Die Andeutungen auf Höheres in den untergeordneten Tierarten können dagegen nur verstanden werden, wenn das Höhere selbst schon bekannt. (*Werke*, XIII, 636.)

The English translation of this work (*A Contribution to the Critique of Political Economy*) includes the original introduction as an appendix, but the passage here in question suffers in the translation. (It appears on page 300 of the translation.) In this passage it is of interest to note not only the similarity between

Marx's contention and Hegelian modes of explanation, but also the fact that, when this introduction was written, Marx apparently accepted an evolutionary account of biological forms. The date of the introduction was 1857–58 (cf. *Werke*, XIII, 707, n. 402); it was therefore written prior to the publication of the *Origin of Species*.

As we have already seen (pp. 68–69, above) Comte held a view essentially the same as that endorsed by Marx in the foregoing passage.

29. For a passing remark to this effect, cf. *Phenomenology of Mind*, p. 692.

30. This view was, for example, characteristic of Savigny in his treatment of law:

Diese Erscheinungen [i.e., law, language, etc.] haben kein abgesondertes Dasein, es sind nur einzelne Kräfte und Tätigkeiten des einen Volkes, in der Natur untrennbar verbunden, und nur unserer Betrachtung als besondere Eigenschaften erscheinend. Was sie zu einen ganzen verknüpft, ist die gemeinsame Überzeugung des Volkes, das gleiche Gefühl innerer Notwendigkeit, welches allen Gedanken an zufällige und willkürliche Entstehung ausschliesst" (*Grundgedanken*, p. 3).

That which binds the people into an enduring spiritual substance was held by Savigny, and was generally held by others, to be *tradition*. (For example, cf. Savigny's essay "Die historische Schule in der Rechtswissenschaft," in *Grundgedanken*, p. 15; also, cf. Hegel's introduction to his *Lectures on the History of Philosophy*, I, 2–3.)

31. A similar view was sometimes held with respect to the proper form of a Universal History: such a history was not to be a composite picture of each of the great periods of civilization, but was to be conceived as having a single subject-matter, the development of mankind as a whole. For example, in his letter to the contributors to the *Cambridge Modern History*, Lord Acton wrote:

By Universal History I understand that which is distinct from the combined history of all countries, which is not a rope of sand, but a continuous development, and is not a burden on the memory, but an illumination of the soul. It moves in a succession to which the nations are subsidiary. Their story will be told, not for their own sake, but in reference and subordination to a higher series, according to the time and the degree in which they contribute to the common fortunes of mankind. (*Apud* Fritz Stern, *Varieties of History*, p. 249.)

32. The fact that I confine myself to *empirical* difficulties should not be taken as suggesting that there do not also exist methodological and ontological difficulties in the views which I am about to criticize. However, if I were to raise these further difficulties, it would be necessary to offer more detailed analyses of the variant forms of this general type of position, and to take cognizance of differences in the basic philosophic presuppositions which were often connected with these forms. By considering only empirical difficulties, these complications can be avoided.

33. Comte was absolutely explicit on this point:

La plus importante de ces restrictions logiques, et qui comprend implicitement toutes les autres, consiste à concentrer essentiellement notre analyse scientifique sur une seule série sociale, c'est-à-dire, à considérer exclusivement le développement effectif des populations les plus avancées, en écartant, avec une scrupuleuse persévérance, toute vaine et irrationelle digression sur les divers autres centres de civilisation indépendante, dont l'évolution a été, par des causes quelconques, arrêtée jusqu'ici à un état plus imparfait; à moins que l'examen comparatif de ces séries accessoires ne puisse utilement éclairer le sujet principal, comme je l'ai expliqué en traitant de la méthode sociologique. Notre exploration historique devra donc être presque uniquement réduite à l'élite ou l'avant-garde de l'humanité, comprenant la majeure partie de la race blanche ou les nations européennes, en nous bornant même, pour plus de précision, surtout dans les temps modernes, aux peuples de l'Europe occidentale. (*Cours de philosophie positive*, V, 3-4.)

34. A clear instance of this is to be found in his treatment of the Syriac civilization, as can be seen in the following statement which appears in the Somervell abridgment of *A Study of History:*

The Syriac process of decline and fall was suspended for a thousand years by an Hellenic intrusion ... the 'Abbasid Caliphate merely picks up the thread of Syriac history where the Achaemenian Empire had been compelled to drop it in the fourth century B.C. (I. 263.)

For fuller discussion, cf. the original unabridged edition, I, 72-77.

35. While the foregoing does in fact constitute a criticism of the manner in which Marx and Marxists have actually interpreted the relationship between the substructure and the superstructure of a society, that relationship might be reformulated as a functional law which would not be subject to the same criticism. Such a law would merely state that there do exist forms of covariation between the substructure and all elements in the superstructure, regardless of the sources of the changes which occur in the substructure. Since this would leave open the possibility that many substructural changes arose out of superstructural elements (as well as having in some cases been due to events in nature, or to historical contacts), the legitimate scope of historical inquiry would be left unaffected by such a law.

Whether in fact such a law could be formulated raises other questions, which I do not wish to raise here. I have merely attempted to show that, if one admits that historical change is not always initiated by some tendency inherent in the substructure, this would not necessarily lead one to abandon all distinctions between what Marx considered to be the substructure and what he termed the superstructure.

36. In an address entitled "Historical Determinism and the Gospel of Freedom," I briefly discussed this fact with relation to what I termed "the time-table of history"; in the same place, I also discussed "the retrospective fallacy," to which I shall shortly turn. (Cf. *Journal of General Education*, VI [1951], 7-16.)

37. As one further striking illustration of this conviction, I might cite the following statement from Comte:

The chronological order of historic epochs is not their philosophical order. In place of saying: the past, the present, and the future, we should say the past, the future, and the present. In truth it is only when we have conceived the future by the aid of the past that we can with advantage revert to the present so as to seize its true character. (*System of Positive Polity*, IV, 563.)

38. Letter to Carlyle, dated 2nd February, 1833, in *Earlier Letters*, I, 139. It is worth taking note of Mill's position, since he has sometimes mistakenly been criticized for espousing historicism, and also for having confused "ought" and "is."

39. As one typical example of this point of view I may cite a passage from Hegel:

Justice and virtue, wrongdoing, power and vice, talents and their achievements, passions strong and weak, guilt and innocence, grandeur in individual and national life, autonomy, fortune and misfortune of individuals, all these have their specific significance and worth in the field of known actuality; therein they are judged and therein they have their partial, though only partial justification. World-history, however, is above the point of view from which these things matter. Each of its stages is the presence of a necessary moment in the Idea of the world-mind, and that moment attains its absolute right in that stage. (*Philosophy of Right*, p. 217.)

PART III—THE MALLEABILITY OF MAN

CHAPTER 8.   CHALLENGES TO CONSTANCY

1. For some, the transformation of men's natures was a precondition for reform; for others, such as Marx, changes in human nature presupposed changes in social conditions. In either case, man's malleability was stressed; when it was denied, that denial was coupled with scepticism regarding the feasibility of radical reform.

2. In contrasting eighteenth-century thought with what he took to be typical of the thought of his age, F. D. Maurice remarked:

We may easily confound the *Human Nature* which was the favorite and common subject of study in the last age with the *Humanity* which has begun to be so much spoken of in ours. If we do, I suspect we shall not appreciate the step we have taken in advance of our immediate predecessors. (*Social Morality*, p. 415.)

3. As I have pointed out, Popper's claim that John Stuart Mill accepted the historicist mode of explanation rests on a misinterpretation of the text which he cited. (Cf. p. 391, n. 44, above.) With respect to the evaluative thesis of historicism it is clear that Mill absolutely rejected it. (For example, cf. his letter to Carlyle, cited on p. 419, n. 38 above.)

CHAPTER 9.   GENETICISM: THE ASSOCIATIONIST TRADITION

1. The acceptance of a pluralism of native propensities was an important aspect of Bishop Butler's analysis of morality; Thomas Reid's listing of twenty-four active powers of the mind was a second extremely influential source of the pluralistic nativism against which later geneticism reacted.

2. Descartes's theory of the passions of the soul had relied heavily upon a doctrine of conditioning, and thus tended, on the whole, toward geneticism in this particular branch of psychology; however, later forms of a physiologically oriented psychology tended toward nativism. This is evident in La Mettrie's *L'homme machine*; in Diderot's criticism of Helvétius (cf. Diderot, *Oeuvres*, II, 263-456); and most particularly in Cabanis's *Les rapports du physique et du moral*.

One may also note that one of the major aspects of Gall's phrenological psychology was his attempt to overcome the geneticist assumptions of Helvétius (cf. Gall, *Sur les fonctions du cerveau*, I, 6-8). In this connection, it is worth noting that the influence of phrenology was of sufficient importance throughout the first half of the nineteenth century for Bain to have devoted considerable attention to criticizing it in a series of articles which he republished in 1861 in his volume entitled *On the Study of Character, Including an Estimate of Phrenology.*

3. On these points, see my *Philosophy, Science, and Sense Perception*, pp. 46–47. One may also note how his discussion of the complex idea of power leads directly to a long discussion of freedom, and the many points at which theologically relevant issues arise in connection with his treatment of the human mind and of personal identity.

4. Cf. Locke's dedicatory epistle prefaced to *Thoughts Concerning Education,* which was originally published in 1693.

5. In those portions of Locke's papers which have been edited by Lough (Locke, *Travels in France . . .*), one finds numerous references to Bernier, who had traveled extensively in the Orient, and in Book I, Ch. III, Sect. 9 of the *Essay* we find that Locke cites numerous other accounts of travelers, all of them designed to show the variability in moral and religious practices. In this connection we may note that Locke compiled "A Catalogue and Character of Most Books of Voyages and Travels," which is truly extensive: it covers just over fifty pages in the last volume of the 1823 edition of Locke's *Works.*

6. With respect to the body, cf. Section 7; for a discussion of the need for training in conduct, cf. Sections 32 to 36.

7. In an essay on "The Malleability of Man in Eighteenth-Century Thought," J. A. Passmore discussed many of the figures with whom we shall here be concerned; he too emphasized the importance of Locke in this development. What seems to me to be of particular importance in that essay is the emphasis placed on the theological background of Locke's position, and the influence of this background on others as well. However, Passmore's concern with the role which Locke ascribed to custom seems to me to have led to a failure to lay sufficient stress on the contrast which one finds in Locke between the merely customary and the true.

8. Consequently, this chapter postdates *Thoughts Concerning Education,* and the doctrine of malleability stressed in Locke's educational theory cannot be regarded as superseding his dichotomy of custom *vs.* reason.

9. There is, in principle, a fundamental difference between those theories of the association of ideas which rely on the principle of contiguity only, and those in which resemblance also plays a fundamental part. As we shall note, Hume's view differed from the views of most other eighteenth-century associationists in the great importance which he attached to resemblance. Recently, this issue has been revived and has been placed in a more extended context by some Gestalt psychologists. For example, cf. W. Köhler, "On the Nature of Associations," *Proceedings of the American Philosophical Society,* v. 84 (1941), 489–502, and Solomon E. Asch, "A Reformulation of the Problem of Associations," *American Psychologist,* v. 24 (1969), 92–102.

10. *Essay,* Bk. II, Ch. XXXIII, Sect. 6.

11. *Ibid.,* Sect. 9. However, a more cautious manner of speaking is really de-

manded by some of the associations by contiguity which Locke cited. For example, the case of the musician which he cites in Section 6, and the grief of a mother at the thought of her dead child, cited in Section 13, are cases of association by contiguity rather than resemblance, but the characterization of the ideas as "a wrong connexion" could surely not be maintained. What Locke evidently had in mind were, in the main, the effects of chance and the effects of custom due to human agency, not the effects of experience which is founded on a natural order independent of us.

12. Abraham Tucker, who was by no means one of the more radical innovators in this connection, altered Locke's theory at precisely this point (cf. his theory of judgment in *The Light of Nature Pursued*, First Part, Ch. XI). On this basis he was led to say:

> I conceive that all our stores of knowledge, and skill in discerning between one thing and another, was acquired, not born with us, but learned by practice: if we had judgments any other way than those above mentioned in our infancy, we have lost them, and possess nothing now which was not once a new acquisition (I, 334).

13. *Treatise of Human Nature*, Bk. I, Part I, Sect. vii.

14. Cf. his *Histoire moderne*, Livre XIX, Ch. XII, where he says of Locke:

> Il n'a pas imaginé de chercher la génération des operátions de l'âme: il n'a pas vu qu'elles viennent de la sensation, ainsi que nos idées, et qu'elles ne sont que la sensation transformée (*Oeuvres*, XX, 528).

15. In the introduction to his *Essai sur l'origine des connoissances humaines* (his first work), Condillac criticized Locke in the following way:

> Il a passé trop légèrement sur l'origine de nos connoissances, et c'est la partie qu'il a le moins approfondie. Il suppose, par exemple, qu'aussi-tôt que l'âme reçoit des idées par les sens, elle peut, à son gré, les répéter, les composer, les unir ensemble avec une variété infinie, et en faire toutes sortes de notions complexes (*Oeuvres*, I, 14).

16. It is of interest to compare the views of Condillac with those of both Buffon and Bonnet, whose relevant works belong to the same period.

In Buffon's *Histoire naturelle*, when he considers man's senses in general, he imagines a man fully equipped with the powers of sensation, alone at creation, and describes what such a man would experience (III, 364-70). Although this account is not wholly consistent with his earlier account of the role played by experience in the case of sight, he did include the perception of *objects* among the initial experiences of such a man; thus, he took as *given* much that Condillac assumed to be gradually acquired through successive experiences. One may note that Condillac, in his *Traité des animaux*, stood in open opposition to Buffon's views.

Bonnet's view in his *Essai analytique sur les facultées de l'âme* (1760), is closer to the position of Condillac; and he too utilizes the fiction of the statue endowed with powers of sensation. (As he informs us, he hit upon this method of exposition independently of Condillac, but the latter's *Traité des sensations* was published before Bonnet had written his *Essai*.) Bonnet shares Condillac's view that sensation is the sole source of our ideas (cf. *Oeuvres*, VI, xvi), and that abstract ideas are always sensible in character (*ibid.*, p. 112); however, he does grant to the mind active powers which Condillac's theory of judgment would not have included (cf. *ibid.*, p. 135-36). At the same time, his account of sensations, and of their effects, is far more heavily dependent upon physiological hypotheses.

17. As examples from Helvétius and d'Holbach, cf. the former's *De l'esprit*, Discourse I, Ch. I, or his *De l'homme*, Sect. II, Ch. IV; and the latter's *Système de la nature*, Ch. VIII.

It is interesting to note how quickly the first works of Condillac, Hartley, and Helvétius followed one another, appearing in 1746, 1749, and 1758 respectively. While it may be argued that Helvétius was indebted to Condillac, it is probably correct to view each of the three as independent of the others; however, each of the three acknowledges the heavy debt owed to Locke, and each can be regarded as among Locke's successors.

18. As is evident in the introduction to *Observations on Man*, the only simple ideas which Hartley admits into his system are "Ideas of Sensation." As Priestley says in contrasting Hartley with Locke, "Dr. Hartley supposes that our external senses furnish the materials of all the ideas of which we are ever possessed, and that those which Mr. Locke calls ideas of reflection, are only ideas of so very complex a nature, and borrowed from so many ideas of sense, that their origin cannot easily be traced" (*Hartley's Theory of the Human Mind*, p. xxxiii). This was also Priestley's own view (*ibid.*, p. xxxv). However, in his *Examination of Dr. Reid's Inquiry*, Priestley had misconstrued Locke's doctrine, treating it as if Locke had not taken our ideas of reflection to be as original as ideas of sensation (cf. *op. cit.*, pp. 4–5).

19. The relation of Hobbes to associationism was pointed out by Reid (cf. *Works*, I, 386a), but I know of no earlier mention of him in this connection. The term "association of ideas" (as the use of the word "idea" suggests) seems to stem from Locke himself.

20. Gay himself was obviously indebted to Locke for his general theory of knowledge, and presumably also for his use of the term "association." How dependent his own views were upon Locke's analysis of ideas can be seen in the following statement:

> The ideas themselves about which morality is chiefly conversant . . . are all mixed modes, or compound ideas, arbitrarily put together, having at first no archetype or original existing, and afterwards no other than that which exists in other men's minds.

Gay's dissertation, entitled "Concerning the Fundamental Principle of Virtue or Morality," was prefixed to Archbishop King's *Essay on the Origin of Evil* (1731); it is now most readily available in volume II, of Selby-Bigge, *British Moralists*. The above quotation is taken from paragraph 850 of Selby-Bigge. It is to be compared with Locke's *Essay*, Bk. II, Ch. XXVIII, Sect. 4 and (for Locke's doctrine of mixed modes) with Bk. II, Ch. XXII, Sects. 1 and 8.

21. The memoir of Hartley's son is prefixed to later editions of the *Observations on Man*, and the son says that his father "had received his first principles of logic and metaphysics from the work of that good and great philosopher Locke." (It is to be noted that the term "metaphysics" was commonly used, at that time, to refer to what we should now designate as "psychology.")

22. *Observations on Man*, I, 5–6.

In 1747 (therefore two years before the *Observations*) an anonymous author published *An Enquiry into the Origin of the Human Appetites and Affections, shewing how each arises from Association*. (This is most readily available in Samuel Parr, *Metaphysical Tracts by English Philosophers of the Eighteenth*

Century [London, 1837].) Whether or not he was one of "the ingenious Persons" referred to by Hartley, I cannot say. However, the anonymous author explicitly acknowledges his debt to Locke. It is also virtually certain that he was acquainted with Gay's work, since he refers to Archbishop King's *Essay on the Origin of Evil* to which Gay's dissertation served as introduction.

23. My interpretation of Gay's contribution to the formation of Hartley's system is consonant with the account given by Priestley, who attributes to Gay the attempt "to show the possibility of deducing all our passions and affections from association" (*Hartley's Theory of the Human Mind*, p. xxiii).

Gay's influence on moral theory appears to be greater than is sometimes recognized. For example, Bentham's specific classification of the sanctions of morality seems to be derivative from Gay (cf. Selby-Bigge, par. 863 for Gay's treatment; and Selby-Bigge, vol. I, par. 379 for Bentham's treatment of the same topic).

One may also note that Gay's associational account of the desire for wealth (Selby-Bigge, paragraph 884) is echoed in Hartley's *Observations on Man* in 1749 (cf. Ch. IV, Sect. III; vol. I, p. 458 of the first edition), and subsequently finds its way into Priestley (*Examination of Dr. Reid's Inquiry*, 1774, pp. xxix–xxx), into Godwin (*Enquiry Concerning Political Justice*, 1793, I, p. 425), into James Mill (*Analysis of the Phenomena of the Human Mind*, II, 210), and into John Stuart Mill (*Utilitarianism*, Ch. IV, pp. 34–5). This sequence is surely not accidental, since each of these writers obviously knew the relevant works of his predecessors. For a different, independent explanation of the origin of miserliness, cf. Helvétius: *De l'Esprit*, Discours III, Ch. X.

24. Selby-Bigge, par. 852.

25. Introduction to Part I, Ch. I of *Observations on Man*, I, 6.

In the *Treatise of Human Nature*, Hume drew an analogy between the association of ideas and gravitational attraction (Selby-Bigge edition, pp. 12–13); and in his *Examination of Dr. Reid's Inquiry* (p. 2), Priestley compared Hartley's accomplishment with that of Newton.

The comparison between the principle of association as the basis of all mental phenomena and the law of gravitation continued throughout the history of the movement. One finds it explicitly stated at two points in John Stuart Mill's preface to his father's *Analysis of the Phenomena of the Human Mind*.

26. These are the disciplines he specifically mentions in his introduction to the *Treatise*. One may note how lightly he passes over questions concerning the general principles of association in Section IV of Part I, contrasting this discussion with the detailed account of the *results* of associations which he offers in Book II, when he discusses the passions.

27. The title of Hartley's major work indicates this interest: *Observations on Man. His Frame, His Duty, and His Expectations.* In that work, a considerable portion of the first part is devoted to discussions of our "intellectual pleasures," which are of direct moral significance, and to the question of liberty and necessity. The whole of the second part of the work is devoted to theology.

28. *Examination of Dr. Reid's Inquiry*, p. xiii.

29. *Observations on Man*, Part I, Ch. I, Sect II, Prop. 14, Cor. 5.

30. An interest in practice may also have been responsible (in part, at least) for the emphasis which was later placed on association theory in the United States in the first decades of the twentieth century. (Cf. E. S. Robinson, *Association Theory To-Day*, pp. 4–5.)

31. Locke's use of the principle stressed the relations of *thoughts* to one another, and, as we have seen, he only utilized the principle in those cases in which the connections were established by custom rather than reason. The radical nature of associationism after Hume can be seen in the fact that both Hartley and Helvétius (and their successors) attempted to explain almost every aspect of thought, as well as feeling and action, in terms of the single principle: associations among that which was given in sensation.

32. *An Examination of Dr. Reid's Inquiry*, p. 18 f. This is a point to which Priestley frequently returns. (For example, *op. cit.*, p. xx and p. 110; also cf. his preface to his abridgment of Hartley, entitled *Hartley's Theory of the Human Mind*, p. xxiv and p. xxxii.)
    One finds the same point made in more theological terms by the anonymous author of *An Enquiry into the Origin of the Human Appetites and Affections* (in Samuel Parr, *Metaphysical Tracts*, p. 48).

33. Their assumption that this was the case rested on the fact that they, unlike Hume, believed that they understood the general nature of the process by means of which associations came to be formed: they all appealed to neurological hypotheses of a mechanical sort, of which the Hartleian vibrations were the most famous.

34. One may also relevantly note the fact that, in Hume and in Hartley, for example, associationism tended to stress the continuity between animal learning and the association of ideas in man. An affinity of this sort could not help but throw doubt on the thesis that certain truths were directly known through the native capacities of the human mind.

35. Hartley, *Observations on Man*, Part I, Prop. 14.

36. *Ibid.*, Cor. 12.

37. Hartley's account of the psychological basis of morality is more complex than Gay's, and does not, in the same sense, rest on self-interest. The elementary basis of his theory (cf. *Observations on Man*, Part I, Ch. III, Sect. III) is to be found in the pleasure or the pain which accompany other sensations, and which—through association—generate desire or aversion for particular objects. The desires thus engendered lie at the basis of all of the passions, and Hartley uses the existence of these acquired passions to explain what he terms "the intellectual pleasures." Each of the types of intellectual pleasure bears some relation to the moral life, but the highest among them is the pleasure attaching to "the Moral Sense," that is, pleasure associated with moral self-approbation (or the approbation of others) and pain attaching to feelings of moral guilt (or to the evidence of vice in others).
    It is worthy of note that, in spite of accounting for all of the intellectual pleasures through the effects of association, Hartley takes no cognizance of the fact that there might be differences in the experience of persons of different cultures, and therefore differences in at least the forms in which these pleasures

manifest themselves. One may note, for example, how closely tied to his own times he was in his account of the fear of death (cf. *Observations on Man*, Part I, Ch. IV, Sect. III, "Of Rational Self-Interest").

38. Cf. *Treatise of Human Nature*, Bk. III, Part II, Sect. II (especially pp. 486–95 of the Selby-Bigge edition).

39. Cf. *Treatise of Human Nature*, Bk. III, Part II, Sect V.

40. *Treatise of Human Nature*, Bk. III, Part III, Sect. VI (Selby-Bigge edition, p. 620).

41. One may note such a divergence between the implications drawn from associationism in fields other than moral theory. For example, Martin Kallich, in "The Association of Ideas and Critical Theory" classifies associationist theories with respect to their effects on literary criticism: some tend to stress uniformity and uphold neoclassical standards, others tend to emphasize diversity and pave the way for a romantic esthetic. While there are a number of points to criticize in this article, it does document the widespread effect of associationism on criticism, and also has relevance to the problem with which we are here concerned.

42. *Hartley's Theory of the Human Mind*, p. xxxii.

43. *Hartley's Theory of the Human Mind*, p. xliii.

44. Cf. *De l'Esprit des lois*, Bk. XIV, Ch. I.

45. In the first and second Discourses of that work, Helvétius laid down his epistemological presuppositions, and his doctrine of interests, which served as the basis of his social psychology. In these Discourses one can note how his sensationalistic presuppositions separate him from the views which Montesquieu held concerning the nature of man. (For example, the views of "l'esprit" and of "les plaisirs de l'âme" which one finds in Montesquieu's *Essai sur le goût* contrast sharply with those expressed by Helvétius.) It is not until the Third Discourse that Helvétius reaches the theses for which his previous analyses were written, and from that point forward his views must be seen in relation to those of Montesquieu, whose work—even while still in manuscript form—he had long studied with care (cf. Albert Keim, *Helvétius*, pp. 154–55).

46. Cf. *De l'esprit*, Discours III, Ch. I; also, *De l'homme*, Sect. I, Ch. I and II.
   Such was also the implication of Mill's characterization of education in his rectoral address at the University of St. Andrews. (Cf. p. 448, n. 16, below.)

47. "Chaque nation a sa manière particulière de voir et de sentir, qui forme son caractère; et, chez tous les peuples, ce caractère ou change tout-à-coup, ou s'altère peu-à-peu, selon les changements subits ou insensibles survenus dans la forme de leur gouvernement, par conséquent dans l'éducation publique" (*De l'homme*, Sect. IV, Ch. II; *Oeuvres*, VIII, 216). To this passage Helvétius added the following footnote: "La forme du gouvernement où l'on vit, fait toujours partie de notre éducation."

48. *De l'esprit*, Discours III, Ch. XXX (*Oeuvres*, V, 69–70). For extended analyses

of the effects of interests and of custom as causes of variability, cf. Discours II, Ch. VII, XVIII, and XX.

49. Cf. *De l'esprit*, Discours II for Helvétius's recognition of a marked degree of pluralism in the standards within any one society.

50. Cf. his remarks on the differences in that to which the search for glory becomes attached in different times and places, *ibid.*, Disc. III, Ch. XVI.

51. *De l'esprit*, Discours III, Ch. XXX (*Oeuvres*, V, 93); cf. Discours III, Ch. I–IV; also Ch. XXVI. It was on the ground that he overlooked differences in the inherited organization of individuals that many of Diderot's criticisms of Helvétius turned (cf. Diderot, "Réflexions sur le livre *De l'esprit*" and "Réfutation suivie de l'ouvrage d'Helvétius intitulé *De l'homme*," *Oeuvres*, II, 263–456).

52. *De l'homme*, Introduction (*Oeuvres*, VII, 22).

53. *De l'homme*, Sect. II, Ch. I (*Oeuvres*, VII, 155).

54. It is worth noting, however, that Rousseau's view was considerably less extreme than that of Helvétius in this respect. In Section V of *De l'homme*, Helvétius attacked Rousseau for believing that there are native differences in temperament among men. While Rousseau had stressed the effects of education, and while he was regarded by Godwin, among others, as belonging in the camp of those who, like the associationists and sensationalists, attributed all formative influences to education, Helvétius's interpretation of Rousseau (including his attack on him for inconsistencies) seems wholly justified. As the opening chapter of *Émile* makes abundantly clear, Rousseau regarded human beings as being born, like all living things, with inherent tendencies, and the education which a human being receives through the actions of others is only one part of his education. According to Rousseau, a good education is that in which the effects due to man are in harmony with those which spring from nature and from experience with objects. Thus, even though he did emphasize a native equality in men, Rousseau's view did not, in general, belong within the tradition in which Helvétius stood.

55. This statement appears at the beginning of the fourth paragraph of Hume's essay "Of the Original Contract," in *Essays, Moral, Political, and Literary*, p. 454.

56. *The Wealth of Nations*, Bk. I, Ch. II (I, 14).

57. In the preface to his *Enquiry Concerning Political Justice* (1793), Godwin says that he "derived great additional instruction from reading the most considerable French writers upon the nature of man in the following order, *Système de la nature*, Rousseau and Helvétius." [The precise wording of this passage is slightly altered in the third edition, cf. vol. I, p. ix.] In a new chapter introduced in the second edition (1795), i.e. Bk. I, Ch. 4, Godwin again acknowledged his debt to Helvétius and to Rousseau, and on page 275 of that edition, he commended Hume, Hartley, Rousseau, and Helvétius. For comments on the relationship between the thought of Godwin and those with whom we are here concerned, cf. the commentary of F. E. L. Priestley in volume III of his edition of Godwin's *Enquiry Concerning Political Justice*.

The close relationship between the general theoretical framework of Godwin's views and those of Helvétius can be seen when Godwin says: "The actions and dispositions of men are not the offspring of any original bias that they bring into the world in favour of one sentiment or character rather than another, but flow entirely from the operation of circumstances and events acting upon a faculty of receiving sensible impressions." (Enquiry Concerning Political Justice, I, 26–27.)

58. As is well known, Bentham acknowledged Helvétius to be his precursor (e.g., Works, X, 70–71); and James Mill's respect for Helvétius was extremely high. As he said:

> The degree in which the useful qualities of human nature are, or are not, under the powers of education ... is the subject of a famous controversy, with names of the highest authority on both sides of the question. Helvétius, it is true, stands almost alone, on one side. But Helvétius, alone, is a host. No one man, perhaps, has done so much towards perfecting the *theory* of education" (Education, p. 18).

59. In the first essay of that book, Owen described this statement as a self-evident principle (cf. p. 16), and it is indeed the foundation of his theory of social reform.

60. An analogue to twentieth-century totalitarianism can be found in the St. Simonian movement. However, the St. Simonians did not, of course, share the presuppositions of those with whom we are here concerned. In fact, as we shall note, they were more closely identified with those tendencies of thought which supplanted this form of the doctrine of man's malleability, and this form of interventionism.

61. Godwin, Enquiry Concerning Political Justice I, p. 5.

CHAPTER 10.   ORGANICISM: CULTURE AND HUMAN NATURE

1. Cf. the following statement made by Gladys Bryson:

> Hume cannot escape his century. In spite of his feeling for history, in spite of his much writing of it, his historical method is vitiated by a fundamental assumption. This assumption, shared by all his contemporaries, is that the starting point for all humanistic study, including history, is man's nature, his psychology. (Man and Society, p. 109.)

And, in the same connection, Miss Bryson said: "The Scottish moralists were convinced that there could be no sound science of man unless it were built on 'the facts of human nature'." (Man and Society, p. 114.)

(For more general statements relevant to these points, cf. pp. 25 and 242–43 of the same work.)

2. "Une nation n'est que l'assemblage des citoyens qui la composent." (De l'esprit, Disc. II, Ch. VIII; in Oeuvres, II, 105.)

This view may be contrasted with that which came to characterize the German Historical School, which Savigny enunciated in 1815 when he stated the principles on which the new Zeitschrift für geschichtliche Rechtswissenschaft was founded:

> Es war eine Zeit, wo die Absonderung des Einzelnen vom Ganzen streng und mit grossen Selbstvertrauen durchgeführt wurde, nicht bloss die Absonderung der Gegenwart von der gering geschätzten Vorzeit, sondern auch des einzelnen Bürgers vom Staate. (Grundgedanken, p. 16.)

It was against the assumptions of that period that his program was directed.

3. The fact that Mill also represents the tradition of associationism did not prevent him from responding to this new and fundamentally antagonistic current

in the thought of his times. However, as we shall see, his own views regarding human nature are not identical with traditional geneticism nor, it is clear, with organicism; they constitute a form of the doctrine that man is essentially a progressive being whose developing capacities depend both upon the principles of association and the effects of culture.

With respect to the actual history of the concept of a "spirit of the age," the following points may be noted:

a) The first entry given in Grimm's *Wörterbuch* for the term *"Zeitgeist"* dates from 1789; it is there pointed out that the term was also frequently used by Herder and Goethe. In 1790 Reinhold published his *Briefe über die Kantische Philosophie* and the heading of the first letter includes the phrase "Der Geist unsers Zeitalters." That the term was being used in a sense which is at least connected with subsequent uses of the term "Zeitgeist" is especially clear on pp. 10–12 of that letter. (I am indebted to Professor M. H. Abrams for calling my attention to this passage.)

Although Hegel did not use the term itself in his *Phenomenology of Mind* (1807), the concept of a *Zeitgeist* was assuredly implicit at many points in that work, and particularly in Hegel's characterization of the spirit of his own time, which we have already quoted. (Cf. above, p. 4.)

b) The Oxford English Dictionary cites uses of the term "spirit" as applied to a period of time (*Spirit*, entry 10-b), by Shelley in 1820 and by Landor in 1824. One should also note Hazlitt's portraits of literary figures, published in 1825 under the title *The Spirit of the Age*. However, Hazlitt's portraits do not provide illustrations of an attempt to depict a *Zeitgeist*; for such an attempt one may note Coleridge's *Lectures*. (Cf. the *résumé* of the first lecture of the 1818 series, which was entitled "General Character of the Gothic Mind in the Middle Ages," *Complete Works*, IV, 232–34.)

c) The spread of the concept of a spirit of the age could scarcely have been so rapid had there not previously been concepts such as *Nationalgeist*, *Geist des Volkes*, *Nationalcharakter*, and the like. Sir Isaiah Berlin attributes the concept of *Nationalgeist* to Karl Friedrich von Moser, and cites a variety of passages in which these concepts were used by Herder. (Cf. Berlin, "Herder and the Enlightenment," pp. 75, 77, and 79.) Earlier attempts to understand the essence of the Greek spirit, such as one finds in Winckelmann and also in Lessing, had assuredly paved the way for a wider extension of these concepts, as had Montesquieu's analysis of forms of government and their relation to the people in *L'esprit des lois*. The most developed philosophic use of the concept of a Nation as a spiritual entity prior to Hegel is undoubtedly to be found in Fichte. (Cf. Lask, *Fichtes Idealismus und die Geschichte*, pp. 255–67.) It is to be noted, however, that neither in Herder nor in Fichte does an emphasis on the Nation as a spiritual whole lead to an abandonment of a standard in which the self-realization of the individual, as individual, is the highest moral goal. (On Fichte's complex views regarding this matter, cf. Part III, Ch. 2 of Lask's book, especially pp. 204–6 and 210.)

4. From the third section of *The Spirit of the Age*, pp. 47–48.

5. Bentham's essay entitled "Of the Influence of Time and Place in Matters of Legislation" (*Works*, I, 169–94) does not constitute an exception to this statement. In that essay he raised the question of whether the same laws which would be perfect in England would also be perfect in other countries (e.g., in Bengal). While he acknowledged that any differences in circumstances which affected differences in sensibility would have to be taken into account, and that variations in

customs and beliefs would also have to be taken into account if happiness were not to be sacrificed, he held that the goals of primitive peoples are not different from the goals of people in more advanced societies. Thus, he would not have held, as Mill came to hold, that "human nature must proceed step by step"; on the contrary, he believed that, apart from specific differences in circumstances, "the laws which are best for a civilized [age] would also have been best for a rude age" (I, 190). For Mill's opposition to this view, cf. the early draft of his *Autobiography*, p. 142.

It is worth noting at this point that Mill also held that the generalizations of political economy must be "relative to a given stage of social advancement," and that political economists should not assume that "their present experience of mankind [is] of universal validity" (*Positive Philosophy of Auguste Comte*, p. 76 and p. 77). He then continues (p. 77), pointing out the error of "mistaking temporary or local phases of human character for human nature itself; having no faith in the wonderful pliability of the human mind; deeming it impossible, in spite of the strongest evidence, that the earth can produce human beings of a different type from that which is familiar to them in their own age, or even, perhaps, in their own country."

6. *Works of Lord Macaulay*, V, 266. James Mill's *Government* was written for the Supplement to the fifth edition of the *Encyclopaedia Britannica* (1820); Macaulay's attack appeared in the *Edinburgh Review* in 1829. In his *Autobiography*, John Stuart Mill tells us that it was this particular attack which forced him to depart more radically than he had previously thought necessary from the views held by his father and by Bentham on the theory of government. (Cf. *Autobiography, Early Draft*, pp. 134–35. Hereafter, parallel references to this work appear in brackets following the main citation.)

7. *Works of Lord Macaulay*, V, 268.

8. Cf. "Westminster Reviewer's Defence of Mill," *Works of Lord Macaulay*, V, 290.

9. Cf. *Autobiography*, Ch. V [*Early Draft*, pp. 134–40].

10. Cf. *Autobiography*, Ch. V [*Early Draft*, pp. 131–37] for a discussion of this set of influences, and its relation to the effect which Macaulay's attack on his father had upon Mill's views.

To be sure, Mill's essay "Coleridge," published in 1840, is an earlier account which is relevant to the German influence on him. However, in his attempt to present a fair intellectual portrait of Coleridge, Mill was not in a position to show precisely how his own thought had been affected by Coleridge. Mill always remained unalterably opposed to what he took to be the most essential feature of the latter's philosophic position: its nativistic view of the human mind. (Cf. *Dissertations*, II, 21.)

11. In *The Earlier Letters of John Stuart Mill* one notes that, in a letter to Carlyle in 1832, it is clear that much of Mill's knowledge of Goethe had come from what Carlyle had told him (cf. I, 111–12); though, it is also evident through later letters to Comte that he had first-hand knowledge of Goethe's lyrics (cf. II, 576 f. and 582).

12. *Dissertations*, II, 15.

13. *Dissertations*, II, 37.

14. *Dissertations*, II, 40. (In this passage Mill was using the term "metaphysician" to refer to those who adopted a psychological approach. As I have elsewhere pointed out [cf. *Journal of the History of Philosophy*, VI (1968), 39], this was a not uncommon usage, and is frequently to be found in Mill's writings.)

With respect to the recognition of the diversity and particularity of cultures, also note Mill's praise of Michelet for his skill in portraying "the collective mind" of the people of a time, and for recognizing that "each period has a physiognomy and character of its own" (*Dissertations*, II, 217 and 219).

15. Herder's works were not only available in several editions, but his *Ideen* had been translated into English and had gone through two editions, as well as having been translated into French.

In his essay on Coleridge, Mill praised Herder along with Michelet, and this connection between French historians and the Germano-Coleridgian school became explicit at the end of the passage just cited. (Cf. *Dissertations*, II, 41.) The members of "the French school" of historians undoubtedly included Thierry and Guizot, along with Michelet. (Cf. Mill's review of Michelet's *History of France* in the same volume of the *Dissertations*.)

16. *Earlier Letters*, II, 576.

17. Cf. *Autobiography*, Ch. V [*Early Draft*, pp. 137–40; also pp. 187–88].

For an extended discussion of Mill's relation to the Saint-Simonians and to Comte, cf. Iris W. Mueller, *John Stuart Mill and French Thought* (1956).

18. Cf. Comte's *Plan des travaux scientifiques nécessaires pour réorganiser la société*, in *System of Positive Polity*, IV, 530, *et passim*.

19. *Positive Philosophy of Auguste Comte*, p. 78.

The point of view here expressed has a parallel in Macaulay's attack on the Benthamite theory, which we have already mentioned. In his rejoinder to the *Westminster Review*'s defense of James Mill, in a passage which we have already quoted in part, Macaulay said:

> Our knowledge of human nature, instead of being prior in order to our knowledge of the science of government, will be posterior to it. And it would be correct to say, that by means of the science of government, and of other kindred sciences—the science of education, for example, which falls under exactly the same principle—we arrive at the science of human nature. (*Works*, V, 290.)

For "the science of government" Comte would, of course, substitute "sociology." Furthermore, as we shall note, Macaulay's science of government might be regarded (and was regarded by John Stuart Mill) as wholly lacking in scientific method.

20. *Positive Philosophy of Auguste Comte*, p. 80.

21. Cf. *Autobiography*, Ch. V [*Early Draft*, pp. 134 and 136].

22. Mill said:

> The *fons errorum* in M. Comte's later speculations is this inordinate demand for "unity" and "systematization." This is the reason why it does not suffice to him that all

should be ready, in case of need, to postpone their personal interests and inclinations to the requirements of the general good: he demands that each should regard as vicious any care at all for his personal interests, except as a means to the good of others. (*Positive Philosophy of Auguste Comte*, p. 127.)

In opposition to this conception Mill briefly outlined his own Utilitarian standard of evaluation (pp. 131–32).

23. Lévy-Bruhl, in his preface to the *Lettres inédites* of Mill and Comte (pp. xxvi–xxxvi), takes a view similar to that which follows. The crucial letter in which Mill's break with Comte over questions of psychology finally becomes clear was dated October 30, 1843. (Cf. *Lettres inédites*, pp. 259–71, or *Earlier Letters*, II, 604–11.)

We may also note that, in the first of his two essays on Comte, when he was discussing Comte's rejection of psychology as an independent science, Mill said, "This great mistake is not a mere hiatus in M. Comte's system, but the parent of serious errors in his attempt to create a Social Science" (*Positive Philosophy of Auguste Comte*, p. 62).

24. Cf. "On Interpreting Mill's *Utilitarianism*," *Journal of the History of Philosophy*, VI (1968), 35–46, and "Two Moot Issues in Mill's *Utilitarianism*," in J. B. Schneewind (ed.), *Mill: A Collection of Critical Essays* (Garden City: Doubleday, 1968).

25. The clearest expressions of his view on this point are to be found in an early essay, "Examen du traité de Broussais sur l'irritation." (Cf. especially, *System of Positive Polity*, IV, 646–47.)

26. For Comte's most comprehensive discussion of the relations of his views to those of Gall, cf. *System of Positive Polity*, I, 543–51.

27. For a discussion of Comte's social statics, which are crucial in this regard, the reader may be referred to Paul Barth's *Philosophie der Geschichte als Soziologie*, pp. 165–72.

28. In characterizing the cluster of views most frequently referred to as "organicism," Isaiah Berlin said:

Thus nations or cultures or civilizations for Fichte or Hegel (and Spengler; and one is inclined, though somewhat hesitantly, to add Professor Arnold Toynbee) are certainly not merely convenient collective terms for individuals possessing certain characteristics in common; but are more 'real' and more 'concrete' than the individuals who compose them. Individuals remain 'abstract' precisely because they are mere 'elements' or 'aspects, 'moments' artificially abstracted for *ad hoc* purposes, and literally without existence (or at any rate, 'historical' or 'philosophical' or 'real' being) apart from the wholes of which they form a part. (*Historical Inevitability*, p. 8.)

29. In 1886, in an essay entitled "The Historical Method," Henry Sidgwick stated this criticism of the earlier individualistic forms of social theory when he criticized one passage in Mill:

It does not follow that, as Mill conceives, a psychology exists or can be constructed independent of sociology. . . . In saying that "men in a state of society are *still* men," it is implied that we have some means of knowing them adequately *out* of a state of society. . . . But I cannot perceive that we have any such means of knowing the properties of men in this supposed elementary, non-social, condition,—so far, at least, as the most important and interesting departments of their mental life are concerned" (*Mind*, XI [1886], 212).

However, it is to be noted that Sidgwick's chief purpose in this article was to criticize the evaluative implications which were frequently drawn by those who accepted what he defined as "the historical method."

30. I have attempted to defend this thesis in "Societal Facts," *British Journal of Sociology*, VI (1955), 305–17. [Reprinted in Patrick Gardiner, *Theories of History* (New York: Free Press, 1959) and in Edward H. Madden, *Structure of Scientific Thought* (Boston: Houghton Mifflin, 1960).]

31. For example, cf. *Cours de philosophie positive*, VI, 668 and 680.

32. *System of Positive Polity*, IV, 582.

33. For an example of a twentieth-century anthropologist who used this contrast as a means of establishing the difference between the organic and the super-organic, cf. Kroeber, "The Superorganic," *American Anthropologist*, XIX (1917), 163–213.

The notion of a social inheritance was basic in Comte, and received its most extreme expression in the sacerdotal aspects of the positivist cult. It was summed up by Comte in a famous phrase when he said, "The fundamental principle of human *Order* is this: The Living are essentially and increasingly governed by the Dead." (*System of Positive Polity*, III, xxix).

34. *Cours de philosophie positive*, VI, 692.

There are two passages in Comte's correspondence with Mill which are worth quoting in the same connection, and which are all the more forceful in that Comte does not employ the concept of the collective being, Humanity, in formulating his anti-individualistic position. In one he speaks of "la haute irrationalité que présente toute théorie quelconque sur l'homme, quand on s'y borne au point de vue individuel" (*Lettres inédites*, p. 63), and in the other he says,

... j'ai nettement reconnu ... que l'étude intellectuelle et morale ne saurait être convenablement instituée en pure biologie, parce que l'homme individuel constitue, à cet égard, un point de vue bâtard et même faux; c'est seulement par la sociologie que cette opération doit être dirigée, puisque notre évolution réelle est inintelligible sans la considération continue et prépondérante de l'état social, où tous les aspects quelconques sont d'ailleurs pleinement solidaires" (p. 75–76).

35. *System of Positive Polity*, I, 268. (Also, cf. the quotation given in note 24, p. 389, above.)

36. On Comte and the doctrine of emergence, cf. p. 379, n. 48, above.

37. In comparison with Spencer and with a number of post-Darwinian sociologists, and in conformity with his strict use of the concept of emergence, Comte tended to be moderately cautious with respect to drawing detailed comparisons between societies and individual organisms. For one point at which he expresses the need for caution, cf. *System of Positive Polity*, II, 239.

38. The clearest and at the same time most succinct expression of this point of view is to be found in his *Cours de philosophie positive*, IV, 324–62, from which the following passage is taken:

Mais on doit, à ce sujet, reconnaître, en principe, que le consensus devient toujours d'autant plus intime et plus prononcé qu'il s'applique à des phénomènes graduellement plus complexes et moins généraux.... c'est surtout aux systèmes organiques, en vertu de leur plus grande complication, que conviendra toujours essentiellement la notion scientifique de solidarité et de consensus, malgré son universalité nécessaire. C'est seulement alors que cette notion, jusque-là purement accessoire, constitue directement la base indispensable de l'ensemble des conceptions positives; et sa preponderance y devient toujours aussi d'autant plus prononcée qu'ils s'agit d'organismes plus composés ou des phénomènes plus complexes et plus éminents. Ainsi, par example, le consensus animal est bien plus complet que le consensus végétal: de même, il se développe evidemment à mesure que l'animalité s'élève, jusqu'à son maximum dans la nature humaine.... En pursuivant rationellement cette marche philosophique, d'après l'ensemble fondamental de nos connaissances positives, cette grande notion devait donc, à priori, acquérir, dans l'étude générale de l'organisme social, une prépondérance scientifique encore supérieure à celle que tous les bons esprits lui attribuent maintenant sans hésitation en biologie (IV, 350–51).

Comte dealt with social statics at greater length in volume II of his *Système de politique positive,* but the theoretical foundations of his views were less fully developed there; that work placed greater emphasis upon questions of normative political philosophy which Comte believed were entailed by his theoretical system.

39. On the history of functionalism in anthropology—which has, of late, often been misinterpreted—cf. my article "Functionalism in Social Anthropology," in *Philosophy, Science, and Method: Essays in Honor of Ernest Nagel* (ed. S. Morgenbesser, P. Suppes, M. G. White), New York: St. Martin's Press, 1969.

40. Cf. the following statement:

The true theory of the human Family may be treated from two aspects, differing essentially but both natural, the one being the moral, the other the political.... Under both of these aspects we shall regard the Family as the direct constituent of Society, that is to say, as the simplest and most spontaneous form of association. To analyse societies into individuals, strictly so called, as the anarchical schools insist, would be no less unreasonable than immoral and would tend rather to dissolve, than to explain, our social life, for the theory only holds good when association ends. It would be in Sociological reasoning an error as great, as in Biological reasoning it would be, to analyse the body chemically into ultimate molecules, which have no separate existence during life. (*System of Positive Polity,* II, 152.)

For a further statement concerning the growth of a more complex form of political and social organization out of an original basis in familial organization, cf. *System of Positive Polity,* II, 222.

41. His praise of Aristotle is interesting in this respect:

The incomparable Aristotle laid down the true principle of every collective organism, when he described it as the distribution of functions, and the combination of labour. (*System of Positive Philosophy,* II, 234.)

42. *Cours de philosophie positive,* IV, 327. This was one of the bases on which Comte sometimes attacked political economists: they attempted to separate one aspect of social life from all others. (For example, cf. *Cours de philosophie positive,* IV, 353–54.) Another basis was that they purportedly used metaphysical concepts. Nevertheless, Comte had a high regard for Adam Smith's analysis of the importance of the division of labor, and he viewed Smith (along with Hume) as an important social philosopher, not subject to the same criticisms as were other economists. (On these points, cf. *Cours de philosophie positive,* IV, 266–72, and on Smith and Hume, his letters to Mill: *Lettres inédites,* pp. 162 and 366.)

43. Cf. *Cours de philosophie positive*, IV, 358–61. The same point of view had been stated in his *Plan des travaux scientifiques* in 1822. (Cf. *System of Positive Polity*, IV, 587.)

44. For example, in the chapter entitled "That There Is, or May Be, A Science of Human Nature," in his *System of Logic*, Mill discussed the formation of character and remarked: "nothing which has happened to the person throughout his life being without its portion of influence" (p. 588).

45. For this reason, as we shall later have occasion to note, Mill advocated the introduction of a new science, Ethology, into the system of the moral sciences.

46. For those who may tend to place primary emphasis on Comte's evaluational attitudes, I would suggest a consideration of Comte's discussion of historical necessity in the forty-eighth lesson of his *Cours de philosophie positive* (cf. especially, IV, 324–99). His doctrines of a consensus in the social organism, his emphasis on the leading role of intellectual development in social change, and the requirements of what constitutes a positive science, loom far larger in that discussion than his views regarding what constitutes a good state of society or a proper fulfilment of human nature.

47. In anticipation of our treatment of Hegel, I might merely cite the following passages from Comte's discussion of the necessity inherent in the developmental process.

> Pour achever ici de caractériser sommairement cette conception préliminaire du développement humain, qui constitue le sujet propre de toute la sociologie dynamique, j'y dois encore signaler, sous un dernier point de vue, la disposition générale qu'elle doit spontanément produire à toujours considérer l'état social, envisagé sous tous ses divers aspects principaux, comme ayant été essentiellement aussi parfait, à chaque époque, que le comportait l'âge correspondant de l'humanité (*Cours de philosophie positive*, IV, 387).

And, with respect to political institutions:

> Il n'y a pas d'influence perturbatrice, soit extérieure, soit humaine, qui puisse faire co-exister, dans le monde politique réel, des élémens antipathiques, ni altérer, à aucun titre, les vraies lois naturelles du développement de l'humanité (*ibid.*, p. 394).

And, with respect to man's moral nature:

> On n'en saurait douter davantage, au fond, à l'égard même du développement moral de notre nature, dont le caractère est certainement réglé surtout, à chaque époque, par l'état correspondant de l'évolution sociale, quelles que soient les modifications volontaires derivées de l'éducation, et même les modifications spontanées relatives à l'organisation individuelle. Chacun des modes fondamentaux de l'existence sociale détermine un certain système de moeurs co-relatives, dont la physionomie commune se retrouve aisément chez tous les individus, au milieu de leurs différences caractéristiques (*ibid.*, p. 398).

48. Page 81 (Baillie translation).

49. For example, near the outset of his treatment of the individual mind in his *Enzyklopädie der philosophischen Wissenschaften* he said:

> Die Frage um die Immaterialität der Seele kann nur dann noch eine Interesse haben, wenn die Materie als ein Wahres einerseits, und der Geist als ein *Ding* anderseits vorgestellt wird. (*Sämtliche Werke*, VI, 232, Section #309.)

50. In criticizing traditional modern cosmology, Hegel said:

Nature they regard as subject in its workings to necessity; Mind they hold to be free. No doubt there is a real foundation for this distinction in the very core of Mind itself: but freedom and necessity, when thus abstractly opposed, are terms applicable only in the finite world to which, as such, they belong. A freedom involving no necessity, and mere necessity without freedom, are abstract and in this way untrue formulae of thought. Freedom is no blank indeterminateness. . . . Necessity . . . in the ordinary acceptation of the term in popular philosophy, means determination from without only—as in finite mechanics, where a body moves only when it is struck by another body, and moves in the direction communicated to it by the impact. This however is a merely external necessity, not the real inward necessity which is identical with freedom. (*Enzyklopädie der philosophischen Wissenschaften*, Section 35. I quote the passage from page 71 of the Wallace translation of *The Smaller Logic*, which constituted the first part of the *Enzyklopädie*.)

51. Baillie translation, p. 336. (The original is to be found at II, 239 in the *Sämtliche Werke*.)

It is also worth noting that Hegel inveighs bitterly against that form of an inner-outer dichotomy which attempts to distinguish the true nature of a man's inner character from his acts. He says, "The true being of a man is, on the contrary, his act." And, again, "It [the act] *is* such and such, and its being is not merely a symbol, it is the fact itself. It *is* this, and the individual human being *is* what the act *is*." (Cf. *Phenomenology of Mind*, Baillie translation, pp. 349 and 350; in *Sämtliche Werke*, II, 250.) In another place (*Philosophy of Right*, p. 83, Section 124) he says, "What the subject is, is the series of his actions."

52. Cf. *Phenomenology of Mind*, pp. 331–36, and *Enzyklopädie der philosophischen Wissenschaften*, in *Werke*, VI, 259.

53. I am here taking these terms in a general and non-technical sense, and I am not attempting to make my usage conform to that which is to be found in Hegel when he gives his dialectical account of the successive stages in the development of the soul and of consciousness. (Cf. *Enzyklopädie*, Sections 311–43. These passages are translated by Wallace in Hegel's *Philosophy of Mind*, pp. 14–53; however, they there bear section numbers 391–423.)

54. *Philosophy of Right*, p. 43 (Section 47).

This passage stresses the concept of willing, but the importance of feeling in distinguishing self from not-self becomes clear in the remark added to Section 48 (cf. p. 44) where Hegel says: "If my body is touched or suffers violence, then, because I feel, I am touched myself actually, here and now." He uses this as a means of distinguishing between personal injury and damage to one's external property; while property is an extension of the self, it is not included in the core of the self, for in external property one's *will* "is not actually present in [the same] direct fashion."

55. *Philosophy of Right*, p. 41 (Section 44).

It is to be noted that the right of appropriation is absolute only with respect to things, not persons, according to Hegel. On this basis he rejected all attempts to justify slavery as a social institution. (Cf. *Philosophy of Right*, p. 48, Section 57.) Furthermore, it is to be noted that Hegel rejected the view that marriage rests on contract: contract applies to property, and only things—not human beings—are to be conceived of as property. (Cf. *Philosophy of Right*, p. 58, Section 75.)

It is to be noted in passing that the famous discussion which is often referred to as "Master and Slave" (which is a dubious translation of *"Herrschaft und Knechtschaft"*) in Section B, 4A, of Hegel's *Phenomenology of Mind* should not be interpreted as a discussion of a concrete form of social institution: it relates to the development of the consciousness of self through consciousness of the other.

56. *Philosophy of Right*, p. 57 (Section 71).

57. The structure of Hegel's *Philosophy of Right* leaves much to be desired, and one may note that in his *History of Political Theory* (p. 631 f.) G. H. Sabine explicitly abandoned any attempt to present its major theses in conformity with its ostensible structure. Plamenatz, however, bases his exposition on the structure which Hegel appears to have suggested in Section 33 of the *Philosophy of Right* (cf. *Man and Society*, II, 227–32). However, Plamenatz fails to show how the two triads with which he deals are related to one another. One may note that Hegel's own later addition to Section 33 (cf. *Philosophy of Right*, p. 234, or *Sämtliche Werke*, VII, 86) suggests that the second triad is to be understood as the concrete embodiment of the first, that is, as a working-out of the ethical life in the concrete materials of existence—*not* as a distinct triad. If this is taken to be so, the order of exposition which I have adopted needs no further justification.

I shall, however, omit consideration of Hegel's treatment of the family. If Plamenatz is correct in thinking that Hegel may have had the extended family or clan structure in mind, then the criticism he offers (*Man and Society*, II, 231–35) is more than justified. However, I am inclined to believe that the family, as Hegel actually discussed it, can only be construed in terms of the nuclear family; as such it cannot be considered as *historically* prior to civil society. Hegel was not speaking of the historical past. From the point of view of its impact on the personality of the individual, the family can be thought of as "prior" to civil society. Furthermore, had Hegel omitted a separate consideration of the family, his lectures on the philosophy of law would not have covered all of the materials expected at that time in a treatise which, when published, bore the double title *Naturrecht und Staatswissenschaft im Grundrisse* and *Grundlinien der Philosophie des Rechts*.

58. In other words, we shall have gone immediately from Hegel's discussion of "Abstract Right" to his discussion of the concrete embodiments of "The Ethical Life," omitting at this point a consideration of the materials in Sections 105 to 155. Since we shall also omit consideration of Hegel's treatment of the Family, for reasons suggested in the preceding note, we shall proceed immediately to Section 182, which is the beginning of his discussion of "Civil Society."

59. I have attempted to state Hegel's conception of Civil Society in terms more familiar to the contemporary reader than those which he himself uses; it may be that I have overextended his meaning, although I do not believe so. For his own explicit definition the reader may wish to consult *Philosophy of Right*, p. 110 (Section 157).

60. *Philosophy of Right*, p. 123 (Section 182).
In his foreword to this volume (cf. pp. x–xi), T. M. Knox has a brief but helpful characterization of Civil Society as Hegel conceived of it.

61. For one of the clearest expressions of this view, cf. *Phenomenology of Mind*, pp. 375–77.

It may also be helpful to cite G. H. Sabine's description of this aspect of Hegel's doctrine:

> Neither society nor the state can be said to depend merely on individual consent; they are too deeply ingrained in the whole structure of needs and satisfactions that make up personal self-realization. The highest of all human needs is a need for participation, to be an organ of causes and purposes larger than private wants and satisfactions. (*History of Political Theory,* p. 651.)

62. As we have already noted, Hegel contends that the individual's world is not an external reality, "given *per se*," independent of his thought and his will (cf. above, p. 176). Once this is acknowledged, the individual's world is not primarily the world of nature but the world of spirit, that is, the social world.

63. From the Preface to *Philosophy of Right,* p. 10. (*Sämtliche Werke,* VII, 33.)

64. From *The Smaller Logic,* Wallace translation, p. 11. This passage is particularly appropriate here, since in the immediately preceding paragraph Hegel had cited his earlier dictum that "what is rational is actual and what is actual is rational," and it was as an elucidation of that dictum that he inveighed against contrasting an ideal "ought to be" with the actual nature of the real.

He expressed the same position throughout his writings; for example, in the *Phenomenology of Mind* he said:

> What is universally valid is also universally effective: what *ought to be,* as a matter of fact, *is* too; and what merely *should* be, and is *not,* has no real truth (p. 289).

65. *Philosophy of History,* p. 9.

The following comparable passage appears in the Preface to the *Philosophy of Right:*

> If [a philosopher's] theory really goes beyond the world as it is and builds an ideal one as it ought to be, that world exists indeed, but only in his opinions, an unsubstantial element where anything you please may, in fancy, be built (p. 11).

In many passages in which Hegel rejected the separation of that which ought to be from that which truly is, he obviously had Kant's views in mind. This becomes perfectly explicit in another passage in the *Philosophy of Right* (p. 90, Section 135), where he claims that his *Phenomenology of Mind* had shown the antinomies in which "the moral way of thinking" tends to become entrapped.

66. *Philosophy of History,* p. 36.

With respect to Hegel's theological position, we may point out that the preceding quotation is immediately followed by this sentence: "This *Good,* this *Reason,* in its most concrete form, is God." (For the original, cf. *Sämtliche Werke,* XI, 67.)

67. Cf. Ch. 1, pp. 31–32, above.

68. *Philosophy of Right,* p. 10.

69. *Philosophy of History,* p. 36.

70. Cf. *Philosophy of History,* p. 15. (The passage should, however, be read in the context supplied by pages 12 through 16.)

71. *Philosophy of History*, p. 39. Also, cf. *Philosophy of Right*, p. 285 (an addition to Section 272), where he speaks of the State as "a secular deity."

72. Cf. the following statements from the addition to Section 258:

The march of God in the world, that is what the state is. The basis of the state is the power of reason actualizing itself as will. In considering the Idea of the state, we must not have our eyes on particular states or on particular institutions. Instead we must consider this Idea, this actual God, by itself. On some principle or other, any state may be shown to be bad, this or that defect may be found in it. . . . Since it is easier to find defects than to understand the affirmative, we may readily fall into the mistake of looking at isolated aspects of the state and so forgetting its inward organic life. The state is no ideal work of art; it stands on earth and so in the sphere of caprice, chance, and error, and bad behavior may disfigure it in many respects. But the ugliest of men, or a criminal, or an invalid, or a cripple, is still always a living man. The affirmative, life, subsists despite his defects, and it is this affirmative factor which is our theme here (*Philosophy of Right*, p. 279).

It should not be thought that, in this passage, Hegel is admitting that he has abstracted an ideal essence common to all states, and can understand that essence without understanding its actual embodiments in their particularity. His conception of "the Idea" was not Platonic. To understand *the State* one must, on Hegel's view, understand states in their concreteness. What he was arguing was that such an understanding will show that some features of actual states are merely accidental and thus irrelevant to an understanding of the state as a fundamental form of human existence.

73. In this connection it must be borne in mind that Hegel rejected the doctrines of contract and of consent as the foundations of the state. For one especially clear example of his rejection of the contract theory, note the remark and the addition to Section 75 of the *Philosophy of Right* (pp. 59 and 242); as an example of his rejection of a theory stressing consent, note the following passage:

Unfortunately, however, as Fichte did later, he [Rousseau] takes the will only in a determinate form as the individual will, and he regards the universal will not as the absolutely rational element in the will, but only as a 'general' will which proceeds out of this individual will as out of a conscious will. The result is that he reduces the union of individuals in the state to a contract and therefore to something based on their arbitrary wills, their opinion, and their capriciously given express consent. (*Philosophy of Right*, p. 157, Section 258.)

As Marcuse has remarked, in Hegel's theory "the general will is the result and not the origin of the state" (*Reason and Revolution*, p. 84).

74. In some fundamental respects, the Hegelian doctrine of morality may be compared with those presently espoused views in which morality is taken to be based upon *practices* which have their justification in their necessity for social life. For example, for Hegel, the ethical life (*Sittlichkeit*) is based upon custom (*Sitte*), and individual virtue is a mode of behavior which, through habit, has become a fixed element in that individual's character. (Cf. *Philosophy of Right*, pp. 107–9 and 260, Sections 150 and 151 with their additions.)

75. *Philosophy of History*, p. 38.

In F. H. Bradley's essay, "My Station and its Duties," one finds an even more conservative form of Hegelian doctrine than that which I am here attributing to Hegel. Bradley's emphasis on one's station in a society, and one's duties as being defined in terms of one's station, does build on concepts which Hegel frequently used (e.g., *Philosophy of Right*, p. 107–8, Section 150). However, Hegel was viewing morality as part of the self-development of the World-Spirit, whereas Bradley's essay was concerned with what constitutes the duty of an individual. When one considers Hegel's views of the role of individual passion, the inevitability of suffering, and the character of world-historical individuals, his emphasis on the ultimate dominance of the state shows more sensitivity to the values which frequently bring individuals into conflict with their societies than is to be found in Bradley's ethical theory.

76. *Philosophy of History*, p. 77. Also, cf. *Philosophy of History*, p. 38 and *Phenomenology of Mind*, p. 378.

It is to be noted that "freedom," as applied to an individual, may have a variety of meanings, and therefore a variety of different polar opposites. The manner in which Hegel's contrast of freedom and caprice is related to other meanings of freedom is not of present concern. We need merely note that this particular contrast was dominant in his treatment of the individual and the state.

77. *Philosophy of History*, p. 52.
Also, cf. p. 74, where Hegel says:

> Every Englishman will say: We are the men who navigate the ocean, and have the commerce of the world; to whom the East Indies belong and their riches; who have a parliament, juries, etc.—The relation of the individual to that Spirit is that he appropriates to himself this substantial existence; that it becomes his character and capability, enabling him to have a definite place in the world.

78. This doctrine was characteristic of *organicism* in its nineteenth-century forms, and is to be found in Comte and in Spencer as well as in Hegel. The biological doctrine that "ontogeny recapitulates phylogeny," when applied to psychological capacities, was sometimes taken as lending support to the position. However, it is to be noted that this widely held position was not easy to reconcile with *geneticism*, for the assumptions of geneticism demand that one account for the complex forms of any individual's experience in terms of the effects of earlier, simpler experiences. We may note that Herbert Spencer reconciled organicism and geneticism by postulating an inheritance of the effects which experience had had on earlier generations.

79. For example, one may note the passage in which Hegel holds that the individual traverses the same road as had the race, but that the cultural achievements of the past, which originally demanded great efforts, become a second nature to those who had inherited them. In part, that passage reads as follows:

> The particular individual, so far as content is concerned, has also to go through the stages through which the general mind has passed, but as shapes once assumed by mind but now laid aside, as stages of a road which has been worked over and levelled out. Hence it is that, in the case of various kinds of knowledge, we find that what in former days occupied the energies of men of mature ability sinks to the level of information, exercises, and even pastimes, for children; and in this educational progress we can see the history of the world's culture delineated in faint outline. This bygone mode of existence has already become an acquired possession of the general mind, which constitutes the substance of the individual. (*Phenomenology of Mind*, pp. 89–90.)

80. *Philosophy of History*, p. 52.

81. *Philosophy of Right*, p. 11.

82. His treatment of the early manifestations of the German spirit provides a notable exception to what I here characterize as having been his dominant view. (Cf. *Philosophy of History*, pp. 341–43 and 347–55.)

83. Cf. *Phenomenology of Mind*, p. 334:

By the way . . . in which the state of the world has affected in particular any individual . . . it must itself have assumed a particular shape on its own account, and have operated upon the individual in the specific character which it assumed. Only so could it have made the individual the specific particular individual he is.

84. If I am not mistaken, his later doctrine is also suggested in the *Phenomenology of Mind* in the discussion of "Spirit in its self-estrangement" and in the introductory remarks to "Culture and its realm of actual reality" (cf. pp. 513–19).

The more specifically sociological discussions with which we shall here be concerned are the two works entirely devoted to the realm of objective spirit: the *Philosophy of Right* and the *Philosophy of History*. (In this connection, it is to be noted that the *Phenomenology of Mind* moves directly from the ethical life to religion; therefore, civil society, the state, and the role of the nation in world-history receive almost no consideration in it.)

85. *Philosophy of Right*, pp. 179 and 287 (Section 276, with its addition).

86. *Philosophy of Right*, p. 164 (Section 269); cf. also p. 282 (the addition to Section 269).

In the same connection we may note that, in discussing civil society, Hegel held that "the sanctity of marriage and the dignity of Corporation membership are the two fixed points round which the unorganized atoms of civil society revolve" (*Philosophy of Right*, p. 154, Section 255). As the addition to this section makes clear, these "unorganized atoms" are individual persons: it is not through them, but out of the families and corporations engendered by their wills, that civil society achieves its unity. (Cf. also the translator's note to this particular passage.)

87. Cf. *Philosophy of History*, p. 33. In general, on the role of individual passion and private reason in historical change, cf. pp. 20–24.

88. *Ibid.*, p. 27.

89. A comparable passage appears in Section 441 of the *Enzyklopädie* (*Werke*, VI, 296–97).

90. *Philosophy of History*, p. 46.

91. *Ibid.*, p. 49.

92. *Ibid.*, p. 63–64. The most concise and explicit statement of Hegel's position on this point is to be found in Sections 448–50 of the *Enzyklopädie* (*Werke*, VI, 298–99).

93. Cf. Ch. 4, pp. 70–71.

94. *Economic and Philosophical Manuscripts*, p. 105.

95. *Ibid.*, p. 145.

For a brief discussion of Feuerbach's emphasis on direct interpersonal relationships (and in particular his emphasis on the love of man and wife, which is echoed in Marx's *Manuscripts*), cf. Jodl, *Feuerbach*, pp. 34–36.

96. In this connection, I should like to point out the oddity which develops if one fails to draw any distinction between Marx's views in the *Economic and Philosophic Manuscripts* and his later views. Marcuse, after quoting Marx's theory of the fetishism of commodities from *Capital*, goes on to ask

> What does this reification accomplish? It sets forth the actual social relations among men as a totality of objective relations, thereby concealing their origin, their mechanisms of perpetuation, and the possibility of their transformation. Above all, it conceals their human core and content.... The laws of supply and demand, the fixing of value and prices, the business cycles, and so on, would be amenable to study as objective laws and facts, regardless of their effect on human existence....
>
> Marxian theory rejects such a science of economics and sets in its place the interpretation that economic relations are existential relations between men. (*Reason and Revolution*, pp. 280–81.)

But what does it mean to "reject such a science of economics"? Is one to interpret Marx as if he did not take himself to be a political economist, analyzing the economic forces which explain and predict events occurring within the capitalist system? In effect, this is Marcuse's interpretation, for he immediately goes on to appeal to the doctrines of the *Economic and Philosophic Manuscripts*, and to precisely that passage which I have already quoted, in which Marx rejects "society" as an abstraction (cf. note 94). To be sure, Marcuse is not wrong in thinking that Marx conceived of the future classless society in terms very similar to, or identical with, the relationships to be found among men who suffered no alienation, and in which there was no fetishism of commodities. However, to discuss Marx as if his sole concern were the existential state of the individual— and not at all a question of understanding the structure of societies, and the dependence of that structure on concrete instruments of production—is to offer a portrait of Marxian thought which entirely fails to do justice to Marx's position in the history of the social sciences.

97. There is at least one earlier passage which may be taken as expressing the same point of view as that which Marx states in his *Theses on Feuerbach*; it occurs in his essay, *Zur Kritik der Hegelschen Rechtsphilosophie (Einleitung)*:

> Aber *der Mensch*, das ist kein abstraktes, ausser der Welt hockendes Wesen. Der Mensch, das ist *die Welt des Menschen*, Staat, Sozietät. (*Werke*, I, 378.)

However, in this particular passage Marx is speaking as a critic of the other-worldliness of religion, and it is not clear from the context that his views were, at this time, different from those of Feuerbach with respect to man. (They were, however, utterly different with respect to religion: it is in this passage that the phrase "religion is the opium of the people" occurs.)

98. I quote these theses in the translation given by Sidney Hook (*From Hegel to Marx*, p. 296), for they more clearly reproduce the original than does the standard translation given as an appendix to Engels's *Ludwig Feuerbach*. However, it is worth notice that there are some points in this document at which the text given by Engels (and followed by Hook) deviates slightly from the presently available form in which the theses were formulated by Marx. For Marx's original version, cf. Marx-Engels, *Werke*, III, 5 ff.; for Engels's published version, *ibid.*, 533 ff.

I might add that, in his discussion of this document, Hook lays less stress on these two theses than I should be inclined to do. (Cf. *From Hegel to Marx*, pp. 296–98.)

99. Engels, *Ludwig Feuerbach*, p. 51.

The most thorough discussion of the "Theses on Feuerbach" is that of Nathan Rotenstreich. In discussing Theses VI and VII, he too comments on the difference between Marx's view of the social nature of man and Feuerbach's conception of social relationships as being primarily I–Thou relationships. (Cf Rotenstreich's second article, p. 486 f.) However, Rotenstreich does not place the emphasis which I have placed on the existence of a definite break in Marx's thought at this time. On my interpretation, it was at this point that Marx no longer regarded social institutions as "abstractions" and men as the true agents of history; instead, he began to analyze history in institutional terms, and recognized that men were historically determined by the institutions themselves.

100. Engels attributed the step to Marx alone, citing his work in the *Holy Family* (cf. *Ludwig Feuerbach*, p. 51). It is to be recalled that the *German Ideology* had not at the time been published, and was published only long after Engels's death.

As Engels stated in the foreword to his book on Feuerbach, there were defects in the views which he and Marx held regarding economic history when they wrote the *German Ideology*; it was for this reason that he subsequently decided not to publish that early work. In spite of this fact, the *German Ideology* contains the clearest expression of their views regarding the nature of man in relation to the forms of his social existence. With respect to this particular relationship their views did not subsequently change.

101. Cf. *German Ideology*, p. 7, for this characterization of man. In *Capital* (I, 200), Marx cites the not unrelated characterization of man suggested by Benjamin Franklin, that man is a tool-making animal. Also, cf. *Capital*, I, 197–98 for another passage in which Marx contrasts human nature with the nature of animals.

102. The foregoing summarizes the doctrine to be found in *Werke*, III, 20–21. The key passage reads as follows:

> Die Weise, in der die Menschen ihre Lebensmittel produzieren ... ist nicht bloss nach der Seite hin zu betrachten, dass sie die Reproduktion der physischen Existenz der Individuen ist. Sie ist vielmehr schon eine bestimmte Art der Tätigkeit dieser Individuen, eine bestimmte Art, ihr Leben zu äussern, eine bestimmte *Lebensweise* derselben. Wie die Individuen ihr Leben äussern, so sind sie. Was sie sind, fällt also zusammen mit ihrer Produktion, sowohl damit, *was* sie produzieren, als auch damit, *wie* sie produzieren. Was die Individuen also sind, das hängt ab von den materiellen Bedingungen ihrer Produktion (p. 21).

A translation of this passage appears in the last paragraph of page 7 of the *German Ideology*. The fact that this translation fails to convey the meaning of the original is as much a function of the original mode of expression, and the nuances of the language, as it is attributable to the translator.

103. Cf. *German Ideology*, p. 13.

For other instances in which Marx emphasized the fact that the productive relationships into which individuals enter are independent of their wills, cf. his letter to Annenkov (especially pp. 152–53, as reprinted in the *Poverty of Philosophy*) and the famous passage in his preface to *A Contribution to the Critique*

NOTES TO PAGES 187-88

of Political Economy, "In the social production which men carry on they enter into definite relations that are indispensable and independent of their will; these relations of production correspond to a definite stage of development of their material powers of production" (p. 11). Also, cf. the emphasis which he placed on understanding the effects of the division of labor in societies (*Capital,* I, 386–87, *et passim*).

This conception of the relation between individuals and social structures may be contrasted with Marx's earlier views when he *rejected* "society" as an abstraction, and spoke of social relationships as "man to man" relationships. (Cf. above, p. 186.)

104. From *German Ideology,* pp. 13–15. (For the original, cf. *Werke,* III, 26–27.)

Echoes of this very language are to be found throughout the later works of both Marx and Engels. For example, in the preface to his *Contribution to the Critique of Political Economy* (p. 11 f.), Marx says: "It is not the consciousness of men that determines their existence, but, on the contrary, their social existence determines their consciousness."

105. In the *Economic and Philosophic Manuscripts* Marx had said, "Man's individual and species life are not different" (p. 105), a phrase which Cornu has placed in its proper context when he said:

Comme l'existence de l'individu est indissolublement liée à la société, on ne peut ni le séparer de celle-ci, ni l'opposer à elle. Si l'homme est, en effet, un individu particulier, possédant un caractère spécifique et par là-même une singularité, qui le distingue des autres hommes, il incarne en même temps, par sa pensée et par ses actes, la totalité idéale de la société. (*Marx et Engels,* III, p. 162.)

However, no such identity could be claimed between an individual belonging to one *class* and his society as a whole; nor could an identity between particular individuals belonging to different stages in social life be assumed. Thus, the following passage from the *German Ideology* can be read as if it were an explicit answer to these earlier quasi-Feuerbachian views of Marx, especially when one recalls that the earlier statement appeared in the context of a discussion of the individual's consciousness-of-self and of others:

Where speculation ends—in real life—there real, positive science begins.... Empty talk about consciousness ceases, and real knowledge has to take its place. When reality is depicted, philosophy as an independent branch of activity loses its medium of existence. At the best its place can only be taken by a summing-up of the most general results, abstractions which arise from the observation of the historical development of men. Viewed apart from real history, these abstractions have in themselves no value whatsoever. (*German Ideology,* p. 15.)

106. *German Ideology,* pp. 19–20. (*Werke,* III, 30–31).

107. *German Ideology,* p. 29 (*Werke,* III, 38).

Also, cf. *German Ideology,* p. 68 (*Werke,* III, 69).

108. For example, in the *Poverty of Philosophy* one finds Marx saying, "M. Proudhon does not know that all history is nothing but a transformation of human nature" (p. 124); and in the *Communist Manifesto* (p. 28) one reads:

Does it require deep intuition to comprehend that man's ideas, views, and conceptions, in one word, man's consciousness, changes with every change in the conditions of his material existence, in his social relations and in his social life?

109. Cf. *Poverty of Philosophy*, p. 93.

110. *Communist Manifesto*, p. 26. Also, cf. Marx's letter to Annenkov, in *Poverty of Philosophy*, pp. 160–61.

111. For example, cf. Hook, *From Hegel to Marx*, pp. 257–59.

112. *Phenomenology of Mind*, p. 336. (Cf. above, p. 176.)
   In the original, Hegel's remark reads: "Die Individualität ist, was *ihre* Welt als die *ihrige* ist" (*Werke*, II, 239).

113. Marx contrasted his materialism, which stresses activity, or *praxis*, with Feuerbach's "contemplative" materialism (*der anschauende Materialismus*), and in his Fifth Thesis he criticized Feuerbach's interpretation of sensory knowledge in saying "er fasst die Sinnlichkeit nicht als *praktische* menschlich-sinnliche Tätigkeit" (*Werke*, III, 6).
   For discussions of this aspect of Marx's thought, cf. Hook, *From Hegel to Marx*, Ch. VIII and Rotenstreich, "Marx' Thesen über Feuerbach."

114. Cf. the opening paragraph of the original preface to the *Critique of Political Economy* (*Werke*, XIII, 615). This preface is added as an appendix to the English translation of that work, but unfortunately the translation is unreliable.
   For a later, parallel discussion, cf. *Capital*, I, 87–89. For Engels's criticism of Adam Smith from the same point of view, cf. *Anti-Dühring*, p. 167–68.

115. "Je tiefer wir in der Geschichte zurückgehen, je mehr erscheint das Individuum, daher auch das produzierende Individuum, als unselbständig, einem grössren Ganzen angehörig. . . . Erst in dem 18. Jahrhundert, in der 'bürgerlichen Gesellschaft,' treten die verschiedenen Formen des gesellschaftlichen Zusammenhangs dem Einzelnen als blosses Mittel für sein Privatzwecke entgegen, als äusserliche Notwendigkeit" (*Werke*, XIII, 616).

116. This, as we have seen, was also the view held by Hegel. (Cf. p. 439, n. 72, above.)
   We may note the following statement by Marx:

   Wenn also von Produktion die Rede ist, ist immer die Rede von Produktion auf einer bestimmten gesellschaftlichen Entwicklungsstufe—von der Produktion gesellschaftlicher Individuen. (*Werke*, XIII, 616.)

   In the section entitled "The Method of Political Economy" in the same (unpublished) preface to the *Critique of Political Economy*, Marx wrestled with the problem of legitimate and illegitimate forms of abstraction from the concrete nature of social institutions. Unfortunately, the English translation of this important, difficult, and often unclear, section is particularly weak.

117. *Contribution to the Critique of Political Economy*, p. 11.

118. This statement appears in his Third Observation on Proudhon in the *Poverty of Philosophy*, p. 93. In that observation he takes Proudhon to task for dislocating the limbs (*Glieder*) of the social system, and for overlooking the fact that in the structure of society "all relations coexist simultaneously and support one another" (p. 94).

119. *Contribution to the Critique of Political Economy*, p. 12.

120. "At a certain stage of their development, the material forces of production in society come in conflict with the existing relations of production, or—what is but a legal expression for the same thing—with the property relations within which they had been at work before. From forms of development of the forces of production these relations turn into their fetters. Then comes the period of social revolution. With the change of the economic foundation the entire immense superstructure is more or less rapidly transformed." (*Contribution to the Critique of Political Economy*, p. 12.)

121. *Poverty of Philosophy*, p. 93.

CHAPTER 11.   MAN AS A PROGRESSIVE BEING

1. P. G. Guizot, *Cours d'histoire moderne: Leçons du cours de 1828*, p. 15.
   In the light of what is to follow, it is significant to note Mill's admiration for Guizot, which comes out in numerous of the *Earlier Letters of John Stuart Mill*, and is also expressed, though less clearly, in Mill's review of Guizot's *Essays* and his *Lectures on History*, reprinted in *Dissertations and Discussions*, II, 297–362.

2. "I regard utility as the ultimate appeal on all ethical questions; but it must be utility in the largest sense, grounded on the permanent interests of man as a progressive being." (*On Liberty*, p. 74.)

3. Cf. above, pp. 166–67.

4. Cf. his essay on Coleridge, *Dissertations and Discussions*, II, 20–22.

5. Cited in *Life and Letters of F. D. Maurice*, I, 80. (The quotation dates from 1828, when Maurice and Mill were fellow-members of the Debating Society.)

6. In his *Autobiography*, when speaking of the period during which his views underwent change due to the influence of the Germano-Coleridgians, Mill stated that even though he had "found the fabric of my old and taught opinions giving way in many fresh places, I never allowed it to fall to pieces, but was incessantly occupied in weaving it anew" [*Early Draft*, p. 133].

7. I have examined this problem in more detail in an article entitled "On Interpreting Mill's *Utilitarianism*," *Journal of the History of Philosophy*, VI (1968), 35–46. For further documentation of the interpretation which follows, the reader is referred to that article.

8. After praising Bentham for his method as a critical philosopher, and for the reform which this method had brought to philosophy, Mill continued:

Human nature and human life are wide subjects; and whoever would embark in an enterprise requiring a thorough knowledge of them has need both of large stores of his own, and of all aids and appliances from elsewhere. His qualifications for success will be proportional to two things,—the degree in which his own nature and circumstances furnish him with a correct and complete picture of man's nature and circumstances, and his capacity of deriving light from other minds.
   Bentham failed in deriving light from other minds. His writings contain few traces of the accurate knowledge of any schools of thinking but his own. . . .
   Bentham's contempt, then, of all other schools of thinkers . . . was his first disqualification as a philosopher. His second was the incompleteness of his own mind as a

representative of universal human nature. In many of the most natural and strongest feelings of human nature he had no sympathy; from many of its graver experiences he was altogether cut off; and the faculty by which one mind understands a mind different from itself, and throws itself into the feelings of that other mind, was denied by his deficiency of imagination. (*Dissertations and Discussions*, I, 375 and 378.)

9. This essay was entitled "Remarks on Bentham's Philosophy," and it was published as an appendix to E. L. Bulwer's *England and the English* in 1833. Fortunately, it is now readily available in *Mill's Ethical Writings*, edited by J. B. Schneewind (New York, 1965). For Mill's own references to this anonymous article, cf. the early draft of his *Autobiography*, p. 157, and *Earlier Letters*, pp. 152, 172, and 236.

10. This doctrine, which is a subspecies of the doctrine that men always act in accordance with pleasure or for an avoidance of pain, is sometimes termed "psychological hedonism of the present moment." It had antecedents in Locke, and among recent philosophers was defended by A. O. Lovejoy in his *Reflections on Human Nature*. It may be illustrated by a statement of James Mill, which was then elucidated in a comment by John Stuart Mill.
   James Mill said:

It not unfrequently happens, that the idea of the unfavourable sentiments of mankind, becomes more intolerable than all the consequences which could result from them; and men make their escape from life, in order to escape from the tormenting idea of certain consequences, which, at most, would only diminish the advantages of living.

To which John Stuart Mill's note added the following:

They do not seek death to escape from the idea of any *consequences* of the unfavourable sentiments of mankind. The mere fact of having incurred those unfavourable sentiments has become, by the adhesive force of associations, so painful in itself, that death is sometimes preferred to it. There is often no thought of the consequences that may arise from the unfavourable sentiments. . . . it is true that a vague conception of the many unpleasant consequences liable to arise from the evil opinion of others, was the crude matter out of which the horror of the thing itself was primitively formed: but once formed, it loses its connexion with its original source.

The last sentence also illustrates what I shall refer to as Mill's doctrine of functional autonomy, immediately below.
   (The two foregoing quotations are to be found in James Mill, *Analysis of the Phenomena of the Human Mind*, II, 296–97.)

11. "Remarks on Bentham's Philosophy," p. 55.

12. In Note 45, to James Mill, *Analysis of the Phenomena of the Human Mind*, II, 233. Also, cf. the beginning of the first paragraph of Note 58 (II, 307–8), and in another context, Mill's *System of Logic*, Book VI, Ch. II, Sect. 4.

13. Cf. *Utilitarianism*, pp. 34–35.

14. Dr. Thomas Brown provides the most notable exception to this generalization. Unlike Hartley, and unlike Bentham and James Mill, Brown believed that associationism entailed historical variability, which also entailed variability in individual human nature. (Cf. Lecture XLIV of his *Lectures on the Philosophy of the Human Mind*, especially pp. 423–26.)

15. Two quotations from his *System of Logic* will serve to illustrate this important aspect of Mill's thought:

> It is one of the characters, not absolutely peculiar to the sciences of human nature and society, but belonging to them in a peculiar degree, to be conversant with a subject-matter whose properties are changeable. I do not mean changeable from day to day, but from age to age; so that not only the qualities of the individuals vary, but those of the majority are not the same in one age as in another. (Book VI, Ch. X, Sect. 3, pp. 631–32.)

And, in the following section, he said:

> After the first few terms of the series, the influence exercised over each generation by the generations which preceded it becomes . . . more and more preponderant over all other influences; until at length what we now are and do is in a very small degree the result of the universal circumstances of the human race, or even of our own circumstances acting through the original qualities of our species, but mainly of the qualities produced in us by the whole previous history of humanity (p. 633).

16. This, of course, presupposes that human beings are strongly responsive to the feelings of others, which Mill firmly believed. Cf. what he said concerning "the social feelings of mankind" in the third chapter of *Utilitarianism* (p. 29), and the role played by sympathy in his account of justice in the fifth chapter of the same work (pp. 47–48).

Granted this responsiveness, most so-called moral education need not, on Mill's view, be planned or deliberately inculcated. In this connection we may note how broadly he defined "education":

> Whatever helps to shape the human being—to make the individual what he is, or hinder him from being what he is not—is part of his education. (*Dissertations and Discussions*, IV, 333.)

We may also note that in the original draft of his thoughts on the emancipation of women, which he wrote for Harriet Taylor, and which long afterwards was published in the form of his essay, *The Subjection of Women*, Mill stressed the fact that the education of the feelings and the conscience of children derives in large measure from their association with their mothers, but that this most important aspect of education arises naturally and without conscious design. (Cf. Hayek, *John Stuart Mill and Harriet Taylor*, p. 67.)

17. Cf. the following passage:

> Like the other acquired capacities above referred to, the moral faculty, if not a part of our nature, is a natural outgrowth from it; capable, like them, in a certain small degree, of springing up spontaneously; and susceptible of being brought by cultivation to a high degree of development. Unhappily it is susceptible, by a sufficient use of the external sanctions and of the force of early impressions, of being cultivated in almost any direction: so that there is hardly anything so absurd or so mischievous that it may not, by means of these influences, be made to act on the human mind with all the authority of conscience. . . .
>
> But moral associations which are wholly of artificial creation, when intellectual culture goes on, yield by degrees to the dissolving force of analysis. (*Utilitarianism*, Chapter III, pp. 28–29.)

18. I do not wish to be interpreted as belittling the social importance which Mill attached to progress in belief; as he said with respect to intellectual activity and the pursuit of truth:

> Notwithstanding the relative weakness of this principle among other sociological

agents, its influence is the main determining cause of the social progress; all the other dispositions of our nature which contribute to that progress being dependent upon it for the means of accomplishing their share of the work. (*System of Logic*, Book VI, Ch. X, Sect. 7, p. 641.)

My only point is that Mill did not hold that in acquiring more adequate beliefs the fundamental motivation of men was changed; however, such a change *did* occur when the effects of experience on their feelings led men to seek virtue and justice, rather than the satisfaction of their own immediate interests.

19. Cf. *System of Logic*, Book VI, Ch. V.

20. From *Ibid.*, Ch. V, Sect. 6, p. 605.

21. Cf. *Ibid.*, Ch. IX, Sect 3, p. 623.

22. *Ibid.*, Ch. IX, Sect. 4, p. 627.

23. *Ibid.*, Ch. IX, Sect. 4, p. 626. It is to be noted that very early in his career Mill had rejected the views of the St. Simonians (among whom Comte was at the time included), for not having recognized diversity in the character of different nations which stood at the same stage of advance in general civilization. (Cf. *Earlier Letters*, I, 43.)

24. *System of Logic*, Book VI, Ch. IX, Sect. 4, pp. 626–27. (Also, cf. *The Positive Philosophy of Comte*, pp. 76–77, quoted in note 5 of the preceding chapter.)

25. This passage was explicitly directed against the views of progress characteristic of continental thought (but, oddly enough, exempted Comte from its criticism); it proceeds as follows:

It is conceivable that those laws [i.e., of psychology and ethology] might be such, and the general circumstances of the human race such, as to determine the successive transformations of man and society to one given and unvarying order. But even if the case were so, it cannot be the ultimate aim of science to discover an empirical law. Until that law could be connected with the psychological and ethological laws on which it must depend . . . it could not be relied on for the prediction of future events, beyond, at most, adjacent cases. (*System of Logic*, Book VI, Ch. X, Sect. 3, p. 633.)

As Lévy-Bruhl recognized and indicated, Mill's position with respect to there being a science of ethology provided a point of fundamental disagreement between his views and those of Comte. For Comte, a knowledge of the character of men is derivative from sociology, and not from the laws of the human mind. In this connection, Lévy-Bruhl quotes Comte as saying, "Il ne faut pas expliquer l'humanité par l'homme, mais au contraire l'homme par l'humanité." (Cf. preface to *Lettres inédites de J. S. Mill*, p. xxxv.)

26. In his essay, "The Utility of Religion," Mill wrote:

The power of education is almost boundless; there is not one inclination which it is not strong enough to coerce and, if needful, to destroy by disuse. (*Three Essays on Religion*, p. 82.)

27. *The Subjection of Women*, Ch. I, pp. 39–41.

In this connection we may note that one of the circumstances which played a role in the growing separation between Mill and Comte was, as one can see in their correspondence, their quite different estimates of the nature and potentialities of women. This difference reflected the differences in their views regarding precisely those matters with which we are here concerned. (Cf. Lévy-Bruhl's remarks on the same subject in his preface to *Lettres inédites de J. S. Mill*, pp. xxiv–xxx).

28. A clear statement of Mill's view is to be found in his *System of Logic*, Book VI, Ch. IV, Sect. 4:

Unfortunately the reaction of the last and present generation against the philosophy of the eighteenth century produced a very general neglect of this great department of analytical inquiry [viz. the general laws of the mind].... The majority of those who speculate on human nature prefer dogmatically to assume that the mental differences which they perceive, or think they perceive, among human beings are ultimate facts, incapable of being either explained or altered, rather than take the trouble of fitting themselves, by the requisite processes of thought, for referring those mental differences to the outward causes by which they are for the most part produced, and on the removal of which they would cease to exist. The German school of metaphysical speculation, which has not yet lost its temporary predominance in European thought, has had this among other injurious influences; and at the opposite extreme of the psychological scale, no writer, either of early or of recent date, is chargeable in a higher degree with this aberration from the true scientific spirit than M. Comte (pp. 595–96).

29. Once again it may be useful to point out that the use of organic analogies with respect to the relationships among the institutional elements within a society, and with respect to society as a whole, need not involve organicism with respect to the relations between individuals and the society. This is particularly evident in Mill, who, in mentioning the impossibility of insulating any feature of a society from its other features, said:

Whatever affects, in any appreciable degree, any one element of the social state, affects through it all the other elements. (Cf. *System of Logic*, Book VI, Ch. IX, Sect. 2, p. 622.)

In fact, in this section, and in the following section of the same chapter, as well as in Chapter X, Sect. 2, he used the Comtean term *"consensus"* to refer to the organic relationships among the elements in a society. However, there were two features of the cluster of doctrines often termed "organicism" to which he was unalterably opposed: (1) the organicist rejection of constant psychological principles such as the laws of association; and (2) the use of organic analogies with respect to social institutions which suggested that these institutions were not, to any degree, subject to human control. (Cf. *Representative Government*, Ch. I, pp. 175–77.)

30. In this connection one may note that each used De Tocqueville's picture of democracy in America in portraying some of the contemporary threats to culture. Mill's essays on De Tocqueville are well known. While Arnold mentioned De Tocqueville not infrequently, it was only in the essay entitled "Democracy" that he did so in this special connection. (Cf. *Complete Prose Works*, II, 9.) However, in the same essay (pp. 16 and 25), as well as elsewhere, he used the expression "Americanize." For a comparison of the views of Arnold and Mill on the United States, cf. Alexander, *Matthew Arnold and John Stuart Mill*, pp. 224–29.

31. That there is a connection between their two essays on the proper scope of state authority is unmistakable; one of the clearest signs is the way in which Arnold discusses Mill's use of Wilhelm von Humboldt's book, *The Sphere and Duties of Government*. Cf. Mill, *On Liberty*, Ch. III, pp. 115–16, and Arnold, *Culture and Anarchy*, Ch. III (*Complete Prose Works*, V, 160–61.)

32. On the problem of race in Arnold's thought, cf. Trilling, *Matthew Arnold*, pp. 232–42. However, there are passages in which Arnold tends to modify his usual view; perhaps most strikingly in his essay "Democracy," which served as the introduction to his book *The Popular Education of France*, but which he republished eighteen years later as an independent essay. There, in speaking of "*the modern spirit*," he says that it is

... gradually making its way everywhere, removing old conditions and imposing new, altering long-fixed habits, undermining venerable institutions, even modifying national character. (*Complete Prose Works*, II, 29.)

33. On "Millism" as a degenerate form of Hellenism, cf. Arnold's preface to the first edition of *St. Paul and Protestantism* (*Complete Prose Works*, VI, 126). However, as Edward Alexander points out (pp. 30–32), Arnold later withdrew this epithet, and at some points was generous in his praise of Mill. In this connection Alexander remarks that "Arnold and Mill never fully comprehended each other personally, but they came close to comprehending each other spiritually" (p. 32). Even so, Arnold never softened his criticism of Bentham, and in the preface to *Essays in Criticism*, there is a delightful sketch of Benthamism as the religion of the English middle class. (Cf. *Complete Prose Works*, III, 288–89.)

34. Alexander acknowledges a debt to Lionel Trilling, M. H. Abrams, F. R. Leavis, G. L. Nesbitt, and also W. E. Houghton in this connection. Like Alexander, I am inclined to reject the distinction which Houghton tends to draw between Arnold as "Goethean" and Mill as "Romantic." (Cf. Houghton, *Victorian Frame of Mind*, pp. 287–91; Alexander, pp. 26–27.) However, I should like to cite a passage from Houghton which wholly agrees with the distinction I am using in the present chapter between those who, like Fichte and Green, stress effort and vision as the basis for the self-transformation of man, and those who stress the cultivation of the higher, nobler forms of sensibility. In Houghton, this general distinction is phrased in terms of a contrast between "earnestness" and "enthusiasm"; he says:

In significant contrast with that of moral earnestness, the ethic of enthusiasm assumes that ... the organ of virtue is the sensibility rather than the conscience; and that the moral life depends, not on the arduous struggle to master the passions and compel the will to a life of duty, but on the vitality of the noble emotions, inspiring the delighted service of a high ideal (p. 264).

In my opinion—as is obvious—Matthew Arnold, no less than Mill, belonged primarily in the latter camp. Houghton, however, places him (along with Thomas Arnold) primarily in the former. As a preliminary defense of my own view I might cite the extent to which Arnold's sympathies lay with what he termed Hellenism, and in this connection we may recall that he said, "the governing idea of Hellenism is *spontaneity of consciousness*; that of Hebraism, *strictness of conscience*" (*Culture and Anarchy*, Ch. IV; in *Complete Prose Works*, V, 165).

35. "A French Eton," *Complete Prose Works*, II, 322.
In this connection we may note that Arnold believed that the growth and development of new classes was a natural tendency in history. As he said in speaking of the rise of democracy,

This change has been brought about by natural and inevitable causes, and neither the great nor the multitude are to be blamed for it. The growing demands and audaciousness of the latter, the encroaching spirit of democracy, are, indeed, matters of loud complaint with some persons. But these persons are complaining of human nature itself, when they thus complain of its native and ineradicable impulse. Life itself

consists, say the philosophers, in the effort *to affirm one's own essence* ... Democracy
is trying to affirm its own essence; to live, to enjoy, to possess the world, as aristocracy
has tried, and successfully tried, before it. Ever since Europe emerged from barbarism,
ever since the condition of the common people began a little to improve, ever since
their minds began to stir, this effort of democracy has been gaining strength; and the
more their condition improves, the more strength this effort gains. So potent is the
charm of life and expansion upon the living; the moment men are aware of them, they
begin to desire them, and the more they have of them, the more they crave. (From
"Democracy," *Complete Prose Works*, II, 7.)

36. "A French Eton," *Complete Prose Works*, II, 324.

37. From "The Literary Influence of Academies," *Complete Prose Works*, III,
236.

38. *Culture and Anarchy*, Ch. VI, in *Complete Prose Works*, V, 219.

39. From the preface to the first edition of *St. Paul and Protestantism* (*Complete
Prose Works*, VI, 125).
    While a strong affinity with self-realizationism, rather than hedonism, is sug-
gested by this quotation, and by the two preceding it, cf. my discussion of this
issue in note 34, above.

40. From "My Countrymen" in *Friendship's Garland* (*Complete Prose Works*,
V, 19).

41. *Complete Prose Works*, III, 283. (Also, cf. pp. 268 and 280.)

42. From "The Function of Criticism," *Complete Prose Works*, III, 269.
    Arnold contrasted epochs of *expansion* with those of *concentration*, and this
contrast has sometimes been compared with the Saint Simonian and Comtean
contrast between "organic" and "critical" periods, which was adopted by Mill in
The Spirit of the Age. (For such a comparison, cf. Alexander, *Matthew Arnold
and John Stuart Mill*, p. 41.) However, the comparison is defective, for as Arnold's
use of Burke and his estimate of his own age suggest, his own contrast lay between
epochs which were directed at conserving and concentrating their heritages, and
those which were progressive and expansive. The notion of a period which is
critical (rather than organic) does not fit into Arnold's dichotomy.

43. *Complete Prose Works*, V, 88.

44. *Culture and Anarchy*, Ch. II, in *Complete Prose Works*, V, 134–35.

45. Cf. Trilling, *Matthew Arnold*, p. 275, and Alexander, *Matthew Arnold and
John Stuart Mill*, p. 141.

46. From "Democracy," *Complete Prose Works*, II, 8.
    Nor was Arnold incapable of indignation at insensibility to suffering, as we may
note in his impassioned advocacy of restriction in the size of the population as a
means of preventing the suffering of children. (Cf. *Culture and Anarchy*, Ch. VI,
in *Complete Prose Works*, V, 217–20.)

47. In discussing his phrase "sweetness and light" (which he borrowed from
Swift's simile of the bee's production of honey and of wax), Arnold said:

If I have not shrunk from saying that we must work for sweetness and light, so
neither have I shrunk from saying that we must have a broad basis, must have sweetness

and light for as many as possible. Again and again I have insisted how those are the happy moments of humanity, how those are the marking epochs of a people's life, how those are the flowering times for literature and art and all the creative power of genius, when there is a *national* glow of life and thought, when the whole of society is in the fullest measure permeated by thought, sensible to beauty, intelligent and alive." (*Culture and Anarchy*, Ch. I, in *Complete Prose Works*, V, 112.)

48. Cf. his discussion of "the Barbarians" (i.e., of aristocracy) in *Culture and Anarchy*, Ch. III, and his comparison of aristocracy and democracy in the essay "Democracy," prefixed to his *Popular Education of France*.

Furthermore, it is noteworthy that Arnold holds that in an epoch of expansion (as opposed to epochs of concentration), the very virtues of the aristocracy are likely to prove socially harmful. (Cf. *Complete Prose Works*, V, 125 and 126.)

49. *Culture and Anarchy*, Ch. I, in *Complete Prose Works*, V, 94.

50. I should not expect this characterization of Mill's ideal to be challenged, but in case it should be, I would refer the reader to the second chapter of *Utilitarianism* in which the qualitative differences among pleasures are discussed, and to my analysis of Mill's doctrine of virtue in the *Journal of the History of Philosophy*, VI (1968), 42–46.

51. *Culture and Anarchy*, in *Complete Prose Works*, V, 94.

52. *Ibid.*, p. 91.

53. *Ibid.*, p. 94.

54. *Ibid.*, pp. 164–65.

55. For example, *ibid.*, pp. 170–71; and vol. VI, 124–25.

56. For example, *Complete Prose Works*, V, 175, 176–77, 178, 181, and 185.

57. *Ibid.*, p. 165; also, p. 180.

58. We may note that, when Arnold returned to a discussion of his contrast between Hellenism and Hebraism in the conclusion of *Literature and Dogma*, he did in fact identify Hellenism and culture. To be sure, he pointed out that culture was only one-fourth of life, whereas *conduct* constituted three-fourths. However, he insisted that conduct must be informed by culture if it is not to go astray. (Cf. *Complete Prose Works*, VI, 407–8.)

59. *Culture and Anarchy*, Ch. IV (*Complete Prose Works*, V, 167). Also, cf. Ch. V, where Arnold says, "To say we work for sweetness and light, then, is only another way of saying that we work for Hellenism" (p. 178).

60. From *Culture and Anarchy*, Ch. I (*Complete Prose Works*, V, 108).

61. At one point Arnold states this doctrine in saying, "the great end of society is perfecting the individual, the fullest, freest, and worthiest development of the individual's activity"; these are words with which Mill could have wholly agreed. (The quotation is from "A French Eton," *Complete Prose Works*, II, 312.)

Similarly, when in the third chapter of *On Liberty* (the very chapter Arnold chose to criticize) Mill made the following statement, it might have been Arnold speaking:

It really is of importance, not only what men do, but also what manner of men they are that do it. Among the works of man, which human life is rightly employed in perfecting and beautifying, the first in importance surely is man himself (p. 117).

62. It is important to note that, as Alexander points out, both Mill and Arnold were aware of themselves as living in an age of transition, and one which posed grave threats to the ideals in which they believed:

They knew their epoch to be undergoing a tremendous and irresistible revolution, and they felt a moral obligation to use their great gifts to facilitate the transition and to ensure that the great imminent change would be change for the better and not the worse. (*Matthew Arnold and John Stuart Mill*, p. 14.)

63. For Arnold's most explicit praise of Burke in this particular connection, cf. "The Function of Criticism," *Complete Prose Works*, III, 266–67, and the letter which R. H. Super quotes (pp. 475–76) in his note to this passage. In two other critical notes (*ibid.*, II, 377 and V, 425), Super indicates how closely Arnold's characterization of "the State" followed Burke's views.

64. *Ibid.*, V, 221.

65. We have noted the emphasis which Mill placed upon *education*, and how he included the effects of all experience within that term; it is necessary to note that Arnold was professionally engaged in education, not only (for a time) as a professor, but as one who, early in his career, was designated by a Royal Commission on Education to survey the lower schools in France, Switzerland, and Holland, and who later, over a long period of time, served as an inspector of schools in England.

In the same general connection we may note that in Mill's essay "Civilization," and in his "Inaugural Address" as Rector of St. Andrews University, Mill—like Arnold—argued for the importance of classical education. In this respect Arnold (who became engaged in a controversy with Huxley regarding this point) expressed himself as being wholly in accord with Mill. (For a brief discussion, cf. Alexander, *Matthew Arnold and John Stuart Mill*, pp. 31–32.)

66. It is often assumed that, in the latter part of the nineteenth century, those who regarded man as capable of self-improvement had been led to that conviction by the Darwinian theory of evolution. Such is definitely not the case, as we shall later have ample opportunity to see. In the present connection, however, it may be pointed out that neither Mill nor Arnold had been influenced in this way. Mill's reservations with respect to Darwinian theory are evident in his appraisal of the argument from design in his essay on "Theism." With respect to Arnold we may note that, in the first six volumes of the most recent edition of his prose works, he does not discuss evolutionism at all, in spite of his concern with issues centering in religious dogma; in fact, he mentions Darwin only once, and that with reference to the latter's book on the expression of emotion in animals and men. (Cf. *Complete Prose Works*, VI, 314.) In fact, a progressivist view of man outgrowing his animal nature is not, as we shall see, characteristic of Darwinism.

In connection with progressivist views which were independent of Darwinian views, we may cite the last stanzas (save two) of Tennyson's "In Memoriam":

A soul shall draw from out the vast
And strike his being into bounds,

And, moved thro' life of lower phase,
Result in man, be born and think,

And act and love, a closer link
Betwixt us and the crowning race

Of those that eye to eye, shall look
　On knowledge; under whose command
　Is Earth and Earth's, and in their hand
Is Nature like an open book;

No longer half-akin to brute,
　For all we thought and loved and did,
　And hoped, and suffer'd, is but seed
Of what in them is flower and fruit.

67. This is obvious in the case of Arnold. With respect to Mill one may say that his psychology was almost as insulated from the influence of any physiological considerations as his father's had been. However, Alexander Bain's psychology was not, and in this respect Bain had some effect upon Mill. (Cf. Mill's essay on Bain, and also his criticism of his father's views of the emotions in a note to *Analysis of the Phenomena of the Human Mind*, II, 234–36.) Nevertheless, even though Mill acknowledged that future physiological discoveries might play a larger role in understanding mental phenomena, his own systematic approach left relatively little room for such possible influences.

One of Mill's most explicit comments regarding this question suggests that his position was not only a consequence of his remaining within the general tradition of associationism, but that he was strongly reacting against Comte's physiologically-oriented views. (Cf. *System of Logic*, Book VI, Ch. IV, Sect. 4, p. 596.)

68. For example, in "Evolution and Ethics" Huxley said:

> For his successful progress, throughout the savage state, man has been largely indebted
> to those qualities which he shares with the ape and the tiger. . . . But in proportion
> as men have passed from anarchy to social organization, and in proportion as civilization
> has grown in worth, these deeply ingrained qualities have become defects. After the
> manner of successful persons, civilized man would gladly kick down the ladder by which
> he has climbed. He would only be too pleased to see 'the ape and tiger die.' But they
> decline to suit his convenience. (*Collected Essays*, IX, 51–52.)

Also, cf. *Collected Essays*, IX, 205.

69. Cf. "Emancipation—Black and White," written in 1865. (*Collected Essays*, III, 66–75.) In the course of a later essay entitled "The Aryan Question," in which he was concerned with philological issues, Huxley made passing remarks which showed that he had not altered his views regarding the differences between races with respect to inherited mental characteristics. (Cf. *Collected Essays*, VII, 279–80. Particularly relevant is the fact that he in no way challenged the quite extreme quotation which he introduced as a footnote to his discussion. Also, cf. II, 172 on the inheritance of moral tendencies.)

70. Cf. *Collected Essays*, III, 67–68 and 75.

All three men, we may note, had strong egalitarian sympathies, and all three showed special concern for the education of the working class. For example, both Mill and Arnold went out of their way to ensure that inexpensive editions of their most relevant works were available (cf. Alexander, *Matthew Arnold and John Stuart Mill*, p. 18; also, Arnold's preface to the Popular Edition of his *Literature and Dogma*, *Prose Works*, VI, 141–42); Huxley's concern led him to give regular courses of lectures to working-class groups and to help organize technical schools directed toward their needs. (For example, cf. *Life and Letters*, I, 149–50 and

507–10, as well as the last three essays in the volume entitled *Science and Education* and the latter half of his essay on "The Struggle for Existence in Human Society.")

71. "A Liberal Education; and Where to Find It" represents the best single source for understanding Huxley's views on these issues. For the place which, in that essay, he assigns to the classics, cf. *Collected Essays*, III, 97–101. For a specific discussion of Arnold's views, cf. Huxley's essay "Science and Culture," III, 141–44.

The best single statement of Mill's views on the same topic is to be found in his "Inaugural Address" as Rector of St. Andrew's University, published in the fourth volume of *Dissertations and Discussions*. With respect to Mill's views on literature, and on poetry in particular, the materials contained in J. W. M. Gibbs's *Early Essays of John Stuart Mill* are particularly helpful.

72. For example, in *Friendship's Garland* Arnold has Bottles, the pupil of the modern educator Archimedes Silverpump, Ph.D., say:

"Original man, Silverpump! fine mind! fine system! None of your antiquated rubbish—all practical work—latest discoveries in science—mind constantly kept excited—lots of interesting experiments—lights of all colors—fizz! fizz! bang! bang! That's what I call forming a man." (*Complete Prose Works*, V, 71.)

73. In at least one passage he did express a fear of demagoguery in politics (*Collected Essays*, IX, 22–23); in another, there is some fear that so-called leaders might merely follow a popular trend, and that universal suffrage among an unenlightened populace might have disastrous results (V, 252).

74. Cf. *Complete Prose Works*, VI, 168. However, among the letters which Arnold wrote to Huxley, there is one in which he expressed some regret that the differences between them in this matter appeared to be so great. (Cf. Armytage, "Matthew Arnold and T. H. Huxley," p. 352.)

75. For Arnold's two letters to Huxley concerning these volumes, cf. the article by Armytage, pp. 346–47 and 350; also, cf. the letter given by Armytage on pp. 350–51.

76. Armytage's article, and the letters he quotes, as well as Huxley's letter to Arnold after the death of the latter's son (*Life and Letters*, I, 398–99) make this clear. One may also note the good-natured banter between Huxley and Arnold which Super points out in his critical note to the opening paragraph of the preface to *Culture and Anarchy* (*Complete Prose Works*, V, 231 and 447).

Unfortunately, a great deal of Huxley material remains unpublished. The papers housed in the Muniments Library of the Imperial College of Science and Technology in London were catalogued in *The Huxley Papers*, published for the Imperial College by Macmillan (London, 1946). This catalogue has been supplemented by *T. H. Huxley: A List of his Scientific Papers*, and by a list of his correspondence (1847–54) with his future wife. (Both lists were published by the Imperial College, in 1968 and 1969 respectively.) Having used these papers in the past, I regret that I have not been able to do so again while preparing this book for publication.

77. For example, cf. "Evolution and Ethics," in *Collected Essays*, IX, 80–81, as well as the "Prolegomena" to that essay (IX, 4, including his note). Also, cf. *Life and Letters*, II, 284.

78. *Collected Essays*, IX, 81. This passage continues:

> The practice of that which is ethically best—what we call goodness or virtue—involves a course of conduct which, in all respects, is opposed to that which leads to success in the cosmic struggle for existence.

And, in a later essay, he wrote:

> The course shaped by the ethical man—the member of society or citizen—necessarily runs counter to that which non-ethical man—the primitive savage, or man as a mere member of the animal kingdom—tends to adopt. (*Collected Essays*, IX, 203.)

79. *Collected Essays*, IX, viii. The Prolegomena was written a year after the original lecture. As Huxley confesses (p. vii), the lecture had not been correctly understood because he had presupposed a better acquaintance with the actual nature of the evolutionary process than was shown by those who criticized him. We may therefore take the Prolegomena to be Huxley's attempt to make unmistakably clear what he actually believed concerning evolution, in so far as it related to an understanding of man's moral standards.

80. *Ibid.*, IX, 9–10. In a slightly earlier essay, "The Progress of Science," Huxley had stated the same thesis (cf. I, 51–52).

81. *Collected Essays*, IX, 11.

82. *Ibid.*, p. 13.

83. *Ibid.*, p. 14.
In referring to utility and beauty, Huxley was in this passage still speaking in terms of his simile of the gardener. However, if "the beautiful" is not taken in too narrow a sense, this twin standard provided Huxley with criteria which he often used in his judgments of value. This fact is clearly indicated in a letter which he wrote outlining his ethical views (*Life and Letters*, II, 324–25), as well as in a number of his essays on education. In the latter we frequently find him insisting on the appreciation of beauty as one of the final ends to be sought. (For examples, cf. *Collected Essays*, III, 86, 130, and 205.)

84. The foregoing account parallels that given in the Prolegomena with which we have been dealing. (Cf. *Collected Essays*, IX, 26 and 28–30.)
For Darwin's view on this topic, cf. especially his summary statement near the outset of the third chapter of *Descent of Man* (I, 68–70); however, the whole of the chapter is relevant, as are some portions of that section of the fifth chapter which bears the sub-heading "Natural Selection as affecting Civilized Nations."

85. Mill's concern with the population problem was by no means confined to that early occasion on which he was arrested for distributing birth-control information. Packe doubtless overstates the case, but he goes so far as to say, "Malthus' main contention ... the invariable tendency of population to overrun the means of subsistence, remained, as it had always been, the foundation of the entire social philosophy of Mill" (*Life of John Stuart Mill*, p. 302). (For an account of the episode involving Mill's arrest, cf. Packe, pp. 56–59.)
For Arnold's concern with the population problem, cf. *Complete Prose Works*, V, 216–20 and 211–12.

86. Cf. *Collected Essays*, IX, 20–23, and 34; also, 209. It is to be noted that in this

discussion Huxley takes cognizance of proposals for eugenic controls, but rejects them. (Also, cf. pp. 36–37.)

87. For example, cf. "The Struggle for Existence in Human Society," *Collected Essays*, IX, 214–16.

88. Huxley was well aware of the philosophical objections which were being raised against state action; in his essay on "Administrative Nihilism" he sought to show that these objections were wholly unfounded in so far as they were being applied to the field of education. In the closing pages of "The Struggle for Existence in Human Society," he returned to the same point, but focused attention on the moral justification of levying taxes for the benefit of educating other people's children. In both of these essays he alluded to Mill's views in *On Liberty*. He did not disparage Mill's aim of defending personal liberty, but he clearly showed that he did not believe that Mill's argument in any way served to justify laissez-faire individualism. (Cf. *Collected Essays*, I, 269 and IX, 227–28.) Nor did Mill claim that it would.

89. Cf. "A Liberal Education; and Where to Find it," *Collected Essays*, III, 81–83.

90. *Ibid.*, I, 38. It is worth notice that Huxley later admitted a trace of Spencer's influence in this passage, but he was, of course, on the whole opposed to Spencer's systematic form of positivism. In this connection I refer the reader to his brief footnote in "Agnosticism and Christianity" where, after saying that he does not like to use the term "unknowable" in connection with that which is not known, Huxley remarks: "I confess that, long ago, I once or twice made this mistake; even to the waste of a capital 'U'." (*Ibid.*, V, 311.)

91. This contrast is Huxley's own: cf. *ibid.*, I, 41.

92. We owe the term to Huxley; however, as will become immediately clear, he himself used it in a different sense from that in which it is currently prevalent. For his coinage of the term, see his account in "Agnosticism" (*ibid.*, V, 239–40).

93. "Agnosticism and Christianity," *ibid.*, V, 310. For another summary statement of how Huxley used the term, cf. "Agnosticism" (*ibid.*, V, 246).

94. Wace had said, "It is, and it ought to be, an unpleasant thing for a man to have to say plainly that he does not believe in Jesus Christ." For the indignation with which Huxley replied, cf. *ibid.*, V, 240–41.

95. This was also the view stated by W. K. Clifford, in his essay, "The Ethics of Belief," which William James attempted to refute in "The Will to Believe."

Clifford's essay was published in 1877, thus antedating Huxley's "Agnosticism" by twelve years. However, Huxley's position had already been clearly formulated in 1866, in his essay "On the Advisableness of Improving Natural Knowledge." Given the close relations between Huxley and Clifford, it must be supposed that each was well aware of the other's views.

96. From "Agnosticism and Christianity" (*ibid.*, V, 310).

97. One perfectly explicit theoretical statement of this justification is to be found in his essay "On the Study of Biology," where he said:

I judge of the value of human pursuits by their bearing upon human interests; in
other words, by their utility.... I think that knowledge of every kind is useful in
proportion as it tends to give people right ideas, which are essential to the foundation
of right practice, and to remove wrong ideas, which are the no less essential foundations
and fertile mothers of every description of error in practice. And inasmuch as, whatever
practical people may say, this world is, after all, absolutely governed by ideas, and
very often by the wildest and most hypothetical ideas, it is a matter of the very
greatest importance that our theories of things, and even of things that seem a long
way apart from our daily lives, should be as far as possible true, and as far as possible
removed from error. (*Collected Essays*, III, 272–73.)

This conviction, which he repeats in a brief autobiographical statement (*Collected Essays*, I, 16), could have served as Huxley's justification of his refusal,
after the death of his son, to abandon his former beliefs in favor of others which
would have been more consoling. In a long, intimate, and obviously anguished
letter to Charles Kingsley at the time, he maintained his position. With all the
emphasis at his command, he said, "... I have searched over the grounds of my
belief, and if wife and child and name and fame were all to be lost to me one
after the other as penalty, still I will not lie" (*Life and Letters*, I, 233). The same
demand of his conscience was reiterated near the conclusion of that letter (p.
238).

One is reminded of Mill's famous lines of indignation against Mansel:

If ... I am informed that the world is ruled by a being whose attributes are infinite,
but what they are we cannot learn, nor what are the principles of his government,
except that "the highest human morality which we are capable of conceiving" does not
sanction them; convince me of it, and I will bear my fate as I may. But when I am
told that I must believe this, and at the same time call this being by the names which
express and affirm the highest human morality, I say in plain terms that I will not.
Whatever power such a being may have over me, there is one thing which he shall not
do; he shall not compel me to worship him. I will call no being good who is not what I
mean when I apply that epithet to my fellow creatures; and if such a being can
sentence me to hell for not so calling him, to hell I will go. (*Examination of Hamilton*,
p. 123–24.)

98. From "Administrative Nihilism," *Collected Essays*, I, 281. It is important to
note that in this particular statement of his standard, and elsewhere, Huxley
characterized social well-being in terms of individual well-being. As he said in
"The Struggle for Existence in Human Society,"

I am unable to see that civil society is anything but a corporation established for a
moral object—namely the good of its members. (*Collected Essays*, IX, 227.)

In this respect, as in others, he clearly belongs within the Utilitarian tradition,
and stands opposed to the assumptions of organicism. He seems also to have
accepted psychological hedonism as a theory of motivation. For example, in
answering one of Darwin's critics who had said that Darwin could only recognize
the existence of three motives relevant to morals—fear of punishment, the anticipation of pleasure, and affection—Huxley accepted these motives as adequate,
and suggested that they might be further reduced. (Cf. *Collected Essays*, II, 169–
70.) The form of psychological hedonism which this suggests is a so-called psychological hedonism of the present moment, such as I have attributed to Mill.
(Cf. above, pp. 194–95, and *Journal of the History of Philosophy*, VI [1968],
35–46.)

99. From "The Struggle for Existence in Human Society," *Collected Essays*, IX,
205. (Also, cf. *Life and Letters*, II, 300.)

There is some reason for astonishment in Huxley's too facile assumptions concerning the development of social life in the early history of the race. These assumptions are not only present here, but almost wherever he speaks of "savages."
Not only might one challenge his use of such assumptions on the basis of the
principle of agnosticism which he had formulated, but he must surely have been
aware of less crude views which were developing in his own generation among
those concerned with social evolution. He was a friend of Lubbock, and certainly
acquainted with Spencer's work. While he had investigated some questions in the
field of physical anthropology, and had been concerned with the history of
language (cf. the last three papers in the seventh volume of *Collected Essays*), the
widespread interest in ancient law and family organization, in the origins and
evolution of religion, etc., seem to have had no impact on his thought. Had he
taken cognizance of these problems, his speculations concerning the early history
of man might have been less crude than they generally appear to be.

100. For example, cf. the whole of his discussion of the simile of the gardener
(especially, *Collected Essays*, IX, 17), as well as the following passage from "Evolution and Ethics":

> Ethical nature may count upon having to reckon with a tenacious and powerful enemy
> as long as the world lasts. But, on the other hand, I see no limit to the extent to which
> intelligence and will, guided by sound principles of investigation, and organized in
> common effort, may modify the conditions of existence, for a period longer than that
> now covered by history. And much may be done to change the nature of man himself.*
> The intelligence which has converted the brother of the wolf into the faithful guardian
> of the flock ought to be able to do something towards curbing the instincts of savagery
> in civilized men. (*Ibid.*, IX, 85.)

The note which is designated by the asterisk in the above quotation reads:

> The use of the word "nature" here may be criticized. Yet the manifestation of the
> natural tendencies of men is so profoundly modified by training that it is hardly too
> strong. Consider the suppression of the sexual instinct between near relations (p. 116).

Two minor observations are necessary at this point if Huxley's beliefs are to be
correctly interpreted. First, he did not believe that the physical, mental, or moral
characteristics of individuals had substantially changed over a considerable length
of time, at least not in England over a period of several hundred years (cf. *ibid.*,
IX, 38 and 40), and, as we have remarked (note 86, above), he did not believe in
eugenic programs. Thus, it had to be through advances in knowledge, and in the
diffusion of knowledge, that more rapid improvements must come. Second, he
did not believe in the possibility of *indefinite* progress, not only because he was
sometimes saddened by the knowledge of past history and aware of the fairly
narrow limits within which nature allowed men to operate, but because of the
ultimate fate assigned to our solar system by accepted principles in thermodynamics. (On these various points, cf. ibid., V, 256–57; IX, 14; and III, 33.)

101. In Chapter 5, above, we have discussed this issue and have noted that Darwin
was reluctant to share the dominant view, but none the less tended to accept it.
In this connection it is relevant to note that, unlike Darwin, Huxley was well
aware of the confusion implicit in contemporary uses of the concept of nature's
laws, and explicitly warned against treating a law as if it could make things
happen, as if it were more than a record of experience. (Cf. "Scientific and
Pseudo-Scientific Realism," in *Collected Essays*, V, 76–81; also, "Science and
Pseudo-Science," V, 108 ff.)
In an essay on "Natural Rights and Political Rights," Huxley sought to remove

another associated confusion: that in which "the Law of Nature" was taken to be relevant to moral and political issues. (Cf. *ibid.*, I, 342–52.)

102. At this point we may call the reader's attention to Mill's essay "Nature," posthumously published in *Three Essays on Religion* in 1874. The parallels between it and Huxley's "Evolution and Ethics" (and the Prolegomena to the latter) are striking, even though Huxley's whole argument was phrased in terms of a criticism of specifically evolutionary theories.

The term "meliorism" apparently originated in 1854, but I have not noticed its occurrence in either Mill or Huxley. It seems not to have received wide use until after 1877, when George Eliot used it. Mill and Huxley must be reckoned among those most unambiguously sharing a meliorist view. On the whole, the designation may also appropriately be applied to Arnold.

103. For example, cf. *Collected Essays*, IX, 214–16. We have already noted Arnold's sensitivity to the same problem. However, Mill's meliorism was even more confident than was that which either Arnold or Huxley expressed. In Chapter II of *Utilitarianism*, he said:

All the grand sources, in short, of human suffering are in a great degree, many of them almost entirely, conquerable by human care and effort (p. 14).

104. This characterization comes from "Agnosticism" (*Collected Essays*, V, 249); we have already cited Huxley's earlier characterization of religion in terms of "cherishing the noblest and most human of man's emotions, by worship . . . at the altar of the Unknown." These two characterizations illustrate the extent to which religion tended to be defined—often by the same persons—in terms either of morality or of feeling by those nineteenth-century writers who championed liberalism against orthodoxy. What they rejected was any claim on the part of religion to the possession of special truths concerning the nature of man or the world. (For two passages characteristic of Huxley on this subject, cf. *Collected Essays*, IV, 162–63 and I, 284.)

105. From "Evolution and Ethics," in *ibid.*, IX, 51.

106. It is obvious that both Mill and Huxley were determinists. We have already cited one relevant passage from Huxley on this point (cf. note 81) and many more might be found. Mill developed his position in Book VI, Chapter II of his *System of Logic*, and he also discussed it in Chapter XXVI of his *Examination of Hamilton*. Not surprisingly, Arnold is less explicit on this philosophical issue; however, an acceptance of determinism seems to be implicit in what he accepted from Spinoza, and in the lack of contradictory passages. For example, Arnold showed no lack of sympathy with Spinoza's criticism of teleology and with his deterministic view of nature in "Spinoza and the Bible" (cf. *Complete Prose Works*, III, 175–77). Furthermore, in his diary for July 17, 1870, there is a deterministic passage from the *Ethics* (cf. Super's note in *ibid.*, VI, 423–24), and one also notes that as early as 1860 Arnold had made tacit reference to a related passage in the *Ethics* (cf. *ibid.*, II, 7).

107. With respect to some of the points with which I shall deal, there is a continuity between Fichte's thought and that of some of his eighteenth-century predecessors. For example, in the famous choice between whether it is preferable to possess the truth or constantly pursue it, Lessing's answer foreshadowed Fichte's position. Furthermore, Fichte's concern with the growth of humanity, and

especially his lectures entitled "The Characteristics of the Present Age," belong within the same strong current of philosophic reflection on history which included Lessing and Schiller, as well as Kant and Herder. However, the radical nature of Fichte's conception of man, and his use of that conception as the basis for a metaphysical idealism, separated him from others with whom his thought might be compared; it places him as the first exemplar of what—in less extreme form—came to be one of the dominant ways in which man's progressive nature was conceived during much of the latter half of the nineteenth century.

108. In quoting from Fichte's theory of knowledge, I shall use the English translation, entitled *The Science of Knowledge*, which brings together parts of several of these expositions. For our purposes, the materials which are included in that volume are adequate.

109. Kant himself had suggested the primacy of the practical reason, but had done so only in the most carefully restricted ways. For example, cf. his discussion of the *positive* value of his critical position in the Preface to the second edition of the *Critique of Pure Reason* (B xxiv–B xxx), and that section of the same work which is entitled "The Canon of Pure Reason."

110. This is taken to be "the absolute, first, and unconditioned fundamental principle of human knowledge" by Fichte. (Cf. *Science of Knowledge*, p. 63.)

111. *Popular Works*, I, 419. Also, cf. "The Vocation of the Scholar," where he says that "the ultimate purpose of each individual man, as well as of all society . . . is the moral elevation of all men" (*ibid.*, I, 192).

112. Quoted by W. T. Harris in his preface to the translation of Fichte's *Science of Knowledge*, p. xii. Also, cf. Harris's preface to the translation of Fichte's *Science of Rights*, pp. v–viii.

It may occasion surprise to note that, in the first-mentioned preface, Harris, who was a highly influential American idealist, should have said of Fichte: "He is the greatest genius in psychology to be found in the history of philosophy" (p. vii). This statement, made in 1888 by one who was not, strictly speaking, a follower of Fichte, should serve to suggest the influence of a Fichtean view of human nature in the United States during the last decades of the nineteenth century.

In this connection we may also note that Mill, in his essay on Bain, referred to Fichte (along with Cousin) as a *psychologist*. (Cf. *Dissertations and Discussions*, IV, 109.)

113. From "The Vocation of the Scholar," *Popular Works*, I, 153. Also, cf. the following paean to man's freedom from "The Vocation of Man":

I desire to possess an inward and peculiar power of manifestation,—infinitely manifold like those powers of Nature. . . .
I would exercise my voluntary power freely, for the accomplishment of aims which I shall have freely adopted; and this will, as its own ultimate ground, determinable by nothing higher, shall move and mould, first my own body, and through it the surrounding world. My active powers shall be under the control of my will alone, and shall be set in motion by nothing else than by it. Thus it shall be. There shall be a Supreme Good in the spiritual world; I shall have the power to seek this with freedom until I find it, to acknowledge it as such when found, and it shall be my fault if I do not find it. This Supreme Good I shall be able to desire merely because I desire it; and if I desire anything else instead of it, the fault shall be mine. My actions shall be the results of this will, and without it there shall absolutely no action of mine ensue, since there

shall be no other power over my actions but this will. Then shall my powers, determined by, and subject to the dominion of, my will, invade the external world. I will be the lord of Nature, and she shall be my servant. I will influence her according to the measure of my capacity, but she shall have no influence over me. (*Ibid.*, I, 347–48.)

114. From "The Way towards the Blessed Life," Lect. VII, *ibid.*, II, 417.

115. *Ibid.*, I, 155. Fichte also put this doctrine in a theological context when he said:

I hope that I have already laid my foundation so deep, that I shall not fail of my subsidiary purpose of taking away all possible subterfuge from the common practice of confounding together Blessedness and Happiness (*ibid.*, II, 438).

116. *Ibid.*, I, 415.

117. *Ibid.*, I, 423–24.

118. *Science of Rights*, p. 60. In "The Vocation of the Scholar" Fichte states the same position in other terms:

The social impulse thus belongs to the fundamental impulses of man. It is man's vocation to live in Society—he *must* live in Society;—he is no complete man, but contradicts his own being, if he lives in a state of isolation. (*Popular Works*, I, 163.)

These passages suggest that there may have been a connection between Fichte's thought and that of Feuerbach; a suggestion made more plausible by the role which the concept of love plays in the ethics of both. That issue need not occupy us here, since in other respects Feuerbach's views do not seem to belong within the self-realizationist tradition with which I am dealing.

119. From "Characteristics of the Present Age," Lect. III (*ibid.*, II, 36–37).
One later finds evolutionists adopting an analogous view, and holding that the standard of value should be the good of the race which emerges from the struggle of individuals. Satirizing this evolutionary optimism, Huxley said:

There would be something in this argument if, in Chinese fashion, the present generation could pay its debts to its ancestors; otherwise it is not clear what compensation the *Eohippus* gets for his sorrows in the fact that, some millions of years afterwards, one of his descendents wins the Derby. (*Collected Essays*, IX, 198–99.)

It should be equally obvious that neither Mill nor Arnold would have been willing to adopt a standard for judging value which was not meant to be applicable to the welfare of particular persons.

120. These phrases come from "The Vocation of the Scholar," Lect. II, *Popular Works*, I, 166.

121. From "The Vocation of Man," in *ibid.*, I, 430.

122. From "The Vocation of the Scholar," Lect. II, in *ibid.*, I, 166.

123. For a discussion of Fichte's theory of education, and a translation of selections other than those which come from the *Speeches*, cf. G. H. Turnbull, *The Educational Theory of J. G. Fichte* (University of Liverpool Press, 1926).
In many ways, the educational theory of Friedrich Froebel, the originator of the *Kindergarten*, resembled that of Fichte, and there may have some measure of in-

fluence. Froebel had begun his studies at the University of Jena in 1799. Even though his formal studies were confined to the sciences, his early background showed an interest in religious issues and he could scarcely have been unaware of the religious controversy which led to Fichte's dismissal from the University in that year. Furthermore, his first wife, whom he married in 1818, had been a student of Fichte's in Berlin. Therefore, although I find no mention of Fichte in Froebel's work, there may well have been some measure of influence. (On these biographical points, cf. his *Autobiography*, pp. 13, 25, 28–29, and 123 n.)

While not sharing Fichte's view of how Nature is related to man, Froebel's conception of spiritual progress, and his metaphysically based confidence in that progress, are very similar to Fichte's position. For example, he said:

> Man, humanity in man, as an external manifestation, should, therefore, be looked upon not as perfectly developed, not as fixed and stationary, but as steadily and progressively growing, in a state of everliving development, ever ascending from one stage of culture to another toward its aim which partakes of the infinite and eternal.
>
> It is unspeakably pernicious to look upon the development of humanity as stationary and completed, and to see in its present phases simply repetitions and greater generalizations of itself. For the child, as well as every successive generation, becomes thereby exclusively imitative, an external dead copy—as it were, a cast of the preceding one— and not a living ideal for its stage of development which it had attained in human development as a whole, to serve future generations in all time to come. (*Education of Man*, p. 17.)

124. *Science of Rights*, pp. 121–25.

Froebel also frequently made use of imagery drawn from botany, and in his *Autobiography* he said:

> An intimate communion with Nature for more than thirty years . . . has taught me that plants, especially trees, are a mirror, or rather a symbol, of human life in its highest spiritual relations (p. 12).

He also frequently cited the forces involved in the growth of crystals, a branch of *Naturphilosophie* much cultivated at the time. In his *Education of Man* he developed the principles of crystallography at great length (pp. 167–97); but what was involved in this analogy, as in his analogies from botany, was an emphasis upon a natural unfolding due to inner spontaneous energy and self-fulfilling activity. As he said of his crystallographic studies,

> My duties busied me the greater part of the day amongst minerals, dumb witnesses to the silent thousand-fold creative energy of Nature . . . even in these so-called lifeless stones and fragments of rock, torn from their original bed, there lay germs of transforming, developing energy and activity (*Autobiography*, pp. 96–97).

125. A similar contrast between man's plasticity and animal instinct was pointed out by Herder, and he too attributed the possibility of Mankind's progress to it. (Cf. *Ideen*, Book IX, Sect. 1, in *Sämmtliche Werke*, XIII, 345.)

126. The specific aspect of Coleridge's thought which is here of primary importance was his attack on associationism. For that, cf. *Biographia Literaria* (*Complete Works*, v. III), Ch. V–VII and XIII, especially pp. 228–29 and 363–64.

127. "Mr. James Ward's 'Psychology'," p. 461–62.

For an extended reply to some of the current criticisms of associationism, cf. Bain's article "On 'Association'-Controversies," *Mind*, XII (1887), 161–82.

128. "On Some Omissions of Introspective Psychology," p. 16.

129. *Mind*, XII (1887), 357. The fact that this article postdates James's is not of importance: Bradley's chapter entitled "The Theory of Association of Ideas" which appeared in the first edition of his *Principles of Logic* in 1883 contained the same general type of criticism. In that discussion, his attack was not primarily psychological, but was directed against the association of ideas as "the battle cry of a school, and a metaphysical doctrine and theory of things" (p. 274) which offers a false view of the nature of inference.

130. Cf. *Prolegomena to Ethics*, p. 21.

131. Cf. "Mr. F. H. Bradley's Analysis of Mind," p. 564, *et passim*.

132. Ward's psychological views, as stated in this period, are primarily to be found in his *Encyclopaedia Britannica* article, to which reference has already been made, and to a series of articles entitled "Psychological Principles" which appeared in *Mind* in 1883 and in 1887. His book, also bearing the title *Psychological Principles*, did not appear until 1918.

To avoid misunderstanding, it should probably be noted that Ward did seek to establish and defend a pluralistic idealism, but he always attempted to separate psychological from metaphysical questions.

133. In Bosanquet's *Logic*, which was published in 1888, there is a brief criticism of the associationist doctrine (cf. II, 15); and all of his subsequent work developed an alternative theory of mind.

Bosanquet deserves special mention at this point because he was a student of Green, and because there was a much greater similarity between his moral and political thought and that of Green than existed between the thought of Green and the other idealists who have been mentioned. However, even between Bosanquet and Green there would appear to have been an appreciable distance. While there are passages in which Green may sound as if he stood in about the same relationship to Hegel's position as Bosanquet usually did, there also are passages, such as Sections 184 and 185 of the *Prolegomena to Ethics*, in which it is clear that Green wished to hold fast to the point of view of the individual, claiming that no wider social appeal transcended that point of view. We shall have occasion to return to this issue.

134. *Prolegomena to Ethics*, p. 58.

135. Cf. *Prolegomena to Ethics*, Bk. I, Ch. III, especially Sections 75–76 and 82, as well as Bk. II, Ch. I, which bears the heading "The Freedom of the Will."

136. Cf. *Prolegomena to Ethics*, Sect. 87.

137. *Prolegomena to Ethics*, p. 194.

138. In Germany, hedonism had already been all but universally rejected as a standard of value, and self-realizationism was dominant. In Britain, self-realizationism had not been an important alternative to other moral theories until the period with which we are here concerned. Since ethical hedonism had been linked to psychological hedonism, it was entirely relevant for Green to be attacking the hedonistic interpretation of desire.

Sidgwick, of course, continued to uphold a hedonistic standard of value, but not on the basis of psychological hedonism. In his own moral psychology (although

it was not fully developed), he not only rejected a hedonistic account of motivation, but rejected any account which attempted to make all forms of motivation
instances of an attempt to achieve some one end. However, Sidgwick's primary
influence is not to be found in his criticism of psychological hedonism, nor in his
defense of ethical hedonism, but in his sharp separation of these questions, and
in the appeal to intuition which he consequently had to make in order to support
an ethical hedonism. The separation between normative questions and all matters
of fact (which, for a time, dominated English philosophy because of G. E. Moore's
influence and, for the same period, all but dominated American ethical theory)
can be traced to Sidgwick. Although a similar separation of moral and factual
questions was characteristic of Kant's ethical theory, it was not through his influence that it entered into the mainstream of Anglo-American thought.

It should go without saying—though, unfortunately, it does not—that Hume's
distinction between normative and descriptive *statements* is not decisive with
respect to questions concerning the relationships between ethical theory and
psychology. Hume's own ethical theory should suffice to show this to be the case.

139. This position, which resembled that of Fichte, was of course based on
Green's metaphysics. However, he could not wholly avoid taking cognizance of
views which, on the basis of evolutionary theory, linked man's nature to the
capacities and tendencies of animals. While he did not discuss this issue in specific
terms, it is clear from his introduction to the *Prolegomena to Ethics* that he had it
much in mind. (Cf. especially Section 2.) The general manner in which he solved
it was to hold that in so far as there are resemblances to an animal nature in man,
such characteristics are transformed and, indeed, superseded by man's spiritual
development; as a consequence, taken as one finds them in the animal world, they
are not relevant to man's self-development as a moral being. (Cf. Sections 5–6, 18,
and 67 of the *Prolegomena to Ethics*, as well as much that he says in Book II, Ch.
II of the same work, when he discusses desire, intellect, and will.)

140. *Prolegomena to Ethics*, p. 203.
Green's metaphysical views, it may be remarked, included the concept of an
eternal consciousness which is at once God and an inclusive reality of which all
finite selves are fragmentary parts. It is not essential for us to trace this aspect of
his system.

141. This passage comes from the concluding paragraph of Section 172 (p. 197),
but the other paragraphs of that section are also concerned with how we are to
discern that which is morally good. (Also, cf. Section 180, pp. 206–7.)

142. Cf. *Prolegomena to Ethics*, Sections 200–202.

143. For example, cf. *Prolegomena to Ethics*, pp. 217–18.
This was also fundamental in his political philosophy; for example, in his
Lectures on the Principles of Political Obligation he said:

But in truth it is only as members of a society, as recognizing common interests and
objects, that individuals come to have these attributes and rights; and the power, which
in a political society they have to obey, is derived from the development and systematisa-
tion of those institutions for the regulation of a common life without which they
would have no rights at all. (*Works*, II, 428.)

In his historical analyses he also recognized the fact that social institutions
could not be understood in terms of individual formative powers alone. For example, in *Four Lectures on the English Revolution* he said:

In reaction from the latter [the 'dry light' of judicious historians] has appeared a mode of treatment, worked with special force by Mr. Carlyle, which puts personal character in boldest relief, but overlooks the strength of circumstance, the organic life of custom and institution, which acts on the individual from without and from within, which at once informs his will and places it in limits against which it breaks itself in vain. (*Works*, III, 277.)

His position, then, was one in which individual personality and social institutions must be said to imply one another. On this point, cf. *Prolegomena to Ethics*, Sections 190 and 191.

144. Cf. *Prolegomena to Ethics*, pp. 218–19 and p. 242.

145. Cf. *ibid.*, p. 242.

146. *Ibid.*, p. 430.

147. Cf., above, Chapter 5, p. 77, and note 2. Also, for a more extensive treatment, cf. the article referred to in note 1 of Chapter 5.

148. It is to be noted that Darwin not only does not attempt to explain intelligence in the same terms as instinct, but tends to contrast them. (For example, cf. *Descent of Man*, I, 36–37.) This point separates his thought concerning intelligence and the nature of reason from that of many who took themselves to be his followers.

149. For this, and for what immediately follows, cf. *Origin of Species*, p. 268.

150. This was a characteristic belief at the time. As we shall see, it was fundamental to Spencer's psychology; even Bain, whose associationism led him to challenge it, found himself forced to assume that in some extremely simple cases, due to the effects of unremitting practice, it did occur. (Cf. *Emotions and the Will*, pp. 48–54; and, on Bain, cf. note 188, below.)

However, by 1890 when a significant portion of Weismann's work was known, we find Huxley saying:

I absolutely disbelieve in use-inheritance as the evidence stands. Spencer is bound to it *a priori*—his psychology goes to pieces without it. (*Life and Letters*, II, 285.)

151. Cf. *Descent of Man*, I, 48–49.

152. Darwin's own view seems to have been that both habit and chance variations played an important role in the development of new forms of behavior, at least under conditions of domestication. Since he was not inclined to draw a sharp distinction between the factors involved in the development of new forms under natural conditions and under conditions of domestication, we may take the following statement as an accurate depiction of his views on the subject:

Hence, we may conclude that under domestication instincts have been acquired and natural instincts have been lost, partly by habit and partly by man selecting and accumulating, during successive generations, peculiar mental habits and actions, which at first appeared from what we must in our ignorance call an accident. In some cases compulsory habit alone has sufficed to produce inherited mental changes. In other cases compulsory habit has done nothing, and all has been the result of selection, pursued both methodically and unconsciously; but in most cases habit and selection have probably concurred. (*Origin of Species*, pp. 274–75.)

It should go without saying that in attributing this role to habit in the development of instinctive forms of behavior, Darwin was not necessarily committing
himself to a comparable position with respect to the effects of use on the development of bodily structures.

153. *Descent of Man*, I, 76. The account of the relations between pleasure and
desire which Darwin gives on this page, and on the following pages, must be
acknowledged to suffer from confusions. These were in some measure due to his
failure to distinguish between two different types of question: (1) whether, in the
cases with which he was concerned, pleasure was a by-product of the satisfaction
of desire, or whether it was the object of the desire; and (2) whether the pleasure
accompanying the past satisfaction of desire does or does not serve as the cause of
the arousal of such desires on later occasions.

With respect to the first of these questions, Darwin should assuredly have taken
the view that, in the exercise of instinct, pleasure was a by-product, not the object
of desire; his language, however, was unclear with respect to this point. It was in
fact the second of these questions to which he was addressing himself. His answer
was that there are cases in which past satisfaction *is* the cause of the arousal of
present desire, but there also are cases in which it is not. Thus, it is fair to say
that he rejected a consistently hedonistic psychology in any form.

With respect to this point, as it affected his moral theory, we may also note the
following passage in which he was criticizing the moral standard proposed by
Mill:

... as all wish for happiness, the "greatest happiness principle" will have become a most
important secondary guide and object; the social instincts, including sympathy, always
serving as the primary impulse and guide. (*Descent of Man*, I, 94.)

In spite of its unclarity, one may assuredly say of this passage that in it Darwin
is rejecting a hedonistic psychology. He is holding that while we may, in a derivative sense, all be said to desire happiness, this happiness is correlated with our
fulfilling our wants; it is not for the sake of happiness that we strive to fulfil them.

154. *Descent of Man*, I, 102. Whether Darwin's acceptance of this standard as the
foundation of morality is consistent with the standard of the general good which
he also espoused, is not our present concern. Unfortunately, this is not the only
respect in which Darwin's moral theory was rather poorly worked out.

155. *Descent of Man*, I, 68–69.

156. Darwin does not deny that love and sympathy are often related in specific
cases; he merely argues that they are to be distinguished, as being capable of
operating independently of each other. (Cf. *Descent of Man*, I, 77–79.)

157. Cf. *Descent of Man*, I, 77.

158. Darwin himself mentions self-preservation as an instinct, placing it alongside
specific instincts such as hunger and lust. (Cf. *Descent of Man*, I, 85.) However,
it was not a factor which he specifically took into account in his discussions of
evolutionary change, as one would expect him to have done had he really thought
of it as a separate instinct. In spite of this fact, popular evolutionary thought
took "an instinct of self-preservation" to be one of the essential building-blocks
of Darwinian theory.

159. Cf. *Descent of Man*, I, 86–87.

160. It is interesting to note that contrary to many theories (including some contemporary theories) Darwin does not find the origins of conscience in praise and blame, which he regarded as presupposing language. (Cf. the sequence of stages which he gives in summarizing his theory: *Descent of Man*, I, 69.)

It is also of interest to note that although Darwin did not wholly exclude a calculation of advantage to the self from the causes of cooperative behavior (cf. *Descent of Man*, I, 157), he assuredly minimized the influence of this factor when compared with the power of the social instincts.

161. *Descent of Man*, I, 93–94.

162. Bagehot's influential book, *Physics and Politics; or, Thoughts on the Application of the Principles of "Natural Selection" and "Inheritance" to Political Society*, first appeared in the form of articles in the *Fortnightly Review*, in 1867, 1868, and 1869. For Darwin's references to them, cf. *Descent of Man*, I, 89 n., and 156.

163. For example, cf. *Descent of Man*, I, 99 and 159.

164. We have already indicated the reservations which Darwin had concerning a universal law of progress (cf. Ch. 5, pp. 82–83); for an application of such reservations to social evolution, cf. *Descent of Man*, I, 171.

165. From *Descent of Man*, I, 177. (Quoted above, Ch. 6, p. 104.) In this statement, as was often the case, Darwin had clearly abandoned the primarily biological orientation of his original definition of the general good. That definition read:

> The term, general good, may be defined as the means by which the greatest possible number of individuals can be reared in full vigor and health, with all their faculties perfect, under the conditions to which they are exposed. (*Descent of Man*, I, 94.)

Unfortunately, he never tried to reconcile these two apparently divergent tendencies in his ethical theory.

166. In *Inquiries into Human Faculty*, Galton said:

> It has been the privilege of this generation to have had fresh fields of research pointed out to them by Darwin, and to have undergone a new intellectual birth under the inspiration of his fertile genius (p. 179).

As we shall shortly note, Darwin's work had exactly this influence on the thought of W. K. Clifford, among others.

167. *Inquiries into Human Faculty*, p. 332.

168. For example, one reads with a sense of astonishment that Darwin was even willing to attribute characteristics such as a tendency to lie or to steal to the effects of heredity. (Cf. *Descent of Man*, I, 98.)

169. *Inquiries into Human Faculty*, pp. 1–2. (Also, cf. pp. 334–36.)

170. Cf. Pollock's "Biographical Introduction" to Clifford's *Lectures and Essays*, I, 42.

At this point Pollock also mentions Clifford's indebtedness to Spencer, an indebtedness which Clifford himself acknowledged. (Cf. the letter reprinted in *Lectures and Essays*, I, 117–19; also, II, 292–93.) The relationship between Clifford and Spencer depended primarily upon Spencer's emphasis on the concept of evolution as applying to all phases of nature, and to the associated analogy of societies with organisms—two points which are not to be found in Darwin. As we shall see, the mechanism of the evolutionary process which Clifford invoked was much closer to that of Darwin (although it was not an orthodox Darwinism) than it was to Spencer's view. (Cf. note 180, below.)

171. *Lectures and Essays*, I, 114. This lecture, entitled "On Some of the Conditions of Mental Development," was delivered in 1868, the year in which Clifford became a fellow of Trinity College. His later essays on moral topics place little or no emphasis on this aspect of evolutionary change, though he does take it up again in the essay "Cosmic Emotion."

172. Cf. Pollock's introduction to Clifford's *Lectures and Essays*, I, 43–44, as well as II, 94.

173. In the early essay here under consideration, Clifford says:

> To recapitulate. The mind is changing so constantly that we only know it by its changes. The law of these changes, which we call character, is also a thing which is continually changing, though more slowly. And that law of force which governs all the changes in a given people at a given time, which we call the Spirit of the Age, this also changes, though more slowly still (I. 85).

Clifford discussed the same point again in his late essay on "Cosmic Emotion" (*Lectures and Essays*, II, 282).

174. Cf. *Lectures and Essays*, I, 98–100.

175. Cf. *Lectures and Essays*, II, 84–85. Galton also accepted Darwin's view as well established. (Cf. *Inquiries into Human Faculty*, p. 212.)

176. Cf. his reference to Darwin in "Right and Wrong: The Scientific Ground of their Distinction," *Lectures and Essays*, II, 149–50.

177. *Lectures and Essays*, II, 83–84.

178. In that section of "The Scientific Basis of Ethics" which is entitled "The Final Standard," Clifford said:

> Ethic is a matter of the tribe or community, and therefore there are no "self-regarding virtues." The qualities of courage, prudence, etc., can only be *rightly* encouraged in so far as they are shown to conduce to the efficiency of a citizen.... Any diversion of conscience from its sole allegiance to the community is condemned *a priori* in the very nature of right and wrong. (*Lectures and Essays*, II, 93–94.)

179. *Lectures and Essays*, II, 94.
In the same discussion of "The Final Standard" he said:

> The end of Ethic is not the greatest happiness of the greatest number. Your happiness is of no use to the community, except in so far as it tends to make you a more efficient citizen—that it to say, happiness is not desired for its own sake, but for the sake of something else. If any end is pointed to, it is the end of increased efficiency in each man's special work, as well as in the social functions which are common to all (II, 94).

180. *Principles of Biology*, I, 80.

As Spencer pointed out, these chapters were largely taken over from the first edition of his *Principles of Psychology*. It may be useful to quote a further passage from that work:

Thus then we find variously illustrated in detail, the truth enunciated at the outset, that all vital phenomena are directly or indirectly in correspondence with phenomena in the environment. Whether the kind of Life contemplated be that embraced by Physiology, or that of which Psychology treats, it equally consists of internal changes that mediately or immediately conform to external coexistence and sequences (p. 482).

Spencer's stress on adaptation to the environment was in striking contrast to the evolutionary view which, as we have noted, Clifford had developed in his early writings: progress, he had claimed, depended upon the spontaneity of organisms, not on their capacities to react to conditions imposed by the environment. (Cf. *Lectures and Essays*, I, 111-13.)

181. *Principles of Biology*, I, 462.

We may note that Spencer considered it a weakness in the theories of Darwin and of Lamarck that they did not give a more ultimate explanation of organic evolution, an explanation which made it but one manifestation of a total evolutionary process. (Cf. *Principles of Biology*, I, 409-10.)

182. The whole of Section 166 of *Principles of Biology* was written to establish this point, as against Darwin; the words quoted are to be found on page 455 of volume I.

Also, cf. *Principles of Psychology* (2nd ed.), I, 423 n., in which this section is referred to.

183. While Darwin did admit that some instincts might have developed out of habitual actions, he specifically rejected that hypothesis as being an adequate account in most cases. (Cf. *Origin of Species*, pp. 228-29.)

184. Cf. *Principles of Psychology* (2nd ed.), I, 439.

185. Cf. in particular Section 189 of the chapter entitled "The Growth of Intelligence" in *Principles of Psychology* (2nd ed.), 419-25. (This doctrine was also contained in the same form in the earlier edition of that work.)

186. Cf. *Principles of Psychology* (2nd ed.), I, 422.

187. *Emotions and Will*, p. 53.

188. Bain's caution in this respect may be indicated by the following remark:

Darwin and others have adduced facts which appear to show the inheritance of acquired or educated peculiarities. Few of them, however, if any, are decisive to the degree that we should wish for such an enormous issue. (*Emotions and Will*, p. 51-52.)

189. For example, he expressed the belief that national characteristics could become inherited, "so that the French child grows into a French man even when brought up among strangers" (*Education*, p. 123). Nor was this only a passing and inadvertent remark, as is evident in his discussion of the inheritance of the effects of practice in the development of musical ability (*Principles of Biology*, I, 249-50).

190. In Chapter 5 of *The Descent of Man*, where Darwin dealt with "The Development of the Intellectual and Moral Faculties During Primeval and Civilized Times," even the indirect effects of most social institutions were passed over without mention, the inheritance of wealth and primogeniture being the only notable exceptions. (Cf. *Descent of Man*, I, 162–64.)

Galton's mode of inquiry was specifically directed to questions concerning individual abilities, but his interest in the problem of "nature vs. nurture" should have led to a consideration of the effects of different social institutions on individuals. A similar criticism can be leveled against Bain. Like Bentham and James Mill, Bain tended to treat all societies as if their institutions could be described simply by saying, as he said,

> The major part of every community adopt certain rules of conduct necessary for the common preservation, or ministering to the common well-being. They find it not merely their interest, but the very condition of their existence, to observe a number of maxims of individual restraint, and of respect to one another's feelings in regard to person, property, and good name.... (*Emotions and Will*, p. 467).

As this passage should be sufficient to indicate, Bain had failed to grasp how important the concrete nature of historically developing institutions should be considered to be by any adherent of associationism.

On the other hand, Clifford accepted a doctrine of "the social organism," and he said of Spencer that it was to him that one owed

> ... the first clear and rational statement of the analogy between the individual and the social organism, which indeed, is more than an analogy, being in many respects a true identity of process and structure and function. (*Lectures and Essays*, II, 292–93).

However, Clifford only used this doctrine with respect to the existence of a tribal self: he did not himself carry out analyses of social structure in relation to social functions, nor was he concerned to relate changes in the social organism to changes in the natures of individuals.

191. On this specific point, cf. *Principles of Sociology*, I, 4 where Spencer is discussing the rearing of offspring.

Spencer's own account of the matters with which I am here primarily concerned will chiefly be found in the *Principles of Sociology*, Part I, Ch. 1, 2, and 27; and in Part II of the same work. His essay "The Social Organism" is also relevant.

192. Cf. above, pp. 169–70.

193. *Principles of Sociology*, I, 11–12.
This doctrine paralleled what Spencer held with respect to biological development, as can be seen in the following statement:

> Beginning with the low life of plants and of rudimentary animals, the progress to life of higher and higher kinds essentially consists in a continual improvement of the adaptation between organic processes and processes which environ the organism. (*Principles of Psychology*, 2nd ed., I, 294.)

194. *Data of Ethics*, p. 275. (For an earlier statement of this corollary, cf. p. 73 of the same work.)

195. *Social Statics*, p. 32. This was published in 1850, and therefore before Spencer was acquainted with von Baer's work and before he had written "The Development Hypothesis."

196. In general, those who accepted geneticism used "man" as a collective term, and were not referring to mankind as a developing historical reality. However, some among them—of whom Robert Owen was probably one—may very possibly be said to have shared the view which we have here been discussing.

197. Herder was very explicit with respect to this point. Cf. *Ideen*, Book IX, 1 (*Sämmtliche Werke*, XIII, 345-47). Also, cf. *Ideen*, Book VII, 1 (*Sämmtliche Werke*, XIII, 252 ff.)

198. It may be desirable to quote the original in order to illustrate what I have briefly paraphrased:

... so würde durch eine solche Erziehung allerdings eine ganz neue Ordnung der Dinge und eine neue Schöpfung beginnen. Zu dieser neuen Gestalt würde nun die Menschheit sich selber durch sich selbst, eben indem sie als gegenwärtiges Geschlecht sich selbst als zukünftiges Geschlecht erzieht, erschaffen.... Dies sei die eigentliche Bestimmung des Menschengeschlechts auf der Erde ... dass es mit Freiheit sich zu dem mache, was es eigentlich ursprünglich ist. (Fichte, *Sämmtliche Werke*, VII, 305-6.)

199. Also, cf. the following remark from the *Philosophy of Right*, in which Hegel is speaking of the education of the individual, but which holds also of the race:

Education is the art of making men ethical. It begins with pupils whose life is at the instinctive level and shows them the way to a second, spiritual [*geistige*] nature, and makes this spiritual level habitual to them (p. 260).

200. For example, it was the view of Renan, in his synthesis of Hegelian and Comtean modes of thought. (Cf. p. 70, above.)
  I take it that Comte's own doctrine on this point is sufficiently familiar not to demand discussion. However, it is worth citing a point to which Lévy-Bruhl has called attention:

Presque jamais, dans la statique sociale, (et moins encore dans la dynamique), Comte ne dit *les* sociétés, comme il disait, en biologie, *les* animaux et *les* végétaux. Il dit *l'organisme collectif*: organisme unique, immense dont la vie s'étend indéfinement dans le passé et dans l'avenir, d'un mot, l'humanité. (*Philosophie d'Auguste Comte*, pp. 299-300.)

  To grasp how prevalent the conception of Humanity as one individual was in France at the time, one should note that it was not only to be found in Renan and the Comteans, but was a conception which Cousin shared. (Cf. Bréhier, *Histoire de la philosophie*, II, 663.)

201. Cf. *The Positive Philosophy of Comte*, pp. 122-24. Of Comte's doctrine of the *Grand Être*, Mill said:

For this M. Comte has been subjected to unworthy ridicule, but there is nothing truer or more honorable to him in the whole body of his doctrines (p. 124).

202. *Study of Psychology*, p. 5-6. (This work constitutes the first volume in the Third Series of Lewes' posthumous *Problem of Life and Mind*.)

203. *Study of Psychology*, p. 71.

204. Cf. the following quotation from Chapter 9 of *The Study of Psychology*, a chapter entitled "The General Mind":

Because Psychology is interpreted through Sociology, and Experience acquires its development mainly through social influences, we must always take History into account (p. 153).

205. The transformation in empirical psychology which this doctrine would entail, were it to be actually carried out, can be seen in the following quotation, where Lewes speaks of

... the experience of the race in its influence on the experience of the individual; that is to say, the direction impressed by the General Mind on the feelings and opinions of particular minds. This influence is implied in the familiar use of such terms as *the* Mind, Common Sense, Collective Consciousness, Thought (*Das Denken*), Reason, Spirit of the Age, etc. Obviously these terms indicate something over and above the individual mind. (*Study of Psychology*, p. 159.)

206. Cf. Wundt's original preface, I, viii.

207. *Ethics*, I, 330. Wundt's doctrine of the heterogeny of ends, like Mill's doctrine that whatever serves as a means to an end may itself become an end, is a psychological principle which can be used to justify a belief in the possibility of constantly expanding goals of human endeavor.

208. Cf. *Ethics*, III, 77–80.

209. *Ethics*, III, 85. At this point, Wundt also rejects hedonism, happiness being "a secondary result brought about in the subjective consciousness by these psychical products."

210. *Ethics*, III, 90.

211. *Lectures and Essays*, II, 296.

CHAPTER 12.   CONSTANCY AND CHANGE IN HUMAN NATURE: A CRITICAL ACCOUNT

1. It may be prudent once again to call attention to the fact that the term "organicism" is here being used with reference to a doctrine concerning man's nature, not with reference to a type of theory concerning social structure. (Cf. above, p. 170.) In the discussion which follows we shall see why these two forms of the doctrine often exhibit a natural affinity with one another.

2. A brief but comprehensive historical account of this development is given in Kimble, *Hilgard and Marquis' Conditioning and Learning*, Ch. II. Of particular importance is the convincing account of why the concept of conditioning spread so rapidly among professional psychologists. Its more general spread must be attributed to Watson's popular expositions of the doctrine, and especially to the fact that these expositions called attention to his theory of molding behavior through childhood training. In addition, Watson's popular expositions had the same appeal as various of the other forms of "debunking" prevalent at the time.

3. In his earlier experimental work, Pavlov had appealed to "psychic factors," but as he developed his theory of conditioned reflexes, he completely broke away from that view, placing as much emphasis as did Watson on explaining behavior in terms of nerve connections, without appeal to consciousness. For Pavlov's own account of this transformation, cf. his *Lectures on Conditioned Reflexes*, pp. 37–40.

4. It is at this point that one sees the difference between the views of Dewey and Cooley and those of Sumner and Westermarck. For example, cf. Dewey's *Human Nature and Conduct*, pp. 58–60, and his criticism of Sumner on page 77 of the same work.

5. For Pavlov's most explicit discussion of the pluralism of unconditioned reflexes, cf. his discussion of the reflex of freedom (especially, *Lectures on Conditioned Reflexes*, pp. 282–83). For the fact that his view of reflexes did not commit him to a hostility toward the concept of instinct, cf. the opening of his lecture, "The Reflex of Purpose." For what are perhaps his most helpful general statements of his theoretical position, cf. his Huxley Lecture of 1906 and his 1909 lecture on "Natural Science and the Brain" (*Lectures on Conditioned Reflexes*, pp. 81–96 and 120–30, respectively).

6. It is to be recalled that, during this period, anthropologists had shown that most previously accepted views of race-differences were untenable. Since differences in culture were not attributable to biological inheritance, it was necessary to regard them as having been socially acquired. Because of the loose way in which the concept of conditioning was being used, all socially acquired differences in attitudes and beliefs were therefore said to be socially conditioned.

7. For the contrast between the assumptions of classical conditioning and of instrumental conditioning, cf. Kimble, *Hilgard and Marquis' Conditioning and Learning*, pp. 44–47, 65–66, 73, 74–77, *et passim*. (Also, cf. p. 40 and pp. 207–8.)
  These two types of conditioning are referred to by Skinner as Types S and R, the first being primarily concerned with respondent behavior, the second with operant behavior. (Cf. Skinner's *Behavior of the Organism*, especially pp. 18–22 and 438–39.)

8. In addition, at least one other factor may sometimes be involved as a precondition of the occurrence of the process of conditioning. As Kimble points out in discussing Thorndike's experiments, the type of activity on the part of an animal in its cage which leads to a successful instrumental response may not be purely random. (Cf. *Hilgard and Marquis' Conditioning and Learning*, p. 73.) However, for the sake of simplicity this factor need not be discussed in the present analysis.

9. Cf. *Behavior of Organisms*, pp. 10–12.

10. Lovejoy's description of the theory, in which he himself believed, makes it clear that the theory is restricted in scope. He said:

> It is not with "passions" in the etymological sense . . . that we shall be concerned in this lecture. It is with the question what affective states operate as the distinctive *springs of action* in man and how they so operate. We are more specifically to consider, first of all, the nature of what are commonly called desires and motives, and the ways in which they appear to determine more or less deliberate voluntary choices, decisions by human agents to act in one or another manner, when the thought of the act and its alternative is—though it may be but dimly and momentarily—present to consciousness before the act takes place. (*Reflections on Human Nature*, p. 70.)

Shortly thereafter, in discussing the concept of drive, Lovejoy admitted that there are cases in both human and animal behavior in which acts are done automatically, without conscious reference to the future, but he dismissed their possible relevance to his theory in saying, "but they are assuredly not the only modes, nor, in man, the most distinctive" (p. 75).

We may also note that the general positions to which Locke and Mill were committed by their theories of knowledge made it relatively easy for them to have accepted an analysis of human motivation in purely mentalistic terms.

11. I do not wish to deny that there may be some physiological concept, such as homeostasis, which is applicable in the analysis of both hunger and thirst, serving to explain why each is an unconditioned propensity. It might be claimed that such a concept could also be applied in all other cases of unconditioned propensities, such as shock-avoidance. Even were this true, the general factors of homeostatic tendency would not be that which served as the agent of conditioning: rather, the effective agent would be the particular deprivation which had been present, and it would be the removal of that deprivation through eating or through drinking, that was the conditioning factor.

12. Skinner himself did not insist on reducing the number of drives to any particular number; as we have noted, the task which he had set himself did not involve classifying ("botanizing") reflexes. And we may here note what he specifically said with respect to this point:

There is a natural tendency to reduce the drives of an organism to the smallest possible number because of the simplicity that is achieved, but we may go only so far in the matter as behavior itself will allow. (*Behavior of Organisms*, p. 371.)

This commendable dictum should, however, be applied to all instances of behavior, and not restricted to those which lend themselves to the usual types of conditioning procedures in animal experimentation.

13. *Introduction to Comparative Psychology*, p. 53.

14. The fact also becomes explicit in his answer to one objection. (Cf. *Introduction to Comparative Psychology*, pp. 54-55.)

15. The example of "verbal behavior" is one of the most obvious which might be cited in this connection. Whether the capacities requisite for learning a language can be explained solely in terms of stimulus-response conditioning is one of the major questions in this general field. An important contribution to that discussion was Chomsky's review of Skinner's *Verbal Behavior*, in *Language*, XXXV (1959), 26-58. An interesting more recent discussion is David McNeill's paper "On Theories of Language Acquisition."

16. To cite merely one instance of this tendency, we may note that in Otto Klineberg's criticism of instinctivist theories he used three criteria to determine whether a particular component of behavior was unlearned (i.e., innate). One of them (which is that here in question) is to discover a definite biochemical or physiological basis for such a component. (Cf. *Social Psychology*, p. 69 and, especially, p. 164.) We may note that another of his criteria was that which was denied by us in the preceding paragraphs: that any innate component in behavior will have to be continuous with components present in other biological species. [The passages here cited are identical with those in the first edition of Klineberg's very widely used text.]

17. Though I do not believe that this is the case, were I mistaken it should be possible to find some other tendency with respect to which the following remarks

are undoubtedly true. In fact, I am reasonably confident that sympathy—to which we shall immediately turn—constitutes an indisputable case in point.

Were the reader to doubt what I later say concerning sympathy, I suggest that he consider the views of Darwin and Huxley with reference to this point, or the fact that John Stuart Mill and Westermarck (neither of whom was inclined to underestimate the effects of social conditioning) found it necessary to regard sympathy as a fundamental and underived propensity in the human species.

In his recent book, *Conduct and Conscience*, Justin Aronfreed offers evidence to show that sympathy is an acquired form of behavior. However, as he points out (p. 149), he is using the term "sympathy" in a sense which is different from that in which it is often used, denoting by that term not a particular affective state, but a disposition to act in a way that will relieve the distress of another. As he notes, empathic experience (of a sort often designated as "sympathy") is a precondition of the overt form of behavior with which he is concerned.

18. Hume, however, did so. (Cf. *Treatise of Human Nature*, Book II, Part I, Ch. XII.)

19. Cf. *Lectures on Conditioned Reflexes*, pp. 282–85.

20. This is not a supposition that I would be inclined to make. However, for the sake of the argument I have attempted to analyze conditioning procedures in a way that does not involve the introduction of any factors which conditioning-theorists would not themselves accept. (For a discussion of conditioning-theory and some alternatives, the reader may wish to consult K. W. Spence, "Theoretical Interpretations of Learning," in S. S. Stevens' *Handbook of Experimental Psychology* [1951].)

21. There also are grave difficulties in associationism when taken as a general theory of learning, especially in those cases in which associations by contiguity, rather than by resemblance, are stressed. (Cf. note 9 to Ch. 9, above.)

22. This is an assumption which I would reject, but against which I have not here attempted to argue. To do so would involve a careful analysis of the meanings of "pleasure" and "pain," and of the forms of pleasurable experience.

23. To be sure, some anthropologists have tended to emphasize organicism and have also used the concept of "social conditioning," relying on the latter to explain how society molds the individual. Ruth Benedict's work provides a quite clear example of such a view. In such cases, both the preceding argument and the argument which is to follow will apply.

24. To be sure, Durkheim did seek to establish certain general conclusions regarding the evolutionary development of social institutions; however, his arguments in favor of organicism, which were most clearly stated in his *Rules of Sociological Method*, were independent of his theories of social development. Furthermore, although he himself did not cite his important distinction between questions of *origin* and questions of *function* in this specific connection, that distinction does entail that we can investigate the impact of institutions on individuals without tracing the origins of those institutions. (On the separation of origins and functioning, cf. *Rules of Sociological Method*, pp. 89–97.)

25. However, I should like to point out that there is a strong *ad hominem* argu-

ment which can be used against those who seek to establish organicism by appealing to the great differences in culture between earlier ages and our own: unless we can assume common modes of feeling and thinking, regardless of differences in culture, we have no right to assume that we can understand the nature of any culture other than our own. In short, the evidence which allegedly proves how different others are from ourselves rests on the assumption that there are fundamental respects in which they are *not* different, but similar.

26. Cf. "Societal Facts," *British Journal of Sociology*, VI (1955), 305–17. [Also available in the anthologies cited in note 30, p. 433, above.]

27. Cf. pp. 171–72, above.

28. The term "societal" is not used by Durkheim, but I use it in preference to "social" in order to call attention to the institutional character of the facts with which Durkheim was concerned: some facts which might be termed "social" relate to interpersonal relationships of a non-institutionalized sort.

29. *Rules of Sociological Method*, p. 1. Also, in this connection, cf. pp. 104–6 of the same work.

30. *Rules of Sociological Method*, p. 2. The whole of the chapter is relevant, as is Durkheim's preface to the second edition of this work. (Cf. especially, pp. xliii–xlvii.)

31. It has often been assumed that, in speaking of "collective representations," Durkheim was necessarily accepting the doctrine of a group mind, in the sense of a single collective consciousness of the sort sometimes attributed to crowds, or to social groups possessing an exceptional *esprit de corps*. Because of his concern with the moral aspects of the social order (in which, of course, religious phenomena were of fundamental importance), and because of his concern with questions of social solidarity, this aspect of what he termed "collective representations" was frequently very conspicuous in his work. However, if one examines the theory which he held concerning the nature of an *individual*'s mind—a theory which he formulated in opposition to both epiphenomenalism and metaphysical dualism—one finds that a mind is simply a system of representations. If interpreted in this way, some of the misleading connotations of "collective representations" tend to disappear. Nonetheless, the term is surely not wholly fortunate, and will be avoided in both our defense and our criticism of Durkheim's point of view.

The basic text for an analysis of Durkheim's position with respect to this subject is an article entitled "Individual and Collective Representations" (1898), which is included in the volume of essays entitled *Sociology and Philosophy*. (Cf. especially, pp. 23–28.)

32. For example, cf. *Rules of Sociological Method*, pp. xlvii–xlix.

In this connection it should be recalled that the doctrine of emergence was also held—though not necessarily in the same form—by Comte, by Hegel, and by Marx.

33. While Durkheim never put the matter in this way, it is a way which is consonant with his own attempt to state the difference between the psychological and the sociological in terms of the doctrine of emergence. There he said:

Social facts do not differ from psychological facts in quality only: *they have a*

NOTES TO PAGES 253-58

different substratum; they evolve in a different milieu. (*Rules of Sociological Method*, p. xlix.)

34. Cf. above, p. 171.

35. Cf. *Rules of Sociological Method*, p. 1.

36. Were someone to argue that the class status of a person's progenitors often affects his biological inheritance because of societal restrictions on permitted marriages, one can agree with the point. However, it would have no relevance to the malleability thesis of organicism: the individual's capacities would have been biologically inherited, rather than having been formed in him by the social institutions under which he lived.

37. Cf. *Elementary Forms of the Religious Life*, pp. 13–18, *et passim*.

38. *Ibid.*, p. 440.

39. Cf. *ibid.*, pp. 10–12, for such remarks concerning time and space.

40. Cf. *ibid.*, pp. 441–42.

41. Cf. *ibid.*, pp. 432–34.

42. *Ibid.*, p. 439.

43. "The Dualism of Human Nature," p. 327. (Also, cf. pp. 337 and 338.)

44. *Elementary Forms of the Religious Life*, p. 37.

45. *Ibid.*, p. 227.

46. Both of the foregoing statements are from *ibid.*, p. 230.

47. For the maxims which he establishes regarding social integration and egoistic suicide, cf. *Suicide*, pp. 208–9. For his account of the mediating psychological factor, cf. pp. 213–15.
   In the second type of suicide which Durkheim analyzed, i.e., altruistic suicide, it is less clear that psychological generalizations serve as the mediating factors. However, in anomic suicide, the third type which Durkheim distinguished, the psychological presuppositions of his theory are exceedingly clear. (Cf. *ibid.*, pp. 246–48.)

48. It will be recalled that one form of Marxian argument against a traditional psychological approach to human nature derived from the philosophical argument that there is a necessary interpenetration of the self and the world. (Cf. p. 189, above.) I shall not deal with that Hegelian form of argument here. I shall confine myself to what I take to be the more important sociological thesis: that the forms of individual consciousness derive from forms of social organization.

49. This generalization would clearly apply to Freud, as well as to psychologists who do not belong within the psychoanalytic tradition; whether it would apply to Jung is perhaps more doubtful. In this respect, Jung's later work may well stand quite outside the traditions of psychology.

50. In my opinion, these theses may also serve to limit some of the disputes which have characterized the functionalist movement in anthropology. For a discussion of that movement which concentrates on the views of Malinowski and of Radcliffe-Brown, cf. my article "Functionalism in Social Anthropology" in *Philosophy, Science, and Method: Essays in Honor of Ernest Nagel* (ed. S. Morgenbesser, P. Suppes, M. G. White), New York: St. Martin's Press, 1969.

51. Cf. above, Ch. 7, pp. 134–36.

52. Cf. *Ethical Studies*, pp. 66–69.
   In his early *Outlines of a Critical Theory of Ethics* (1891), John Dewey spoke in a somewhat similar way, saying:

> A desire, taken as a desire for its own apparent or direct end *only*, is an abstraction.
> It is a desire for an entire and continuous activity, and its satisfaction requires that
> it fitted into this entire and continuous activity; that it be made conformable to the
> conditions which will bring the whole man into action. It is this fitting-in which, is the
> the law of the desire—the 'universal' controlling its particular nature. This 'fitting-in' is
> no mechanical shearing off, nor stretching out, but a reconstruction of the natural
> desire till it becomes an expression of the whole man. The problem then is to find
> that special form of character, of self, which includes and transforms all special desires.
> This form of character is at once the Good and the Law of man (p. 96).

By 1908, when Dewey and Tufts wrote their *Ethics*, we find Dewey speaking in the following manner, which directly contradicts Bradley's view:

> Every moral act in its outcome marks a development or fulfillment of selfhood. But
> the very nature of right action forbids that the self should be the end in the sense
> of being the conscious aim of moral activity. For there is no way of discovering the
> nature of the self except in terms of objective ends which fulfill its capacities, and there
> is no *way* of realizing the self except as it is forgotten in devotion to these objective
> ends (pp. 391–92).

It is the latter position which expresses a point of view identical with that here adopted.

53. The following listing will serve to suggest how widely these texts were distributed:

> Friedrich Paulsen, *System der Ethik*, 1889; fifth edition 1900; tenth edition 1913;
> English translation, 1899.
> John H. Muirhead, *The Elements of Ethics*, 1892; second edition 1894; six reprintings prior to the third edition of 1910.
> John Stuart MacKenzie, *A Manual of Ethics*, 1893; fourth edition 1900.
> James Seth, *A Study of Ethical Principles*, 1894; fourth edition 1898; tenth edition 1908.

54. This tendency toward consistency is what many moralists refer to as *reasonableness* or *rationality* in conduct. (For example, cf. the critical reinterpretation of Kant in Dewey and Tufts, *Ethics*, pp. 314–17.) However, since that terminology tends to suggest that there must be a specifically logical or intellectual component in our avoidance of inconsistency, I prefer not to use these terms.
   I have elsewhere discussed the importance of the standard of consistency in a somewhat different context. (Cf. my *Phenomenology of Moral Experience*, pp. 263–77.)

55. If the point here being made is not sufficiently clear to the reader, he may

consult an unusually cogent exposition of the same thesis in Goldenweiser, *Anthropology*, Ch. XXXI.

Concerning the role of the comparative method in evolutionary theory in general, cf. pp. 78–80, above.

The Boas article, cited above, is most readily available in his collected essays, *Race, Language, and Culture*. (Cf. especially pp. 275–76.)

PART IV—THE LIMITS OF REASON

CHAPTER 13. CRITIQUES OF THE INTELLECTUAL POWERS OF MAN: THE IDEALIST STRAND

1. The traditional dichotomous division of the faculties of the mind is to be found in Aristotle, Descartes, and Wolff, among others.

For reasons which will become obvious in the text, Rousseau must be recognized as one of the chief sources of the view that Feeling constitutes a separate faculty. One can also find anticipations of later uses of the concept of "feeling" in eighteenth-century British thought, particularly in Shaftesbury. However, the trichotomous division of the aspects of mental life into the faculties of Feeling, the Understanding, and the Will was not formalized until Tetens and Kant. It was primarily through Kant's *Critique of Judgment* that this classification became influential. (For an extended discussion of this development in German psychology, cf. Robert Sommer, *Grundzüge einer Geschichte der deutscher Psychologie und Aesthetik von Wolff-Baumgarten bis Kant-Schiller* [Würzburg, 1892].)

2. Vico's thought would provide an earlier starting point, but in my opinion the dominant aspects of nineteenth-century criticisms of man's intellectual powers are not, at most points, congruent with Vico's views. On the other hand, Kant's system exerted a direct and important influence on almost every thinker with whom we shall here be concerned.

3. For the importance of Jacobi's influence on the period, cf. Lovejoy, *The Reason, the Understanding, and Time*, pp. 4–7.

I should like at this point to note that the particular tendencies in nineteenth-century thought with which Lovejoy was dealing in discussing *The Reason, the Understanding, and Time*, are not identical with the views with which we shall here be concerned, even though they frequently overlap. Lovejoy was especially interested in analyzing and criticizing those philosophers who laid stress on an inner sense as the most penetrating organ of knowledge, and thus, for example, Schelling's early thought belonged squarely within the tradition which he discussed. Nonetheless, Schelling does not properly fall within the stream of thought with which we are here concerned. For example, he bitterly attacked Jacobi's view that all philosophic systems and intellectual constructions are necessarily misleading (cf. *Sämmtliche Werke*, I, viii, 54), and at some points he put forward views which must be regarded as wildly exaggerated claims concerning the depths which systematic philosophy could plumb. (For example, cf. the introduction to his *System des transcendentalen Idealismus*, in *Sämmtliche Werke*, I, iii, 339–52.) Conversely, because of this difference in theme, we shall be dealing with some figures in nineteenth-century thought with whom Lovejoy, quite properly, was not concerned.

4. This contrast between his view and Kant's is implicit in the title of Jacobi's treatise: *Ueber das Unternehmen des Kriticizmus, die Vernunft zu Verstande zu bringen.* (For Jacobi's own comments on this title, cf. *Werke*, III, 81–83.)

5. In 1815, in a foreword to the second volume of his collected works, Jacobi himself called attention to this fact (*Werke*, II, 7–8 and 10–11). This lengthy foreword was designed to serve as an introduction to all of his philosophical writings, and it is without question the clearest exposition of most aspects of his position.

For a discussion of the harmony between Jacobi's earlier and later terminology, cf. Lévy-Bruhl, *La philosophie de Jacobi*, pp. 51–57.

6. In the foreword to the fourth volume of Jacobi's collected works, we find the following account of what he wished to establish in his letters concerning Spinoza:

> Meine Briefe über die Lehre des Spinoza wurden desshalb nicht geschrieben um Ein System durch das Andre zu verdrängen, sondern um die Unüberwindlichkeit des Spinozismus von seiten des logischen Verstandesgebrauches darzuthun. (*Werke*, IV¹, xxxvii.)

While this foreword was posthumous, and is dependent upon fragmentary manuscripts, there is no reason to challenge the accuracy with which it reflects Jacobi's own estimate of the import of his early work.

7. In his attack on Schelling, Jacobi called attention to the difference between his view of Reason and Kant's. He explicitly rejected the view that what Kant termed Ideas of Reason depend upon an extension of the concepts of the Understanding; for Jacobi, they were "ursprüngliche Erkenntnisse von objectiver Gültigkeit." (*Werke*, III, 376–77.)

8. For example, in the 1815 exposition of the basic principles of his thought, Jacobi said:

> Und so gestehen wir denn ohne Scheu, dass unsere Philosophie von dem Gefühle, dem *objectiven* nämlich und *reinen*, ausgeht. . . . Das Vermögen der Gefühle ist im Menschen das über alle andere erhabene Vermögen; dasjenige, welches allein ihn von dem Thiere specifisch unterscheidet; . . . es ist, behaupten wir, mit der Vernunft Einer und Dasselbe." (*Werke*, II, 61.)

The adjectives *"objectiv"* and *"rein"* are insisted upon in other passages as well (e.g., *Werke*, II, 105). Kant had, of course, used these two adjectives in connection with moral incentives, and that may have been a source for Jacobi's use of them. However, in Jacobi's thought, as I shall now point out, Reason is actually a medium through which something is given, a suprasensible sensibility, rather than being related to Kant's "practical Reason."

9. One passage in which this phrase is used runs as follows:

> Ich berufe mich auf ein unabweisbares unüberwindliches Gefühl als ersten und unmittelbaren Grund aller Philosophie und Religion; auf ein Gefühl, welches den Menschen gewahren und inne werden lässt: er habe einen Sinn für das Uebersinnliche. Diesen Sinn nenne ich *Vernunft*, zum Unterschiede von den Sinnen für die sichtbare Welt. (*Werke*, IV¹, xxi.)

10. Jacobi, in opposition to Kant, accepted a version of "direct realism." For an analysis of his realism, the reader may wish to consult Alexander W. Crawford's doctoral dissertation, *The Philosophy of F. H. Jacobi*, in *Cornell Studies in Philosophy*, No. 6 (1905).

11. For example, cf. the following passage:

> Die Vernunft schafft keine Begriffe, erbaut keine Systeme, urtheilet auch nicht, sondern ist, *gleich den äusseren Sinnen*, bloss offenbarend, positiv verkündend.
>
> Diess vor allem anderen ist fest zu halten: Wie es eine sinnliche Anschauung giebt, eine *Anschauung* durch denn *Sinn*, so giebt es auch eine rationale Anschauung durch die *Vernunft*.... Der *sinnlichen Anschauung* entgegen gilt keine Demonstration, indem alles Demonstriren nur ein Züruckführen des Begriffes auf die ihn bewährende... *sinnliche Anschauung* ist.... Aus demselben Grunde gilt auch keine Demonstration wider die *rationale* oder *Vernunftanschauung*, die uns der Natur jenseitige Gegenstände zu erkennen giebt. (*Werke*, II, 58–59.)

On the following page, he continues:

> Wenn jemand spricht, er wisse, so fragen wir mit Recht, woher er wisse? Unvermeidlich muss er dann am Ende auf eins von diesen beyden sich berufen: entweder auf *Sinnes-Empfindung*, oder auf *Geistes-Gefühl*.

12. It is precisely at this point that we must note one fundamental difference between the position of Schleiermacher and that of Jacobi. While he, too, stressed the autonomy of the religious, and also insisted that feeling constitutes the religious dimension of experience, Schleiermacher defended the claims of the intellect, and refused to accept the view that conclusions reached by the Understanding were not to be relied upon in the search for truth. (For example, cf. his discussion of Jacobi in a letter to his friend K. G. Brinkmann, and his letter dated March 30, 1818 to Jacobi himself; in Schleiermacher's *Briefe*, pp. 94–95 and 337–40, respectively.)

We may therefore again point out that the tendencies of thought with which we are here concerned are not in all respects identical with those which Lovejoy selected for attention in *The Reason, the Understanding, and Time*. (Cf. above, note 3.)

13. That Jacobi had a strong and direct influence upon Kierkegaard is entirely clear from reference to him in Kierkegaard's *Concluding Unscientific Postscript*. (Cf. especially pp. 92 and 224.) While all of these references allude to only one of Jacobi's books (his letters to Mendelssohn concerning Spinoza), it was the only work immediately relevant in that particular context. We may note, however, that when Kierkegaard cites passages from this book he refers the reader to Jacobi's collected works; Jacobi's influence upon him may therefore have been fairly extensive. In this connection it is to be noted that in Jacobi one finds frequent philosophic use made of the disjunct *"entweder-oder"* and, in one place at least, of *"noch-weder."* (For example, cf. *Werke*, II, 74–75 and 88–92; also, III, 377–78.) One of these passages occurs in *Von den Göttlichen Dingen und ihrer Offenbarung*, which was Jacobi's attack on Schelling. It would surely be surprising if Kierkegaard had not been well-acquainted with this particular controversy. Given these facts, I should think that a study of the possible influences of Jacobi upon Kierkegaard might be of interest; so far as I know, no extended study of this sort has been made.

14. In his general account of his position, he said:

> Die Annahme einer wirklichen und wahrhaften Vorsehung und Freiheit, nicht nur in dem höchsten sondern in jedem vernünftigen Wesen, und die Behauptung, dass diese zwey Eigenschaften sich einander gegenseitig voraussetzen, ist das, was meine Philosophie von allen andern, seit Aristoteles bis auf diesen Tag entstandenen, Philosophien unterscheidet. (*Werke*, II, 46–47.)

In this connection we must of course note that Plato is exempted from Jacobi's generalization. His relation to Plato's philosophy, as he interpreted it, was extremely close.

15. In this respect one is reminded of Kierkegaard's attitude toward the Hegelian system, which he regarded as the greatest of all systems, but as being only a thought-experiment which did not touch existence. (Cf. below, Ch. 15, pp. 334–36.) The more specific points with which we shall now be concerned will also be noticed to resemble much that was more trenchantly put by Kierkegaard.

16. Jacobi's position is well expressed in one passage in which he criticizes Kant's own system, explaining why that system appeals to philosophers:

> So führt der Kantischen Lehre nothwendig zu einem System absoluter Subjectivität, gefällt aber eben desswegen dem erklärenden Verstande, den man den philosophirenden nennt, und der zuletzt doch nicht erklärt, sondern nur vertilgt; und hat *wider* sich nur die von diesem Wege abmahnende, nicht erklärende, sondern positiv offenbarende, unbedingt entscheidende Vernunft, oder den *natürlichen Vernunftglauben.* Der Weg der Jacobischen Lehre, indem er zu einen System absoluter Objectivität eben so nothwendig führt, missfällt dem an dem Begreiflichen allein sich haltenden Verstande . . . und hat für sich nur die nicht erklärende, unmittelbar offenbarende Vernunft. (*Werke,* II, 36–37.)

The contrast with which this passage ends may suggest to the reader a parallel between Jacobi and Dilthey. While Dilthey was thoroughly familiar with Jacobi's work (for he was perhaps the most eminent of all who have investigated the intellectual history of Germany in this period), Dilthey's own distinction between *erklären* and *verstehen* must be regarded as having arisen in connection with the problems of the humane sciences (*die Geisteswissenschaften*), rather than having been derived from the issues which chiefly concerned Jacobi and his contemporaries.

17. The passage in the letter to Fichte reads:

> Unsere Wissenschaften, blos als solche, sind Spiele, welche der menschliche Geist, zeitvertreibend, sich ersinnt. Diese Spiele ersinnend, organisirt er nur seine Unwissenheit, ohne einer Erkenntniss des Wahren auch nur um ein Haar breit näher zu kommen. (*Werke,* III, 29.)

The lengthier, later passage is to be found in *ibid.,* III, 305–6.

We may note that, in other contexts, Jacobi is sometimes even more critical of those forms of philosophy which rely upon the Understanding, rather than upon the Reason:

> Also erfand sich der Verstand den doppelten Unglauben, erst an eine materielle, dann auch an eine immaterielle, geistige Welt, und nannte die Kunst alle Wahrheit zu verlieren—denn das war seine Erfindung—*Philosophie. (Ibid.,* II, 99–100.)

18. *Ibid.,* III, 306.

19. For this contrast, cf. *ibid.,* III, 306–7.

20. Cf. *ibid.,* II, 65–66.

21. The passage criticizing Kant from this point of view is to be found in *ibid.,* III, 175–79.

22. In the concluding paragraphs of his treatise on Kant, Jacobi said:

Dahin muss es kommen mit den grossen Gegenständen der Sittenlehre und Religion, wenn man sie aus blosen *Begriffen*, aus einer verständigen Zusammensetzung für die philosophierende Vernunft, in ihrer Wahrheit begründen will. Freyheit wird zum Gespenste, göttliche Vorsehung zum Problem. Aber im Geiste des lebendigen Menschen sind sie kein Gespenst und kein Problem, sondern das Wahrhafteste und Ursprünglichste alles Gedankes und aller Empfindung. (*Ibid.*, III, 192.)

23. In 1815, in looking back upon the reception accorded his letters to Mendelssohn, Jacobi said:

Die in dem Werke über Spinoza von dem Verfasser aufgestellte Behauptung: *Alle menschliche Erkenntniss gehe aus von Offenbarung und Glauben*, hatte in der deutschen philosophischen Welt ein allgemeines Aergerniss erregt. Es sollte durchaus nicht wahr seyn, dass es ein Wissen aus der ersten Hand gebe, welches alles Wissen aus der zweyten (die Wissenschaft) erst bedinge, ein Wissen *ohne Beweise*, welches dem Wissen *aus Beweisen* nothwendig vorausgehe, es begründe, es fortwährend und durchaus beherrsche. (*Ibid.*, II, 3-4.)

For a discussion of this point in the letters themselves, cf. *ibid.*, IV[1], 210.

24. On the relationships between them, cf. Lévy-Bruhl, *La philosophie de Jacobi*, pp. 205-23, and Léon, *Fichte et son temps*, II (Part I), 146-56, 165-67, and 222-26.

25. In the preface to the *Vocation of Man* he says:

This book is therefore not intended for philosophers by profession, who will find nothing in it that has not already been set forth in other writings of the same author.... [But] it ought to attract and animate the reader, and to elevate him from the world of sense into a region of transcendental thought. [Es sollte anziehen und erwärmen, und den Leser kräftig von der Sinnlichkeit zum Uebersinnlichen fortreissen.] (*Popular Works*, I, 321-22.)

26. Once again, it is well to point out that neither Schelling nor Schleiermacher should be classed along with Jacobi and Fichte when the issue is one concerning the limits of human understanding, and the role of the intellect in the search for truth. Of course, there were many other respects in which their views were similar, as one would expect from the personal ties and common concerns which related them to one another.

27. *Ibid.*, I, 411.

28. Almost immediately after the passage just quoted, Fichte says:

I will not suffer myself to entertain the desire of pressing this conviction on others by reasoning, and I will not be surprised if such an undertaking should fail. I have adopted my mode of thinking first of all for myself, not for others, and before myself only will I justify it. He who possesses the honest, upright purpose of which I am conscious, will also attain a similar conviction,—without that, such a conviction can in no way be attained. (*Ibid.*, I, 411-12.)

29. Cf. *Ibid.*, I, 413-14. A comparison with statements to be found in James's "Dilemma of Determinism" is here in order. James introduced his argument by telling his readers:

I thus disclaim openly on the threshold all pretension to prove to you that the freedom of the will is true. The most I hope is to induce some of you to follow my own example in assuming it true, and acting as if it were true. If it be true, it seems

is involved in the strict logic of the case. Its truth ought not to be
lly down our indifferent throats. It ought to be freely espoused by men
ly well turn their backs upon it. In other words, our first act of freedom,
ought in all inward propriety to be to affirm that we are free. (*The*
t, and Other Essays, p. 46.)

30. These studies were published in the second volume (1802) of the *Critical Journal of Philosophy*, which Schelling and Hegel edited; the full title of the series was "Glauben und Wissen, oder die Reflexionsphilosophie der Subjetktivität, in der Vollständigkeit ihrer Formen, als Kantische, Jacobische und Fichtesche Philosophie" (*Sämtliche Werke*, I, 279–433).

31. Cf. *ibid.*, I, 280; for a further comparison of their views, also cf. I, 392–3.

32. Cf. *ibid.*, I, 431.

33. For example, cf. *ibid.*, I, 411–13 and 419–22.

34. This is a statement already quoted (cf. p. 179, above). Hegel himself used it twice, in the prefaces to *The Smaller Logic* and to the *Philosophy of Right*.

35. This, he tells us, is the hypothesis which philosophy establishes, and which it brings to the consideration of history: cf. *Philosophy of History*, p. 9.

36. For example, cf. *ibid.*, pp. 32–34.

37. *Philosophy of Right*, pp. 12–13.

38. *The Smaller Logic*, translated by Wallace, Sect. 45, p. 92.

39. Cf. Hegel's discussion of how Sense leads to Conception, and how Conception needs to be superseded by Thought, in *The Smaller Logic*, translated by Wallace, Sect. 20, pp. 36–39.

40. *The Smaller Logic*, translated by Wallace, Sect. 80, p. 143.

41. *The Smaller Logic*, translated by Wallace, Sect. 80, p. 144.

42. Cf. above, Ch. 10, pp. 175–76.
   One particularly helpful discussion of the dialectic is to be found in *The Smaller Logic*, Wallace translation, Sect. 81, pp. 147–51. In that section (p. 148), we find the following statement:

Wherever there is movement, wherever there is life, wherever anything is carried into effect in the actual world, there Dialectic is at work. It is also the soul of all knowledge which is truly scientific.

43. In *The Smaller Logic* he even warns us against identifying the term *thought* as referring to a "subjective activity—one amongst many similar faculties, such as memory, imagination, and will." Thought, as the subject of logic, is not to be interpreted as an activity which is tied to individual persons at all. (Cf. Wallace translation, p. 39.)

44. Hegel said of the history of philosophy:

The stages in the evolution of the Idea seem to follow each other by accident, and to present merely a number of different and unconnected principles, which the several systems of philosophy carry out in their own way. But it is not so. For these thousands of years the same Architect has directed the work: and that Architect is the one living Mind whose nature is to think, to bring to self-consciousness what is, and, with its being thus set as object before it, to be at the same time raised above it, and so to reach a higher stage of its own being. (*The Smaller Logic*, Wallace translation, Sect. 13, p. 22.)

45. Cf. Hegel's larger *Science of Logic*, translated by Johnston and Struthers, I, 56.

Hegel's most drastic criticism of the Understanding is directed against the abstractness of mathematical thought. (For example, cf. the preface to the *Phenomenology of Mind*, pp. 100–105.) However, the more familiar world of common sense also provides an instance in which what passes for "thought" is not, according to Hegel really thought. In the preface to the *Phenomenology of Mind* (p. 92) he states the point pithily: "What is 'familiarly known' is not properly known, just for the reason that it is 'familiar'." ("*Das Bekannte überhaupt ist darum, weil es bekannt ist, nicht erkannt.*") He proceeds as follows:

When engaged in the process of knowing, it is the commonest form of self-deception, and a deception of other people as well, to assume something to be familiar, and give assent to it on that very account. Knowledge of that sort, with all its talk, never gets from the spot, but has no idea that this is the case. . . . Apprehending and proving consist similarly in seeing whether every one finds what is said corresponding to his idea too. . . .

46. For example, what Hegel said concerning Kant's treatment of the antinomies, *The Smaller Logic*, Wallace translation, Sect. 48, pp. 97–99, and Sect. 81, p. 149. Also, cf. the more general remarks in the preface to *Phenomenology of Mind*, p. 93.

47. Cf. *Sämtliche Werke*, VI, 260–72, (Sect. 368–87); in Wallace, *Hegel's Philosophy of Mind*, pp. 64–90 (Sect. 445–68).

48. *Sämtliche Werke*, VI, 260–61. (In Wallace, *Hegel's Philosophy of Mind*, p. 64.)

49. This is from Wallace's translation, p. 91. In *Sämtliche Werke*, VI, 273 (Sect. 388), the same basic view is expressed in other terms.

50. Cf. *Science of Logic*, translated by Johnston and Struthers, I, 40. Their translation at this point is opaque: cf. *Sämtliche Werke*, IV, 21.

51. Cf., respectively, pp. 184 and 178, above.

52. In analyzing early nineteenth-century thought, Dilthey also called attention to the fact that Maine de Biran bears comparison in certain respects with Fichte and Jacobi: all three exemplified forms of idealism founded on notions of personality and freedom. (Cf. *Gesammelte Schriften*, IV, 533–36; also, II, 314, and VIII, 107–12.)

53. The best treatment of Maine de Biran's knowledge of Kant is to be found in Gouhier, *Les conversions de Maine de Biran*. (For example, cf. pp. 211, 230, and, especially, pp. 256–59 and 354–55 of that work.)

54. There was one point at which he expressed a definite debt to Kant rather than merely offering a comparison of their views: this concerned the necessity for drawing a distinction between the "I" and the concept of a soul-substance. (Cf. *Oeuvres*, X, 377-78.)

For relatively brief references to Kant's theory of knowledge in those works in which Maine de Biran was developing his own analysis of experience, cf. *ibid*., III, 119 and 124, and *ibid*., VIII, 2 and 140-42; also, cf. *Journal*, III, 29-32.

55. Cf. *Journal*, II, 129 and 159.

Other late French philosophers also emphasized this side of Kant's system, rather than his theory of knowledge. For example, one may note Ravaisson's interpretation of what Kant had contributed to modern thought (*La philosophie en France*, pp. 7-8).

56. Cf. his introduction to *Influence de l'habitude* (*Oeuvres*, II, 20-22).

57. A brief statement of this essential aspect of his position is to be found in the introduction to the above mentioned essay (*ibid*., II, 24-27).

58. Maine de Biran himself gives two retrospective accounts of the developments implicit in his earlier psychological works (cf. *Oeuvres*, VIII, 1-13, and XIV, 202-21).

59. As Gouhier showed in *Les conversions de Maine de Biran*, Maine de Biran had originally been influenced by the attempts of Charles Bonnet and by Cabanis to relate psychological phenomena and physiology; however, by 1811, when he wrote his *Mémoire sur les rapports du physique et du moral de l'homme* for the Copenhagen Academy, he had wholly rejected their views. (Cf. *Oeuvres*, XIV, 219; for an account of this *Mémoire*, cf. *ibid*., III, cxxxvi-cxxxix.)

60. In somewhat shortened form, this passage reads as follows:

Je dis qu'il y a une sorte de sensations qui peuvent être considérées comme *fondées* dans le sujet unique *moi*.... C'est là, peut-être, et non point dans une impression *reçue* quelconque, qu'il faudrait chercher l'origine spéciale de nos facultés actives, le point d'appui de l'existence et le fondement de toutes les idées simples, que nous pouvons acquérir de nous-mêmes et de nos actes intellectuels....

On peut concevoir au contraire des affections *simples*, toutes *fondées* dans l'organisation matérielle, ou dans une cause quelconque étrangère au *moi*, réduites par conséquent à le *matière*, et plus ou moins denuées des formes de la personnalité.... (*Oeuvres*, III, 126.)

He continues his contrast between these two forms of primitive elements within experience, by speaking of them in the following terms: "l'*effort* produit d'une volonté, inséperable de *moi*," and "l'affection résultat *impersonnel* d'une propriété organique" (*ibid*., p. 127).

61. Cf. the following passage:

J'ajouterai encore, comme une dernière réflexion sur les abus ou écarts des méthodes, que les limites où me paroit devoir s'arrêter celle que l'on nomme *analogie* des physiciens se trouvent fixées par la nature même des moyens qu'elle peut employer, et surtout par la nature de l'objet à qui elle est appropriée. Ces moyens, en effet, ne peuvent être qu'empruntés des sciences externes et de l'imagination ou faculté représentative; son objet exclusif consiste dans les apparences ou phénomènes représentés hors du *moi*; elle ne pourra donc avoir aucune prise sur cette espèce de faits primitifs qui ne tombent que sous le sens le plus intime, et s'il y a une sorte d'observation ou de sens particulièrement approprié à des faits élémentaires de cet ordre, les analogies ou ressemblances phénoménales qui s'offrent à un point de vue extérieur ou physique ne pourront rentrer dans le champ intérieur où l'être pensant assiste comme temoin reflechi à ses opérations les plus exactes, à ses modifications les plus intimes. Ici tout se simplifie et s'individualise, là, au contraire, tout se généralise et se compose. *Les classifications et les lois,* qui sont, après l'observation des effets, les deux grands mobiles des sciences naturelles, ne trouveront donc guère d'emploi utile dans la connoissance des faits primitifs ou des vérités de sentiment qui s'en déduisent de la manière la plus immédiate. (*De l' aperception immédiate* [ed. by J. Echeverria], p. 53.)

On the contrast between abstract, generalizing, classificatory knowledge and that which seeks to grasp inner, psychological fact, cf. *Oeuvres*, VIII, 9–10.

62. Cf. *ibid.*, VIII, 82–83.

63. P. Tisserand, in his introduction to the volume of the collected works which includes this study, pointed out that under the influence of the circle of philosophers in which Maine de Biran found himself in Paris after 1813, his theory of knowledge expanded into a theory of Reason, or a faculty of that which grasps the absolute (*Oeuvres*, VII, xi). This involved an even more explicit rejection of abstractive generalization (*ibid.*, pp. xvi–xvii), and a sharper separation of our knowledge and our belief from the elements of experience which were presented to us through sense experience (*ibid.*, xx-xxi).

64. Cf. the following passage, here given in a shortened form:

Vient-il à tourner ses regards sur lui-même? L'homme ne se considère d'abord que comme objet de cette nature phénoménique dont il fait partie dans le point de vue extérieur où il se trouve placé....

Ainsi il se voit ou se sent entraîné dans ce cercle fatal où roulent tous les êtres passifs, animés comme inanimés, soit qu'ils sentent ou connaissent le mouvement nécessaire auquel ils obéissent, soit qu'ils le suivent d'une manière tout à fait aveugle sans le sentir ni le connaître.

Comme les corps célestes suivent sans la savoir dans l'espace et le temps absolus les lois constantes de l'attraction qui déterminent les formes de leurs orbites, comme les molécules infinitésimales de la matière obéissent aussi constamment aux affinités *électives* qu'elles ignorent, les machines organisées ... paraissent également soumises à certaines attractions, sympathies ou antipathies, que les lois de la sensibilité organique rendent plus obscures et plus compliquées encore, en les laissent également sous l'empire du *fatum*....

Mais, en sa qualité d'être intelligent, voulant et pensant, l'homme se place lui-même en dehors et au-dessus de cette nature qui lui est donnée comme objet de son intuition; il la domine en effet par sa pensée et par sa volonté.... Non seulement il sent ou a des sensations, mais de plus il sait qu'il sent, il a l'idée ou la connaissance de ses sensations; non seulement il a des rapports avec les divers agents ou objets de la nature, mais encore il aperçoit ces rapports et peut se rendre compte; de plus, il les modifie, les étend, les complique ou les multiplie sans cesse, ou s'en crée de nouveaux à chaque instant par l'exercice d'une puissance, d'une force agissante qui l'affranchit les liens du *fatum* et le constitue individu, personne morale, intellectuelle et libre. (*Oeuvres*, X, 64–65.)

65. Cf. *ibid.*, XIV, 200–201, and (earlier) in *De l'aperception immédiate* (*Mémoire de Berlin*), p. 115.

As Maine de Biran's *Journal* shows, he was a close student of Pascal, but what received most emphasis in his journal were points of disagreement rather than agreement. (For a discussion of Maine de Biran and Pascal, cf. Gouhier, *Les conversions de Maine de Biran.*)

66. Cf. *Oeuvres*, XIV, 195.

67. "Il y a donc plus qu'une différence de degré entre l'homme et la brute"
is the sentence with which his section on "Vie animale" closes, and which therefore introduces the section entitled "Vie humaine." (Cf. *ibid.*, XIV, 268.)

68. *Ibid.*, XIV, 234–35.

69.

"Cette clarté [he charged] tient plutôt à l'emploi d'une certaine méthode abstraite et
hypothétique, fondée sur le besoin et le parti pris d'avance de simplifier le langage, ou
de n'avoir recours qu'au plus petit nombre de termes et de formules les plus
symétriques, pour former ce qu'on appelle la science: science logique ou conventionnelle
où l'on croit tout expliquer à force d'abstraire, de dissimuler ou de dénaturer les choses
ou les faits rebelles aux catégories formées d'avance." (*Ibid.*, XIV, 301.)

70. Cf. *ibid.*, XIV, 235.

71. Cf. *ibid.*, XIV, 222–23, and 369 ff.

72. Maine de Biran said:

Quand tout serait d'accord et en harmonie entre les facultés sensitives et actives qui
constituent l'homme, il y aurait encore une nature supérieure, une troisième vie,
qui ne serait pas satisfaite, et ferait sentir qu'il y a un autre bonheur, une autre sagesse,
une autre perfection, au-delà du plus grand bonheur humain, de la plus haute sagesse
ou perfection intellectuelle et morale dont l'être humain soit susceptible. (*Ibid.*, XIV,
397.)

73. For two of many examples of this Platonic tendency in Maine de Biran's
later thought, cf. *Journal*, II, 351, and *Oeuvres*, XIV, 397–98.

74. Ravaisson, we may note, after having sketched the fact that sensationalism
had placed an overwhelming burden upon philosophy, attributed its regenera-
tion to two men: Maine de Biran and Ampère. (Cf. *La philosophie en France*,
p. 14.)

75. Henri Gouhier has explored the question of the possible influence of Maine
de Biran on Bergson's thought, in his essay on "Maine de Biran and Bergson."
What is significant for us in this connection is not the question of actual influence, but the very close parallel between Maine de Biran's position and
Bergson's critique of the intellectual powers of man (cf. below, p. 353). Bergson
himself indicated the close relations which existed between the position of
Maine de Biran and Janet, and of the whole of the French spiritualist tradition
in the ninenteenth century. (Cf. Gouhier, "Maine de Biran et Bergson," p. 141.)

76. In Gouhier, "Maine de Biran et Bergson," p. 146. One may note that
Ravaisson, too, regarded the inner sense of effort as a privileged experience, transcending the phenomenal world. In a passage which not only shows his relation
to Maine de Biran, but to Bergson as well, Ravaisson argued against Kant's
phenomenalism on the ground that any *motion* presupposes an underlying force
to give it its unitary character. He identified this transphenomenal source as an
inner tendency or effort:

... l'effort, qui n'est pas, comme le mouvement par lequel il se manifeste, un objet des

sens et de l'imagination, mais que nous fait seule connaître, dans le type unique de
la volonté, notre plus intime conscience. (*La philosophie en France*, p. 239.)

The transcendence of the limits of Kantian phenomenalism through turning
inward was, of course, characteristic of Bergson himself. For example, he said:

> Kant had proved, so it was said, that our thought exerts itself upon a matter previously
> scattered in Space and Time, and thus prepared especially for man: the "thing in
> itself" escapes us; to comprehend it we would need an intuitive faculty which we do
> not possess. On the contrary, from my analysis the result was that at least a part of
> reality, our person, can be grasped in its natural purity. Here, at any rate, the materials
> of our knowledge have not been created, or ground out of shape and reduced to
> powder. . . . Our person appears to us just as it is "in itself," as soon as we free ourselves
> of the habits contracted for our greater convenience. (*A Study in Metaphysics*, p. 28.)

This passage, taken from the first introduction to *La pensée et le mouvant*,
is paralleled by other Bergsonian discussions of Kant. For example, in his Oxford
Lecture on "The Perception of Change," Bergson said that the greatest service
that Kant had rendered to speculative philosophy lay in the fact that "he definitively established that, if metaphysics is possible, it can be so only through an
effort of intuition" (*A Study in Metaphysics*, p. 140). As Bergson makes clear,
this intuition involves breaking with those modes of knowing which Kant had
characterized as the Understanding.

CHAPTER 14. IGNORAMUS, IGNORABIMUS: THE POSITIVIST STRAND

1. From "An Autobiographical Sketch," in *Popular Lectures*, II, 284–85. The
same theme is also to be found, phrased in a slightly different way, in his lecture
"On Thought in Medicine," in *ibid.*, II, 233–34.

2. I shall *not* be using the term "phenomenalism" in what has recently become
one of its standard senses: that all material-object statements are to be considered as analyzable into statements concerning groups or sequences of sensa.
Instead, I shall use it to designate the general view that *if* there is a reality
which is independent of experience, we cannot know it. Obviously, some phe-
nomenalists, such as Kant, do affirm such a reality (an Unknown-X); others,
such as Hume, do not. Helmholtz and Spencer, as well as DuBois-Reymond,
adopt a position similar to Kant's, and unlike Hume's, on this particular issue.

3. That there often are closer connections between the sciences and epistemology than philosophers generally grant is a point I attempted to establish in
Philosophy, Science, and Sense Perception. Thus, I do not find physiologically
oriented arguments for an epistemological position unusual. Whether the actual
arguments with which we shall deal were or were not adequate is, of course,
another question.

4. For Helmholtz's account of German intellectual life in the post-Kantian
period, cf. *Popular Lectures*, II, 13–15.

5. The lecture, "Ueber die Grenzen des Naturerkennens" was originally given
in 1872, and can be said to have become almost immediately world-famous. A
companion-piece is the lecture "Die sieben Welträthsel," given eight years later,
in which DuBois-Reymond's views remained unchanged.

6. Cf. Helmholtz's autobiographical sketch in *Popular Lectures*, II, 275–77.

7. As Helmholtz indicated in the autobiographical passage just cited, DuBois-Reymond, who had been a fellow-student in Müller's physiological laboratory, was one who defended his essay on the conservation of energy.

8. In the concluding paragraph of his rectoral address, Kirchhoff said:

Wir müssen hiernach gestehen . . . dass unser Verständniss der Naturerscheinungen, selbst derjenigen, die die unorganische Körperwelt darbietet, bis jetzt ein sehr unvollkommenes ist. In höherem Maasse noch gilt das von den viel complicirteren Vorgängen, welch in den Pflanzen und Thierkörperen stattfinden. Hier wie dort ist das wahre Verständiss nicht gewonnen, so lange die Zurückführung auf die Mechanik nicht gelungen ist." (*Ueber das Ziel der Naturwissenschaften*, p. 24.)

9. For example, cf. Helmholtz's dicussion of vitalism *versus* the principle of the conservation of energy in *Popular Lectures*, I, 335–37; also, note that he regarded his teacher G. Magnus, the physicist, as having dealt vitalism a death blow through his investigations of gases in the blood, laying correct foundations for the theory of respiration. (*Ibid.*, II, 15–16.) Cf. DuBois-Reymond's rejection of vitalism in "Die Grenzen das Naturerkennens," *Reden*, I, 115–17.

10. In this connection we may cite the following passage:

Dass es in Wirklichkeit keine Qualitäten giebt, folgt aus der Zergliederung unserer Sinneswahrnehmungen . . . Das mosaïsche: "Es ward Licht," ist physiologisch falsch. Licht war erst als der erste rothe Augenpunkt eines Infusoriums zum ersten Mal Hell und Dunkel unterschied. Ohne Seh- und ohne Gehörsinn-substanz wäre diese farbenglühende tönende Welt um uns finster und stumm. (*Reden*, I, 109–10.)

11. *Popular Lectures*, II, 234.

12. For example, in the introduction to his great book, *On the Sensations of Tone*, he says:

In the inorganic world the kind of motion we see, reveals the kind of moving force in action, and in the last resort the only method of recognizing and measuring the elementary powers of nature consists in determining the motions they generate ⟨p. 2⟩.

13. *Popular Lectures*, I, 226.
In this connection we may recall that not only was this the view of DuBois-Reymond, but that he had been a fellow-student in Müller's laboratory.

14. *Popular Lectures*, I, 343. Also, cf. the following from his relatively early inaugural address as professor at Koenigsberg:

Wir können das Verhältniss vielleicht am schlagendsten bezeichnen, wenn wir sagen: Licht- und Farbenempfindungen sind nur Symbole für Verhältnisse der Wirklichkeit; sie haben mit den letzteren ebenso wenig und ebenso viel Aehnlichkeit oder Beziehung, als der Namen eines Menschen, oder der Schriftzug für den Namen mit dem Menschen selbst. (*Wissenschaftliche Abhandlungen*, II, 608.)

We shall return to this passage shortly.

15. *Popular Lectures*, I, 176.

16. *Ibid.*, I, 343.

17. In the paragraph from which I have already quoted in note 14, Helmholtz says:

Der wesentlichste Unterschied zwischen der Symbolik der menschlichen Sprache und dieser Symbolik unserer Sinnesnerven scheint mir der zu sein, dass jene ein Erzeugniss der Willkür, letztere uns von der Natur selbst, welche unseren Körper in der bestimmten Weise aufgebaut hat, mitgegeben ist. Die Sprache unserer Sinnesnerven kennt keine Sprachstämme und Dialekte, sie ist für die ganze Menschheit dieselbe. (*Wissenschaftliche Abhandlungen*, II, 608.)

18. *Physiological Optics*, III, 4.

19. *Popular Lectures*, I, 268. Cf. *Physiological Optics*, III, 2-4 and 533-34.

20. *Popular Lectures*, I, 269. In discussing implicit inference as involved in space perception, Helmholtz compared such inferences with inferences based on a knowledge of the laws of optics:

The psychic activities that lead us to infer that there in front of us at a certain place there is a certain object of a certain character, are generally not conscious activities but unconscious ones. In their result they are equivalent to a *conclusion* . . . What seems to differentiate them from a conclusion, in the ordinary sense of that word, is that a conclusion is a conscious act of thought. An astronomer comes to real conscious conclusions of this sort when he computes the positions of the stars in space, their distances, etc. from the perspective images he has had of them at various times and as they are seen from different parts of the orbit of the earth. In ordinary acts of vision this knowledge of optics is lacking. Still it may be permissible to speak of the psychic acts of ordinary perception as *unconscious conclusions*. (*Physiological Optics*, III, 4.)

To be sure, he did admit that it may be open to doubt whether the psychic processes which are involved are entirely similar in the two cases; what he makes clear, however, is that whatever such psychic processes may be, inference from past experience is essential in both: no strictly physiological explanation of the judgment of distance, and no other form of nativistic theory, is to be accepted. (Cf. *ibid.*, III, 4-5 and 541-44.)

21. Cf. *ibid.*, III, 24-27.

22. One of these essays is to be found in the second volume of *Popular Lectures*; three others are included in the second volume of *Wissenschaftliche Abhandlungen*.

23. *Popular Lectures*, I, 242. Also, cf. *Physiological Optics*, III, 18-19 and 24.

24. This passage comes near the beginning of Helmholtz's most systematic account of his theory of scientific method, and of what constitutes a proper interpretation of that method (*Popular Lectures*, I, p. 324). For a discussion of the relationships between mathematical and experimental methods within physics, cf. his memorial address for his teacher Gustav Magnus (*ibid.*, II, especially pp. 14-21).

25. *Ibid.*, I, 324.

26. *Ibid.*, I, 325-26. Also, cf. II, 231-32.

27. *Ibid.*, I, 326-27. There is a passage in *Physiological Optics* (III, 34-35) which also deals with the difference between classifications according to "general notions" and scientific explanations, but it was written several years earlier and is less clear. It also suggests a stronger Kantian influence because it involves the

suggestion that the search for objective regularities within experience is attributable to a fundamental impulse of the human mind.

28. Cf. *Popular Lectures*, II, 233–34 and 284–85. The epigraph of the present
chapter comes from the latter passage.

29. Helmholtz argued that whatever we regard as a property of an object really
consists in a relationship: "All properties attributable to [objects in the external
world] may be said to be simply *effects* exerted by them either on our senses or
on other natural objects." (*Physiological Optics*, III, 20.) Also, cf. *Popular Lectures* II, 260–61.

30. In this connection, we may note Helmholtz's discussion of the systematic
connections among the "signs" which give us knowledge concerning an individual object. The same sorts of systematic connections are established among the
laws of the various sciences, giving us knowledge of nature as a whole. (For
example, cf. *ibid.*, I, 293–94.) With respect to the adequacy of our knowledge
of individual objects he says:

The idea of a single individual table which I carry in my mind is correct and exact,
provided I can deduce from it correctly the precise sensations I shall have when my
eye and my hand are brought into this or that definite relation with respect to the
table. Any other sort of similarity between such an idea and the body about which the
idea exists, I do not know how to conceive. One is the mental symbol of the other.
The kind of symbol was not chosen by me arbitrarily, but was forced on me by the
nature of my organ of sense and of my mind. This is what distinguishes this sign-
language of our ideas from the arbitrary phonetic signs and alphabetical characters
that we use in speaking and writing. A writing is correct when he who knows how to
read it forms correct ideas by it. And so the idea of a thing is correct for him who
knows how to determine correctly from it in advance what sense-impressions he will get
from the thing when he places himself in definite external relations to it. Incidentally,
it does not matter at all what sort of mental symbols we employ, provided they constitute a sufficiently varied and ordered system. Nor does it matter either how the words
of a language sound, provided there are enough of them, with sufficient means of
denoting their grammatical relations to one another. (*Physiological Optics*, III, 23.)

It was clearly Helmholtz's view that, without the physical instruments of the
sciences, our *vocabulary* would be insufficient to deal with the processes of
nature and that, without experimental inference, we should never learn the
grammar of nature.

31. Cf. the following statement of DuBois-Reymond:

Je unbedingter aber der Naturforscher die ihm gesteckten Grenzen anerkennt, und
je demüthiger er in seine Unwissenheit sich schickt, um so tiefer fühlt er das Recht, mit
voller Freiheit, unbeirrt durch Mythen, Dogmen und alterstolze Philosopheme, auf
dem Wege der Induction seine eigene Meinung über die Beziehung zwischen Geist
und Materie sich zu bilden. ("Die Grenzen des Naturerkennens," in *Reden* I, 126.)

32. In his *Autobiography* (I, 546 ff.) Spencer wrote a mock-review of the first
edition of the *Principles of Psychology*, showing how a hostile reviewer should
have reviewed that work in order to give a fair account of its nature. In his
mock-review he stated (p. 547) that the order of exposition was faulty: that
Part III, which emphasized the adaptive nature of mental processes and the
evolution of intelligence, should have been placed first. This can be taken
as reflecting Spencer's own opinion. In the preface to the first edition, he himself
had said that the order of the sections was an arbitrary one. Actually, however,

the order which he adopted reflected the fact that, up to that time, the science of psychology had usually been oriented toward an analysis of cognitive processes. This cognitive bias is evident in the organization of Spencer's book, for its first part deals with the question of what constitutes the criterion of valid belief, and the second part, which consisted in an analysis of mental operations, started with a discussion of complex forms of quantitative reasoning, ultimately proceeding to the foundations of sense-perception in impressions. In the second edition, the latter discussion was not introduced until Part VI, and the original criterion of valid belief, and the epistemological discussions associated with it, became Part VII.

[In general, I shall be citing the second edition, as will be evident from the fact that references will include a volume number. When I cite the first edition, I shall do so by referring to it as *Principles of Psychology (A)*.]

33. Cf. *Principles of Psychology (A)*, Part III, Ch. IV (specifically, p. 374). For the second edition, which refers back to the *Principles of Biology*, see Sect. 131 (*Principles of Psychology*, I, 293–94).

34. Cf. *ibid.*, I, 47–48 (Sects. 17 and 18).

35. Cf. *ibid.*, I, 98 (Sect. 41).

36. Cf. *ibid.*, I, 109 and 117–18 (Sects. 45 and 47).

37. Cf. *ibid.*, I, 120 ff. (Sect. 48).
Because Spencer, like other associationists, had assumed that it was possible to analyze all processes of thought into the relationship between more ultimate sensory components, he did not regard it as necessary to include any special treatment of thought-processes within aestho-physiology.

For relevant passages concerning his views regarding the processes of thought, cf. his chapters on "Reason" and "The Feelings" in Part IV of the first edition, which also constitutes Part IV of the second edition.

38. *Ibid.*, I, 130 (Sect. 52).

39. *Ibid.*, I, 132–33 (Sect. 53).

40. *Ibid.*, I, 140 (Sect. 56). Also, cf. the following statement:

Can we then think of the subjective and objective activities as the same? Can the oscillation of a molecule be represented in consciousness side by side with a nervous shock, and the two be recognized as one? No effort enables us to assimilate them. That a unit of feeling has nothing in common with a unit of motion, becomes more than ever manifest when we bring the two into juxtaposition. (*Ibid.*, I, 158 [Sect. 62].)

On nerve shocks as the ultimate units of consciousness, and on particular sensations as resulting from waves of such shocks, cf. *ibid.*, I, 151 and 184 (Sects. 60 and 74).

41. For example, cf. *ibid.*, I, 85–86 (Sect. 36), or the concluding sentence of Sect. 47 (I, 120).

42. *Ibid.*, I, 194 (Sect. 78). At the beginning of the following chapter he summarizes what he has established, in saying:

In the last chapter, it was shown that the kinds and amounts of feelings are determined by the nature of the subject—exist, as we know them, only in consciousness, and
have no resemblance to the agents beyond consciousness which cause them (I, 210).

43. The general structure of the arguments of which I made use in the third
essay of *Philosophy, Science, and Sense Perception* had been anticipated by
Spencer, but I was unaware of that fact at the time. For Spencer's arguments
against Berkeley and Hume, cf. *Principles of Psychology (A)*, Part I, Ch. III,
especially pp. 36–40 and 49, and the more extended treatment in Part VII of
the second edition.

As one basic argument in Spencer's rejection of the subjectivistic position, the
following brief passage may be cited:

All the foregoing arguments, and all arguments of kindred natures, set out by
assuming objective existence.... The proposition that whatever we feel has an existence
which is relative to ourselves only, cannot be proved, nay cannot even be intelligibly
expressed, without asserting, directly or by implication, an external existence which is
not relative to ourselves.... If, after finding that the same tepid water may feel warm
to one hand and cold to the other, it is inferred that warmth is relative to our own
nature and our own state; the inference is valid only supposing the activity to which
these different sensations are referred, is an activity out of ourselves which has not been
modified by our own activities. (*Principles of Psychology*, I, 208 [Sect. 88].)

For a parallel passage to that just quoted, cf. *ibid*. I, 226–27 (Sect. 95).

44. *Ibid.*, II, 494 (Sect. 472).

45. *Ibid.*, II, 494–99 (Sect. 473).

46. In this connection we may note that Spencer says:

Indeed the primitive belief that redness exists as such out of the mind, and that sound
possesses apart from ourselves that quality which it has for our perception, is thus
rendered as hard for the psychologist to entertain as its opposite is hard to entertain
for the uncultivated. (*Ibid.*, I, 205 [Sect. 86].)

47. Cf. Helmholtz, *Popular Lectures*, II, 233 and 284–86.

48. For example, cf. Spencer's *Principles of Psychology*, I, 158–62 (Sect. 63) or
the concluding section of *First Principles*.

In this connection, we may note Helmholtz's remark: "Our generation has
had to suffer under the tyranny of spiritualistic metaphysics; the newer generation will probably have to guard against that of materialistic hypotheses."
(*Popular Lectures*, II, 230.)

49. This illustration and the implications drawn from it, will be found in *First
Principles*, pp. 26–30 (Sect. 9).

50. On Spencer's fundamental law of development, cf. pp. 89–90, above.

51. In Lotze's *Logic*, which was the first volume of his *System of Philosophy*,
published in 1874, one finds precisely the same acceptance of an experiential
starting point in which all that we can know are our own ideas, and an
acceptance of correspondence as the meaning of truth. The task of establishing
what propositions are true was one of distinguishing coherent associations of
ideas from associations which were merely coincidental; truth for Lotze was

defined in terms of agreements between the relationships among ideas and relationships existing among the objects of these ideas. (Cf. *Logic*, Sect. I–III, pp. 1–2.)

It may be remarked that the psychologically oriented manner in which Lotze developed this doctrine had no counterpart in his earlier and much briefer *Logik*, which had been published in 1843.

52. Karl Pearson's position was assuredly more like that of Mach than it was like that of Helmholtz or Spencer. A few of these points of resemblance will be noticed in passing.

Heinrich Hertz may also be regarded as offering an alternative to the view held by Helmholtz, whose student he had been. As one notes in both the preface and the introduction to *Principles of Mechanics*, his praise of Mach may be taken as referring to Mach's historical-critical analyses, not to his epistemological views.

For a brief discussion of Hertz's philosophy of science, and for the contrast between his views and those of Mach, Robert S. Cohen's preface to the Dover edition of Hertz's *Principles of Mechanics* (New York, 1956) is to be recommended. For Mach's own views regarding Hertz's philosophy of science, cf. Appendix XXI of Mach's *Science of Mechanics*, pp. 548–55.

53. I shall confine myself to using what Mach himself tells us in his published works concerning this development. The stages here traced are compatible with other accounts of the development of Mach's philosophic views, but avoid the differences in interpretation and emphasis to be found in them. Mention may be made of three studies of Mach which contain accounts of his intellectual development: Hans Henning, *Ernst Mach, Als Philosoph, Physiker, und Psycholog* (Leipzig, 1915); Robert Bouvier, *La pensée d'Ernst Mach* (Paris, 1923); and K. D. Heller, *Ernst Mach, Wegbereiter der modernen Physik* (Vienna/New York, 1964).

54. For his account of this, cf. his *Analysis of Sensations*, p. 30, n. 1, and p. 367.

55. Cf. *Analysis of Sensations*, p. 368.

56. In support of this conjecture we may note that the influence of Herbart's views is mentioned, and that Mach's most frequent references to Hume concern the problem of the ego. Apart from one passing reference (cf. *Science of Mechanics*, p. 484), I have noticed only one occasion on which Mach discusses Hume's analysis of causation (cf. the chapter entitled "Causalität und Erklärung" in *Principien der Wärmelehre*, pp. 430 ff.). Obviously, his attack on realism derived from Berkeley, and was not directly related to any arguments which can be specifically connected with Hume.

In further substantiation of the conjecture that Mach was here referring to Hume's rejection of a substantial self, rather than to any other aspect of his thought, we may note that, in the *Analysis of Sensations*, he quotes Lichtenberg's attack on the notion of such a self (cf. pp. 28–29) and then links the names of Hume and of Lichtenberg (p. 256 n.).

57. Cf. *Die Leitgedanken meiner naturwissenschaftlichen Erkenntnislehre*, p. 3, and *Science of Mechanics*, pp. 579–80. We may note that Karl Pearson attributed the views which were fundamental to his own position to attempting "to think how the elements of dynamical science could be presented free from metaphysics

to young students." This was in 1882. (Cf. preface to the first edition of *The Grammar of Science*, p. 4.)

58. Cf. *Analysis of Sensations*, pp. 370–71. Although the bibliography in Henning's *Ernst Mach* dates these lectures as 1861, Mach himself sets the date at 1863, and this is correct. (The most adequate bibliography is that compiled by Joachim Thiele and published in *Centaurus* in 1963.)

59. The doctrine was fully present in the first edition of that work, which was entitled *Beiträge zur Analyse der Empfindungen* (1885). The second edition (1900) contained additional essays, and carried a revised title which explicitly called attention to the fact that it proposed a solution to the problem of the mind-body relationship: *Die Analyse der Empfindungen und das Verhältnis vom Physischen zum Psychischen*. Both forms of the book have been translated; it is the later, expanded form that I shall here use.

60. In referring to his psychophysical works of this period, Mach himself states that he had originally put forward his views regarding the unification of psychological and physical conceptualizations only as a heuristic principle for research (cf. *Analysis of Sensations*, p. 60). In this connection we may note that the implications of his position were not greatly stressed in the popular lectures which he gave on acoustics and on optics during this period, although at one point he did reject the view that the various sciences deal with disparate phenomena (*Popular Scientific Lectures*, pp. 86–88). What led to the development of his heuristic principle into a full-fledged epistemological doctrine seems to have been Mach's desire to overcome any form of psycho-physical dualism. For example, cf. his replies to the criticisms of Paul Carus in the *Monist*, I (1890–91), 398–99, and II (1891–92), 198–199 and 206–8.

For the manner in which he later utilized this point of view in his systematic exposition of the foundations of a science of optics, cf. *Principles of Physical Optics*, pp. 1–7.

61. Cf. *Die Leitgedanken meiner naturwissenschaftlichen Erkenntnislehre*, pp. 3–4.

62. *Popular Scientific Lectures*, p. 63. This lecture was originally published in 1867.

63. Cf. *Die Leitgedanken meiner naturwissenschaftlichen Erkenntnislehre*:

In kürzester Art ausgedruckt erscheint dann als Aufgabe der wissenschaftlichen Erkenntnis: *Die Anpassung der Gedanken an die Tatschen und die Anpassung der Gedanken aneinander*. Jeder förderliche biologische Prozess ist ein Selbsterhaltungsvorgang, als solcher zugleich ein Anpassungsprozess und ökonomischer als ein dem Individuum nachteiliger Vorgang. Alle förderlichen Erkenntnisprozesse sind Spezialfälle oder Teile biologisch günstiger Prozesse. Denn das physische biologische Verhalten der höher organisierten Lebewesen wird mitbestimmt, ergänzt durch den inneren Prozess des Erkennens, des Denkens. An dem Erkenntnisprozess mögen sonst noch die verschiedensten Eigenschaften zu bemerken sein; wir charakterisieren diesen zunächst als *biologisch* und als *ökonomisch*, d. h. zwecklose Tätigkeit ausschliessend (p. 4).

64. *Popular Scientific Lectures*, p. 190.

65. I shall not hereafter pay particular attention to the chronology of Mach's works, for by 1882–83 his position on this matter had become relatively fixed.

Instead, I shall follow what seems a logically convenient order in discussing his views regarding the organization of experience.

66. Cf. the following passage:

My coat may receive a stain, a tear. My very manner of expressing this shows that we are concerned here with a sum-total of permanency, to which the new element is added and from which that which is lacking is subsequently taken away.

Our greater intimacy with this sum-total of permanency, and the preponderance of its importance for me as contrasted with the changeable element, impel us to the partly instinctive, partly voluntary and conscious economy of mental presentation and designation, as expressed in ordinary thought and speech. That which is presented in a single image receives a single designation, a single name. (*Analysis of Sensations*, p. 3.)

Karl Pearson's account of our conceptions of external objects is similar, but not identical. (Cf. *Grammar of Science*, pp. 38ff.) Although he used Mach's *Analysis of Sensations* at one point in his exposition (p. 59), he also expressed reservations regarding Mach's conception of what constitute the ultimate elements of experience (p. 62, n. 2).

67. *Analysis of Sensations*, p. 13.

68. Cf. *Space and Geometry*, especially, pp. 10–13 and 32–33. Also cf. *Analysis of Sensations*, Ch. IX ("Biologico-Teleological Considerations concerning Space"). Pearson made similar remarks concerning all sense perception. (For example, cf. *Grammar of Science*, p. 90.)

69. *Popular Scientific Lectures*, p. 190.

70. Cf. *Analysis of Sensations*, pp. 13–14 and *Erkenntnis und Irrtum*, pp. 12–15.

71. Cf. *Science of Mechanics*, p. 490. Problems of this type were of special interest to Mach as a physicist. (For example, cf. *ibid.*, p. 460.)

For a summary of the ways in which the methods of science contribute to the economy of thought, cf. "The Economical Nature of Physical Inquiry" (1882), in *Popular Scientific Lectures*, especially pp. 191–206.

72. *Analysis of Sensations*, p. 37. For a general discussion of truth and error from the point of view of adaptation, cf. the chapter "Erkenntnis und Irrtum" in the book of essays which bears the same title (pp. 108 ff.).

73. From "Facts and Mental Symbols," *Monist*, II (1891–92), 201. Also, cf. the following passage in *Science of Mechanics*:

In the reproduction of facts in thought, we never reproduce the facts in full, but only that side of them which is important to us, moved to this directly or indirectly by a practical interest (p. 482).

A related passage, although differing in several respects, is to be found in *Analysis of Sensations*, pp. 333–40.

74. From "The Economical Nature of Physical Inquiry," *Popular Scientific Lectures*, p. 199.

One may also note that, in concluding a lecture on the development of the principle of the conservation of energy, Mach held that underlying this development there was *first* "a formal need of a very simple, palpable, substantial conception of the processes in our environment," and that our conception of nature was subsequently gradually adapted to that need. (Cf. *Popular Scientific Lectures*, p. 184.)

75. Cf. pp. 18–19 of Part I, above.

76. Mach frequently mentions DuBois-Reymond's point of view in an almost entirely disparaging way. For example, cf. *Analysis of Sensations*, pp. 313–14 and 366; *Monist*, II (1891–92), 199; and *Erkenntnis und Irrtum*, p. 12 n.

Pearson also rejected DuBois-Reymond's position (*Grammar of Science*, pp. 24 and 233–34), and he set up a contrary axiom, *ignoramus, laborandum est*, with which his work closes (p. 335).

CHAPTER 15. THE REBELLION AGAINST REASON

1. In what follows we are no longer concerned with the Kantian distinction between the Understanding and the Reason, since that distinction is not of importance in the thought of Schopenhauer, Kierkegaard, or Nietzsche. I shall be using the term "reason" and the term "the intellect" in roughly interchangeable ways.

With respect to a rebellion against reason, i.e., against the intellect, there was one anti-intellectualist strand in nineteenth-century thought of which I should here like to take note, for I shall not have any other occasion to call attention to it. It consisted in the claim that the critical intellect was not only incapable of providing a stable base for social life, but that any reliance upon it was inimical to the social good. This claim was associated with organicism in social theory, and was greatly enhanced by the conservative reaction against the French Revolution. Thus we find Burke writing as follows:

> We are afraid to put men to live and trade each on his own private stock of reason; because we suspect that this stock in each man is small, and that individuals would do better to avail themselves of the general bank and capital of nations and ages. Many of our men of speculation, instead of exploding general prejudices, employ their sagacity to discover the latent wisdom which prevails in them. If they find what they seek, and they seldom fail, they think it more wise to continue the prejudice, with the reason involved, then to cast away the coat of prejudice, and to leave nothing but the naked reason; because prejudice, with its reason, has a motive to give action to that reason, and an affection which will give it permanence. Prejudice is of ready application in an emergency; it previously engages the mind in a steady course of wisdom and virtue, and does not leave the man hesitating in the moment of decision, sceptical, puzzled and unresolved. (*Reflections on the Revolution in France*, p. 84.)

Furthermore, in the case of Comte, whose fundamental aim was to establish a *science* of society, we find the following conviction constantly reiterated:

> In the treatment of social questions Positive science will be found utterly to discard those proud illusions of the supremacy of reason, to which it had been liable during its preliminary stages. Ratifying, in this respect, the common experience of men even more forcibly than Catholicism, it teaches us that individual happiness and public welfare are far more dependent upon the heart than upon the intellect. . . .
> . . . The only position for which the intellect is permanently adapted is to be the servant of the social sympathies. If, instead of being content with this honourable post, it aspires to become supreme, its ambitious aims, which are never realized, result simply in the most deplorable disorder. (*System of Positive Polity*, I, 11.)

Among the many other similar passages in which Comte claims that affection must preponderate over intellect, cf. *ibid.*, I, 4, 9, 11–12, 164, 183, and 257.

As these quotations suggest, the positions of Burke and of Comte were more radical than that which has been described by W. E. Houghton as Victorian "anti-intellectualism." (Cf. *The Victorian Frame of Mind*, Ch. 5.) Nevertheless, both involved a distrust of the intellect when it is to be used as a guide for conduct. However, the form of "anti-intellectualism" which I wish to denominate as "a rebellion against reason" is not primarily concerned to warn against the consequences of granting precedence to the intellect in practical affairs; rather, it consists in denying that the intellect is autonomous, and can ever be free of the control of the will.

2. This sentence comes from a notebook written in Dresden in 1814. (Cf. *Sämtliche Werke*, XI, 206.) The passage from which it is taken reads as follows:

> Jeder einzelne Willensakt ist ein *specimen* des Wollens, worin sich das ganze Wollen offenbart: es kann nicht anders sichtbar werden als in solchen einzelnen *speciminibus*: der Leib ist zwar sein Abbild, erhält aber von den einzelnen Willensakten Erläuterung seiner Bedeutung.

3. For example, Patrick Gardiner's *Schopenhauer*, although an admirable book, adopts the interpretation which I wish to reject. In his discussion of Schopenhauer's views regarding science, Gardiner makes interesting use of some doctrines characteristic of contemporary analytic philosophy; for example, he interprets Schopenhauer's rejection of the applicability of causal explanation to self-knowledge in terms of them. Though it is surely appropriate to draw some sort of parallel here, the differences seem to me fundamental. Schopenhauer's view, as I shall show, presupposed a physiologically oriented epistemology, and thus had quite different foundations from the much simpler view which Gardiner, in line with contemporary discussions, attributes to him. (Cf. Gardiner, *Schopenhauer*, pp. 124–33 and pp. 56–57. Pages 152–58 are also relevant.)

The only discussion of which I am aware which emphasizes the scientific orientation of Schopenhauer as much as I incline to do, is K. Schewe's doctoral dissertation, *Schopenhauers Stellung zu der Naturwissenschaft* (1905); however, there is a considerable difference between his interpretation and mine.

The contrast between the two types of view is to be seen in the following quotations. In speaking of the basis of Schopenhauer's metaphysical view of the world as Will, Gardiner said:

> Since [Schopenhauer] had already argued that all scientific reasoning and theorizing proceeded in conformity with the principle of sufficient reason, the application of that principle being limited exclusively to the phenomenal sphere, it followed directly that the employment of scientific procedures could have no place in what he was now trying to accomplish (p. 125).

On the other hand, Schewe contends:

> Die Naturwissenschaft war für [Schopenhauer] der Ausgangspunkt und die stete Begleiterin seiner philosophischen Studien; die Interpretation der Natur ist die Absicht seiner Metaphysik; die Ergebnisse der Naturwissenschaften werden von ihm überall als Beweismittel und Bestätigungen seiner philosophischen Theorien benutzt (p. 5).

4. *World as Will and Representation*, I, 3 [*WWI*, I, 3].

In what follows I shall quote from the Payne translation because it is somewhat preferable to the older three-volume translation of Haldane and Kemp. However, since the latter is likely to be more readily accessible to many readers, I shall also add in brackets, as above, page references to it.

One difference between the translations is that "*Vorstellung*," as it appears in the title of the book, is translated as "representation" by Payne, rather than by the now more familiar term "idea."

5. *Ibid.*, I, 4 and 5 [*WWI*, I, 5].

6. *Ibid.*, II, 195 [*WWI*, II, 404–5].
As early as Schopenhauer's doctoral dissertation, he had contrasted *knowing* and *willing* in a way which is strongly reminiscent of Fichte, claiming that we can only grasp the nature of the subject in acts of will, not through acts of knowledge:

> Erkannt wird das Subjekt nur als ein *Wollendes*, eine Spontaneität, nicht aber als ein *Erkennendes*. (*Sämtliche Werke*, III, 71. Also, cf. 71–72 and 75–76. For his later revisions of these passages, cf. III, 249 and 251.)

At this point it is well to recall that Schopenhauer had attended Fichte's lectures in Berlin. Also, he had previously heard G. E. Schulze in Göttingen. It was, of course, Schulze's *Aenesidemus* (1792) which had charged the Kantian system with leading to skepticism; and it was in reviewing that book that Fichte had argued that only through the will can skepticism be overcome. It is difficult to suppose that Schopenhauer would have been unaware of this important episode in the discussion of Kant's views.

7. For example, cf. his curriculum vitae, *Sämtliche Werke*, XIV, 289–90.
It is not possible to tell from Schopenhauer's notebooks just how many of the works which he later cited in corroboration of his theories were read by him before he wrote *The World as Will and Representation*. Nonetheless, it is to be noted that many of the materials cited in the second edition of that work, as well as in *On the Will in Nature*, were already available during his student years.

8. *Sämtliche Werke*, III, 26. The same doctrine is expressed in an early notebook entry, where he speaks of ". . . der Leib, das unmittelbare Object des Erkennens das alles Erkennen vermittelt . . ." (*Sämtliche Werke*, XI, 126). This doctrine is, of course, crucial in *The World as Will and Represenation*, cf. I, 11 and 19–20 [*WWI*, I, 14 and 23–24].

9. In this connection we may note that Section 21 of Chapter IV of the *Fourfold Root* had no counterpart in the dissertation as originally written; yet this is the section in which his theory of perception is stated as it was also stated in *The World as Will and Representation*.

10. Cf. his entry in his early notebooks on this point:

> Licht und alle Sichtbarkeit ist nur in Beziehung aufs Auge. Wir gehn also bei Betrachtung der Farben am besten vom Auge aus und sagen: Roth ist die lebhafteste Affektion des Auges und demnach der eine, der positive Pol: Grün ist die Erholung des Auges von der lebhaften Affektion und folglich der negative Pol. . . .
> Wir sehn dass man, nach Göthens Art vom *Objekt* ausgeht, man darauf kommt Blau und Gelb für die Pole zu halten: Roth und Grün aber, wenn man, nach meiner Art, vom Subjekt ausgeht. (*Sämtliche Werke*, XI, 96.)

The above was written in Weimar in 1814; a year later, in Dresden, Schopenhauer returned to the same point:

> Man muss ausgehen vom *Auge*, also von den *physiologischen Farben*, d.h. von der Affektion der *retina*, nicht von den Mitteln durch welche diese Affektion hervorgebracht wird. . . . (*Sämtliche Werke*, XI, 311.)

Naturally, when he did publish his theory of colors it was not well received by Goethe. (Cf. the exchange of letters in *Sämtliche Werke*, XIV, 186–213.)

11. Cf. *Sämtliche Werke*, VI, 8.

12. Cf. the following statement:

Es ist unbezweifelte Lehre der Physiologie, das Sensibilität nie reine Passivität sei, sondern Reaktion auf emfangenen Reiz." (*Sämtliche Werke*, VI, 20.)

In the light of what we shall later have to say concerning Schopenhauer's evolutionary views, and their similarities to those of Lamarck, it is interesting that to this statement he appended a reference to Erasmus Darwin.

13. For the early passage in which Schopenhauer connected irritability with the Will, cf. *Sämtliche Werke*, XI, 186–87. For one passage in *The World as Will and Representation*, cf. II, 248–49 [*WWI*, II, 472–73].

Haller's classic statement of the distinction between irritability and sensibility is to be found in his *Dissertation on the Sensible and Irritable Parts of Animals* (Baltimore: Johns Hopkins Press, 1936).

14. This is evident at many points in the Appendix on Kant, which appeared in the first edition of *World as Will and Representation*. For example, cf. I, 431 and 452–53. [*WWI*, II, 24 and 53.]

15. Cf. *World as Will and Representation*, I, 6, 23, and 39–40. [*WWI*, 7, 28–29 and 50–52.]

In his doctoral dissertation, in 1813, Schopenhauer had already made the same point: perception is to be found in all forms of life which have a sufficiently complex nervous system, but only man has the capacity to form abstract concepts. There he explicitly called attention to what he regarded as the contrast between this view and earlier conceptions of the nature of the Understanding and of Reason. (Cf. *Sämtliche Werke*, III, 51–53.)

16. *World as Will and Representation*, II, 285 [*WWI*, III, 22–23]. This passage comes from a chapter entitled "Objective View of the Intellect" which was added to the second edition. Similar statements are common in *On the Will in Nature* and in other additions to the second edition of *The World as Will and Representation*. However, it was also present in the first edition, coming out strikingly in the critical discussion of Kant, where the formative powers of the mind to which Kant appealed were identified with brain-functions by Schopenhauer. (Cf. I, 418 and 421 [*WWI*, II, 7, and 11].) Other passages which can be cited from the first edition are: I, 150, 175, 203, and 230 [*WWI*, I, 196, 228, 262, and 426].

17. For example:

What is *knowledge*? It is above all else and essentially *representation*. What is *representation*? A very complicated *physiological* occurrence in an animal's brain, whose result is the consciousness of a *picture or image* at that very spot. (*World as Will and Representation*, II, 191 [*WWI*, II, 400].)

18. *World as Will and Representation*, I, 107 and 108, respectively [*WWI*, I, 139 and 141]. Schopenhauer's Berlin lectures were, in general, a less concise and polished presentation of *The World as Will and Representation*. For that reason they frequently provide helpful elucidations of his views. For his lengthier

discussions of animal organs as objectifications of will in these lectures, cf. *Sämtliche Werke*, X, 51-54.

19. *Two Essays*, pp. 259-65. I have not been able to establish at what point Schopenhauer became acquainted with *Philosophie zoologique* (1809); I have found no references to Lamarck's views prior to the first edition of *On the Will in Nature* (1836). Therefore, whether Lamarck's position exerted a formative influence on Schopenhauer's doctrine of bodily organs as objectifications of will is not clear. The first statements of this doctrine which I recall having found in Schopenhauer date from 1814; they appear in repeated entries in his notebook during that year. (For example, cf. *Sämtliche Werke*, XI, 102-3, 145-48, 179.)

20. *Two Essays*, p. 255.

21. *Two Essays*, p. 261.

22. For an early expression of the manner in which Schopenhauer attributes will to plants and to minerals, cf. *Sämtliche Werke*, XI, 146-48.
  For later expressions of the same point of view, see the chapters on "The Physiology of Plants" and on "Physical Astronomy" in his essay *On the Will in Nature*. According to Deussen, the editor of the *Sämtliche Werke* (cf. III, v), Schopenhauer regarded these chapters as among the clearest expressions of his views. (On this point, cf. *World as Will and Representation*, I, 119 n. [*WWI*, I, 154 n.].

23. For one passage of this sort, which dates from the first edition, cf. *World as Will and Representation*, I, 159 [*WWI*, I, 208].

24. Whether Schopenhauer actually believed in "evolution," in the sense that a series of new forms successively arose, rather than that all forms were present at all times, is a point which has been frequently debated. One of the best known of these discussions is that of A. O. Lovejoy, who answers the question affirmatively. However, as Lovejoy tells us, when he originally published his article, "Schopenhauer as an Evolutionist," in *The Monist* in 1911 (XXI, 195-222), he was not able to answer some questions concerning the chronology of the views which Schopenhauer held. Shortly thereafter volume three of the *Sämtliche Werke* was published, and in its third appendix it collates changes in the various editions of *On the Will in Nature*. With this help it is relatively easy to date the various passages cited by Lovejoy, and to say with some assurance that Schopenhauer rejected "evolution" (as defined above) until some time after 1836, but accepted it by 1851. Precisely what form of evolutionary theory is to be ascribed to him is not clear, even with the help of Lovejoy's article.
  It would appear to me that a line of inquiry that might help answer this question would be to compare Schopenhauer's views on morphological explanation in general, and on biology in particular, with Goethe's biological theories. In other respects at least, there appear to be strong affinities between these aspects of their views regarding nature.

25. At one point, in remarking on the maxim *natura non facit saltus*, Schopenhauer admits that on rare occasions animals may rise above mere perception and show signs of conceptualization. Cf. *World as Will and Representation*, II, 82 [*WWI*, II, 232-33].
  For a use of the phrase "representations of representations," cf. *World as Will*

and Representation, I, 40 [*WWI*, I, 52, where the translation of course reads "ideas of ideas"].

26. *World as Will and Representation*, I, 35 [*WWI*, I, 45].

At the beginning of the following section, he also says: "The concepts form a peculiar class, existing only in the mind of man, and differing entirely from the representations of perception." (*World as Will and Representation*, I, 39 [*WWI*, I, 50].)

27. For our present purposes, this brief statement concerning Schopenhauer's views on abstraction and its relation to various types of thought will have to suffice. Its basic contours may be followed in Sections 8 to 14 of *The World as Will and Representation*, and in Chapter VI and VII of the additions to its second edition.

28. Cf. *World as Will and Representation*, I, 421 [*WWI*, II, 11], where Schopenhauer is discussing Kant's critical philosophy as demonstrating the falsity of rationalist metaphysics. As we previously noted, Schopenhauer identified what Kant said about "the human mind" with what is to be said about the functioning of *the brain*.

29. For example, cf. *World as Will and Representation*, I, 150; II, 201, 245, 273, and 279 [*WWI*, I, 196; II, 411 and 468; III, 6–7 and 14]; also, in *Parerga und Paralipomena, Sämtliche Werke*, V, 54.

30. This appears as early as 1814, in an interesting passage in his notebooks, when he speaks of both the use and the limitations of abstract thought:

> Die *Vernunft* setzt uns zu den Thieren in eben das Verhältniss, in welchem alle sehenden Geschöpfe zu den augenlosen (Polypen, Würmer, Zoophyten) stehn. Diese nämlich erkennen, durch blosses Fühlen, allein die ihnen im *Raum* unmittelbar gegenwärtigen (sie berührenden) Gegenstände; die Sehenden aber einen ganzen weiten Kreis von Entfernteren. Eben so sind die vernunftlosen Thiere auf die ihnen in der *Zeit* unmittelbar gegenwärtigen vollständigen Vorstellungen beschränkt: wir aber, mittelst des Vermögens der Begriffe (Vernunft) umfassen alle möglichen Vorstellungen, haben eine völlige *Uebersicht* des Lebens, unabhängig von der Zeit, haben gleichsam immer einen verkleinerten, farblosen, abstrakten, mathematischen Riss der ganzen Welt. Was also in Hinsicht auf den Raum und für den äussern Sinn das Auge, das ist in Hinsicht auf die Zeit und für den innern Sinn die Vernunft. Wie aber die Sichtbarkeit der Gegenstände nur wichtig ist indem sie die Fühlbarkeit derselben verkündet, so liegt der ganze Werth der Begriffe doch zuletzt in den vollständigen Vorstellungen auf die sie sich beziehn. (*Sämtliche Werke*, XI, 92–93.)

31. For example, *World as Will and Representation*, I, 203, 330; II, 510 [*WWI*, I, 262, 426; III, 310].

In this connection one may also note his discussion of the fact that in human beings in contrast to animals, the head is distinct from the trunk of the body. (*World as Will and Representation*, I, 177–78 [*WWI*, I, 230].)

32. For example, *World as Will and Representation*, II, 571 [*WWI*, III, 380].

33. *World as Will and Representation*, II, 279 [*WWI*, III, 14–15].

34. This immediately follows the preceding quotation. Also, cf. passages which

occur in Schopenhauer's discussion of Lamarck in *On the Will in Nature* (*Two Essays*, p. 265 and p. 269; in addition, *ibid.* p. 292).

35. This passage reads:

The understanding projects the sensation, by means of its form of space, as something external and different from its own person. But with man the spontaneity of the brain's activity, conferred in the last instance by the will, goes farther than mere *perception* and immediate apprehension of causal relations. It extends to the formation of abstract concepts from these perceptions, and to operating with them, in other words, to *thinking*, as that in which man's *reason* (*Vernunft*) consists. The *ideas*, therefore, are farthest removed from the body.... (*World as Will and Representation*, II, 276 [*WWI*, III, 9–10].)

36. It appears to me that Patrick Gardiner, in *Schopenhauer*, fails to recognize this point. (For example, cf. his discussion on page 119.)

37. Cf. the following passage:

As I have often explained, the necessity of consciousness is brought about by the fact that, in consequence of an organism's enhanced complication and thus by its manifold and varied needs, the acts of its will must be guided by *motives*, no longer by mere stimuli, as at the lower stages. For this purpose it had now to appear furnished with a knowing consciousness, and so with an intellect as the medium and place of its motives. (*World as Will and Representation*, II, 250–51 [*WWI*, II, 475].)

This intellect, as we have seen, and as Schopenhauer immediately goes on to state, is the manner in which the brain functions: it is in the brain that all rays of stimuli to which our sensory organs react come to a single focus.

38. For example, cf. *World as Will and Representation*, II, 284. [*WWI*, III, 21.] In a similar connection, we may note that this is how Schopenhauer interpreted the fact that a world of representations arises:

... with this expedient [the objectification of need in the form of a brain] the *world as representation* now stands out at one stroke with all its forms, object and subject, time, space, plurality, and causality. The world now shows its second side; hitherto mere *will*, it is now at the same time *representation*, object of the knowing subject. The will, which hitherto followed its tendency in the dark with extreme certainty and infallibility, had at this stage kindled a light for itself. This was a means that was necessary for getting rid of the disadvantage which would result from the throng and the complicated nature of its phenomena, and would accrue precisely to the most perfect of them. The hitherto infallible certainty and regularity with which the will worked in inorganic and merely vegetative nature, rested on the fact that it alone in its original inner being was active as blind urge, as will, without assistance, but also without interruption, from a second and entirely different world, namely the world as representation. Indeed, such a world is only the copy of the will's own inner being, but yet is of quite a different nature, and now intervenes in the sequence of the phenomena of the will. Thus that infallible certainty comes to an end. (*World as Will and Representation*, I, 150–51 [*WWI*, I, 196–97].)

39. For example, in a frequently cited passage on billiards, fencing, shaving, etc. Cf. *World as Will and Representation*, I, 56 [*WWI*, I, 72–73].

40. *World as Will and Representation*, I, 53 [*WWI*, I, 68–69]. Also, cf. II, 68 [*WWI*, II, 241], as well as his discussion of the difference between animal behavior and human action (I, 297–300 [*WWI*, I, 383–88]).

41. He so classifies it twice in speaking of the advantages which abstraction confers: cf. *World as Will and Representation*, I, 37 and 62 [*WWI*, I, 48 and 80].

42. Cf. *World as Will and Representation*, I, 62-69 [*WWI*, I, 80-90].

43. *World as Will and Representation*, II, 63 [*WWI*, II, 234].

44. *World as Will and Representation*, II, 64 [*WWI*, II, 235].

45. The passage from which I cite is worth quoting more fully:

All men also know quite well how to recognize the manifestation of this faculty [reason], and to say what is rational and what is irrational, where reason appears in contrast to man's other faculties and qualities, and finally what can never be expected even from the cleverest animal, on account of its lack of this faculty. The philosophers of all times speak on the whole with one voice about this universal knowledge of reason, and moreover stress some particularly important manifestations of it, such as the control of the emotions and passions, the capacity to make conclusions and to lay down general principles. . . . (*World as Will and Representation*, I, 37-38 [*WWI*, I, 48-49].)

46. Cf. *World as Will and Representation*, II, 245 [*WWI*, II, 468] for an explicit statement on this point.

47. *World as Will and Representation*, II, 208 [*WWI*, II, 420].

48. *World as Will and Representation*, II, 136 [*WWI*, II, 328].

49. For a variety of examples, cf. Chapter XIX, "On the Primacy of the Will in Self-Consciousness," which was added in the second edition of *The World as Will and Representation*.

50. In characterizing his philosophy, Schopenhauer said:

It sticks to the actual facts of outward and inward experience as they are accessible to everyone, and shows their true and deepest connexion, yet without really going beyond them to any extramundane things, and the relations of these to the world. Accordingly, it arrives at no conclusions as to what exists beyond all experience, but furnishes merely an explanation and interpretation of what is given in the external world and in self-consciousness. (*World as Will and Representation*, II, 640 [*WWI*, III, 468].)

51. For example, cf. *World as Will and Representation*, II, 571-72. [*WWI*, III, 380-81].

52. For example, cf. *World as Will and Representation*, I, 294 and II, 149 [*WWI*, I, 379-80 and II, 347].
Also, compare his remarks on the power of ideas to control so-called involuntary bodily functions, I, 116. [*WWI*, 150-51].

53. *World as Will and Representation*, II, 269 [*WWI*, III, 2]. The whole of this brief chapter, entitled "Retrospect and More General Consideration," is directly relevant to the point I am here making.

54. The parallels between Bergson and Schopenhauer are frequent and striking,

and do not consist solely in this general and fundamental resemblance. The reader may have noticed some of them in connection with quotations used in the foregoing discussion, and there are others, such as Schopenhauer's doctrine of the ludicrous, or his remarks on the mosaic character of the products of the intellect. (Cf. *World as Will and Representation*, I, 57 [*WWI*, I, 74].) However, that is not an investigation which need be undertaken here.

55. This is the testimony of *The Point of View for my Work as an Author*; see pp. 5–6 for this point's basic enunciation.

56. Jolivet adopts a more cautious posture with reference to the acceptability of Kierkegaard's own testimony in *The Point of View*, and his interpretation is not itself implausible. (Cf. *Introduction to Kierkegaard*, pp. 111–12.) However, what is to follow would not be affected by an acceptance of Jolivet's view.

57. In this connection we may cite an interesting contrast between Pascal and Kierkegaard, to which Jolivet calls attention:

"If the principles of reason are shaken," Pascal writes, "our religion will be absurd and ridiculous." For Kierkegaard on the other hand, faith is properly speaking a "leap into absurdity"; which Pascal will not admit, for faith to him is above reason, not contrary to it (*Pensées*, fr. 265) . . . The opposition between Pascal and Kierkegaard is no less noticeable in another connection. "One must first show," says Pascal (*Pensées*, fr. 187), "that religion is not contrary to reason; nor that it can be presented to the non-believer as something lovable, nor that it can be shown to be true." (*Introduction to Kierkegaard*, pp. 62–63, n. 17.)

58. For example, cf. *Concluding Unscientific Postscript*, pp. 249–51 on *Docents*. The following entry (#1052) in the *Journals* is also to be noted:

. . . Hegel was a don, a professor of philosophy, not a thinker; and moreover he must have been very insignificant as a person, making no real impression—but as a professor quite exceptional, that I do not deny.
   The day will certainly come when the idea "Don" will stand for a comic person (pp. 372–73).

In this connection it is amusing to note that Professor Martensen, a Hegelian, had attacked Kierkegaard's *Philosophical Fragments* as being "unscientific," "unsystematic," and "unprofessorial." (Cf. Collins, *The Mind of Kierkegaard*, p. 17.)

59. Cf. *Journals*, entry 1354 (p. 524), where he charges Schopenhauer with sharing the failings of "donnish philosophy."

60. Cf. *ibid.*, entry 723 (pp. 227–28), which was later elaborated in the second of two notes entitled "That Individual," and published after twelve years as an appendix to *The Point of View for my Work as an Author*.
   It is worth pointing out how different Kierkegaard's position is from that of Schopenhauer, with respect to the ultimacy of individuality. Schopenhauer's rejection of the premises of rationalism was coupled with his acceptance of the Will as ultimate reality: not will in this or that creature, but *the* Will as a single underlying reality. All individuation therefore belonged only to the realm of manifestations; for Kierkegaard, however, that which is real is always and only that which exists as an individual.

61. *The Present Age*, p. 33.

62. *Ibid.*, p. 42–43.

63. *Ibid.*, p. 68.

64. *Ibid.*, p. 69.

65. The relationship which Kierkegaard believed to hold between the principle of contradiction and the individuality and distinctness of existing beings can be suggested by citing the following sentence from one of his attacks on the Hegelian notion of an inclusive system: "Existence separates, and holds the various moments of existence discretely apart." (*Concluding Unscientific Postscript*, p. 107; also, cf. p. 112.)

66. This is not only true with respect to his manner of treating Socrates in his dissertation, *The Concept of Irony* (cf. especially, Chapter III, and the supplement on Hegel's conception of Socrates); it is equally true of the recurrent use of Socrates in *Philosophical Fragments*.

67. Kierkegaard frequently discusses his relationship to his readers, and the need for having used pseudonyms; he refers to this relationship as being based on "doubly reflected communication." In speaking of "a direct or personal form of communication," I am not contradicting what he says on this point. (Cf. *Concluding Unscientific Postscript*, pp. 70–74, and the chapter entitled "Appendix. A Glance at a Contemporary Effort in Danish Literature," especially pp. 246–47.)

68. These are the introduction to *The Concept of Dread* (1844), *Philosophical Fragments* (1844), and, above all, *Concluding Unscientific Postscript* (1846).

69. The first portion of that which has been quoted is to be found on page 124 of *The Point of View*; the remainder comes from pp. 131–32.

70. Kierkegaard was a splendid satirist of what he took to be the lack of insight brought about by a conforming mentality which placed reliance on "the Public," being guided by what this faceless entity might allegedly think. However, his social criticism went deeper than that, and explicitly challenged most of the major social ideals of the age. He was, for example, extremely hostile to attaching importance to material progress, to the ideal of social equality, and to the value of knowledge. Furthermore, as *The Present Age* shows (cf. p. 79), he even denied that individuals could be strengthened, and could better achieve important ends, through a community based on mutually supportive actions: this he regarded as a leveling and weakening of men. In fact, in the end, his attitude became one that can only be described as rage against whatever could be identified as "the crowd," that is, against whatever form of human existence was not characteristic of an individual in moments of almost desolate isolation:

> Wherever there is a crowd there is untruth, so that (to consider for a moment the extreme case), even if every individual, each for himself in private, were to be in possession of the truth, yet in case they were all to get together in a crowd . . . untruth would at once be in evidence. . . .
>
> A crowd—not this crowd or that, the crowd now living or the crowd long deceased, a crowd of humble people or of superior people, of rich or of poor, &c.—a crowd in its very concept is the untruth, by reason of the fact that it renders the individual completely impenitent and irresponsible, or at least weakens his sense of responsibility

by reducing it to a fraction. (From "That Individual," in *The Point of View*, pp. 112 and 114.)

Truth only comes when, like Abraham, the individual stands alone before God. (Cf. the preface to *The Sickness unto Death* as quoted below, p. 332.) This, it appears to me, is one of the points at which special problems inherent in the structure of Kierkegaard's own personality intrude into his work and where his work is not understood apart from the distortions present in his life. Among these distortions, none seems to me to have been more important than whatever led him to seek, with all deliberateness, to alienate himself from his society, rejecting any vocation within it.

71. *Concluding Unscientific Postscript*, p. 99.

72. For example, cf. *ibid.*, pp. 273 and 288. In his *Journals*, Kierkegaard explicitly refers to the distinction between essence and existence in relation to the ontological argument as found in Spinoza and in Leibniz, and to Kant's criticism of it. (Cf. entry 1027, pp. 357-58.) Also, compare his lengthy note on Spinoza concerning this question, in *Philosophical Fragments*, pp. 33-34.

73. For example, he argues in this way in the section on "Becoming" in *Philosophical Fragments* (pp. 60-62) and in the introduction to *The Concept of Dread* he says of the Hegelian school: "In logic they use *the negative* as the motive power which brings movement into everything. And movement in logic they must have, any way they can get it, by fair means or foul." He seeks to rebut this position by saying, "In logic no movement can *come about*, for logic *is*, and everything logical simply is, and this impotence of logic is the transition to the sphere of being where existence and reality appear" (pp. 11-12). To this he adds a footnote: "The eternal expression of logic is that which the Eleatic School transferred by mistake to existence: Nothing comes into existence, everything is."

In the same place he also said: "The contingent, which is an integral part of reality, cannot be permitted to slip into logic" (*ibid.*, p. 9).

74. Cf. the following passage:

Hegel is utterly and absolutely right in asserting that viewed eternally, *sub specie aeterni*, in the language of abstraction, in pure thought and pure being, there is no either-or. How in the world could there be, when abstract thought has taken away the contradiction, so that Hegel and the Hegelians ought rather to be asked to explain what they mean by the hocus-pocus of introducing contradiction, movement, transition, and so forth, into the domain of logic. If the champions of an either-or invade the sphere of pure thought and there seek to defend their cause, they are quite without justification.... On the other hand, Hegel is equally wrong when, forgetting the abstraction of his thought, he plunges down into the realm of existence to annul the double *aut* with might and main. It is impossible to do this in existence. (*Concluding Unscientific Postcript*, pp. 270-71.)

75. For example, cf. *ibid.*, pp. 97-98.

76. *Ibid.*, pp. 16-17. (Also, cf. p. 169 and pp. 291-92.)

77. *Ibid.*, p. 34 n.

78. For example, *ibid.*, pp. 102-3. Also, cf. *Concept of Dread*, pp. 12-13.

79. *Concluding Unscientific Postscript*, pp. 274–75.

80. Cf. Part III, Ch. 2, pp. 181–82, above.

81. *Concluding Unscientific Postscript*, pp. 119–20.

82. *Ibid.*, p. 121. Also, cf. the following passage:

Even if the contemplative individual is not demoralized in this fashion, nevertheless, when the ethical is confused with the world-historical, so that it becomes essentially different when it has to do with millions from when it has to do with one, another confusion readily arises: namely, that the ethical first finds its concrete embodiment in the world-historical, and becomes in this form a task for the living. The ethical is thus not the primitive, the most primitive of all that the individual has within him, but rather an abstraction from the world-historical experience. We contemplate universal history, and seem to see that every age has its own moral substance. We become objectively puffed up, and though existing individuals, we refuse to be content with the so-called subjective-ethical (p. 129).

83. From the preface to *Sickness unto Death*, p. 142.

84. According to Collins, the chief document on which Kierkegaard relied for Hegel's philosophy of religion was the last section of the *Encyclopedia* (cf. *The Mind of Kierkegaard*, p. 105); however, he apparently also studied the theological controversies of the following generation of Hegelians (*ibid.*, pp. 103–4 and 210).

For Jean Wahl's analysis of the relationship between Kierkegaard and Hegel's philosophy of religion, cf. *Etudes kierkegaardiennes*, pp. 125–30 and pp. 164–68.

85. *Concluding Unscientific Postscript*, pp. 335.

86. *Ibid.*, p. 339. Also, cf. the following statement:

If Christianity were a doctrine, the relationship to it would not be one of faith, for only an intellectual type of relationship can correspond to a doctrine. Christianity is therefore not a doctrine, but the fact that God has existed.

The realm of faith is thus not a class for numskulls in the sphere of the intellectual, or an asylum for the feeble-minded. Faith constitutes a sphere all by itself, and every misunderstanding of Christianity may at once be recognized by its transforming it into a doctrine, transferring it to the sphere of the intellectual. (*Ibid.*, pp. 290–91.)

87. *Journals*, entry 88 (p. 35).

88. *Concluding Unscientific Postscript*, p. 339.

89. We may note the preface to the *Fragments* where Kierkegaard says that this work "does not make the slightest pretension to share in the philosophical movement of the day, or to fill any of the various roles customarily assigned in this connection: transitional, intermediary, final, preparatory, participating, collaborating, volunteer follower, hero, or at any rate relative hero, or at the very least absolute trumpeter" (p. 1). On the next page he refers to "the howling madness of the higher lunacy recognizable by such symptoms as convulsive shouting; a constant reiteration of the words 'era,' 'epoch,' 'era and epoch,' 'epoch and era,' 'the System' . . . "

Also, cf. the serious reference to the *Fragments* in the *Concluding Unscientific*

Postscript, p. 52, where Kierkegaard denies that Christianity is an historical phenomenon.

90. James Collins characterizes this doctrine in the following way:

The main consequence which Kierkegaard drew from this discussion, concerns the difference between the various generations of believers. God Himself gives the power to share in the Instant, and God is master of the temporal process. Hence the very same condition of faith is given immediately by God to all who believe in Christ, even though they live at a later time. What Christ's own earthly presence was to His first disciples— an occasion for receiving faith, but not faith itself—is now supplied by the testimony of believers, the tradition "handed down from the fathers." The power to believe, however, is God's direct gift to each individual disciple, and makes every believer, of whatever historical period, contemporaneous with Christ in His unique historical actuality. (*The Mind of Kierkegaard*, p. 226.)

The term "the Instant" is Collins' rendering of what the original translator, D. F. Swenson, rendered as "the Moment."

91. *Fear and Trembling*, p. 130.

92. For example, cf. the conclusion of the *Concluding Unscientific Postscript* on both "childish Christianity" and "objective Christianity."

93. *Concluding Unscientific Postscript*, p. 536. Also, cf. p. 223.

94. *Ibid.*, p. 537. (Italics added.)

95. *Ibid.*, pp. 99 ff.

96. *Ibid.*, p. 107.

97. *Philosophical Fragments*, pp. 31–32.

98. For example, cf. *Concluding Unscientific Postscript*, pp. 267, 273, 274; *Journals*, entry 465, p. 127.

99. *Concluding Unscientific Postscript*, p. 111.

100. Cf., especially, *ibid.*, p. 109; also, pp. 50, 99, 107, 267, and 268. For the famous remark on Hegel as a comic figure, cf. *Journals*, entry 497, p. 134.

101. This is the manner in which Kierkegaard formulates the delusive Hegelian ideal of a system: *The Concept of Dread*, p. 9.

102. For example, cf. *Concluding Unscientific Postscript*, p. 18 and p. 279.

103. Cf. *Journals*, entry 552 (p. 148). The passage from the *Logische Untersuchungen* which he there cites criticized Hegel's use of the concept of "immediacy" (*das Unmittelbare*). The passage is to be found in the more readily accessible third edition of Trendelenburg's *Logische Untersuchungen* (Leipzig, 1870), in Part II, p. 302.

Also, cf. Trendelenburg, *Geschichte der Kategorienlehre*, pp. 360–61; this book also influenced Kierkegaard. For his further references to Trendelenburg, cf. *Journals*, entries 502 and 636 (pp. 136 and 194), and *Concluding Unscientific Postscript*, p. 100, as well as p. 267 n.

NOTES TO PAGES 336-37

104. *Ibid.*, p. 103. Similarly, he says:

Whenever a beginning is *made* ... unless through being unaware of this the procedure stamps itself as arbitrary, such a beginning is not the consequence of an immanent movement of thought, but is effected through a resolution of will, essentially in the strength of faith (p. 169).

105. For example, in the *Journals* he said:

Socrates did not first of all get together some proofs of the immortality of the soul in order then to live in that belief, on the strength of the proofs. The very reverse is the case; he said: the possibility of there being an immortality occupies me to such a degree that I unquestionably stake my whole life upon it as though it were the most certain of all things. And so he lived—and his life is a proof of the immortality of the soul. He did not believe merely on the strength of the proofs and then live: no, his life is the proof, and only with his martyr's death is the proof complete. (*Journals*, entry 1044, p. 367.)

106. *Concluding Unscientific Postscript*, p. 268 and 268 n.

107. *Ibid.*, pp. 178 and 179-80. (Italics in the original.)

108. The term "appropriated" is significant. Kierkegaard's definition of truth reads: *"An objective uncertainty held fast in an appropriation-process of the most passionate inwardness is the truth,* the highest truth attainable for an *existing* individual." (*Ibid.*, p. 182. Italics in the original.)

109. Kierkegaard holds that one can only understand the ethical element in and through one's own personal experience: the observation of others is always likely to be deceptive. (Cf. *Ibid.*, p. 127.) In seeking better to understand ourselves through a comparison of our experience with men of the past, we are led to read our misunderstandings of them into our own experience, and thus falsify that experience (*ibid.*, p. 131). To appeal to the history of "the human race" is, of course, to use a phrase which lacks meaning: the race is an abstraction, only individuals exist. (Cf. *ibid.*, p. 138; also, *Journals*, entry 1050, page 370.)

110. While not directly involving this comparison, the following passage is apposite:

As soon as subjectivity is eliminated, and passion eliminated from subjectivity, and the infinite interest eliminated from passion, there is no decision at all. ... All decisiveness, all essential decisiveness, is rooted in subjectivity. A contemplative spirit, and that is what the objective subject is, feels nowhere any infinite need of a decision, and sees no decision anywhere. (*Concluding Unscientific Postscript*, p. 33.)

111. Cf. the following assertion:

The only reality that exists for an existing individual is his own ethical reality. To every other reality he stands in a cognitive relation. (*Ibid.*, p. 280.)

112. Here I refer to what Kierkegaard says in his own voice concerning value, not to his portrayal of the ethical stage of life. It was this conception of value that he attributed to Lessing, but which he himself put forward in a far more violent form. In this conception he bears a much closer resemblance to Fichte. (Cf. p. 461, n. 107, above.)

113. *Concluding Unscientific Postscript,* p. 110.

114. *Ibid.,* p. 84.

115. Cf. *ibid.,* p. 79, on the renunciation; and pp. 267 and 273 for two examples of the characterization of the existent with becoming.

116. A long and important journal entry, written in 1835 at the age of twenty-two, includes the following passage:

> What I really lack is to be clear in my own mind *what I am to do,* not what I am to know. . . . The thing is to understand myself, to see what God really wishes *me* to do; the thing is to find a truth which is true *for me,* to find *the idea for which I can live and die.* What would be the use of discovering so-called objective truth, of working through all systems of philosophy and of being able, if required, to review them all and show up the inconsistencies within each system;—what good would it do me to be able to explain the meaning of Christianity if it had *no* deeper significance *for me and for my life;*—what good would it do me if truth stood before me, cold and naked, not caring whether I recognized her or not . . . ? *(Journals,* entry 22, p. 15.)

117. I say "cherished," for it was essential to Nietzsche that his thought should be engaged in battle. Walter Kaufmann's comments on the use of the term "war" in Nietzsche are helpful in this respect. (Cf. entries under "war" in his *Nietzsche.*) Also, cf. *Ecce Homo,* Part I, Sect. 7 *(Basic Writings,* p. 687–88). [In citing Nietzsche's works, I shall, wherever possible, use Walter Kaufmann's translations, rather than the *Complete Works* as edited by Oscar Levy; however, I shall always attempt to give references which are identifiable regardless of what translation is used. I shall use Kaufmann's anthologies of his translations, rather than their separately published parts, since that is the form in which they are likely to be most widely available.]

118. *Beyond Good and Evil,* Sect. 23. *(Basic Writings,* p. 222.)

119. According to Kaufmann *(Nietzsche,* p. 125), Nietzsche had heard of Kierkegaard through Georg Brandes, but too late to have knowledge of his work. Brandes was, of course, one of the most important sources through whom both Kierkegaard and Nietzsche came to be more widely known.

120. The affinities between the thought of Nietzsche and of Feuerbach have not, to my knowledge, been commented upon. One might, I should think, have expected such comments in some of the more recent accounts of nineteenth-century theological views, particularly in those by Barth and Tillich.

Although Nietzsche's works contain only two references to Feuerbach, neither of which is suggestive, one can scarcely overlook the similarities between them when one studies Jaspers's very suggestive and enlightening *Nietzsche.* As contrasted with any form of trans endence, the doctrine of immanence which one finds in Nietzsche is, at most points, similar to views held by Feuerbach. (On "immanence," cf. Jaspers, *Nietzsche,* pp. 319–30 and 429–34.)

121. *Basic Writings,* p. 193.

122. Furthermore, Nietzsche attacked not merely what Kierkegaard referred to as "Christendom," but any belief in a transcendent being, or any acceptance of Christian dogma, as a monstrous indecency. For example, in *The Antichrist,* we find passages such as the following:

My attitude to the past, like that of all lovers of knowledge, is one of great
tolerance.... I am careful not to hold mankind responsible for its mental disorders.
But my feeling changes, breaks out, as soon as I enter modern times, *our* time. Our
time *knows better*.

What was formerly just sick is today indecent—it is indecent to be a Christian today.
And here begins my nausea. I look around: not one word remains of what was formerly
called "truth." If we have even the smallest claim to integrity, we must know today
that a theologian, a priest, a pope, not merely is wrong in every sentence he speaks,
but *lies*—that he is no longer at liberty to lie from "innocence" or "ignorance"....

All the concepts of the church have been recognized for what they are, the most
malignant counterfeits that exist, the aim of which is to devalue nature and natural
values.... We know, today our *conscience* knows, what these uncanny inventions of the
priests and the church are really worth, *what ends they served* in reducing mankind
to such a state of self-violation that its sight can arouse nausea.... (from *Portable
Nietzsche*, p. 611).

123. Apparently, Nietzsche's first formulation of the phrase "God is dead" is
to be found in Section 125 of *The Joyful Wisdom* (pp. 167–69); it recurs in
Section 343 (pp. 275–76), which was added in the second edition.

In connection with Nietzsche's doctrine that man is the creator of all values,
we can once again note a conection between his views and those of Feuerbach.

124. *Beyond Good and Evil*, Sect. 2 (*Basic Writings*, pp. 199–200).

125. *Will to Power*, Sect. 493 (p. 272). [Italics added.] This entry is dated 1885,
which places it in the same period as *Beyond Good and Evil*. [Here, as elsewhere,
I shall accept the dating of the entries as given in the Musarion edition, and
followed in the Kaufmann translation.]

126. *Beyond Good and Evil*, Sect. 4 (*Basic Writings*, p. 201). Among the many
passages in *The Will to Power* which bear on the same theme, perhaps Section
584 (pp. 314–16) is the most suggestive.

127. For example, cf. *Will to Power*, Sects. 555 and 556 (pp. 301–2). These entries,
which are dated 1885–86, belong to the same period as does *Beyond Good and
Evil*. Also, cf. *Will to Power*, Sect. 481 (p. 267).

On the notion of "thing" as applied to the thing-in-itself, cf. *Will to Power*,
Sect. 569, item 4 (p. 307).

128. The interrelation and interpenetration of apparent opposites was a basic
principle of interpretation for Nietzsche in all of his writings. One finds it as
early as his interpretation of Greek culture in *The Birth of Tragedy* and in his
fragmentary essay "Homer's Contest." Its relation to his doctrine of perspectives
and his theory of truth is suggested in the following entry in *The Will to Power*,
which dates from 1887, and is here given in its entirety:

My purpose: to demonstrate the absolute homogeneity of all events and the application of moral distinctions as conditioned by perspective; to demonstrate how
everything praised as moral is identical in essence with everything immoral and was
made possible, as in every development of morality, with immoral means and for
immoral ends—; how, on the other hand, everything decried as immoral is, economically
considered, higher and more essential, and how a development toward a greater
fulness of life necessarily also demands the advance of immorality. "Truth" the extent
to which we permit ourselves to understand this fact. (Sect. 272, p. 155.)

129. The bibliography of Kaufmann's *Nietzsche* contains references to two

papers by Freud which concern Nietzsche. The text of that volume also cites other materials which are relevant to the connections between Nietzsche and Freud.

One might give many examples of particular cases in which Nietzsche seems to anticipate Freudian doctrines, but I shall only choose one explicit statement to illustrate a basic similarity in their views. It is a passage in which Nietzsche contrasts former assumptions with his own moral psychology:

> A calamitous new superstition, an odd narrowness of interpretation, thus became dominant: the origin of an action was interpreted in the most definite sense as origin in an *intention*; one came to agree that the value of an action lay in the value of the intention. . . .
> But today—shouldn't we have reached the necessity of once more resolving on a reversal and fundamental shift in values, owing to another self-examination of man, another growth in profundity? . . . After all, today at least we immoralists have the suspicion that the decisive value of an action lies precisely in what is *unintentional* in it, while everything about it that is intentional, everything about it that can be seen, known, "conscious," still belongs to its surface and skin—which, like every skin, betrays something but *conceals* even more. In short, we believe that the intention is merely a sign and symptom that still requires interpretation. . . . (*Beyond Good and Evil*, Sect. 32 [*Basic Writings*, p. 234].)

130. *Beyond Good and Evil*, Sect. 3 (*Basic Writings*, p. 201).
Nietzsche's doctrine of the unconscious is also relevant here, as when he says:

> For a very long time conscious thinking was regarded as thinking proper: it is now only that the truth dawns upon us that the greater part of our intellectual activity goes on unconsciously and unfelt by us. (*Joyful Wisdom*, Sect. 333, page 257.)

131. Cf. *Beyond Good and Evil*, Sect. 5 (*Basic Writings*, pp. 202-3), where he speaks of the "Tartuffery" of Kant and the "timidity" of Spinoza, whom he characterizes as "a sick hermit."

132. *Beyond Good and Evil*, Sect. 6 (*Basic Writings*, p. 203). As will immediately become clear, this passage—when it is thus taken out of context—is apt to be misleading.

133. From *Portable Nietzsche*, p. 485. Also, cf. the following passage from *The Will to Power*:

> *Why philosophers are slanderers.*—The treacherous and blind hostility of philosophers toward the senses—how much of mob and middle class there is in this hatred! . . . It is a miserable story: man seeks a principle through which he can despise men—he invents a world so as to be able to slander and bespatter this world. . . . The history of philosophy is a secret raging against the preconditions of life, against the value feelings of life, against partisanship in favor of life. (Sect. 461, p. 253.)

Nietzsche frequently reverts to this point in *The Will to Power*; for examples, cf. Sects. 579 and 585 (A) (pp. 310-11 and 316-19). It also appears in *Beyond Good and Evil*, Sect. 10. (*Basic Writings*, pp. 206-7).

134. Perhaps the last expression of that point of view is to be found in *The Joyful Wisdom*. (Cf. the end of Sect. 335—"Cheers for Physics!"—pp. 262-63.)

135. *Beyond Good and Evil*, Sect. 14 (*Basic Writings*, p. 211).

136. *Will to Power*, Sect. 503 (p. 274).

137. *Ibid.*, Sect. 515 (p. 278).

138. Cf. the following staccato (and incomplete) paragraph:

The so-called drive for knowledge can be traced back to a drive to appropriate and conquer: the senses, the memory, the instincts, etc. have developed as a consequence of this drive. The quickest possible reduction of the phenomena, economy, the accumulation of the spoils of knowledge (i.e., of world appropriated and made manageable).... (*Will to Power*, Sect. 423 [p. 227].)

139. *Beyond Good and Evil*, Sect. 206 (*Basic Writings*, p. 315). Also, cf. *Will to Power*, Sect. 424 (p. 229).

140. *Will to Power*, Sect. 600 (p. 326).

141. *Portable Nietzsche*, p. 46.

142. *Will to Power*, Sect. 521 (p. 282). Among the many other similar passages, the following may be noted: Sects. 513, 520, and 569 (pp. 277, 281, and 306-7).

143. Cf. *Beyond Good and Evil*, Sects. 12 and 17 (*Basic Writings*, pp. 209-10 and 214).
Also, cf. *Will to Power*, Sects, 624 and 636 (pp. 334 and 339).

144. *Beyond Good and Evil*, Sect. 21 (*Basic Writings*, p. 219).
In an entry entitled "Causalism" in *The Will to Power*, which was written at approximately the same time, Nietzsche said:

Within the mechanistic view of the world (which is logic and its application to space and time), that concept ["cause and effect"] is reduced to formulas of mathematics— with which, as one must emphasize again and again, nothing is ever comprehended, but rather designated and distorted. (Sect. 554, pp. 300-301.)

This entry of course describes how Nietzsche himself thought the mechanical view of the world should be interpreted, not the way it was being interpreted by his opponents. (Also, cf. *Will to Power*, Sect. 636 [p. 339].)

145. *Will to Power*, Sect. 628 (p. 335). Also, cf. Sects. 624 and 629 (pp. 334 and 335-36).

146. *Beyond Good and Evil*, Sect. 21 (*Basic Writings*, p. 219).

147. *Beyond Good and Evil*, Sect. 22 (*Basic Writings*, p. 220).

148. *Will to Power*, Sect. 605 (p. 327).

149. For three relevant instances among Nietzsche's many anti-Darwinian remarks, cf. *Joyful Wisdom*, Sect. 349 (pp. 289-90), *Beyond Good and Evil*, Sect. 13 (*Basic Writings*, p. 211) and *The Will to Power*, Sect. 647 (pp. 343-44).

150. *Beyond Good and Evil*, Sect. 211 (*Basic Writings*, p. 326).

151. The full title of *The Twilight of the Idols* is *Götzendämmerung oder Wie man mit dem Hammer philosophiert.*

152. *Beyond Good and Evil*, Sect. 43 (*Basic Writings*, p. 243).

153. *Beyond Good and Evil*, Preface (*Basic Writings*, p. 193); also, cf. Sect. 34 (pp. 236–37).

154. *Beyond Good and Evil*, Sect. 207 (*Basic Writings*, pp. 316–17 and 318).

155. From Sections 567 and 568 of *The Will to Power* (pp. 305 and 306). Also, cf. Sects, 481, 616, 636, and 637 (pp. 267, 330, and 339–40).

156. *Ibid.*, Sect. 534 (p. 290).

CHAPTER 16.   THE LIMITS REAPPRAISED

1. Cf. below, pp. 353–55.

2. Although the position here adopted has been most explicitly and clearly emphasized by Gestalt psychologists, it can also be found in James J. Gibson's analysis of visual perception in terms of the gradients of stimulation in *The Perception of the Visual World*, and it is basic to his theoretical approach in *The Senses Considered as Perceptual Systems*. Similarly, it is an essential aspect of an information-theory approach to perception, such as that to be found in W. E. Garner's *Uncertainty and Structure as Psychological Concepts*.

3. Cf. *Logic* I, 174–75, *et passim*.

4. For this statement in its entirety, cf. p. 344, above.

5. From "Introduction to Metaphysics," in *A Study in Metaphysics: The Creative Mind*, p. 167.

6. *Ibid.*, p. 175.

7. Although this assumption was not shared by positivists, we shall soon see that their accounts of the role of concepts in organizing experience led to conclusions similar to those of their opponents with whom we are here concerned. (Cf. pp. 363, below.)

8. This is merely one of the ways in which Darwin's views have been used to challenge the autonomy of thought. In the following section (pp. 366–67), I shall suggest some of the reasons why such interpretations involve a misapplication of evolutionary theory.

9. The translation of this general assumption into concrete terms becomes most explicit in Chapter IV of *Analysis of Sensations* where Mach discusses "The Chief Points of View for the Investigation of the Senses."

10. The above remarks apply, for example, to discussions in the *Analysis of Sensations*, pp. 16 and 17.

11. For example, cf. *ibid.*, pp. 32–34.
Mach's clearest expression of the point of view that our everyday experience is to be interpreted in terms of adaptive needs is to be found in his 1883 essay "On Transformation and Adaptation in Scientific Thought." Cf. *Popular Scientific Lectures*, pp. 216–17 and 218–20, in particular.

12. For further discussion of this point, cf. pp. 366–67, below.

13. One should note that this is *not* the familiar argument from "the egocentric predicament:" that we cannot verify what lies outside of experience because we must experience it in order to verify it. Neither Helmholtz nor Spencer used this Berkeleian form of argument; in fact, they could not have done so, since they did not hold that verification must be "direct," i.e., non-inferential.

(It was Ralph Barton Perry who coined the term "the ego-centric predicament," and who showed it to be inconclusive as an argument for subjective idealism. Cf. *Present Philosophical Tendencies*, pp. 129–31).

14. For example, cf. Helmholtz on our sensations as *signs* rather than *images*, discussed on pp. 293–94, above. Also, the equivalent doctrine as held by Spencer discussed on pp. 300–303, above.

15. It has been suggested by Professor Peter Bien of the English Department of Dartmouth College that the present unrest among students in our colleges and universities is linked to an acceptance of Bergsonian modes of thought. On the basis of my own recent experience in teaching Bergson in introductory courses, this suggestion seems to me less unlikely than it might initially appear to be. However, it is probable that one should speak of affinities rather than of influences in this particular case.

16. For example, if one were to expunge Schopenhauer's Lamarckianism, or his substantival view of what "the will" is, little would be left of his psychology. Similarly, if one were to examine Nietzsche's views regarding the sexes, or his psychology of national characteristics, or his contempt for hedonistic forms of motivation, one would not (I should think) place much reliance on him as a psychological theorist.

17. For the discussion of this point in relation to the theory of conditioning, cf. pp. 243–44, above; for a discussion of it in opposition to the view that there is a general principle of self-realization, cf. pp. 263–64.

18. Cf. p. 244, above.

19. In fact, I am inclined to say that I am over-emphasizing it, for I am not taking into account the role of external stimuli in evoking curiosity or exploratory behavior. In an account which would do justice to them, the assumption that curiosity is an expression of some deeper motivational factor becomes even less plausible.

For one account in which it is extremely clear that the nature of the stimulus is of great importance in evoking drives, cf. B. P. Wiesner and N. B. Sheard, *Maternal Behavior in the Rat (Biological Monographs and Manuals, XI)*, Edinburgh, 1933.

I shall return to this topic shortly, after dealing with issues supposedly raised by the theory of evolution.

20. To say that a drive is autonomous is not necessarily to say that it—along with all other drives—cannot be explained with reference to some general physiological principle, such as homeostasis. An explanation of that type would not reduce one drive to another, but would account for all in the same terms. Thus, if applied to our present problem, it would (if adequate) explain thought

in terms of homeostasis, just as it would explain any instance of wish-fulfilment in terms of homeostasis; it would not explain thought as wish-fulfilment.

21. Cf. above, p. 17 and the accompanying note numbered 37.

22. Cf. *How We Think*, pp. 69 ff.

23. As Locke noted, the association of ideas can also lead to error. In this connection, it is interesting to note that Freud, in his early paper "On the Forgetting of Proper Names," offered a wholly voluntaristic account of one case of this phenomenon, but that he never considered the possibility that, at some points at least, the standard principles of the association of ideas would have given a plausible but quite different explanation of it.

24. I have attempted to justify one reason for this dissatisfaction with more recent tendencies in the concluding chapter of *Philosophy, Science, and Sense-Perception*.

The following bibliography does not, of course, make any claim to being exhaustive; it does not even include all works to which the text and footnotes make reference. Only those works are included to which specific page references are given.

Wherever possible, references have been phrased in a manner that will allow discovery of the cited passage regardless of the edition being used.

In all primary sources which were issued in more than one edition and in which a later edition or a translation is here cited, the date of the first edition is given in brackets. Works by individual authors are listed in chronological order, according to the original date of publication rather than in accordance with the editions here cited, except in the case of collected works.

Abrams, M. H. *The Mirror and the Lamp: Romantic Theory and the Critical Tradition*. New York: Oxford, 1953.

Ackerknecht, Erwin H. "On the Comparative Method in Anthropology," in *Method and Perspective in Anthropology*, ed. Robert F. Spencer. Minneapolis: University of Minnesota, 1954.

Acton, H. B. *What Marx Really Said*. New York: Schocken, 1967.

Alexander, Edward. *Matthew Arnold and John Stuart Mill*. New York: Columbia University Press, 1965.

Aliotta, Antonio. *The Idealistic Reaction against Science*. London: Macmillan, 1914.

Aristotle. *Physica*, trans. R. P. Hardie and R. K. Gaye. Oxford: Clarendon Press, 1930.

Armytage, W. H. G. "Matthew Arnold and T. H. Huxley: Some New Letters, 1870–80," *Review of English Studies*, n.s. IV (1953), 346–53.

Arnold, Matthew. *The Complete Prose Works of Matthew Arnold*, ed. R. H. Super. Vols. I–[VI]. Ann Arbor: University of Michigan Press, 1960–[1967].

Aronfreed, Justin. *Conduct and Conscience: The Socialization of Internalized Control over Behavior*. New York: Academic Press, 1968.

Avebury, Lord. [See Lubbock, John]

Bain, Alexander. *The Emotions and the Will* [1859]. 3rd ed., New York: Appleton, 1888.

————. *On the Study of Character, Including an Estimate of Phrenology.* London: Parker, 1861.

————. "Mr. James Ward's 'Psychology'," *Mind*, XI (1886), 457–77.

————. "On Physiological Expression in Psychology," *Mind*, XVI (1891), 1–22.

————. "On 'Association'-Controversies," *Mind*, XII (1887), 161–82.

Balfour, Arthur James, Earl of. *Foundations of Belief.* New York: Longmans, 1895.

Barth, Paul. *Die Philosophie der Geschichte als Soziologie. Erster Teil: Grundlegung und Kritische Uebersicht.* [No subsequent volume published.] 2nd ed., Leipzig: Reisland, 1915.

Benrubi, Isaac. *Les sources et les courants de la philosophie contemporaine en France.* 2 vols. Paris: Alcan, 1933.

Bentham, Jeremy. *Works,* ed. J. Bowring. 11 vols. New York: Russell and Russell, 1962.

Bergmann, Gustav. *Philosophy of Science.* Madison: University of Wisconsin Press, 1957.

Bergson, Henri. *A Study in Metaphysics: The Creative Mind* [*La pensée et le mouvant*], trans. M. L. Andison. Totowa, N.J.: Littlefield, Adams, 1965.

Berlin, Isaiah. *Historical Inevitability.* London: Oxford University Press, 1955.

————. "Herder and the Enlightenment," in *Aspects of the Eighteenth Century,* ed. Earl R. Wasserman. Baltimore: Johns Hopkins Press, 1965.

Bernard, Claude. *An Introduction to the Study of Experimental Medicine* [1865]. New York: Dover [1957].

————. *Leçons sur les phenomènes de la vie communs aux animaux et aux végétaux.* Paris: Baillière, 1878.

Biran, Maine de. *Oeuvres,* ed. P. Tisserand. 14 vols. Paris: Alcan, 1920–49.

————. *Journal,* ed. H. Gouhier. 3 vols. Neuchatel: Editions de la Baconnière, 1954–57.

————. *De l'aperception immédiate (Mémoire de Berlin, 1807),* ed. J. Echeverria. Paris: Vrin, 1963.

Bloomfield, Leonard. *Language.* New York: Holt, 1933.

Boas, Franz. *Race, Language, and Culture.* New York: Macmillan, 1940.

Bober, M. M. *Karl Marx's Interpretation of History.* 2nd ed.; Cambridge: Harvard University Press, 1948.

Bock, Kenneth E. *The Acceptance of Histories: Toward a Perspective for Social Science.* University of California Publications in Sociology and Social Institutions, vol. III, no. 1, pp. 1–132. Berkeley: University of California Press, 1956.

————. "Darwin and Social Theory," *Philosophy of Science,* XXII (1955), 123–34.

Boltzmann, Ludwig. *Populäre Schriften.* Leipzig: Barth, 1905.

Bonnet, Charles. *Oeuvres d'historie naturelle et de philosophie.* 8 vols. Neuchatel: Fauche, 1779–83.

Bosanquet, Bernard. *Logic, or The Morphology of Knowledge.* Oxford: Clarendon Press, 1888.

Boutroux, Émile. *Science and Religion in Contemporary Philosophy* [1908]. London: Duckworth, 1909.

Bradley, Francis Herbert. *Principles of Logic.* London: Kegan Paul, 1883.

————. "Association and Thought," *Mind*, XII (1887), 35–81.

Bréhier, Émile. *Histoire de la philosophie.* 2 vols. Paris: Alcan, 1929–35.

Brown, Thomas. *Lectures on the Philosophy of the Human Mind* [1820]. 2 vols. 16th ed.; Edinburgh: Tait, 1846.

Bryson, Gladys. *Man and Society: The Scottish Inquiry of the Eighteenth Century.* Princeton: Princeton University Press, 1945.

Büchner, Ludwig. *Force and Matter, or Principles of the Natural Order of the Universe* [1855]. Translated from 15th German ed. New York: Eckler, 1891.
———. *Die Darwin'sche Theorie von der Entstehung und Umwandlung der Lebe-Welt.* [Originally published in 1868 as *Sechs Vorlesungen über die darwinische Theorie.*] 5th ed.; Leipzig: Thomas, 1890.
———. *Am Sterbelager des Jahrhunderts* [1898]. 2nd ed.; Giessen: Roth, 1900.
Buckle, Henry Thomas. *History of Civilization in England* [1857]. 2 vols. 2nd ed.; New York: Appleton, 1888.
Buffon, G. L. L., Comte de. *Histoire naturelle, générale et particulière.* 15 vols. Paris: Imprimerie Royale, 1749–67.
Bukharin, Nikolai. *Historical Materialism: A System of Sociology.* New York: International Publishers, 1925.
Burke, Edmund. *Reflections on the Revolution in France* [1790]. (Everyman's Library) London/New York: Dent/Dutton, 1935.
Burrow, J. W. *Evolution and Society: A Study in Victorian Social Theory.* Cambridge: University Press, 1966.

Campbell, Lewis, and Garnet, William. *The Life of James Clerk Maxwell.* London: Macmillan, 1884.
Cassirer, Ernst. *The Problem of Knowledge: Philosophy, Science, and History since Hegel.* New Haven: Yale University Press, 1950.
Chambers, Robert. *Vestiges of the Natural History of Creation* [1844]. London: Routledge, 1887.
Chomsky, Noam. Review of *Verbal Behavior* by B. F. Skinner. *Language,* XXXV (1959), 26–58.
Clifford, William Kingdon. *Lectures and Essays,* ed. Leslie Stephen and Sir Frederick Pollock. 2 vols. 3rd ed.; London: Macmillan, 1901.
Coleridge, Samuel Taylor. *Complete Works,* ed. W. G. T. Shedd. 7 vols. New York: Harper, 1854.
Collins, James. *The Mind of Kierkegaard.* Chicago: Regnery, 1953.
Comte, Auguste. *Cours de philosophie positive.* 6 vols. Paris: Bachelier, 1830–42.
———. *System of Positive Polity* [1851–54]. 4 vols. New York: Franklin, 1967. [Reproduced from London edition of 1875.]
———. [For correspondence with J. S., Mill, see Mill, John Stuart, *Lettres inédites . . .*]
Condillac, Etienne Bonnot de. *Oeuvres.* 23 vols. Paris: Hovel, 1798.
Condorcet, Marquis de. *Oeuvres* ed. O'Connor and Arago. 10 vols. Paris: Didot, 1847.
Cornu, Auguste. *Karl Marx et Friedrich Engels. Leur vie et leur oeuvre.* 3 vols. Paris: Presses Universitaires, 1955–62. [Volume 4 appeared in 1970, too late to be taken into account in the present book.]

Danto, Arthur C. *Nietzsche as Philosopher.* New York: Macmillan, 1965.
Darwin, Charles Robert. *Journal of Researches into the Natural History and Geology of the Countries Visited during the Voyage of H. M. S. Beagle* [1839]. 2nd ed.; London: Murray, 1889.
———. *The Foundations of the Origin of Species* [Drafts written in 1842 and 1844]; ed. Francis Darwin. Cambridge: University Press, 1909.
———. *The Origin of Species, by Means of Natural Selection, or The Preservation of Favoured Races in the Struggle for Life* [1859]. *6th ed.;* "The World's Classics"; London: Oxford University Press, 1902.
———. *Descent of Man and Selection in Relation to Sex.* 2 vols. New York: Appleton, 1871.

————. *The Life and Letters of Charles Darwin*, ed. Francis Darwin. 2 vols. New York: Basic Books, 1959.

————. *More Letters of Charles Darwin*, ed. Francis Darwin. 2 vols. New York: Appleton, 1903.

Dewey, John. *Outlines of a Critical Theory of Ethics* [1891]. New York: Hillary House, 1957.

————. *How We Think*. Boston: Heath, 1910.

————. *Human Nature and Conduct: An Introduction to Social Psychology*. New York: Holt, 1922.

————, and Tufts, James H. *Ethics*. New York: Holt, 1908.

Diderot, Denis. *Oeuvres complètes*. 20 vols. Paris: Garnier, 1875–77.

Dilthey, Wilhelm, *Gesammelte Schriften*. 12 vols. Leipzig/Berlin: Teubner, 1913–36.

DuBois-Reymond, Emil. *Reden*. 2 vols. Leipzig: Veit, 1886–87.

Dühring, Eugen. *Das Werth des Lebens* [1865]. 8th ed.; Leipzig: Reisland, 1922.

————. *Cursus der Philosophie*. Leipzig: Koschny, 1875.

Durkheim, Émile. *The Rules of Sociological Method* [1895]. Glencoe: Free Press, 1938.

————. *Suicide: A Study in Sociology* [1897]. Glencoe: Free Press, 1951.

————. *Sociology and Philosophy* [Essays written 1898–1911]. Glencoe: Free Press, 1953.

————. *The Elementary Forms of the Religious Life* [1912]. London: Allen & Unwin, 1915.

————. "The Dualism in Human Nature and its Social Conditions," [1914], reprinted in *Essays on Sociology and Philosophy*, ed. Kurt H. Wolff, pp. 325–40. New York: Harper Torchbooks, 1960.

Edwards, Paul. [See *Encyclopedia of Philosophy*.]

Encyclopedia of Philosophy, ed. Paul Edwards. 8 vols. New York: Macmillan and Free Press, 1967.

Engels, Friedrich. *Herr Eugen Dühring's Revolution in Science (Anti-Dühring)* [1878]. Marxist Library, XVIII. New York: International Publishers, 1939.

————. *The Origin of the Family, Private Property and the State* [1884]. New York: International Publishers, 1942.

————. *Ludwig Feuerbach and the Outcome of Classical German Philosophy* [1888]. Marxist Library, XV. New York: International Publishers, 1935.

————. [Cf. Marx, Karl, and Engels, Friedrich.]

Evans-Pritchard, E. E. *Anthropology and History: A Lecture*. Manchester: University Press, 1961.

Feuerbach, Ludwig. *Sämtliche Werke*. 10 vols. Leipzig: Wigand, 1846–66.

————. *Briefwechsel und Nachlass*, together with an essay entitled *Ludwig Feuerbach's Philosophischen Charakterentwicklung*, ed. Karl Grün. 2 vols. Leipzig: Winter, 1874.

Fichte, Johann Gottlieb. *The Science of Knowledge* [1794]. London: Trübner, 1889.

————. *The Science of Rights* [1796]. London: Trübner, 1889.

————. *Popular Works*. 2 vols. London: Trübner, 1889.

————. *Sämtliche Werke*, ed. J. H. Fichte. 8 vols. Berlin: Veit, 1845–46.

Fiske, John. *Outlines of Cosmic Philosophy*. [1874]. 4 vols. (*The Miscellaneous Writings of John Fiske*, I–IV.) Boston/New York: Houghton Mifflin, 1902.

————. *A Century of Science* [1899]. (*The Miscellaneous Writings of John Fiske*, X.) Boston/New York: Houghton Mifflin, 1902.

Flavell, John H. *The Developmental Psychology of Jean Piaget.* Princeton: Van Nostrand, 1963.

Forbes, Duncan. *The Liberal Anglican Idea of History.* Cambridge: University Press, 1952.

Froebel, Friedrich. *The Education of Man.* [1826]. New York: Appleton, 1891.

———. *Autobiography* [1886]. Syracuse, N.Y.: Bardeen, 1889. [F. did not publish an autobiography; the materials translated date from 1828 and after.]

Gall, Franz Joseph. *Sur les fonctions du cerveau.* 6 vols. Paris: Baillière, 1825.

Galton, Francis. *Inquiries into Human Faculty and its Development.* London: Macmillan, 1883.

Gardiner, Patrick. *Schopenhauer.* Baltimore: Penguin, 1963.

Garnet, William [See Campbell, Lewis]

Gay, John. "Concerning the Fundamental Principle of Virtue or Morality," originally prefixed to Archbishop King, *Essay on the Origin of Evil* [1731], but reprinted in Selby-Bigge, *British Moralists* [q.v.].

Ginsberg, Morris. "Social Evolution," in *Darwinism and the Study of Society,* ed. Michael Banton. London: Tavistock, 1961.

Godwin, William. *Enquiry Concerning Political Justice and Its Influence on Morals and Happiness* [1793], ed. F. E. L. Priestley. 3 vols. Toronto: University of Toronto Press, 1946.

Goldenweiser, Alexander A. *Anthropology.* New York: Crofts, 1937.

Goldstein, Leon J. "Theory in Anthropology: Developmental or Causal?" in Llewellyn Gross, *Sociological Theory: Inquiries and Paradigms.* New York: Harper & Row, 1967.

Gooch, G. P. *History and Historians in the Nineteenth Century.* London: Longmans, Green, 1920.

Gossman, Lionel. *Mediaevalism and the Ideologies of the Enlightenment: The World and Work of La Curne de Sainte-Palaye.* Baltimore: Johns Hopkins Press, 1968.

Gouhier, Henri. *Les conversions de Maine de Biran.* Paris: Vrin, 1947.

———. "Maine de Biran et Bergson," in *Les Études Bergsoniennes,* I, 130–73. Paris: Michel, 1948.

Green, Thomas Hill. *Prolegomena to Ethics.* [1883]. Oxford: Clarendon Press, 1906.

———. *Works,* ed. R. L. Nettleship. 3 vols. London: Longmans, Green, 1885–88.

Grote, John. *Exploratio Philosophica,* Part I (no further parts published). Cambridge: Deighton, Bell Co., 1865.

Guizot, François P. G. *Cours d'histoire moderne: Leçons du cours de 1828. (Histoire générale de la civilisation en Europe depuis la chute de l'Empire romain jusqu'à la Révolution française).* Paris: Pichon et Didier, 1828.

Haeckel, Ernst. *The History of Creation: or, the Development of the Earth and Its Inhabitants by the Action of Natural Cause* [1868]. 2 vols. New York: Appleton 1876.

Hartley, David. *Observations on Man. His Frame, His Duty, His Expectations.* 2 vols. London: Richardson, 1749.

Hayek, F. A. von. *John Stuart Mill and Harriet Taylor: Their Correspondence and Subsequent Marriage.* Chicago: University of Chicago Press, 1951.

———. *The Counter-Revolution of Science: Studies in the Abuse of Reason.* Glencoe: Free Press, 1952.

Haym, Rudolf. *Hegel und seine Zeit.* Berlin: Gaertner, 1857.

Hegel, G. W. F. *Sämtliche Werke* (Jubiläums Ausgabe), ed. Hermann Glockner. 20 vols. Stuttgart: Frommans, 1928.

———. *Dissertatio philosophica de orbitis planetarum* [1801]. In *Sämtliche Werke*, ed. G. Lasson, I (*Erste Druckschriften*), 347–401. Leipzig: Meiner, 1928.

———. *The Phenomenology of Mind* [1807], trans. J. B. Baillie. Introduction by George Lichtheim. New York: Harper Torchbooks, 1967.

———. *Science of Logic* [1812], trans. W. H. Johnston and L. G. Struthers. 2 vols. New York: Macmillan, 1929.

———. *Logic (The Smaller Logic)* [1817], Translated from the *Enzyclopädie der philos. Wissenschaften im Grundrisse* by William Wallace. 2nd ed. Oxford: Clarendon Press, 1892.

———. *Philosophy of Mind* [1817], Translated from the *Enzyclopädie der philos. Wissenschaften im Grundrisse*, with Five Introductory Essays, by William Wallace. Oxford: Clarendon Press, 1894.

———. *Philosophy of Right* [1821], trans. T. M. Knox. Oxford: Clarendon Press, 1952.

———. *Lectures on the History of Philosophy* [1833–36], trans. E. S. Haldane and Frances H. Simson. 3 vols. London and New York: Routledge & Kegan Paul, and Humanities Press, 1963.

———. *The Philosophy of History* [1837], trans. J. Sibree. New York: Dover, 1956.

Helmholtz, Hermann. *Helmholtz's Treatise on Physiological Optics* [*Handbuch der Physiologischen Optik*, 1856–66]. 3 vols. Rochester: Optical Society of America, 1924.

———. *On the Sensations of Tone* [*Die Lehre von den Tonempfidungen als physiologischer Grundlage für die Theorie der Musik*, 1863]. London: Longmans, Green, 1885.

———. *Die Thatsachen in der Wahrnehmung*. Berlin: Hirschwald, 1879.

———. *Wissenschaftliche Abhandlungen*. 3 vols. Leipzig: Barth, 1882–95.

———. *Popular Lectures on Scientific Subjects*. 2 vols. London: Longmans, Green, 1884.

Helvétius, Claude Adrien. *Oeuvres complètes*. 14 vols. Paris: Didot, 1796.

Hempel, Carl G. *Aspects of Scientific Explanation, and Other Essays in the Philosophy of Science*. New York: Free Press, 1965.

———. *Philosophy of Natural Science*. Englewood Cliffs: Prentice-Hall, 1966.

Herder, J. G. *Sämtliche Werke*, ed. B. Suphan. 33 vols. Berlin: Weidmann, 1877–1913.

———. *God: Some Conversations*, trans. F. H. Burkhardt. New York: Veritas Press, 1940.

Herschel, John F. W. *Preliminary Discourse on the Study of Natural Philosophy* [1831]. London: Longman, Green, Brown, Longmans, 1851.

Hertz, Heinrich Robert. *Principles of Mechanics* [1894]. London: Macmillan, 1899.

———. *Miscellaneous Papers*. London: Macmillan, 1896.

Hilgard, Ernest R. [See Kimble, Gregory A.]

Hodgen, Margaret T. "The Doctrine of Survivals: The History of an Idea," *American Anthropologist*, XXXIII (1931), 307–24.

Höffding, Harald. *History of Modern Philosophy*. 2 vols. New York: Dover, [n.d.].

———. *Modern Philosophers*. London: Macmillan, 1915.

———. *Sören Kierkegaard als Philosoph*. 3rd German ed.; Stuttgart: Fromann, 1922.

Hofstadter, Richard. *Social Darwinism in American Thought, 1860–1915*. Philadelphia: University of Pennsylvania Press, 1945.

Holton, Gerald. "Johannes Kepler's Universe: Its Physics and Metaphysics," in Robert S. Palter, *Toward Modern Science*, II, 192–216. New York: Noonday Press, 1961.

Hook, Sidney. *From Hegel to Marx: Studies in the Intellectual Development of Karl Marx*. New York: Reynal and Hitchcock, [n.d.].

———. *Reason, Social Myths, and Democracy*. New York: Humanities Press, 1950.

Houghton, Walter E. *The Victorian Frame of Mind, 1830–70*. New Haven: Yale University Press, 1957.

Hume, David. *A Treatise of Human Nature* [1739], ed. L. A. Selby-Bigge. Oxford: Clarendon Press, 1896.

———. *Essays, Moral, Political, and Literary*. World's Classics, XXXIII. London: Richards, 1903.

Hutton, Richard Holt. *Criticism on Contemporary Thought and Thinkers*. London: Macmillan, 1894.

———. *Aspects of Religious and Scientific Thought*. London: Macmillan, 1899.

Huxley, Thomas Henry. *Collected Essays*. 9 vols. New York: Appleton, 1894.

———. *Life and Letters of Thomas Henry Huxley*, ed. Leonard Huxley. 2 vols. New York: Appleton, 1900.

Hyppolite, Jean. *Genèse et structure de la phénoménologie de l'esprit de Hegel*. 2 vols. Paris: Aubier (Éditions Montaigne), 1946.

Jacobi, Friedrich Heinrich. *Werke*. 6 vols. Leipzig: Fleischer, 1812–25.

James, William. "On Some Omissions of Introspective Psychology," *Mind*, IX (1884), 1–26.

———. *Principles of Psychology*. 2 vols. New York: Holt, 1890.

———. *The Will to Believe, and Other Essays in Popular Philosophy*. New York: Longmans, Green, 1897.

Jaspers, Karl. *Nietzsche: An Introduction to the Understanding of his Philosophical Activity*. Tucson: University of Arizona Press, 1965.

Jodl, Friedrich. *Ludwig Feuerbach*. Stuttgart: Fromann, 1921.

Johnson, William Ernest. *Logic*. 3 vols. Cambridge: University Press, 1921–24.

Jolivet, Regis. *Introduction to Kierkegaard*. New York: Dutton, [n.d.]

Kallich, Martin. "The Association of Ideas and Critical Theory," *ELH: A Journal of English Literary History*, XII (1945), 29–315.

Kaufmann, Walter. *Nietzsche: Philosopher, Psychologist, Antichrist*. 3rd ed.; Princeton: Princeton University Press, 1968.

———. *Hegel: Texts and Commentary*. New York: Anchor, 1966.

Keim, Albert. *Helvétius, sa vie et son oeuvre*. Paris: Alcan, 1907.

Kelvin, Lord [Sir William Thomson]. *Mathematical and Physical Papers*, vol. I. Cambridge: University Press, 1882.

Kidd, Benjamin. *Social Evolution*. New York: Macmillan, 1894.

Kierkegaard, Sören. *The Concept of Irony* [1841]. New York: Harper & Row, 1966.

———. *Fear and Trembling* [1843]. Princeton: Princeton University Press, 1954.

———. *Philosophical Fragments* [1844]. Princeton: Princeton University Press, 1936.

———. *The Concept of Dread* [1844]. Princeton: Princeton University Press, 1944.

———. *The Present Age* [1846]. New York: Harper & Row, 1962.

———. *Concluding Unscientific Postscript* [1846]. Princeton: Princeton University Press, 1941.

———. *The Point of View for my Work as an Author* [completed 1848; posthumously published]. London: Oxford University Press, 1939.

———. *The Sickness unto Death* [1849]. [Included with *Fear and Trembling*, q.v.]

———. *Journals.* Selected and translated by A. Dru. London: Oxford University Press, 1938.

Kimble, Gregory A. *Hilgard and Marquis' Conditioning and Learning.* (2nd ed.) New York: Appleton-Century-Crofts, 1961.

Kirchhoff, Gustav. *Ueber das Ziel der Naturwissenschaften.* Heidelberg: Mohr, 1865.

Klineberg, Otto. *Social Psychology* [1940]. 2nd ed.; New York: Holt, 1954.

Kolakowski, Leszek. *The Alienation of Reason: A History of Positivist Thought.* Garden City: Doubleday, 1968.

Kroeber, Alfred L. "Evolution, History, and Culture," in *The Evolution of Man*, ed. S. Tax, vol. II, pp. 1–16. Chicago: University of Chicago Press, 1960.

———. "The Superorganic," *American Anthropologist* XIX (1917), 163–213.

Kroner, Richard. *Von Kant bis Hegel.* 2 vols. Tübingen: Mohr, 1921.

Laas, Ernst. *Idealismus und Positivismus.* 3 vols. Berlin: Wiedmann, 1879–84.

Lamarck, J. B. *Zoological Philosophy* [1809], trans. H. Elliot. New York/London: Hafner, 1963.

Lask, Emil. *Fichtes Idealismus und die Geschichte.* Tübingen: Mohr, 1902.

Leo, Heinrich. *Lehrbuch der Universalgeschichte.* 6 vols. Halle: Anton, 1840–51.

Léon, Xavier. *Fichte et son temps.* 2 vols., of which the second has two parts. Paris: Colin, 1922–27.

Lévy-Bruhl, Lucien. *La philosophie de Jacobi.* Paris: Alcan, 1894.

———. *La philosophie d'Auguste Comte.* Paris: Alcan, 1900.

———. [Also, see Mill, John Stuart, *Lettres inédites . . .*]

Lewes, George Henry. *Biographical History of Philosophy.* 2 vols. 3rd ed.; London: Longmans, Green, 1867.

———. *Problems of Life and Mind* [1874–75]. Third Series, vol. I: *The Study of Psychology.* Boston: Houghton, Osgood, 1879.

Lewin, Kurt. "The Conflict between Aristotelian and Galilean Modes of Thought in Contemporary Psychology," *Journal of General Psychology*, V (1931), 141–76.

Lichtheim, George. *Marxism: An Historical and Critical Study.* London: Routledge & Kegan Paul, 1961.

Locke, John. *Essay Concerning the Human Understanding* [1690], ed. A. C. Fraser. 2 vols. Oxford: Clarendon Press, 1894.

———. *Some Thoughts Concerning Education* [1693], in *Works*, vol. IX, pp. iii–v, 1–205. London: Printed for Thomas Tegg et al., 1823.

———. *Travels in France, 1675–1679, as Related to His Journals, Correspondence, and Other Papers* (ed., with introduction, by John Lough). Cambridge: University Press, 1953.

Lotze, Hermann. *Logic (System of Philosophy, Part I)* [1874]. Oxford: Clarendon Press, 1884.

Lough, John. [See Locke, *Travels in France*.]

Lovejoy, Arthur O. *The Great Chain of Being.* Cambridge: Harvard University Press, 1936.

———. "Schopenhauer as an Evolutionist," in *Forerunners of Darwin, 1745–1859*, ed. B. Glass, O. Temkin, W. Straus, Jr. Baltimore: Johns Hopkins Press, 1959.

———. *The Reason, the Understanding, and Time.* Baltimore: Johns Hopkins Press, 1961.

———. *Reflections on Human Nature*. Baltimore: Johns Hopkins Press, 1961.

Lowie, Robert H. *The History of Ethnological Theory*. New York: Rinehart, 1937.

Lubbock, John [Lord Avebury]. *Pre-Historic Times, as Illustrated by Ancient Remains and the Manners and Customs of Modern Savages* [1865]. 2nd ed.; New York: Appleton, 1872.

———. *The Origin of Civilization and the Primitive Condition of Man* [1870]. New York: Appleton, 1871.

Lyell, Charles. *The Geological Evidences of the Antiquity of Man*. Philadelphia: Childs, 1863.

Macaulay, Thomas Babington [Baron Macaulay]. *The Works of Lord Macaulay*. ed. Lady Trevelyan. 8 vols. London: Longmans, Green, 1866.

Mach, Ernst. *Popular Scientific Lectures* [1864–94]. Chicago: Open Court, 1894.

———. *Science of Mechanics: A Critical and Historical Account of its Development* [1883]. 3rd ed.; Chicago: Open Court, 1907.

———. *Contributions to the Analysis of Sensations* [1886]. 5th ed.; New York: Dover, 1959.

———. "Some Questions of Psycho-Physics," *Monist*, I (1890–91), 393–420.

———. "Facts and Symbols," *Monist*, II (1891–92), 198–208.

———. *Die Prinzipien der Wärmelehre*. Leipzig: Barth, 1896.

———. *Space and Geometry, in the Light of Physiological, Psychological, and Physical Inquiry* [1901–3]. Chicago: Open Court, 1906.

———. *Erkenntnis und Irrtum, Skizzen zur Psychologie der Forschung* [1905]. 2nd ed.; Leipzig: Barth, 1906.

———. *Die Leitgedanken meiner naturwissenschaftlichen Erkenntnislehre und ihre Aufnahme durch die Zeitgenossen* [1910]. Leipzig: Barth, 1919.

———. *Principles of Physical Optics* [1913]. New York: Dover, [n.d.].

McClennan, John Ferguson. *Studies in Ancient History, Comprising a reprint of Primitive Marriage, etc.* [1865 and 1876]. London: Macmillan, 1886.

McNeill, David. "On Theories of Language Acquisition," in *Verbal Behavior and General Behavior Theory*, ed. T. R. Dixon and D. L. Horton. Englewood Cliffs: Prentice-Hall, 1968.

Marcuse, Herbert. *Reason and Revolution: Hegel and the Rise of Social Theory*. 2nd ed.; New York: Humanities Press, 1954.

Marković, Mihailo. "Gramsci on the Unity of Philosophy and Politics," *Praxis (édition internationale)*, III (1967), 333–39.

Marquis, Donald G. [See Kimble, Gregory A.]

Marx, Karl. *Economic and Philosophic Manuscripts of 1844*. Moscow: Foreign Languages Publishing House, 1961.

———. *The Poverty of Philosophy* [1847]. Marxist Library, XXVI. New York: International Publishers, [n.d.].

———. *A Contribution to the Critique of Political Economy* [1859]. Chicago: Kerr, 1904.

———. *Capital: A Critique of Political Economy* [1867–94]. 3 vols. Chicago: Kerr, 1906.

Marx, Karl and Engels, Friedrich. *Werke*. Institut für Marxismus-Leninismus beim ZK der SED. 33 vols. Berlin: Dietz, 1956–66.

———. *Selected Works*. Prepared by Marx-Engels-Lenin Institute, Moscow. 2 vols. New York: International Publishers, [n.d.].

———. *The German Ideology* [written in 1846]. Marxist Library, VI. New York: International Publishers, 1947.

————. *Manifesto of the Communist Party* [1848]. New York: International Publishers, 1932.

Marx, Melvin H. *Psychological Theory: Contemporary Readings*. New York: Macmillan, 1951.

Maurice, Frederick Denison. *Social Morality: Twenty-One Lectures*. London: Macmillan, 1869.

————. *Life and Letters of Frederick Denison Maurice* [1884]. 2 vols. (4th ed.) London: Macmillan, 1885.

Maxwell, James Clerk. *Scientific Papers*. 2 vols. Cambridge: University Press, 1890.

Mayer, Robert. *Ueber die Erhaltung der Energie: Briefe an Wilhelm Griesinger* [written 1842–45], ed. W. Preyer. Berlin: Paetel, 1889.

Meinecke, Friedrich. *Die Entstehung des Historismus*. 2 vols. München/Berlin: Oldenbourg, 1936.

Mill, James. *Education* [1814]. Reprinted from *Encyclopaedia Britannica*, Supplement to the Fifth Edition. London: J. Innes, [n.d.].

————. *Analysis of the Phenomena of the Human Mind* [1829]. A new edition ... edited with additional notes by John Stuart Mill. 2 vols. London: Longmans, Green, Reader, and Dyer, 1869.

Mill, John Stuart. *The Spirit of the Age* [1831], ed. F. A. von Hayek. Chicago: University of Chicago Press, 1942.

————. "Remarks on Bentham's Philosophy," [1833] in J. B. Schneewind, *Mill's Ethical Writings*, pp. 45–61. New York: Collier, 1965.

————. *A System of Logic, Ratiocinative and Inductive* [1843]. 2 vols. 8th ed.; New York: Harper, 1879.

————. *On Liberty* [1859]. [See *Utilitarianism*, below.]

————. *Dissertations and Discussions: Political, Philosophical, and Historical* [original publication in 2 vols., 1859]. 5 vols. New York: Holt, 1874–82.

————. *Representative Government* [1861]. [See *Utilitarianism*, below].

————. *Utilitarianism, On Liberty, Representative Government*. [*Utilitarianism* first appeared in 1861]. Everyman's Library. London & Toronto: Dent. New York: Dutton, [n.d.].

————. *An Examination of Sir William Hamilton's Philosophy* [1865]. 3rd ed.; London: Longmans, Green, Reader, and Dyer, 1867.

————. *The Positive Philosophy of Auguste Comte* [1865]. Boston: Spencer, 1867.

————, edited and annotated James Mill, *Analysis of the Phenomena of the Human Mind* [q.v.].

————. *The Subjection of Women* [1869]. New York: Appleton, 1869.

————. *Autobiography* [1873]. New York: Columbia University Press, 1924.

————. *Autobiography, Early Draft*. [See Stillinger, Jack.]

————. *Three Essays on Religion* [1874]. 2nd ed.; London: Longmans, Green, Reader, and Dyer, 1874.

————. *Lettres inédites de John Stuart Mill à Auguste Comte*, ed. L. Lévy-Bruhl. Paris: Alcan, 1899.

————. *Letters of John Stuart Mill*, ed. Hugh Elliot. 2 vols. London: Longmans, Green, 1910.

————. *The Earlier Letters of John Stuart Mill, 1812 to 1848*. 2 vols. (Being volumes XII and XIII of the *Collected Works*). ed. F. E. Mineka. Toronto: University of Toronto Press, 1963.

————. [For correspondence with Harriet Taylor, see entry under Hayek, F. A. von.]

Morgan, C. Lloyd. *An Introduction to Comparative Psychology*. London: Scott, 1894.

Morgan, Lewis H. *Ancient Society* [1877], ed. Leslie A. White. Cambridge: Harvard University Press, 1964.

Morley, John. *On Compromise* [1874]. London: Macmillan, 1898.

Mueller, Iris W. *John Stuart Mill and French Thought*. Urbana: University of Illinois Press, 1956.

Murphy, Gardner. *Historical Introduction to Modern Psychology*. Revised ed.; New York: Harcourt, Brace, 1949.

Nagel, Ernest. *The Structure of Science: Problems in the Logic of Scientific Explanation*. New York: Harcourt, Brace and World, 1961.

Nietzsche, Friedrich. *The Portable Nietzsche*, trans. and ed. Walter Kaufmann. New York: Viking, 1954. (Includes: *Thus Spake Zarathustra* [1883-4]; *The Twilight of the Idols* [1888]; *The Anti-Christ* [1888]; *Nietzsche contra Wagner* [1888]; etc.)

———. *Basic Writings*. Trans. and ed. Walter Kaufmann. New York: Modern Library, 1968. (Includes: *Birth of Tragedy* [1872]; *Beyond Good and Evil* [1886]; *Genealogy of Morals* [1887]; *The Case of Wagner* [1888]; *Ecce Homo* [1888]; etc.)

———. *The Joyful Wisdom*. [1882]. *Complete Works of Nietzsche*, vol. X., trans. Thomas Common, ed. Oscar Levy. New York: Macmillan, 1924.

———. *The Will to Power* [notes written 1883-88, posthumously published], trans. Walter Kaufmann and R. J. Hollingdale, ed. Walter Kaufmann. New York: Vintage Books, 1967.

Owen, Robert. *A New View of Society, and Other Writings; Essays on the Principle of the Formation of the Human Character* [1813]. Everyman Library. New York: Dutton, 1949.

Packe, Michael St. John. *The Life of John Stuart Mill*. London: Secker and Warburg, 1954.

Parodi, Dominique. "Le criticisme de Cournot," *Révue de métaphysique et de morale*, XIII (1905), 451-84.

———. *La philosophie contemporaine en France*. Paris: Alcan, 1919.

Parr, Samuel. *Metaphysical Tracts by English Philosophers of the Eighteenth Century*. 2 vols. London: Lumley, 1837.

Passmore, John A. "The Malleability of Man in Eighteenth-Century Thought," in *Aspects of the Eighteenth Century*, ed. Earl R. Wasserman, pp. 21-46. Baltimore: Johns Hopkins Press, 1965.

Pavlov, Ivan. *Lectures on Conditioned Reflexes: Twenty-five Years of Objective Study of Higher Nervous Activity of Animals*. [1923], trans. H. W. Gantt. New York: International Publishers, 1928.

Pearson, Karl. *The Grammar of Science* [1892]. Everyman's Library. London: Dent, 1937.

Perry, Ralph Barton. *Present Philosophical Tendencies*. New York: Longmans, Green, 1925.

Pfleiderer, Otto. *Development of Theology*. London: Swan, Sonnenschein, 1893.

Plamenatz, John. *Man and Society*, vol. II. (*Political and Social Theory: Bentham through Marx*). New York: McGraw-Hill, 1963.

Popper, Karl. "What is Dialectic?" *Mind*, XLIX (1940), 403-25.

———. *The Poverty of Historicism* [1944-45]. New York: Basic Books, 1960.

———. *The Open Society and its Enemies* [1945]. 2 vols. Princeton: Princeton University Press, 1950.

Priestley, Joseph. *Examination of Dr. Reid's Inquiry*. London: J. Johnson, 1774.

———. *Hartley's Theory of the Human Mind*. London: [no publ.], 1775.

Ranke, Leopold von. *Ueber die Epochen der neueren Geschichte: Vorträge, dem König Maximilian II. von Bayern gehalten* [1854], ed. Alfred Dove, in *Weltgeschichte*, VIII (4th ed.). München/Leipzig: Duncker und Humblot, 1921.

Rankine, William J. M. "Outline of the Science of Energetics," in *Miscellaneous Scientific Papers*. London: Griffin, 1881.

Ravaisson, Félix. *La philosophie en France au XIXᵉ siècle*. Paris: Imprimerie Impériale, 1868.

Reid, Thomas. *Works*, ed. Sir William Hamilton. 2 vols. 8th ed.; Edinburgh: Maclachlan and Stewart, 1895.

Reinhold, Karl Leonhard. *Briefe über die Kantische Philosophie* [1786]. 2 vols. Leipzig: Göschen, 1790.

Renan, Ernest. *L'Avenir de la science* [1848]. Paris: Calman-Lévy, [n.d.].

Robinson, Edward S. *Association Theory To-Day: An Essay in Systematic Psychology*. New York: Century, 1932.

Rostow, W. W. *The Process of Economic Growth*. New York: Norton, 1952.

Rotenstreich, Nathan. "Marx' Thesen über Feuerbach," *Archiv für Rechts- und Sozialphilosophie*, XXXIX (1950–51), 338–60 and 482–510.

Rufus, W. Carl. "Kepler as an Astronomer," *Johann Kepler, 1571–1630*. Special Publication No. 2 of the History of Science Society. Baltimore: Williams & Wilkins, 1931.

Sabine, George H. *A History of Political Theory*. 3rd ed.; New York: Holt, Rinehart, Winston, 1961.

Sahlins, Marshall D., and Service, Elman R., eds. *Evolution and Culture*. Ann Arbor: University of Michigan Press, 1960.

Saint-Simon, Claude-Henri de. *Oeuvres*. 6 vols. [Reproduced from the Enfantin-Dentu edition, plus a reproduction of those writings which had been excluded from the former edition.] Paris: Editions Anthropos, 1966.

Sapir, Edward. *Selected Writings*, ed. D. G. Mandelbaum. Berkeley: University of California Press, 1951.

Savigny, Friedrich Carl von. *Grundgedanken der historischen Rechtsschule 1814/40*, Deutsches Rechtsdenken, ed. Erik Wolf, Heft 8. Frankfurt: Klostermann, 1948.

Schelling, F. W. J. *Sämmtliche Werke*. Abtheilung I, 10 vols; Abtheilung II, 4 vols. Stuttgart/Augsburg: Cotta, 1856–61.

Schewe, Karl. *Schopenhauers Stellung zu der Naturwissenschaft*. (Inaugural dissertation: Berlin, 1905).

Schleiermacher, Friedrich. *Briefe Schleiermachers*, ed. H. Mulert. Berlin: Propyläen-Verlag, 1923.

Schopenhauer, Arthur. *Sämtliche Werke*, ed. P. Deussen. 16 vols. München: Piper, 1911–42.

———. *The World as Will and Idea*. Translated by Haldane and Kemp. 3 vols. London: Truebner, 1883.

———. *The World as Will and Representation*, trans. E. J. Payne. 2 vols. New York: Dover, 1966.

———. *Two Essays: I. On the Fourfold Root of the Principle of Sufficient Reason* [1st ed., 1813; 2nd ed. 1847]; *II. On the Will in Nature* [1836]. London: Bell, 1889.

Selby-Bigge, L. A. *British Moralists*. 2 vols. Oxford: Clarendon Press, 1897.

Service, Elman R. [*See* Sahlins, Marshall D.]

Sidgwick, Henry. "The Historical Method," *Mind*, XI (1886), 203–19.

Simon, Ernst. "Ranke und Hegel," *Historische Zeitschrift*, Beiheft #15. München/Berlin: Oldenbourg, 1928.

Skinner, B. F. *The Behavior of Organisms: An Experimental Analysis*. New York: Appleton-Century-Crofts, 1938.

Smith, Adam. *An Inquiry into the Nature and Causes of the Wealth of Nations*. [1776]. (Everyman Edition). 2 vols. New York: Dutton, 1912.

Spencer, Herbert, *Social Statics, or the Conditions Essential to Human Happiness* [1850]. New York: Appleton, 1865.

————. *The Principles of Psychology*. 1st ed.; London: Longman, Brown, Green, & Longmans, 1855.

————. *The Principles of Psychology* [1870–72]. 2 vols. 2nd ed.; New York: Appleton, 1871–73.

————. *Essays: Scientific, Political, and Speculative* [1858–63; 1885]. 3 vols. New York: Appleton, 1892.

————. *Education: Intellectual, Moral and Physical* [1861]. New York: Appleton, 1866.

————. *First Principles* [1862]. 4th ed.; New York: Appleton, 1898.

————. *Principles of Biology* [1864–67]. 2 vols. New York: Appleton, 1891.

————. *Principles of Sociology* [1876–96]. 3 vols. 3rd ed.; New York: Appleton, 1896.

————. *Data of Ethics*. New York: Appleton, 1879.

————. *An Autobiography*. 2 vols. New York: Appleton, 1904.

Stern, Fritz (ed.). *Varieties of History: From Voltaire to the Present*. New York: Meridian, 1956.

Stillinger, Jack (ed.). *The Early Draft of John Stuart Mill's "Autobiography"*. Urbana: University of Illinois Press, 1961.

Steward, Julian H. *Theory of Culture Change: The Methodology of Multilinear Evolution*. Urbana: University of Illinois Press, 1955.

Strauss, Leo. *Natural Right and History*. Chicago: University of Chicago Press, 1953.

Taine, Hippolyte. *Les philosophes français du XIXᵉ siècle*. Paris: Hachette, 1857. [Subsequent editions entitled *Les philosophes classiques du XIXᵉ siècle*.]

————. *Histoire de la littérature anglaise* [1864]. 5 vols. 3rd ed.; Paris: Hachette, 1873–74.

Teggart, Frederick J. *The Idea of Progress, A Collection of Readings*. Berkeley: University of California, 1949.

Thiele, Joachim. "Ernst Mach—Bibliographie," *Centaurus, International Magazine of the History of Science and Medicine*, VIII [1963], 189–237.

Tillich, Paul. "Existential Philosophy," *Journal of the History of Ideas*, V (1944), 44–70.

Toynbee, Arnold J. *A Study of History*. 12 vols. London & New York: Oxford University Press, 1934–61.

————. *A Study of History*, abridged by D. C. Somervell. 2 vols. New York & London: Oxford University Press, 1946–57.

Trendelenburg, Adolf. *Logische Untersuchungen* [two parts, issued in one volume]. Berlin: Bethge, 1840.

————. *Geschichte der Kategorienlehre* [1846]. Hildesheim: Olms, 1963.

Trilling, Lionel. *Matthew Arnold*. New York: Norton, 1939.

Troeltsch, Ernst. *Der Historismus und seine Probleme*. Tübingen: Mohr, 1922.

Tucker, Abraham. *The Light of Nature Pursued* [1768–78]. 7 vols. 2nd ed.; London: Faulder, 1805.

Tucker, Robert C. *Philosophy and Myth in Karl Marx*. Cambridge: University Press, 1961.

Tufts, James H. [*See* Dewey, John and Tufts, James H.]

Tulloch, John. "Modern Scientific Materialism," in *Modern Theories in Philosophy and Religion*. Edinburgh: Blackwood, 1884.

Turgot, Anne Robert Jacques. *Oeuvres*. 9 vols. Paris: Berlin, Delance, 1808–11.

Tylor, Edward B. *Researches into the Early History of Mankind* [1865]. New York: Holt, 1878.

———. "On Traces of the Early Mental Condition of Man," *Annual Report of the Board of Regents of the Smithsonian Institution* (1867), pp. 390–98. [Reprinted from the *Proceedings of the Royal Institution of Great Britain*.]

———. *Primitive Culture* [1871]. 2 vols. New York: Holt, 1889.

———. *Anthropology* [1881]. New York: Appleton, 1899.

———. "How the Problems of American Anthropology Present Themselves to the English Mind," *Transactions of the Anthropological Society of Washington*, III (Nov. 6, 1883 to May 19, 1885), 81–94. [Published as *Smithsonian Miscellaneous Collections*, No. 630.]

Tyndall, John. "The Scope and Limit of Scientific Materialism," in *Fragments of Science*. New York: Appleton, 1872.

———. *Address Delivered before the British Association in Belfast*. New York: Appleton, 1875.

Vaihinger, Hans. *Hartmann, Dühring, und Lange*. Iserlohn: Baedeker, 1876.

Wahl, Jean. *Études kierkegaardiennes*. 2nd ed.; Paris: Vrin, 1949.

Wallace, William. [See Hegel, G. W. F. *Philosophy of Mind*.]

Ward, James. "Psychological Principles," *Mind*, VIII (1883), 153–69 and 465–86; XII (1887), 45–67.

———. "Mr. F. H. Bradley's Analysis of Mind," *Mind*, XII (1887), 564–75.

Wundt, Wilhelm. *Ueber den Einfluss der Philosophie auf die Erfahrungswissenschaften*. Leipzig: Engelmann, 1876.

———. *Ethics: An Investigation of the Facts and Laws of the Moral Life*. [1886]. 3 vols. London: Swan, Sonnenschein, 1897–1901.

Zilsel, Edgar. "Physics and the Problem of Historico-Sociological Laws," *Philosophy of Science*, VIII (1941), 567–79.

To avoid repetitive entries, notes which merely serve as documentation and elaboration of the text are not separately indexed. However, when a note refers to an author or subject not explicitly mentioned in the discussion to which that note is appended, the index will carry the appropriate entry.